LEONARD E. MORRISSEY

Professor of Accounting

Amos Tuck School of Business Administration

Dartmouth College

Contemporary
Accounting Problems

Text and Cases

PRENTICE-HALL, INC.
Englewood Cliffs, N. J.

Current printing (last digit):

12 11 10 9 8 7 6 5 4

PRINTED IN THE UNITED STATES OF AMERICA

LIBRARY OF CONGRESS CATALOG CARD NO.:
63-19439
C–16958

Foreword

It has become commonplace to refer to accounting as the "language of business." This designation correctly recognizes the important role of accounting in communicating financial information to various levels of management as a basis for making effective administrative decisions, and to a growing number of corporate owners as a basis for making wise investment decisions. In fact, a vast network of communication based on accounting data has developed. This communication network is of national interest for "without adequate information about the results of business operations no one could make intelligent decisions, and our economy would fall apart." [1]

Yet, it is frightening to realize how seldom accounting is treated as a "language" in actual practice. Difficulties arise because it is not recognized that accounting, as a language, is subject to the problems of any language such as irregularities, inexactness, change, and variations of meaning. Generally, the character of accounting is not fully understood either by the people who use it as a means of communicating the results of operations for which they are responsible (business managers) or by the people to whom such results are communicated (stockholders, investors, labor, general management and others). Those at both ends of this communication process often believe that somewhere in the middle the accountant, through application of mysterious specialized techniques, can translate the facts and judgments underlying business transactions into quantitative terms, predigest them, and come out at the end of the process with figures which precisely measure the results of business operations.

This concept of accounting is an illusion. Among the more serious implications of this illusion is the general failure of those who use the communication process of accounting to understand the real meaning of the financial information upon which they base their decisions or actions. When one thinks about the vast impact of decisions based on reported

---

[1] Marquis G. Eaton, "Financial Reporting in a Changing Society," *Journal of Accountancy*, Vol. 104, August 1957, p. 25.

accounting data, it should arouse considerable alarm to ponder the realism and implications of the late Marquis Eaton's observation: "I suspect it would come as something of a shock to some people to realize that two otherwise identical corporations might report net income differing by millions of dollars simply because they followed different accounting methods—and that the financial statements of both companies might still carry a certified public accountant's opinion stating that the reports fairly presented the results in accordance with 'generally accepted accounting principles.'" [2]

The lack of appreciation for the communication aspects of accounting has resulted in a serious dilemma for the accounting profession. An important function of the profession is to provide an independent viewpoint in the form of an opinion as to the fairness and integrity of the financial presentations of management. Yet, paradoxically, the opinions of independent public accountants on financial statements perpetuate misconceptions about the nature of accounting. The customary reference in such opinions to generally accepted accounting principles "suggests to the ordinary reader the existence of some authoritative code of accounting which when applied consistently will produce precise and comparable results." [3] Thus, the auditor's opinion produces a false sense of complacency which insulates those who present and use accounting information from an awareness of their need to penetrate and understand the substance of the accounting language in terms of the significance and limitations of the data being communicated.

I believe that misunderstanding of the phrase *generally accepted accounting principles* extends beyond the "ordinary reader." My observations have led to a feeling that it exists across the whole spectrum of business activity. It even exists to a surprising degree—wittingly or unwittingly—within the accounting profession itself and in the ranks of teachers of accounting and business administration.

At the heart of this misunderstanding is a failure to recognize the meaning of the word "accepted" in the concept "generally accepted accounting principles." In using "acceptance" as part of the criterion of "fairness," the accounting profession has relied upon business management and others actively involved in the communication process to develop, from the actual business practices and the prevailing modes of thought of society, the standards by which the fairness of financial presentations would be judged.

The accounting profession quite properly visualized its role as being more of a catalyst than a prescriber of standards. Beginning in the early 1930's, the profession undertook to stimulate the resolution and crystalliza-

---

2 Eaton, pp. 26-27.
3 Eaton, p. 26.

tion of generally accepted standards of accounting in areas where divergent concepts and practices existed. In this endeavor, the profession consistently exercised restraint in trying unilaterally to impose standards of its own on the business community. Instead, the profession sought to identify standards generally accepted by the business community and to facilitate such identification through the efforts of the professional committees of the American Institute of Certified Public Accountants. In this task, the profession has brought about much improvement in the quality and the amount of financial information available to users of accounting statements.

It was to be expected that in a dynamic and constantly changing environment there would always be some areas where common modes of thought and business practices had not evolved to the point where it was possible to identify generally accepted uniform standards. The profession's approach in these unsettled areas has been (1) to require supplemental disclosure, through footnotes or otherwise, which would enable the reader to place the reported results in perspective, and (2) to reduce the number of unsettled areas by the development, exposure to the business community, and ultimate issuance of *Accounting Research Bulletins* for the guidance of accountants and business management. Even here, however, it was made clear that the authority of these *Bulletins* rested on their *acceptance*.

Notwithstanding the inherent soundness of this approach, a realistic analysis of how it is working in actual practice gives cause for great concern. For example, the supplemental footnote disclosures which accountants so carefully provide to deal with problems in unsettled areas all too frequently either drop out of the communication process or are not given the attention they warrant by the great number of readers of financial reports.

This condition has given rise to a strong feeling that the accounting profession should develop its own set of accounting principles, against which independent accountants can judge the fairness of the businessman's financial presentations. There is no question that the seriousness of the situation demands a great sense of urgency on the part of the profession to take a vigorous role of leadership in bringing about correction of these serious communication problems. However, in seeking solutions to these problems, I am convinced that acceptance must be retained as a substantial element in the determination of generally accepted accounting principles, for without a substantial degree of acceptance fairness in a full sense cannot be achieved. In fact, efforts to dissociate acceptance and fairness run the risk of narrowing the areas of difference in accounting principles in form only rather than in substance. Such a result could bring about even greater problems.

The profession's reliance upon acceptance recognizes the primacy of the businessman's responsibility for publishing informative financial statements. It further recognizes that in actual practice the accountant's function must be, in large measure, one of providing guidance to the businessman in achieving a meaningful matching of costs and revenues. This matching—assuming good faith all around—is largely a matter of reflecting business judgment in distributing the impact of business events over time. If alone for this reason, we must recognize the need for great restraint in abandoning a philosophy which permits reflection in financial statements of the judgments of businessmen as to the facts which guided their decision making.

In my opinion, the present dilemma of the accounting profession stems from widespread misunderstanding of the profession's long-standing philosophy toward exercising its responsibilities, not from a basic weakness in the philosophy itself. There are many possible reasons for this misunderstanding. I am sure that to a substantial degree the roots of the problem lie in the failure of business and accounting education to develop in students an understanding and awareness of the significance and limitations of generally accepted accounting principles, as well as a respect for the long-run value of the philosophy which underlies the profession's approach to the problem of narrowing the differences in accounting practice.

Traditionally, students of accounting learn their subject in an atmosphere of specialization. Early in their careers they develop an attitude that accounting principles and techniques somehow have validity in themselves. Students are not made sufficiently aware that accounting is in a state of continuing evolutionary change, and they graduate blissfully unaware of the broader dimensions of accounting—its function in society and its heavy reliance upon management's judgment, participation, and integrity.

If the far-reaching significance of accounting is discussed at all, it is usually in introductory lectures presented early in the student's program. Understandably, the impact of these lectures is soon forgotten as the student becomes immersed in the technical aspects of intricate and demanding problems. Technical skills are, of course, a necessary and fundamental part of any future accountant's education. My quarrel is with the failure to maintain and develop the student's appreciation of the severe limitations of what he is doing in relation to the responsibilities, needs, and modes of thought of management and others directly involved in the use of accounting data.

All of the blame does not rest with us teachers of accounting, however. Other courses in business administration aggravate the problem further. Seldom do such courses as finance, production, and business policy examine the nature of the concepts and assumptions which underlie the accounting data they incorporate so freely in their analyses. As a result, the nonaccounting business graduate is not made conscious of the need to involve himself, either as a manager or other user of accounting data, in the accounting process. Typically, he is unaware of his vital role in the development and application of accounting principles and of the subtle ways that decisions made by accountants influence his actions.

Thus, the illusion is perpetuated. Future accountants enter the business world with exaggerated notions regarding the extent to which they can provide meaningful, responsive information on the basis of generally accepted accounting principles. Those who sometime in the future will either issue or use financial reports accept unquestionably the accounting information presented to them by accountants. The two ends of the communication process remain unaware of the significance and limitations of the "language" upon which they base their decisions, and in the middle the accountant acts as a technician rather than a catalyst seeking to develop a language based on "acceptance" which will more closely measure and communicate the financial aspects of business activity.

I believe Professor Morrissey's book will provide a basis for helping to correct this disturbing weakness in accounting and business education. Wisely used, the book can provide students with the kind of perspective and understanding they need to deal intelligently with the accounting function when they enter the business world.

The significant difference between this book and conventional accounting texts and case books lies in the way the author develops—through text and related cases—a framework for teaching the communication aspects of the accounting process and the evolutionary nature of the principles which underlie this process. Nearly every chapter consists of text which analyzes one or more *Accounting Research Bulletins.* Following the text are cases illustrating how various managements employed the accounting principles previously discussed in the text. In most instances, it should be noted, the cases and text focus upon contemporary and controversial accounting issues such as the capitalization of long-term leases and accounting for business combinations and deferred income taxes.

The current nature of the material discussed generates a high level of student interest. The liberal reproduction and discussion of the *Accounting Research Bulletins* makes the student familiar with the most authoritative written statement of generally accepted accounting principles in existence. At the same time, the text highlights the profession's heavy reliance upon the evolutionary development of accounting principles through authorship and acceptance by the business community. The cases make students aware of the role of users of financial reports in the development of accounting principles, and of the crucial part management judgment plays in the choice of accounting techniques to apply in particular instances.

Professor Morrissey's book is timely. Today the challenge in accounting education is to develop perspective among compilers, issuers, and users of financial reports regarding their roles in both the development and use of the accounting communication process. We educators have not met this challenge in the past. This book provides us with an opportunity to respond more effectively to this educational need of our time.

Walter F. Frese
Professor of Business Administration
Graduate School of Business Administration
Harvard University

Soldiers Field
Boston, Massachusetts

Preface

In his Foreword to this book, Professor Walter F. Frese admirably describes the development of financial accounting in the past thirty years and the impact of this development on teachers and students of accounting and business administration. While there is much upon which accountants now agree—at least as much as in most other fields typically included in the business administration curriculum—there are still vast areas of disagreement.

One of the purposes of this book is to make students aware both of the areas of substantial agreement and of those troublesome areas in which the accounting profession is currently attempting to achieve some uniformity. In addition, this book should enable the student to understand and appreciate the evolutionary process which leads to the establishment of so-called "generally accepted accounting principles." Because a number of the current problems faced by the accounting profession bring into particularly sharp relief both the need for generally accepted accounting principles and the difficulty often encountered in defining and applying such principles, much of the material in this book pertains to these current problems.

The cases are presented to show how accounting principles were applied in a variety of situations and not to illustrate good or bad accounting practices. To conserve the student's time and to focus his attention on the relevant issues, each case is followed by a series of questions. Many of these questions require journal entries or computations of various kinds. The student will find it helpful to scan these questions before reading the case.

All of the cases have been used at the Tuck School with students in the second year of a two-year MBA program, and a majority of the cases have been similarly used by Professor Frese at the Harvard Business School. Advanced undergraduate students as well should find the cases interesting and challenging. Several of the cases have been discussed in management development programs. When used with such groups, questions calling for journal entries or other accounting techniques have been omitted.

The material in this book is more than ample for a semester-length course. If students are assigned some readings from the *References* following each chapter, there is adequate material for two semesters. At Tuck, the book is used in a course of approximately sixty class meetings extending over two terms.

Acknowledgments

Erik Jorgensen, a graduate of the Tuck School, offered extremely valuable help at every stage in the preparation of the manuscript. Other former Tuck students who made significant contributions include C. Bennett Brown, Donald F. Moran, Alfred W. Roberts, and William C. Sadd.

Professor Frese, in addition to contributing the Foreword and several cases, offered wise counsel and constant encouragement. Helpful suggestions and comments were made by Professor Homer A. Black of the Florida State University who reviewed the entire manuscript and by Professor George I. Prater of Tuck who reviewed all of the text material. Dean Karl A. Hill of Tuck granted the author substantial relief from burdensome committee assignments in the final year of the project and provided funds for the support of various assistants. Professor Arthur Schleifer, also of Tuck, provided mathematical assistance.

The American Institute of Certified Public Accountants was most generous in granting permission to use its publications, including many of the *Accounting Research Bulletins* issued by the Committee on Accounting Procedure. Numerous other organizations and individuals kindly granted permission to quote from various sources.

Seven of the cases (listed on the back of the title page) are used with permission of the President and Fellows of Harvard College. Of these cases, "Rocky Mountain Construction Company" and "Trans World Airlines" were written by Professors Neil E. Harlan and Richard F. Vancil of the Harvard Business School. Professor Frese contributed four of the Harvard cases, and one case is based upon materials used to teach consolidated financial statements at the Harvard Business School. "Vitreometals, Inc.," was written by Professor Henry Key of Texas Christian University.

The following members of Tuck's secretarial staff carefully and cheerfully typed the manuscript: Constance W. Elder, Deborah H. Warren, Delia M. Clark, Polly J. Greene, and Elizabeth S. Pease.

Leonard E. Morrissey

Hanover, New Hampshire

Table of Contents

8 *Inventories* (Cont.):

9 *Plant and Equipment—Depreciation* 243

10 *Price-Level Adjustments* 308

11 *Long-Term Leases* 367

PART ONE

Introduction

CHAPTER ONE

Financial Reporting

Corporate financial statements disclose management's stewardship of the resources provided by stockholders, creditors, and by society itself. The increasing separation of corporate management and ownership has made financial statements essential for appraisals of management's actions by stockholders. In addition to stockholders, to whom public financial statements are primarily directed, a number of other parties rely extensively on such statements. Creditors base lending decisions on both the historic and projected financial statements of current and prospective borrowers. Potential stockholders use financial statements to estimate future corporate earnings and dividends. Government agencies use corporate financial statements for various tax and regulatory purposes and for analyzing economic trends. Labor unions examine such statements to establish a corporation's "ability to pay" increased wages.

According to modern concepts, business has an obligation to produce socially acceptable results from its activities. The right to do business is granted by society, and society will grant this right only so long as its best interests are served. The free-market mechanism of allocating society's limited resources receives guidance from the relative profitability of alternative goods and services. Financial statements facilitate resource allocation according to relative profitability.

TYPES OF FINANCIAL STATEMENTS

There are four basic types of financial statements: the income statement, the statement of retained earnings, the balance sheet, and the funds statement. The income statement discloses the amount of income or loss realized during an accounting period as measured by *matching* the revenues obtained from sales during the period and the expenses incurred to create these sales. The difference between these revenues and expenses represents an increase or decrease in assets resulting from operations as well as being the measure of income or loss for the period.

Assets derived from profitable operations increase the owners' equity and are legally available for distribution to owners. Such additions to the owners' equity and dividend distributions are disclosed in a second financial statement, the statement of retained earnings. This statement is also frequently used to disclose the results of various extraordinary or non-recurring transactions. Some accountants, who oppose this means of disclosure, believe that all revenue or expense items, whether attributable to normal operations or to extraordinary events, should be included in the income statement. This controversy is considered in Chapter 3.

The balance sheet is a *static* statement showing a corporation's financial position as of a specific date. It is usually divided into two parts, one part showing the assets, and the second part showing the three *sources of assets:* (a) creditors (liabilities), (b) owners (capital stock and other paid-in capital), and (c) the results of past operations (retained earnings).

The funds statement presents a summary of the firm's financial activities during a fiscal period. Among other things, it reflects transactions with creditors and owners which do not affect the income statement and are not readily apparent in the balance sheet. The form and content of this statement, as well as the definition of "funds," varies considerably. These differences and their significance are discussed in Chapter 4.

Of the four statements, the income statement is generally regarded as the most important because a record of past income is often a useful guide in forecasting future income. The balance sheet and the funds-flow statement are useful in estimating a corporation's ability to pay dividends and repay maturing debt.

GENERALLY ACCEPTED ACCOUNTING PRINCIPLES

The conventions followed in preparing financial statements are embodied in so-called "generally accepted accounting principles." While the American Institute of Certified Public Accountants and other professional bodies have published bulletins and monographs on generally accepted accounting principles, the acceptability of these principles does not follow from the authority of such groups. Rather, the authoritative status of these principles flows from their general acceptance and use by the business world in financial reporting.

The most influential pronouncements have been the Accounting Research Bulletins issued by the Committee on Accounting Procedure of the American Institute of Certified Public Accountants. Between 1939 and 1959, the committee issued 51 Accounting Research Bulletins in an endeavor "to narrow areas of difference and inconsistency in accounting practices, and to further the development and recognition of generally accepted accounting principles."[1] Many of these bulletins are reproduced in this book.

The bulletins of the Committee on Accounting Procedure are guides to appropriate accounting practice. The effective application of these guides requires a knowledge of accounting theory, an appreciation of the unique business characteristics of a particular corporation and its industry, and an understanding of the information needs of the major users of a corporation's financial statements. Application of principles without regard for these factors seldom leads to useful financial statements.

In the *Introduction* to Accounting Research Bulletin No. 43, a revision and restatement published in 1953 of the first 42 bulletins issued from 1939 through 1953, the Committee on Accounting Procedure stated:

Accounting and the Corporate System

1. Accounting is essential to the effective functioning of any business organization, particularly the corporate form. The test of the corporate system and of the special phase of it represented by corporate accounting ultimately lies in the results which are produced. These results must be judged from the standpoint of society as a whole—not merely from that of any one group of interested persons.

2. The uses to which the corporate system is put and the controls to which it is subject change from time to time, and all parts of the machinery must be adapted to meet changes as they occur. In the past fifty years there has been an increasing use of the corporate system for the purpose of converting into readily transferable form the ownership of large, complex, and more or less permanent business enterprises. This evolution has brought in its train certain uses of the processes of law and accounting which have led to the creation of new controls, revisions of the laws, and reconsideration of accounting procedures.

3. As a result of this development, the problems in the field of accounting have increasingly come to be considered from the standpoint of the buyer or seller of an interest in an enterprise, with consequent increased recognition of the significance of the income statement and a tendency to restrict narrowly charges and credits to surplus. The fairest possible presentation of periodic net income, with neither material overstatement nor understatement, is important, since the results of operations are significant not only to prospective buyers of an interest in the enterprise but also to prospective sellers. With

---

[1] Committee on Accounting Procedure, American Institute of Certified Public Accountants, *Restatement and Revision of Accounting Research Bulletins* (New York: The Institute, 1953), p. 8.

the increasing importance of the income statement there has been a tendency to regard the balance sheet as the connecting link between successive income statements; however this concept should not obscure the fact that the balance sheet has significant uses of its own.

4. This evolution has also led to a demand for a larger degree of uniformity in accounting. *Uniformity* has usually connoted similar treatment of the same item occurring in many cases, in which sense it runs the risk of concealing important differences among cases. Another sense of the word would require that different authorities working independently on the same case should reach the same conclusions. Although uniformity is a worthwhile goal, it should not be pursued to the exclusion of other benefits. Changes of emphasis and objective as well as changes in conditions under which business operates have led, and doubtless will continue to lead, to the adoption of new accounting procedures. Consequently diversity of practice may continue as new practices are adopted before old ones are completely discarded.

Applicability of Committee Opinions

5. The principal objective of the committee has been to narrow areas of difference and inconsistency in accounting practices, and to further the development and recognition of generally accepted accounting principles, through the issuance of opinions and recommendations that would serve as criteria for determining the suitability of accounting practices reflected in financial statements and representations of commercial and industrial companies. In this endeavor, the committee has considered the interpretation and application of such principles as appeared to it to be pertinent to particular accounting problems. The committee has not directed its attention to accounting problems or procedures of religious, charitable, scientific, educational, and similar non-profit institutions, municipalities, professional firms, and the like. Accordingly, except where there is a specific statement of a different intent by the committee, its opinions and recommendations are directed primarily to business enterprises organized for profit.

Voting Procedure in Adopting Opinions

6. The committee regards the representative character and general acceptability of its opinions as of the highest importance, and to that end has adopted the following procedures:

(a) Any opinion or recommendation before issuance is submitted in final form to all members of the committee either at a meeting or by mail.

(b) No such opinion or recommendation is issued unless it has received the approval of two-thirds of the entire committee.

(c) Any member of the committee dissenting from an opinion or recommendation issued under the preceding rule is entitled to have the fact of his dissent and his reasons therefor recorded in the document in which the opinion or recommendation is presented.

7. Before reaching its conclusions, the committee gives careful consideration to prior opinions, to prevailing practices, and to the views of professional and other bodies concerned with accounting procedures.

Authority of Opinions

8. Except in cases in which formal adoption by the Institute membership has been asked and secured, the authority of opinions reached by the com-

mittee rests upon their general acceptability. The committee recognizes that in extraordinary cases fair presentation and justice to all parties at interest may require exceptional treatment. But the burden of justifying departure from accepted procedures, to the extent that they are evidenced in committee opinions, must be assumed by those who adopt another treatment.

9. The committee contemplates that its opinions will have application only to items material and significant in the relative circumstances. It considers that items of little or no consequence may be dealt with as expediency may suggest. However, freedom to deal expediently with immaterial items should not extend to a group of items whose cumulative effect in any one financial statement may be material and significant.

Opinions Not Retroactive

10. No opinion issued by the committee is intended to have a retroactive effect unless it contains a statement of such intention. Thus an opinion will ordinarily have no application to a transaction arising prior to its publication, nor to transactions in process of completion at the time of publication. But while the committee considers it inequitable to make its statements retroactive, it does not wish to discourage the revision of past accounts in an individual case if it appears to be desirable in the circumstances.

The Company and Its Auditors

11. Underlying all committee opinions is the fact that the accounts of a company are primarily the responsibility of management. The responsibility of the auditor is to express his opinion concerning the financial statements and to state clearly such explanations, amplifications, disagreement, or disapproval as he deems appropriate. While opinions of the committee are addressed particularly to certified public accountants whose problem it is to decide what they may properly report, the committee recommends similar application of the procedures mentioned herein by those who prepare the accounts and financial statements.

In September, 1959, the Committee on Accounting Procedure was superseded by the Accounting Principles Board.[2] This new Institute group was formed to direct an expanded accounting research program and, from time to time, to issue pronouncements related to proper accounting practice. In its first three years, this new group had neither revised nor revoked any of the earlier committee's publications. The Accounting Principles Board has published, for discussion purposes only, the results of several of its research projects.[3]

Whether the Accounting Principles Board will enjoy the influence

---

[2] The Accounting Principles Board also superseded the Committee on Accounting Terminology, which between 1940 and 1957 issued a series of bulletins on accounting terminology.

[3] As of May, 1963, the following Accounting Research Studies had been published by the American Institute of Certified Public Accountants: No. 1, *The Basic Postulates of Accounting*, Maurice Moonitz; No. 2, *"Cash Flow" Analysis and the Funds Statement*, Perry Mason; No. 3, *A Tentative Set of Broad Accounting Principles for Business Enterprises*, Robert T. Sprouse and Maurice Moonitz; and No. 4, *Reporting of Leases in Financial Statements*, John H. Myers.

of the former Committee on Accounting Procedure remains to be seen. The board must cope with a basic controversy among accountants concerning the methods of applying accounting principles. Some accountants advocate that the board set forth an authoritative list of uniform accounting methods to apply in most cases, even where two or more acceptable alternatives now exist. These methods, it is proposed, would be binding on management and accountants alike. Supporters claim that greater accounting uniformity would facilitate comparison of corporations' financial statements.

Others question the wisdom of this approach on three counts. First, the Institute lacks authority to impose its will on management; second, such uniformity would lead to artificial and misleading results because the unique characteristics of each corporation would not be reflected in its financial statements; and, third, accounting flexibility is necessary for the development of accounting principles and practices appropriate to the ever-changing needs of the business world.

The United States Securities and Exchange Commission (SEC) has published a number of Accounting Series Releases. These apply only to financial statements *filed with the Commission.*[4] In general, the SEC has agreed with the opinions expressed in the Institute's Accounting Research Bulletins. Relations between the SEC and the Institute have been extremely close and cooperative. The American Accounting Association, the professional association of accounting teachers, has also issued a number of statements on accounting principles. Accounting principles and their relevance to the cases in this book are discussed in Chapter 2, *Underlying Concepts and Conventions.*

THE INDEPENDENT PUBLIC ACCOUNTANT'S REPORT

Financial statements prepared by management for stockholders, credit institutions, and regulatory agencies are often accompanied by the report of a certified public accountant. The Committee on Terminology of the American Institute of Certified Public Accountants described this report as follows:

The report (or certificate) of an independent accountant (or auditor) is a document in which he indicates the nature and scope of the examination (or audit) which he has made and expresses the opinion which he has formed in respect of the financial statements.[5]

---

[4] Companies having securities listed on a national securities exchange must file periodic financial statements with the SEC. With some exceptions, companies offering securities to the public must also file specified financial statements.

[5] Committee on Terminology, American Institute of Certified Public Accountants, *Accounting Terminology Bulletin* No. 1, p. 19.

One form of audit report reads as follows:

February 11, 1964

To the Stockholders and Board of Directors of Warren Corporation:

We have examined the balance sheet of Warren Corporation as of December 31, 1963 and the related statements of income and retained earnings for the year then ended. Our examination was made in accordance with generally accepted auditing standards, and accordingly included such tests of the accounting records and such other auditing procedures as we considered necessary in the circumstances.

In our opinion, the accompanying balance sheet and statements of income and retained earnings present fairly the financial position of Warren Corporation at December 31, 1963, and the results of its operations for the year then ended, in conformity with generally accepted accounting principles applied on a basis consistent with that of the preceding year.

D. Clark & Co.
Certified Public Accountants

The first paragraph in this form of audit report describes the *scope* of the auditor's examination, while the second paragraph contains his *opinion* of the financial statements. The auditor's report adds credibility to management's financial statements. This credibility flows from the public's confidence that certified public accountants, as professionally trained experts, are independent, dependable, thorough, and objective.

An independent auditor may render one of four types of opinions on the financial statements. He may give an *unqualified opinion,* as in the example above, indicating that the statements present fairly the corporation's financial position and the results of its operations. A *qualified opinion* is sometimes given. The auditor's examination may be narrower in scope than he believes appropriate, but still sufficient for him to express a partial opinion. In this case, he should describe any limitations in his examination in the "scope" paragraph and indicate the effect of such limitations on his opinion in the second paragraph. Similarly, if the auditor decides that management's financial statements are not prepared "in conformity with generally accepted accounting principles" or "on a basis consistent with that of the preceding year," he is obligated to note such variations and describe their effect on the financial statements. In these cases, the auditor is said to have qualified his opinion or taken an exception. Such a qualification or exception does not necessarily indicate the auditor's disapproval. The corporation may have merely changed from one acceptable accounting practice to another acceptable practice. For this reason, auditors often give some expression of approval such as "in which we concur," "which we approve," or "to an acceptable alternative method."

A third possibility is the so-called *disclaimer of opinion.* This is a positive denial of an opinion by the auditor because he cannot determine the effect, which he believes to be material, of variations from generally accepted accounting principles, inconsistencies in the application of accounting principles, or limitations in the scope of his audit.

Finally, the independent auditor may express an *adverse opinion* and state that the financial statements *do not* present fairly the company's financial position or the results of its operations in conformity with generally accepted accounting principles. If the auditor has an adverse opinion, he should state it rather than disclaim any opinion.

THE USE OF CASES

This book consists of cases and related text material. The cases focus on controversial topics such as accounting for income taxes, business combinations, stock options, pensions, long-term leases and other areas in which the application of accounting principles is difficult. The study of such cases develops judgment and perspective in applying and interpreting accounting principles.

The cases present examples of one or more financial reporting practices used by *particular* corporations. Every corporation is a unique organization with its own peculiar characteristics—products, industry, management, owners, and prospects. The reader should consider the appropriateness of the accounting practices employed in each of these unique case examples. Hopefully, these cases will help the reader develop an appreciation of the usefulness and limitations of financial reporting.

REFERENCES

Anreder, Steven S., "Pitfalls for the Unwary," *Barron's*, 42 (Dec. 24, 1962), 3 ff.

Barr, Andrew, "Accountants and the Securities and Exchange Commission," *Journal of Accountancy*, 113 (Apr. 1962), 31–37.

_____, "Financial Reporting for Regulatory Agencies," *Journal of Accountancy*, 105 (Feb. 1958), 26–32.

Bedford, Norton M., "Accounting Measurements of Economic Concepts," *Journal of Accountancy*, 103 (May 1957), 56–62.

Bevis, Herman W., "The Accounting Function in Economic Progress," *Journal of Accountancy*, 106 (Aug. 1958), 27–34.

_____, "The CPA's Attest Function in Modern Society," *Journal of Accountancy*, 113 (Feb. 1962), 28–35.

Blough, Carman G., "Challenges to the Accounting Profession in the United States," *Journal of Accountancy*, 108 (Dec. 1959), 37–42.

_____, "Responsibility to Third Parties," *Journal of Accountancy*, 109 (May 1960), 58–65.

Brundage, Percival F., "Milestones on the Path of Accounting," *Harvard Business Review*, 29 (Jul. 1951), 71–81.

_____, "Roadblocks in the Path of Accounting," *Harvard Business Review*, 29 (Sept. 1951), 110–19.

Cannon, Arthur M., "Accounting as a Social Force," *Journal of Accountancy*, 99 (Mar. 1955), 60–66.

Carey, John L., "The Place of the CPA in Contemporary Society," *Journal of Accountancy*, 106 (Sept. 1958), 27–32.

Crane, Nicholas E., "A Security Analyst Looks at Annual Reports," *Journal of Accountancy*, 105 (Mar. 1958), 31–36.

Dohr, James L., "What They (Economists) Say About Us (Accountants)," *Journal of Accountancy*, 96 (Aug. 1953), 167–75.

Eaton, Marquis G., "Financial Reporting in a Changing Society," *Journal of Accountancy*, 104 (Aug. 1957), 25–31.

_____, "What Is an Accountant?" *Journal of Accountancy*, 99 (Feb. 1955), 46–51.

Higgins, Thomas G., "Professional Ethics: A Time for Reappraisal," *Journal of Accountancy*, 113 (Mar. 1962), 29–35.

_____, "Professional Ethics and Public Opinion," *Journal of Accountancy*, 106 (Nov. 1958), 34–39.

Jennings, Alvin R., "Accounting Research," *Accounting Review*, 33 (Oct. 1958), 547–54.

Knauth, Oswald W., "An Executive Looks at Accountancy," *Journal of Accountancy*, 103 (Jan. 1957), 29–32.

May, George O., "Income Accounting and Social Revolution," *Journal of Accountancy*, 103 (Jun. 1957), 36–41.

_____, "Retrospect and Prospect," *Journal of Accountancy*, 112 (Jul. 1961), 31–36.

Pillsbury, Wilbur F., "Organized Labor's Views of Corporate Financial Information," *Journal of Accountancy*, 105 (Jun. 1958), 46–56.

Powell, Weldon, "Report on the Accounting Research Activities of the American Institute of Certified Public Accountants," *Accounting Review*, 36 (Jan. 1961), 26–31.

Seidman, J. S., "What is the Future of the Accounting Profession?" *Journal of Accountancy*, 107 (Mar. 1959), 29–36.

Smith, L. Hartley, "A Security Analyst Looks at Financial Statements," *Journal of Accountancy*, 108 (Aug. 1959), 37–41.

A Symposium, "What's Wrong With Financial Reporting?" *Journal of Accountancy*, 112 (Aug. 1961), 28–33. A Symposium of views on financial reporting presented at the 1960 annual meeting of the American Institute of Certified Public Accountants.

Werntz, William W., "Accountant's Responsibility in Reporting Corporate Profits," *Journal of Accountancy*, 107 (Mar. 1959), 42–49.

West, Phillip L., "The Reporting of Earnings to Stockholders," *Journal of Accountancy*, 107 (Feb. 1959), 27–32.

Wise, T. A., "The Auditors Have Arrived," *Fortune*, 62 (Nov. 1960), 151 ff.; (Dec. 1960), 144 ff.

CHAPTER TWO

Underlying Concepts and Conventions

A basic accounting framework has evolved to facilitate communication between the compilers and the users of financial statements. Without such a framework, reliance on financial statements would be virtually impossible unless each user had extensive knowledge of the assumptions and procedures used by each compiler.

The basic framework of accounting is not static; it is still developing. There are numerous controversies among accountants concerning some aspects of this framework. Many of the cases in this book focus on these controversies. There is also disagreement concerning the terminology used to describe this framework. Terms such as *concepts, conventions, postulates, principles, assumptions, standards, doctrines, propositions,* and others are used in accounting literature.

The term "principles" appears in a number of the Accounting Research Bulletins issued between 1939 and 1959 by the Committee on Accounting Procedure of the American Institute of Certified Public Accountants. In keeping with its name, this committee made recommendations applicable to specific *accounting procedures,* such as accounting for inventories or intangibles. The committee did not formally consider whether there are broad principles which form a foundation or framework underlying all accounting.

Since 1934, "principles" has appeared in the usual form of auditor's report, which states that a corporation's financial statements present fairly its financial position and results of operations "in conformity with generally accepted accounting principles." Here, also, "principles" refers primarily to generally accepted procedures or practices rather than to any broad underlying concepts and conventions.

In contrast to the emphasis of the Committee on Accounting Procedure on specific problems, committees of the American Accounting Association have issued several statements dealing with the basic foundation or framework of accounting. These are: *A Tentative Statement of Accounting Principles Underlying Corporate Financial Statements* (1936), *Accounting Principles Underlying Corporate Financial Statements* (1941), *Accounting Concepts* and *Standards Underlying Corporate Financial Statements* (1948), and *Accounting and Reporting Standards for Corporate Financial Statements* (1957).[1] It is interesting to note the changes in the titles of these four statements. Only the first two, issued in 1936 and 1941, included the term "principles." As accounting "principles" acquired a narrower meaning, closer to that of accounting procedures or practices, later American Accounting Association committees dropped "principles" in favor of "concepts and standards," used in the title of the 1948 statement, and "standards" only, used in the 1957 report. Notice, also, that the title of the 1957 statement refers to both *accounting* and *reporting* standards.

The Institute's new Accounting Principles Board has sponsored two research studies dealing with basic accounting postulates and broad accounting principles.[2,3] These studies, which have been published for discussion purposes only, do not represent the official position of the Accounting Principles Board.

The remainder of this chapter consists of comments on twelve underlying or basic accounting concepts and conventions. Since these concepts and conventions are more easily seen in real situations, such as in the cases described in later chapters, the comments in this chapter are very brief. The author claims no authority for this list. Some accountants might expand it, while others would probably delete or combine some items. Also, the author has made no attempt to distinguish among postulates, principles, concepts, conventions or the numerous other terms used in describing the basic framework or foundation of accounting.

---

[1] All of these statements appear in *Accounting and Reporting Standards for Corporate Financial Statements and Preceding Statements and Supplements* (Columbus, Ohio: American Accounting Association, 1957).

[2] Maurice Moonitz, *The Basic Postulates of Accounting*, Accounting Research Study No. 1 (New York: American Institute of Certified Public Accountants, 1961). The Summary, Conclusions and Recommendations of this Accounting Research Study were reprinted in the *Journal of Accountancy*, 112 (Nov. 1961), 71-72.

[3] Robert T. Sprouse and Maurice Moonitz, *A Tentative Set of Broad Accounting Principles for Business Enterprises*, Accounting Research Study No. 3 (New York: American Institute of Certified Public Accountants, 1962). The Summary of this Accounting Research Study was reprinted in the *Journal of Accountancy*, 113 (May 1962), 61-63.

THE ACCOUNTING ENTITY

The accountant regards a business as a separate unit or entity, distinct and apart from its owners and other suppliers of capital. Accounting transactions are analyzed from the viewpoint of the business entity; it is the center of attention. Financial statements present the entity's operating results and financial position, not those of stockholders, partners, proprietors, creditors or other interested parties. Assets devoted to business purposes are regarded as entity assets, and claims against the business as entity liabilities. Similarly, revenue and expense transactions and any resulting income or loss are associated with the entity. Owners do not realize such income until it is distributed to them from the accounting entity.

Occasionally problems arise in defining the limits of an accounting entity. For example, useful financial statements may often be developed by treating two or more corporations subject to common control or ownership as a single accounting entity. Such financial statements, known as consolidated statements, are discussed in Chapter 5.

Another problem involving the entity concept may occur when two corporations combine. A combination may result in the survival of one or both of the combining entities, or the creation of an entirely new entity. The significant accounting implications of these possible results are considered in Chapter 16, *Business Combinations*.

CONTINUITY OF OPERATIONS

In the absence of contrary evidence, the life of an accounting entity is assumed to be indefinite. This assumption, often called the going-concern concept, conforms to the usual expectations of business owners and managers; possible liquidation is not the usual expectation.

A number of common accounting practices derive their justification from the going-concern concept. Examples are found in accounting for various long-lived assets whose services are normally rendered through future *use* rather than through *liquidation*. Continuity of operations is assumed whenever the useful life of such assets is estimated in calculating depreciation or amortization.

MONEY MEASUREMENT

Accounting is concerned only with those events which can be measured in terms of money. Money is the *common denominator* of accounting.

Many accountants contend that money measurements are often defective because changes in the relative value of the monetary unit itself make it an unsatisfactory common denominator. Frequent challenges have been made to the use of money as the standard of accounting measurement, particularly during the period of inflation since World War II. These challenges are considered in Chapter 10, *Price-Level Adjustments.*

THE FISCAL PERIOD

The ultimate success of a business unit can be determined only after it ceases to exist. However, periodic "test readings" of an entity's progress and its financial status are needed by management, owners, creditors, taxing authorities and other interested parties. Such "test readings" are usually made at least once a year. In addition to annual, audited financial statements, many companies issue interim statements to their stockholders, usually at quarterly intervals. For internal management purposes, even shorter accounting periods of a week or a month are often used.

The periodic financial statements of most business entities are of a *tentative* or *provisional* character. Financial statements are usually based upon an assumed course of future events involving such uncertainties as the collectibility of receivables, the salability of inventory, or the future usefulness of plant and equipment.

Periodic financial statements are especially difficult to prepare for long-term contractors whose work on buildings, highways, dams, ships, power stations and other projects may extend over several fiscal periods. These accounting problems are discussed in Chapter 7, *Revenue and Income Recognition.*

VERIFIABLE, OBJECTIVE EVIDENCE

Accounting is based upon verifiable, objective evidence. This underlying convention, which implies a high degree of reliability in accounting data, obviously cannot be applied in an absolute sense. For example, there is no completely objective way of determining the probable life of an asset or the most appropriate depreciation method.

As used by the accountant, "objective" means free from personal bias. Objective evidence has been defined as "impersonal and external to the person most concerned in contrast with that person's unsupported opinion or desire."[4]

---

[4] W.A. Paton and A.C. Littleton, *An Introduction to Corporate Accounting Standards* (Chicago: American Accounting Association, 1940).

Accounting data which are objectively determined are usually verifiable. That is, their accuracy or fairness can be determined or tested by examining documents such as invoices and cancelled checks. Sometimes the judgment of an independent expert, such as an actuary, is required in verifying accounting data.

A fascinating, unsolved problem concerns the place of index numbers in establishing verifiable, objective evidence for accounting purposes. Accounting has accepted the use of index numbers in one situation, while rejecting their use in another. These contradictory attitudes towards index numbers are considered in Chapter 8, *Inventories*, and Chapter 10, *Price-Level Adjustments*.

THE COST BASIS

The acquisition cost of an asset is generally an objective amount, readily verified. Cost data are usually the result of market transactions, sometimes called "arm's-length" transactions. Assets are recorded initially at cost and subsequent accounting is based upon this initial cost. No attempt is normally made to reflect later changes in market values. Depreciation, for example, represents allocation of original cost, not an attempt to recognize current market values. An apparent exception to the accountant's general reliance on cost is found in the lower of cost or market rule applied to inventories. Supporters of this rule, which is discussed in Chapter 8, *Inventories*, contend that it is not inconsistent with the cost concept.

REALIZATION

The term "realization" is customarily used by accountants in reference to revenue, although it may refer to earnings, losses, expenses, assets, or liabilities. Revenue is usually considered realized, and consequently recognized in the accounts, at the time of a sale. At this time the amount of revenue can be objectively determined and verified.

Under an alternative approach used in accounting for some long-term construction contracts extending over two or more fiscal periods, revenue is recognized from time to time in accordance with estimated progress towards completion of a contract. This departure from the point of sale as the appropriate time to recognize revenue is rejected in most other instances because there is no comparable assurance concerning ultimate salability.

In contrast to long-term construction contracts, where the point of sale is often considered *too late* for revenue realization, the point of sale is considered *too early* in other instances. Examples of the latter situation may occur in accounting for various types of installment sales.

Long-term construction contracts, installment sales, and other problems in accounting for revenue are considered in Chapter 7, *Revenue and Income Recognition.*

MATCHING COSTS AND REVENUES

Many accountants consider the periodic matching of costs and revenues as the most fundamental concept of accounting. The end result of such a matching is, of course, net income or earnings. Despite constant warnings from accountants concerning the tentative and uncertain nature of earnings data, such data are understandably of great interest to all parties concerned with corporate financial affairs.

Under ideal conditions, all costs would be identified with some element of revenue. This ideal is often impractical, or even impossible, and many costs must be assigned or allocated to the fiscal period rather than to elements of revenue. The assignment of some costs to specific fiscal periods may be extremely difficult. An example is accounting for research and development costs.

Appropriate matching of costs and revenues usually requires use of the *accrual method* of accounting instead of the *cash method.* Under the accrual method, the actual receipts and disbursements of cash do not affect the measurement of revenues and expenses; the receipt of cash may precede or follow the realization of revenue, while the disbursement of cash may precede or follow the incurrence of an expense. The distinction between the two methods occasionally becomes hazy. A current example is accounting for pension costs where the amount of *cash* disbursed during a fiscal period is often treated as pension expense, even though this amount differs significantly from the amount which would be recorded under the accrual method. This problem is considered in Chapter 14, *Pensions.*

CONSERVATISM

The concept of conservatism, while still widely acknowledged in accounting, has diminished in importance. This concept was formerly applied to balance-sheet valuations by minimizing assets and maximizing liabilities with little regard for related income statement effects. Since the early 1930's, greater emphasis has been given to the income statement as the prime indicator of earning capacity, and it is now generally accepted that "conservative" balance-sheet accounting in one fiscal period may lead to "unconservative" income statements in subsequent periods. For example, a write-down of assets subject to depreciation or amortization, made simply to achieve a "conservative" balance sheet, will reduce current earnings (unless the write-down is charged against retained earnings), but will increase future earnings through lower depreciation or amortization charges.

The concept of conservatism is used today as a guide. For example, if an accountant must select from one of two acceptable alternatives, he will normally choose the more conservative one. In the case of a going concern, conservatism should play a minor role in most accounting decisions.

CONSISTENCY

The importance of the consistency standard in accounting is indicated by specific reference to it in the customary form of auditor's report, which states that the financial statements present fairly a corporation's financial position and the results of its operations "in conformity with generally accepted accounting principles applied on a basis consistent with that of the preceding year."

A material change between fiscal periods in the accounting principles employed, or in the method of their application, must be described in the auditor's report with an indication of the effect of such a change on the financial statements. The latter information may be given either in the auditor's report or in a note to the financial statements cited in the auditor's report. While the consistency standard facilitates comparison of successive periods' financial statements, lack of comparability may arise for other reasons. For example, the nature of the business may change because of the sale of an important operating division. Such a change, since it does not involve the application of generally accepted accounting principles, would not be noted in the auditor's report. However, the standard of full disclosure, as discussed below, might well require a note to the financial statements describing such a transaction.

FULL DISCLOSURE

The concept or standard of full disclosure, which has been receiving increasing attention, holds that management should disclose all significant financial data on the premise that an informed person will not be misled. Since corporate financial statements are directed primarily to stockholders, the information needs of existing and potential stockholders are considered paramount in applying the concept of full disclosure.

Some areas, considered later in this book, in which important questions of disclosure arise include long-term leases, stock options and business combinations.

MATERIALITY

The concept of materiality is closely related to several of the preceding concepts and conventions. As stated by the Committee on Accounting Procedure in the *Introduction* to its Accounting Research Bulletins, "items of little or no consequence may be dealt with as expediency may suggest."[5]

A problem often arises, however, in determining what is an immaterial item. This is entirely a matter of professional judgment. Questions concerning materiality occur in a number of the cases in this book. In each instance, the reader should ask himself if the decisions of a reasonable person, particularly investment decisions, might have been influenced by different accounting for the item in question.

CONFLICTING CONCEPTS AND CONVENTIONS

Identifying the relevant concepts or conventions in a particular situation is often comparatively easy. The real problem frequently lies in determining which of two or more relevant, but conflicting, concepts or conventions has governing priority. This problem is encountered in many of the cases in this book.

REFERENCES

American Accounting Association, Committee on Accounting Concepts and Standards, "Accounting and Reporting Standards for Corporate Financial Statements—1957 Revision," *Accounting Review*, 32 (Oct. 1957), 536–46. This statement also appears in *Accounting and Reporting Standards for Corporate Financial Statements and Preceding Statements and Supplements.* Columbus, Ohio: American Accounting Association, 1957.

Andersen, Arthur, & Co., *The Postulate of Accounting—What It Is, How It Is Determined, How It Should Be Used.* Chicago: Arthur Andersen & Co., 1960.

"The Approach to Accounting Principles," (Editorial) *Journal of Accountancy*, 113 (May 1962), 37–38.

---

[5] See paragraph 9 on page 7.

Arnett, Harold E., "What Does 'Objectivity' Mean to Accountants?" *Journal of Accountancy*, 111 (May 1961), 63–68.

Bastable, C. W., "Tomorrow's Accounting?" *Journal of Accountancy*, 107 (Jun. 1959), 52–58.

Bevis, Herman W., "Riding Herd on Accounting Standards," *Accounting Review*, 36 (Jan. 1961), 9–16.

Blough, Carman G., "Principles and Procedures," *Journal of Accountancy*, 111 (Apr. 1961), 51–53.

Bordner, H. W., "Fund Concepts as Accounting Postulates," *Journal of Accountancy*, 112 (Jul. 1961), 52–60.

Bows, Albert J., "The Urgent Need for Accounting Reforms," *N. A. A. Bulletin*, 42 (Sept. 1960), section 1, 43–52.

Broad, Samuel J., "The Applicability of Generally Accepted Accounting Principles," *Journal of Accountancy*, 104 (Sept. 1957), 31–37.

Cannon, Arthur M., "Discussion Notes on 'The Basic Postulates of Accounting,'" *Journal of Accountancy*, 113 (Feb. 1962), 42–53.

Catlett, George R., "Factors that Influence Accounting Principles," *Journal of Accountancy*, 110 (Oct. 1960), 44–50.

_____, "Relation of Acceptance to Accounting Principles," *Journal of Accountancy*, 109 (Mar. 1960), 33–38.

Corbin, Donald A., "The Revolution in Accounting," *Accounting Review*, 37 (Oct. 1962), 626–35.

Dein, Raymond C., "The Future Development of Accounting Theory," *Accounting Review*, 33 (Jul. 1958), 389–400.

Gaa, Charles J., "Uniformity in Accounting 'Principles,'" *Journal of Accountancy*, 111 (Apr. 1961), 47–51.

Grady, Paul, "The Quest for Accounting Principles," *Journal of Accountancy*, 113 (May 1962), 45–50.

Heaton, Herbert, "'Postulates and Principles'—Unsupported and Unrestrained," *New York Certified Public Accountant*, 32 (Oct. 1962), 658–64.

Herrick, Anson, "A Review of the Work of the Accounting Procedure Committee," *Journal of Accountancy*, 98 (Nov. 1954), 627–38.

Hicks, Ernest L., "Materiality: A Useful Audit Tool," *Journal of Accountancy*, 114 (Jul. 1962), 63–67.

Hylton, Delmer P., "Current Trends in Accounting Theory," *Accounting Review*, 37 (Jan. 1962), 22–27.

_____, "Some Comments on Materiality," *Journal of Accountancy*, 112 (Sept. 1961), 61–64.

Jennings, Alvin R., "Present-Day Challenges in Financial Reporting," *Journal of Accountancy*, 105 (Jan. 1958), 28–34.

_____, "International Standards of Accounting and Auditing," *Journal of Accountancy*, 114 (Sept. 1962), 36–42.

Kelley, Arthur C., "Comments on the 1957 Revision of Corporate Accounting and Reporting Standards," *Accounting Review*, 33 (Apr. 1958), 214–15.

Kraayenhof, Jacob, "International Challenges for Accounting," *Journal of Accountancy*, 109 (Jan. 1960), 34–38.

Lawrence, Charles and Floyd Windal, "Audit Opinions and Accounting Principles—A Problem of Alternatives," *New York Certified Public Accountant*, 32 (Sept. 1962), 597–99.

Leonard, W. G., "Comments on 'Accounting and Reporting Standards for Corporate Financial Statements—1957 Revision,'" *Accounting Review*, 33 (Jul. 1958), 401–2.

Lewis, Charles A., Jr., "Are There 'Principles' of Accounting?" *Accounting Review*, 34 (Apr. 1959), 239–41.

Littleton, A. C., "The Search for Accounting Principles," *New York Certified Public Accountant*, 28 (Apr. 1958), 247–56.

Mautz, R. K., "The 1957 Statement of Accounting and Reporting Standards," *Accounting Review*, 32 (Oct. 1957), 547–53.

May, George O., "Generally Accepted Principles of Accounting," *Journal of Accountancy*, 105 (Jan. 1958), 23–27.

Moonitz, Maurice, *The Basic Postulates of Accounting*, Accounting Research Study No. 1. New York: American Institute of Certified Public Accountants, 1961. The Summary, Conclusions and Recommendations of this Accounting Research Study were reprinted in the *Journal of Accountancy*, 112 (Nov. 1961), 71–72.

Moonitz, Maurice and Carl L. Nelson, "Recent Developments in Accounting Theory," *Accounting Review*, 35 (Apr. 1960), 206–17.

Nielsen, Oswald, "New Challenges in Accounting," *Accounting Review*, 35 (Oct. 1960), 583–89.

Odmark, V. E., "Current Challenges to Accounting Principles," *Accounting Review*, 35 (Apr. 1960), 272–77.

Peloubet, Maurice E., "Is Further Uniformity Desirable or Possible?" *Journal of Accountancy*, 111 (Apr. 1961), 35–41.

Powell, Weldon, "The Challenge to Research," *Journal of Accountancy*, 109 (Feb. 1960), 34–41.

Queenan, John W., "Postulates: Their Place in Accounting Research," *Journal of Accountancy*, 114 (Aug. 1962), 29–33.

———, "The Process of Developing Accepted Accounting Standards," *Journal of Accountancy*, 98 (Jul. 1954), 58–65.

Raby, William L., "The Two Faces of Accounting," *Accounting Review*, 34 (Jul. 1959), 452–61.

Research Division of the American Institute of Certified Public Accountants, "Comments on 'The Basic Postulates of Accounting'" (Accounting Research Study No. 1), *Journal of Accountancy*, 115 (Jan. 1963), 44–55.

Spacek, Leonard, "Are Accounting Principles Generally Accepted?" *Journal of Accountancy*, 111 (Apr. 1961), 41–46.

_____, "Can We Define Generally Accepted Accounting Principles?" *Journal of Accountancy*, 106 (Dec. 1958), 40–47.

_____, "Challenge to Public Accounting," *Harvard Business Review*, 36 (May-June 1958), 115–24.

_____, "The Need for an Accounting Court," *Accounting Review*, 33 (Jul. 1958), 368–79.

Sprouse, Robert T. and Maurice Moonitz, *A Tentative Set of Broad Accounting Principles for Business Enterprises*, Accounting Research Study No. 3. New York: American Institute of Certified Public Accountants, 1962. The Summary of this Accounting Research Study was reprinted in the *Journal of Accountancy*, 113 (May 1962), 61–63.

Staubus, George J., "Comments on 'Accounting and Reporting Standards for Corporate Financial Statements—1957 Revision,'" *Accounting Review*, 33 (Jan. 1958), 11–24.

"Uniformity and Flexibility " (Editorial), *Journal of Accountancy*, 111 (Apr. 1961), 33–34.

Vatter, William J., "Another Look at the 1957 Statement," *Accounting Review*, 37 (Oct. 1962), 660–69.

Werntz, William W., "Accounting in Transition: The Statements Sponsored by the American Accounting Association," *Journal of Accountancy*, 105 (Feb. 1958), 33–36.

_____, "Dilemmas in Today's Reporting," *Journal of Accountancy*, 100 (Nov. 1955), 44–50.

PART TWO

Financial Statements

CHAPTER THREE

Income Statement and Balance Sheet

From 1940 until it was superseded by the Accounting Principles Board in 1959, the Committee on Accounting Procedure issued several bulletins dealing with the presentation of financial information. These included bulletins on *Income and Earned Surplus*, *Form of Statements*, *Earnings per Share*, and *Working Capital*.

Net income and related earnings per share have assumed increasing significance in our society as many millions of people have acquired a direct or indirect interest in corporate affairs as owners, employees, and creditors. While accountants are fully aware of the growing public need for reliable financial information, they have faced an increasing number of problems in measuring the operating results of a modern, dynamic corporation with the degree of precision assumed by many businessmen and investors. Many of these contemporary accounting problems are considered in this book.

INCOME STATEMENT

There are two main types of income statements, classified according to the items included in net income: (1) the all-inclusive type, and (2) the current operating performance type. The distinction between these two types and the advantages and disadvantages of each are discussed in Chapter 8, *Income and Earned Surplus*, of Accounting Research Bulletin No. 43, issued in June, 1953. This chapter, which brought together three separate bulletins issued between 1947 and 1951, follows:

1. The purpose of this chapter is to recommend criteria for use in identifying material extraordinary charges and credits which may in

some cases and should in other cases be excluded from the determination of net income and to recommend methods of presenting these charges and credits.

2. In dealing with the problem of selecting the most useful form of income statement, the danger of understatement or overstatement of income must be recognized. An important objective of income presentation should be the avoidance of any practice that leads to income equalization.

3. Attention is directed to certain facts which serve to emphasize that the word *income* is used to describe a general concept, not a specific and precise thing, and that the income statement is based on the concept of the *going concern*. It is at best an interim report. Profits are not fundamentally the result of operations during any short period of time. Allocations to fiscal periods of both charges and credits affecting the determination of net income are, in part, estimated and conventional and based on assumptions as to future events which may be invalidated by experience. While the items of which this is true are usually few in relation to the total number of transactions, they sometimes are large in relation to the other amounts in the income statement.

4. It must also be recognized that the ultimate distinction between *operating* income and charges and *non-operating* gains and losses, terms having considerable currency in the accounting profession, has not been established. The former are generally defined as recurrent features of business operation, more or less normal and dependable in their incidence from year to year; the latter are generally considered to be irregular and unpredictable, more or less fortuitous and incidental. The committee is also mindful that the term *net income* has been used indiscriminately and often without precise, and most certainly without uniform, definition in the financial press, investment services, annual reports, prospectuses, contracts relating to compensation of management, bond indentures, preferred stock dividend provisions, and many other places.

5. In the committee's view, the above facts with respect to the income statement and the income which it displays make it incumbent upon readers of financial statements to exercise great care at all times in drawing conclusions from them.

6. The question of what constitutes the most practically useful concept of income for the year is one on which there is much difference of opinion. On the one hand, net income is defined according to a strict proprietary concept by which it is presumed to be determined by the inclusion of all items affecting the net increase in proprietorship during the period except dividend distributions and capital transactions. The form of presentation which gives effect to this broad concept of net income has sometimes been designated the *all-inclusive* income statement. On the other hand, a different concept places its principal emphasis upon relationship of items to the operations, and to the year, excluding from the determination of net income any material extraordinary items which are not so related or which, if included, would impair the significance of net income so that misleading inferences might be drawn therefrom. This latter concept would require the income statement to be designed on what might be called a *current operating performance* basis, because its chief purpose is to aid those primarily interested in what a company was able to earn under the operating conditions of the period covered by the statement.

7. Proponents of the *all-inclusive* type of income statement insist that annual income statements taken for the life of an enterprise should, when added together, represent total net income. They emphasize the dangers of possible manipulation of the annual earnings figure if material extraordinary items

may be omitted in the determination of income. They also assert that, over a period of years, charges resulting from extraordinary events tend to exceed the credits, and the omission of such items has the effect of indicating a greater earning performance than the corporation actually has exhibited. They insist that an income statement which includes all income charges or credits arising during the year is simple to prepare, is easy to understand, and is not subject to variations resulting from the different judgments that may be applied in the treatment of individual items. They argue that when judgment is allowed to enter the picture with respect to the inclusion or exclusion of special items, material differences in the treatment of borderline cases develop and that there is danger that the use of *distortion* as a criterion may be a means of accomplishing the equalization of income. With full disclosure of the nature of any special or extraordinary items, this group believes the user of the financial statements can make his own additions or deductions more effectively than can the management or the independent accountant.

8. Those who favor the *all-inclusive* income statement largely assume that those supporting the *current operating performance* concept are mainly concerned with establishing a figure of net income for the year which will carry an implication as to future earning capacity. Having made this assumption, they contend that income statements should not be prepared on the *current operating performance* basis because income statements of the past are of only limited help in the forecasting of the earning power of an enterprise. This group also argues that items reflecting the results of unusual or extraordinary events are part of the earnings history of the company, and accordingly should be given weight in any effort to make financial judgments with respect to the company. Since a judgment as to the financial affairs of an enterprise should involve a study of the results of a period of prior years, rather than of a single year, this group believes that the omission of material extraordinary items from annual income statements is undesirable since there would be a greater tendency for those items to be overlooked in such a study.

9. On the other hand, those who advocate the *current operating performance* type of income statement generally do so because they are mindful of the particular business significance which a substantial number of the users of financial reports attach to the income statement. They point out that, while some users of financial reports are able to analyze a statement and eliminate from it those unusual and extraordinary items that tend to distort it for their purposes, many users are not trained to do so. Furthermore, they contend, it is difficult at best to report in any financial statement sufficient data to afford a sound basis upon which the reader who does not have an intimate knowledge of the facts can make a well-considered classification. They consider it self-evident that management and the independent auditors are in a better position than outsiders to determine whether there are unusual and extraordinary items which, if included in the determination of net income, may give rise to misleading inferences as to current operating performance. Relying on the proper exercise of professional judgment, they discount the contention that neither managements nor the independent auditors, because of the absence of objective standards to guide them, have been able to decide consistently which extraordinary charges and credits should be excluded in determining earning performance. They agree it is hazardous to place too great a reliance on the net income as shown in a single annual statement and insist that a realistic presentation of current performance must be taken for what it is and should not be construed as conveying an implication as to future accomplishments. The net income of a single year is only one of

scores of factors involved in analyzing the future earnings prospects or potentialities of a business. It is well recognized that future earnings are dependent to a large extent upon such factors as market trends, product developments, political events, labor relationships, and numerous other factors not ascertainable from the financial statements. However, this group insists that the net income for the year should show as clearly as possible what happened in that year under that year's conditions, in order that sound comparisons may be made with prior years and with the performance of other companies.

10. The advocates of this *current operating performance* type of statement join fully with the so-called *all-inclusive* group in asserting that there should be full disclosure of all material charges or credits of an unusual character, including those attributable to a prior year, but they insist that disclosure should be made in such manner as not to distort the figure which represents what the company was able to earn from its usual or typical business operations under the conditions existing during the year. They point out that many companies, in order to give more useful information concerning their earning performance, make a practice of restating the earnings of a number of prior years after adjusting them to reflect the proper allocation of items not related to the years in which they were first reported. They believe that material extraordinary charges or credits may often best be disclosed as direct adjustments of surplus. They point out that a charge or credit in a material amount representing an unusual item not likely to recur, if included in the computation of annual net income, may be so distorting in its results as to lead to unsound judgments with respect to the current earning performance of the company.

11. The committee has indicated elsewhere[1] that in its opinion it is plainly desirable that over the years all profits and losses of a business be reflected in net income, but at the same time has recognized that, under appropriate circumstances, it is proper to exclude certain material charges and credits from the determination of the net income of a single year, even though they clearly affect the cumulative total of income for a series of years. In harmony with this view, **it is the opinion of the committee that there should be a general presumption that all items of profit and loss recognized during the period are to be used in determining the figure reported as net income. The only possible exception to this presumption relates to items which in the aggregate are material in relation to the company's net income and are clearly not identifiable with or do not result from the usual or typical business operations of the period.** Thus, only extraordinary items such as the following may be excluded from the determination of net income for the year, and they should be excluded when their inclusion would impair the significance of net income so that misleading inferences might be drawn therefrom:[2]

(a) Material charges or credits (other than ordinary adjustments of a recurring nature) specifically related to operations of prior years, such as the elimination of unused reserves provided in prior years and adjustments of income taxes for prior years;

(b) Material charges or credits resulting from unusual sales of assets not acquired for resale and not of the type in which the company generally deals;

(c) Material losses of a type not usually insured against, such as those

---

[1] See Chapter 2 (b), paragraph 3 [p. 33].

[2] See Chapter 10 (b) with respect to the allocation of income taxes [pp. 123-27].

resulting from wars, riots, earthquakes, and similar calamities or catastrophes except where such losses are a recurrent hazard of the business;

(d) The write-off of a material amount of intangibles;[3]

(e) The write-off of material amounts of unamortized bond discount or premium and bond issue expenses at the time of the retirement or refunding of the debt before maturity.

12. The following, however, should be excluded from the determination of net income under all circumstances:

(a) Adjustments resulting from transactions in the company's own capital stock;

(b) Amounts transferred to and from accounts properly designated as surplus appropriations, such as charges and credits with respect to general purpose contingency reserves;

(c) Amounts deemed to represent excessive costs of fixed assets, and annual appropriations in contemplation of replacement of productive facilities at higher price levels;[4] and

(d) Adjustments made pursuant to a quasi-reorganization.

13. Consideration has been given to the methods of presentation of the extraordinary items excluded in the determination of net income under the criteria set forth in paragraph 11. One method is to carry all such charges and credits directly to the surplus account with complete disclosure as to their nature and amount. A second method is to show them in the income statement after the amount designated as net income. Where the second method is used, misconceptions are likely to arise as to whether earnings for the period are represented by the amount actually designated as net income or by the final, and often more prominent, amount shown on the income statement after deduction or addition of material extraordinary items excluded from the determination of net income. Having in mind the possibility of such misconceptions where the second method is employed, the committee believes that the first method more clearly portrays net income. It should be noted that the Securities and Exchange Commission, in its revised Regulation S-X issued in December, 1950, made provision in item 17 of Rule 5–03 for the addition to or deduction from net income or loss, at the bottom of income statements filed with the Commission, of items of profit and loss given recognition in the accounts during the period and not included in the determination of net income or loss. The change in Rule 5–03 does not affect the determination of the amount to be reported as net income or earnings for the year. Furthermore, the additions or deductions at the foot of the income statement after determination of net income are equivalent to direct credits or charges to earned surplus. In view of the foregoing, and although the committee strongly prefers the first method, it considers the second method of presentation described above to be acceptable provided care is taken that the figure of net income is clearly and unequivocally designated so as not to be confused with the final figure in the income statement. Thus it is imperative that the caption of the final figure should precisely describe what it represents, e.g., *net income and special items, net income and refund of 1945 excess profits taxes, net loss and special items,* or *profit on sale of subsidiary less net loss.* A company may use the first method

---

[3] See Chapter 5, paragraphs 8 and 9, for conditions under which a material portion or the entire amount of intangibles described therein as type (b) may be written off [pp. 393–94].

[4] See Chapter 9 (a) and dissents thereto [pp. 309–11].

of presentation in one statement and the second method in another like statement covering the same fiscal period. The committee wishes to make clear that neither of the above-described methods of presentation precludes the use of the combined statement of income and earned surplus.[5] However, where such combined statement is utilized, the committee's preference is that the figure of net income be followed immediately by the surplus balance at the beginning of the period. It is also the committee's opinion that deduction of the single item of dividends from net income on the income statement would not be subject to misconception.

14. In its deliberations concerning the nature and purpose of the income statement, the committee has been mindful of the disposition of even well-informed persons to attach undue importance to a single net income figure and to *earnings per share* shown for a particular year. The committee directs attention to the undesirability in many cases of the dissemination of information in which major prominence is given to a single figure of *net income* or *net income per share*. However, if such income data are reported (as in newspapers, investors' services, and annual corporate reports), the committee strongly urges that any determination of *income per share* be related to the amount designated in the income statement as net income and that where material extraordinary charges or credits have been excluded from the determination of net income, the corresponding total or per-share amount of such charges and credits also be reported separately and simultaneously. In this connection the committee earnestly solicits the cooperation of all organizations, both governmental and private, engaged in the compilation of business earnings statistics from annual reports.

In paragraph 2 the committee states: "An important objective of income presentation should be the avoidance of any practice that leads to income equalization." The possibility of such a practice is also mentioned in paragraph 7. A company with a record of growing or stable earnings is often considered more attractive by investors than a company with an erratic earnings record, even if the latter indicates underlying long-term growth. For this reason, there is a natural tendency for management to favor some equalization of reported income to the extent possible within the relatively loose constraints imposed by generally accepted accounting principles.

Paragraph 13 describes two methods of presenting extraordinary items excluded from the determination of net income under the criteria set forth in paragraph 11. The first method, carrying all such charges and credits directly to the retained earnings account, was used by ACF Industries, Incorporated in its report for the fiscal year ended April 30, 1962. This company reported net income of $6,010,000 in its 1962 annual report. Direct reductions of earned surplus in the net amount of $6,206,000 were described as follows in a note accompanying the financial statements:

---

[5] See Chapter 2 (b) [pp. 32–33].

SPECIAL ADJUSTMENTS OF EARNED SURPLUS:

During the year the Company sold its investment in 214,500 shares of Republic Aviation Corporation common stock. Also, during the year the Company announced its intention of closing and disposing of the Berwick plant. These transactions are not related to the Company's normal business operations and the results thereof, less estimated present and future federal income tax effects, have been charged to earned surplus:

Profit on sale of Republic Aviation Corporation stock	$(3,772,000)
Estimated loss on disposition of Berwick plant assets not transferrable to other ACF locations	2,405,000
Estimated pensions and retirement benefits to be paid in future years to Berwick plant employees, less portion already funded. Payable 1963–$384,000, 1964–$269,000, 1965–$286,000, 1966–$262,000, 1967–$257,000, etc.	5,918,000
Other expenses of closing the Berwick plant (primarily transferring equipment and personnel to other ACF locations)	1,655,000
	$ 6,206,000

A second method of presenting extraordinary items is to show them in the income statement *after* the amount designated as net income. This method is illustrated by the American Brake Shoe Company's 1961 statement of consolidated earnings, which is presented in Figure 1.

Income:	
Shipments	$165,503,959
Other Income—net	479,376
Total	165,983,335
Costs and Expenses:	
Materials, wages, and other costs	117,539,476
Selling, administrative, and research expense	21,566,870
Depreciation and amortization of intangibles	7,662,040
Repairs and maintenance of plant and equipment	4,714,992
Property, excise, and miscellaneous taxes	2,411,968
Interest expense	818,284
Total	154,713,630
Earnings before Taxes on Income	11,269,705
Provision for taxes on income	5,900,000
Net Earnings	5,369,705
Special Item:	
Federal excess profits tax refund for the years 1950-1953	995,000
Net Earnings and Special Item	$ 6,364,705
Per Share of Common Stock Outstanding at End of Year:	
Net earnings	$ 3.29
Special item	.61
Total Net Earnings And Special Item	$ 3.90

Figure 1. Statement of Consolidated Earnings

The committee prefers the first method, carrying extraordinary items directly to retained earnings, because under the second method "misconceptions are likely to arise as to whether earnings for the period are represented by the amount actually designated as net income or by the final, and often more prominent, amount shown on the income statement after deduction or addition of material extraordinary items excluded from the determination of net income." In contrast to the committee's position, the SEC favors disclosing extraordinary items arising from *current-year* events in the income statement, either in the calculation of net income, or as special items following net income. The SEC does permit material *prior-year* adjustments to be carried directly to retained earnings.[6] The committee concludes that the second method is equivalent to carrying such items directly to retained earnings and is therefore acceptable, "provided care is taken that the figure of net income is clearly and unequivocally designated so as not to be confused with the final figure in the income statement." Observe that the American Brake Shoe Company conformed to this recommendation.

Paragraph 14 expresses the committee's concern with the "undue importance" attached to *earnings per share*. This concern was even more strongly expressed in 1958 in a separate bulletin, which is considered later in this chapter. The American Brake Shoe Company followed the committee's recommendation, as given in paragraph 14, concerning disclosure of the per-share amount of extraordinary items.

COMBINED STATEMENT OF INCOME AND RETAINED EARNINGS

In paragraph 13 of the statement above on *Income and Earned Surplus*, the committee stated that neither of the methods described for presenting extraordinary items "precludes the use of the combined statement of income and earned surplus." The combined statement was the subject of Accounting Research Bulletin No. 8, issued in February, 1941, and later included in ARB No. 43 as Section B of Chapter 2, *Form of Statements*. This section follows:

1. Attention has already been called in the introduction to the increased significance attributed to the income statement by users of financial statements and to the general tendency to regard the balance sheet as the connecting link between successive income statements [see paragraph 3, pp. 5–6]. It therefore becomes important to consider the problems presented by the practice of combining the annual income statement with the statement of earned surplus.

2. The combining of these two statements, where possible, will often be found to be convenient and desirable. Where this presentation is contempla-

---

[6] The SEC has jurisdiction only over financial statements filed with it, not over the financial statements included in annual reports or elsewhere.

ted, however, certain considerations should be borne in mind if undesirable consequences are to be avoided.

Advantages of the Combined Statement

3. Over the years it is plainly desirable that all costs, expenses, and losses, and all profits of a business, other than decreases or increases arising directly from its capital-stock transactions, be included in the determination of income. If this principle could in practice be carried out perfectly, there would be no charges or credits to earned surplus except those relating to distributions and appropriations of final net income. This is an ideal upon which all may agree, but because of conditions impossible to foresee it often fails of attainment. From time to time charges and credits are made to surplus which clearly affect the cumulative total of income for a series of years, although their exclusion from the income statement of a single year is justifiable. There is danger that unless the two statements are closely connected such items will be overlooked, or at any rate not given full weight, in any attempt on the part of the reader to compute a company's long-run income or its income-earning capacity.

4. There is a marked tendency to exaggerate the significance of the net income for a single year, particularly the degree to which the net income can be identified exclusively with that year. In so far as the combined form calls attention to the character of the income statement as a tentative instalment in the long-time financial results it serves a useful purpose.

5. To summarize, the combined income and earned surplus statement serves the purpose of showing in one statement both the earnings applicable to the particular period and modifications of earned surplus on a long-run basis. It distinguishes current charges and credits related to a company's more usual or typical business operations from material extraordinary charges and credits[7] which may have arisen during the period by placing them in different sections of a continuous statement.

Disadvantages and Limitations

6. In the combined statement, net income for the year appears somewhere within the statement and not at the end. Such wording and arrangement should be used as will make this item unmistakably clear and leave the reader in no doubt as to the point at which the net income has been determined.

7. While it is true that the net income amount, when expressed as earnings per share, is often given undue prominence and its significance exaggerated, there nevertheless remain the responsibility for determination of net income by sound methods and the duty to show it clearly. The adoption of the combined statement provides no excuse for less care in distinguishing charges and credits to income from charges and credits to surplus than would be required if separate statements of income and surplus were presented. Failure to exercise care in the use of this form of statement would immediately discredit it.

The combined statement of income and retained earnings is illustrated in Figure 2 which shows the Caterpillar Tractor Company's 1961 Consolidated Results of Operations.

---

[7] See Chapter 8, paragraphs 11, 12, and 13 [pp. 28–30].

Sales		**$734,317,505**
Costs:		
Inventories brought forward from previous year	$227,116,780	
Materials, supplies, services purchased, etc.	370,515,161	
Wages, salaries and contributions for employee benefits	229,242,195	
Portion of original cost of buildings, machinery and equipment allocated to operations (depreciation and amortization)	31,642,485	
Interest on borrowed funds	8,128,068	
United States and foreign taxes based on income	51,558,379	
	918,203,068	
Deduct: Inventories carried forward to following year	239,131,352	
Costs allocated to year		679,071,716
		55,245,789
Profit of Caterpillar Credit Corporation		577,056
Profit for year—consolidated		**55,822,845**
Add:		
Profit employed in the business at beginning of year		197,025,251
		252,848,096
Deduct:		
Dividends paid in cash during year:		
Preferred stock—$4.20 per share	746,183	
Common stock—$1.00 per share	27,188,563	
		27,934,746
Profit employed in the business at end of year		$224,913,350

Figure 2. Consolidated Results of Operations Year 1961

The reader's attention is directed to Caterpillar Tractor's unusual treatment of inventories and the terminology used for depreciation and retained earnings. This corporation has frequently been cited as a pioneer in financial reporting.

EARNINGS PER SHARE

In paragraph 14 of Chapter 8, ARB No. 43, quoted above, the Committee on Accounting Procedure noted the undue emphasis often given to earnings per share data. Because of continuing emphasis on such data, the committee issued ARB No. 49, *Earnings per Share*, in April, 1958. In this bulletin the committee reaffirmed and expanded its earlier position as follows:

1. Statistical presentations of periodic net income (or loss) in terms of earnings per share[8] are commonly used in prospectuses, proxy material, and

---

[8] As used herein, the term *earnings per share* connotes either earnings or losses per share.

annual reports to shareholders, and in the compilation of business earnings statistics for the press, statistical services, and other publications. This bulletin deals with a number of problems arising in the computation and presentation of such statistics.

2. The committee has previously considered certain aspects of this matter[9] and now reaffirms its earlier conclusions that:

(a) It is, in many cases, undesirable to give major prominence to a single figure of earnings per share;

(b) Any computation of earnings per share for a given period should be related to the amount designated in the income statement as net income for such period; and

(c) Where material extraordinary charges or credits have been excluded from the determination of net income, the per-share amount of such charges and credits should be reported separately and simultaneously.

3. Not only does the use of a single figure for earnings per share involve the same limitations of usefulness as does a single figure for net earnings, but also, in many circumstances, the computation of earnings per share involves unique problems. While it is desirable to achieve as much uniformity as is feasible, clear explanation and disclosure of methods used are especially important in this area of financial reporting.

4. The committee suggests the following general guides to be used in computing and presenting earnings per share:

(a) Where used without qualification, the term *earnings per share* should be used to designate the amount applicable to each share of common stock or other residual security outstanding.

(b) Earnings per share, and particularly comparative statistics covering a period of years, should generally be stated in terms of the common stock position as it existed in the years to which the statistics relate, unless it is clear that the growth or decline of earnings will be more fairly presented, as for example, in the case of a stock split, by dividing prior years' earnings by the current equivalent of the number of shares then outstanding.

(c) *In all cases in which there have been significant changes in stock during the period to which the computations relate, an appropriate explanation of the method used should accompany the presentation of earnings per share.*

SINGLE-YEAR COMPUTATIONS

5. In the computation of earnings per share for a single year, minor increases or decreases in the number of shares outstanding during the year may be disregarded, and it is appropriate to base the computation on the number of shares outstanding at the end of the year. In the case of a substantial increase or decrease in the number of shares resulting from the issuance or reacquisition of stock for cash or other property during the year, it is generally appropriate to base the computation of earnings per share on a weighted average of the number of shares outstanding during the year. Where there has been little or no opportunity to utilize the proceeds from the issuance of such shares, as would most clearly be the case when the shares were

---

[9] Accounting Research Bulletin No. 43, *Restatement and Revision of Accounting Research Bulletins* (1953), Chapter 8, par. 14. Also see Chapter 2 (b), par. 4 [See pp. 30 and 33 in this chapter].

issued shortly before the end of the year, such shares may be disregarded in the computation. When an increase in the number of shares outstanding results from a stock dividend or a stock split, or a reduction in the number of shares outstanding results from a reverse split, without proceeds or disbursements, the computation should be based on the number of shares outstanding at the end of the year. For purposes of determining the number of shares outstanding, reacquired shares should be excluded.

6. If there has been a stock split[10] or a reverse split after the balance-sheet date but before the issuance of the financial report, it is desirable to base the computation of earnings per share on the new number of shares, since the reader's primary interest is presumed to be in the present stock position. Similar considerations may apply to stock dividends,[10] although a relatively small stock dividend may properly be disregarded. In these cases of changes after the balance-sheet date, it is preferable to choose the more useful and informative basis of computation rather than to present two simultaneous and possibly confusing computations on different bases. When computations of earnings per share reflect changes in the number of shares after the balance-sheet date, it is important that this fact be clearly disclosed since there may be a presumption that earnings per share are based on the number of shares shown on the balance sheet. It is equally important that significant changes in the number of shares after the balance-sheet date be disclosed when such changes are not reflected in the computation of earnings per share.

7. Where there are shares outstanding senior to the common stock or other residual security, the claims of such securities on net income should be deducted from net income or added to net loss before computing per-share figures, since the term *earnings per share* is ordinarily used to designate the amount applicable to each share of common stock or other residual security outstanding. In arriving at net income applicable to common stock for purposes of the per-share computations, provision should be made for cumulative preferred dividends for the year, whether or not earned. In the case of a net loss, the amount of the loss should be increased by any cumulative preferred stock dividends for the year. Where such dividends are cumulative only if earned, no adjustment of this nature is required except to the extent of income available therefor. In all cases the effect that has been given to dividend rights of senior securities in arriving at the earnings per share of common stock should be disclosed.

8. The following special considerations relate to convertible securities:

(a) When debt capital, preferred stock, or other security has been converted into common stock during the year, earnings per share should ordinarily be based on a weighted average of the number of shares outstanding during the year. When the weighted average is used in such cases, adjustments for the year in respect of interest or other related factors are not made.

(b) When capitalizations consist essentially of two classes of common stock, one of which is convertible into the other and is limited in its dividend rights until conversion takes place as, for example, when certain levels of earnings are achieved, two earnings-per-share figures, one assuming conversion, are ordinarily necessary for full disclosure of the situation.

---

[10] See Accounting Research Bulletin No. 43, Chapter 7 (b) [pp. 591–94].

COMPARATIVE STATISTICS

9. Presentations of earnings-per-share data for a period of several years should be governed basically by the criteria for single year presentations, but may involve a number of special considerations in view of changes in conditions during the period, and the purpose for which the data are to be used. It should be recognized that any tabulation of earnings per share for a period of years may have little bearing on the present position, and may fail to give any indication of present expectations. Variations in the capital structure may have substantial effects on earnings per share. The usefulness of such statistics depends in large measure on collateral historical information and disclosure of methods of computation used. The committee's recommendations which follow are intended as guides to general uniformity but not as substitutes for explanations and disclosures or as cures for the inherent defects in statistical presentations of earnings per share.

10. When computations of earnings per share for a period of years, such as are submitted in annual reports and in prospectuses, include periods in which there have been stock splits or reverse splits, the earnings for periods prior to the dates of the splits should be divided by the current equivalent of the number of shares outstanding in the respective prior periods in order to arrive at earnings per share in terms of the present stock position. Similar treatment should be accorded to stock dividends; however, it is permissible not to extend such treatment to small recurrent stock dividends, although in a prospectus or when such dividends in the aggregate become material, consideration should be given to recognizing the cumulative effect thereof. On the other hand, where, during the period of years for which data are given, there have been issuances or reacquisitions of stock for cash or other property, or, issuances in connection with conversions of debt capital, preferred stock, or other security, the computations of earnings per share for the years prior to such changes are not affected; it follows that earnings per share for these years should be based on the number of shares outstanding in the various years. When both situations have occurred, the effect of each should be reflected in accordance with the foregoing recommendations.

11. When equity securities are being publicly offered:

(a) If there have been significant conversions of debt capital, preferred stock, or other security during the period of years for which data are given, it is appropriate to present supplementary calculations revising past figures to reflect subsequent conversions, on a pro forma basis.

(b) If the securities being offered, or their proceeds, are to be used to retire outstanding securities in circumstances which assure such retirement, it may be useful to present, in addition to otherwise appropriate calculations, supplementary computations to show pro forma earnings per share for at least the most recent year as if such substitution of securities had been made. When this is done, the basis of the supplementary computations should be clearly disclosed. Where, however, the securities being offered, or their proceeds, are to be used, not to retire existing securities, but for such purposes as expansion of the business, earnings per share should be computed without adjustment for any increase in the number of shares anticipated as a result of such offering.

12. Where there has been a pooling of interests[11] during the period of

---

[11] See Accounting Research Bulletin No. 48, *Business Combinations* (1957) [pp. 560–63].

years for which data are given, in connection with which the number of shares outstanding or the capital structure in other respects has been changed, the method used in computing earnings per share for those years prior to the pooling of interests should be based on the new capital structure. When there is to be a pooling of interests in connection with which the number of shares outstanding or the capital structure in other respects will be changed, earnings per share for any period for which income statements of the constituent companies are presented in combined form should be computed on a basis consistent with the exchange ratio to be used in the pooling of interests. In either case earnings per share should, in all other respects, be computed in conformity with the principles set forth in the foregoing paragraphs.

EARNINGS COVERAGE OF SENIOR SECURITIES

13. Where periodic net income is related to outstanding shares of senior securities, such as preferred stock, the committee believes that, under most circumstances, the term *earnings per share* is not properly applicable in view of the limited dividend rights of such senior securities. In such cases it may be helpful to show the number of times or the extent to which the requirements of senior dividends have been earned, but such information should not be designated as earnings per share.

MISCELLANEOUS

14. It is impracticable to deal, in this bulletin, with all of the possible conditions and circumstances under which it may be necessary or desirable to compute data in terms of earnings per share—for example, acquisitions, mergers, reorganizations, convertible and participating securities, outstanding stock options, retirements, and various combinations of these circumstances. While such situations should be dealt with in harmony with the recommendations made in this bulletin, they call for especially careful consideration of facts and the exercise of judgment in the light of all the circumstances of the case and the purposes for which the data are prepared. In such complex situations as those mentioned in this paragraph, a clear disclosure of the basis on which the computations have been made is essential.

DIVIDENDS PER SHARE

15. Although this bulletin deals primarily with earnings per share, certain considerations may apply comparably to dividends per share. In general, dividends per share constitute historical facts and should be so reported. However, in certain cases, such as a stock split as mentioned in paragraph 10, a presentation of dividends per share in terms of the current equivalent of the number of shares outstanding at the time of the dividend is necessary so that dividends per share and earnings per share will be stated on the same basis. When dividends per share are stated on any other than the historical basis, it is generally desirable that such statement be supplemental to the historical record, and its basis and significance should be fully explained.

The statement entitled "Earnings per Share" was unanimously adopted by the twenty-one members of the committee.

BALANCE SHEET

The Committee on Accounting Procedure has issued two bulletins dealing with the classification and presentation of current assets and current liabilities in the balance sheet. One of these, originally issued in 1947 as ARB No. 30, was later included in ARB No. 43 as Section A, *"Current Assets and Current Liabilities,"* of Chapter 3, *Working Capital.* This section follows:

1. THE WORKING CAPITAL of a borrower has always been of prime interest to grantors of credit; and bond indentures, credit agreements, and preferred stock agreements commonly contain provisions restricting corporate actions which would effect a reduction or impairment of working capital. Many such contracts forego precise or uniform definitions and merely provide that current assets and current liabilities shall be determined in accordance with generally accepted accounting principles. Considerable variation and inconsistency exist, however, with respect to their classification and display in financial statements. In this section the committee discusses the nature of current assets and current liabilities with a view toward a more useful presentation thereof in financial statements.

2. The committee believes that, in the past, definitions of current assets have tended to be overly concerned with whether the assets may be immediately realizable. The discussion which follows takes cognizance of the tendency for creditors to rely more upon the ability of debtors to pay their obligations out of the proceeds of current operations and less upon the debtor's ability to pay in case of liquidation. It should be emphasized that financial statements of a going concern are prepared on the assumption that the company will continue in business. Accordingly, the views expressed in this section represent a departure from any narrow definition or strict *one year* interpretation of either current assets or current liabilities; the objective is to relate the criteria developed to the operating cycle of a business.

3. Financial position, as it is reflected by the records and accounts from which the statement is prepared, is revealed in a presentation of the assets and liabilities of the enterprise. In the statements of manufacturing, trading, and service enterprises these assets and liabilities are generally classified and segregated; if they are classified logically, summations or totals of the *current* or *circulating* or *working* assets, hereinafter referred to as *current assets*, and of obligations currently payable, designated as *current liabilities*, will permit the ready determination of working capital. *Working capital*, sometimes called *net working capital*, is represented by the excess of current assets over current liabilities and identifies the relatively liquid portion of total enterprise capital which constitutes a margin or buffer for meeting obligations within the ordinary operating cycle of the business. If the conventions of accounting relative to the identification and presentation of current assets and current liabilities are made logical and consistent, the amounts, bases of valuation, and composition of such assets and liabilities and their relation to the total assets or capital employed will provide valuable data for credit and management purposes and

afford a sound basis for comparisons from year to year. It is recognized that there may be exceptions, in special cases, to certain of the inclusions and exclusions as set forth in this section. When such exceptions occur they should be accorded the treatment merited in the particular circumstances under the general principles outlined herein.

4. For accounting purposes, the term *current assets* is used to designate cash and other assets or resources commonly identified as those which are reasonably expected to be realized in cash or sold or consumed during the normal operating cycle of the business. Thus the term comprehends in general such resources as (a) cash available for current operations and items which are the equivalent of cash; (b) inventories of merchandise, raw materials, goods in process, finished goods, operating supplies, and ordinary maintenance material and parts; (c) trade accounts, notes, and acceptances receivable; (d) receivables from officers, employees, affiliates, and others, if collectible in the ordinary course of business within a year; (e) instalment or deferred accounts and notes receivable if they conform generally to normal trade practices and terms within the business; (f) marketable securities representing the investment of cash available for current operations; and (g) prepaid expenses such as insurance, interest, rents, taxes, unused royalties, current paid advertising service not yet received, and operating supplies. Prepaid expenses are not current assets in the sense that they will be converted into cash but in the sense that, if not paid in advance, they would require the use of current assets during the operating cycle.

5. The ordinary operations of a business involve a circulation of capital within the current asset group. Cash is expended for materials, finished parts, operating supplies, labor, and other factory services, and such expenditures are accumulated as inventory cost. Inventory costs, upon sale of the products to which such costs attach, are converted into trade receivables and ultimately into cash again. The average time intervening between the acquisition of materials or services entering this process and the final cash realization constitutes an *operating cycle*. A one-year time period is to be used as a basis for the segregation of current assets in cases where there are several operating cycles occurring within a year. However, where the period of the operating cycle is more than twelve months, as in, for instance, the tobacco, distillery, and lumber businesses, the longer period should be used. Where a particular business has no clearly defined operating cycle, the one-year rule should govern.

6. This concept of the nature of current assets contemplates the exclusion from that classification of such resources as: (a) cash and claims to cash which are restricted as to withdrawal or use for other than current operations, are designated for expenditure in the acquisition or construction of noncurrent assets, or are segregated[12] for the liquidation of long-term debts; (b) investments in securities (whether marketable or not) or advances which have been made for the purposes of control, affiliation, or other continuing business advantage; (c) receivables arising from unusual transactions (such as the sale of capital assets, or loans or advances to affiliates, officers, or employees) which are not expected to be collected within twelve months; (d)

---

[12] Even though not actually set aside in special accounts, funds that are clearly to be used in the near future for the liquidation of long-term debts, payments to sinking funds, or for similar purposes should also, under this concept, be excluded from current assets. However, where such funds are considered to offset maturing debt which has properly been set up as a current liability, they may be included within the current asset classification.

cash surrender value of life insurance policies; (e) land and other natural resources; (f) depreciable assets; and (g) long-term prepayments which are fairly chargeable to the operations of several years, or deferred charges such as unamortized debt discount and expense, bonus payments under a long-term lease, costs of rearrangement of factory layout or removal to a new location, and certain types of research and development costs.

7. The term *current liabilities* is used principally to designate obligations whose liquidation is reasonably expected to require the use of existing resources properly classifiable as current assets, or the creation of other current liabilities. As a balance-sheet category, the classification is intended to include obligations for items which have entered into the operating cycle, such as payables incurred in the acquisition of materials and supplies to be used in the production of goods or in providing services to be offered for sale; collections received in advance of the delivery of goods or performance of services[13]; and debts which arise from operations directly related to the operating cycle, such as accruals for wages, salaries, commissions, rentals, royalties, and income and other taxes. Other liabilities whose regular and ordinary liquidation is expected to occur within a relatively short period of time, usually twelve months, are also intended for inclusion, such as short-term debts arising from the acquisition of capital assets, serial maturities of long-term obligations, amounts required to be expended within one year under sinking fund provisions, and agency obligations arising from the collection or acceptance of cash or other assets for the account of third persons.[14]

8. This concept of current liabilities would include estimated or accrued amounts which are expected to be required to cover expenditures within the year for known obligations (a) the amount of which can be determined only approximately (as in the case of provisions for accruing bonus payments) or (b) where the specific person or persons to whom payment will be made cannot as yet be designated (as in the case of estimated costs to be incurred in connection with guaranteed servicing or repair of products already sold). The current liability classification, however, is not intended to include a contractual obligation falling due at an early date which is expected to be refunded,[15] or debts to be liquidated by funds which have been accumulated in accounts of a type not properly classified as current assets, or long-term obligations incurred to provide increased amounts of working capital for long periods. When the amounts of the periodic payments of an obligation are,

---

[13] Examples of such current liabilities are obligations resulting from advance collections on ticket sales, which will normally be liquidated in the ordinary course of business by the delivery of services. On the contrary, obligations representing long-term deferments of the delivery of goods or services would not be shown as current liabilities. Examples of the latter are the issuance of a long-term warranty or the advance receipt by a lessor of rental for the final period of a ten-year lease as a condition to execution of the lease agreement.

[14] Loans accompanied by pledge of life insurance policies would be classified as current liabilities when, by their terms or by intent, they are to be repaid within twelve months. The pledging of life insurance policies does not affect the classification of the asset any more than does the pledging of receivables, inventories, real estate, or other assets as collateral for a short-term loan. However, when a loan on a life insurance policy is obtained from the insurance company with the intent that it will not be paid but will be liquidated by deduction from the proceeds of the policy upon maturity or cancellation, the obligation should be excluded from current liabilities.

[15] There should, however, be full disclosure that such obligation has been omitted from the current liabilities and a statement of the reason for such omission should be given. Cf. note 12.

by contract, measured by current transactions, as for example by rents or revenues received in the case of equipment trust certificates or by the depletion of natural resources in the case of property obligations, the portion of the total obligation to be included as a current liability should be that representing the amount accrued at the balance-sheet date.

9. The amounts at which various current assets are carried do not always represent their present realizable cash values. Accounts receivable net of allowances for uncollectible accounts, and for unearned discounts where unearned discounts are considered, are effectively stated at the amount of cash estimated as realizable. However, practice varies with respect to the carrying basis for current assets such as marketable securities and inventories. In the case of marketable securities where market value is less than cost by a substantial amount and it is evident that the decline in market value is not due to a mere temporary condition, the amount to be included as a current asset should not exceed the market value. The basis for carrying inventories is stated in chapter 4 [pp. 187–94]. It is important that the amounts at which current assets are stated be supplemented by information which reveals, for temporary investments, their market value at the balance-sheet date, and for the various classifications of inventory items, the basis upon which their amounts are stated and, where practicable, indication of the method of determining the cost—e.g., *average cost, first-in first-out, last-in first-out*, etc.

> *One member of the committee, Mr. Mason, assented with qualification to adoption of section (a) of chapter 3.*

Mr. Mason does not accept the view implied in paragraph 6 that unamortized debt discount is an asset. Also, referring to paragraph 9, he believes that the market value is the most significant figure in connection with marketable securities held as temporary investments of cash, and would prefer to show such securities in the accounts at their market value, whether greater or less than cost. He would accept as an alternative the use of cost in the accounts with market value shown parenthetically in the balance sheet.

The second bulletin on the classification and presentation of current assets and current liabilities, originally issued as ARB No. 14 in 1942, was later included in ARB No. 43, as Section B of Chapter 3, *Working Capital*. This section, *"Application of United States Government Securities Against Liabilities for Federal Taxes on Income,"* follows:

1. IT IS A GENERAL PRINCIPLE of accounting that the offsetting of assets and liabilities in the balance sheet is improper except where a right of set-off exists. An example of such exception was the showing of United States Treasury Tax Notes, Tax Series A-1943 and B-1943, as a deduction from the liability for federal taxes on income, which the committee approved in 1942.

2. In view of the special nature of the terms of the 1943 tax notes, the intention of the purchaser to use them to pay federal income taxes could be assumed, since he received no interest or other advantage unless they were so used. Some purchasers doubtless viewed their purchase of the notes as being, to all intents and purposes, an advance payment of the taxes.

3. In the absence of evidence of a contrary intent, it was considered acceptable, and in accordance with good accounting practice, to show the notes in the current liability section of the balance sheet as a deduction from federal

taxes on income in an amount not to exceed the accrued liability for such taxes. The full amount of the accrued liability was to be shown with a deduction for the tax payment value of the notes at the date of the balance sheet.

4. It also was recognized as clearly proper to show the notes in the current asset section of the balance sheet as any other temporary investments are shown. If at the balance-sheet date or at the date of the independent auditor's report there was evidence that the original intent was changed, the notes were to be shown in the current asset section of the balance sheet.

5. Government securities having restrictive terms similar to those contained in the 1943 tax series notes are no longer issued, although certain other types of government securities have since been issued which are acceptable in payment of liabilities for federal taxes on income. However, because of the effect on the current position of large tax accruals and the related accumulations of liquid assets to meet such liabilities, many companies have adopted the practice of acquiring and holding government securities of various issues in amounts related to the estimated tax liability. In their financial statements these companies have often expressed this relationship by showing such securities as a deduction from the tax liability, even though the particular securities were not by their terms acceptable in payment of taxes. If the government securities involved may, by their terms, be surrendered in payment of taxes, the above practice clearly falls within the principle of the permissive exception described in paragraph 1. The committee further believes that the extension of the practice to include the offset of other types of United States government securities, although a deviation from the general rule against offsets, is not so significant a deviation as to call for an exception in an accountant's report on the financial statements.

6. Suggestions have been received that similar considerations may be advanced in favor of the offset of cash or other assets against the income and excess profits tax liability or against other amounts owing to the federal government. In the opinion of the committee, however, any such extension or application of the exception, recognized as to United States government securities and liabilities for federal taxes on income, is not to be regarded as acceptable practice.

> *One member of the committee, Mr. Calkins, assented with quali-*
> *fication to adoption of section (b) of chapter 3.*

Mr. Calkins does not approve the concluding sentence of paragraph 5, which states that the offset of other types of United States Government securities, although a deviation from the general rule against offsets, is not so significant a deviation as to call for an exception in an accountant's report. He believes that the significance of such a deviation is a matter for judgment based on the facts of a particular case; that the broader language of the statement constitutes a condonation of the practice of offsetting against tax liabilities United States Government obligations which are not by their terms acceptable in payment of federal taxes; and that the condonation of such a practice is inconsistent with the opinion of the committee expressed in paragraph 6, with which he agrees, that cash and other assets should not be offset against liabilities for federal taxes.

Note that offsetting United States Government securities against an estimated tax liability has no effect on the amount of a company's working capital. However, this practice may have a very significant effect on the current ratio (the ratio of current assets to current liabilities), or on any ratio using total assets, such as return on total assets.[16]

There have been no bulletins on the form of the balance sheet. Two forms are in common use. In one, known as the *account* form, the assets are presented on the left and the sources of assets (liabilities and stockholders' equity) are presented on the right. In the second common form, known as the *report* form, the assets are presented first followed by the sources of assets. A third form, which is favored by some companies, displays working capital as a single figure and emphasizes the owners' equity. This form is illustrated by the Consolidated Statement of Financial Position of the General Foods Corporation at March 31, 1962, as given in Figure 3.

(All dollar amounts expressed in thousands)

	At March 31, 1962
Cash	$ 8,933
Marketable Securities (at cost, which approximates market)	81,928
Receivables (less provisions of $2,153)	107,465
Inventories, at Lower of Cost (primarily average) or Market	183,498
Expenses Paid in Advance (advertising, insurance, taxes, and others)	4,946
Current Assets	**$386,770**
Notes and Accounts Payable	43,318
Accrued Liabilities	30,041
Income Taxes	68,027
Current Liabilities	**$141,386**
Working Capital (Current Assets less Current Liabilities)	**$245,384**
Long-Term Receivables and Sundry Assets, Less Provisions	6,676
Land, Buildings, and Equipment (at cost, less accumulated depreciation)	193,184
Intangibles (at purchased cost):	
Patents, Licenses, and Formulas, Less Amortization	994
Goodwill (on acquisitions since fiscal 1954)	14,631
Working Capital and Other Assets	**$460,869**
Less Non-Current Liabilities:	
Long-term Debt	35,434
Other	6,680
	42,114
Excess of Assets over Liabilities	**$418,755**
Represented by Stockholders' Interest:	
Common Stock Issued	157,794
Earnings Retained in the Business	260,961
	$ 418,755

Figure 3. Consolidated Statement of Financial Position

While the form of the balance sheet illustrated in Figure 3 prominently discloses working capital and the owners' equity, it does not disclose

---

[16] As an example of this practice, see the Consolidated Balance Sheet as of December 31, 1961, of E.I. du Pont de Nemours & Company, Inc., p. 450.

as a separate figure the total resources used by management. It is suggested that the reader calculate this amount from Figure 3.

COMPARATIVE FINANCIAL STATEMENTS

In one of its first statements, ARB No. 6, issued in 1940, the Committee on Accounting Procedure recommended the presentation of comparative financial statements. In 1953, this early statement was included in ARB No. 43, Chapter 2, *Form of Statements*, as Section A, *"Comparative Financial Statements."* This section follows:

1. THE PRESENTATION OF comparative financial statements in annual and other reports enhances the usefulness of such reports and brings out more clearly the nature and trends of current changes affecting the enterprise. Such presentation emphasizes the fact that statements for a series of periods are far more significant than those for a single period and that the accounts for one period are but an instalment of what is essentially a continuous history.

2. In any one year it is ordinarily desirable that the balance sheet, the income statement, and the surplus statement be given for one or more preceding years as well as for the current year. Footnotes, explanations, and accountants' qualifications which appeared on the statements for the preceding years should be repeated, or at least referred to, in the comparative statements to the extent that they continue to be of significance. If, because of reclassifications or for other reasons, changes have occurred in the manner of or basis for presenting corresponding items for two or more periods, information should be furnished which will explain the change. This procedure is in conformity with the well recognized principle that any change in practice which affects comparability should be disclosed.

3. It is necessary that prior-year figures shown for comparative purposes be in fact comparable with those shown for the most recent period, or that any exceptions to comparability be clearly brought out.

4. Circumstances vary so greatly that it is not practicable to deal here specifically with all situations. The independent accountant should, however, make very clear what statements are included within the scope of his report.

NOTES TO FINANCIAL STATEMENTS

The income statement and the balance sheet usually contain only limited space for any elaboration on certain significant data, transactions, or changes in accounting methods. Such information is given in notes to the financial statements. Notes are also used to disclose material contingencies, commitments, and restrictions or liens. Significant events occurring between the date of the financial statements and the date of the audit opinion should be disclosed in notes. These notes are an *integral part* of the financial statements and are covered by the audit report. Notes to the financial statements should never be used as a substitute for adequate disclosure in the body of the financial statements themselves.

REFERENCES

American Accounting Association, Committee on Concepts and Standards Underlying Corporate Financial Statements, "Standards of Disclosure for Published Financial Reports—Supplementary Statement No. 8," *Accounting Review*, 30 (Jul. 1955), 400–404. This statement also appears in *Accounting and Reporting Standards for Corporate Financial Statements and Preceding Statements and Supplements.* Columbus, Ohio: American Accounting Association, 1957.

Andersen, Arthur, & Co., *Accounting and Reporting Problems of the Accounting Profession*, 2nd ed. Chicago: Arthur Andersen & Co. (Oct. 1962), 39–44, 161–67.

Blough, Carman G., "Proper Treatment of Losses on Cuban Assets," *Journal of Accountancy*, 111 (Jan. 1961), 76–77.

Bullock, Clayton L., "Footnotes in Financial Statement Preparation," *Journal of Accountancy*, 102 (Jul. 1956), 39–44.

Chan, Stephen, "Notes to Financial Statements," *Journal of Accountancy*, 111 (Mar. 1961), 54–58.

Chetkovich, Michael N., "Standards of Disclosure and Their Development," *Journal of Accountancy*, 100 (Dec. 1955), 48–52.

Flowers, W. Baker, "Some Criteria for Post-Statement Disclosure," *Journal of Accountancy*, 111 (Jan. 1961), 48–58.

Forderhase, F. B., "Notes to Financial Statements," *Journal of Accountancy*, 100 (Oct. 1955), 50–55.

Griffin, Charles H. and Thomas H. Williams, "Measuring Adequate Disclosure," *Journal of Accountancy*, 109 (Apr. 1960), 43–48.

Marple, Raymond P., "The Balance Sheet—Capital Sources and Composition," *Journal of Accountancy*, 114 (Nov. 1962), 57–60.

Mauriello, Joseph A., "The Working Capital Concept—A Restatement," *Accounting Review*, 37 (Jan. 1962), 39–43.

Myers, John H., "Footnotes," *Accounting Review*, 34 (Jul. 1959), 381–88.

Rice, Marilyn Young, "Sketch for a Universal Accounting Statement," *Accounting Review*, 37 (Jan. 1962), 6–21.

Staubus, George J., "The Residual Equity Point of View in Accounting," *Accounting Review*, 34 (Jan. 1959), 3–13.

Thacker, Ronald J., "Income Statement Form and Classification," *Accounting Review*, 37 (Jan. 1962), 51–55.

Trumbull, Wendell P., "The All-Inclusive Standard," *Accounting Review*, 27 (Jan. 1952), 3–14.

Werntz, William W., "The Resurgence of the Balance Sheet as a Useful Element in Financial Analysis," *Journal of Accountancy*, 96 (Nov. 1953), 555–69.

Witte, Arthur E., "The Income Statement as a Management Tool," *Journal of Accountancy*, 108 (Oct. 1959), 44–48.

The Kratter Corporation

The Kratter Corporation, a publicly owned real estate finance company, was incorporated in February, 1959. Following its organization, Kratter acquired the capital of seven predecessor real estate partnerships on a share exchange basis. Kratter owns hotels, office and apartment buildings, shopping centers and other properties throughout the United States and Canada. Kratter's 1959 and 1960 financial statements are given in Exhibits 1 and 2.

In an interim report issued for the period May 1, 1959 through April 30, 1960, Kratter presented the following case history to illustrate its operations:

In order to illustrate in an easily understood form certain of the essential techniques that characterize the operations of The Kratter Corporation, the following imaginary case history is presented. While it greatly simplifies actual situations, it is generally representative of the company's approach and policy.

In this hypothetical transaction, the seller of the building and the land is a large corporation presently occupying the premises. This firm will remain as the tenant under a net leaseback arrangement with The Kratter Corporation. That means the tenant will be responsible for and be required to pay all building operating expenses, including real estate taxes and assessments, insurance premiums, maintenance and repairs, alterations, fuel, supplies and the like.

As owner of the property, The Kratter Corporation receives a regular, definite and contractually predetermined monthly rental income which is not normally subject to fluctuation in occupancy or uncontrolled changes in expenses, real estate taxes, insurance rates, or increases in the cost of supplies and labor. These are all the legal obligations of the tenant under the terms of the net leaseback, in addition to the monthly net rental payment.

FINANCING THE PURCHASE

Of the $10,000,000 cost, $2,000,000 is paid in cash and represents the company's equity capital investment in the property and $6,000,000 is paid by taking the property subject to an institutional mortgage (life insurance company, pension fund or bank) and $2,000,000 is paid by giving back to the seller-tenant a purchase money mortgage (a second mortgage), which is pledged back to the company as security for the seller-tenant's performance of his obligations under the leaseback to him. These mortgages have total constant payment carrying charges at the rate of 8 per cent or $640,000 per annum of which the first payment at the annual rate of 5 per cent, or $400,000, is interest and 3 per cent, or $240,000, is repayment on the mortgage (amortization-debt reduction).

RENTAL DETERMINATION

The company's aim in entering into this theoretical transaction was to obtain a 12 per cent usable cash flow yield on its $2,000,000 equity investment—or $240,000 annually. The rental must be sufficient to cover not only this $240,000 but the $640,000 annual mortgage servicing charges as well. Therefore, an annual net leaseback rental of $880,000 is established.

CASH FLOW

Income: Rental Receipts	$880,000
Outgo: Interest on Mortgage	400,000
	$480,000
Outgo: Repayment on Mortgage	240,000
Net Cash Operating Receipts	$240,000

INCOME TAX LOSS

The $10,000,000 cost was divided: $9,000,000 for the building, $1,000,000 for the land.

The building has a remaining "life" of 20 years. Using the "declining balance" method for determining depreciation, $7\frac{1}{2}$ per cent of the building's cost can be charged off during the first year, or $675,000.[1]

For Income Tax Purposes:	
Revenues: Rental Receipts	$880,000
Expenses: Interest on Mortgage	400,000
	$480,000

(The $240,000 repayment on the mortgage is not classified as a current expense for income tax statement purposes.)

Deduct: Depreciation Allowable	675,000
Net loss for Income Tax Purposes	$195,000

(This net operating loss can be used to offset other current corporate income and can also be carried forward against future corporate income.)

---

[1] In this case history a depreciation rate of $1\frac{1}{2}$ times the straight-line rate (5 per cent per year) is used. This is an acceptable depreciation method for tax purposes, first allowed in 1939. Beginning in 1954, a "declining balance" rate of twice the straight-line rate could be used for most *new* assets. Note that the $7\frac{1}{2}$ per cent rate in the case is applied each year to a declining amount. In the first year, $7\frac{1}{2}$ per cent of $9,000,000 equals $675,000; in the second year, $7\frac{1}{2}$ per cent of $8,325,000 ($9,000,000 − $675,000) equals $624,375. This subject is more fully discussed in Chapters 6 and 9.

AS A RESULT

Cash distributions received by shareowners are not in the usual case subject to federal income taxes because the company for income tax purposes reported a bookkeeping loss. Under such circumstances, any distribution to shareowners is not considered income, and these cash distributions are treated as a "return of capital" (reduction in cost basis to the shareowner) and as such are not subject to normal income taxation.

However, the cost basis of the shareowner's investment in the company is reduced by the amount of the distribution, and thus the basis for determining any future capital gain upon the sale of his stock is accordingly lowered.

"Dividend" Policy

Kratter's "dividend" policy is unique inasmuch as it is not based on income or retained earnings, as defined in the usual accounting sense, but on cash flow. The policy calls for distribution to stockholders of substantially all of the corporation's net cash operating receipts. In the 1960 interim report under the heading "Earnings and Cash Flow," management stated:

For the twelve-month period from May 1, 1959 through April 30, 1960, your company had consolidated income, before depreciation of properties and amortization of leaseholds and organization expenses for federal income tax purposes, (cash flow) of $4,473,230. This is equivalent to $1.59 per share on the average number of shares of common stock outstanding at each monthly dividend record date from May 15, 1959 to April 15, 1960, and before adjustment for the 10 per cent common stock distribution made in May 1960. Payments to reduce mortgages totaled $1,256,181 or 45 cents per share, including voluntary prepayments of $93,677 or 3 cents per share. Thus, $3,119,319 or $1.11 per share was available for distribution to common shareholders, of which $2,790,146 or $0.99 actually was distributed. Cash flow is the important measurement used by management of real estate companies, for it indicates the actual amount that is available for debt reduction, cash dividends, and other corporate purposes.

Elsewhere in the report management disclosed a "Summary of Income Available for Distribution to Common Shareholders," shown as Exhibit 3. The following opinion by Kratter's independent accountants accompanied the summary:

We have examined, to the extent we considered necessary for the purposes of this report, the accompanying Summary of Income Available for Distribution to Common Shareholders of The Kratter Corporation for the twelve months ended April 30, 1960.

In our opinion, the accompanying Summary of Income Available for Distribution to Common Shareholders of The Kratter Corporation for the twelve months ended April 30, 1960, presents fairly the information contained therein.

Cost vs. Market Value

In the annual report for the year ended December 31, 1960, Mr. Marvin Kratter, President and Chairman of the Board, commented on the Corporation's balance sheet as follows:

Inasmuch as the balance sheet of real estate companies, including The Kratter Corporation, is somewhat different from the usual type of balance sheet encountered by investors, it might prove helpful if several explanatory comments were made.

The balance sheet of a real estate company usually shows properties at cost and then deducts a figure representing "allowances for depreciation and amortization." Inasmuch as prices for major income-producing properties such as those owned by The Kratter Corporation have been trending sharply upward during the past few years, this accounting practice has resulted in gross understatements of current values in the balance sheets of many companies. One major company has adopted the policy of including its officers' estimates of current market values of properties in its reports. While it has been decided not to include such estimates in the report of The Kratter Corporation, it should be apparent that market values of the company's properties are substantially in excess of cost and most certainly are in excess of values carried in the balance sheet...

Mortgage Debt

Mr. Kratter noted further in the 1960 annual report that substantial amounts of the corporation's liabilities "do not constitute debt in the usual sense." He stated:

The largest single liability item on the balance sheet is "Mortgages on Properties." Although listed as liabilities of the company, these mortgages are, in actuality, only liens against specific properties. A holder of a mortgage could not proceed to collect against The Kratter Corporation if payments on the mortgage were to be discontinued, and must look only to the property.

Also, included in the total of $58,895,192 of "Mortgages on Properties" as of December 31, 1960 were $23,560,833 of purchase money mortgages used as security for payments by tenants of their lease obligations to The Kratter Corporation. If leases were to be defaulted by tenants, these purchase money mortgages, which have been assigned to the Corporation, are cancellable or reducible. Also, rent payments to the corporation were calculated to include charges payable on the purchase money mortgages. Thus, it can be seen that these purchase money mortgages outstanding do not constitute debt in the usual sense. First mortgages against properties (as opposed to purchase money mortgages) are in a very low ratio to the total property values (28 per cent of undepreciated book value).

"Retained Earnings"

In an interim report, dated September 1, 1960, Mr. Kratter made the following comment on the corporation's "retained earnings:"

In the real estate industry, a substantial part of "retained earnings" is generally represented by reductions in mortgages and other indebtedness. To the extent that these repayments are made, it is usually possible after a period of time to refinance the mortgages and thereby provide the company with new funds (tax-free) for the acquisition of other properties. Presently, the company's "retained earnings," in the form of mortgage reduction, are accumulating at a substantial rate.

As presently constituted, the company's existing portfolio of properties creates increasing amounts of retained earnings each year. This is possible where there is a "constant" or "level" payment mortgage servicing charge. With each payment, larger portions of the payments are allocated to the reduction of the debt, as the interest cost decreases.

At the annual meeting, held in San Francisco on April 19, 1961, Mr. Kratter stated that the corporation's conventional financial statements failed to reflect (1) the enhancement in market values of the corporation's properties, (2) the unique nature of Kratter's debt, and (3) the amount of retained earnings represented by mortgage payments. He stated:

I have no doubt that in the future the accepted accounting practice will catch up to development in the real estate industry so that there may be presented to you a more practical picture of the financial position of the company.

EXHIBIT 1

The Kratter Corporation
Balance Sheets as of December 31, 1960 and 1959

	1960	1959
ASSETS		
Cash	$ 4,739,557	$ 2,868,149
Receivables:		
Rentals	152,567	86,555
Other	476,123	1,286,083
	$ 628,690	$ 1,372,638
Prepaid expenses	223,714	176,060
Investments	7,578,661	
Properties:		
Real properties, leaseholds, etc.	$ 99,297,930	$ 57,812,183
Equipment for rental	4,000,000	3,340,000
Office furniture, fixtures, etc.	179,967	87,912
	$103,477,897	$ 61,240,095
Less allowances for depreciation and amortization	12,520,983	5,664,819
	$ 90,956,914	
Deposits on properties	77,606	
Total properties	$ 91,034,520	$ 55,575,276
Deferred Charges	404,544	200,387
	$104,609,686	$ 60,192,510

LIABILITIES

Notes payable	$ 10,682,617	$ 2,000,000
Accounts payable and accrued expenses	1,274,873	379,357
Deposits and rents received in advance	412,970	264,258
Distributions payable to stockholders	686,049	261,914
Mortgages on properties	58,895,192	37,733,859
Total Liabilities	$ 71,951,701	$ 40,639,388

DEFERRED INCOME	2,525,711	
MINORITY INTEREST	734,195	3,548,394

STOCKHOLDERS' EQUITY

Preferred stock, par value $1 a share	$ 973,251	
Common stock, par value $1 a share		
Class A	3,234,936	$ 2,626,933
Class B	183,470	300,000
Capital surplus[1]	28,189,392	12,621,599
Earned surplus (deficit)	(1,306,044)	456,196
	$ 31,275,005	$ 16,004,728
Less treasury stock	1,876,926	
	$ 29,398,079	
	$104,609,686	$ 60,192,510

---

[1] Increased in 1960 by $21,418,567, the excess over par value of proceeds from sale of 1,174,799 shares of $1.20 Cumulative Convertible Preferred Stock. (Note: The annual dividend on this issue of preferred stock was $1.20 per share; the par value was $1.00 per share.)

EXHIBIT 2

The Kratter Corporation
1960 and 1959 Income Statements

	Year Ended 12/31/60	Eight Months Ended 12/31/59
Revenues:		
Rentals	$9,346,848	$5,063,229
Services, utilities, etc. charged to tenants	88,944	66,407
Interest on mortgages receivable	295,487	41,376
Gain on sales of properties		746,173
Other revenues	265,764	
Total revenues	$9,997,043	$5,917,185
Deductions:		
Operating expenses	$1,437,416	$ 365,978
Leasehold and ground rents	715,403	768,076
Interest on mortgages and notes payable	1,709,828	830,742
Income applicable to minority interest	142,416	152,200
Administrative expenses, etc.	831,608	393,146
Total deductions	$4,836,671	$2,510,142
Income before depreciation and amortization	$5,160,372	$3,407,043
Depreciation and amortization	6,922,612	2,950,847
Net income (loss)	($1,762,240)	$ 456,196

EXHIBIT 3

The Kratter Corporation
Summary of Income Available for Distribution to
Common Shareholders
(Twelve Months ended April 30, 1960)

	Amount	*Per Share*
Income of The Kratter Corporation and subsidiaries and affiliated partnerships before depreciation of properties and amortization of leaseholds and organization expenses	$4,473,230	$1.59
Deduct:		
Payments to reduce mortgages:		
Required by mortgage agreements	1,162,504	.42
Prepayments made at corporation's option	93,677	.03
	$1,256,181	$ .45
Cash distribution provided for preferred shareholders—$.083 per share (paid in May 1960)	97,730	.03
	$1,353,911	$ .48
Available for distribution to common shareholders	$3,119,319	$1.11
Cash distributions paid to common shareholders	2,790,146	.99
Balance retained by the corporation	$ 329,173	$ .12

QUESTIONS:

1. As a common shareholder in The Kratter Corporation, how would you look upon Kratter's distributions? Are such payments really dividends? Explain carefully.

2. Using data from Exhibits 1 and 2, determine Kratter's apparent accounting treatment in recording distributions to shareholders. In 1960, these distributions consisted of cash, $5,560,849, and common stock with a par value of $289,925. Do you agree with the corporation's accounting treatment of these distributions? Explain.

3. Contrast the usefulness of the statements presented in Exhibits 2 and 3 to existing and potential stockholders. Should more corporations present statements similar in form to the one shown in Exhibit 3?

4. Do you agree with Kratter's independent accountants' opinion on the "Summary of Income Available for Distribution to Common Shareholders"?

5. What is Kratter's concept of retained earnings? Is this concept consistent with your reply to question 1 above? Do you agree with Kratter's concept of retained earnings?

6. Do you believe Kratter's balance sheet should reflect the increase in the market value of its properties? Would this provide "a more practical

picture of the financial position of the company"? What problems would you anticipate in developing such a presentation?

7. Do you believe that substantial amounts of Kratter's liabilities "do not constitute debt in the usual sense"? Would you suggest any change in the accounting presentation of these obligations? Does the quotation under *Mortgage Debt* imply a different way of disclosing such obligations?

The Iowa Grain Company

The Iowa Grain Company buys grain and other agricultural products which it stores for later processing and sale. The company owns mills and storage facilities in Iowa, Colorado, Idaho, Illinois, Ohio and Michigan. Exhibits 1 and 2 show Iowa's statements of earnings, retained earnings, and capital in excess of par value for the fiscal years ended August 31, 1960 through 1962, as they appeared in the company's annual reports to its stockholders. Exhibit 3 shows the company's condensed balance sheet at August 31, 1962.

Early in 1963, the Board of Directors became increasingly concerned about trends and conditions that were developing in the organization under the existing management. A careful survey was undertaken and it was deemed vital to the company's welfare that an immediate change be made. The President and two Vice-Presidents resigned and a new management took over. At the same time, new auditors were engaged to review the company's activities and examine the accounts for the year ended August 31, 1963.

The audit review of plant and properties indicated that certain mills were idle while other facilities had been dismantled or abandoned. The loss on such properties scrapped or abandoned in the 1962-1963 fiscal year was $443,105. In addition, similar losses of $208,780 were incurred in the previous fiscal year, but not recognized in the accounts.

During the 1961-1962 fiscal year, annual depreciation rates had been reduced as follows: buildings from 3 to 2 per cent, machinery and equipment from 7.5 to 5 per cent, and harvesting equipment from 15 to 7.5 per cent. The new management felt that the old rates were more appropriate. It was estimated that the reductions in depreciation rates had caused an understatement of $288,589 in depreciation expense for the year 1961–1962.

On August 31, 1962, the Company held 45,000 tons of barley, including 4,000 tons held for delivery to Central Warehouse Company. On August 30, 1962, an entry had been made in the books recording the sale of 4,000 tons to Central Warehouse Company, delivery to be made in September. Iowa owned 40 per cent of Central's outstanding common stock. Subsequent to August 31, the books indicated that 3,200 tons were repurchased from Central at approximately the original sales price. In the early fall of 1962, sales in excess of 50,000 tons were made at substantial losses. It was impossible for the auditors to identify sales by individual lots, but, on the assumption that sales were made first from the year-end inventory and later from subsequent purchases, the estimated loss on the 45,000 tons held prior to the sale to Central approximated $297,500.

In the annual report for the fiscal year ended August 31, 1963, it was decided to include not only the 1962–1963 financial statements, but also the restated statements for the previous year reflecting the necessary corrections and adjustments.

The following data pertain to the 1962–1963 fiscal year only:

Cost of goods sold	$15,802,382
Write-off of worthless patents	59,152
Loss from operations	563,803
Gain on retirement of debentures	77,428
Net sales	16,546,734
Gain on sale of Illinois storage facility	221,721
Selling, general and administrative expenses	1,308,155
Other expenses (interest)	444,382
Loss on sale of Ohio storage facility	421,160

No tax refund was available in 1963.

EXHIBIT 1

The Iowa Grain Company
Statement of Earnings, Years Ended August 31, 1962, 1961 and 1960

	1962	1961	1960
Net sales	$13,885,716	$15,057,791	$12,871,334
Cost of goods sold	13,331,174	13,267,259	13,072,970
Gross profit (loss)	$ 554,542	$ 1,790,532	$ (201,636)
Selling, general and administrative expenses	1,229,564	999,751	952,920
Profit (loss) from operations	$ (675,022)	$ 790,781	$(1,154,556)
Other income:			
Gain (loss) on disposal of plant and equipment	$ 42,826	$ (12,697)	$ 224
Other	58,259	33,006	48,584
	$ 101,085	$ 20,309	$ 48,808
	$ (573,937)	$ 811,090	$(1,105,748)
Other charges			
Interest	372,863	113,558	212,721
Earnings (loss) before Federal income tax	$ (946,800)	$ 697,532	$(1,318,469)
Provision for Federal income tax (refundable)	(346,469)	160,140	(475,708)
Net earnings (loss) before special credit	$ (600,331)	$ 537,392	$ (842,761)
Special credit—gain on sale of storage facility, less applicable Federal income tax, $179,860	—	169,544	—
Net earnings (loss) and special credit	$ (600,331)	$ 706,936	$ (842,761)

EXHIBIT 2

The Iowa Grain Company
Statement of Retained Earnings, Years Ended August 31, 1962, 1961 and 1960

	1962	1961	1960
Amount at beginning of period (deficit)	$ 162,578	$ (544,358)	$ 298,403
Add net earnings (loss) and special credit	(600,331)	706,936	(842,761)
Amount at the end of period (deficit)	$ (437,753)	$ 162,578	$ (544,358)

Statement of Capital in Excess of Par Value, Years Ended
August 31, 1962, 1961 and 1960

	1962	1961	1960
Amount at beginning of period	$ 5,743,215	$ 5,743,215	$ 5,649,880
Add excess of par value over cost of 13,160 shares of 5 per cent cumulative preferred stock retired	—	—	93,335
	$ 5,743,215	$ 5,743,215	$ 5,743,215
Deduct transfer to common stock account resulting from increase of par value of 1,343,000 shares of common stock from $1 to $3	2,686,000	—	—
Amount at end of period	$ 3,057,215	$ 5,743,215	$ 5,743,215

EXHIBIT 3

The Iowa Grain Company
Balance Sheet, August 31, 1962 (Condensed)

ASSETS

Current assets	$ 3,907,557
Investment in Central Warehouse Company	255,850
Property, plant and equipment at cost	$18,294,467
Less accumulated depreciation	7,225,553
	$11,068,914
Deferred charge—unamortized debt expense	66,057
Patents, less amortization	59,152
	$15,357,530

LIABILITIES AND STOCKHOLDERS' EQUITY

Current liabilities	$ 2,299,765
Long-term debt	5,952,525
Capital and retained earnings:	
Common stock, $3 par value; authorized 1,700,000 shares; issued and outstanding 1,343,000	$ 4,029,000
Capital in excess of par value	3,057,215
Excess of book value of net assets of subsidiary at acquisition over cost of investment	456,778
Retained earnings (deficit)	(437,753)
	$ 7,105,240
	$15,357,530

QUESTIONS:

1. Prepare the 1963 income statement and the restated 1962 income statement to be included in the 1963 annual report.

2. What form of income statement did you use in question 1? Note its advantages and disadvantages. Note the advantages and disadvantages of other acceptable forms you might have used.

3. Prepare the 1963 retained earnings statement.

4. Restate the 1962 balance sheet. What assumptions have you made in accounting for the loss on idle, abandoned or dismantled mills?

5. What was Iowa Grain's apparent objective in the sale of barley to the Central Warehouse Company in August, 1962?

6. Prepare the audit report you would give in the 1963 annual report to stockholders.

Unexcelled Chemical Corporation

The Unexcelled Chemical Corporation, which succeeded the Central Fireworks Company, was incorporated in 1915 as the Unexcelled Manufacturing Company. The present name was adopted in 1946.

From 1950 through 1956, the corporation realized a profit in only two years. The cumulative loss for these seven years exceeded profits by almost $1 million. In 1957 and 1958, the corporation reported small profits.

A new management assumed operating control of the corporation in late 1958. At that time, Unexcelled produced industrial paints and varnishes, bronze and aluminum powder and paints, insect repellents, and aluminum extrusions.

The new president described his task as "weeding out unprofitable investments, finding new investment opportunities and re-selling some of them on profitable terms, and otherwise streamlining the procedures of the company." In keeping with these objectives, the corporation began an aggressive program of acquiring and selling subsidiaries and divisions.

1959 Acquisitions and Disposals

Three acquisitions were made in 1959. In April, Unexcelled acquired the assets of the Aylward Chemical Company and its affiliates in exchange for 35,500 shares of Unexcelled common stock. Aylward, a producer of fertilizer, became the Aylco Division of Unexcelled.

In July of 1959, the assets of Bennett and Clayton Co., a manufacturer of lawn and turf products, were purchased for $130,000 cash. Bennett and Clayton products are sold to the general public through garden centers, hardware and chain stores.

The third and most important transaction in 1959 occurred in December when 103,682 Unexcelled common shares were

59

exchanged for all of the outstanding common stock of R. R. Williams, Inc.[1] This company, which specialized in manufacturing pre-moistened, disposable towelettes sold under the names of "Wash'n Dri" and "Baby Bottom Bath," was designated the Consumer Products Division of Unexcelled. Management believed that the growth potential of this division in terms of new products, increased volume, and profitability was outstanding.

In June, 1959, Unexcelled sold a wholly-owned subsidiary, the Ohio Bronze Powder Company, at a gain of $259,291.

1960 Acquisitions and Disposals

Early in 1960, Unexcelled exchanged 2,352 of its common shares for the Trav Company, a producer of packaged detergents designed principally as a travel accessory. This company, which was operated as a wholly-owned subsidiary, was added to Unexcelled's Consumer Products Division.

In April, 1960, Unexcelled acquired 58.3 per cent (5,511 shares) of the outstanding common stock of Oneida Paper Products, Inc., together with 61.1 per cent ($152,778 principal amount) of Oneida's outstanding 8 per cent debenture bonds due January 1, 1972. The purchase price was approximately $2,150,000, payable in cash, 6 per cent notes and shares of Unexcelled common stock. Oneida has its office and main plant in Clifton, New Jersey, with other plants in Maryland, California, and Illinois. It is a major manufacturer of specialty packaging materials used principally in the food industry. Products produced by Oneida include a complete line of glassine, cellophane, and polyethylene bags.

Following the Oneida purchase, Unexcelled acquired a printing company in Switzerland. Excellent growth was anticipated for this company and Unexcelled's management intended to seek additional investment opportunities in Europe.

Three sales of divisions or subsidiaries were reflected in the 1960 financial statements, although one sale didn't actually take place until January 3, 1961. Because of uncertainties in the agricultural economy, the corporation disposed of its Aylco Fertilizer Division in April, 1960, in exchange for 33,230 shares of Unexcelled common stock. No gain or loss was recognized on this transaction. The book

---

[1] For accounting purposes, this exchange of shares was treated as a pooling of interests (described in Chapter 16). In accordance with this concept, the deficits of Unexcelled and R. R. Williams were combined as of January 1, 1959, and R. R. Williams' operating results for the entire year were included in Unexcelled's Consolidated Statement of Income and Deficit (see Exhibit 2).

value of the Aylco Division on Unexcelled's books was assigned as the cost of the 33,230 shares of treasury stock received in the exchange.

On July 31, 1960, a gain of $214,214 was realized from sale of the company's Jasco Aluminum Products Division to Irving Air Chute Co., Inc. in return for cash and 42,000 shares of Irving. This division had been established in 1957 when Unexcelled purchased the Jasco Aluminum Products Corporation of New Hyde Park, New York. It was sold by the new management because of the low earnings potential of the extruded aluminum industry.

Effective as of January 3, 1961, the company sold substantially all the assets of its Consumer Products Division, including the Trav Company, to the Colgate-Palmolive Company for $3,129,400 in cash, payable on February 28, 1961. A gain of $2,123,740 was realized on this sale. The sales and profits of the Consumer Products Division in 1960 had been somewhat disappointing to Unexcelled's management. The division's plant and equipment had been expanded during 1960 and considerable outlays had been made for advertising. At the close of the year the advertising program had not resulted in a sales volume large enough to justify its cost. Colgate-Palmolive, with its established distributorship organization, was in a better position to develop the potential of the division. Colgate's offer for the division was so attractive that Unexcelled's management and directors felt it could not be refused.

Financial Statements

In its 1959 annual report, Unexcelled presented, in comparative form, the company's Consolidated Balance Sheet at December 31, 1959 and 1958, and comparative Consolidated Statement of Income and Deficit for the years 1959 and 1958. These statements are given in Exhibits 1 and 2. On page 2 of the 1959 annual report, under the heading "Financial Highlights," the following data were presented:

	1959	1958
Net sales	$7,003,344	$3,747,139
Costs and expenses	6,501,701	3,624,769
Net income and gain on sale of subsidiary	760,934	122,370
Per share	1.44	.34
Working capital	1,572,078	1,348,196
Property, plant and equipment, less depreciation	1,134,015	369,174
Long-term debt	96,879	55,000
Shareholders' equity	3,855,041	2,592,848
Per share	7.06	6.47

Comparative statements were not given in the 1960 annual report. The Consolidated Balance Sheet at December 31, 1960, and the Consolidated Statement of Income and Retained Earnings for the year were presented as shown in Exhibits 3 and 4. The "Financial Highlights" section of the 1960 annual report contained the following information:

	1960	1959
Net income*	$1,370,831	$ 760,934*
Net income per share	2.40	1.44
Working capital	3,111,685	1,572,078
Shareholders' equity	5,814,075	3,855,041
Shareholders' equity per share	10.02	7.06

* A footnote in the annual report read, "Restated for purposes of comparison."

The gain of $2,123,740 on the sale of assets to Colgate-Palmolive was treated as a 1961 transaction *for income tax purposes*. However, since the effect of the transaction was recognized in the company's 1960 financial statements, the estimated tax liability of $630,000 resulting from the transaction was also shown in the 1960 financial statements. Because of operating loss carryovers, no income taxes were actually payable for the years 1958 through 1960.

Stockholders' Criticism of Annual Report

At a meeting of stockholders early in 1961, a stockholder termed the annual report "highly unsatisfactory." He contended that the 1960 financial statements gave no indication of whether the company made or lost money from its operations, although he stated the indication was that the company lost money. A second shareholder asked: "What do we have to do to get a report that shows operating figures?"

In reply to a stockholder's suggestion that Unexcelled be reincorporated as an investment company under the Investment Company Act, the president stated that it was not the company's intention to act as a "holding" company, but to get a broader base for operations. "Our eventual plan," he said, "is to create one big, fine business instead of spending all our efforts on burdensome negotiations to sell off our assets."

One of the critical stockholders asked if Unexcelled was still a chemical company, to which the president replied, "That's a good question."

EXHIBIT 1

Unexcelled Chemical Corporation
Consolidated Balance Sheet at December 31, 1959 and 1958

	1959	1958
ASSETS		
Current assets:		
Cash	$ 604,901	$ 603,239
Trade accounts receivable, less allowance for doubtful accounts of $122,407—1959; $74,105—1958	828,710	500,665
Other accounts and notes receivable	248,892	31,508
Inventories, at lower of cost or market	1,140,224	493,937
Prepaid expenses	42,127	38,600
Total current assets	$2,864,854	$1,667,949
Property, plant and equipment, at cost, less accumulated depreciation of $594,480—1959; $445,269—1958	1,134,015	369,174
Land not used in operations, at cost of $150,263 plus writeup of $930,295 to 1956 appraised value	1,080,558	1,080,558
Other assets:		
Deferred charges and noncurrent receivables	66,869	—
Excess of investment cost over equity in net assets acquired	216,320	—
	$ 283,189	—
Total assets	$5,362,616	$3,117,681
LIABILITIES AND SHAREHOLDERS' EQUITY		
Current liabilities:		
Notes payable	$ 109,575	$ —
Accounts payable	1,054,275	206,541
Accrued expenses	91,455	61,962
Current portion of mortgages payable	37,471	51,250
Total current liabilities	$1,292,776	$ 319,753
Mortgages payable	96,879	55,000
Deferred rental income	117,920	150,080
Shareholders' equity:		
Common stock — authorized 1,000,000 shares of $5 par value; shares issued and outstanding: 546,413—1959; 400,731—1958	2,732,065	2,003,655
Capital surplus	787,090	862,998
Appraisal surplus	930,295	930,295
Deficit	(594,409)	(1,204,100)
Total shareholders' equity	$3,855,041	$2,592,848
Total liabilities and shareholders' equity	$5,362,616	$3,117,681

EXHIBIT 2

Unexcelled Chemical Corporation
Consolidated Statement of Income and Deficit, Years Ended
December 31, 1959 and 1958

	1959	*1958*
Net sales	$7,003,344	$3,747,139
Costs and expenses:		
Cost of operations	$5,084,180	$2,846,877
Selling, general and administrative expenses	1,300,753	729,627
Provision for depreciation	126,793	49,669
Other (income) and deductions, net	(10,025)	(1,404)
	$6,501,701	$3,624,769
Net income	$ 501,643	$ 122,370
Gain on sale of subsidiary	259,291	—
Net income and gain on sale of subsidiary	$ 760,934	$ 122,370
Deficit at beginning of year	(1,204,100)	(1,326,470)
Deficit of R. R. Williams, Inc. as of January 1, 1959	(151,243)	—
Deficit at end of year	$ (594,409)	$(1,204,100)

EXHIBIT 3

Unexcelled Chemical Corporation
Consolidated Balance Sheet at December 31, 1960

ASSETS

Current assets:	
Cash	$ 55,092
Investment in marketable securities, at lower of cost or market	724,676
Receivable from Colgate-Palmolive Company	3,129,400
Accounts and notes receivable, less reserve	113,404
Inventories, at lower of cost or market	74,478
Prepaid expenses	24,388
Total current assets	$4,121,438
Property, plant and equipment, at cost, less accumulated depreciation of $325,725	$ 357,452
Land not used in operations, at cost of $150,263 plus writeup of $930,295 to 1956 appraised value	1,080,558
Investments at cost:	
Oneida Paper Products, Inc.	2,247,140
Foreign subsidiaries	48,000
	$2,295,140
Total assets	$7,854,588

LIABILITIES AND SHAREHOLDERS' EQUITY
Current Liabilities:

Notes payable to banks	$ 253,611
Other notes payable	232,453
Accounts payable and accrued expenses	458,689
Current portion of long-term debt	65,000
Total current liabilities	$1,009,753
Long-term debt, net of installments due within one year	$ 315,000
Deferred rental income	85,760
Estimated taxes on income	630,000

Shareholders' Equity:

Common stock—$5 par, authorized 1,000,000 shares; issued 609,125; outstanding 580,395, after deducting 28,730 in treasury	3,045,625
Capital surplus	1,700,309
Appraisal surplus	930,295
Retained earnings	776,422
	$6,452,651
Deduct—cost of 28,730 shares in treasury	638,576
Total shareholders' equity	$5,814,075
Total liabilities and shareholders' equity	$7,854,588

EXHIBIT 4

Unexcelled Chemical Corporation
Consolidated Statement of Income and Retained Earnings
Year Ended December 31, 1960

Revenue:

Gain on sale of assets	$2,337,954
Net sales	3,597,528
Dividends from Oneida Paper Products, Inc.	55,110
	$5,990,592

Costs and expenses:

Cost of sales	$2,601,985
Selling, general and administrative	1,297,175
Taxes on income	630,000
Other deductions, net	90,601
	$4,619,761
Net income for the year	$1,370,831
Deficit at beginning of year	(594,409)
Retained earnings at end of year	$ 776,422

QUESTIONS:

1. Do you agree with the stockholders' criticism of the 1960 financial statements? Would you revise the 1960 statements in any way? Do you believe comparative statements should have been presented in 1960? Explain.

2. Compare the "Financial Highlights" sections from the 1959 and 1960 annual reports. Do you approve of the restatement of 1959 results in the 1960 "Financial Highlights"? Explain.

3. What total dollar amounts were used to calculate the per share results of $2.40 and $1.44 included in the 1960 "Financial Highlights"? Do you agree with the use of these amounts? Explain. In calculating the 1960 and 1959 per share results, what number of shares was used as the denominator each year? Compare these numbers with the shares outstanding at the close of 1960 and 1959, as indicated on the respective balance sheets. How do you explain the differences?

4. Do you approve of giving effect in 1960 to the sales transaction with Colgate-Palmolive, when the transaction did not actually take place until January 3, 1961? Explain.

5. Do you approve of recording in 1960 the estimated tax liability of $630,000 resulting from the Colgate transaction, when Unexcelled intended to treat it as a 1961 transaction for tax purposes? Explain.

6. What is your opinion of the $930,295 writeup of land to its 1956 appraised value? To what extent does this writeup affect data included under "Financial Highlights"?

CHAPTER FOUR

Funds Statements

In addition to the conventional financial statements (the balance sheet, income statement, and statement of changes in retained earnings), which were considered in Chapter 3, another financial statement has received increasing attention in recent years. The description, form, and content of this statement vary. It is frequently called the "Funds Statement," and usually reveals the sources and uses of working capital (current assets less current liabilities) *during a fiscal period.* While most funds statements found in corporate annual reports focus on working capital, other definitions of "funds" are occasionally used in such reports. These will be discussed in a later section of this chapter.

Figure 1 is an example of a funds statement taken from the 1961 annual report of the Eastman Kodak Company.

Funds Became Available from :	
Net earnings	$130,203,447
Provision for depreciation	44,467,175
Miscellaneous items—net	2,348,362
Total	$177,018,984
Funds Were Used for :	
Dividends declared	$ 86,581,941
Expenditures for additions and improvements to properties and equipment	70,659,058
Additional investments in foreign subsidiaries	7,340,693
Total	$164,581,692
Increase in working capital	$ 12,437,292

Figure 1. Sources and Uses of Funds

In Figure 1, "funds" and "working capital" are used interchangeably. The two parts of the statement are described in terms of "Funds available" and "Funds used," but the final amount is labeled "Increase in working capital."

EARLY FUNDS STATEMENTS

The first attempt to report on the sources and uses of funds was made in 1908 by William Morse Cole.[1] This crude beginning consisted merely of comparing net changes in the accounts between two balance-sheet dates, no attempt being made to analyze cause and effect relationships. In the past fifty years, business firms have grown rapidly in size and complexity, top management has become increasingly separated from the details of day-to-day operations, and the number of stockholders has grown at a phenomenal rate.[2] These changes have emphasized the need for financial information not readily apparent, if indeed even determinable, from an examination of the usual financial statements.

RECENT EMPHASIS ON FUNDS STATEMENTS

More recently, inflation and other forces have caused increased interest in funds statements. These statements, unlike income statements, are less subject to distortions in reporting caused by inflation because the dollar values listed in a funds statement are relatively current. Also, the growing use of alternative accounting procedures with varying impacts on reported earnings has made it increasingly difficult to compare different companies' results. Since some of these alternative procedures, such as in depreciation accounting, do not directly affect the flow of funds, the funds statement may facilitate comparability among a group of corporations.[3]

These two considerations, inflation and a growing lack of uniformity in accounting, have led security analysts and others interested in accounting comparability to look with increasing favor on the funds statement. Management has also emphasized the funds statement in explaining to stockholders why it is necessary for the corporation to retain a significant portion of earnings. In addition to questions about dividend policy, a funds statement may help answer such questions as the following: How was the expansion of plant and equipment financed? How were the proceeds from the sale of stock, bonds, or various assets used? How was the retirement of debt or preferred stock financed?

---

[1] William Morse Cole, *Accounts: Their Construction and Interpretation* (Boston: Houghton Mifflin Co., 1908).

[2] In July, 1962, according to a New York Stock Exchange estimate, there were 17 million American stockholders, up from 6.5 million in 1952.

[3] Depreciation accounting may affect the amount of funds required for income taxes. This indirect influence of depreciation on the flow of funds is considered later.

FORM OF FUNDS STATEMENT

One common form of the funds statement was given in Figure 1. Another form, which reconciles the funds statement with the beginning and ending balance of working capital, appeared in the 1961 annual report of the Inspiration Consolidated Copper Company. This statement is shown in Figure 2.

Working Capital—December 31, 1960			$18,049,962
1961:			
Sources of Funds:			
Net income			3,469,677
Depreciation and amortization			1,270,776
Other			154,893
Total funds made available			4,895,346
Application of Funds:			
Dividends paid to stockholders		$2,956,768	
Capital expenditures			
Plant and equipment	$5,337,757		
Mines, mining claims and lands	1,509	5,339,266	8,296,034
Decrease in working capital			3,400,688
Working Capital —December 31, 1961			$14,649,274

Figure 2. Working Capital and Sources and Application of Funds

As another example, Figure 3 shows a funds statement taken from the 1961 annual report of the Armstrong Cork Company.

Funds Became Available from:	
Net earnings	$18,506,000
Depreciation and amortization	11,679,000
Sale of common stock	1,175,000
Deferred federal income tax	1,000,000
	$32,360,000
These Funds Were Used for:	
Expenditures for property, plant and equipment	$19,405,000
Dividend payments to stockholders	9,307,000
Increasing working capital	2,125,000
Other items—principally investments	1,523,000
	$32,360,000

Figure 3. Source and Use of Funds—1961

The differences among the three funds statements illustrated in Figures 1, 2, and 3 may appear minor since one form can be readily converted to another. However, the message to the reader is quite different. The forms illustrated in Figures 1 and 2 draw attention to working capital, particularly the status of working capital at the close of the fiscal period. The messages to the reader are: "By the close of the fiscal period, working capital had increased (or decreased) by $..." (Figure 1); or, "at the close of the fiscal period, the balance of working capital was $..., compared to $... at the beginning of the period" (Figure 2). The message in Figure 3 is: "These amounts of working capital became available during the year and here is how they were used." This last form of funds statement is favored by some accountants because it emphasizes the movement of funds and not the net effect of these movements.

COMPARATIVE AND CUMULATIVE FUNDS STATEMENTS

The usefulness of the funds statement is enhanced by presenting comparative data for the current and one or more prior periods. Although the amount of a company's earnings or loss may change abruptly from year to year, the *nature* of the revenue and expense transactions will usually be similar from one period to the next. This is less true of the financial activities reported in the funds statement. For example, a corporation may infrequently borrow on a long-term basis or sell additional capital stock, but these financing transactions are significant events with important future implications, whether they occurred in the present or a recent past period.

In addition to comparative funds statements, a cumulative statement may even more effectively summarize financial management activities over many years. Figure 4 is a combined two-year comparative and ten-year cumulative funds statement of the Addressograph-Multigraph Corporation.

	FISCAL YEARS ENDED JULY 31		10 YEARS ENDED JULY 31, 1962
	1962	1961	
Funds Provided:			
Net income	$13,151,000	$12,177,000	$ 89,110,000
Depreciation and amortization	4,330,000	3,858,000	25,426,000
In exchange for common stock		496,000	11,657,000
Bank loans			5,000,000
Total funds provided	$17,481,000	$16,531,000	$131,193,000
Funds Applied:			
Cash dividends paid	$ 5,890,000	$ 5,759,000	$ 39,880,000
Net additions to properties	9,122,000	5,414,000	47,720,000
Miscellaneous (Net)	541,000	55,000	895,000
Repayment of bank loans			5,000,000
Total funds applied	$15,553,000	$11,228,000	$ 93,495,000
Excess:			
Net increase in working capital	$ 1,928,000	$ 5,303,000	$ 37,698,000

Figure 4. Application of Funds Statement

TECHNICAL PROBLEMS

In each of the funds statements illustrated so far in this chapter, the first "source" listed is net earnings or net income. The implication is clear that funds or working capital must have been increased during the period by the amount of net earnings. Since net earnings is simply the excess of revenues over expenses, it would seem to follow that revenue transactions must have increased funds while expense transactions decreased funds. Revenue transactions *may* increase funds and expense transactions *may* decrease funds, but some revenue and expense transactions have no current effect on the flow of funds.

Depreciation is the most common and usually the most significant expense which does not result in an outlay of funds. The mere recording of depreciation, while it does reduce net earnings, does not *directly* diminish funds. Depreciation does have an *indirect* impact on the flow of funds because of its deductibility for tax purposes and the resulting reduction in funds required for tax payments. It is customary in the funds statement to "add back" depreciation to net earnings, *not* because depreciation is a source of funds, but rather because net earnings understates the flow of funds from operations. The actual outflow of funds occurs when depreciable assets are acquired.

It may prove helpful to the reader of the funds statement and also clarify the relationship between depreciation and funds flow if funds derived from operations are grouped together with an appropriate subtotal disclosed. The Armco Steel Corporation used this presentation in 1960:

Working capital provided from operations:		
Net income for the year	$70,459,000	
Depreciation	40,163,000	$110,622,000

One form of funds statement which avoids the problem of "adding back" depreciation and hence eliminates the tendency to consider depreciation as a source of funds is illustrated in Figure 5, a funds statement from the Gulf Oil Corporation's 1961 annual report.

There are other expenses in addition to depreciation which reduce net earnings, but do not currently diminish funds. In Figure 3, for example, net earnings were reduced by recording $1,000,000 of income tax expense, the payment of which was deferred. Such deferred taxes are classified as a liability outside the working capital section on the balance sheet. At some future date the actual payment of these taxes will reduce funds, but will have no effect on earnings.

Funds Were Received from:	
Sales and other revenues	$3,285,663,000

Funds Were Paid for:	
Purchased crude oil, petroleum products, and other merchandise	1,011,128,000
Taxes on income and general taxes	711,769,000
Wages, salaries, and employee benefits	294,662,000
Other expenses	686,040,000
Total	2,703,599,000

Funds Left from Operations	582,064,000
Additional Funds Were Received from:	
Sale of Union Oil Company of California debentures	120,000,000
Sale of properties and other items—net	21,600,000
Total Funds Provided For The Year	723,664,000

These Funds Were Used for:	
Properties, plants, and equipment	288,209,000
Related business investments	56,236,000
Retirement of long-term debt	28,261,000
Cash dividends to Gulf shareholders	112,907,000
Cash dividends to minority shareholders	10,325,000
Total	495,938,000

Balance Added to Working Capital	$ 227,726,000

Figure 5. Employment of Funds—1961

Disclosing the sale of property in the funds statement may create problems. Generally such property will not be sold at precisely its book value; some gain or loss will be realized on the sale. If such a gain is included in net earnings for the period, only the balance of the proceeds (the book value of the property sold) will be shown separately among the sources of funds. The 1961 funds statement of the Hooker Chemical Corporation, shown in Figure 6, illustrates this method of disclosing the sale of plant and equipment.

Funds Available:		
Net income for year		$11,986,500
Charges against income not affecting working capital:		
Depreciation and amortization	$8,987,800	
Deferred income taxes	871,000	9,858,800
Book value of plant and equipment sold or retired (gain or loss included in net income)		288,500
Sale of common stock under stock option and stock purchase plans		720,500
		22,854,300
Applied as Follows:		
Additions to plant and equipment	26,479,500	
Dividends on capital stocks	7,574,800	
Reduction in long-term debt	2,680,000	
Increase in other assets	577,100	37,311,400
Decrease in Working Capital		$14,457,100

Figure 6. Source and Application of Funds

If the method used in Figure 6 might prove misleading, deduction of the gain from net earnings and separate disclosure of the entire proceeds from the sale is an acceptable alternative.

If a loss on the sale of property is reflected in net earnings, the loss would be "added back" because it does not decrease funds. The total proceeds from the sale would then be shown as a separate source of funds.

NET VS. GROSS CHANGES

Although funds statements presumably depict the flow of working capital, rather often certain inflows and outflows occurring *within* the fiscal period are offset against one another without disclosure of the separate amounts. This practice is objectionable unless the amounts involved are immaterial. This problem may arise in showing additions and retirements of long-term debt, the issuance and reacquisition of capital stock, and the sale and acquisition of property. The word "net" will usually indicate when this has been done, as in the following examples: "Increase in long-term debt, net of re-payments," or "Additions to properties, net of disposals." In the latter case it may not be clear whether the gross additional investment has been reduced by the total proceeds from the sale of property or the book value of such property. Figure 7 shows the 1961 funds statement of the Kendall Company in which gross changes in funded debt are disclosed, while other less material changes are designated, "Other items—net."

Source of Funds:	
Net earnings after taxes	$ 5,012,000
Depreciation	2,861,000
Additional funded debt	7,000,000
Other items net	845,000
	$15,718,000
Use of Funds:	
Expenditures for plant and related facilities	$ 8,596,000
Cash dividends common and preferred stock	2,596,000
Reduction in funded debt	618,000
	$11,810,000
Increase in Working Capital	$ 3,908,000

Figure 7. Source and Use of Funds in 1961

The type of offsets noted above will typically involve increases and decreases in the same class of item, such as long-term debt. An attempt to relate a particular source and a particular use of funds results in another type of offset. Usually the two amounts, and not just the net difference, are disclosed. A common case is the disclosure of dividends as a deduction from net earnings. As an example, see the 1961 funds statement of the United States Rubber Company, shown in Figure 10. Similarly, depreciation may be shown as a deduction from expenditures for property, plant and equipment. These types of offsets are of doubtful validity, since it is usually difficult to identify what specific resources were applied to specific uses.

CHANGES WITHIN WORKING CAPITAL

While the word "funds," when used in the description of "funds statements," usually means working capital, there are other definitions used by accountants. None of the funds statements illustrated so far indicates changes in the components of working capital. Changes in cash, accounts receivable, inventories, or current liabilities may often be of greater significance and magnitude than the changes in non-working capital items disclosed in the typical funds statement. One method of disclosing such information is to supplement the funds statement with a separate schedule of changes within working capital. This method is illustrated in Figure 8(a)–8(b) by the funds state-

Funds Provided by:	
Net income	$3,000,016
Depreciation and amortization charged to income	917,933
Proceeds from the sale of capital stock under Stock Option Plan	132,571
Other	4,794
Total funds provided	$4,055,314
Funds Used for:	
Property, plant and equipment	$ 800,138
Purchase of capital stock for Treasury	1,002,613
Dividends	1,567,034
Total funds used	$3,369,785
Increase in Working Capital	$ 685,529

Figure 8(a). Sources and Uses of Funds

	1961	1960	Increase (Decrease)
Current Assets:			
Cash and marketable securities	$ 5,797,325	$ 5,562,870	$234,455
Notes and accounts receivable, net	6,800,976	6,074,855	726,121
Inventories	12,621,090	12,844,766	(223,676)
Deposits and prepayments	547,681	728,656	(180,975)
Total current assets	$25,767,072	$25,211,147	$555,925
Current Liabilities:			
Accounts payable	$ 1,584,127	$ 1,518,601	$ 65,526
Federal income taxes	1,037,143	1,333,644	(296,501)
Accrued liabilities	1,993,604	1,892,233	101,371
Total current liabilities	$ 4,614,874	$ 4,744,478	($129,604)
Working capital	$21,152,198	$20,466,669	$685,529

Figure 8(b). Changes in Working Capital

ment and schedule of changes in working capital included in the 1961 annual report of Ametek, Inc.

A more condensed, yet satisfactory, disclosure of the significant changes within working capital is shown in Figure 9 from the 1960 annual report of the Pittsburgh Plate Glass Company.

Working Capital at Beginning of Year		$159,559,000
Source of Working Capital:		
Net Earnings	$47,631,000	
Depreciation and Depletion	35,766,000	
Federal Income Taxes Deferred	2,200,000	
Total		$ 85,597,000
Application of Working Capital:		
Expenditures for Plant and Equipment	$25,056,000	
Cash Dividends Paid	22,291,000	
Retirement of Long-term Debt	6,255,000	
Other (Net of Other Sources)	277,000	
Total		$ 53,879,000
Increase in Working Capital*		$ 31,718,000
Working Capital at End of Year		$191,277,000
*The increase in working capital is represented by the following:		
Additions:		
Increase in cash and marketable securities	$23,206,000	
Increase in inventories	1,311,000	
Decrease in current liabilities	12,852,000	$ 37,369,000
Deductions:		
Decrease in current receivables	$ 5,375,000	
Decrease in prepaid expenses	276,000	5,651,000
		$ 31,718,000

Figure 9. Source and Application of Funds

In contrast to Figure 8(a)–8(b), only the net changes, not the opening and closing balances, are revealed in Figure 9, and the details of changes in current liabilities are not disclosed. However, such details are normally disclosed in the balance sheet.

A second method of disclosing significant changes within working capital, which eliminates the need for a supplementary schedule, is to change the definition of funds so that such changes will appear in the funds statement itself. Funds may be defined as cash, or, more frequently, as cash plus short-term securities. This latter definition is used in Figure 10, the 1961 funds statement of the United States Rubber Company, although the changes in current items other than cash and short-term securities are shown in a single net figure.

A funds statement revealing working capital changes in greater detail was included in the 1961 annual report of the Continental Can Company. This is given in Figure 11.

Funds Provided:
Net income $27,096,000
Less—cash dividends to stockholders   17,860,000 $ 9,236,000
Depreciation of property   25,711,000
Increase in current liabilities in excess of increase in
    receivables and inventories   3,566,000
Sale of common stock—exercise of stock options   581,000

Total $39,094,000

Funds Required:
Property additions, net of retirements $35,789,000
Purchases of 2 ⁵/₈ per cent debentures   3,483,000
Investments in affiliated companies   2,060,000
Purchase of preferred stock for retirement   868,000
Miscellaneous   521,000

Total $42,721,000

Cash and Short-Term Securities:
December 31, 1960 $57,635,000
December 31, 1961   54,008,000

Decrease—excess of requirements over funds provided
    in 1961 $ 3,627,000

Figure 10. Sources and Uses of Funds

Source of Funds	1961	1961	Use of Funds
	in millions	in millions	
Income, before income taxes	$ 76.9	$ 40.8	Income taxes
Depreciation and depletion	39.6	47.8	Capital expenditures
Increase in payables and accruals	2.9	22.8	Dividends on Preferred and
Increase in tax accruals	15.9		Common stocks
Increase in reserves	5.4	6.3	Increase in receivables
Sale of Common stock to		13.2	Increase in inventories
employees	2.5	.7	Purchase of Preferred and Common stocks
Net value capital assets disposed			
of, etc.	3.1	2.2	Decrease in long-term debt
	146.3	11.6	Decrease in current portion of
Net decrease in cash and short-			long-term debt
term securities	4.2	4.4	Provision for prior year taxes
		.7	Increase in other assets
	$150.5	$150.5	

Figure 11. Sources and Uses of Funds

Continental Can emphasizes the amount of income taxes by listing income before income taxes among the sources of funds, while listing income taxes first among the uses of funds.

BROADENING THE CONCEPT OF FUNDS

So far two definitions of funds have been discussed. The first is working capital and the second is cash and short-term securities. Use of the latter definition may result in improved disclosure of changes within working capital, although such changes may be disclosed by a separate schedule.

Occasionally there are other significant financial events which would not be revealed in the funds statements described above because they have no impact on cash and short-term securities or any other item within working capital. Examples are the conversion of bonds into stock or the receipt of property, plant or equipment in exchange for long-term bonds or capital stock.

In Accounting Research Study No. 2, *"Cash Flow" Analysis and The Funds Statement*,[4] Perry Mason recommended a definition of "funds" as "all financial resources" or as spending or purchasing power. In addition to the type of information disclosed in the usual funds statements, in which funds is defined as working capital, this definition would result in disclosing *both* important changes within working capital and movements of financial resources wholly outside of working capital such as those mentioned above. The conclusions and recommendations of Dr. Mason's study of the funds statement, which are presented later in this chapter, contain suggestions to prevent the proposed form of statement from becoming excessively detailed.

Figure 12, from the 1961 annual report of the Pittsburgh Plate Glass Company, illustrates the type of statement recommended by Dr. Mason. This statement should be carefully compared with this company's more conventional 1960 funds statement given in Figure 9.

Sources of Funds:	
From operations*	$69,819,000
Decrease in cash and marketable securities	5,316,000
From miscellaneous sources (net)	4,436,000
Total	$79,571,000
Uses of Funds:	
Additions to plant and equipment	$30,280,000
Cash dividends paid	22,693,000
Retirement of long-term debt (including current maturities)	6,045,000
Increase in working capital (exclusive of working capital items included above)	20,553,000
Total	$79,571,000

*Composed of Net Income, $34,627,000, and depreciation and depletion, $35,192,000.

Figure 12. Summary of Financial Activities—1961

"CASH-FLOW" ANALYSIS

Many corporations present so-called "cash-flow earnings" in their annual reports. The term "cash-flow earnings" is a misnomer since the amounts so designated usually correspond with "funds from operations" in the funds statements. Often this is merely the sum

---

[4] See References, page 81.

of net earnings and depreciation although, as noted earlier in this chapter, other "non-fund" expense or revenue items may influence the determination of funds derived from operations. Cash-flow data are frequently expressed in both per share and total amounts.

"Cash flow," or funds derived from operations, is a useful measurement in appraising a corporation's ability to finance expansion, pay dividends, or retire debt. However, such data are more appropriately shown as part of the sources side of a funds statement in which *both* the sources and uses of financial resources are disclosed.

The accounting profession has become increasingly concerned with the growing use of such presentations, particularly when the data are presented apart from the funds statements. "Cash-flow earnings" may substantially exceed earnings computed by the usual accrual method, and, by implication, the reader may feel that "cash earnings" are more significant in revealing operating results than net earnings properly determined. In any case, it is confusing to encounter two earnings figures.

In his research study, *"Cash Flow" Analysis and The Funds Statement,"* Dr. Mason was equally concerned with these two closely related subjects. His conclusions and recommendations are reproduced below.

Conclusions and Recommendations—Part I: "Cash Flow" Analysis

1. "Cash flow" in financial analysis means net income after adding back expense items which currently do not use funds, such as depreciation. (It may also involve deducting revenue items which do not currently provide funds, such as the current amortization of deferred income.) This concept of "cash flow" as the amount of assets or funds made available after meeting the current requirements of revenue-earning operations is a valid and useful analytical tool. It can be used effectively as one of the major factors in judging, for example, the ability to meet debt-retirement requirements, to maintain regular dividends, and to finance replacement and expansion costs.

2. Depreciation and other similar "non-fund" charges to operations are not "sources" of funds. The amount of the "non-fund" items, however, can properly be used, together with the net income or net loss, in the *measurement* of the cash flow if operations are successful, or of the drain on current resources if operations are unsuccessful. This is a convenient or short-cut means of computing the funds provided by operations.

3. It is possible under some circumstances that an expansion of physical plant and equipment can take place without additional equity or debt financing, where depreciation and other similar factors are present. There is a strong presumption, however, that the major portion of the retained funds associated with depreciation accounting will be needed to finance replacements, and that the funds required for expansion must in large part be provided by the retention of earnings or other additional invested capital.

4. In no sense can the amount of cash flow or cash income be considered as a substitute for or an improvement upon the net income, properly determined, as an indication of the results of operations or the change in

financial position. Under some circumstances, especially where the accounting methods used are significantly different, cash-flow calculations may improve the comparability of operating statistics from one company to another. There are, however, many other differences between companies which make effective comparisons extremely difficult. For example, in a rate-of-return computation, the elimination of depreciation would not avoid the lack of comparability of the cost of the plant and equipment where the acquisitions were made at different price levels.

5. The presentation of cash-flow data in annual reports of corporations can be greatly improved. The inclusion of a well-designed comparative funds statement in the annual report should become a generally accepted practice. It should be accompanied by interpretive comments and charts which would provide the reader with useful information as to the conduct of financial affairs by the management during the period covered by this type of operating statement. Isolated comments or statistics concerning cash flow should be avoided since they are generally meaningless and often misleading.

Conclusions and Recommendations—Part II: The Funds Statement

1. The funds statement should be treated as a major financial statement. It should be presented in all annual reports of corporations and be covered by the auditor's short-form report.

2. The statement should be broad enough in scope and in its concept of "funds" to make it a report of all financial management operations. It should not be merely a reconciliation of cash or working capital. The definition of "funds" as "all financial resources," or as spending or purchasing power, comes closest to this conception of the function of the funds statement. The title need not be uniform, but should be as descriptive as possible. "Summary of Financial Activities" or some similar title is recommended.

3. It should be standard practice for the management to include in the annual report interpretive comments related directly to the funds statement which assist the reader in understanding the financial policies, plans, and operations of the company. As indicated in Part I, comments and statistics of "cash flow" should not be presented apart from or without reference to the funds statement.

4. There should be no standard arrangement of the items within the funds statement. Instead, it should be designed to disclose and emphasize the more important financial events of the period covered by the statement. Related items may be shown together when the result contributes to the clarity of the statement. Unimportant items may be combined. The change in working capital should not be shown as a single item unless the changes in individual current assets and liabilities are immaterial.

5. The more popular form of the statement which begins with net income is recommended for general use, but great care should be taken to avoid giving the impression that depreciation and other such adjustments are "sources" of funds. The best way to accomplish this is to begin the statement with the adjusted net income, the "funds provided from operations," and show the details of the calculation in a footnote.

6. The form which begins with total revenue instead of net income is acceptable and has certain advantages, but it is not recommended as a preferable arrangement. If it is used, disclosure of the non-fund items which have been omitted in the computation of the amount derived from operations is desirable.

7. Gross changes in capital stock and in liabilities should be shown where the amounts are material. The proceeds from an issue of securities should appear as a separate source of funds.

8. Where significant in amount, the proceeds from the sale of property should be disclosed and shown separately from the acquisition of noncurrent assets.

9. The consolidated funds statement should present the combined financial operations as though a single business unit were involved.[5] The significant net income figure, therefore, is not the net income after deducting the share of the minority interest, if there is such, but is the consolidated net income or the net income of the group of companies as a whole. Dividends to minority shareholders should be combined or grouped with dividends to parent-company shareholders.

10. Comparative and cumulative funds statements should be encouraged. Except at the end of the first year of operations of a new or reorganized company, a two-year comparative statement should be presented as one of the group of major financial statements. Comparative funds statement data for longer periods, such as five or ten years, should also be included in the annual report, following the pattern adopted by the company for other financial summaries.

REFERENCES

Anton, Hector R., *Accounting for the Flow of Funds*. Boston: Houghton Mifflin Co., 1962.

Bierman, Harold, Jr., "Measuring Financial Liquidity," *Accounting Review*, 35 (Oct. 1960), 628–32.

Blough, Carman G., "'Cash Flow Earnings'—A Dangerous Concept," *Journal of Accountancy*, 106 (Oct. 1958), 77–78.

Castenholz, W. B., "That Application of Funds Statement," *Accounting Review*, 31 (Jul. 1956), 431–34.

Corbin, Donald A., "Proposals for Improving Funds Statements," *Accounting Review*, 36 (Jul. 1961), 398–405.

Corbin, Donald A., and Russell Taussig, "The AICPA Funds Statement Study," *Journal of Accountancy*, 114 (Jul. 1962), 57–62.

Horngren, Charles T., "The Funds Statement and Its Use by Analysts," *Journal of Accountancy*, 101 (Jan. 1956), 55–59.

_____, "Increasing the Utility of Financial Statements," *Journal of Accountancy*, 108 (Jul. 1959), 39–46.

Kempner, Jack J., "Funds Statement Practices of Certified Public Accounting Firms," *Accounting Review*, 32 (Jan. 1957), 71–82.

Mann, Everett J., "Cash Flow Earnings—New Concept in Security Analysis," *Accounting Review*, 33 (Jul. 1958), 423–26.

Mason, Perry, "'Cash Flow' Analysis and Funds Statements," *Journal of Accountancy*, 111 (Mar. 1961), 59–72. Letters regarding this article appeared in 111 (May 1961), 37, and 111 (Jun. 1961), 31.

---

[5] Consolidated financial statements are considered in Chapter 5.

_____, *"Cash Flow" Analysis and The Funds Statement*, Accounting Research Study No. 2. New York: American Institute of Certified Public Accountants, 1961. The conclusions and recommendations from this Accounting Research Study were reprinted in the *Journal of Accountancy*, 112 (Dec. 1961), 66–68.

Moonitz, Maurice, "Reporting on the Flow of Funds," *Accounting Review*, 31 (Jul. 1956), 375–85.

Research Division of the American Institute of Certified Public Accountants, "Comments on *'Cash Flow' Analysis and The Funds Statement"* (Accounting Research Study No. 2), *Journal of Accountancy*, 114 (Sept. 1962), 63–67.

Stone, Williard E., "The Funds Statement as an Analysis Tool," *Accounting Review*, 34 (Jan. 1959), 127–30.

Zannetos, Zenon S., "Depreciation and Fund Statements," *Accounting Review*, 37 (Apr. 1962), 300–307.

Farm Machinery Company

Farm Machinery has over 75,000 stockholders including many large institutions such as pension funds and investment trusts. Because of the widespread investor interest in its securities, the company has made every effort to present understandable and useful financial information to its shareholders and others interested in its financial affairs. In the annual report for the fiscal year ended October 31, 1962, the following information was presented:

Statement of Income for the Years Ended October 31, 1962 and 1961 (Exhibit 1);

Statement of Financial Condition at October 31, 1962 and 1961 (Exhibit 2);

Summary of Net Income Retained for Use in the Business for the Years Ended October 31, 1962 and 1961 (Exhibit 3);

Summary of Changes in Net Assets During the 1962 and 1961 Fiscal Years (Exhibit 4);

Changes in Property Accounts During the 1962 and 1961 Fiscal Years (Exhibit 5); and

Notes to the 1962 Financial Statements (Exhibit 6).

The company did not present a statement of "funds flow" in its 1962 annual report. However, the following explanation was included in the "Financial Review" section of the report under the heading, "Working Capital and Cash Flow":

Working capital is the difference between current assets (cash, marketable securities, receivables and inventories) and current liabilities. As its name implies, it represents the funds which support the regular operations of the business. Thus, it is distinguished from fixed assets, whose cost is charged against operations gradually over a period of years as depreciation, and from other assets which generally consist of investments and other non-current items.

During 1962, working capital increased from $105,095,000 to $116,779,000, an increase of $11,684,000. This compares with an increase of $6,371,000 in 1961.

The major internal sources of increased working capital are the company's income from operations and depreciation charged in the determination of income from operations. (The latter represents in effect a conversion of a part of the fixed assets into working capital form.) To these are added the dividends received from subsidiaries to arrive at the amount to be regarded as the increase in working capital generated by the regular operations of the business.

Working capital is also increased or decreased by changes in the balances of other assets and of long-term debt, as well as by fixed asset disposals, by the deferral of tax liability due to depreciation deductions for tax purposes in excess of depreciation charged against income, and certain other items.

The total working capital inflow in 1962, sometimes called cash flow, can be displayed as follows:

	1962
Net income (excluding dividends from subsidiaries)	$14,896,000
Depreciation	10,134,000
Dividends from subsidiaries	4,208,000
Other increases	847,000
Total	$30,085,000
Per share of common stock outstanding at October 31	$ 8.15

Working capital is depleted mainly by the payment of dividends and by capital expenditures. Dividends were $8,713,000 in 1962, and capital expenditures were $7,627,000, representing 29.0 per cent and 25.4 per cent respectively of the working capital inflow.

EXHIBIT 1

Farm Machinery Company
Statement of Income for the Years Ended October 31, 1962 and 1961
(000 omitted)

	1962	*1961*
NET SALES		
To dealers and users in the United States	$294,039	$231,596
Defense products	6,309	5,036
To subsidiary companies	36,223	34,314
Total	$336,571	$270,946
DEDUCT		
Cost of goods sold	$270,615	$224,871
Selling and administrative expenses	35,564	31,361
Total	$306,179	$256,232
INCOME FROM OPERATIONS	$ 30,392	$ 14,714
OTHER INCOME CREDITS AND (CHARGES)		
Dividends received from subsidiary companies	$ 4,208	$ 4,355
Interest earned	960	309
Interest paid	(881)	(896)
Gain (loss) on property sold and scrapped	385	(102)
Total	$ 4,672	$ 3,666
INCOME BEFORE FEDERAL INCOME TAXES AND PROVISION FOR DEFERRED CREDIT—FEDERAL INCOME TAXES	$ 35,064	$ 18,380
PROVISION FOR FEDERAL INCOME TAXES	(15,332)	(6,798)
PROVISION FOR DEFERRED CREDIT—FEDERAL INCOME TAXES (Note 1)	(628)	(834)
NET INCOME	$ 19,104	$ 10,748

84   FARM MACHINERY COMPANY

EXHIBIT 2

Farm Machinery Company
Statement of Financial Condition at October 31, 1962 and 1961
(000 omitted from column figures)

NET ASSETS IN WHICH CAPITAL WAS INVESTED

	1962	1961
CURRENT ASSETS		
Cash	$ 15,508	$ 15,774
United States government securities, at lower of cost or market	31,456	22,258
Accounts receivable (less reserves for losses: 1962—$812,803; 1961—$845,753)	16,757	14,889
Trade accounts with subsidiary companies	7,740	5,396
Inventories	97,720	80,305
Total current assets	$169,181	$138,622
LESS CURRENT LIABILITIES		
Current invoices, payrolls, etc.	$ 28,473	$ 18,010
Accrued taxes	20,995	13,207
Dividends payable	2,438	2,092
Trade accounts with subsidiary companies	496	218
Total current liabilities	$ 52,402	$ 33,527
NET CURRENT ASSETS (WORKING CAPITAL)	$116,779	$105,095
PROPERTY		
Buildings, machinery and equipment	$154,588	$152,432
Deduct reserve for depreciation	79,323	74,277
Net depreciable property	$ 75,265	$ 78,155
Land	5,117	4,953
Net property	$ 80,382	$ 83,108
INVESTMENT IN SUBSIDIARY COMPANIES	$ 33,493	$ 31,760
OTHER ASSETS	$ 3,263	$ 2,935
TOTAL NET ASSETS IN WHICH CAPITAL WAS INVESTED	$233,917	$222,898

SOURCES FROM WHICH CAPITAL WAS OBTAINED

	1962	1961
CONVERTIBLE DEBENTURES		
Twenty-year, $3^1/_2$ per cent, dated October 1, 1957; convertible into common stock beginning October 1, 1962 (Note 2)	$ 16,128	$ 25,000
DEFERRED CREDIT—FEDERAL INCOME TAXES (Note 1)	$ 2,786	$ 2,158
EQUITY CAPITAL		
Preferred stock, authorized 248,350 shares, 7 per cent cumulative $100 par value; issued 204,181 shares	$ 20,418	$ 20,418
Common stock, authorized 4,377,385 shares, no par value; issued 1962—3,690,673 shares; 1961—3,468,873 shares	147,627	138,755
Net income retained	46,958	36,567
Total equity capital	$215,003	$195,740
TOTAL CAPITAL INVESTED	$233,917	$222,898

EXHIBIT 3

Farm Machinery Company
Summary of Net Income Retained for Use in the Business for the Years
Ended October 31, 1962 and 1961
(000 omitted)

	1962	1961
Balance at beginning of year	$36,567	$34,186
Changes during the year		
Net income	$19,104	$10,748
Cash dividends declared		
Preferred stock—$7.00 per share	$(1,429)	$(1,429)
Common stock—1962, $2.10 per share; 1961, $2.00 per share	(7,284)	(6,938)
Total	$(8,713)	$(8,367)
Net increase	$10,391	$ 2,381
Balance at end of year	$46,958	$36,567

EXHIBIT 4

Farm Machinery Company
Summary of Changes in Net Assets During the 1962 and 1961 Fiscal Years
(000 omitted)

	1962	1961	Increase or (Decrease)
Cash and marketable securities	$ 46,964	$ 38,032	$ 8,932
Receivables (net)	16,757	14,889	1,868
Trade accounts with subsidiary companies	7,740	5,396	2,344
Inventories	97,720	80,305	17,415
Total current assets	$169,181	$138,622	$30,559
Less current liabilities	52,402	33,527	18,875
Net current assets (working capital)	$116,779	$105,095	$11,684
Property (net)—see Exhibit 5	80,382	83,108	(2,726)
Investment in subsidiary companies	33,493	31,760	1,733
Other assets	3,263	2,935	328
Total net assets in which capital was invested	$233,917	$222,898	$11,019

EXHIBIT 5

Farm Machinery Company
Changes in Property Accounts During the 1962 and 1961 Fiscal Years
(000 omitted)

	1962	1961
Land, Buildings, Machinery and Equipment		
Balance at beginning of year	$157,385	$151,220
Additions	7,627	11,851
Sold, scrapped, etc.	(5,307)	(5,686)
Balance at end of year	$159,705	$157,385
Reserve for Depreciation		
Balance at beginning of year	$ 74,277	$ 69,630
Provision for depreciation	10,134	9,739
Charges for property sold, scrapped, etc.	(5,088)	(5,092)
Balance at end of year	$ 79,323	$ 74,277
Net Property	$ 80,382	$ 83,108

EXHIBIT 6

Farm Machinery Company
Notes to the 1962 Financial Statements

1. The company, for federal income tax purposes only, and in accordance with the Internal Revenue Code, continued to apply increased rates of depreciation to certain capital additions. This had no effect on net income because of a provision made for "Deferred Credit—Federal Income Taxes" in an amount equivalent to the tax savings applicable to the additional depreciation. The provision for 1962 was $628,000, and the accumulated amount totaled $2,786,000 as of October 31, 1962.
2. Effective October 1, 1962, the twenty-year, $3^1/_2$ per cent debentures, dated October 1, 1957, are convertible into shares of common stock in the ratio of 25 shares of common stock for each $1,000 of debentures. As of October 31, 1962, debentures in the amount of $8,872,000 had been converted into 221,800 shares of common stock.

QUESTIONS:

1. Consider carefully the explanation, "Working Capital and Cash Flow," quoted in the case. Which parts, if any, particularly appeal to you? What changes, if any, would you make? Explain.

2. What two items compose the $847,000 of other increases in the 1962 working capital inflow? Explain why these items are included.

3. Prepare a Sources and Uses of Funds statement for 1962, defining "funds" as working capital. Design your statement so that the total sources of funds are equal to the total uses, as in Figure 3, page 69.

4. Make the necessary changes in the statement prepared in question 3 to convert it to a Sources and Uses of Funds statement in which "funds" is defined as the sum of cash and United States government securities.

5. Prepare a Summary of Financial Activities statement for 1962 showing the significant sources and uses of funds. Define "funds" broadly as all financial resources. Begin the statement with a single figure for funds provided from operations, and indicate the details of this figure in a footnote.

6. Compare the three statements you have prepared for questions 3, 4 and 5. Which one would most assist you in understanding the company's financial policies, operations and plans? Explain. What additional information, if any, would you find helpful?

The Jorgensen Manufacturing Company[1]

The president of the Jorgensen Manufacturing Company has reviewed the 1962 financial statements and is unable to determine the reasons for the changes in working capital during the year. He requests your assistance.

You obtain the 1962 income statement (Exhibit 1) and post-closing trial balances at December 31, 1962 and 1961 (Exhibit 2). In addition, you obtain the following information concerning 1962 transactions:

1. Old machinery which cost $10,800 was scrapped and written off the books. Accrued depreciation on this machinery was $7,920.
2. Stock was sold during the year at $90.00 per share. The discount was charged to the goodwill account.
3. A two per cent cash dividend was declared and paid on the capital stock outstanding at January 1, 1962.
4. There were no purchases or sales of tools.
5. Bad debt expense was included in selling expenses. Taxes were included in general expenses.
6. No unusual items were included in the income or expense accounts in Exhibit 1.

EXHIBIT 1
The Jorgensen Manufacturing Company
Statement of Income for the Year 1962

Sales (net)		$3,110,000
Operating charges:		
Materials and supplies	$660,000	
Direct labor	554,000	
Manufacturing overhead, excluding depreciation	435,600	
Depreciation—buildings, machinery and tools	296,400	
Selling expenses	588,000	
General expenses	552,000	
Interest expense (net)	18,000	
Total		3,104,000
Net income		$ 6,000

[1] Adapted with permission from a Uniform CPA Examination.

EXHIBIT 2

The Jorgensen Manufacturing Company
Post-Closing Trial Balances at December 31, 1962 and 1961

	1962	1961	Increase (Decrease)
Cash	$ 4,800	$ 21,600	$ (16,800)
Accounts receivable	432,000	220,800	211,200
Notes receivable—trade	50,400	64,800	(14,400)
Inventories	504,000	523,200	(19,200)
Prepaid insurance	2,880	3,360	(480)
Land	336,000	360,000	(24,000)
Buildings	1,944,000	1,344,000	600,000
Machinery	792,000	480,000	312,000
Tools	96,000	168,000	(72,000)
Bond investment	43,200	36,000	7,200
Deferred bond discount	5,040	6,000	(960)
Goodwill	—0—	480,000	(480,000)
	$4,210,320	$3,707,760	$ 502,560
Bank overdraft	$ 9,600	$ —0—	$ 9,600
Accounts payable	139,200	124,800	14,400
Notes payable—trade	21,600	24,000	(2,400)
Bank loans—short-term	13,200	16,320	(3,120)
Accrued interest	24,000	14,400	9,600
Accrued taxes	12,000	7,200	4,800
Allowance for bad debts	10,800	5,520	5,280
Bonds payable	360,000	240,000	120,000
Allowance for depreciation	650,880	434,400	216,480
Capital stock ($100 par)	1,680,000	960,000	720,000
Retained earnings	1,289,040	1,881,120	(592,080)
	$4,210,320	$3,707,760	$ 502,560

QUESTIONS:

1. Prepare a Statement of Sources and Applications of Funds for 1962 in which "funds" is defined as working capital. Prepare a supporting schedule of working capital changes.

2. Prepare a Statement of Cash Flow for 1962. Compute the net cash inflow from operations by adjusting sales and operating expenses to reflect the *actual* cash collections from customers and the *actual* cash payments made to suppliers and employees and for other operating expenditures. To the net cash inflow from operations add other cash receipts and deduct other cash disbursements. The excess of cash disbursements for the year over cash receipts should be $16,800, the decline in the cash balance from December 31, 1961 to December 31, 1962.

3. Comment on the appropriateness of the company's apparent accounting for land, tools, goodwill, old machinery, and capital stock.

CHAPTER FIVE

Consolidated Statements

Consolidated financial statements show the operating results and the financial position of related corporations as though they were a single company. Consolidated statements do not represent a *legal* entity; instead they represent an *economic* entity subject to common ownership and control. This economic entity consists of a *parent* corporation and one or more *subsidiary* corporations in which the parent has a controlling interest.

Consolidated financial statements are prepared by integrating the parent's and the subsidiaries' separate financial statements. The techniques for integrating or *consolidating* these separate statements are best understood after the major differences between consolidated and parent company financial statements are recognized. The annual reports of the International Harvester Company (Harvester) for the fiscal years ended October 31, 1959 and 1960, describe some of these differences. The 1959 report contained the following statement:

> The financial statements of the report are presented on a non-consolidated basis; that is, the assets and liabilities of subsidiary companies and their operating results are not included. Instead, the investment of International Harvester Company in subsidiaries is carried in the statement of financial condition as an asset, and only the dividends received from subsidiaries are included in the statement of income.

Although Harvester presented financial statements for the *parent* company only, it revealed elsewhere in the annual report the parent's interest in the net assets[1] of its 31 subsidiaries and the parent's interest in the amount of 1959 earnings retained by these subsidiaries. On its Statement of Financial Condition at October 31,

---

[1] The term *net assets* appears several times in this chapter. It means total assets less total liabilities. Note that this is the same as stockholders' equity.

1959, Harvester disclosed the carrying value (essentially the *cost*) of its "Investment in Subsidiary Companies" at $134.0 million. In contrast to this amount, the parent's interest in the net assets of these subsidiaries, as shown by the books of the subsidiaries, was $320.5 million. The difference, $186.5 million, represented earnings retained by the subsidiaries from the time the parent company acquired its controlling interests. The parent company's interest in the subsidiaries' 1959 earnings was $28.3 million, but only the amount of dividends actually received from the subsidiaries, $17.8 million, was included in the parent's net income.

In its 1960 annual report, Harvester for the first time presented consolidated financial statements. The reason for this change in policy and the effects of the change were explained as follows:

In order to provide an even more comprehensive picture of Harvester activities, the Company has decided to report henceforth on a consolidated basis beginning with this report. As a consequence, the statement of financial condition reflects the net assets of subsidiaries instead of the Company's investment therein; and the statement of income includes the net income of subsidiaries instead of the dividends received therefrom.

INSTITUTE PRONOUNCEMENT

In August, 1959, just before it was superseded by the Institute's new Accounting Principles Board, the Committee on Accounting Procedure issued Accounting Research Bulletin No. 51, *Consolidated Financial Statements*. Paragraphs 1 through 18 of this bulletin follow:[2]

Purpose of Consolidated Statements

1. The purpose of consolidated statements is to present, primarily for the benefit of the shareholders and creditors of the parent company, the results of operations and the financial position of a parent company and its subsidiaries essentially as if the group were a single company with one or more branches or divisions. There is a presumption that consolidated statements are more meaningful than separate statements and that they are usually necessary for a fair presentation when one of the companies in the group directly or indirectly has a controlling financial interest in the other companies.

Consolidation Policy

2. The usual condition for a controlling financial interest is ownership of a majority voting interest, and, therefore, as a general rule ownership by one company, directly or indirectly, of over fifty per cent of the outstanding

---

[2] Paragraphs 19 through 24 and the related qualified assents are reproduced in Chapter 13, *Investments in Unconsolidated Subsidiaries and Jointly-Owned Companies*, pages 435–37.

voting shares of another company is a condition pointing toward consolidation. However, there are exceptions to this general rule. For example, a subsidiary should not be consolidated where control is likely to be temporary, or where it does not rest with the majority owners (as, for instance, where the subsidiary is in legal reorganization or in bankruptcy). There may also be situations where the minority interest in the subsidiary is so large, in relation to the equity of the shareholders of the parent in the consolidated net assets, that the presentation of separate financial statements for the two companies would be more meaningful and useful. However, the fact that the subsidiary has a relatively large indebtedness to bondholders or others is not in itself a valid argument for exclusion of the subsidiary from consolidation.

3. In deciding upon consolidation policy, the aim should be to make the financial presentation which is most meaningful in the circumstances. The reader should be given information which is suitable to his needs, but he should not be burdened with unnecessary detail. Thus, even though a group of companies is heterogeneous in character, it may be better to make a full consolidation than to present a large number of separate statements. On the other hand, separate statements or combined statements would be preferable for a subsidiary or group of subsidiaries if the presentation of financial information concerning the particular activities of such subsidiaries would be more informative to shareholders and creditors of the parent company than would the inclusion of such subsidiaries in the consolidation. For example, separate statements may be required for a subsidiary which is a bank or an insurance company and may be preferable for a finance company where the parent and the other subsidiaries are engaged in manufacturing operations.

4. A difference in fiscal periods of a parent and a subsidiary does not of itself justify the exclusion of the subsidiary from consolidation. It ordinarily is feasible for the subsidiary to prepare, for consolidation purposes, statements for a period which corresponds with or closely approaches the fiscal period of the parent. However, where the difference is not more than about three months, it usually is acceptable to use, for consolidation purposes, the subsidiary's statements for its fiscal period; when this is done, recognition should be given by disclosure or otherwise to the effect of intervening events which materially affect the financial position or results of operations.

5. Consolidated statements should disclose the consolidation policy which is being followed. In most cases this can be made apparent by the headings or other information in the statements, but in other cases a footnote is required.

Consolidation Procedure Generally

6. In the preparation of consolidated statements, intercompany balances and transactions should be eliminated. This includes intercompany open account balances, security holdings, sales and purchases, interest, dividends, etc. As consolidated statements are based on the assumption that they represent the financial position and operating results of a single business enterprise, such statements should not include gain or loss on transactions among the companies in the group. Accordingly, any intercompany profit or loss on assets remaining within the group should be eliminated; the concept usually applied for this purpose is gross profit or loss. (See also paragraph 17.) However, in a regulated industry where a parent or subsidiary manufactures or constructs facilities for other companies in the consolidated group,

the foregoing is not intended to require the elimination of intercompany profit to the extent that such profit is substantially equivalent to a reasonable return on investment ordinarily capitalized in accordance with the established practice of the industry.

Elimination of Intercompany Investments

7. Where the cost to the parent of the investment in a purchased[3] subsidiary exceeds the parent's equity in the subsidiary's net assets at the date of acquisition, as shown by the books of the subsidiary, the excess should be dealt with in the consolidated balance sheet according to its nature. In determining the difference, provision should be made for specific costs or losses which are expected to be incurred in the integration of the operations of the subsidiary with those of the parent, or otherwise as a result of the acquisition, if the amount thereof can be reasonably determined. To the extent that the difference is considered to be attributable to tangible assets and specific intangible assets, such as patents, it should be allocated to them. Any difference which cannot be so applied should be shown among the assets in the consolidated balance sheet under one or more appropriately descriptive captions. When the difference is allocated to depreciable or amortizable assets, depreciation and amortization policies should be such as to absorb the excess over the remaining life of related assets. For subsequent treatment of intangibles, see Chapter 5 of Accounting Research Bulletin No. 43, [pages 391–94].

8. In general, parallel procedures should be followed in the reverse type of case. Where the cost to the parent is less than its equity in the net assets of the purchased subsidiary, as shown by the books of the subsidiary at the date of acquisition, the amount at which such net assets are carried in the consolidated statements should not exceed the parent's cost. Accordingly, to the extent that the difference, determined as indicated in paragraph 7, is considered to be attributable to specific assets, it should be allocated to them, with corresponding adjustments of the depreciation or amortization. In unusual circumstances there may be a remaining difference which it would be acceptable to show in a credit account, which ordinarily would be taken into income in future periods on a reasonable and systematic basis. A procedure sometimes followed in the past was to credit capital surplus with the amount of the excess; such a procedure is not now considered acceptable.

9. The earned surplus or deficit of a purchased[3] subsidiary at the date of acquisition by the parent should not be included in consolidated earned surplus.

10. When one company purchases two or more blocks of stock of another company at various dates and eventually obtains control of the other company, the date of acquisition (for the purpose of preparing consolidated statements) depends on the circumstances. If two or more purchases are made over a period of time, the earned surplus of the subsidiary at acquisition should generally be determined on a step-by-step basis; however, if small purchases are made over a period of time and then a purchase is made which results in control, the date of the latest purchase, as a matter of convenience, may be considered as the date of acquisition. Thus there would generally be included in consolidated income for the year in which

---

[3] See Accounting Research Bulletin No. 48, *Business Combinations*, for the difference in treatment between a purchase and a pooling of interests, [pages 560–63].

control is obtained the postacquisition income for that year, and in consolidated earned surplus the postacquisition income of prior years, attributable to each block previously acquired. For example, if a 45% interest was acquired on October 1, 1957 and a further 30% interest was acquired on April 1, 1958, it would be appropriate to include in consolidated income for the year ended December 31, 1958, 45% of the earnings of the subsidiary for the three months ended March 31, and 75% of the earnings for the nine months ended December 31, and to credit consolidated earned surplus in 1958 with 45% of the undistributed earnings of the subsidiary for the three months ended December 31, 1957.

11. When a subsidiary is purchased during the year, there are alternative ways of dealing with the results of its operations in the consolidated income statement. One method, which usually is preferable, especially where there are several dates of acquisition of blocks of shares, is to include the subsidiary in the consolidation as though it had been acquired at the beginning of the year, and to deduct at the bottom of the consolidated income statement the preacquisition earnings applicable to each block of stock. This method presents results which are more indicative of the current status of the group, and facilitates future comparison with subsequent years. Another method of prorating income is to include in the consolidated statement only the subsidiary's revenue and expenses subsequent to the date of acquisition.

12. Where the investment in a subsidiary is disposed of during the year, it may be preferable to omit the details of operations of the subsidiary from the consolidated income statement, and to show the equity of the parent in the earnings of the subsidiary prior to disposal as a separate item in the statement.

13. Shares of the parent held by a subsidiary should not be treated as outstanding stock in the consolidated balance sheet.

Minority Interests

14. The amount of intercompany profit or loss to be eliminated in accordance with paragraph 6 is not affected by the existence of a minority interest. The complete elimination of the intercompany profit or loss is consistent with the underlying assumption that consolidated statements represent the financial position and operating results of a single business enterprise. The elimination of the intercompany profit or loss may be allocated proportionately between the majority and minority interests.

15. In the unusual case in which losses applicable to the minority interest in a subsidiary exceed the minority interest in the equity capital of the subsidiary, such excess and any further losses applicable to the minority interest should be charged against the majority interest, as there is no obligation of the minority interest to make good such losses. However, if future earnings do materialize, the majority interest should be credited to the extent of such losses previously absorbed.

Income Taxes

16. When separate income tax returns are filed, income taxes usually are incurred when earnings of subsidiaries are transferred to the parent. Where it is reasonable to assume that a part or all of the undistributed earnings of a subsidiary will be transferred to the parent in a taxable distribution, provision for related income taxes should be made on an estimated basis at the time the earnings are included in consolidated income, unless these taxes

are immaterial in amount when effect is given, for example, to dividend-received deductions or foreign-tax credits. There is no need to provide for income tax to the parent company in cases where the income has been, or there is evidence that it will be, permanently invested by the subsidiaries, or where the only likely distribution would be in the form of a tax-free liquidation.

17. If income taxes have been paid on intercompany profits on assets remaining within the group, such taxes should be deferred or the intercompany profits to be eliminated in consolidation should be appropriately reduced.

Stock Dividends of Subsidiaries

18. Occasionally, subsidiary companies capitalize earned surplus arising since acquisition, by means of a stock dividend or otherwise. This does not require a transfer to capital surplus on consolidation, inasmuch as the retained earnings in the consolidated financial statements should reflect the accumulated earnings of the consolidated group not distributed to the shareholders of, or capitalized by, the parent company.

*   *   *

Mr. Bedford objects to the provision in paragraph 2 that ownership of over fifty per cent of the outstanding voting stock is the general rule governing consolidation policy. He believes the over fifty per cent ownership requirement is at best only one of several criteria evidencing the existence of a consolidated entity.

Messrs. Graese and Hoyler do not agree with the statement made in the last sentence of paragraph 8. Mr. Graese believes there are cases in which the crediting of a capital surplus account with the "excess credit" will result in a more appropriate presentation of consolidated operations and financial position, particularly in (but not limited to) situations where the acquisition of control of the subsidiary has been accomplished over an extended period of time or where there are acquisitions of minority interest at a date considerably after obtaining control. Mr. Hoyler is of the opinion that there have been, and probably will be, circumstances under which credits to capital surplus of the excesses referred to in this paragraph will be appropriate.

Messrs. Halvorson and Werntz object to the relative emphasis given to the recommendations in paragraph 10, which they believe should be reversed. They believe that the date of the purchase which results in control should generally be considered to be the date of acquisition; however, if a limited number of purchases are made over a period of time pursuant to a plan or program which culminates in control, they agree that the earned surplus of the subsidiary at acquisition may be determined on a step-by-step basis.

Mr. Halvorson disagrees with the recommendation in paragraph 18. In his view, the usual subsidiary is a closely held corporation, and consequently is under no pressure to declare stock dividends and is under no compulsion to follow the "fair value" method of accounting for them if it does. If it does capitalize earned surplus by means of a stock dividend or otherwise, particularly "otherwise," he feels that it must have been done with a purpose relating to its financial position, at the direction of, and with the acquiescence of, the parent company, and that the capitalization should carry through into the consolidated surplus accounts. If the subsidiary is one in which there is a publicly held minority interest, and a stock dividend is issued and accounted for on a fair-value basis in the manner of an independent publicly owned corporation, the accounting for earned surplus in respect of the majority interest would be the same as that for the minority interest, and again he believes that the capitalization should follow through into the consolidated surplus accounts. Mr. Powell also disagrees with the conclusion expressed in this paragraph. He believes that if a parent causes a subsidiary to freeze a part or all of its earned surplus through the payment of a stock dividend or otherwise, thus making such surplus unavailable for ordinary dividends, it should follow a similar procedure on consolidation.

Consolidated statements are prepared primarily for the benefit of parent company shareholders and creditors. Consolidated statements, rather than the separate statements of the parent company and its subsidiaries, are generally more meaningful to these groups. Consolidated statements do not ordinarily meet the information needs of a subsidiary's creditors or its minority shareholders. These parties usually look to the subsidiary's own financial statements.

Paragraphs 2 and 3 of the bulletin deal with the question of what subsidiaries should be included in consolidated statements. This is a matter of some disagreement among accountants, although the trend is towards consolidation of most subsidiaries. In addition to the reasons for excluding some subsidiaries from consolidation cited in paragraphs 2 and 3, foreign subsidiaries often present unique problems. For example, following is a note to the 1961 financial statements of the American Radiator and Standard Sanitary Corporation explaining its consolidation policy:

All subsidiaries are included in the consolidated financial statements except the Brazilian subsidiary which has been excluded because of the instability of that country's currency.

The concluding sentence of paragraph 2 is particularly applicable to the real estate subsidiaries established by some department store and supermarket chains. Such subsidiaries, which acquire or construct properties for long-term lease to the parent or other consolidated subsidiaries, are typically financed by a limited amount of equity capital supplied by the parent and substantial amounts of long-term debt supplied by outside creditors. Contrary to the view expressed in the bulletin, some real estate subsidiaries are excluded from consolidation.

Combined statements, which are mentioned in paragraph 3, are sometimes prepared for a group of *unconsolidated* subsidiaries. Management may feel that the usual criteria for consolidation exist *within* a group of subsidiaries, but do not exist between the group and the parent company. In this case, combined statements, the result of *consolidating* the separate financial statements of a group of unconsolidated subsidiaries, may be presented instead of the separate financial statements of the subsidiaries. For example, the General Electric Company's 1961 annual report includes combined statements of operations and financial position for the company's unconsolidated foreign subsidiaries (see page 444). Combined financial statements are considered further in Chapter 13.

PREPARING CONSOLIDATED FINANCIAL STATEMENTS

The remainder of this chapter is devoted to the techniques of preparing consolidated statements. Only the more common consolidation problems will be described and illustrated. A few additional problems, not specifically mentioned in the text material, are included in Case 5-1, Problems in Consolidation. Since the topics considered in this discussion will correspond to those presented in paragraphs 6 through 18 of ARB No. 51, reproduced above, the reader may find it helpful to refer to these paragraphs.

In consolidating the accounts of related *legal* entities to prepare financial statements for the single *economic* entity, various intercompany account balances and transactions must be eliminated. Only transactions between the consolidated entity and *outsiders* should be reflected in the consolidated statements. Assume that a chemical company (P) established a subsidiary (S) on January 1, 1963, and invested $400,000 in the capital stock of S, and $100,000 in S's 10-year, 5 per cent debentures, interest payable June 30 and December 31. S sold an additional $200,000 of these debentures to outsiders. S was formed primarily to supply raw materials to its parent (P), but some sales were also made to others.

The preparation of consolidated financial statements for P and S at December 31, 1963, is facilitated by a consolidation work sheet, one form of which is illustrated in Figure 1. This form provides eight money columns: two each for P's and for S's 1963 account balances as taken from their separate financial statements (or pre-closing trial balances), two columns for eliminations and adjustments, and two columns for items which will be used in preparing the 1963 consolidated statements. Normally *all* items from each company's separate financial statements (or pre-closing trial balances) would be listed in the first four columns. However, items requiring no eliminations or adjustments are *omitted* from the work sheet illustrated in Figure 1 because they present no accounting problem. For example, the balances of the two cash accounts would merely be added together and extended to the debit column under "Items for Consolidated Statements."

The following comments, which are keyed to Figure 1, describe certain reciprocal relationships between P and S.

	Parent		Subsidiary		Eliminations and Adjustments		Items for Consolidated Statements	
	Debit	Credit	Debit	Credit	Debit	Credit	Debit	Credit
(1) Accounts receivable	1,123,018		181,382			147,626	1,156,774	
Accounts payable		931,987		202,485	147,626			986,846
(2a) Investment in S capital stock	400,000					400,000		
Capital stock				400,000	400,000			1,000,000
(2b) Investment in S debentures	100,000					100,000		
Debentures due 1/1/73				300,000	100,000			200,000
(3) Purchases	3,010,982		596,312			956,387	2,650,907	
Sales		9,103,408		1,206,718	956,387			9,353,739
(4) Interest expense			15,000			5,000	10,000	
Interest income		5,000			5,000			
(5) Inventory	1,082,431		86,551			18,231	1,150,751	
Retained earnings		1,853,875		32,121	18,231			1,867,765

Figure 1. Partial Consolidation Work Sheet, December 31, 1963

(1) At December 31, 1963, P and S have open account balances as follows:

	P	S
Accounts receivable	$1,123,018	$181,382
Accounts payable	931,987	202,485

Included in S's accounts receivable and P's accounts payable is $147,626 arising from sales made by S to P. The elimination of this amount and the appropriate extensions to the "Items for Consolidated Statements" columns is shown in Figure 1. The post-elimination amounts of accounts receivable, $1,156,774, and accounts payable, $986,846, represent the status of these accounts at December 31, 1963, with regard to customers and suppliers *outside* the consolidated entity.

(2) P holds all of S's outstanding capital stock and one-third of S's 10-year debentures. Assuming that P has outstanding capital stock of $1,000,000, the proper eliminations are illustrated in Figure 1 by (2a) and (2b). Observe that the $200,000 of subsidiary debentures held by *outsiders* will appear as a liability on the consolidated balance sheet.

(3) During 1963, total sales and purchases by P and S are as follows:

	P	S
Sales	$9,103,408	$1,206,718
Purchases	3,010,982	596,312

Included in S's sales and P's purchases is $956,387 of sales made by S to P. The elimination of these intercompany transactions is shown in Figure 1. Observe that the amounts extended to the final two columns reveal the consolidated entity's purchases from *outsiders*, $2,650,907, and its sales to *outsiders*, $9,353,739.

(4) In 1963, S incurred $15,000 of interest expense on its $300,000 of debentures, and P recorded $5,000 of interest income on the $100,000 of S debentures held by it. P's interest income is eliminated and only $10,000 of S's interest expense, representing the amount paid to *outsiders*, will appear on the consolidated income statement. S declared no dividends in 1963, its first year of operation.

(5) At the close of 1963, P's inventory includes materials purchased from S on which S realized a gross profit of $18,231. In consolidating the accounts of P and S, this profit should be eliminated from S's retained earnings at December 31, 1963, because, from the viewpoint of the consolidated entity, this profit is not realized until the materials are sold to *outsiders*.

Similarly, for consolidation purposes, this profit should be eliminated from P's inventory at December 31, 1963. The consolidated balance sheet will then reflect inventory at *cost* to the consolidated entity. The corporations' inventories and retained earnings, as reported on their separate balance sheets at December 31, 1963, and entered in the consolidation work sheet, are as follows:

	P	S
Inventory	$1,082,431	$ 86,551
Retained earnings	1,853,875	32,121

Some managements do not eliminate intercompany profit in inventories or other assets, either because the amount is impractical to determine or is considered immaterial. Others follow a policy similar to that described in the following note to International Shoe Company's 1961 consolidated financial statements:

All subsidiaries with a 51% or greater ownership are included in the consolidated financial statements in accord with the established policy of the company. Operating results from acquisition date of newly acquired subsidiaries are included in consolidated income. Insofar as practicable, all intercompany accounts, transactions, and unrealized profit in inventories have been eliminated in consolidation.

EXCESS OF INVESTMENT OVER EQUITY IN NET ASSETS

In the example above, the subsidiary corporation was organized by the parent corporation. As a result, the elimination of the intercompany investment was straightforward because the reciprocal accounts, "Investment in S Capital Stock" (on P's books) and "Capital Stock" (on S's books), had identical balances of $400,000.

Assume that instead of organizing a subsidiary, a corporation *purchased* 100 per cent of a second corporation's stock from the second corporation's former stockholders for $200,000. According to the purchased corporation's books at the date of acquisition, it had net assets of $170,000, represented by $100,000 of capital stock and $70,000 of retained earnings. Thus, P paid $30,000 in excess of the equity it acquired in S's net assets. Such a purchase, which is not uncommon, may reflect factors such as: (1) the influence of inflation, (2) conservative practices used by S in accounting for such items as inventories or fixed assets, or (3) a willingness by P to pay for goodwill which S appears to have developed in the successful conduct of its business.

Paragraph 7 of ARB No. 51 recommends that a debit excess should be dealt with in the consolidated balance sheet "according to its nature." In agreeing to pay $200,000 for the S corporation's capital stock, P's management may have considered specific assets to be undervalued on S's books, or it may have considered the entire $30,000 excess as a payment for goodwill. Allocation of such a debit excess to specific tangible and intangible assets, to the extent there is some reasonable basis for such an allocation, is recommended in the bulletin.

Any difference which cannot be applied to specific assets "should be shown among the assets in the consolidated balance sheet under one or more appropriately descriptive captions." Captions such as "goodwill" or "goodwill arising from consolidation," widely used in the past, have been gradually replaced by more informative captions such as "cost of investment in subsidiary in excess of underlying net assets at date of acquisition." The subsequent accounting treatment of such an account is discussed in Chapter 12, *Intangible Assets*.

EXCESS OF EQUITY IN NET ASSETS OVER INVESTMENT

Paragraph 8 of ARB No. 51 is concerned with the purchase of a subsidiary for less than the acquired equity, as shown on the subsidiary's books at date of acquisition. Such a purchase may occur when the subsidiary has a poor earnings record or is in financial difficulty. In preparing a consolidated balance sheet, this credit excess should be allocated to reduce specific subsidiary assets. Such allocations may be based on values assigned to specific assets in arriving at the purchase price paid by the parent. In accordance with the generally accepted accounting principle that assets should be recorded at *cost*, a subsidiary's assets should not be carried in the consolidated financial statements in excess of the parent's cost.

In "unusual circumstances," even after downward restatement of the subsidiary's assets, a credit difference may remain. This credit is usually classified on the consolidated balance sheet between the liability and the stockholders' equity sections. It is described by a caption such as "excess of equity in subsidiary's net assets at date of acquisition over cost." The credit is sometimes loosely called "negative goodwill," but this is hardly an informative description.

The bulletin recommends that a remaining credit difference "ordinarily would be taken into income in future periods on a reasonable and systematic basis." The timing of such transfers to income, a matter of judgment, would be based on considerations such as the following:

(1) If there is little prospect of change in the subsidiary's earning power and no unusual expenses are anticipated in integrating

the subsidiary, the transfers to income might be related to the estimated remaining lives of the subsidiary's depreciable assets.

(2) Extraordinary short-term expenses may be necessary to improve a recently-acquired subsidiary's operating performance. If these extraordinary expenses were anticipated by the parent, and were a factor in determining the price paid for the subsidiary, the credit might be transferred to income during the readjustment period.

(3) If other subsidiaries have been acquired at a cost in excess of the parent's equity in the subsidiaries' net assets at dates of acquisition, and an excess debit balance remains in the consolidated balance sheet from such acquisitions, it is considered acceptable to offset the excess debit and the excess credit. Such an offset is described in the following note to the 1961 Consolidated Balance Sheet of Textron, Inc.:

The book value of the net assets of Spencer Kellogg and Sons, Inc. at date of acquisition exceeded the market value of the Textron common stock issued therefor. This excess was charged with expenses of acquisition and losses in connection with the reorganization of the business, including the sale of its three soybean crushing plants. The balance ($6,858,960) is being taken into income ratably over a period of ten years from date of acquisition.

In prior years, Textron purchased several companies at costs which were in excess of the book value of the underlying net tangible assets. These excess costs are being amortized by charges to income over a ten-year period. In the accompanying balance sheet at December 30, 1961, the unamortized balance ($4,783,436) of excess cost of companies acquired has been offset against the deferred credit resulting from the purchase of the Spencer Kellogg business.

PARENT'S INTEREST IN SUBSIDIARY'S EARNINGS AND RETAINED EARNINGS

The phrase *date of acquisition* has appeared throughout this chapter. The date of acquisition of a parent's interest in a subsidiary is of major significance because only the subsidiary's earnings and retained earnings *after* that date are properly included in the consolidated statement of earnings and the consolidated balance sheet. In accordance with paragraph 9, a subsidiary's retained earnings at *date of acquisition* is eliminated in preparing consolidated statements. A subsidiary can contribute to the earnings and retained earnings of the consolidated entity only *after* its acquisition by the parent corporation.

Observe in paragraph 10 that various acquisition *dates,* rather than

Current Liabilities:	
Accounts payable	$ 1,690,932
Accrued wages and additional compensation, commissions, sundry taxes, etc.	2,058,070
United States and foreign taxes on income—estimated	3,276,386
Total Current Liabilities	$ 7,025,388

►Minority Interest in a Consolidated Subsidiary   56,854

Shareowners' Equity:	
Common stock—par value $0.625 per share:	
Authorized 8,000,000 shares	
Issued and outstanding 3,911,067 shares	$ 2,444,417
Additional capital in excess of par value of shares	4,384,479
Undistributed earnings used in the business	21,022,388
Total Shareowners' Equity	$27,851,284
	$34,933,526

Credit Side of Consolidated Balance Sheet at December 31, 1961

Net sales	$48,226,159
Interest, royalties, and sundry income	973,896
	$49,200,055

Deductions from income:	
Cost of products sold	$11,135,090
Selling, advertising, shipping, administrative and general expenses	23,936,134
Discount expense, less discount income	696,917
Additional compensation to key personnel under profit sharing plan	621,425
Interest	6,695
►Minority interest in net income of a consolidated subsidiary	20,068
	$36,416,329
Income Before Income Taxes	$12,783,726
United States and foreign taxes on income—estimated	6,407,789
Net Income	$ 6,375,937

Statement of Consolidated Income for Year Ending December 31, 1961

Figure 2. The Norwich Pharmacal Company

the single *date* on which control is finally obtained, may be significant in the preparation of consolidated statements.

Paragraphs 11 and 12 are concerned with methods of presenting a subsidiary's operating results in the consolidated income statement when the subsidiary is purchased or disposed of during the year.

In accordance with paragraph 13, shares of the parent held by a subsidiary are usually treated as reacquired (treasury) stock, and are shown as a deduction in the stockholders' equity section of the consolidated balance sheet.

MINORITY INTERESTS

In the examples presented earlier in this chapter, the subsidiary corporation was assumed to be wholly-owned. Frequently a minority portion of a consolidated subsidiary's outstanding voting stock is held by shareholders outside of the controlling group. These minority shareholders may be other corporations or individual investors. The equity interest of these shareholders in the consolidated subsidiary is called a *minority interest.*

In preparing consolidated financial statements, subsidiaries with minority shareholders are treated in essentially the same manner as wholly-owned subsidiaries. However, the minority's equity in the subsidiary's net assets is disclosed separately on the consolidated balance sheet. Similarly, the minority's share of the subsidiary's current earnings or loss is shown as a deduction on the consolidated statement of income. Examples of such disclosure from the 1961 consolidated financial statements of The Norwich Pharmacal Company are given in Figure 2.

Observe that the minority interest, while usually shown on a consolidated balance sheet as a single figure, really consists of the minority's interest in the subsidiary's capital stock and in its retained earnings. If the minority interest is relatively large, these amounts may be shown separately on the consolidated balance sheet. However, the distinction is usually not significant to the parent corporation's stockholders to whom consolidated statements are primarily directed.

Assuming that a subsidiary with a minority interest has operated profitably since control was acquired by the majority, its retained earnings will be allocated three ways in the preparation of a consolidated balance sheet:

(1) The parent's interest in the subsidiary's retained earnings *as of the date of acquisition* will be eliminated in consolidation.

(2) The parent's interest in the subsidiary's retained earnings *since the date of acquisition* will be included in consolidated retained earnings.

(3) The minority's interest in the subsidiary's retained earnings *as of the date consolidated financial statements are prepared* will be allocated to "minority interest."

Assume that on June 30, 1962, P corporation purchased 80 per cent of S corporation's capital stock for $240,000. On that date S had net assets of $270,000, represented by capital stock of $150,000 and retained earnings of $120,000. Thus, P paid $24,000 in excess of the 80 per cent equity interest it acquired in the net assets of S (as shown on the books of S), determined as follows:

Amount paid by P	$240,000
Less P's equity in subsidiary's net assets at date of acquisition (.80 × $270,000)	216,000
Excess paid over equity in subsidiary's net assets at date of acquisition	$ 24,000

One year later, on June 30, 1963, the amount of the subsidiary's capital stock outstanding was unchanged, but it then had $140,000 of retained earnings. This amount would be allocated as follows in preparing a consolidated balance sheet:

$96,000 eliminated (.80 × $120,000 = $96,000, P's interest in S's retained earnings *as of the date of acquisition*).

$16,000 included in consolidated retained earnings (.80 × $20,000 = $16,000, P's interest in S's retained earnings *since the date of acquisition*).

$28,000 included in minority interest (.20 × $140,000 = $28,000, minority's interest in S's retained earnings *as of the date consolidated financial statements are prepared*).

The total minority interest on the consolidated balance sheet at June 30, 1963, would be $58,000 consisting of the minority's interest in retained earnings *as of the date consolidated financial statements are prepared*, $28,000, plus the minority's interest in the subsidiary's outstanding capital stock, $30,000.

Most accountants agree with the view expressed in paragraph 14 that the elimination of intercompany profit, for purposes of preparing consolidated statements, should not be influenced by the existence of a minority interest. For example, a subsidiary's profit on goods sold to its parent, to the extent that such goods remain in the parent's inventory at the date of consolidation, should be *completely* eliminated, even though such profit is realized from the standpoint of the subsidiary's minority shareholders.

There is disagreement among accountants concerning how eliminated intercompany profit should be allocated between majority and minority interests. It may be allocated entirely to the majority interest, thus reducing consolidated earnings for the fiscal period and consolidated retained earnings at the close of the period by the *full* amount of the eliminated profit. Under an acceptable alternative, mentioned in the concluding sentence of paragraph 14, the eliminated profit is allocated proportionately between the majority and the minority interests.

INCOME TAXES

Paragraphs 16 and 17 concern income taxes which would become payable upon the transfer of a subsidiary's undistributed earnings to its parent, and income taxes already paid on intercompany profits applicable to assets remaining within the group at the close of a fiscal period. In the latter case, the recognition of such taxes as an expense should be deferred until the intercompany profit, eliminated in consolidation, is realized in subsequent fiscal periods. From the standpoint of the consolidated entity such taxes may be considered as prepaid.[4]

An alternative method, mentioned in paragraph 17, is to eliminate only the amount of *after-tax* intercompany profits. Either method produces the same consolidated earnings. The second method is followed by the Caterpillar Tractor Co., as explained in the following note to its 1962 consolidated financial statements:

All of the Company's subsidiaries are wholly owned, and the results of their operations are included in the consolidated results of operations. Intercompany profits in inventories (less the applicable income taxes) have been eliminated.

PERSPECTIVE

The preparation of consolidated financial statements can be an extremely complicated task. A number of difficult technical problems may occur, including several not discussed in this chapter and not mentioned in Accounting Research Bulletin No. 51. However, the essential logic of consolidated financial statements is not difficult to understand.

---

[4] Accounting problems related to timing differences between the *accrual* of income-tax expense and the *actual payment* of income taxes are considered at length in Chapter 6, *Income Tax Reporting in Financial Statements.*

REFERENCES

American Accounting Association, Committee on Accounting Concepts and Standards, "Consolidated Financial Statements—Supplementary Statement No. 7," *Accounting Review*, 30 (Apr. 1955), 194–97. This statement also appears in *Accounting and Reporting Standards for Corporate Financial Statements and Preceding Statements and Supplements*. Columbus, Ohio: American Accounting Association, 1957.

Campbell, J. D., "Consolidation vs. Combination," *Accounting Review*, 37 (Jan. 1962), 99–102.

Kelley, James A., "Should a Corporation Consolidate its Foreign and Domestic Accounts?" *New York Certified Public Accountant*, 26 (Oct. 1956), 585–87.

Moonitz, Maurice, *The Entity Theory of Consolidated Statements*. Bloomington, Ind.: American Accounting Association, 1944.

Newlove, G. H., "New Techniques in Consolidations," *Accounting Review*, 28 (Oct. 1953), 500–504.

Peoples, John, "The Preparation of Consolidated Statements," *Journal of Accountancy*, 104 (Aug. 1957), 32–36.

Research Department of the American Institute of Accountants, "Some Problems Regarding Consolidated and Parent Company Statements," *Journal of Accountancy*, 96 (Nov. 1953), 570–76.

Sapienza, S. R., "The Divided House of Consolidations," *Accounting Review*, 35 (Jul. 1960), 503–10.

Simon, Sidney I., "Consolidated Statements and the Law," *Accounting Review*, 28 (Oct. 1953), 505–14.

Survey of Consolidated Financial Statement Practices. New York: American Institute of Accountants, 1956.

Problems in Consolidation[1]

The problems below, which gradually increase in complexity, are designed to cover the main types of eliminations and adjustments in consolidation.

Analyze each problem separately on a consolidation work sheet by entering the proper eliminations and/or adjustments. Several problems may be analyzed on a single work sheet. Use nine worksheet columns—a column for account titles plus eight money columns. This provides a debit column and a credit column for each of the following: (a) Parent Company, (b) Subsidiary Company, (c) Eliminations and Adjustments, and (d) Items for Consolidated Statements.

1. Among the current assets of a parent company and its subsidiary on the date of consolidation were marketable securities of $178,442, and $41,348, respectively. These securities represented the investment of excess funds. None of them was issued by either of the companies concerned.

2. A subsidiary company had loaned $85,000 to its parent company. On the books of the latter were $116,000 of notes payable, which included amounts owed to the subsidiary.

3. A parent company had on its books $10,750 of notes receivable, $5,000 of which arose from loans to its subsidiary. The parent company had discounted $8,000 of its notes receivable and on its books had debited Cash and credited Notes Receivable Discounted. The notes receivable from the subsidiary were among those discounted by the parent. Notes payable of the subsidiary were $11,000.

4. A subsidiary had $4,000,000 of bonds outstanding which were issued at par. Subsequent to the date of issue, the parent

---

[1] Problems 1 through 14 are adapted with permission from problems originally prepared for use at the Graduate School of Business Administration, Harvard University. Problems 15 through 18 are adapted with permission from a Uniform CPA Examination.

bought $500,000 of these bonds in the open market for $525,000. These bonds were carried on the parent's books at cost. Retained earnings of the parent were $15,103,284.

5. At the end of an accounting period, a wholly-owned subsidiary's inventory included goods purchased from the parent for $69,258. It was estimated that this amount contained intercompany profit of $13,850. Retained earnings of the parent were $407,369, and those of the subsidiary were $211,382. Total inventory of the subsidiary was $118,312 and inventory of the parent was $283,172.

6. A parent company bought a 100 per cent interest in a subsidiary for $173,578. At the date of acquisition, the capital stock of the subsidiary was $150,000 and its retained earnings were $23,578.

7. A parent paid $1,369,129 in acquiring 100 per cent of the stock of a subsidiary with par value of $975,000 and retained earnings at date of acquisition of $306,784. What additional information, if any, would be helpful to you? Explain.

8. A parent paid $584,564 in acquiring 100 per cent of the stock of a subsidiary with par value of $500,000 and retained earnings at date of acquisition of $153,392. What additional information, if any, would be helpful to you? Explain.

9. A parent paid $456,376 in acquiring 100 per cent of the stock of a subsidiary with par value of $325,000 and retained earnings at date of acquisition of $102,261. A year later retained earnings of the subsidiary were $111,379. Show consolidation entries at this time. Retained earnings of the parent were $266,483. Assume in this problem, and in the remaining problems, that the parent carries its investment in the subsidiary at cost.

10. A parent purchased 75 per cent of the capital stock of a subsidiary for $1,725,232. At date of acquisition the capital stock of the subsidiary was $2,000,000 and its retained earnings were $840,240. Consolidation was to take place at date of acquisition.

11(a). A parent company purchased a 60 per cent interest in a subsidiary company for $1,604,925. At the time of acquisition the capital stock and retained earnings of the subsidiary were $1,800,000 and $775,091, respectively. One year later, at the time of the present consolidation, the retained earnings of the subsidiary were $908,327, while retained earnings of the parent were $6,181,912.

11(b). On December 31, 1961, a parent company purchased a 70 per cent interest in a subsidiary company for $895,703; the capital stock and retained earnings of the subsidiary were $900,000 and $442,198, respectively. One year later, at the time of the present consolidation, the retained earnings of the parent and of the subsidiary were $3,280,174 and $393,756, respectively.

11(c). The original facts are the same as those given in 11(b).

On December 31, 1963, the parent company purchased an additional 15 per cent interest in the capital stock of the subsidiary for $188,162. At that time retained earnings of the subsidiary were $410,645, and retained earnings of the parent were $3,342,861. Consolidation was to take place on December 31, 1963.

12. A parent company owned 80 per cent of the stock of a subsidiary. The subsidiary had declared, but not yet paid, dividends of $28,850. The parent company had not recorded its share of the dividends prior to the time of consolidation. The retained earnings of the parent were $873,369 and those of the subsidiary, after recording the dividend declaration, were $204,862.

13(a). Ninety per cent of the stock of a subsidiary was owned by the parent. At December 31, 1962, the balance sheets of the two companies were as follows:

	Parent Company	Subsidiary
Cash	$ 79,351	$ 28,806
Accounts and Notes Receivable	109,462	40,570
Inventories	142,240	39,681
Advances to Subsidiary	21,247	—
Net Plant	545,355	101,136
Investment in Subsidiary	165,218	—
	$1,062,873	$210,193
Accounts and Notes Payable	$ 107,844	$ 20,525
Advances from Parent	—	21,247
Capital Stock:		
Parent ($10 par)	760,000	—
Subsidiary ($25 par)	—	110,000
Retained Earnings:		
Parent	195,029	—
Subsidiary	—	58,421[1]
	$1,062,873	$210,193

Prepare the consolidation working papers at December 31, 1962.

13(b). During 1963, the parent acquired the 10 per cent minority interest in its subsidiary, paying $40 per share for the 440 shares held by minority shareholders. At the end of 1963, the balance sheets of the two companies were as follows:

	Parent Company	Subsidiary
Cash	$ 87,286	$ 36,687
Accounts and Notes Receivable	170,408	49,627
Inventories	206,464	43,649
Advances to Subsidiary	19,122	—
Net Plant	490,819	95,022
Investment in Subsidiary	182,818	—
	$1,156,917	$224,985

---

[1] At date of acquisition retained earnings of the subsidiary were $37,698.

Accounts and Notes Payable	$ 179,979	$ 20,569
Advances from Parent	—	19,122
Capital Stock:		
Parent ($10 par)	760,000	—
Subsidiary ($25 par)	—	110,000
Retained Earnings:		
Parent	216,938	—
Subsidiary	—	75,294[2]
	$1,156,917	$224,985

Prepare the consolidation working papers at December 31, 1963.

14. In the fall of 1962, a wholly-owned subsidiary constructed a building for its parent, realizing a profit of $3,620 on the contract. The parent entered the building on its books at the contract price of $72,400. A life of 25 years and no salvage was estimated, and at the end of 1963 the parent recorded depreciation for the first year of $2,896. The retained earnings accounts of the two companies at the date of consolidation, December 31, 1963, after closing the revenue and expense accounts for 1963, were $43,519 and $21,709, respectively. The parent had acquired the subsidiary two years earlier for a cash payment equal to the subsidiary's net asset value at that time. This consisted of $50,000 of outstanding capital stock and $8,760 of retained earnings.

In problems 15 through 18, which follow, assume that a parent (P) owns 100 per cent of the outstanding common stock of a subsidiary (S). Analyze each problem on a consolidation work sheet at December 31, 1963.

15. Marketable securities of S include $100,000 (at cost) of P's stock purchased on a stock exchange for payment of S company executive bonuses.

16. On December 26, 1963, P purchased from S for $16,000 certain equipment which was carried on the books of S at a cost of $30,000 with accumulated depreciation of $16,000. S, which acquired the equipment in early 1956, was depreciating it over 15 years. S recorded $2,000 of depreciation for 1963 since it had used the equipment for all but the last few days of the year.

17. On January 1, 1958, S issued $200,000 of ten-year, 4 per cent bonds. These were sold at 98 and expenses of issue were $2,400. Interest is payable on January 1 and July 1. On March 31, 1963, P purchased on the market $100,000 face value of S bonds at 90 and accrued interest.

18. On January 2, 1961, S sold some machinery it had manufactured to P for $60,000. This machinery, which cost S $51,000 to manufacture, has an estimated useful life of 15 years.

[2] Retained earnings at date of acquisition of 90 per cent interest, $37,698; of 10 per cent interest, $67,170.

The Hartford Corporation

The Hartford Corporation is engaged in the whole-sale grocery business in central Connecticut. During 1962, the corporation expanded its operations by two major investments. One of these was the purchase of the Waterbury Company, which extended Hartford's distribution into western Connecticut and added the Red Clover brand to Hartford's famous Lilac label. Hartford acquired all of the outstanding capital stock of Waterbury for $2,186,947 in cash and $1,202,003 principal amount of 4.5 per cent promissory notes payable in 10 substantially equal annual installments commencing March 31, 1963. At the date of acquisition, the net assets of Waterbury were $3,981,252. Waterbury continued to operate under its own name as a wholly-owned subsidiary.

The second investment was the purchase of 58 per cent of the voting stock of Seaside Farms, Inc., a processer of quick-frozen seafood specialties. It was purchased for $3,000,000 by a cash payment of $500,000 and a collateral note issued for $2,500,000, payable July 15, 1963. Hartford's equity in the net assets of Seaside Farms, Inc. at the date of acquisition exceeded the purchase price by $1,769,009.

Mr. G. I. Prater, Hartford's controller and a CPA, had recently read Accounting Research Bulletin Number 51, "Consolidated Financial Statements." Following the recommendations made in this bulletin, he believed it would be possible in preparing Hartford's consolidated financial statements to take the excess of net assets acquired over the cost of these purchases into income over a number of years. He requested his chief accounting officer to prepare various acceptable methods and specify which procedure he considered the most realistic.

In 1961, Hartford reported net income of $254,000. At the close of the 1961 fiscal year it had total assets of $13,230,000, and Stockholders' Equity of $5,223,000.

QUESTIONS:

1. As the chief accounting officer, prepare the acceptable method(s) of accounting for the excess of the book value of net assets acquired over the cost of these purchases in Hartford's consolidated financial statements. Select one method, and support your choice in terms of generally accepted accounting principles.

2. If Hartford decided to show the excess of net assets acquired over cost as a credit account on the consolidated balance sheet, would you recommend classifying this account within or outside the stockholders' equity section? Explain.

CHAPTER SIX

Income Tax Reporting
In Financial Statements

Determining the amount of federal income tax expense to report in a company's income statement often involves controversial accounting procedures. The basic question is whether the amount shown as Federal Income Tax Expense should be:

(1) the amount of tax *actually payable* for the period as computed in the current *income tax return*;

(2) the amount of tax applicable to the company's current *book income*, whether actually payable in the current, a past, or a future period;

(3) or some other amount.

Differences between *book income* for a year, as reported in a company's income statement, and *tax return income* for that year may arise for three reasons. First, certain items are specifically excluded by law from the calculation of income taxes. Some revenues, such as interest on municipal, state, and other nonfederal government securities, are excluded from taxable income. Likewise, some expenses, such as amortization of goodwill, are not allowed as tax deductions. If material, the amount of such revenues and expenses should be separately disclosed. These items seldom create accounting problems and they are not considered in this chapter.

A second difference between *book income* and *tax return income* may occur in accounting for extraordinary transactions. Generally, the income tax effect of recurring transactions is not separately disclosed. Instead, income taxes are identified with the combined effect of *all* revenue and expense transactions for the period—that is, with net income. However, when extraordinary transactions are excluded from the determination of net income and either

113

(a) shown as special items in the income statement following after-tax net income from usual operations, or (b) carried directly to retained earnings, the income tax effect of such transactions should be treated in the same manner as the transactions themselves—either as special items in the income statement or as direct adjustments of retained earnings. Thus, the amount deducted in the income statement as Federal Income Tax Expense is the amount which would have been accrued without the special items. These procedures, which are illustrated later in this chapter, result in *intraperiod* income tax allocation because the total amount of income taxes payable for the period is *allocated within the period* between sections of the income statement, or between the income statement and the statement of retained earnings.

The third reason for differences between book income and tax return income concerns the *timing* of revenue and expense recognition. A number of underlying accounting concepts and conventions, discussed in Chapter 2, influence the timing of revenue and expense recognition for financial reporting purposes. For various political, social, economic, and other reasons, the tax laws frequently do not observe these concepts and conventions, and consequently some revenues or expenses may be included in tax return income before or after their inclusion in book income. As a result, the actual payment of income taxes is either advanced or postponed. Procedures used to account for such differences in *timing* result in *interperiod* income tax allocation. That is, the income tax effects of these revenues and expenses are *allocated* to the fiscal periods in which the revenues or expenses are recognized for book purposes.

This chapter will consider *intraperiod* income tax allocation and the basic procedures of *interperiod* income tax allocation. Some aspects of *interperiod* income tax allocation, particularly those related to the use of accelerated depreciation for income tax purposes, are considered in Chapter 9, *Plant and Equipment—Depreciation*, and Chapter 18, *Classification of Deferred Income Taxes as Equity*. Since problems of accounting for income taxes are widespread, they arise in a number of the cases throughout this book.

Intraperiod Income Tax Allocation

Intraperiod income tax allocation between the income statement and the statement of retained earnings is illustrated by the following example. In 1961, the Curtiss-Wright Corporation incurred an extraordinary loss of $17,389,490 which was charged to earned surplus and disclosed as follows in the Consolidated Statement of Earned Surplus:

Loss on disposition of divisions, less $9,000,000 reduction in federal income taxes resulting therefrom $8,389,490

In its Consolidated Statement of Income, Curtiss-Wright included the following deduction:

Provision for Federal Income Taxes $8,275,000
([This] amount . . . represents the tax that would have been payable had not the loss on disposition of divisions (charged to earned surplus) resulted in a $9,000,000 reduction in federal income taxes.)

Since the $9,000,000 tax reduction arising from the loss on disposition of divisions exceeded the tax of $8,275.000 which would otherwise have been payable, Curtiss-Wright claimed a federal income tax refund under the loss carryback provisions of the Internal Revenue Code. These provisions are discussed later in this chapter.

An example of *intraperiod* income tax allocation between sections of the income statement is found in the Raytheon Company's 1960 Statement of Income.

Net sales	$539,974,777
Less:	
Cost of sales	$472,362,988
Administrative and selling expenses	47,447,421
Interest expense	4,561,112
Other deductions (income)—net	(242,183)
	$524,129,338
	$ 15,845,439
Federal and foreign income taxes—estimated	7,740,000
Net income before special items	$ 8,105,439
Special items:	
Income from grant of certain patent and proprietary rights for production of Hawk Missile in Europe (after provision for taxes of $1,680,000)	5,040,000
Loss from price reductions on components used in certain government contracts from 1956 through 1959 (after tax credit of $1,750,000)	(1,608,687)
Net income	$ 11,536,752

Observe that the first special item qualified as a long-term capital gain, and, as a result, the tax rate used to determine the provision for taxes was the maximum rate applicable to corporate long-term capital gains, 25 per cent. The rate used in computing the tax credit allocated to the second item was approximately 52 per cent.[1] *Intraperiod* income tax allocation involves little controversy and has become a generally accepted practice. Methods of applying this practice, in addition to the two methods illustrated above, are considered in case 6–1.

Interperiod Income Tax Allocation

Some revenue and expense items are taxable or tax-deductible in an earlier or later fiscal period than the period in which they are recognized for financial reporting purposes. Compared to the amount of income taxes which *would be payable* based on current book income, the amount of taxes *actually payable* currently is increased by (1) recognizing revenue earlier in the income tax return than in the books, or (2) deducting expenses later in the tax return than in the books. In either situation, income taxes are *prepaid*. That is, more tax is currently payable than is properly allocable to the book income of the period.

The amount of taxes *actually payable* currently, compared to the amount which *would be payable* based on book income, is decreased by (1) recognizing revenue later in the tax return than in the books, or (2) deducting expenses earlier in the tax return than in the books. In these situations, the payment of income taxes is *postponed*. That is, less tax is currently payable than is properly allocable to the book income of the period.

If no accounting adjustments are made for these differences between book income and tax return income, the initial effect on reported (book) income is reversed in subsequent fiscal periods. For example, assume $2,000,000 for two years' rent is received from a tenant at the beginning of a year. The following journal entries would be made by the owner of the property:

Upon receipt of the tenant's prepayment

Cash	$2,000,000	
Unearned Rental Income		$2,000,000

At the close of both the first and second years

Unearned Rental Income	$1,000,000	
Rental Income		$1,000,000

---

[1] Many of the cases in this book refer to a 52 per cent corporate income tax rate. From 1951 through 1962 the corporate tax rate consisted of two parts: a normal tax of 30 per cent of total taxable income plus a surtax of 22 per cent of taxable income in excess of $25,000. The tax for corporations with taxable income exceeding $25,000 is easily computed by applying the 52 per cent rate to total taxable income and then deducting $5,500, the amount of surtax *not* payable on the first $25,000 (22 per cent of $25,000 equals $5,500).

The *total* amount of rental income, including that part applicable to the second year, must be included in taxable income when received. Assume the rented property is owned by a corporation subject to a 52 per cent income tax rate. The tax effect of this transaction might be recorded by the following entry, made at the close of the first year:[2]

Income Tax Expense	$1,040,000	
Income Tax Currently Payable		$1,040,000

As a result of the preceding entries, one-half of the rental income, $1,000,000, is recognized each year, but the *total* tax effect of the transaction, $1,040,000, is charged to Income Tax Expense in the first year. To achieve proper *matching* of Rental Income and related Income Tax Expense, the entry immediately above would not be made. Instead, the following entries would be recorded (in addition to the entries at the close of each year charging Unearned Rental Income and crediting Rental Income):

At the close of the first year

Income Tax Expense	$520,000	
Prepaid Income Tax Liability of Future Years	520,000	
Income Tax Currently Payable		$1,040,000

At the close of the second year

Income Tax Expense	$520,000	
Prepaid Income Tax Liability of Future Years		$ 520,000

These two entries have *allocated* the $1,040,000 of income tax to the two fiscal periods in which the rental income is recognized, even though the entire amount of rentals must be included in the first year's income tax return.

In the preceding illustration of interperiod income tax allocation, the amount of tax actually payable in the first year exceeds the tax which would be payable based on current book income. A similar situation arises when expenses or losses, properly recognized in the books during the current fiscal period, are not tax-deductible until a later fiscal period. This situation is considered in case 6–2, Norwich-Springfield Company, Inc.

---

[2] This entry would not be made separately, but would simply be part of the entry made to record total income tax for the period.

INCOME TAX POSTPONEMENT

Interperiod income tax allocation may involve either the prepayment or postponement of income taxes. Situations involving tax postponement, rather than tax prepayment, occur more frequently and usually involve more material amounts.

For example, in the early part of an asset's life, depreciation for tax purposes, computed by using accelerated depreciation methods permitted by the Internal Revenue Code, frequently exceeds depreciation charged for financial reporting purposes. In the later years of the asset's life, depreciation for tax purposes is less than depreciation in the financial reports. This type of tax postponement is considered at length in Chapter 9, *Plant and Equipment—Depreciation.*

The payment of taxes is also postponed if income, recognized currently for financial reporting purposes, is not included in the tax return until a later fiscal period. The following note accompanying the 1961 financial statements of the Brunswick Corporation explains such a tax postponement:

> The Company and subsidiaries have consistently followed, for book purposes, the practice of recording income from sales financed by long-term instalment notes receivable when customers take delivery of bowling lanes, automatic pinsetters and other products. This practice, which is known as the "accrual basis," is the income-reporting method followed by most business concerns. Accrued Federal and Canadian income taxes included in the accompanying financial statements have been provided for on the basis of book income. As permitted by Federal and Canadian income tax regulations, the Company and subsidiaries follow the instalment basis of reporting income from such sales for income tax purposes and as a result, accrued Federal and Canadian income taxes of $112,000,000 at December 31, 1961, will not be payable until future years.

When income taxes are postponed, interperiod income tax allocation is achieved by the following entry:

Income Tax Expense	xxx	
Income Tax Currently Payable		xxx
Income Tax Payable in Future Years		xxx

As in the earlier illustration involving prepayment of income tax, the debit to "Income Tax Expense" is the amount of tax accrued —that is, the amount which would be payable on book income. In later years, when less income tax expense is accrued than is payable (because taxable income then exceeds book income[3]), the following entry is required:

---

[3] The possibility that this condition may never materialize because of continuing additional tax postponements is considered in Chapter 9.

Income Tax Expense	xxx	
Income Tax Payable in Future Years	xxx	
Income Tax Currently Payable		xxx

TERMINOLOGY AND PRESENTATION PROBLEMS

In the preceding illustrations, the accounts, "Prepaid Income Tax Liability of Future Years" and "Income Tax Payable in Future Years," were used to achieve interperiod income tax allocation. Unfortunately, these account titles are rarely found in practice, and the term "Deferred Income Taxes" is widely used to describe both the asset when taxes are prepaid and the liability when payment of taxes is postponed. For example, this terminology is used by the Armstrong Cork Company to describe the effect of postponed taxes in its 1961 "Source and Use of Funds" statement, shown on page 69.

Frequently the amounts of prepaid income taxes or taxes payable in future years are not presented separately in the balance sheet. Instead, these amounts are offset against a related asset or liability. For example, research and development costs may be deducted as incurred for income tax purposes even though capitalized and amortized over the estimated periods benefited for *book* purposes. The resulting difference between *book* and *tax return* income causes the payment of taxes to be postponed. The following two entries are consistent with those given in previous illustrations:

Unamortized Research and Development Costs	xxx	
Cash, Various Payables, etc.		xxx
Income Tax Expense	xxx	
Income Tax Currently Payable		xxx
Income Tax Payable in Future Years		xxx

An alternative to the second entry, which has the same effect on the amount of net income reported in the current fiscal period and in subsequent periods, is the following entry:

Income Tax Expense	xxx	
Income Tax Currently Payable		xxx
Unamortized Research and Development Costs		xxx

The effect of this alternative entry is to show the Unamortized Research and Development Costs net of the reduction in income taxes realized by the immediate deduction of all Research and Development Costs on the tax return. The reduced balance of Unamortized Research and Development Costs will then be amortized over future periods. Note that these future periods will bear smaller charges for the amortization of Unamortized Research and Development Costs, but Income Tax Expense in future periods will be charged with the full amount of taxes *actually payable* because there will be no account, "Income Taxes Payable in Future Years," to absorb part of the charge.

In summary, the effects of this procedure are (1) to offset the liability for income taxes payable in future years against unamortized research and development costs, and (2) to increase income tax expense and reduce amortization expense by identical amounts in future periods. The justification for such a procedure is that an asset which has already been "expensed" for income tax purposes has less future utility than an asset whose tax deductibility has not been fully exhausted. Therefore, the presentation of such an asset in the balance sheet should reflect its tax status. Despite this seemingly logical justification, the method does violate the accounting convention against offsetting assets and liabilities in the balance sheet.

This method of disclosing interperiod income tax allocation is illustrated by the following comment from the 1959 annual report of the Minneapolis-Honeywell Regulator Company:

> Our electronic data processing activity is a long-range undertaking which requires substantial investment. Since April 1955, we have invested approximately $38,000,000 to establish ourselves in this business. Of this, approximately $14,000,000 represents engineering and development costs which have been deferred on our books and are being amortized over the life of rental equipment. These engineering costs have been deducted currently for tax purposes, and the resulting credit equal to approximately half this amount is an offset in the property account.

Sometimes liabilities are also disclosed "net of income tax." For example, manufacturers of automobiles and appliances usually provide free repair service to their customers for a stated warranty period. In accordance with the matching concept, the expense of meeting such warranties is estimated in the period of sale and an appropriate liability established. However, no tax deduction is allowed until expenditures are actually incurred to fulfill such warranties. Instead of recording prepaid income taxes, some companies disclose the estimated liability net of the income tax deductions which will arise when expenditures are made. The rationale for this treatment is similar to the justification for showing an asset, such as Unamortized Research and Development Costs, net of income taxes. A liability whose payment will result in a tax deduction is less of a future burden than the usual liability whose payment is not tax deductible. The appropriate journal entries are considered in case 6–2, Norwich-Springfield Company, Inc.

INTERPERIOD INCOME TAX ALLOCATION VS.
INCOME TAX ACCRUAL

Some accountants object to the expression "interperiod income tax allocation." They contend that the entire process is nothing more than ordinary accrual accounting which is essential to the proper matching of revenue and expense. They claim the process simply results in *accruing* the amount of taxes related to a fiscal period's book income, regardless of whether such taxes have been paid in the past, are currently payable, or will become payable in the future. They fear that the expression, "interperiod income tax allocation," implies some different form of accounting peculiar to income taxes, which, of course, is not true. While such criticism has considerable merit, the expression has become firmly entrenched in accounting practice and literature. Also, as will be discussed in Chapter 9, other accountants argue that income tax allocation is not always consistent with accrual accounting.

Loss Carrybacks And Carryforwards

The Internal Revenue Code permits operating losses to be carried back for three years and carried forward for five years as an offset against otherwise taxable income. For example, an operating loss in 1963 would first be carried back and offset against taxable income, if any, of 1960. If the 1963 loss exceeded 1960 taxable income, the balance of the loss would then be applied against 1961 and 1962 taxable income. If the business did not operate before 1963, or if the 1963 loss exceeded the cumulative taxable income of 1960, 1961 and 1962, the 1963 operating loss may be carried forward to the years 1964 through 1968. Exhibit 2 of case 6-3, American Motors Corporation, page 142, contains excerpts from the Internal Revenue Code explaining the Net Operating Loss Deduction. Note that the operating loss carryback and carryforward are not offset against the amount of taxes paid or payable, but are offset against the *taxable income* of previous or subsequent fiscal periods.

A loss carryback results in a claim for refund of income taxes previously paid. A receivable, such as "Income Tax Refund Receivable," is debited, while the current year's reported loss is reduced by a credit to an account such as "Special Credit—Refundable Federal Income Taxes." Thus, in the case of a *loss carryback*, the tax reduction is usually identified with the loss year.[4]

---

[4] Under a strict definition of the current operating performance type of income statement, it might be argued that the refund should be credited to retained earnings.

When losses are carried forward, the resulting tax reductions are seldom identified with the loss year, but instead with the year in which the tax benefit is realized. As a result, reported income may be virtually doubled if income taxes otherwise payable are eliminated in a profitable year by tax loss carryforwards. Some accountants believe that such tax reductions should be credited to retained earnings when realized instead of being used to reduce current income tax expense. This is the policy followed by the Carpenter Steel Company in accounting for a subsidiary's tax loss carryforward. The losses were incurred by the subsidiary before its acquisition by Carpenter. The following note accompanied Carpenter's financial statements for the fiscal year ended June 30, 1961:

> Income of the subsidiary has been charged in each year with a provision for federal income taxes computed at applicable rates. Federal income taxes of $2,512,000 for fiscal 1961 and $2,202,000 for fiscal 1960 are not payable because of losses carried forward from prior years. It is the company's policy to credit reinvested earnings with the tax reduction resulting from the application of these loss carryforwards, since misleading inferences might be created if they were credited to income.

Some accountants propose that an asset be recorded in a loss year to the extent that estimated future profits make it likely that part or all of a tax loss carryforward benefit will be realized. Others object to this proposal as unconservative. They argue it is impossible to project the future profitability of a business with any certainty. These opposing views are considered at greater length in case 6-3.

INSTITUTE PRONOUNCEMENTS

The Committee on Accounting Procedure first referred to income tax allocation in ARB No. 18, *Unamortized Discount and Redemption Premium on Bonds Refunded* (Supplement), issued in December, 1942. When bonds are refunded before maturity, a current tax deduction is allowed for any unamortized discount or for any redemption premium paid to bondholders. For *book* purposes these items are preferably written off immediately by either a charge to income or a charge to retained earnings, or they may be amortized over the remainder of the original life of the retired bond issue.

The committee recommended *intraperiod* income tax allocation when the write-off is made to retained earnings and *interperiod* income tax allocation when the charge is amortized over the remainder of the original life of the retired issue. In the latter case, it recommended that a portion of the charge "equal to the reduction in current income tax resulting from the refunding" should be deducted in the income statement and only the remainder of the unamortized discount should be apportioned over the future period, or, alternatively, "another method would be to create a reserve for future taxes by a charge in the income statement equal in amount to such tax deduction."

Two years later, in December, 1944, the committee issued ARB No. 23, *Accounting for Income Taxes*. This bulletin, somewhat revised, appeared in ARB No. 43, as Section B of Chapter 10, *Income Taxes*.[5] Portions of this bulletin are best understood through illustrations. Case 6-1, page 131, illustrates paragraphs 9, 10, 12 and 13 of Chapter 10B. The reader may find it helpful to refer to these illustrative problems when reading the bulletin, which is reproduced below:

1. This section deals with a number of accounting problems which arise in the reporting of income and excess-profits taxes (hereinafter referred to as *income taxes*) in financial statements. The problems arise largely where (a) material items entering into the computation of taxable income are not included in the income statement and where (b) material items included in the income statement do not enter into the computation of taxable income. The section does not apply where there is a presumption that particular differences between the tax return and the income statement will recur regularly over a comparatively long period of time.

2. Basic difficulties arise in connection with the accounting for income taxes where there are material and extraordinary differences between the taxable income upon which they are computed and the income for the period determined in accordance with generally accepted accounting principles. For example, provisions may be made in the income statement for possible losses not yet realized but requiring recognition under generally accepted accounting principles, such losses, however, being deductible for tax purposes only when they occur. On the other hand, deductions may be taken in the tax return which are not included in the income statement, such as charges against an estimated liability account created in a prior period. Likewise, gains subject to income tax may not be included in the income statement, as, for instance, a gain on the sale of property credited to surplus. Also, credits in the income statement may not be includible in taxable income, as when an unneeded past provision for an estimated liability is restored to income.

3. In some cases the transactions result in gains; in others they result in losses or net costs. If all the effects of the transactions (including their effect on income tax) were reflected in the income statement the income would, of course, be increased where the transactions result in a gain and reduced where they result in a loss or net cost. But where the effects are not all reflected in the income statement, and that statement indicates only the income tax actually payable, exactly the opposite effect is produced—where the special transactions result in a gain the net income is reduced; and where they result in a loss, or net cost, the net income is increased. Such results ordinarily detract from the significance or usefulness of the financial statements.

4. Financial statements are based on allocations of receipts, payments,

---

[5] Two other Accounting Research Bulletins pertaining to income tax allocation, Numbers 42 and 44, are considered in Chapter 9.

accruals, and various other items. Many of the allocations are necessarily based on assumptions, but no one suggests that allocations based on imperfect criteria should be abandoned in respect of expenses other than income taxes, or even that the method of allocation should always be indicated. Income taxes are an expense that should be allocated, when necessary and practicable, to income and other accounts, as other expenses are allocated. What the income statement should reflect under this head, as under any other head, is the expense properly allocable to the income included in the income statement for the year.

5. In cases in which transactions included in the surplus statement but not in the income statement increase the income tax payable by an amount that is substantial and is determinable without difficulty, as in the case of a gain credited to surplus, an allocation of income tax between the two statements would ordinarily be made. Objection to allocation in other cases, as where a loss is charged to surplus, has been made on the ground that the amount shown for income taxes in the income statement would be increased beyond the amount of the tax estimated to be actually payable. Further objection has been made on the ground that the amount attributable to accounts other than income is not reasonably determinable.

6. The committee sees no objection to an allocation which results in the division of a given item into two parts one of which is larger than the item itself and is offset by the smaller. The argument that the effect of the special transactions on the amount of tax is not identifiable is usually without substantial merit. The difficulties encountered in allocation of the tax are not greater than those met with in many other allocations of expenses. The allocation procedure recommended here does not, of course, contemplate a determination of the tax effect attributable to every separate transaction. In the committee's view, all that is necessary in making an allocation is to consider the effect on taxes of those special transactions which are not included in the income statement.

7. The cases that are likely to call for allocation are those in which transactions affecting the income tax in a manner which would have a distorting effect on net income are included in (a) surplus accounts, (b) deferred-charge accounts, or (c) estimated liability and similar accounts. Methods of applying the allocation principle in these instances are set forth below.

METHODS OF APPLYING THE ALLOCATION PRINCIPLE

Computation of Tax Effect

8. In most cases, it is appropriate to consider the tax effect as the difference between the tax payable with and without including the item in the amount of taxable income. In certain cases the tax effect attributable to a particular transaction for the purposes indicated above may be computed directly as in the case of transactions subject to the capital gains tax. There may also be cases in which it will be appropriate to use a current over-all effective rate or, as in the case of deferred income, an estimated future tax rate. The estimated rate should be based upon normal and surtax rates in effect during the period covered by the income statement with such changes therein as can be reasonably anticipated at the time the estimate is made.

Credits to Surplus

9. Where an item resulting in a material increase in income taxes is

credited to surplus, the portion of the provision for income taxes which is attributable to such item should, under the principle of allocation, be charged thereto. The committee suggests, however, that the provision for income taxes estimated as due be shown in the income statement in full and that the portion thereof charged to surplus be shown on the income statement either (a) as a separate deduction from the actual tax or (b) as a separate credit, clearly described.

Charges to Surplus

10. Where an item resulting in a material reduction in income taxes is charged to surplus, the principle of allocation may be applied in the income statement in either of two ways: (a) the provision for income taxes may be shown as if the item in question were not deductible (the total amount of tax estimated to be due for the year being indicated) or (b) a special charge representing the portion of such item equal to the tax reduction resulting therefrom may be separately shown. In either case the amount charged to surplus is reduced accordingly.

Deferred-Charge and Estimated Liability Accounts

11. The principle of allocation applies also where an item resulting in a material reduction in income taxes is charged to or carried forward in a deferred-charge account or charged to an estimated liability account.

12. The deduction for tax purposes in a given year of an item which is carried to or remains in a deferred-charge account will involve a series of charges in future income statements for amortization of the deferred charge, and these charges will not be deductible for tax purposes. In the period in which the item is taken as a deduction for tax purposes a charge should be made in the income statement of an amount equal to the tax reduction, in the manner set forth above with respect to charges to surplus, with a corresponding credit in the deferred-charge account. Thereafter amortization of the deferred charge should be based on the amount as adjusted by such tax reduction.

13. Where an item resulting in a material reduction in income taxes is charged to an estimated liability account the principle of allocation may be applied in the income statement in any of three ways: (a) the current provision for income taxes may be shown as if the item in question were not deductible (the total amount of tax estimated to be due for the year being indicated), or (b) a charge may be included for a portion of such item equal to the tax reduction resulting therefrom, or (c) the item in question may be charged in the income statement and a credit made in the income statement representing a portion of the estimated liability account equal to the excess of such item over the related tax reduction.

Special Treatment

14. Where the treatments recommended above are considered to be not practicable, the amount of taxes estimated to be actually payable for the year may be shown in the income statement, provided that the pertinent facts, including the amount of the increase or decrease attributable to other accounts, are clearly disclosed either in a footnote or in the body of the income statement.

ADDITIONAL TAXES AND REFUNDS

15. Adjustments of provisions for income taxes of prior periods, as well as any refunds and any assessments of additional amounts, should be included in the income statement unless they are so material as to have a distorting effect on net income;[6] in such event they may be charged or credited to surplus with indication as to the period to which they relate.

CARRY-BACK OF LOSSES AND UNUSED EXCESS-PROFITS CREDITS

16. While claims for refund of income taxes ordinarily should not be included in the accounts prior to approval by the taxing authorities, a claim based on the carry-back provisions of the Internal Revenue Code presumably has as definite a basis as has the computation of income taxes for the year. Therefore, amounts of income taxes paid in prior years which are refundable to the taxpayer as the result of the carry-back of losses or unused excess-profits credits ordinarily should be included in the income statement of the year in which the loss occurs or the unused excess-profits credit arises. Either of two treatments is acceptable: (a) the amount of taxes estimated to be actually payable for such year may be shown in the income statement, with the amount of the tax reduction attributable to the amounts carried back indicated either in a footnote or parenthetically in the body of the income statement; or (b) the income statement may indicate the results of operations without inclusion of such reduction, which reduction should be shown as a final item before the amount of net income for the period.

CARRY-FORWARD OF LOSSES AND UNUSED EXCESS-PROFITS CREDITS

17. Where taxpayers are permitted to carry forward losses or unused excess-profits credits, the committee believes that, as a practical matter, in the preparation of annual income statements the resulting tax reduction should be reflected in the year to which such losses or unused credits are carried. Either of two treatments is acceptable: (a) the amount of taxes estimated to be actually payable for such year may be shown in the income statement, with the amount of the tax reduction attributable to the amounts carried forward indicated either in a footnote or parenthetically in the body of the income statement; or (b) the income statement may indicate the results of operations without inclusion of such reduction, which reduction should be shown as a final item before the amount of net income for the period. However, where it is believed that misleading inferences would be drawn from such inclusion, the tax reduction should be credited to surplus.

DISCLOSURE OF CERTAIN DIFFERENCES BETWEEN TAXABLE AND ORDINARY INCOME

18. If, because of differences between accounting for tax and accounting for financial purposes, no income tax has been paid or provided as to certain

[6] See Chapter 8, paragraphs 11, 12, and 13 [pages 28–30].

significant amounts credited to surplus or to income, disclosure should be made. However, if a tax is likely to be paid thereon, provision should be made on the basis of an estimate of the amount of such tax. This rule applies, for instance, to profits on instalment sales or long-term contracts which are deferred for tax purposes, and to cases where unrealized appreciation of securities is taken into the accounts by certain types of investment companies.

Two members of the committee, Messrs. Wellington and Werntz,
assented with qualification to adoption of section
(b) of chapter 10.

Mr. Wellington objects to paragraph 17, as he believes that the amount of the reduction in tax of the later year is due to the operations of the prior year, is in effect an adjustment of the net income or net loss previously reported, and, unless it is relatively not significant, should not be included in the income of the current year but should be credited to surplus. In an income statement for several years, he would show this credit to surplus as an addition to the income previously reported for the prior year, with suitable explanation.

Mr. Werntz does not agree with some of the reasoning, particularly paragraph 6, and certain of the conclusions contained in this section. While he believes that in many cases a difference in treatment of items for tax and financial purposes preferably requires a specialized charge or credit in the income account, so that neither a double benefit nor a double deduction results, he believes that the charge or credit may not always be mandatory and should ordinarily be described in terms of the item involved rather than as *taxes.*

The last sentence of paragraph 1, the reference to "material and extraordinary differences" in the first sentence of the next paragraph, and paragraph 14 have been cited frequently in disputes concerning the propriety of interperiod income tax allocation when accelerated depreciation is used for tax purposes only. These disputes are considered in Chapters 9 and 18.

Observe that some of the comments in paragraphs 3 through 6 apply to both intraperiod and interperiod income tax allocation.[7] The heart of the committee's view of income tax allocation, whether intraperiod or interperiod, is stated in the last sentence of paragraph 4—that is, the income statement should reflect, under the heading of income tax expense, the tax "expense properly allocable to the income included in the income statement for the year."

---

[7] Some accountants claim that income tax allocation should not be described in terms of time—intraperiod and interperiod. Income tax allocation, they say, is merely allocation on the balance sheet of the difference between the amount of tax currently payable and the amount of tax properly accrued and charged to income tax expense.

STATEMENTS OF THE AMERICAN ACCOUNTING ASSOCIATION

In 1952, the Committee on Concepts and Standards Underlying Corporate Financial Statements of the American Accounting Association issued its Supplementary Statement Number 4, "Accounting Principles and Taxable Income."[8] This statement did not consider the problem of accounting for differences between book income and tax-return income. Instead, the committee made a strong plea for adherence to generally accepted accounting principles in the determination of book income. It noted that "business has sometimes allowed its accounting practices to be influenced, largely for convenience, by income tax provisions. Corporate accounting practices for purposes of published financial statements should be governed wholly by generally accepted accounting principles, irrespective of measurements of taxable income under provisions of the tax laws."

At the same time, the committee viewed with concern the growing gap between income based upon generally accepted accounting principles and tax-return income. The committee stated that "the public interest will best be served if the differences between taxable income and business income are reduced [and] income subject to tax [is] made as nearly as possible coincidental with net income under generally accepted accounting principles."

The Committee on Concepts and Standards did consider accounting for differences between book income and tax-return income in its 1957 revision, "Accounting and Reporting Standards for Corporate Financial Statements."[9] Differences between book income and tax-return income are often significant, the committee stated, and should be disclosed, particularly since such differences are often followed by offsetting differences in later periods.

However, the committee did not favor the formal accrual of prepaid or deferred taxes—that is, interperiod income tax allocation, because:

...these items do not present the usual characteristics of assets or liabilities; the possible future offsets are often subject to unusual uncertainties; and treatment on an accrual basis is in many cases unduly complicated. Consequently, disclosure by accrual may be more confusing than enlightening and is therefore undesirable.

---

[8] From time to time the committee has issued specific statements to supplement its more general statements such as the general statements issued in 1948, "Accounting Concepts and Standards Underlying Corporate Financial Statements," and in 1957, "Accounting and Reporting Standards for Corporate Financial Statements."

[9] Earlier American Accounting Association statements were: "Tentative Statement of Accounting Principles Affecting Corporate Reports" (1936), "Accounting Principles Underlying Corporate Financial Statements" (1941), and "Accounting Concepts and Standards Underlying Corporate Financial Statements" (1948).

Despite this view, interperiod income tax allocation has become increasingly accepted in practice. Some of the committee's reservations about the characteristics of prepaid or deferred taxes and the unusual uncertainties concerning possible future offsets are discussed in Chapter 9.

In the ten years following the committee's supplementary statement, "Accounting Principles and Taxable Income," the gap between tax-return income and income based upon generally accepted accounting principles increased. This development raised two related questions: (1) to what extent are generally accepted accounting principles violated when certain definitions of taxable income are also applied in determining book income? and (2) when tax definitions are not used to determine book income, what procedures are appropriate in accounting for the resulting difference between book income and tax-return income? This chapter has focused primarily on the second question. Both questions are considered in later chapters, particularly Chapters 8, 9, 14 and 18.

REFERENCES

This list of references includes the more general items dealing with differences between financial reporting in accordance with generally accepted accounting principles and income tax reporting. References primarily concerned with the income tax problems of accelerated amortization and accelerated depreciation are listed following Chapter 9.

American Accounting Association, Committee on Concepts and Standards Underlying Corporate Financial Statements, "Accounting Principles and Taxable Income—Supplementary Statement No. 4," *Accounting Review,* 27 (Oct. 1952), 427–30. This statement also appears in *Accounting and Reporting Standards for Corporate Financial Statements and Preceding Statements and Supplements.* Columbus, Ohio: American Accounting Association, 1957.

Andersen, Arthur, & Co., *Accounting for Income Taxes.* Chicago: Arthur Andersen & Co. (May 1961).

Blough, Carman G., "Provision for Cuban Losses Net of Taxes," *Journal of Accountancy,* 111 (May 1961), 69–70.

Cannon, Arthur M., "Tax Pressures on Accounting Principles and Accountants' Independence," *Accounting Review,* 27 (Oct. 1952), 419–26.

Hendriksen, Eldon S., "The Treatment of Income Taxes by the 1957 AAA Statement," *Accounting Review,* 33 (Apr. 1958), 216–21.

Johns, Ralph S., "Allocation of Income Taxes," *Journal of Accountancy,* 106 (Sept. 1958), 41–50.

Keller, Thomas F., *Accounting for Corporate Income Taxes.* Ann Arbor, Michigan: Bureau of Business Research, School of Business Administration, University of Michigan, 1961.

_____, "The Annual Income Tax Accrual," *Journal of Accountancy*, 114 (Oct. 1962), 59–65.

Lent, George E., "Accounting Principles and Taxable Income," *Accounting Review*, 37 (Jul. 1962), 479–87.

Li, David H., "Income Taxes and Income Tax Allocation Under the Entity Concept," *Accounting Review*, 36 (Apr. 1961), 265–68.

Love, David, "Differences Between Business and Tax Reporting," *Journal of Accountancy*, 110 (Sept. 1960), 44–50.

Miller, Herbert E., "How Much Income Tax Allocation?" *Journal of Accountancy*, 114 (Aug. 1962), 46–51.

Moonitz, Maurice, "Income Taxes in Financial Statements," *Accounting Review*, 32 (Apr. 1957), 175–83.

Powell, Weldon, "Accounting Principles and Income Tax Allocation," *New York Certified Public Accountant*, 29 (Jan. 1959), 21–31.

Ready, Samuel L., "Income Tax Allocation in Financial Statements—Occasions and Opinions," *N.A.A. Bulletin*, 42 (Dec. 1960), section 1, 19–30.

Richardson, Mark E., "The Accountant and the Tax Law," *Journal of Accountancy*, 113 (Feb. 1962), 36–41.

Shield, Hans J., "Allocation of Income Taxes," *Journal of Accountancy*, 103 (Apr. 1957), 53–60.

Steiner, Robert A., "An Analysis of Income Tax Allocation," *Journal of Accountancy*, 111 (Jun. 1961), 64–67.

U. S. Securities and Exchange Commission, "In the Matter of Charges in Lieu of Taxes," *Accounting Series Release*, No. 53 (Nov. 16, 1945).

Problems to Illustrate
Chapter 10 B of Accounting
Research Bulletin No. 43

The problems below, keyed to specific paragraphs in Chapter 10 B, are designed to assist you in understanding the provisions of that Chapter. They illustrate the following types of transactions which may require tax allocation:

1. Credits to surplus.[1]
2. Charges to surplus.
3. Deferred credits to income tax expense.
4. Deferred debits to income tax expense.

Note that 1 and 2 above involve *intraperiod* tax allocation while 3 and 4 involve *interperiod* allocation.

1. *Paragraph 9*—Credits to Surplus

The X Company realized a nonrecurring gain of $100,000 on the sale of one of its plants in 1962. Income from operations before income taxes was $500,000. Income tax payable was computed on the basis of $600,000; that is, $500,000 plus the $100,000 gain. Assume a 50 per cent tax rate on all income other than the $100,000 gain, on which an assumed 25 per cent rate applies. Beginning surplus balance was $1,000,000. No dividends were paid and no other entries were made to surplus during the year. Common shares outstanding were 100,000.

For *each* of the three different accounting treatments listed below: (a) develop the remaining part of the income statement beginning with income from operations of $500,000, (b) develop the statement of surplus, (c) give appropriate earnings per share, and (d) compute the effect (in dollars and in per cent) of the nonrecurring gain on reported net income after taxes.

---

[1] The term "Surplus" is used in these problems to conform to the terminology of Bulletin No. 43; more recent Institute pronouncements favor "Retained Earnings."

(1) The entire gain is credited to surplus and all income taxes actually payable are shown on the income statement as tax expense;

(2) Treatment is as recommended in Paragraph 9 of Chapter 10 B; and

(3) The gain is shown on the income statement.

2. *Paragraph 10*—Charges to Surplus

Assume the same facts as above except that sale of the plant results in a loss of $100,000. Assume the loss is fully tax-deductible, similar to an expense (income taxes are reduced $50,000 as a result of the loss). Prepare (a), (b), (c), and (d) for treatments (1), (2), and (3) above, substituting loss for gain and the applicable provisions of Paragraph 10 for Paragraph 9.

3. *Paragraph 12*—Charges Which are Currently Tax-Deductible, But Recorded in the Books as "Deferred Charges to Future Income"

In 1961, the Y Company incurred $100,000 of research and development costs which it decided to treat on its books and financial statements as a deferred charge applicable in equal amounts to 1961, 1962, 1963, and 1964. However, under current income tax regulations, these costs could be deducted in 1961 and the company took the full $100,000 deduction in determining its 1961 taxable income. Assume net income before taxes for 1961 and 1962 shown on the company's books and financial statements of $500,000 *after* deduction of $25,000 of research and development expense in each year. Use a tax rate of 50 per cent. Common shares outstanding were 100,000.

(1) Develop the amount shown as net income after taxes on the 1961 and 1962 income statements assuming no tax allocation is made. What is the effect of the $100,000 research and development cost on 1961 and 1962 net income after taxes? Give appropriate earnings per share.

(2) Develop journal entries for both 1961 and 1962 to illustrate the income tax allocation recommended in Paragraph 12. What is net income after taxes for 1961 and 1962 under this procedure? Give appropriate earnings per share.

4. *Paragraph 13*—Charging of Tax-Deductible Items to Estimated Liability Accounts

In November, 1961, the ABC Construction Company recognized a profit of $100,000 on a completed contract. Net income for the year 1961 before taxes (including the $100,000) was $460,000, taxable at a rate of 50 per cent. Since ABC agreed to make any necessary repairs during the calendar years 1962 and 1963, it recorded in November an estimated liability of $40,000 for future repairs, charging warranty expense. Net income of $460,000 reflects deduction of this amount on the company's books. However, this amount was not tax-deductible in 1961, but would be deductible in 1962 and 1963 to the extent of actual expenditures incurred.

Note carefully that in Part 4 deduction on the tax return occurs in a period *following* recognition in the company's books, whereas in Part 3 deduction on the tax return *precedes* recognition of research and development expense in the company's books.

(1) Paragraph 13 does not explicitly state what accounting recognition might have been given to the deferred tax deduction in 1961, the year in which the expense and the liability are recorded. It assumes that the expense and liability were recognized in a period prior to the actual tax deductions and appropriate adjustments were made at that time for the deferred tax deduction. Develop an acceptable method for appropriate matching of revenue and expense and give the journal entry or entries you would make in 1961 to reflect this method.

(2) Give the necessary journal entries in 1962 assuming the method you developed in (1) was used in 1961 and actual expenditures in 1962 were $15,000.

(3) Assuming $15,000 was actually expended in 1962, give the three alternatives for disclosing tax expense in the 1962 income statement as outlined in Paragraph 13. Note that Paragraph 13 is concerned *only* with the question of how the tax expense adjustment should be disclosed in the 1962 income statement.

Norwich-Springfield Company, Inc.

Norwich-Springfield is a manufacturer of appliances. In 1954, the company began selling a three-year service and parts warranty contract with most of its appliances at modest additional cost. To utilize the full competitive advantage of its unique warranty contracts, the company intentionally priced these contracts at the estimated cost to fulfill them.

Norwich-Springfield credited income from warranty contract sales to its regular "Sales" account. At the end of each fiscal period it debited "Cost of goods sold" and credited a liability account, "Reserve for warranty contracts," for the full amount of warranty sales during the period. As costs were incurred in fulfilling the warranties, debits were made to the reserve account. As a result of these accounting procedures, the warranty business had no direct effect on the amount of net income *before taxes* reported for a fiscal period. The company was pleased with the increase in appliance sales which it attributed to the warranty contracts. Also, after three years' experience, costs of the warranty program had not exceeded estimates.

For tax purposes, proceeds from warranty contract sales were included in taxable income on the tax return in the year of receipt, whereas the costs incurred in fulfilling these contracts were tax-deductible only as expenditures were actually made. In 1954 and 1955, the amount of income taxes actually payable was shown on the company's books and public reports as "Income tax expense." At December 31, 1956, Norwich-Springfield adopted a policy of deferring income tax expense equal to 52 per cent of the annual increase in the Reserve for warranty contracts. A new ledger account, "Deferred debits to income tax expense," was established. The following analysis of warranty contract sales and *actual* costs incurred in meeting these contracts provided the necessary information for this accounting change.

Analysis of Warranty Contracts
1954-1956

	1954	1955	1956	Three-year Totals
Warranty contract sales	$302,181	$421,982	$503,437	$1,227,600
Cost actually incurred:				
Contracts sold in 1954	$ 46,322	$ 98,476	$106,861	$ 251,659
Contracts sold in 1955		63,121	140,887	204,008
Contracts sold in 1956			80,702	80,702
Total cost actually incurred	$ 46,322	$161,597	$328,450	$ 536,369
Increase in Reserve for warranty contracts (also addition to taxable income)	$255,859	$260,385	$174,987	$ 691,231

On the basis of the analysis, the following journal entries were made on the company's books to record these changes retroactive to 1954:

Deferred debits to income tax expense	$268,447	
Earned surplus		$268,447

To record deferred debits to income tax expense applicable to warranty contract transactions in 1954 and 1955.

Deferred debits to income tax expense	$ 90,993	
Income tax expense[1]		$ 90,993

To record deferred debits to income tax expense applicable to warranty contract transactions in 1956.

The company then reduced the reserve for warranty contracts liability to an amount which reflected the future income tax deductions to be realized as actual warranty costs were incurred:

Reserve for warranty contracts	$359,440	
Deferred debits to income tax expense		$359,440

To reflect reserve for warranty contracts net of future income tax deductions.

Because of intense competition in the appliance industry, Norwich-Springfield had not operated profitably from 1960 through 1962, sustaining the following losses:

Year Ended December 31, 1960	$ 281,444
1961	1,568,801
1962	778,325

[1] This credit assumes that 1956 income tax expense had already been recorded in the company's books, and had been based on the amount of tax actually payable as computed on the *income tax return*, that is, the same procedure had been followed in 1956 as in 1954 and 1955. If, instead, 1956 income tax expense had already been computed under the new policy on the basis of income before taxes as reflected on the *company's books*, then this credit would be to taxes payable.

Management, anticipating another loss year in 1963, had become increasingly concerned about disclosing the warranty reserve net of future income tax deductions because of the losses sustained by the company in recent years and the five-year loss carryover provisions of the Internal Revenue Code.
Exhibits 1 and 2 show the company's 1962 financial statements.

EXHIBIT 1

Norwich-Springfield Company, Inc.
Consolidated Balance Sheet as of December 31, 1962

ASSETS

Current Assets:		
Cash		$ 144,232
Notes and accounts receivable	$ 532,220	
Less: Allowance for bad debts	50,000	482,220
Defense contracts:		
Accounts receivable	$ 806,063	
Raw materials, work in process, finished products and other costs incurred, at cost	1,340,006	2,146,069
Inventories, at the lower of average cost or market		1,801,870
Prepaid expenses		56,782
Total Current Assets		$4,631,173
Land, Buildings and Equipment, at cost	$4,142,672	
Less allowance for depreciation	2,563,321	
	$1,579,351	
Tools and dies, net	26,792	
Construction in progress, at cost	6,239	1,612,382
Patents and goodwill		1
		$6,243,556

LIABILITIES AND NET WORTH

Current Liabilities:		
Notes payable		$1,350,000
Accounts payable		878,253
Accrued wages and other expenses		655,003
Total Current Liabilities		$2,883,256
Notes payable, due 1967		720,000
Reserve for warranty contracts (net of future income tax)		732,292
Other deferred items		169,928
Net Worth:		
Capital stock:		
Cumulative preferred stock, $100 par: Authorized 15,000 shares; issued 8,750 shares	$ 875,000	
Common stock, $1 par: Authorized 400,000 shares; issued 339,374 shares	339,374	
	$1,214,374	
Paid-in and other capital surplus	876,293	
Earned surplus (deficit*)	352,587*	1,738,080
		$6,243,556

EXHIBIT 2

Norwich-Springfield Company, Inc.
Consolidated Statements of Income and Earned Surplus (Deficit*)
for the Year Ended December 31, 1962

Net sales	$11,271,930
Cost of goods sold	10,284,657
	$ 987,273
Selling, research and product development, administrative and general expenses	1,669,220
	$ 681,947*
Other income	32,216
	$ 649,731*
Other deductions:	
Interest paid	$ 116,442
Provision for bad debts	12,152
	$ 128,594
Net loss for the year	$ 778,325*
Earned Surplus (Deficit*)	
Balance, beginning of year	$ 425,738
Net loss for the year	778,325*
Balance, end of year	$ 352,587*

* *denotes red figure.*

QUESTIONS :

1. Assume that Norwich-Springfield sold $720,000 of three-year warranty contracts on January 1, 1957. Ignore contracts sold in earlier and later periods and assume costs of meeting these warranty contracts were incurred at the rate of $20,000 per month for the next 36 months, beginning in January. How would net income after taxes, as determined from the company's books, be affected for the years 1957, 1958 and 1959 under (a) the former accounting treatment and (b) the new treatment? Use a 52 per cent tax rate.

2. In terms of generally accepted accounting principles, do you think the 1956 change in accounting was an improvement?

3. What alternative method of balance-sheet disclosure would be appropriate for the amount of deferred debits to income tax expense? Contrast this with the method of balance-sheet disclosure used by Norwich-Springfield.

4. Why was management particularly concerned about this accounting policy in 1963?

5. How, if at all, would you adjust the accounts at the end of 1963? If you propose any changes, would this call for any action by the auditors?

6. Comment on the balance-sheet classification and terminology used for warranty contracts. Can you suggest preferable alternatives?

American Motors Corporation

American Motors was incorporated in 1916 under the name of Nash Motors Company. In 1937, it merged with the Kelvinator Corporation and on May 1, 1954, Nash-Kelvinator Corporation merged with the Hudson Motor Car Company at which time the present name was adopted. The corporation has two operating divisions: the automotive division which manufactures and sells the Rambler passenger car in the low and medium-priced field, and the appliance division which produces and sells electrical appliances under the trade name "Kelvinator."

Management realized that large automotive operating losses could be expected until the Nash and Hudson lines were thoroughly integrated. In 1954, it was expected that model changes under the integration program would necessitate accelerated amortization of tools. In addition, substantial losses were anticipated from not fully utilizing some inventories. Consequently, management established a reserve of $11,000,000 (accompanied by a debit to retained earnings) against which obsolete tools and inventory items would be written off. Write-offs of $14,856,026 were made against the reserve to absorb tool and inventory charges beyond those applicable to the operations of the current period. The reserve was increased $5,700,000 by refundable federal income taxes resulting from these write-offs. The 1954 "Consolidated Statement of Net Loss" contained tax credits, in addition to the $5,700,000, disclosed as follows:

Consolidated Statement of Net Loss

(including Hudson Motor Car Division from
May 1, 1954, to September 30, 1954, but not including
Hudson Motor Car Company prior to May, 1954)

Year Ended September 30, 1954

Sales			$416,845,731
Less excise taxes			16,502,220
NET SALES			$400,343,511
Other income:			
Dividends received from subsidiaries		$ 1,043,157	
Interest on United States Government securities		120,344	
Sundry other income		1,748,532	2,912,033
			$403,255,544
Costs and expenses:			
Cost of products sold, other than items below		$363,437,544	
Depreciation of plant and equipment		6,342,787	
Cost of pensions for employees		4,267,712	
Selling, advertising, and administrative expenses		48,339,361	
Five-year warranty on refrigerators ($1,084,233), less amount not required for expired warranties ($498,224)		586,009	
Interest and commitment fees on notes payable		2,202,491	
Sundry income deductions		740,877	
Income tax credits:			
Refundable federal normal tax and surtax of prior years resulting from carry-back of operating loss	$17,190,000*		
Less portion applicable to merger charges carried to earnings retained for use in the business	5,700,000	11,490,000*	
Unused provision for state taxes of prior years		100,000*	414,326,781
NET LOSS			$ 11,071,237

* *Credits*

At the end of the 1954 fiscal year, the balance in the merger reserve account was restored to retained earnings, disclosed as follows in the "Consolidated Statement of Earnings Retained for Use in the Business:"

Consolidated Statement of Earnings
Retained for Use in the Business

· Balance at October 1, 1953		$100,941,815
Earned surplus of Hudson Motor Car Company and subsidiaries at date of merger, May 1, 1954		31,107,914
		$132,049,729
Deduct:		
Net loss for the year (including Hudson Motor Car Division from May 1, 1954, to September 30, 1954)		$ 11,071,237
Cash dividends paid ($0.875 a share)		3,965,353
Merger reserve provided at May 1, 1954, date of merger	$ 11,000,000	
Less amount not required	1,843,974	
Merger charges primarily for accelerated amortization of tooling, obsolescence of inventories, and commitment losses resulting from the integration of the automotive lines of Nash and Hudson made possible by the merger, less resulting refundable federal income taxes of prior years of $5,700,000		9,156,026
Merger expenses		391,124
		$ 24,583,740
Balance at September 30, 1954		$107,465,989

Selected income data from 1952 through 1960 are shown in Exhibit 1. Exhibit 2 gives excerpts from the Internal Revenue Code pertaining to loss carrybacks and loss carryovers.

Early in 1955, the integration of Hudson and Nash automotive production in the Wisconsin plants was completed. As a result of the integration, certain older Hudson facilities were vacated and left idle. On its 1955 balance sheet, classified among other assets, American Motors showed "Idle plants and equipment held for sale," $6,376,008, written down from $18,376,008 by a charge of $12,000,000 to retained earnings. In the financial review section of the 1955 annual report, George Romney, President of American Motors, commented on, among other things, the exhaustion of benefits from loss carrybacks:

American Motors incurred a net loss of $6,956,425 for the 1955 fiscal year after applicable tax credits for recoveries of taxes for prior years of $9,700,000. The loss for the 1954 fiscal year, which included Hudson operations for only five months following the merger, was $11,071,237 after tax recoveries of $11,590,000. The reported losses for the two years do not give a fair comparison of operating results because losses from Hudson operations for the seven months of 1954 before the merger are not included in the 1954 loss.

Approximately 85 per cent of the 1955 fiscal year loss was incurred during the first six months, when introduction of new 1955 Nash and Hudson models was delayed by consolidation of production in the Wisconsin plants. With larger shipments to dealers by early Spring, and adequate appliance production after its consolidation in Grand Rapids, the company operated at a profit in the third quarter. The final three months—July, August, September —followed the normal shutdown pattern for vacations, inventory and change-over to new automobile and appliance models for 1956, with production at relatively low levels.

After applying its loss for the 1955 fiscal year, the corporation has now used up its available claims for recovery of income taxes paid in prior years.

The Detroit plants made idle by the removal of Hudson manufacturing were written down in 1955 to estimated realizable values by a charge of $12,000,000 directly against retained earnings of prior years.

American Motors' lower sales in 1956 followed the pattern of the industry as a whole. Management attributed the 1956 loss of $19,746,000 to (1) a decline in automotive sales, (2) excessive cost of using a V-8 engine and transmission made by another company, (3) price reductions involved in liquidating year-end inventories of larger Nash and Hudson 1955 and 1956 models, and (4) extraordinary expenses incurred in introducing the 1956 Rambler a year earlier than originally scheduled. A special credit of $10,662,000 in 1956 arose from a gain on sale of American Motors' investment in Ranco, Inc.

When American Motors moved into a profit position in 1958, the tax credit arising from the carryover of prior years' losses represented an important advantage to the corporation. The total tax loss carryover of $47,000,000 would expire as follows:

September 30, 1958	$ 5,600,000
September 30, 1961	24,800,000
September 30, 1962	16,600,000
Total	$47,000,000

Part of the notes to the 1958 and 1959 financial statements read as follows:

1958:

... No provision for federal and state taxes on income is required because of the carry forward of operating losses of prior years. Without the benefit of such carry forward the provision for federal and state taxes on income of the year would have been approximately $14,000,000, with a corresponding reduction in net earnings. Unused operating losses available for carry forward to future years are approximately $20,000,000.

1959:

The carry forward of unused operating losses of prior years resulted in reduction of the provisions for federal and state taxes on income by approximately $10,800,000 in 1959 and $14,000,000 in 1958, with corresponding increases in net earnings.

In 1960, net sales were $1,057,716,000 compared with $869,850,000 for 1959; net income before taxes, $105,443,000 versus $105,146,000; federal and state income taxes, $57,200,000 versus $45,100,000; and reported net income, $48,243,000 versus $60,046,000.

EXHIBIT 1

American Motors Corporation
Selected Income Data for the Years Ended September 30, 1952-1960
(000 omitted from column figures)

	Net Sales	Income (Loss) Before Income Taxes	Federal and State Income Taxes	Income Tax Credits	Reported Net Income (Loss)
1952	$ 358,401	$ 26,304	$13,700	—	$12,604
1953	478,698	31,143	17,020	—	14,123
1954	400,344	(22,661)	—	$17,290[1]	(11,071)
1955	441,127	(16,656)	—	9,700	(6,956)
1956	408,408	(21,200)	—	1,454[2]	(19,746)
1957	362,234	(12,335)	—	502[2]	(11,833)
1958	470,349	27,170	—	515[2]	27,685
1959	869,850	105,146	45,100	—	60,046
1960	1,057,716	105,443	57,200	—	48,243

[1] Includes $5,700,000 credited to earnings retained for use in the business.

[2] Includes credits arising from offsetting the taxable income of Refrigeration Discount Corp., an unconsolidated subsidiary, against the loss of American Motors in the consolidated tax return—1956: $416,000; 1957: $502,000; 1958: $515,000.

EXHIBIT 2

American Motors Corporation
Excerpts from the Internal Revenue Code,
Section 172.—Net Operating Loss Deduction

Deduction Allowed.—There shall be allowed as a deduction for the taxable year an amount equal to the aggregate of (1) the net operating loss carryovers to such year, plus (2) the net operating loss carrybacks to such year...

Net Operating Loss Carrybacks and Carryovers.—

(1) Years to which loss may be carried.—A net operating loss for any taxable year ending after December 31, 1957, shall be—

(A) a net operating loss carryback to each of the 3 taxable years preceding the taxable year of such loss, and

(B) a net operating loss carryover to each of the 5 taxable years following the taxable year of such loss.

(2) Amount of carrybacks and carryovers.—The entire amount of the net operating loss for any taxable year (hereinafter in this section referred to as the 'loss year') shall be carried to the earliest of the 8 taxable years to which (by reason of sub-paragraphs (A) and (B) of paragraph (1)) such loss may be carried. The portion of such loss which shall be carried to each of the other 7 taxable years shall be the excess, if any, of the amount of such loss over the sum of the taxable income for each of the prior taxable years to which such loss may be carried. . . .

QUESTIONS:

1. Assuming a company is operating profitably, is it realistic for it to report materially higher net income because of a loss in a prior year? How else might this problem be handled?

2. How would you disclose the effect of tax loss carrybacks and carryovers on American Motors' income statements for the years 1954 through 1959?

3. Verify the $20 million of "unused operating losses available for carry forward to future years," as mentioned in the note quoted from the 1958 annual report.

4. Was it appropriate to divide the 1954 federal tax credit of $17,190,000 by crediting the profit and loss statement with $11,490,000 and retained earnings with $5,700,000? Comment.

5. The write-down in 1955 of $12 million of idle Detroit plants did not recognize the future deductibility of such losses for tax purposes. Could this charge to retained earnings have been made net of taxes? Explain.

6. A tax loss carryforward may be of considerable benefit to a company. Can you suggest a way by which this benefit might be reflected in the balance sheet? Show the journal entries you would use. Comment on the appropriateness of such balance-sheet disclosure.

7. What is the justification for tax loss carrybacks and loss carryovers? Do you think the nine-year limit (including the year of loss) is realistic? Explain.

PART THREE

Revenue and
Income Recognition

CHAPTER SEVEN

Revenue and Income Recognition

Periodic determination of net income requires the *matching* of revenues against related expenses. This process involves two steps:

1. Measuring revenues to be recognized in the fiscal period, and
2. Measuring expenses incurred to produce these revenues.

Revenue is usually recognized when goods are sold or a service is rendered. At this time, revenue can be objectively measured in terms of charges made to customers. The actual receipt of cash may precede, follow, or occur simultaneously with the recognition of revenue. Compared to the problems encountered in measuring expenses, considered in Chapters 8 through 15 of this book, problems associated with revenue measurement are less numerous and normally less difficult. This chapter and three of the cases following it deal with two special problems of measuring revenues and determining net income: long-term construction-type contracts and installment sales.

Accounting For Long-Term Construction-Type Contracts

When a contractor has long-term contracts extending over more than a single fiscal period, there is a question whether the recognition of income on each contract should be

1. deferred until the contract is completed, or
2. estimated and recorded periodically as the work progresses.

The Committee on Accounting Procedure discussed this problem of income recognition in ARB No. 45, *Long-term Construction-type Contracts*, issued in October, 1955. This bulletin follows:

1. This bulletin is directed to the accounting problems in relation to construction-type contracts in the case of commercial organizations engaged wholly or partly in the contracting business. It does not deal with cost-plus-fixed-fee contracts ... or contracts such as those for products or services customarily billed as shipped or rendered. In general the type of contract here under consideration is for construction of a specific project. While such contracts are generally carried on at the job site, the bulletin would also be applicable in appropriate cases to the manufacturing or building of special items on a contract basis in a contractor's own plant. The problems in accounting for construction-type contracts arise particularly in connection with long-term contracts as compared with those requiring relatively short periods for completion.

2. Considerations other than those acceptable as a basis for the recognition of income frequently enter into the determination of the timing and amounts of interim billings on construction-type contracts. For this reason, income to be recognized on such contracts at the various stages of performance ordinarily should not be measured by interim billings.

GENERALLY ACCEPTED METHODS

3. Two accounting methods commonly followed by contractors are the percentage-of-completion method and the completed-contract method.

Percentage-of-completion Method

4. The percentage-of-completion method recognizes income as work on a contract progresses. The committee recommends that the recognized income be that percentage of estimated total income, either:
   (a) that incurred costs to date bear to estimated total costs after giving effect to estimates of costs to complete based upon most recent information, or
   (b) that may be indicated by such other measure of progress toward completion as may be appropriate having due regard to work performed.
Costs as here used might exclude, especially during the early stages of a contract, all or a portion of the cost of such items as materials and subcontracts if it appears that such an exclusion would result in a more meaningful periodic allocation of income.

5. Under this method current assets may include costs and recognized income not yet billed, with respect to certain contracts; and liabilities, in most cases current liabilities, may include billings in excess of costs and recognized income with respect to other contracts.

6. When the current estimate of total contract costs indicates a loss, in most circumstances provision should be made for the loss on the entire contract. If there is a close relationship between profitable and unprofitable contracts, such as in the case of contracts which are parts of the same project, the group may be treated as a unit in determining the necessity for a provision for loss.

7. The principal advantages of the percentage-of-completion method are

periodic recognition of income currently rather than irregularly as contracts are completed, and the reflection of the status of the uncompleted contracts provided through the current estimates of costs to complete or of progress toward completion.

8. The principal disadvantage of the percentage-of-completion method is that it is necessarily dependent upon estimates of ultimate costs and consequently of currently accruing income, which are subject to the uncertainties frequently inherent in long-term contracts.

Completed-contract Method

9. The completed-contract method recognizes income only when the contract is completed, or substantially so. Accordingly, costs of contracts in process and current billings are accumulated but there are no interim charges or credits to income other than provisions for losses. A contract may be regarded as substantially completed if remaining costs are not significant in amount.

10. When the completed-contract method is used, it may be appropriate to allocate general and administrative expenses to contract costs rather than to periodic income. This may result in a better matching of costs and revenues than would result from treating such expenses as period costs, particularly in years when no contracts were completed. It is not so important, however, when the contractor is engaged in numerous projects and in such circumstances it may be preferable to charge those expenses as incurred to periodic income. In any case there should be no excessive deferring of overhead costs, such as might occur if total overhead were assigned to abnormally few or abnormally small contracts in process.

11. Although the completed-contract method does not permit the recording of any income prior to completion, provision should be made for expected losses in accordance with the well established practice of making provision for foreseeable losses. If there is a close relationship between profitable and unprofitable contracts, such as in the case of contracts which are parts of the same project, the group may be treated as a unit in determining the necessity for a provision for losses.

12. When the completed-contract method is used, an excess of accumulated costs over related billings should be shown in the balance sheet as a current asset, and an excess of accumulated billings over related costs should be shown among the liabilities, in most cases as a current liability. If costs exceed billings on some contracts, and billings exceed costs on others, the contracts should ordinarily be segregated so that the figures on the asset side include only those contracts on which costs exceed billings, and those on the liability side include only those on which billings exceed costs. It is suggested that the asset item be described as "costs of uncompleted contracts in excess of related billings" rather than as "inventory" or "work in process," and that the item on the liability side be described as "billings on uncompleted contracts in excess of related costs."

13. The principal advantage of the completed-contract method is that it is based on results as finally determined, rather than on estimates for unperformed work which may involve unforeseen costs and possible losses.

14. The principal disadvantage of the completed-contract method is that it does not reflect current performance when the period of any contract extends into more than one accounting period and under such circumstances it may result in irregular recognition of income.

Selection of Method

15. The committee believes that in general when estimates of costs to complete and extent of progress toward completion of long-term contracts are reasonably dependable, the percentage-of-completion method is preferable. When lack of dependable estimates or inherent hazards cause forecasts to be doubtful, the completed-contract method is preferable. Disclosure of the method followed should be made.

COMMITMENTS

16. In special cases disclosures of extraordinary commitments may be required, but generally commitments to complete contracts in process are in the ordinary course of a contractor's business and are not required to be disclosed in a statement of financial position. They partake of the nature of a contractor's business, and generally do not represent a prospective drain on his cash resources since they will be financed by current billings.

> *The statement entitled "Long-term Construction-type Contracts" was adopted unanimously by the twenty-one members of the committee, of whom two, Mr. Coleman and Mr. Dixon, assented with qualification.*

Mr. Coleman and Mr. Dixon do not approve the statements in paragraphs 6 and 11 as to provisions for expected losses on contracts. They believe that such provisions should be made in the form of footnote disclosure or as a reservation of retained earnings, rather than by a charge against revenues of the current period.

Mr. Coleman also questions the usefulness of the refinement of segregating the offset costs and billings by character of excess as set forth in the second sentence of paragraph 12. He suggests that a more useful alternative would be to show in any event total costs and total billings on all uncompleted contracts (a) with the excess shown either as a current asset or a current liability, and (b) with a supporting schedule indicating individual contract costs, billings, and explanatory comment.

Observe that the committee refers to construction-*type* contracts, such as those generally carried on at the job site, but the bulletin may also apply in some cases "to the manufacturing or building of special items on a contract basis in a contractor's own plant."

Interim billings, as mentioned in paragraph 2, are usually subject to an architect's approval and also reflect retainage, a percentage of the amount billed retained by the contractor's customer pending satisfactory completion of the work. Because of these considerations, the committee suggests that interim billings may not be a suitable basis for determining income.

ILLUSTRATION OF PERCENTAGE-OF-COMPLETION METHOD

Assume a long-term construction project with a contract price of $1,000,000. At the end of the fiscal period in which the project is started, $340,000 of costs have been incurred by the contractor, and remaining costs to complete the contract are estimated at $500,000.

Accordingly, the total estimated cost of the completed contract is $840,000 with an estimated profit of $160,000. Since the project is considered to be 40.5 per cent complete ($340,000/$840,000 = 40.5 per cent), this percentage of the estimated ultimate profit, or $64,800, is recognized currently. Also, assume that the contractor's customer has made interim payments of $360,000 during the period.

The following journal entries summarize the period's activities:

Construction Contract in Progress	$340,000	
Cash, Materials, etc.		$340,000
Cash	$360,000	
Customer Advances[1]		$360,000
Construction Contract in Progress	$ 64,800	
Profit on Long-term Construction		
Contract		$ 64,800

Similar entries will be recorded in the following fiscal periods. When the customer has paid the full contract price of $1,000,000 and the contractor has recorded the total profit realized on the contract, both the account "Construction Contract in Progress" and the account "Customer Advances" will contain balances of $1,000,000. An entry is then necessary to eliminate these account balances as follows:

Customer Advances	$1,000,000	
Construction Contract in Progress		$1,000,000

The estimates of total cost and ultimate profit made at the close of the second period may differ from the estimates made at the close of the first period. In this case, retroactive adjustments of the prior year's results are usually not made. Instead, an adjustment is made in the profit recognized at the close of the second period. For example, continuing the preceding illustration, assume that on the basis of incurred costs the contract was considered 80 per cent complete at the close of the second period, and the ultimate profit was then estimated to be $140,000, not $160,000 as estimated in the previous period. The profit recognized at the close of the second period would be $47,200 (80 per cent of $140,000, less $64,800, the amount of profit recognized in the first period). The following excerpt from a note to the 1962 financial statements of Combustion Engineering, Inc. describes such adjustments:

Method of Profit Accrual

Profits on contracts are recorded on the basis of the estimated state of completion .... These contracts extend over a period of from several months

---

[1] This credit may be disclosed on the balance sheet as a current liability or as a deduction from the current asset, "Construction Contract in Progress."

to two or more years, and revisions in cost estimates during the progress of the work under the contracts have the effect of including in subsequent accounting periods adjustments necessary to reflect the results indicated by the revised estimates of final cost.

Although such adjustments are undesirable, they reflect the substantial uncertainty involved in making the required estimates of remaining cost and ultimate profit under the percentage-of-completion method. However, the current recognition of estimated profit on contracts in progress, even though imperfect, may be preferable to deferring recognition of *all* profit until completion of the contract.

In (b) of paragraph 4, the committee states that measures of progress other than cost incurred and estimated remaining costs may be appropriate. An example might be cubic yards of concrete or asphalt laid by a highway contractor in relation to the total requirements of the contract.

The committee suggests in the last sentence of paragraph 4 that costs of materials or subcontracting costs might be excluded when calculating the percentage-of-completion "especially during the early stages of a contract." A significant amount of such costs may be incurred early in a contract and their inclusion in the calculation may produce results indicating a further stage of completion than actually exists. Substantial material costs may even be incurred before *any* construction activity is underway.[2]

Note in paragraph 6 and again in paragraph 11 the committee's attitude towards probable losses, and the dissents to these paragraphs by two members of the committee. When estimated contract costs indicate a loss, the *full* loss should be recognized, regardless of the method of accounting used.

COMPLETED-CONTRACT METHOD

During the performance of a contract, journal entries under the completed-contract method would be similar to those made above for the percentage-of-completion method except that no entries would be made to recognize estimated interim profit. Assuming complete payment has been received from the customer and credited to "Customer Advances," the following entry would be made at the completion of a profitable contract:

Customer Advances	xxx	
Construction Contract in Progress		xxx
Profit on Completed Construction Contract		xxx

---

[2] Such costs may be omitted from both the numerator and denominator in calculating the periodic percentage-of-completion, but must be considered in estimating the the ultimate profit on a contract.

CHOICE OF METHOD

In paragraph 15, the committee expresses a *preference* for the percentage-of-completion method when the essential estimates are *reasonably dependable*. "When lack of dependable estimates or inherent hazards cause forecasts to be doubtful, the completed-contract method is preferable."

Either the percentage-of-completion method or the completed-contract method may be elected for federal income tax purposes.[3] The completed-contract method defers payment of federal income taxes, improving the contractor's working capital position. Also, when payments to the contractor are subject to retainage, the contractor's ability to pay income taxes will be enhanced upon completion of the contract. Some contractors use the completed-contract method for tax purposes only, while using the percentage-of-completion method for financial reporting. If this is done, income tax expense and the related tax liability should be recorded in the accounts for profits recognized in the financial statements on *uncompleted* contracts.

The percentage-of-completion method offers several advantages for financial reporting purposes. Usually the resulting financial statements are

1. more useful to management in appraising progress,
2. more attractive for credit purposes, and
3. more likely to meet certain bid requirements.[4]

Accounting For Installment Sales

Installment selling is widely used in the retail field. Typically, when an installment sale is made, a nominal down payment is required from the customer followed by regular payments, usually monthly, for a period ranging from a few months to 36 or more months. Installment sales generally involve greater collection risks and, also, significant future costs may be incurred in handling installment receivables. However, it is usually possible to estimate future bad debt and collection costs, permitting recognition of the income from installment sales in the fiscal period when the sales are made. As an alternative, some retailers use the "installment method" of accounting for financial reporting purposes, and many more use this method *for tax purposes only*. Under the installment method, *gross profits* on installment sales are recognized as cash is collected from the customer.

---

[3] See the appendix to case 7–2, Charles Crowne Company, page 169, for "Tax Regulations Pertaining to Long-term Construction Contracts."

[4] See case 7–2, Charles Crowne Company, page 164.

ILLUSTRATION OF INSTALLMENT METHOD OF ACCOUNTING

Assume that on August 1, 1963, a customer agrees to pay $400 for a refrigerator as follows: $40 immediately and $10 per month for the following 36 months, beginning September 1, 1963. If the refrigerator cost the dealer $300, the gross profit is $100 and the gross profit percentage is 25 per cent. Assuming the dealer uses the installment method of accounting, the following entries would be recorded:[5]

August 1, 1963
Installment Receivables	$400	
Installment Sales		$400
Cash	$ 40	
Installment Receivables		$ 40

September 1, 1963, and monthly thereafter for 36 months
Cash	$ 10	
Installment Receivables		$ 10

December 31, 1963 (close of dealer's fiscal year in which installment sale was made)[6]
Installment Sales	$400	
Inventory[7]		$300
Deferred Gross Profit on Installment Sales		$100
Deferred Gross Profit on Installment Sales	$ 20	
Recognized Gross Profit on Installment Sales		$ 20

In all, $80, or one-fifth of the sales price, is collected from the customer in 1963. Therefore $20, or one-fifth of the total gross profit from the transaction, is recognized in 1963. The account "Deferred Gross Profit on Installment Sales" will usually appear on the balance sheet as a deferred credit following current liabilities.

In 1964 and in 1965, the customer will pay $120, and $30 of deferred gross profit will be recognized each year. In 1966, the customer will pay the final eight monthly payments of $10, resulting in the recognition of $20 of deferred gross profit.

MATCHING REVENUE AND EXPENSE

Note that only the installment sales account and the cost of the merchandise sold are deferred (rather than defer them separately, only the *difference* between them, gross profit, is deferred). Selling and administrative costs incurred in the period of the sale are not

---

[5] Numerous variations of these entries are possible. The entries given here illustrate *one* way of applying the installment method of accounting.

[6] The first entry might have been recorded at the time of sale.

[7] Assuming perpetual inventory records are maintained.

deferred. If such costs are material, appropriate matching of revenue and expense may not result if the installment method is used. On the other hand, if significant bad debt and collection costs are probable in later fiscal periods and *if* these costs cannot be estimated and provided for at the time of sale, the installment method may provide improved matching of revenue and expense.[8]

GROSS PROFIT PERCENTAGES

The illustration above concerned a single sale. If a retailer uses the installment method for many sales (whether for tax purposes only or for both financial reporting and tax purposes), an average gross profit percentage must be determined for each year's sales. This percentage, which will probably vary somewhat from year to year, will be used to determine the amount of gross profit to be recognized as collections are made in subsequent periods. For example, in 1963, a retailer might receive partial payments on sales made in 1960, 1961, 1962, and 1963. For any amounts collected during 1963 related to 1960 sales, the gross profit percentage of 1960 would be used, and similarly for each other year.

INCOME TAX CONSIDERATIONS

Use of the installment method for income tax purposes may be extremely advantageous, particularly for a growing company.[9] Sears, Roebuck and Co. explained its adoption of the installment method for income tax purposes in a note to its financial statements of January 31, 1962:

> This year, for income tax purposes, Sears adopted the installment method of reporting its income. Under the installment method, the tax on profits from installment sales is payable when the profit is realized by collection from customers or through the sale of accounts. As a result of adopting the installment method for income tax purposes, the company has deferred payment of $178,450,000 of the federal income tax provided at January 31, 1962. However, the company continues to prepare its consolidated statements on the accrual basis wherein the profit on installment sales is included in income at the time of sale, and the provision for federal income tax thereon is charged against income concurrently.

---

[8] According to the American Accounting Association: "There is no sound accounting reason for the use of the installment method for financial statement purposes in the case of closed transactions in which collection is dependent upon lapse of time and the probabilities of realization are properly evaluated." *Accounting Principles and Taxable Income, Supplementary Statement No. 4,* August 1, 1952.

[9] The tax implications of the installment method are considered at length in case 7–1, Spiegel, Inc.

The full impact of Sears' adoption of the installment method for income tax purposes can be better visualized in its funds statement for the 1961–1962 fiscal year. Note the amount of federal income tax deferred.

Source and Application of Working Capital Funds

	Millions	
	1961–62	1960–61
Funds Were Provided by:		
Net income for the year	$220.1	$192.2
Add back expense items not requiring funds:		
Depreciation	36.9	35.2
Amortization of debenture discount and expense	.2	.2
Federal income tax deferred	178.5	—
Proceeds from stock issued under stock option plans	5.7	4.5
Dispositions of property, plant and equipment (net)	2.7	4.8
Sale of stocks of DeSoto Chemical Coatings, Inc., Kellwood Co., and Spencer Press, Inc., less profit of $14,894,057 included in income	4.6	—
Repayment of funds advanced to Latin American subsidiaries	7.7	—
Other decreases in investments and advances	.6	2.0
	$457.0	$238.9
Funds Were Applied to:		
Dividends paid to shareowners	$113.2	$105.4
Expenditures for property, plant and equipment	56.3	69.2
Purchase of properties previously leased from The Supplemental Savings and Retirement Plan of Sears, Roebuck and Co. Employes	61.6	—
Investment and loans—Homart Development Co.	8.4	.7
Investment in Allstate Enterprises, Inc.	14.4	.5
Net increase in working capital	203.1	63.1
	$457.0	$238.9

On its Statement of Income, Sears, Roebuck disclosed $194,350,000 as "Provision for Federal Income Taxes." On the Balance Sheet, $178,450,000 was shown as "Deferred Federal Income Taxes" classified between "Current Liabilities" and "Long-Term Debt."

REFERENCES

Andersen, Arthur, & Co., *Accounting and Reporting Problems of the Accounting Profession*, 2nd ed. Chicago: Arthur Andersen & Co. (Oct. 1962), 65–68, 177–82.

Blackmon, William A., Jr., "Accounting Principles for Long-Term Construction Contracts," *New York Certified Public Accountant*, 30 (Nov. 1960), 759–67.

Blough, Carman G., "An Interpretation of ARB 45 on Construction-type Contracts," *Journal of Accountancy*, 101 (Feb. 1956), 63.

Fess, Philip E. and William L. Ferrara, "The Period Cost Concept for Income Measurement—Can It Be Defended?" *Accounting Review*, 36 (Oct. 1961), 598–602.

Mautz, R. K., "Emphasis on Reporting, Not Calculation, Could Settle Income Statement Controversy," *Journal of Accountancy*, 96 (Aug. 1953), 212–16.

Moonitz, Maurice, "Should We Discard the Income Concept?" *Accounting Review*, 37 (Apr. 1962), 175–80.

Myers, John H., "The Critical Event and Recognition of Net Profit," *Accounting Review*, 34 (Oct. 1959), 528–32.

Paton, William A., "Premature Revenue Recognition," *Journal of Accountancy*, 96 (Oct. 1953), 432–37.

_____, "'Deferred Income'—A Misnomer," *Journal of Accountancy*, 112 (Sept. 1961), 38–40.

Research Department of the American Institute of Accountants, "Construction-Type Contracts," *Journal of Accountancy*, 100 (Dec. 1955), 53–56.

Solomons, David, "Economic and Accounting Concepts of Income," *Accounting Review*, 36 (Jul. 1961), 374–83.

Storey, Reed K., "Cash Movements and Periodic Income Determination," *Accounting Review*, 35 (Jul. 1960), 449–54.

_____, "Revenue Realization, Going Concern and Measurement of Income," *Accounting Review*, 34 (Apr. 1959), 232–38.

Wilcox, Edward B., "Conflicting Methods of Accounting for Construction Contracts," *1954 Annual Meeting Papers*. New York: American Institute of Accountants, 1954. Also included in *Controversial Areas in Accounting*, a booklet published by the Institute, 1954.

Windal, Floyd W., *The Accounting Concept of Realization*. East Lansing, Michigan: Bureau of Business and Economic Research, Graduate School of Business Administration, Michigan State University, 1961.

_____, "The Accounting Concept of Realization," *Accounting Review*, 36 (Apr. 1961), 249–58.

Spiegel, Inc.

Spiegel, Inc., founded in 1865 in Chicago, sells a wide variety of wearing apparel and other merchandise from catalogs. Although originally a retail store business, in the early 1930's Spiegel began to concentrate on catalog selling by featuring a "no charge for credit" time payment plan. This plan was abandoned in 1942 when a charge for credit was instituted because of wartime credit restrictions. By 1957, the company had eliminated its retail store business, which had not been profitable despite considerable expansion during and immediately after the war.

Catalog Merchandising

Spiegel sells through general catalogs of from 600 to 700 pages published twice yearly. Smaller seasonal catalogs and special bulletins are issued from time to time and are mailed to regular and prospective customers.

In addition to direct-mail selling, the company operates over 200 catalog order offices, catalog order desks, and telephone shopping facilities. No merchandise is stocked in these units; the customer either selects his merchandise from catalogs at the catalog order offices or desks, or places his order by telephone. Approximately 28 per cent of total mail order volume is transacted through these facilities.

Credit Operations

Customers are offered three ways to buy: cash with order, 30-day charge, and monthly payment. Spiegel's experience has demonstrated that monthly payment selling is more profitable than selling for cash. Monthly payment customers tend to buy more frequently and in larger amounts than cash customers.

In 1955, the company introduced the Budget Power Plan under which each customer was assigned a line of credit—known as a "credit trust fund." Each Budget Power customer received a monthly statement which listed all transactions affecting his account, including a monthly service charge of 1½ per cent of his balance at the beginning of the month. The statement informed the customer of his currently available buying power and thus permitted more intensive sales promotion.

In January, 1959, longer credit terms, ranging up to 22 months, were offered to the average Spiegel customer. A large part of the growth in sales and profits during recent years is attributed to the Budget Power Plan (See Exhibits 1 and 2).

Sales and service charges were as follows from 1956 through 1960:

Year	Merchandise Sales Cash	Credit	Service Charges
	(thousands)		(thousands)
1956	$31,940	$ 98,007	$ 9,859
1957	32,117	96,148	10,343
1958	33,440	101,402	17,887
1959	39,536	148,844	28,289
1960	43,067	186,049	39,718

Total customer accounts receivable outstanding, the number of active customer accounts, and the average customer account balance were as follows from 1956 through 1960:

December 31	Total Customer Accounts Receivable (thousands)	Number of Customer Accounts (thousands)	Average Customer Account Balance
1956	$ 89,279	921	$ 97
1957	91,605	970	94
1958	103,983	1,043	100
1959	166,566	1,339	124
1960	246,361	1,752	141

Since the merchandising and finance operations are interrelated, their respective profitability can only be a statistical approximation. The company, however, estimated that over the five years, 1956–1960, the profit from credit operations contributed the following percentage of total profit *before* interest charges and income taxes:

1960	1959	1958	1957	1956
55%	43%	47%	30%	17%

In granting credit to new applicants, the company considers particularly family status, home ownership, income, and employment record. Although the maximum credit limit was $1,000, on December 31, 1960, 95.6 per cent of customer accounts had credit limits of $750 or less. If no payment is received for 60 days, an account is considered delinquent, and after 180 days is written off. On December 31, 1960, 69,438 accounts, representing total balances of $6,987,200, were delinquent. Net credit losses have averaged 1.6 per cent of sales.

The company maintains an "Allowance for doubtful accounts and collection expenses" for future bad debt losses and for the estimated expenses of collecting delinquent accounts.

Accounting Procedure

The company's book accounts are maintained on the accrual basis with income from installment sales recognized at the time of sale. For federal income tax purposes, however, income from installment sales is reported as cash is collected. The amount of tax charged against income in any one year on the company's books is based on accrual income and current tax rates; for example, in 1960, the provision for federal income taxes was $11,300,000 on the accrual basis compared with $750,000 on the cash collection basis. The difference between the income tax computed on the accrual basis and income tax computed on the cash basis, $10,550,000, was added to a deferred credit account, classified on the balance sheet between long-term liabilities and shareholders' equity. (See Exhibit 3.)

Spiegel includes all installment receivables in current assets, in accordance with customary trade practice and in compliance with recommendations made by the American Institute of Certified Public Accountants in Accounting Research Bulletin No. 43, Chapter 3.

Prior to 1959, Spiegel had credited selling, general and administrative expenses with service fees charged to installment customers. This charge, which included interest, represented the price differential between cash and credit sales prices. In 1959, the company changed this procedure and included service fees charged to installment customers in net sales.

Financing

The company has financed the extremely rapid growth in its accounts receivable primarily by debt, as indicated in the following tabulation:

	Sources of Assets at December 31 (000 omitted from column figures)				
	1960	1959	1958	1957	1956
Debt:					
Short-term	$ 83,850[1]	$ 40,900	$ 25,800	$ 39,550	$ 46,000
Senior long-term	50,000[2]	50,000	25,000	5,000	
Subordinate long-term	34,668[3]	15,400			
	$168,518	$106,300	$ 50,800	$ 44,550	$ 46,000
Deferred Taxes	$ 37,850	$ 27,300	$ 17,000	$ 13,250	$ 12,625
Shareholders' Equity:					
Common and Preferred Stock	$ 26,336	$ 24,843	$ 25,094	$ 20,791	$ 20,810
Retained Earnings	37,878	30,667	22,386	23,616	22,081
	$ 64,214	$ 55,510	$ 47,480	$ 44,407	$ 42,891
Miscellaneous Current Liabilities	$ 17,219	$ 16,573	$ 11,882	$ 12,875	$ 11,486
Total	$287,801	$205,683	$127,162	$115,082	$113,002

[1] Consisting of $10,050,000 of commercial paper and $73,800,000 of short-term loans from banks at the prevailing prime interest rate.

[2] $5\frac{1}{2}$ per cent promissory note, due July 1, 1979, held by The Prudential Insurance Company of America.

[3] Consisting of $20,000,000 of 5.9 per cent subordinated notes, due 1977 to 1980, held by The Prudential Insurance Company of America; and $14,668,000 of 5 per cent subordinated debentures, due June 1, 1984, convertible into common stock prior to June 1, 1969 (478,271 shares of unissued common stock were reserved at December 31, 1960 for future conversions).

In April, 1961, Spiegel made a public offering of $40,000,000 of $5\frac{1}{4}$ per cent debentures due April 1, 1983. The prospectus for this issue noted that "the net proceeds ... will be added to the general funds of the company to finance the company's increasing accounts receivable." The direct connection between this financing and the expansion in accounts receivable was further indicated by the fact that the debentures were not redeemable before April 1, 1971, *except* under stipulated conditions of declining accounts receivable.

Special Charges in 1954

In 1954, Spiegel made the following disclosure of special charges in its annual report:

Profit before provision for federal income tax	$3,138,462
Provision for federal income tax	1,632,000
PROFIT FOR THE YEAR BEFORE SPECIAL CHARGES	$1,506,462
Special charges (net of applicable tax credits):	
Loss on disposition of certain retail divisions of the company	$1,828,942
Provision for estimated losses on certain other retail divisions of the company to be disposed of	1,680,000[4]
Provision for estimated expenses deductible under 1954 Internal Revenue Code	288,000
	$3,796,942
Loss after special charges transferred to unappropriated earnings invested in the business	$2,290,480

NOTE: In accordance with past practice, the foregoing statement of profit and loss was prepared on the accrual basis, whereas for federal income tax purposes the income arising from installment sales is reported on the cash collection basis. For federal income tax purposes, the company sustained a net loss in 1954 and is, therefore, entitled, under the loss carryback provisions[5] of the Internal Revenue Code, to a refund of a portion of the federal income tax paid in prior years.

On the accrual basis, a tax refund of $585,000 was calculated as follows:
(1) A provision of $1,632,000 for federal income tax was established on profit of $3,138,462 before special charges.
(2) A tax credit of $1,905,000 was established on a loss of $3,733,942 sustained on the disposition of certain retail divisions.
(3) A tax credit of $312,000 was established on the accrual of expenses estimated at $600,000 which are permitted as deductions from taxable income under the Internal Revenue Act of 1954.

Since the income arising from installment sales is reported on the cash collection basis for federal income tax purposes, and the tax loss for 1954 on this basis is greater than on the accrual basis, the refund to be received by the company is $780,000, or $195,000 more than the refund computed on the accrual basis. The refund receivable of $780,000 is included under current assets and the difference of $195,000 referred to above is included in the reserve for federal income taxes on the accrual basis.

Future losses which may be sustained on disposition of retail divisions, to the extent of the gross amount of the reserve provided therefore, will not result in charges against future income. Such losses, however, will be deductible for federal income tax purposes, thereby reducing the amount of taxes payable in future years.

---

[4] Classified on the balance sheet at December 31, 1954, as "Reserve for Estimated Loss on Disposition of Retail Divisions" between Current Liabilities and Stockholders' Equity.

[5] See American Motors Corporation Case, Exhibit 2, page 142, for excerpts from Internal Revenue Code on Net Operating Loss Deduction.

EXHIBIT 1

Spiegel, Inc.
Selected Financial Data for the Years 1950-1960
(000 omitted from column figures)

	Net Sales	*Profit before Provision for Federal Income Tax*	*Provision for Federal Income Tax*[1]	*Net Profit*	*Total Assets*	*Deferred Federal Income Taxes*
1950	$143,517	$ 5,927	$ 2,625	$ 3,302	$ 73,319	$ 5,100
1951	146,308	5,238	2,950	2,288	37,695	6,500
1952	146,054	3,612	1,900	1,712	97,835	7,870
1953	134,082	2,616	1,390	1,226	95,325	8,070
1954	129,202	3,138	1,632	1,506[2]	87,927	8,265
1955	130,434	8,872	4,550	4,322	104,312	11,000
1956	129,947	7,900	4,050	3,850	113,002	12,625
1957	128,265	7,259	3,720	3,539	115,082	13,250
1958	134,842	10,258	5,270	4,988	127,162	17,000
1959	216,669[3]	22,587	11,650	10,937	205,683	27,300
1960	268,834	23,053	11,300	11,753	287,801	37,850

[1] Includes charge equivalent to reduction in federal income taxes arising from use of installment basis for tax purposes.

[2] Before special charges; after special charges a loss of $2,290,480.

[3] Service fees charged to credit customers included beginning in 1959.

EXHIBIT 2

Spiegel, Inc.
Consolidated Statements of Profit and Loss
Years Ended December 31, 1958-1960
(000 omitted from column figures)

	1960	*1959*	*1958*[1]
Net Sales	$268,834	$216,669	$152,729
Deduct:			
Cost of goods sold, including selling, general and administrative expenses	228,054	182,318	135,843
Provision for doubtful accounts and collection expenses	11,063	7,708	4,461
Interest charges	7,019	3,955	2,072
Miscellaneous other income or expense (net)	(355)	101	95
	$245,781	$194,082	$142,471
	$ 23,053	$ 22,587	$ 10,258
Provision for federal income tax	$ 750	$ 1,010	$ 1,760
Charge equivalent to reduction in federal income tax arising from use of installment basis for tax purposes	10,550	10,640	3,510
	$ 11,300	$ 11,650	$ 5,270
Profit for the year transferred to earnings invested in the business	$ 11,753	$ 10,937	$ 4,988

[1] Restated to conform with policy adopted in 1959 of including in Net Sales service fees charged to installment customers. Net Sales for 1958 include $17,887,000 of such fees which were previously deducted from selling, general and administrative expenses.

EXHIBIT 3

Spiegel, Inc.

Consolidated Balance Sheets as of December 31, 1960 and 1959

	1960	1959
ASSETS		
Current Assets:		
Cash	$ 21,880,105	$ 20,685,548
Accounts Receivable—net of allowance for doubtful accounts and collection expenses ($23,620,716 in 1960, $16,081,833 in 1959)	224,950,816	152,333,049
Inventories	21,918,237	17,367,848
Prepaid Expenses	6,488,818	5,833,695
Total Current Assets	$275,237,976	$196,220,140
Properties and Equipment—net	8,960,483	6,892,082
Other Assets	3,602,937	2,570,610
Total Assets	$287,801,396	$205,682,832
LIABILITIES AND EQUITY		
Current Liabilities:		
Notes Payable	$ 83,850,000	$ 40,900,000
Accounts Payable	9,629,479	10,312,612
Due Customers and Accrued Expenses	6,988,304	5,732,457
Federal Income Tax Payable	601,037	528,041
Total Current Liabilities	$101,068,820	$ 57,473,110
Long Term Liabilities:		
Note	$ 50,000,000	$ 50,000,000
Subordinated Notes	20,000,000	—
Subordinated Debentures	14,668,600	15,399,700
Total Long Term Liabilities	$ 84,668,600	$ 65,399,700
Deferred Credit	$ 37,850,000	$ 27,300,000
Shareholders' Equity:		
Cumulative Preferred Stock	$ 7,102,000	$ 7,410,000
Excess of Stated Value Over Cost of Preferred Stock Reacquired	768,653	707,054
Common Stock (without par value)	18,465,014	16,726,172
Total Capital Stock	$ 26,335,667	$ 24,843,226
Earnings Invested in the Business	37,878,309	30,666,796
Total Shareholders' Equity	$ 64,213,976	$ 55,510,022
Total Liabilities and Equity	$287,801,396	$205,682,832

QUESTIONS:

1. Approximately how much taxable income did the company disclose on its 1960 tax return?

2. Explain how it is possible for the company to pay taxes of only $750,000 for 1960 on over $23 million of book income before taxes.

3. What would happen if the company's sales should stabilize over a period of two or three years? If they declined?

4. In addition to the accrual method used by Spiegel, how else might you account for installment sales on the financial statements?

5. From the standpoint of proper financial disclosure, what balance-sheet classifications do you recommend for the accounts related to the installment business, including the deferred tax account? Consider the effect of such classifications on some of the frequently-used financial ratios. For example, at December 31, 1959, the company reported its current ratio as 3.41 to 1.

6. (a) Do you consider the 1959 change in accounting for service charges an improvement? Explain.

   (b) Should the auditors have taken exception with respect to consistency? Explain.

   (c) If your answer to (b) is no, should the auditors have taken exception regarding the application of generally accepted accounting principles in 1958 and prior years?

7. In 1954, the company disclosed a "Provision for federal income tax" of $1,632,000, even though no tax was payable because of Special Charges. Do you agree with this presentation? What tax rate was used in calculating the $1,632,000 provision? In terms of time, what type of tax allocation does this represent? In terms of time, what type of tax allocation is represented by the 1954 addition of $195,000 to the reserve for federal income taxes on the accrual basis?

8. Using the figures given in the quotation from the 1954 annual report, compute the $780,000 tax refund.

9. Calculate the amount of additional estimated gross loss at December 31, 1954, anticipated on the subsequent disposal of "certain other retail divisions of the company." Do you believe this amount should have been disclosed? Contrast the disclosure of the amount of these estimated losses with that of the losses actually recognized in 1954.

10. In 1954, Spiegel included in Special Charges, net of income tax, *both* losses incurred and those anticipated. Consider any alternative procedures which might have been used. Which do you prefer?

11. Assuming the company had 1,600,000 common shares outstanding in 1954 and the dividend requirement on preferred stock was $375,000, what amount would be most appropriate to report as earnings (or loss) per common share? Assume dividends on the preferred stock are cumulative.

12. Compute the debt to equity ratio for each year from 1956 through 1960. What can you say about the leverage in Spiegel's financial structure? Has the company successfully "traded on the equity"?

Charles Crowne Company

In 1926, Mr. Charles Crowne founded his own masonry contracting firm as a single proprietorship. The company grew slowly until 1954 when Mr. Crowne's son John joined the firm after obtaining a degree in architectural engineering. The company then started a gradual move into the general construction field. By 1960, it had become a general contractor devoting its major effort to institutional projects such as municipal garages, churches, and fire stations.

In bidding on projects, the Crowne Co. estimated the cost to complete a project, adding to this estimate a percentage for overhead and profit. A large part of such an estimate was based on the bids of subcontractors for special portions of a job. If the contract was obtained, the company would award subcontracts to those subcontractors who had submitted the lowest bids for portions of the project. Contracts received by Crowne were almost always for a fixed price.

On January 1, 1961, the firm was incorporated with the following stockholders:

	Common Stock
Mr. Charles Crowne, president	$ 60,000
Mr. John Crowne, vice president and treasurer	30,000
Mr. Larry Shane, secretary and office manager	10,000
	$100,000

Crowne performed all masonry work on its contracts. In addition, carpenters were employed to handle rough carpentry work and to assist in supervision of company-employed laborers and subcontractors. Most other work on company projects was performed by subcontractors.

At a meeting held in 1962, John Crowne questioned the corporation's method of recording profits on construction contracts. He stated that a construction company could report its profits either on a percentage-of-dollar-completion basis or on a completed-contract basis, and that the difference between the two methods could have a material effect on a company's financial statements. The other two officers asked for a detailed explanation of the alternatives. The Crowne Co. had always followed the completed-contract method of recording income on its contracts.

John Crowne noted that the company's financial statements were widely used by architects and bonding companies when they appraised Crowne's ability to perform a contract for which it was bidding. The three men agreed they should be aware of the significance of alternatives, since the use of various accounting methods might well influence the firm's success in obtaining contracts from architects and gaining coverage from bonding companies.

The officers were also concerned about the tax aspects of available alternatives and wondered whether one method could be used for tax, and another for financial accounting, purposes. Another factor mentioned was the future prosperity of the company and the construction industry in general. Although over the long run the officers expected to expand the volume of business, the prospects for 1962 did not appear favorable. As a final consideration, John Crowne noted that they would soon have to furnish financial statements with their request to the Second National Bank for assistance in financing a proposed company office and storage building to be constructed in the spring of 1963. He wondered if the amount of bank credit available to Crowne would be influenced by a change in accounting methods.

At the conclusion of the meeting, John Crowne agreed to investigate the available alternatives, to review their application to the Charles Crowne Company, and then to submit his recommendations to the other two officers.

1961 Operating Results

Because of the high volume of institutional construction activity, 1961 was a record year for the Crowne Co. The sales value of contracts completed in 1961 was $1,143,303, compared to the previous high in 1957 of $819,349. Net profit before taxes and officers' compensation in 1961 was estimated at $106,114 compared with $62,809 for 1960. (See Exhibits 1 through 4.)

The status report of contracts in process (see Exhibit 5) as of December 31, 1961 showed that three contracts having a total contract price of $465,164 were in various stages of completion. A total cost of $190,817 had been incurred to date on these contracts. Of the three contracts, two were for fire stations and one for a municipal garage. All contracts had been started after August, 1961 and were expected to be completed in the spring or early summer of 1962. No revenues or costs on these contracts were reflected in the income statement for 1961.

Outlook for 1962

The officers felt that the 1962 construction outlook for their area was not bright. Over-all construction activity seemed likely to remain fairly high, but they believed profit margins would fall. Increasing competition for institutional construction was expected because residential contractors were expanding into the institutional field. As a result, the company had reduced its provision for general overhead and profit in recent bids to approximately 10 per cent of the estimated cost of a project. In the past, it had been company practice to include in its bids 10 per cent for profit plus a provision for general and administrative overhead of 5 per cent. Although the officers realized Crowne Co. might incur losses on one or more contracts as a result of bidding at a lower than normal figure, they hoped volume would tend to wash out any individual loss and give the company a fair profit. Company records showed that past losses had never exceeded 11 per cent of the contract price.

Company officers expected to submit bids in 1962 on projects similar in nature to projects in progress or recently completed. As of January 8, 1962, the company had no backlog of contracts on which it had not started work. Contract awards were usually low in January and February, but customarily picked up in March.

Size of Contracts

For several reasons the company did not bid for contracts in excess of $400,000. The officers desired to spread the risk among a number of contracts and also to keep the company's name before architects in the area. Architects, acting as agents for project owners, were usually responsible for examining the reliability of contractors bidding on a project. Bids from unknown contractors or from contractors not considered reliable were usually eliminated from further consideration. It had taken Crowne several years to acquaint area architects with the company's name and its ability to perform a job. If they committed Crowne Co. to one or two large, long-term contracts, the officers believed they might lose architects' attention for a considerable period of time. They felt it would be difficult to re-establish the company with the architects when the long-term contracts were completed.

A third reason for avoiding contracts over $400,000 was the very important role of bonding companies. Charles Crowne Company, like every contractor, was usually required to post certain bonds with the architect (or the project owner) which stated that it would complete the contract according to specifications. Frequently, a contract clause specified a penalty if the project was not completed by a given date. Nonfulfillment of the stated provisions could result in forfeiture of the bond and a payment by the bonding company to the architect and project owner. To prevent contractors from overextending themselves, bonding companies limited the total sales value of all outstanding contracts at any one time to ten times the contractor's net worth. Thus, the Charles Crowne Company could handle total contracts of $1,232,480—10 times its net worth at December 31, 1961. By taking on contracts over $400,000, the officers believed they could not satisfy the two other considerations outlined above.

Accounting Procedures

(a) Recording Costs

The company's accounting system was not complex. It was designed to provide accurate records of costs incurred for each job. Separate subledgers for each job were kept to facilitate this work.

As costs were incurred, they were journalized and posted to the appropriate job ledger. A voucher was also made out recording the supplier's or subcontractor's name and address and the amount payable. Charges for company-employed labor were compiled at the job site and forwarded to the office. The data specified hours worked, pay rate, and the nature of work performed for each man. These data were also used as a basis for computing payrolls. The total of the balances in the job ledger accounts was the company's "Work in Process."

The job cost accounts tended to be the same for each job. The following major classifications were typical:

1. *Subcontracts:* Separate subaccounts were maintained for each subcontract. For instance, on Job #220, a fire station, there were 20 subcontracts for various portions of the total job. A list of the subcontract accounts on Job #220 is provided in Exhibit 6.
   (The following accounts showed *company*-incurred job costs.)
2. *Masonry:* Separate job accounts were kept for company masonry labor and company-purchased masonry materials.
3. *Carpentry:* Same as for masonry.
4. *Special Projects:* Separate project accounts were provided when unusual portions of a contract were to be completed by the company. For instance, in completing Job #220 the company was to install slide poles to be used in the fire station, and also erect a flag pole. Costs incurred for these purposes would be charged to special slide pole and flag pole accounts.
5. *Supervision:* Used to record the supervisory costs for each job.
6. *Performance Bond and Insurance:* Used to record the bonding charges and insurance required for each job.

7. *General Conditions:* Separate account for each job; used to include all job costs not charged to other accounts. The account contained such items as the cost of the construction shack, telephone and other utilities, general office supplies, wages of timekeeper and watchman, and the wages of laborers not easily separated into other accounts.

(b) Billing

For jobs in process, the company usually submitted a monthly "Application for Payment" to the architect who represented the project owner. Exhibit 7 shows the details provided on the application. Items marked with an asterisk are for company portions of the job, while the remainder are for subcontracted work.

Several steps were involved in determining the amount billed by the contractor. First, a company officer estimated the *physical percentage-of-completion* of each major portion of the contract. In the case of the masonry item on Exhibit 7, it was estimated that masonry work was 90 per cent complete at the end of the month. Since masonry had been estimated at 78 per cent complete at the close of the previous month, 12 per cent of the $51,200 value attached to masonry, or approximately $6,120, was the gross amount to be billed for the current month. It is noteworthy that the extent of physical completion, not costs incurred to date as a percentage of total estimated costs, determined the percentage-of-completion used for billing purposes. Thus, the gross billing of $6,120 for the current month could be equal to, less than, or greater than the actual costs incurred in the month plus the allowances for profit and overhead that were assumed in bidding for the job.

A similar estimating procedure was followed for other items. The items were then summed to obtain the gross billing for the current month. From this total gross billing an amount called retainage, agreed to in the contract as 10 per cent of the gross billing, was deducted to obtain the net billing due the contractor. The application was then forwarded to the architect who verified the percentage of physical completion claimed by the contractor. If the architect considered the percentage billed as valid, he certified the application and requested the project owner to forward the net billing to the contractor. The contractor usually received his progress payment within 15 days after the date of billing.

(c) Recording Income

As mentioned above, the Crowne Co. used the completed-contract method to record income. Contract profit or loss was not booked until completion of the job and its subsequent acceptance by the project owner.

The company recorded the billings, net of retainage, with the following entry:

Billings Receivable—Job #220	xxx	
Work in Process—Job #220		xxx

At December 31, 1961, the credit balance of the work in process account for Job #220 represented billings (net of retainage) in excess of costs.

When the contractor received payment the following entry was made:

Cash	xxx	
Billings Receivable—Job #220		xxx

At the final billing of a contract, the company billed the owner for all retainage, debiting Billings Receivable—Job #220 and crediting Work in Process—Job #220.

When the contract was complete, the credit balance in the Work in Process account gave the profit on the contract. This amount was closed out to profit and loss as follows:

Work in Process—Job #220	xxx	
Profit on Job #220		xxx

APPENDIX

Tax Regulations Pertaining to Long-term Construction Contracts:[1]

Long-term contracts—(a) *Definition.* The term "long-term contracts" means building, installation, or construction contracts covering a period in excess of one year from the date of execution of the contract to the date on which the contract is finally completed and accepted.

(b) *Methods.* Income from long-term contracts (as defined in paragraph (a) of this section), determined in a manner consistent with the nature and terms of the contract, may be included in gross income in accordance with one of the following methods, provided such method clearly reflects income:

(1) *Percentage of completion method.* Gross income derived from long-term contracts may be reported according to the percentage of completion method. Under this method, the portion of the gross contract price which corresponds to the percentage of the entire contract which has been completed during the taxable year shall be included in gross income for such taxable year. There shall then be deducted all expenditures made during the taxable year in connection with the contract, account being taken of the material and supplies on hand at the beginning and end of the taxable year for use in such contract. Certificates of architects or engineers showing the percentage of completion of each contract during the taxable year shall be available at the principal place of business of the taxpayer for inspection in connection with an examination of the income tax return.

(2) *Completed contract method.* Gross income derived from long-term contracts may be reported for the taxable year in which the contract is finally completed and accepted. Under this method, there shall be deducted from gross income for such year all expenses which are properly allocable to the

---

[1] Final Regulations under the 1954 Code—Reg. 1.451-3.

contract, taking into account any material and supplies charged to the contract but remaining on hand at the time of completion.

(c) *In general.* Long-term contract methods of accounting apply only to the accounting for income and expenses attributable to long-term contracts. Other income and expense items, such as investment income or expenses not attributable to such contracts, shall be accounted for under a proper method of accounting.... A taxpayer may change to or from a long-term contract method of accounting only with the consent of the Commissioner.... When a taxpayer reports income under a long-term contract method, a statement to that effect shall be attached to his income tax return.

EXHIBIT 1

Charles Crowne Company
Income Statement for Year Ended December 31, 1961

Sales Value of Contracts Completed		$1,143,303
Cost of Contracts Completed		1,026,112
Gross Income from Contracts		$ 117,191
Add: Discounts Earned		10,833
		$ 128,024
Less:		
General and Administrative Expense	$21,910	
Officers' Compensation	69,140	91,050
Net Income Before Tax		$ 36,974
Federal Taxes		13,726
Net Income		$ 23,248

EXHIBIT 2

Charles Crowne Company
Contracts Completed in 1961

Contract Price	Contract Cost	Gross Income from Contracts
$ 9,061	$ 7,390	$ 1,671
6,970	6,567	403
82,493	72,055	10,438
23,652	24,137	(485)
6,114	4,839	1,275
23,569	22,141	1,428
147,164	141,678	5,486
45,824	41,250	4,574
58,011	53,530	4,481
362,522	320,875	41,647
33,600	32,705	895
43,702	37,266	6,436
27,731	25,872	1,859
3,801	3,110	691
90,200	78,104	12,096
55,314	47,196	8,118
14,071	13,557	514
37,598	29,631	7,967
30,207	28,996	1,211
41,699	35,213	6,486
$1,143,303	$1,026,112	$117,191

EXHIBIT 3

Charles Crowne Company
Sales and Income—1955-1960[1]

	Sales Value of Contracts Completed	Gross Income from Contracts (Including Discounts Earned)	Profit Before Officers' Compensation
1955	$481,302	$63,072	$52,816
1956	548,424	77,799	61,714
1957	819,349	77,424	59,475
1958	581,221	49,487	32,563
1959	340,381	38,200	24,589
1960	661,385	87,566	62,809

[1] During the years 1955-1960 the company was operated as a partnership.

EXHIBIT 4

Charles Crowne Company
Balance Sheet as of December 31, 1961

ASSETS

Current Assets:
Cash		$ 91,132
Billings Receivable		84,559
Deposit Accounts		2,342
Notes Receivable		11,919
		$189,952

Fixed Assets:
Trucks, tools, equipment, and office furniture	$ 12,923	
Less: Reserve for depreciation	2,091	10,832
		$200,784

LIABILITIES AND STOCKHOLDERS' EQUITY

Current Liabilities:
Accounts Payable			$ 43,930
Accrued Taxes			12,531
Accrued Insurance			2,079
Accrued Management Compensation			11,813
Net billings on uncompleted contracts in excess of related costs:			
Gross Billings	$220,000		
Less: Retainage	22,000	$198,000	
Less: Cost to date		190,817	7,183
			$ 77,536

Stockholders' Equity:
Common Stock		$100,000	
Retained Earnings		23,248	123,248
			$200,784

EXHIBIT 5

Charles Crowne Company
Status Report of Contracts

Project	Amount of Contract	Gross Billings Through 12/31/61	Retainage 10 Per Cent	Net Billings Through 12/31/61	Costs to 12/31/61	Cost Estimated to Complete
#220 Fire Station	$232,994	$116,970	$11,697	$105,273	$102,752	$106,230
#221 Municipal Garage	110,220	90,780	9,078	81,702	76,578	9,040
#224 Fire Station	121,950	12,250	1,225	11,025	11,487	100,250
	$465,164	$220,000	$22,000	$198,000[1]	$190,817	$215,520

[1] Of this amount $113,441 had been received by December 31, 1961. The balance was received by January 15, 1962.

EXHIBIT 7

APPLICATION
FOR PAYMENT

AIA FORM 702

FIELD COPY

CONTRACTOR'S APPLICATION NO. **Four (4)**

ARCHITECT'S JOB No. **56133** _____ PERIOD FROM **Dec. 1** TO **Dec. 31**

TO **City of Burriston** _____ OWNER. APPLICATION IS MADE FOR

PAYMENT, AS SHOWN BELOW, IN CONNECTION WITH THE **Architectural** WORK

FOR YOUR **Fire Station** PROJECT

DESCRIPTION OF WORK	CONTRACT AMOUNT	THIS APPLICATION		COMPLETED		BALANCE TO FINISH
		LABOR	MATERIALS	%	TO DATE	
★ Performance Bond	2,400				2,400	-
Site Work	3,500				3,150	350
★ Masonry	51,200	6,120		90	46,080	5,120
Concrete Work	16,140				8,910	7,230
Precast Concrete Panels	25,520	18,520		72.5	18,520	7,000
Aluminum Sash	8,030					8,030
Sash Erection	1,700					1,700
Structural Steel	24,580				19,600	4,980
Glass & Glazing	5,940					5,940
★ Carpentry	8,974					8,974
Finish Hardware	3,080					3,080
Modern Fold Door	740					740
Roofing & Sheet Metal	6,600					6,600
Overhead Doors	21,560					21,560
Hollow Metal Work	6,640				2,000	4,640
Resilient Floor & Base	3,390					3,390
Hard Tile	1,540					1,540
Acoustical Work	3,300					3,300
★ Chalkboard & Tackboards	500					500
★ Caulking & Weatherstrips	1,020					1,020
★ Aluminum Sign Allowance	600					600
★ Plaque Allowance	400					400
★ Exterior Louvers	730				730	-
★ Slide Poles	9,020		8,020	89	8,020	1,000
Asphalt Paving	5,620				2,810	2,810
★ Flag Pole	1,020		750	73.5	750	270
Plastering	4,710					4,710
Painting	3,190					3,190
Toilet Partitions	620					620
★ General Conditions	6,400	1,000		62.5	4,000	2,400
Curtain Wall Panels	4,330					4,330
TOTAL	232,994	25,640	8,770	50	116,970	116,024

THIS IS TO CERTIFY THAT THE WORK AS LISTED ABOVE HAS BEEN COMPLETED IN ACCORDANCE WITH THE CONTRACT DOCUMENTS. THAT ALL LAWFUL CHARGES FOR LABOR, MATERIALS, ETC., COVERED BY PREVIOUS CERTIFICATES FOR PAYMENT HAVE BEEN PAID AND THAT A PAYMENT IS NOW DUE IN THE AMOUNT OF

Thirty Four Thousand, Four Hundred, and 10 $\frac{00}{100}$ DOLLARS ($ 34,410.00)

FROM WHICH RETAINAGE OF **10** % AS SET OUT IN THE CONTRACT DOCUMENTS SHALL BE DEDUCTED. $ 3,441.00

Net Billing $ 30,969.00

Charles Crowne Company CONTRACTOR

DATE **1/3** 19 **62** PER **Larry Shane**

COPYRIGHT 1953 THE AMERICAN INSTITUTE OF ARCHITECTS

EXHIBIT 6

Charles Crowne Company
List of Subcontracts on Job #220

1. Site Work
2. Concrete Work
3. Precast Concrete Panels
4. Aluminum Sash
5. Sash Erection
6. Structural Steel
7. Glass & Glazing
8. Finish Hardware
9. Modern Fold Door
10. Roofing & Sheet Metal
11. Overhead Doors
12. Hollow Metal Work
13. Resilient Floor & Base
14. Hard Tile
15. Acoustical Work
16. Asphalt Paving
17. Plastering
18. Painting
19. Toilet Partitions
20. Curtain Wall Panels

QUESTIONS:

1. Do you have any criticisms or suggestions concerning the company's use of the completed-contract method of accounting? Could the amount of retainage be treated differently? Explain.

2. In light of the facts given in the case, what advantages or disadvantages would Crowne achieve by a change to the percentage-of-completion method?

3. Although Crowne cannot use the percentage-of-completion method for tax purposes, should this preclude the company from using it for accounting purposes? How would you account for the tax effect of the difference between net income reported in the books and on the tax return in 1961 if Crowne used the percentage-of-completion method for book purposes while using the completed-contract method for tax purposes?

4. Develop Crowne's financial statements for 1961 using the percentage-of-completion method. Is the difference significant? Would this method always result in better matching of revenue and expense? Explain.

Ultrasonic Corporation (A)

Ultrasonic Corporation was incorporated in Massachusetts in 1945, at a time when many small electronics firms were being established in the Boston area. In 1954, the corporation's products were divided into three major groups: (1) electronics equipment such as guided-missile controls, sonar systems, computers, gunfire controls, and radar communications systems for the Armed Forces; (2) high-voltage electrical power controls, switching and distribution equipment for public utility and industrial use; and (3) air-conditioning equipment for industrial and home use.

Sale of Common Stock

In the summer of 1954, Ultrasonic filed a registration statement with the SEC for an offering of 200,000 shares of common stock at $12.75 per share. The prospectus for this issue, dated July 21, 1954, included the corporation's audited financial statements for the fiscal year ended September 30, 1953, summaries of earnings for the fiscal years ended September 30, 1949 through 1953, and unaudited statements for the six-month period October 1, 1953 to March 31, 1954.

SEC Hearing

In the late fall of 1955, the SEC challenged the financial statements contained in the prospectus and registration statement, claiming that net income for the six-month period ended March 31, 1954 was overstated because of improper accounting. Hearings were held in Boston before a regional hearing examiner of the SEC to consider three major areas in the accounting procedures of the company:

> (A) Accounting for estimated profits and losses on government contracts in the Electronics Division;

175

(B) Accounting for cost of goods sold in the Monitor Division[1]; and

(C) Accounting for moving expenses incurred in a transfer to new facilities.[2]

The hearings lasted four weeks. Oral testimony totaled 1,462 printed pages plus 800 pages of exhibits. The findings of the hearing examiner and briefs of exceptions to his findings filed by the involved parties added several hundred more pages.

SEC Stop Order Procedures

Depending on the findings at the hearing, the Securities and Exchange Commission might issue a stop order to suspend the effectiveness of the registration statement and prospectus. Ordinarily such an order would block further sale of the stock. However, since all of the Ultrasonic stock had been sold shortly after the offering, a stop order would only aid purchasers of the stock in seeking possible legal action.

When the SEC considers financial statements filed with it to be inadequate or materially misleading, an opportunity is given to the issuing corporation to make suitable changes.[3] Frequently, the corporation, its counsel, and expert witnesses will appear before the Commission in Washington in preliminary, confidential hearings where the deficiencies are discussed and a solution is sought. If an acceptable solution is achieved, these preliminary hearings do not become a part of the public record, and information on the deficiencies is not available to outside parties. However, in cases where a solution is not reached, the SEC begins stop order proceedings which start with a full investigation of the charges.

The case is generally assigned to a regional hearing examiner of the SEC who hears all testimony and briefs in the case. The charges against the corporation are presented by the SEC's Division of Corporation Finance with the corporation represented by its counsel. After hearing all testimony and examining all briefs, the hearing examiner renders his opinion and conclusions on the charges. His findings, plus all testimony and briefs, are forwarded to the Commission in Washington where they are examined before a ruling is made. The hearing examiner's findings are not binding upon the Commission. Only the five-member Commission makes the final decision on whether a stop order shall be issued. If a stop order is issued

---

[1] See Ultrasonic Corporation (B), page 228.

[2] See Ultrasonic Corporation (C), page 409.

[3] Generally, the SEC sends the corporation a "deficiency letter" stating the inadequacies of the financial statements.

and the corporation disagrees with the order, an appeal can be made to the federal courts.

Accounting for Government Contracts in the Electronics Division

In its quarterly report dated December 31, 1953, Ultrasonic recognized a percentage of the estimated total profit on government contract number 174, a contract not subject to price redetermination. Since 44.6 per cent of the contract was complete, that percentage of the estimated profit was considered earned. Total estimated profit was $298,943, 44.6 per cent of which is $133,328. Since the corporation had already recognized $38,928 as income in a prior period, only $94,400 was added to current profit. In addition, $20,000 was added to recognize the percentage of profit estimated as earned on work in process related to this contract. The total of these two items, $114,400, was rounded to $110,000 "in the interests of conservatism." This amount and additional profits recognized in a similar way on other selected contracts were included in the income statement for the six-month period ended March 31, 1954. At the time, there were about 30 contracts in process in the Electronics Division.

At the hearing, the examiner contended that the corporation had selected several potentially profitable contracts for special treatment in order to present favorable operating results, both at December 31, 1953 and at March 31, 1954 (See Exhibit 1). The examiner claimed that the exclusion of certain uncompleted contracts on which losses were probable was not in accordance with currently accepted accounting principles and tended to produce false and misleading statements. To illustrate his point, the examiner referred to contract number 134, which was not reflected in the income statement for the six months ended March 31, 1954.

Contract number 134:
Contract value (selling price)	$477,956
Expenditures through March 31, 1954	484,161[4]
Estimated cost to complete	27,931
Profit recorded prior to October 1, 1953	43,452

In rebuttal, management contended that it looked upon the business of the Electronics Division, which held the government contracts, as an entity. Therefore, it emphasized the total profit expected to be realized on all outstanding contracts net of any estimated losses. At March 31, 1954, a tabulation showed that profits of $549,000 would

---

[4] This is the amount of *actual expenditures* through March 31, 1954. It does not include the profit of $43,452 recorded prior to October 1, 1953.

be achieved upon completion of all outstanding government contracts. Hence, as long as estimated profits exceeded estimated losses in the aggregate, there was no need for any provision for losses or downward profit adjustment (for profits previously recorded on uncompleted contracts) on an individual contract basis.

Reference to Accounting Research Bulletin No. 45

Counsel for the corporation stated that the techniques advocated by the examiner of providing for expected losses on uncompleted contracts rested on the recommendations in Accounting Research Bulletin No. 45, "Long-term Construction-type Contracts," issued in October, 1955. He stated that the corporation had not followed this method and questioned whether the contracts performed by Ultrasonic were covered by the bulletin. He felt that the bulletin referred to large single unit contracts, such as a ship or a bridge. He contrasted this to the large number of relatively small units in the corporation's government contracts. He pointed out that qualifications had been made by members of the committee which prepared the bulletin above, citing the following:

Mr. Coleman and Mr. Dixon do not approve the statements in paragraphs 6 and 11 as to provisions for expected losses on contracts. They believe that such provisions should be made in the form of footnote disclosure or as a reservation of retained earnings, rather than by a charge against revenues of the current period.

The examiner also cited parts of the bulletin, quoting the following from paragraph 6 of the section on the "Percentage-of-completion Method:"

When the current estimate of total contract costs indicates a loss, in most circumstances provision should be made for the loss on the entire contract...

Paragraph 11 of the section on the "Completed-contract Method" was also quoted by the examiner:

Although the completed-contract method does not permit the recording of any income prior to completion, provision should be made for expected losses in accordance with the well established practice of making provision for foreseeable losses. If there is a close relationship between profitable and unprofitable contracts, such as in the case of contracts which are parts of the same project, the group may be treated as a unit in determining the necessity for a provision for losses.

EXHIBIT 1

Ultrasonic Corporation (A)
Summary of Earnings
Years Ended September 30

	1949	1950	1951	1952	1953	6 mos. ended March 31, 1954 (Not Audited)
Net Sales	$183,491	$ 40,135	$679,502	$2,107,503	$5,168,046	$2,443,564
Costs Other than Selling and Administrative	240,482	158,980	580,711	1,679,357	4,111,134	1,803,564
Selling and Administrative	51,920	62,102	70,626	314,115	757,500	499,217
Operating Income or (Loss)	(108,911)	(180,947)	28,165	114,031	299,412	140,783
Interest Charges			3,225	5,459	26,850	36,352
Other Income and Other Deductions (Net)	(17,150)	(36,234)	1,968	(3,131)	(3,744)	(3,716)
Net Income or (Loss) Before Following Charge	(126,061)	(217,181)	26,908	105,441	268,818	100,715
Portion of Moving Expenses						51,000
Net Income or (Loss)	(126,061)	(217,181)	26,908	105,441	268,818	49,715
Shares Outstanding at End of Period	45,430	52,148	81,173	193,056	295,497	332,292
Net Income or (Loss) per Share	(2.77)	(4.16)	.33	.55	.91	.15

The examiner cited several other accounting authorities to support his contention that, regardless of the method used to determine income, losses must be recognized by an appropriate provision as soon as a loss in the foreseeable future becomes reasonably certain.

From the tabulations and forecasts made as of March 31, 1954, the examiner felt that Ultrasonic should have made an adjustment of $220,336, deducting this amount from net income for the six months ended March 31, 1954, in order to make provision for profits recorded and not earned, and also to provide for losses which actual expenditures as of the date above indicated as reasonably certain. The examiner concluded that the accounting treatment for government contracts was inconsistent and against currently accepted accounting principles, and thereby tended to produce false and misleading statements.

QUESTIONS:

1. What method or methods was Ultrasonic using to account for government contracts in the Electronics Division? Do you agree with this accounting? Explain.

2. Do you agree with management's concept of the Electronics Division as an entity for which no losses need be recognized as long as expected profits to be realized on all contracts exceed estimated losses?

3. What was the relevance *to the six-month period ended March 31, 1954* of the $549,000 expected to be earned upon completion of all outstanding government contracts?

4. Was Ultrasonic's counsel correct in his interpretation of contracts covered by ARB No. 45?

5. How would you have accounted for contract number 134 at March 31, 1954?

6. What is the justification for the accountant's attitude towards probable future losses? Is this position consistent with the attitude towards probable future profits?

Russey Electrical Service Company

For many years the Russey Electrical Service Company had done service work on all forms of electrical appliances on a service charge basis. Early in 1961, Russey decided to add a sales organization to market certain appliances under its own brand name. It bought these appliances from various manufacturers who built them to the specifications of the Russey Company. In its sales program the company placed great emphasis on a liberal warranty provision under which Russey's Service Department made all adjustments and repairs for a two-year period, free of charge.

The results exceeded expectations. Sales had risen steadily and management expected a continued increase in subsequent years. There was, however, some growing concern whether the effect of the liberal warranty was given adequate recognition in evaluating the results of operations and a feeling that the company's profits, as shown on its books, were misleading. Many of the appliances sold by the company were in the novelty or gadget category and required frequent adjustment and repair. The company recognized that its increasing sales record was substantially due to the unconditional two-year service guarantee.

Prior to closing the books and preparing the 1963 financial statements, a management conference was held to review the situation. The following summary of the results of operations for the past four years, as shown by the company's books, was reviewed and discussed:

	1960	1961	1962	1963
Appliance Sales		$300,000	$390,000	$ 500,000
Service Dept. Revenue	$600,000	575,000	560,000	580,000
Total Revenues	$600,000	$875,000	$950,000	$1,080,000
Cost of Appliance Sales & Direct Selling Costs		$180,000	$235,000	$ 300,000
Service Dept. Costs	$450,000	447,000	470,000	515,000
Total Direct Costs	$450,000	$627,000	$705,000	$ 815,000
Gross Profit	$150,000	$248,000	$245,000	$ 265,000
General & Administrative Expenses	$ 70,000	$100,000	$120,000	$ 130,000
Federal Income Taxes[1]	32,000	59,200	50,000	54,000
	$102,000	$159,200	$170,000	$ 184,000
Net Profit	$ 48,000	$ 88,800	$ 75,000	$ 81,000

---

[1] For purposes of this case, an arbitrary income tax rate of 40 per cent has been used in determining the annual income tax. You may use this arbitrary rate in dealing with any income tax aspects involved in the case.

The president expressed concern that the total Net Profit and Retained Earnings figures as developed from the company's books and statements were misleading, both to management and to the company's stockholders, since the company recognized revenue from appliance sales at the time of sale, but did not simultaneously provide for the estimated amount of related warranty costs. His attention was called to the fact that the present method of accounting was consistent with federal income tax requirements. The president felt, however, that income tax requirements should not hinder the development of realistic figures in the company's books and statements or prevent application of generally accepted accounting principles in disclosing the results of Russey's operations and its present financial position.

The Service Department manager criticized the company's accounting procedures from the standpoint of management usefulness. He pointed out that Service Department costs included work performed without charge under the warranties and that no provision was made to include anything in Service Department revenues for such work. This made any comparison between Service Department revenues and costs practically meaningless in interpreting the contribution made by that department to the net profit of the company. In fact, he claimed his department had lost some regular business because of the time required for free service work under the warranties. He felt that Service Department revenues should be credited with warranty work on the same basis as regular service work.

The company did not keep formal cost records by jobs. However, informal memoranda kept by the Service Department provided an adequate basis for the following conclusions:

1. From 1960 through 1963, the Service Department maintained a fairly constant markup on its regular (nonwarranty) service work of $33\frac{1}{3}$ per cent on cost.

2. Total warranty service costs incurred on 1961 appliance sales over the warranty period amounted to about 20 per cent of such sales (5 per cent in 1961, 10 per cent in 1962, and 5 per cent in 1963). Similar analyses were made of warranty service costs incurred in 1962 and 1963 on 1962 appliance sales, and costs incurred in 1963 on 1963 appliance sales. These analyses indicated that the pattern of warranty service costs in relation to sales established for 1961 appliance sales would also apply to 1962 and 1963 appliance sales. It was therefore felt that projections of estimated future warranty costs could be made on that basis. The following schedule summarizes the results of these analyses and projections. (You may assume these to be reliable figures for purposes of this case.)

	Warranty Service Costs Incurred in			Projections of Estimated Warranty Service Costs in Future Years Attributable to Past Appliance Sales	
	1961	1962	1963	1964	1965
1961 Sales	$15,000	$30,000	$15,000		
1962 Sales		19,500	39,000	$19,500	
1963 Sales			25,000	50,000	$25,000
Totals[1]	$15,000	$49,500	$79,000	$69,500	$25,000

[1] These amounts are deductible for federal income tax purposes.

QUESTIONS:

1. In 1961, 1962 and 1963, Russey recorded warranty expenses when they were actually incurred. Assume instead that beginning in 1961 the estimated warranty expense and related liability had been recorded at the time of an appliance sale. In summary form, give the appropriate entries which would have been made in 1961, 1962 and 1963 to record the estimated warranty expense and liability and to record the disbursements actually made in fulfilling the warranties. The only accounts required are (a) Warranty expense, (b) Estimated warranty liability, and (c) Cash. Ignore any problem of income tax allocation and ignore the criticism of the Service Department manager—that is, do not attempt to adjust Service Department revenues for work performed in that department under the warranties.

2. In 1961, 1962 and 1963 Russey reported Net Profits of $88,800, $75,000 and $81,000. What amount of Net Profit after taxes would be reported for these years after giving effect to your entries in question 1? Ignore any problem of income tax allocation and use the amounts of federal income taxes given in the case—$59,200 in 1961, $50,000 in 1962, and $54,000 in 1963.

3. Assume that in each year, 1961, 1962 and 1963, Russey had recorded the entries you prepared for question 1. Assume also that in each year the company had recorded a debit to income tax expense and a credit to income taxes payable on the basis of book income. Recognize the difference between the amount of income taxes based on book income and the amount of income taxes based on taxable income by establishing an account, "Deferred charges to income tax expense." Give the entries pertaining to this account as they would have appeared in 1961, 1962 and 1963. What is the balance of this account at the end of each year?

4. What amount of Net Profit after taxes would be reported each year after giving effect to your entries in questions 1 and 3?

5. Assume that Russey had recorded a debit to income tax expense and a credit to income taxes payable on the basis of taxable income rather than book income. What entry is then required each year to achieve interperiod income tax allocation?

6. Instead of establishing an account, "Deferred charges to income tax expense," an alternative procedure would be to reflect the estimated warranty liability established in question 1 net of future income tax deduction. How would your entries in question 3 be changed by this treatment? Which method do you prefer: (a) Establishing a separate account, "Deferred charges to income tax expense," or (b) showing the estimated warranty liability net of future income tax deduction? Explain.

7. Assume the accounts have been maintained as stated in the case and the company has not closed its books nor prepared formal financial statements for 1963. The general ledger account for "Warranty expense" has a balance of $79,000, the amount of expenditures actually incurred in 1963. Assume that management has decided to adopt a policy of providing for warranty expenses in the year of sale. Give the proper entry or entries at December 31, 1963, to adjust the accounts for 1963 and prior years. Recognize income tax allocation either through an account, "Deferred charges to income tax expense," or by showing the estimated warranty liability net of income tax. Justify your choice of accounts to record the portion of the adjustments related to 1961 and 1962 sales.

8. One way of meeting the objections of the Service Department manager and of better matching Service Department revenues with Service Department expenses would be to treat each appliance sale as really consisting of two elements: (1) Sale of an appliance, and (2) Sale of a service contract. Appliance sales revenue from (1) would be recognized at the time of sale, while Service Department revenue from (2) would initially be deferred and later recognized in accordance with the company's past experience in meeting warranty claims—that is, one-fourth in the year of sale, one-half in the following year, and one-fourth in the

second year after the sale. In summary form, give the appropriate entries which would have been made in 1961, 1962 and 1963 for this method. Assume that the portion of each appliance sale credited to "Deferred service department revenue" includes a provision for the rate of markup realized by the Service Department on its regular service work in 1960. Ignore any problem of income tax allocation.

9. What amount of Net Profit would be reported for each of the three years after giving effect to your entries in question 8? Ignore any problem of income tax allocation and use the amounts of federal income taxes given in the case.

10. Assume that the accounting method proposed in question 8 had been adopted in 1961. Assume further that an account, "Deferred charges to income tax expense," had been established in 1961. What would be the balance of this account at the end of 1961, 1962 and 1963? Compare these balances to those determined in question 3. Why are they different?

11. Assume the accounts have been maintained as stated in the case and the company has not closed its books nor prepared formal financial statements for 1963. Management has just decided to adopt the accounting policy described in question 8. Give the proper entry or entries at December 31, 1963, to adjust the accounts for 1963 and prior years. Recognize income tax allocation through an account, "Deferred charges to income tax expense." Justify your choice of accounts to record the portion of the adjustments related to 1961 and 1962 sales.

12. Develop income statements for the years 1961, 1962 and 1963 assuming that estimated warranty expenses had been recognized at the time of sale (as in question 1). Similarly, develop income statements for the three years assuming the deferred revenue approach had been used (as in question 8). In preparing the six statements, separate, to the extent possible, the results of sales activities from service activities. Base the amounts for federal income taxes on *book* income.

13. Contrast the two sets of income statements prepared in question 12 from the standpoint of management usefulness.

PART FOUR

Cost Determination
and Allocation

CHAPTER EIGHT

Inventories

For most manufacturing and mercantile companies, inventory is a major asset, often *the* major current asset, and cost of goods sold is usually the largest single item of expense. Accounting for inventories and cost of goods sold is complicated by the general acceptance of several different accounting methods and numerous variations in applying them. There are few areas of accounting in which such a variety of methods is found and in which the choice of a method may have such a significant effect on the financial statements.

INSTITUTE PRONOUNCEMENT

In July, 1947, after previous attempts to reach substantial agreement on a bulletin had failed, the Committee on Accounting Procedure issued ARB No. 29, *Inventory Pricing.* In 1953, this bulletin appeared in ARB No. 43 as Chapter 4, which follows:

1. Whenever the operation of a business includes the ownership of a stock of goods, it is necessary for adequate financial accounting purposes that inventories be properly compiled periodically and recorded in the accounts.[1] Such inventories are required both for the statement of financial position and for the periodic measurement of income.

2. This chapter sets forth the general principles applicable to the pricing of inventories of mercantile and manufacturing enterprises. Its conclusions are not directed to or necessarily applicable to non-commercial businesses or to regulated utilities.

STATEMENT 1

The term *inventory* is used herein to designate the aggregate of those items of tangible personal property which (1) are held for sale in

---

[1] Prudent reliance upon perpetual inventory records is not precluded.

the ordinary course of business, (2) are in process of production for such sale, or (3) are to be currently consumed in the production of goods or services to be available for sale.

Discussion

3. The term *inventory* embraces goods awaiting sale (the merchandise of a trading concern and the finished goods of a manufacturer), goods in the course of production (work in process), and goods to be consumed directly or indirectly in production (raw materials and supplies). This definition of inventories excludes long-term assets subject to depreciation accounting, or goods which, when put into use, will be so classified. The fact that a depreciable asset is retired from regular use and held for sale does not indicate that the item should be classified as part of the inventory. Raw materials and supplies purchased for production may be used or consumed for the construction of long-term assets or other purposes not related to production, but the fact that inventory items representing a small portion of the total may not be absorbed ultimately in the production process does not require separate classification. By trade practice, operating materials and supplies of certain types of companies such as oil producers are usually treated as inventory.

STATEMENT 2

A major objective of accounting for inventories is the proper determination of income through the process of matching appropriate costs against revenues.

Discussion

4. An inventory has financial significance because revenues may be obtained from its sale, or from the sale of the goods or services in whose production it is used. Normally such revenues arise in a continuous repetitive process or cycle of operations by which goods are acquired and sold, and further goods are acquired for additional sales. In accounting for the goods in the inventory at any point of time, the major objective is the matching of appropriate costs against revenues in order that there may be a proper determination of the realized income. Thus, the inventory at any given date is the balance of costs applicable to goods on hand remaining after the matching of absorbed costs with concurrent revenues. This balance is appropriately carried to future periods provided it does not exceed an amount properly chargeable against the revenues expected to be obtained from ultimate disposition of the goods carried forward. In practice, this balance is determined by the process of pricing the articles comprised in the inventory.

STATEMENT 3

The primary basis of accounting for inventories is cost, which has been defined generally as the price paid or consideration given to acquire an asset. As applied to inventories, cost means in principle the sum of the applicable expenditures and charges directly or indirectly incurred in bringing an article to its existing condition and location.

Discussion

5. In keeping with the principle that accounting is primarily based on cost, there is a presumption that inventories should be stated at cost. The definition of cost as applied to inventories is understood to mean acquisition and production cost,[2] and its determination involves many problems. Although principles for the determination of inventory costs may be easily stated, their application, particularly to such inventory items as work in process and finished goods, is difficult because of the variety of problems encountered in the allocation of costs and charges. For example, under some circumstances, items such as idle facility expense, excessive spoilage, double freight, and rehandling costs may be so abnormal as to require treatment as current period charges rather than as a portion of the inventory cost. Also, general and administrative expenses should be included as period charges, except for the portion of such expenses that may be clearly related to production and thus constitute a part of inventory costs (product charges). Selling expenses constitute no part of inventory costs. It should also be recognized that the exclusion of all overheads from inventory costs does not constitute an accepted accounting procedure. The exercise of judgment in an individual situation involves a consideration of the adequacy of the procedures of the cost accounting system in use, the soundness of the principles thereof, and their consistent application.

STATEMENT 4

Cost for inventory purposes may be determined under any one of several assumptions as to the flow of cost factors (such as first-in first-out, average, and last-in first-out); the major objective in selecting a method should be to choose the one which, under the circumstances, most clearly reflects periodic income.

Discussion

6. The cost to be matched against revenue from a sale may not be the identified cost of the specific item which is sold, especially in cases in which similar goods are purchased at different times and at different prices. While in some lines of business specific lots are clearly identified from the time of purchase through the time of sale and are costed on this basis, ordinarily the identity of goods is lost between the time of acquisition and the time of sale. In any event, if the materials purchased in various lots are identical and interchangeable, the use of identified cost of the various lots may not produce the most useful financial statements. This fact has resulted in the development of general acceptance of several assumptions with respect to the flow of cost factors (such as *first-in first-out, average,* and *last-in first-out*) to provide practical bases for the measurement of periodic income.[3] In some

---

[2] In the case of goods which have been written down below cost at the close of a fiscal period, such reduced amount is to be considered the cost for subsequent accounting purposes.

[3] Standard costs are acceptable if adjusted at reasonable intervals to reflect current conditions so that at the balance-sheet date standard costs reasonably approximate costs computed under one of the recognized bases. In such cases descriptive language should be used which will express this relationship, as, for instance, "approximate costs determined on the first-in first-out basis," or, if it is desired to mention standard costs, "at standard costs, approximating average costs."

situations a reversed mark-up procedure of inventory pricing, such as the retail inventory method, may be both practical and appropriate. The business operations in some cases may be such as to make it desirable to apply one of the acceptable methods of determining cost to one portion of the inventory or components thereof and another of the acceptable methods to other portions of the inventory.

7. Although selection of the method should be made on the basis of the individual circumstances, it is obvious that financial statements will be more useful if uniform methods of inventory pricing are adopted by all companies within a given industry.

STATEMENT 5

A departure from the cost basis of pricing the inventory is required when the utility of the goods is no longer as great as its cost. Where there is evidence that the utility of goods, in their disposal in the ordinary course of business, will be less than cost, whether due to physical deterioration, obsolescence, changes in price levels, or other causes, the difference should be recognized as a loss of the current period. This is generally accomplished by stating such goods at a lower level commonly designated as *market*.

Discussion

8. Although the cost basis ordinarily achieves the objective of a proper matching of costs and revenues, under certain circumstances cost may not be the amount properly chargeable against the revenues of future periods. A departure from cost is required in these circumstances because cost is satisfactory only if the utility of the goods has not diminished since their acquisition; a loss of utility is to be reflected as a charge against the revenues of the period in which it occurs. Thus, in accounting for inventories, a loss should be recognized whenever the utility of goods is impaired by damage, deterioration, obsolescence, changes in price levels, or other causes. The measurement of such losses is accomplished by applying the rule of pricing inventories at *cost or market, whichever is lower.* This provides a practical means of measuring utility and thereby determining the amount of the loss to be recognized and accounted for in the current period.

STATEMENT 6

As used in the phrase *lower of cost or market*[4] the term *market* means current replacement cost (by purchase or by reproduction, as the case may be) except that:

(1) Market should not exceed the net realizable value (i.e., estimated selling price in the ordinary course of business less reasonably predictable costs of completion and disposal); and

(2) Market should not be less than net realizable value reduced by an allowance for an approximately normal profit margin.

---

[4] The terms *cost or market, whichever is lower* and *lower of cost or market* are used synonymously in general practice and in this chapter. The committee does not express any preference for either of the two alternatives.

Discussion

9. The rule of *cost or market, whichever is lower* is intended to provide a means of measuring the residual usefulness of an inventory expenditure. The term *market* is therefore to be interpreted as indicating utility on the inventory date and may be thought of in terms of the equivalent expenditure which would have to be made in the ordinary course at that date to procure corresponding utility. As a general guide, utility is indicated primarily by the current cost of replacement of the goods as they would be obtained by purchase or reproduction. In applying the rule, however, judgment must always be exercised and no loss should be recognized unless the evidence indicates clearly that a loss has been sustained. There are therefore exceptions to such a standard. Replacement or reproduction prices would not be appropriate as a measure of utility when the estimated sales value, reduced by the costs of completion and disposal, is lower, in which case the realizable value so determined more appropriately measures utility. Furthermore, where the evidence indicates that cost will be recovered with an approximately normal profit upon sale in the ordinary course of business, no loss should be recognized even though replacement or reproduction costs are lower. This might be true, for example, in the case of production under firm sales contracts at fixed prices, or when a reasonable volume of future orders is assured at stable selling prices.

10. Because of the many variations of circumstances encountered in inventory pricing, statement 6 is intended as a guide rather than a literal rule. It should be applied realistically in the light of the objectives expressed in this chapter and with due regard to the form, content, and composition of the inventory. The committee considers, for example, that the retail inventory method, if adequate markdowns are currently taken, accomplishes the objectives described herein. It also recognizes that, if a business is expected to lose money for a sustained period, the inventory should not be written down to offset a loss inherent in the subsequent operations.

STATEMENT 7

Depending on the character and composition of the inventory, the rule of *cost or market, whichever is lower* may properly be applied either directly to each item or to the total of the inventory (or, in some cases, to the total of the components of each major category). The method should be that which most clearly reflects periodic income.

Discussion

11. The purpose of reducing inventory to *market* is to reflect fairly the income of the period. The most common practice is to apply the *lower of cost or market* rule separately to each item of the inventory. However, if there is only one end-product category the cost utility of the total stock—the inventory in its entirety—may have the greatest significance for accounting purposes. Accordingly, the reduction of individual items to *market* may not always lead to the most useful result if the utility of the total inventory to the business is not below its cost. This might be the case if selling prices are not affected by temporary or small fluctuations in current costs of purchase or manufacture. Similarly, where more than one major product or operational category exists, the application of the *cost or market, whichever*

is lower rule to the total of the items included in such major categories may result in the most useful determination of income.

12. When no loss of income is expected to take place as a result of a reduction of cost prices of certain goods because others forming components of the same general categories of finished products have a market equally in excess of cost, such components need not be adjusted to market to the extent that they are in balanced quantities. Thus, in such cases, the rule of *cost or market, whichever is lower* may be applied directly to the totals of the entire inventory, rather than to the individual inventory items, if they enter into the same category of finished product and if they are in balanced quantities, provided the procedure is applied consistently from year to year.

13. To the extent, however, that the stocks of particular materials or components are excessive in relation to others, the more widely recognized procedure of applying the *lower of cost or market* to the individual items constituting the excess should be followed. This would also apply in cases in which the items enter into the production of unrelated products or products having a material variation in the rate of turnover. Unless an effective method of classifying categories is practicable, the rule should be applied to each item in the inventory.

14. When substantial and unusual losses result from the application of this rule it will frequently be desirable to disclose the amount of the loss in the income statement as a charge separately identified from the consumed inventory costs described as *cost of goods sold*.

STATEMENT 8

The basis of stating inventories must be consistently applied and should be disclosed in the financial statements; whenever a significant change is made therein, there should be disclosure of the nature of the change and, if material, the effect on income.

Discussion

15. While the basis of stating inventories does not affect the over-all gain or loss on the ultimate disposition of inventory items, any inconsistency in the selection or employment of a basis may improperly affect the periodic amounts of income or loss. Because of the common use and importance of periodic statements, a procedure adopted for the treatment of inventory items should be consistently applied in order that the results reported may be fairly allocated as between years. A change of such basis may have an important effect upon the interpretation of the financial statements both before and after that change, and hence, in the event of a change, a full disclosure of its nature and of its effect, if material, upon income should be made.

STATEMENT 9

Only in exceptional cases may inventories properly be stated above cost. For example, precious metals having a fixed monetary value with no substantial cost of marketing may be stated at such monetary value; any other exceptions must be justifiable by inability to determine appropriate approximate costs, immediate marketability at quoted market price, and the characteristic of unit interchangeability. Where goods are stated above cost this fact should be fully disclosed.

Discussion

16. It is generally recognized that income accrues only at the time of sale, and that gains may not be anticipated by reflecting assets at their current sales prices. For certain articles, however, exceptions are permissible. Inventories of gold and silver, when there is an effective government-controlled market at a fixed monetary value, are ordinarily reflected at selling prices. A similar treatment is not uncommon for inventories representing agricultural, mineral, and other products, units of which are interchangeable and have an immediate marketability at quoted prices and for which appropriate costs may be difficult to obtain. Where such inventories are stated at sales prices, they should of course be reduced by expenditures to be incurred in disposal, and the use of such basis should be fully disclosed in the financial statements.

STATEMENT 10

Accrued net losses on firm purchase commitments for goods for inventory, measured in the same way as are inventory losses, should, if material, be recognized in the accounts and the amounts thereof separately disclosed in the income statement.

Discussion

17. The recognition in a current period of losses arising from the decline in the utility of cost expenditures is equally applicable to similar losses which are expected to arise from firm, uncancelable, and unhedged commitments for the future purchase of inventory items. The net loss on such commitments should be measured in the same way as are inventory losses and, if material, should be recognized in the accounts and separately disclosed in the income statement. The utility of such commitments is not impaired, and hence there is no loss, when the amounts to be realized from the disposition of the future inventory items are adequately protected by firm sales contracts or when there are other circumstances which reasonably assure continuing sales without price decline.

One member of the committee, Mr. Wellington, assented with qualification, and two members, Messrs. Mason and Peloubet, dissented to adoption of chapter 4.

Mr. Wellington objects to footnote (2) to statement 3. He believes that an exception should be made for goods costed on the *last-in first-out* (LIFO) basis. In the case of goods costed on all bases other than LIFO the reduced amount (market below cost) is cleared from the accounts through the regular accounting entries of the subsequent period, and if the market price rises to or above the original cost there will be an increased profit in the subsequent period. Accounts kept under the LIFO method should also show a similar increased profit in the subsequent period, which will be shown if the LIFO inventory is restored to its original cost. To do otherwise, as required by footnote (2), is to carry the LIFO inventory, not at the lower of cost or current market, but at the lowest market ever known since the LIFO method was adopted by the company.

Mr. Mason dissents from this chapter because of its acceptance of the inconsistencies inherent in *cost or market, whichever is lower*. In his opinion a drop in selling price below cost is no more of a realized loss than a rise above cost is a realized gain under a consistent criterion of realization.

Mr. Peloubet believes it is ordinarily preferable to carry inventory at not less than recoverable cost, and particularly in the case of manufactured or partially manufactured goods which can be sold only in finished form. He recognizes that application of the *cost or market* valuation basis necessitates the shifting of income from one period to another, but objects to unnecessarily accentuating this shift by the use, even limited as it is in this chapter, of reproduction or replacement cost as *market* when such cost is less than net selling price.

Throughout this bulletin the Committee on Accounting Procedure emphasizes measurement of periodic income. For example, in paragraph 4 the committee states: "In accounting for the goods in the inventory at any point of time, the major objective is the matching of appropriate costs against revenues in order that there may be a proper determination of the realized income." The bulletin's emphasis on income measurement is significant since the title of the bulletin, *Inventory Pricing*, and the general tendency of accountants to speak of "inventory accounting" and "inventory methods" may imply that the major accounting objective is determination of an appropriate inventory figure on the balance sheet. This terminology has probably become commonplace because it is easier and quicker to refer to "inventory" problems rather than "cost of goods sold" problems.[5]

Lifo Method Of Determining Cost

Statement 3 notes that the primary basis of accounting for inventories is cost, while statement 4 indicates that cost for inventory purposes may be determined under any one of several assumptions as to the flow of cost factors. "The major objective in selecting a method should be to choose the one which, under the circumstances, most clearly reflects periodic income." One method of measuring the flow of cost factors, specifically mentioned by the committee, is the LIFO assumption. While this is often called an *inventory* method, the very words, *last-in, first-out*, denote movement. LIFO therefore more accurately describes a method of measuring or determining *cost of goods sold*.

---

[5] The term "cost of goods sold" may also be criticized. Literally, it should be "expense of goods sold" to reflect the use of assets in obtaining revenues. The word "cost" is more appropriately applied to unexpired assets.

HISTORY OF LIFO

LIFO was advocated in the mid-1930's as a means of reducing the impact of short-term or cyclical price movements on reported income. It was proposed that LIFO would more properly match current costs against current revenues, and simultaneously would minimize so-called "inventory profits" in a period of rising prices and "inventory losses" in a period of declining prices. The likelihood of a long period of price inflation, such as the one beginning in 1941, was not a factor in early considerations of LIFO.

The Revenue Act of 1938 permitted the use of LIFO for specified raw materials in the inventories of tanners and producers and processors of some nonferrous metals. The Revenue Act of 1939 permitted any taxpayer to use LIFO. However, in administering the 1939 Act, the Treasury continued to consider LIFO appropriate only when certain tests, such as the following, were met:

(1) The spread between the *current* purchase cost of merchandise or raw materials and selling prices should be relatively constant. That is, selling prices should be responsive to *current* purchase costs of merchandise or raw materials rather than purchase costs incurred at some earlier date.

(2) The inventory should be fungible (one unit should be physically identical with another) and measurable in physical terms such as barrels, gallons, tons, yards, etc.

(3) Material cost should constitute a significant part of total cost.

(4) The inventory should be relatively large.

Shortly after passage of the Revenue Act of 1939, some department stores adopted LIFO even though their heterogeneous inventories did not meet the second test. These retailers used index numbers, in a manner described later, to apply the LIFO principle. In 1947, these procedures were approved for department stores in a noteworthy Tax Court decision.[6] In 1949, following a 1948 Tax Court decision approving the use of index numbers by retailers other than department stores,[7] amended tax regulations authorized LIFO based on index numbers for all taxpayers.

MECHANICS OF LIFO

Under LIFO, inventory is viewed as consisting of cost "layers."

---

[6] *Hutzler Bros. Co. vs. Commissioner*, 8 T.C. 14 (1947).

[7] *Edgar A. Basse vs. Commissioner*, 10 T.C. 328 (1948).

The basic layer represents the quantities and related costs existing at the time LIFO was adopted. This basic layer is considered to have been acquired at one time at a unit cost equal to the actual cost of the aggregate inventory divided by the number of units on hand. Subsequent inventories are considered to include the basic layer (to the extent it has not been liquidated since the adoption of LIFO) plus the oldest additional layers required to account for the present quantity of goods on hand.

If the inventory is fungible and subject to some common physical measure, such as barrels of crude oil, it is not difficult to compare the quantity of goods in the opening and closing inventory. This comparison is necessary (1) to determine whether an additional LIFO cost layer (or layers) has been added to inventory during the fiscal period, or if an earlier layer (or layers), or possibly a portion of the basic LIFO inventory itself, has been liquidated, and (2) to determine simultaneously the cost of goods sold for the period. When LIFO is used, cost of goods sold may be visualized as consisting of the cost of goods purchased or produced during the period less the cost of any increase in inventory or plus the cost of any decrease in inventory.

As mentioned previously, the inventories of some companies wishing to use LIFO, such as department stores, may not be physically comparable over several fiscal periods. Because of constant changes in materials, colors, styles or packaging, the items in inventory, even just a few years after the adoption of LIFO, may bear little physical resemblance to the items in inventory when LIFO was adopted or when subsequent LIFO cost layers were accumulated. In this case, the dollar amount of such inventories, adjusted to eliminate the effect of price changes, is used to estimate the physical quantity of inventory on hand at the close of a period. This "dollar-value LIFO" method is illustrated by the following hypothetical example:

Assume inventory at December 31, 1962, is $390,000, expressed in current prices. At December 31, 1963, inventory is $440,000, also expressed in (then) current prices. An appropriate price index, which it is believed measures fairly the price change in the type of commodities represented by the inventory,[8] is 100 at December 31, 1962, and 110 at December 31, 1963. The *physical* change in the inventory is measured by comparing the *deflated* inventory values of $390,000/100 and $440,000/110. These are $390,000 and $400,000. Thus, there has been a $10,000 inventory increase, *expressed in 1962 prices*, but under LIFO this increase should be measured in 1963 prices; so this increment must be reinflated, which gives a figure of $11,000 (110 per

---

[8] For both book and income-tax purposes, a published index or one compiled by the individual company, whichever is more appropriate, may be used.

cent × $10,000).[9] The new inventory on a LIFO basis would be $401,000. If inventory shrinks in 1964, this $11,000 increment would be the first layer "peeled off" to become part of cost of goods sold. Although there are many variations in the method of applying dollar-value LIFO, this example illustrates the general principle.

ACCOUNTING ARGUMENTS FOR AND AGAINST LIFO

The basic argument in favor of LIFO (aside from tax considerations which are discussed in the next section) is that it usually states cost of goods sold in relatively current dollars. This matching of sales revenue and cost of goods sold in essentially similar dollars may not result with use of the first-in, first-out or average cost methods. According to LIFO proponents, the latter methods may produce misleading and fictitious profits in a period of rising prices because a portion of such profits must be used to replace—at higher costs— the units sold from inventory. Similarly, LIFO proponents claim that other methods of measuring cost of goods sold tend to overstate losses in a period of falling prices by matching higher acquisition costs incurred earlier against revenue from sales at current reduced prices.

While LIFO may eliminate or reduce the effect of *price* changes, it may not reflect *price-level* changes. That is, the behavior of actual prices for specific items, or the behavior of an index to estimate the price changes in a group of items, may not correspond to changes in the *general* level of prices. Some accountants favor recognizing the effect of *price-level* changes, but not the effect of *price* changes unless the latter happen to correspond to *price-level* changes. This distinction between *price* changes and *price-level* changes is considered further in Chapter 10, *Price-Level Adjustments*.

The arguments against LIFO are numerous. First, it may not result in improved matching of revenues and costs if the quantity of inventory declines. In fact, gross mismatching, and a misleading statement of income, may occur if inventory is depleted after LIFO has been in use for many years. This possibility is discussed further in the next section.

A second objection is that LIFO may permit management to influence reported profits merely by expanding or contracting inventories. If the adoption of LIFO is followed by a period of rising prices in respect to the items in a company's inventory, reported income may be increased by liquidation of earlier LIFO layers, or decreased by significant additions to inventory during the fiscal period. While few managements would manipulate inventories to so affect

---

[9] The year-end price index may not be the most appropriate for reinflating this increment. An average of the index for the year, if available, or some other level of the index, may be more appropriate.

reported income, the possibility of such action is objectionable to opponents of LIFO.

Another argument against LIFO is that the physical flow of goods seldom corresponds to the assumed flow of costs. As a result, the American Accounting Association's Committee on Concepts and Standards Underlying Corporate Financial Statements refers to *artificial* LIFO in its supplementary statement, *Inventory Pricing and Changes in Price Levels.*[10]

A fourth objection to LIFO concerns the balance-sheet disclosure of inventory. Under LIFO, inventory is shown at the prices prevailing when LIFO was adopted and when any additional layers were added. Price inflation following the adoption of LIFO may result in disclosure of inventory at only a small fraction of its current value, thus seriously limiting the usefulness of the inventory figure in measuring performance or appraising financial status. For example, realistic measurements of a company's working capital or of its inventory turnover may be virtually impossible.

A few companies disclose the current value of LIFO inventories. In 1949, such disclosure was favored in the draft of a proposed Accounting Research Bulletin. However, businessmen's comments on this draft were almost wholly unfavorable and the bulletin was never issued by the Committee on Accounting Procedure. Carman Blough, then the Institute's Director of Research, reported that more letters were received from corporate officials disagreeing with this proposed bulletin than had been received in regard to *all* of the 37 bulletins issued prior to 1949. Among the objections were: (1) the cost and difficulty of determining the current value of inventory would be excessive; (2) doubt would be cast on the validity of the LIFO procedure in general; and (3) the significance of the difference between LIFO values and current values is questionable because under LIFO this difference becomes realized income only when inventory is depleted.

Although the proposed Accounting Research Bulletin favoring disclosure of the current value of LIFO inventories was not issued, the statement sponsored by the American Accounting Association recommended that "when LIFO is used there be reported in the financial statements figures showing the inventory valuation and the operating costs (including tax effects) on a realistic basis."[11]

---

[10] American Accounting Association, Committee on Concepts and Standards Underlying Corporate Financial Statements, "Inventory Pricing and Changes in Price Levels—Supplementary Statement No. 6," *Accounting Review*, Vol. 29, April 1954, pp. 188-93. This statement also appears in *Accounting and Reporting Standards for Corporate Financial Statements and Preceding Statements and Supplements* (Columbus, Ohio: American Accounting Association, 1957).

[11] *Ibid.*

INCOME-TAX ASPECTS OF LIFO

LIFO's popularity cannot be attributed to only the accounting arguments in its favor. The favorable income-tax effect of LIFO during an inflationary period has been the major consideration leading to its use by many companies. Other companies have hesitated to adopt LIFO because of possible income-tax disadvantages such as:

(1) A tax-deductible write-down is not allowed when the current market value of inventory falls below LIFO cost. Such write-downs, made in accordance with the lower of cost or market rule and considered later in this chapter, are authorized for taxpayers using the FIFO or average cost methods of determining inventory and cost of goods sold.

(2) Abnormal profits, which may arise when LIFO inventories are temporarily liquidated because of some unusual situation, are taxed currently, even though the taxpayer intends to replenish inventories in a subsequent accounting period.[12] For example, a nationwide steel strike occurred from July until mid-November, 1959. At the end of the strike, the inventories of steel users, including many whose fiscal years ended on December 31, were at a low level. In December, 1959, a steel supplier's advertisement, announcing the availability of certain steel products for immediate delivery, contained the following captions:

Do You Have A LIFO Problem?
Is Your Inventory Below Par?

(3) The LIFO method, if adopted for tax purposes, must also be used in annual reports to stockholders and creditors, regardless of its suitability for such purposes. This requirement led one critic of LIFO to say that "a generally applicable accounting rule was formulated by act of Congress."[13]

Lower Of Cost Or Market Rule

A second controversial aspect of accounting for inventory is the lower of cost or market rule. This is discussed in statements 5, 6, and 7 of the bulletin on *Inventory Pricing*, reproduced above. The term "cost" refers to the actual cost of inventory as determined by

---

[12] Congress has provided for the tax-free replacement of LIFO inventories when inventory liquidation has been caused by war emergencies. These provisions are discussed in case 8-5, Swift & Company (A).

[13] Maurice Moonitz, "The Case Against Lifo as an Inventory-Pricing Formula," *Journal of Accountancy*, Vol. 95, June 1953, p. 684.

FIFO, LIFO, average cost, or some other method.[14] The term "market" normally refers either to replacement cost by purchase from usual suppliers in usual quantities or, in the case of a manufacturer's goods-in-process or finished-goods inventories, to replacement cost by reproduction.

The lower of cost or market rule rests on an assumed relationship between the behavior of a company's selling prices and its replacement costs. Usually a relationship does exist, and a decline in replacement costs will be followed by a decline in selling prices. A decline in replacement costs, therefore, is accepted as tentative evidence of a loss in the utility or usefulness of inventory. Under the lower of cost or market rule, this is a loss of the current period which should be recognized by reducing inventory to the lower market figure, even though the inventory will not be sold until a later period.

"Market" usually means replacement cost in the market in which a company *buys*, but there may be exceptions to this meaning when the assumed relationship between selling prices and replacement costs does not exist. For example, selling prices may decline relatively less than a decline in replacement costs, or selling prices may decline more sharply than replacement costs. To meet these situations, statement 6 provides two exceptions to the usual meaning of *market* as current replacement cost.

The first exception—that *market* should not exceed net realizable value—establishes an upper limit on the amount carried forward in inventory. Net realizable value is defined in statement 6 as "estimated selling price in the ordinary course of business less reasonably predictable costs of completion and disposal." Because of the effect on probable selling prices of style changes, obsolescence while in storage, or other factors, the future utility of some goods in inventory may not be appropriately measured by either original cost or current replacement cost. For example, assume that a toy manufacturer's inventory contains 500 wooden trucks, produced at a cost of $3.40 each. The manufacturer states that recent reductions in lumber and paint prices would cut his production cost to approximately $3.15 per unit. However, he estimates *net realizable value* of only $2.50 per unit because a competitor has just introduced a much lower-priced truck molded from a new, extremely durable plastic. Under exception (1) of statement 6, these goods would be written down to $2.50 per unit, their estimated net realizable value. The resulting inventory value would then be called *market*. Note that in this case anticipated prices in the market in which a company *sells*, not replace-

---

[14] The U.S. Treasury Department prohibits application of the lower of cost or market rule for income tax purposes by taxpayers using LIFO. It does not restrict such applications for book purposes.

ment costs in the market in which it *buys,* are used in applying the lower of cost or market rule.

The second exception—that *market* should not be less than net realizable value reduced by an allowance for an approximately normal profit margin—establishes a lower limit on the amount carried forward in inventory. This exception would apply when a reduction in replacement costs is expected to have only limited effect, or perhaps no effect, on selling prices. For example, assume that goods which cost $60 to buy or produce can now be replaced for $50. Assume also that the original selling price of $100 for these goods will still be realized. The incurred cost of $60, not the current replacement cost of $50, is properly carried forward in inventory because the utility or usefulness of the goods has not been impaired by the reduction in current replacement cost. If it is believed these items will be sold at $95 and not at their original price of $100, a write-down of inventory from $60 to $55 is appropriate to provide for a "normal profit margin" when the goods are sold.[15] Although the actual current market price is $50, the reduced inventory value of $55 would be termed *market* under the lower of cost or market rule. Note in this second exception to the general rule (that *market* means replacement cost), as in the first exception, anticipated prices in the market in which a company *sells* are used in applying the lower of cost or market rule.

When goods are written down below cost to *market,* this reduced amount is considered as *cost* in later fiscal periods. Thus, in subsequent inventories, any of these goods still on hand are not adjusted upward to their original cost even though market returns to the level from which the goods were written down.

OBJECTIONS TO LOWER OF COST OR MARKET RULE

Some accountants object to the lower of cost or market rule, or to some aspects of the rule. One objection, the reason for Mr. Mason's dissent to the chapter on *Inventory Pricing,* concerns the inconsistencies of the rule. The rule is applied in one direction only. The anticipated effect of reduced replacement costs on ultimate selling prices is recognized currently as a loss, but any probable effect of increased replacement costs is not recognized until goods are actually sold. The rule is also criticized as inconsistent in another respect. At the close of one period a company's inventory may be priced

---

[15] This assumes that "normal profit margin" is measured in dollars, not as a per cent of selling price. The Committee on Accounting Procedure did not define "normal profit margin." This was apparently intentional to permit use of whatever measure is most appropriate in a given situation.

largely at cost, while market prices may prevail at the close of another period.

Other accountants, including Mr. Peloubet who dissented to the chapter on *Inventory Pricing*, object to exception (2) of statement 6. They would not reduce inventory below net realizable value to provide for an approximately normal profit margin. These accountants contend that such a write-down accentuates the shift of income from the current to another period, usually the next period.

Other Inventory Accounting Problems

This discussion has focused on two of the more difficult and controversial aspects of accounting for inventory and cost of goods sold. These are the LIFO method of measuring the flow of cost factors during a fiscal period, and the lower of cost or market rule for pricing inventory at the close of a fiscal period. Several other inventory problems have not been considered in this chapter. One problem, the appropriate valuation of a long-term contractor's work-in-process inventory, was discussed in Chapter 7. Another perplexing problem, whether certain overhead costs should be included in inventory or treated as expenses when incurred, is considered in some of the cases included in this chapter.

REFERENCES

American Accounting Association, Committee on Concepts and Standards Underlying Corporate Financial Statements, "Inventory Pricing and Changes in Price Levels—Supplementary Statement No. 6," *Accounting Review*, 29 (Apr. 1954), 188-93. This statement also appears in *Accounting and Reporting Standards for Corporate Financial Statements and Preceding Statements and Supplements.* Columbus, Ohio: American Accounting Association, 1957.

Andersen, Arthur, & Co., *Accounting and Reporting Problems of the Accounting Profession*, 2nd ed. Chicago: Arthur Andersen & Co. (Oct. 1962), 85-89.

Barker, Richard B., "Dollar-Value Lifo and the Klein Chocolate Case," *Journal of Accountancy*, 112 (Sept. 1961), 41-45.

Barron, J.F., "Tax Effects of Inventory Methods," *Journal of Accountancy*, 112 (Aug. 1961), 34-40.

Cerf, Alan R., "Price-Level Changes, Inventory Valuations, and Tax Considerations," *Accounting Review*, 32 (Oct. 1957), 554-65.

Coughlan, John W., "The Guises of Replacement Cost," *Accounting Review*, 32 (Jul. 1957), 434-47.

Engelmann, K., "The 'Lifo-or-Market' Plan," *Accounting Review*, 28 (Jan. 1953), 54-57.

Fremgen, James M., "Involuntary Liquidation of Lifo Inventories," *Journal of Accountancy*, 114 (Dec. 1962), 49-56.

Gordon, Myron J., "The Managerial Use of Data Obtainable in Conjunction with Lifo," *Accounting Review*, 31 (Apr. 1956), 234-43.

Hoffman, Raymond A., *Inventories: A Guide to Their Control, Costing, and Effect Upon Income and Taxes*. New York: The Ronald Press Company, 1962.

Johnson, Charles E., "Inventory Valuation—The Accountant's Achilles Heel," *Accounting Review*, 29 (Jan. 1954), 15-26.

Kempner, Jack J., "A New Look at the Classification of Inventories," *Accounting Review*, 35 (Apr. 1960), 264-71.

McAnly, Herbert T., "The Case for Lifo: It Realistically States Income and Is Applicable to Any Industry," *Journal of Accountancy*, 95 (Jun. 1953), 691-700.

_____, "The Current Status of Lifo," *Journal of Accountancy*, 105 (May 1958), 55-62.

_____, "Inventory Pricing," *Journal of Accountancy*, 114 (Aug. 1962), 34-39.

Moonitz, Maurice, "The Case Against Lifo as an Inventory-Pricing Formula," *Journal of Accountancy*, 95 (Jun. 1953), 682-90.

Myers, John H., "Inventory Disclosure in Annual Reports," *Journal of Accountancy*, 100 (Jul. 1955), 42-45.

Peoples, John, "Disclosure and Accounting for Current Value of Lifo Inventories," *1954 Annual Meeting Papers*. New York: American Institute of Accountants, 1954. Also included in *Controversial Areas in Accounting*, a booklet published by the Institute, 1954.

Rowles, Barry M., "Application of Statistical Sampling Techniques to Lifo Inventory Valuation," *Accounting Review*, 29 (Apr. 1954), 244-50.

Seitelman, Nathan, "Has A.R.B. 29 Settled the Problem of Inventory Valuation?" *Accounting Review*, 28 (Oct. 1953), 550-53.

Simon, Sidney I., "Cost or Market Before the Bar," *Accounting Review*, 31 (Oct. 1956), 621-24.

Spurr, William A., "How to Compile and to Use a Price Index System for Inventory Valuation by the Lifo Method," *Journal of Accountancy*, 93 (Feb. 1952), 204-9.

Suojanen, Waino W., "Lifo as a Spur to Inflation—The Recent Experience of Copper," *Accounting Review*, 32 (Jan. 1957), 42-50.

Van Pelt, John V., III, "Reasons Why the Accounting Profession Should Encourage a Broader Utilization of Lifo," *Journal of Accountancy*, 96 (Oct. 1953), 452-59.

W. T. Grant Company

W. T. Grant Company bears the name of its founder who opened the first Grant Store in Lynn, Massachusetts in 1906. Since then the company has grown rapidly with sales of almost $700 million in the 1962 fiscal year[1] (ended January 31, 1963) from over 1,000 stores in 45 states. It features apparel for women, men, and children, and merchandise for the home. Most sales are for cash, but credit services are available in all stores.

Through the fiscal year ended January 31, 1948, Grant had reported earnings and filed its tax returns based on the retail method of valuing inventories. Following a Tax Court decision that department stores could use the Lifo inventory method, the company adopted Lifo in 1948, retroactively to January 31, 1941.

Lifo's Effect on Earnings

In its report to stockholders for the 1948 fiscal year (ended January 31, 1949), management disclosed the earnings effect of the change to Lifo as follows:

Net earnings amounted to $9,299,167, which, after payment of dividends on preferred stock, are equal to $3.67 per share of common stock.

Had inventories been computed by the method used in previous reports, earnings for the year would have amounted to $7,951,375. To a considerable extent the increase in earnings for the year is brought about, under the Lifo method, by the substantial liquidation of low cost inventories during the year. As inventories reach what may prove to be a more normal level, such credits are not likely to recur.

In the following tabulation there is given a comparison of earnings for the year with those of all prior years involved, both by the use of the present Lifo inventory method as well as by the previous method.

---

[1] The company designates its fiscal year according to the calendar year in which the first eleven months occur. Thus, the 1962 fiscal year began February 1, 1962 and ended January 31, 1963.

Fiscal Year	Earnings Before Taxes		Earnings After Taxes			
	Before Lifo Adjustment	After Lifo Adjustment	Before Lifo Adjustment	Per Common Share*	After Lifo Adjustment	Per Common Share*
1941	$ 9,217,393	$ 7,646,372	$ 4,446,393	$1.72	$4,013,372	$1.54
1942	9,683,723	6,263,775	3,762,223	1.43	3,112,275	1.16
1943	10,406,345	9,146,275	3,810,345	1.46	3,575,275	1.36
1944	14,811,069	12,675,425	4,092,069	1.57	3,782,425	1.44
1945	12,568,092	11,503,905	4,210,092	1.60	4,012,905	1.52
1946	17,557,577	14,859,061	10,877,577	4.33	9,204,061	3.63
1947	13,861,504	10,851,122	8,678,504	3.41	6,812,122	2.63
1948	13,071,375	15,246,167	7,951,375	3.11	9,299,167	3.67

*Based upon 2,378,708 shares outstanding after 2 for 1 stock split in 1945 (after deducting dividends on preferred shares).

Retroactive Effect of Lifo on Inventories and Taxes

In another section of the report to stockholders, management noted its interest in Lifo since 1941 and described the effect of the retroactive change on inventories and taxes:

As noted above, earnings are computed by the Lifo method of inventory valuation, which the Company has adopted retroactively to January 31, 1941, notwithstanding the fact that Treasury Department regulations have not as yet been modified to permit the retroactive use of this method.

The Revenue Act of 1939 extended the use of Lifo to all taxpayers. The Company determined to adopt Lifo in 1941, but was prevented from doing so by the Treasury Department's refusal to permit use of this method by the employment of retail price indices or to issue regulations permitting its practical application by retailers such as your Company.

At the Company's annual meeting held on April 21, 1942, stockholders were informed of the Treasury Department's action, and were advised that the matter was being contested and that, in the event of a favorable decision your Company would adopt Lifo retroactively.

The United States Tax Court, in January 1947, in a test case involving another retailer, sustained the status which your Company originally sought. While the Commissioner of Internal Revenue acquiesced in this decision in 1948, its retroactive application has as yet been permitted to only a limited group of companies, not including your Company.

Nevertheless, amended tax returns and appropriate claims for refund of overpayment of taxes are being processed by your Company.

Without commenting upon the highly technical aspects of Lifo, it may be described as a practical method of minimizing inflationary and deflationary valuations from inventories of unsold goods. Thus, current sales are matched with current costs, and goods remaining on hand, to the extent that they existed at the beginning of the period, are valued at unchanged prices. By removing to a large extent both inflationary and deflationary effects from the

valuation of inventories, realized earnings are more accurately reflected each year.
The effect of Lifo on the Company is further indicated in the table below. The most significant facts are that the valuation of the year-end inventory has been reduced by $12,791,505, and for the eight-year period, federal taxes are reduced by $9,795,000 and net earnings by $3,924,505.

Year-end Inventory

Fiscal Year	Based on Lower of Cost or Market	Based on Lifo	Cumulative Reduction of Inventory	Cumulative Amount of Tax Reduction	Cumulative Reduction of Earnings Used in the Business
1941	$25,482,342	$24,126,564	$ 1,355,778	$1,138,000	$ 340,550*
1942	21,675,697	18,319,855	3,355,842	3,908,000	990,498
1943	24,132,446	20,024,419	4,108,027	4,933,000	1,225,568
1944	21,707,697	17,444,151	4,263,546	6,759,000	1,535,212
1945	26,922,287	21,527,645	5,394,642	7,626,000	1,732,399
1946	37,307,098	26,474,804	10,832,294	8,651,000	3,405,915
1947	41,621,357	26,655,060	14,966,297	9,795,000	5,272,297
1948	32,488,585	19,697,080	12,791,505	9,795,000	3,924,505

* After deducting $92,471 for adjustment in inventory at beginning of Lifo period.

To conform with Treasury Department requirements, the financial reports of the Company to stockholders are being presented on a Lifo basis. Any adjustment in the Company's claim for tax refunds in final settlement would result in a restatement of financial reports. . . .

A note to the financial statements contained essentially the same information as disclosed in the body of the report. Retained earnings were reduced by $5,272,297, labeled "Adjustments applicable to prior years as a result of computing inventories on the last-in, first-out method." On the balance sheet, the company disclosed "Claims for refund of federal taxes on income as a result of the use of the last-in, first-out method," $9,795,000, classified between Current Assets and Other Assets. The company received a qualified audit opinion on its financial statements for the year.

QUESTIONS:

1. Complete the following table for the years 1941 through 1947:

Difference Due to Lifo Adjustment

	In Earnings Before Taxes	In Earnings After Taxes	In Amount of Taxes	Tax Rate Used in Computing Amount of Taxes
1941	$1,571,021	$433,021	$1,138,000	?
1942	3,419,948	649,948	2,770,000	?
↓ 1947	etc.	etc.	etc.	

2. How do you explain the high tax rates you calculated in question 1 for the years 1941 through 1945? Do you suppose these rates applied uniformly to all of Grant's net earnings before taxes? Do these rates help to explain management's great interest in Lifo during World War II and the Korean War? Explain.

3. Using the data from the table in question 1, prove the $9,795,000 of tax claims and the $5,272,297 reduction in earnings used in the business.

4. Do you consider the changes in net earnings per share attributable to Lifo from 1941 through 1948 material? Would these changes have been more or less from 1941 through 1945 had tax rates been lower? Explain.

5. From an examination of the data in the case, do you agree that under Lifo "current sales are matched with current costs"? Explain.

6. Do you agree with the company's 1948 balance-sheet disclosure of the claim for refund of federal taxes on income, $9,795,000? Explain.

Columbia Pictures Corporation

Columbia Pictures was incorporated in New York in 1924. Initially, most of the corporation's revenues were obtained from the production and distribution of motion pictures. Because of television's impact on movie attendance, Columbia later diversified its activities by acquiring television and radio stations in Salt Lake City, and by manufacturing phonograph records on the Colpix label.

In rendering their opinion on the financial statements from 1952 through 1960, Columbia's independent public accountants had to consider several important accounting changes which affected Columbia's net income. Motion picture companies generally include all film production costs in inventories. "Cost of Goods Sold" is determined by one of the following two methods: either (a) the cost-recovery method, or (b) the flow-of-income method. Under the cost-recovery method no profit is recognized until all costs have been recovered (all revenues received are applied to cost recovery). Under the flow-of-income method, costs are amortized over the period during which revenues are expected to be received. Profit is recognized currently to the extent that revenues exceed amortization expense.

Cost Amortization Tables

It is the general practice of the movie industry to lease rather than sell films as they are produced. Normally, Columbia and other producers receive 20 to 40 per cent of the gross revenues of exhibiting theaters. This percentage differs according to the age of and demand for a film. As prints are released, they are first shown in one theater in principal cities in the United States, such as New York, Chicago, San Francisco and Boston, for a period of up to one month. Subsequently, they are released on a nationwide basis and shortly thereafter throughout much of the world. When a film is released widely in the United States, Columbia begins to amortize its production cost by the flow-of-income method. In 1952 these production costs were amortized according to the following tables which reflect Columbia's experience in both domestic and foreign markets:

	Cumulative Percentage of Amortization	
Number of Weeks Released	Black and White Features	Color Features
13	38	32
26	63	60
39	79	75
52	89	85
65	93	89
78	96	92.8
91	98	97
104	100	100

During the 1953 fiscal year, the corporation, on the basis of more recent experience, concluded that relatively more revenues from film rentals were received later in the two-year period than expressed by the tables above. Consequently, the amortization rates were changed as follows:

	Cumulative Percentage of Amortization	
Number of Weeks Released	Black and White Features	Color Features
13	35	28
26	58	52
39	72	67
52	81.5	76.5
65	88	83.4
78	92.8	89
91	96.8	95.5
104	100	100

As a result of this change, income after taxes was increased by approximately $500,000 for the fiscal year ended June 27, 1953. Exhibit 1 shows the consolidated income statement for fiscal 1952 and 1953. A note to the 1953 financial statements explained the change in amortization policy as follows:

The amortization of the cost of released productions is based upon the corporation's latest available experience of film rental income. The larger per-centage of income expected to be earned in foreign territories by productions which comprise the inventory of released features at June 27, 1953, has neces-sitated a revision in the territorial allocation of production cost. Accordingly, the tables ... which have been applied to such inventory at June 27, 1953, reflect allocations against foreign income of 26 per cent for black and white and 31 per cent for color features (each including 8 per cent for Great Britain), instead of 23 per cent and 28 per cent, respectively, heretofore allocated at June 30, 1952.

During the past several years, the corporation has experienced a lengthening of the period during which income is received from feature productions. In order to reflect the inventories on a more realistic basis, the combined world tables . . . amortize cost over a longer period than heretofore. Accordingly, the cost allocated to the domestic territory is now amortized over a period of 104 weeks after release (92 per cent being amortized in the first 52 weeks), instead of 52 weeks as heretofore, and the cost allocated to Great Britain is amortized over a period of 78 weeks, instead of 52 weeks as heretofore, commencing 26 weeks after domestic release. Pursuant to the policy of completely writing off the cost of feature productions in two years after domestic release, the corporation has not lengthened the amortization period applicable to foreign territories other than Great Britain even though substantial rentals are received from these territories after such two-year period. The cost allocated to such other foreign territories continues to be amortized over a period of 91 weeks commencing 13 weeks after domestic release.

In summary, note the following three changes in Columbia's amortization policy: (1) an increase in the allocation of production costs against foreign income, (2) a doubling of the amortization period for cost allocated to the domestic territory from 52 to 104 weeks, and (3) a 50 per cent increase of the amortization period for cost allocated to Great Britain. Between the 1953 and 1960 fiscal years, the company periodically modified its cost amortization tables in accordance with its latest available experience.

Cost of Foreign Prints

As a general policy in the motion picture industry, prints are made available abroad approximately 13 weeks after release on the domestic market. A duplicate of the print is sent to certain central points abroad, such as London or Paris, where prints are made for European markets. Depending on the potential audience, the film is synchronized in the foreign language or subtitles are used. Other necessary changes are made to increase the appeal of a film to various audiences. In relative terms, the industry's revenues from abroad have increased substantially in recent years.

Prior to June 26, 1954, the costs of Columbia's foreign prints were included in inventories and charged to expense by use of the amortization tables. To simplify accounting for foreign operations and to state inventories on a more conservative basis, Columbia charged all such costs directly to expense beginning with the fiscal year ended June 25, 1955. Net profit after taxes was reduced by about $200,000 as a result of this change.

Advances to Other Producers

On its balance sheet at June 25, 1955, the corporation disclosed "Advances to Other Producers, less amortization" of $13,810,830 classified as a current asset. These advances were made to other companies which produced films for Columbia. A change in accounting for such advances, made during the 1955 fiscal year, was explained as follows in a note to the financial statements:

As at June 25, 1955, advances to other producers consist of production costs and domestic print costs, less amortization on released productions computed by the application of amortization tables to the total amounts of such advances.... Except for approximately $840,000 in advances which are collectible from the bank loans to be obtained by the producers, advances to other producers are recoverable only from the proceeds to be derived from the distribution of productions.

Total advances at cost are accounted for as follows:

Released productions, less amortization	$ 6,592,884
Completed productions not yet released	4,292,643
Productions in process	2,925,303
	$13,810,830

For 1954 and prior years, all expenditures for the account of other producers in respect of production and other costs were included in advances and written off by application of amortization tables. As at June 25, 1955, in order to simplify accounting and to state the advances on a more conservative basis, only production costs and domestic print costs continued to be subject to amortization and all other expenditures were charged directly to profit and loss, with the result that net profit for the year then ended was reduced by approximately $875,000 [after taxes].

Licensing Pre-1948 Features to Television

The motion picture industry has leased a number of its older prints to television stations. These leases usually cover a period of five to seven years and typically give the station the right to show the films three times during the lease period. Lease terms, which are usually negotiated individually with each station, are based in part on the size of a station's viewing audience. Payments are generally spread over the lease period, although a substantial amount may be payable when the lease contract is signed.

By June, 1957, Screen Gems, a Columbia television subsidiary, completed its first full year of licensing Columbia's pre-1948 feature films for television use. During a few months of the previous fiscal year, income had been recorded on the basis of cash payments made by the customers. Beginning with the 1957 fiscal year, the accrual method was adopted and income was recognized when prints were delivered or made available to the customers. If this method had been in effect in 1956, $450,000 of 1957 income after taxes would have been recognized in 1956. Comparative net income figures as reported in the 1957 annual report to stockholders were $2,253,103 for 1957 and $2,669,712 (not restated) for 1956.

Television Film Series

Prior to its 1958 fiscal year, Columbia Pictures recognized revenues on films produced specifically for television as billings were made over the term of a contract. In 1958, the corporation partially abandoned this procedure and adopted the practice of accounting for such income, with the exception of newly produced film series being released for the first time, by recording the entire income from an exhibition contract when it was signed. At the same time, a provision was made for shares to independent producers and any other costs to be incurred in fulfilling the contract. This change resulted in an addition to reported net income of approximately $1,900,000, after taxes. Income from new film series being released for the first time continued to be recorded as billings were made over the term of a contract.

Unabsorbed Overhead

Beginning in 1958, Columbia began to make prints primarily for independent producers, who were charged with a fixed percentage of direct costs for studio overhead. Management felt that overhead costs not charged to independent producers should not be applied to the few pictures made directly by the corporation in excess of amounts normally applied. In accordance with this view, management charged 1958 earnings with unabsorbed overhead of $3,837,352, listed as "Studio costs not allocated to productions" on the income statement. In prior years, all overhead costs were allocated to films produced by Columbia and subsequently amortized according to cost amortization tables, such as those shown on page 209. This change was approved by Columbia's auditors, although they did take an exception to consistency. The corporation reported total revenues of $113,624,525 and a net loss of $4,987,330 for the 1958 fiscal year.

World-Wide Advertising and Foreign Print Costs

Previously, Columbia Pictures had charged world-wide advertising and, beginning in the 1954–1955 fiscal year, foreign print costs directly to current income. At the beginning of the 1960 fiscal year, such costs for pictures to be released subsequently were included in inventories to be amortized according to the company's cost amortization tables. As a result of this change, net income for the period was increased by about $3,800,000 after taxes.

Deferred Television Income

During the 1960 fiscal year amortization of feature films was reduced to defer a portion of the cost deemed applicable to future income from television. This increased net income by approximately $350,000 after taxes.

EXHIBIT 1

Columbia Pictures Corporation
Consolidated Income Statement for the Years
Ended June 27, 1953 and June 30, 1952

	June 27, 1953	June 30, 1952
Gross income rentals and sales of film and accessories	$60,273,881	$59,081,213
Deduct:		
Amortization of film costs, other producers' and participants' shares and costs of accessories sold	$38,571,308	$37,806,164
General, administrative, and selling expenses	18,705,741	18,139,579
Taxes, other than income taxes	617,578	910,079
	$57,894,627	$56,855,822
Operating profit	$ 2,379,254	$ 2,225,391
Other income (net) including interest income	306,492	318,464
	$ 2,685,746	$ 2,543,855
Interest expense	535,982	298,192
	$ 2,149,764	$ 2,245,663
Estimated income taxes:		
Federal	$ 500,000	$ 760,000
State and foreign	833,658	682,791
Reduction in Federal taxes on income for 1942	(126,279)	
	$ 1,207,379	$ 1,442,791
Net profit	$ 942,385	$ 802,872

EXHIBIT 2

Columbia Pictures Corporation
Net Income After Taxes for the Fiscal Years 1951-1960

1951	$1,497,814
1952	802,872
1953	942,385
1954	3,594,733
1955	4,948,690
1956	2,669,712
1957	2,253,103
1958	(4,987,330)
1959	151,230
1960	2,106,740

QUESTIONS:

1. Prepare a table as follows:

Year	Changes in Accounting for Revenues	Changes in Accounting for Expenses	Dollar Effect on Reported Net Income	Percentage Effect on Reported Net Income
1952				(Calculate percentage
1953				increase or decrease
1954				from Net Income
				which would have
1955	(Allow enough space to describe			been reported without
1956	briefly each change)			the change).
1957				
1958				
1959				
1960				

2. What type of audit opinion would you give on the financial statements for each year during the period 1953 through 1960? Give reasons for your choice indicating the basis for any qualifications.

3. Do you think management in 1953 should have lengthened the amortization period for production costs allocated to foreign territories other than Great Britain? Explain.

4. What other accounting treatment could have been used in 1958 instead of recording the entire income from an exhibition contract and concurrently making provision for shares to independent producers and other costs to be incurred in fulfilling the contract? Would this result in better matching? Explain.

5. Did the accounting changes tend to stabilize net income from year to year? In general, did they cause net income to be recognized sooner or later? Relate your comments to Exhibit 2 and the table derived in question 1.

Rocky Mountain Construction Company[1]

In 1948, Mr. Roy Benthall and his two sons, all of Boulder, Colorado, incorporated the Rocky Mountain Construction Company as a small masonry and general home improvement business. The company grew rapidly during its first few years, expanding into residential and small plant construction. As additional financing became necessary, common stock was sold to several local Boulder businessmen. Mr. Benthall and his sons retained ownership of 65 per cent of the stock and wished to maintain a controlling interest in the company if possible. However, the need for cash was so pressing that Mr. Benthall and his sons agreed to a public stock offering if this was the only alternative. The company's net profits before taxes had exceeded $50,000 every year since 1953, reaching $70,000 for the year ended December 31, 1960. During the next few years the company expected annual profits of $75,000 to $90,000.

Before 1961, the Rocky Mountain Construction Co. had built private homes and small manufacturing plants in the Boulder-Denver area. The industrial growth of Boulder, which was quite rapid between 1948 and 1960, was expected to continue in the future. The population of Boulder, located 30 miles from Denver via a turnpike, had increased from 20,000 in 1950 to about 40,000 in 1960, and the number of industrial plants in the city had increased over five times. Many national companies were interested in building local branch plants and offices in Boulder because of its ideal geographical location and pleasant living conditions at the foot of the Rocky Mountains.

In late 1960, Mr. Benthall and his sons felt that the development of an industrial park in Boulder would probably be a profitable venture in view of the area's expected growth. They believed that purchase of fully improved, subdivided land would be economic-

---

[1] Adapted with permission from a case prepared by Professors Neil E. Harlan and Richard F. Vancil, copyright by the President and Fellows of Harvard College.

215

ally unsound. Consequently, they established a land development department to develop raw land into plots suitable for industrial plant construction. If this operation proved profitable, they planned similar developments elsewhere in the Boulder-Denver area.

In December, 1960, the company purchased, for $500,000, 65 acres adjoining Route 119, a major highway leading into Boulder. Mr. Rabit, an accountant, was hired to maintain all financial records and to act as office manager for the new land development department, and an architect was employed to draw up plans for the proposed industrial park (See Exhibit 1). Legal fees, title transfer fees, and title insurance premiums of $3,909 were paid at that time.

During 1961, the company began to develop the land into tracts suitable for industrial plants. Some of the work was performed by Rocky Mountain itself while other phases were subcontracted to specialists.

The land was first cleared of trees, brush, rocks and old farm buildings. In some spots, deposits of peat moss had to be removed and replaced with gravel or other solid fill. Grading or leveling was the second step in the land improvement program. Next came the installation of temporary haul roads and storm ditches or drains. When this work had been finished, permanent access roads, storm drains, sewers, and water mains were installed. At December 31, 1961, certain of these operations had been fully completed, while others were only partially completed. Nearly $300,000 had been spent on these operations during 1961.

Exhibit 2 shows total improvement costs incurred through December 31, 1961, for each of the major land development phases and gives the estimated cost to complete each phase. The first column (labor) shows the labor cost of those operations performed directly by Rocky Mountain's land development department while the second column (invoices) shows not only the cost of materials, but also the cost of subcontracted work. This column also includes the charge for equipment rental as determined by the company's construction department. The land development department owned no heavy equipment and thus incurred no depreciation on its books. All equipment was owned and maintained by the construction department which charged a flat rental rate to the land development department for use of equipment. These charges amounted to $30,000 in 1961. The third column gives the total cost of land improvements to December 31, 1961. The remaining columns show the estimated costs of completing the land development project.

Two parcels of land were completed and disposed of during 1961, as indicated in Exhibit 3. One was sold to an industrial organization as a plant site, while the other was transferred to Rocky Mountain's construction department for construction of a plant to be sold or leased to an industrial concern desiring to locate in the Boulder area.

To summarize the operations for 1961, Mr. Rabit prepared a profit and loss statement for the land development department, reproduced as Exhibit 4, and presented it to Mr. Benthall and the board of directors for approval at their February, 1962, meeting. At the meeting, Mr. Benthall expressed concern over this operating statement. Several of the other directors took opposing views concerning the proper presentation of income for the company's land development department. Rocky Mountain's statements were used by management for evaluating operations and were also sent to the company's stockholders. Furthermore, Mr. Benthall realized that the company's statements were going to be presented to the public or to a commercial bank in the near future to raise necessary capital for the recent expansion into land development. Part of the directors' discussion is given below.

MR. BENTHALL:
Our next item of business is the profit and loss statement of the land development department as prepared by Mr. Rabit. As we expected, the department showed a large operating loss for 1961 due to the outlay for land and initial land development costs which were incurred during the first year. However, I'm quite concerned over the prospect of combining this department's $73,000 loss with the construction department's 1961 profit of $68,000, thus disclosing a net loss for the year of $5,000. Not only will our present shareholders be quite concerned over this loss, but the prospects of floating a new stock issue or obtaining a bank loan would be substantially reduced by the presentation of such a statement. As you know, I have already come under fire because of my decision to enter into the land development business, and the picture this statement presents would certainly add fuel to the fire.

FRANK REED (Director of Rocky Mountain and owner of Ledgewood Realty Co.):
Roy [Mr. Benthall], I think we need to take a really close look at Mr. Rabit's statement. I, for one, don't agree with his method of presenting the land development department's results for 1961. He seems to have forgotten that the department has a large inventory of partially improved plots on hand as of the end of the year, but yet, he has deducted from sales income the total cost of the entire tract and all the land development costs to date. Some of this should be deferred as the cost of land that is still available for sale. In my opinion, Mr. Rabit has prepared a very misleading and incorrect statement of the department's profit for 1961, and if certain land costs are deferred, the department will show a profit rather than a loss for 1961.

BILL COLLINS (Rocky Mountain Director and large stockholder):
Now Frank, hold on just a minute. The statement that Mr. Rabit prepared is an honest presentation of the cash flow that took place in the department in 1961. It is essentially a cash statement with certain normal accruals and deferrals. It shows how the company's funds were derived and used in 1961 and should be useful to management for cash budgeting.

MR. BENTHALL:

This may be so, Bill, but the statement still doesn't lend itself to obtaining outside financing. I think Frank had a good idea when he said that certain of these costs could be deferred until future periods of time, but two points about his approach bother me. First, what happens to these deferred costs if our expected future sales don't materialize? We might not sell all of those plots for two or three years yet, even though we have spent the money. And second, how do you propose to allocate the total land costs to the plots which were sold? I'm sure that Mr. Rabit didn't keep track of the costs by individual plots, and, as you know, the plots are at various stages of completion.

JAMES HICKMAN (Director of Rocky Mountain and Vice President of Construction Contracting):

Roy, I think that Frank is making a mistake when he only looks at individual plots. I think we should consider the Park as a complete entity in itself, and recognize income from it based on the percentage-of-completion method used in our construction operation. From the figures Mr. Rabit gave you [Exhibit 2] you can estimate the completed cost of the development. You could also estimate total income which you expect to receive from the development based on sales to date. Then the profit recognized this year would be the percentage of estimated total profit that incurred costs to date bear to estimated total costs. And furthermore, such a statement would show a higher profit than the one which Frank proposes, and thus the earnings per share figure this year would reflect the true profit which the company earned during the year. This would end some of the unfavorable criticism which several of our shareholders expressed when we went into the land development business, and would provide a healthy income statement which could be used to float a stock issue or obtain a bank loan. This method would also eliminate the necessity of trying to assign costs to individual plots, and would answer your question about deferred costs.

MR. BENTHALL:

Jim, I like your idea of the high earnings figure...

FRANK REED:

Now just a second, Roy! Don't let Jim confuse you by his slippery methods of pulling a big profit out of the clear blue! That land hasn't been sold yet and you can't recognize profit on your inventory just because you would like to have a pretty income statement. The only profit we are entitled to show is that profit which we made on actual sales during 1961. Why, Jim's method would have us showing income this year on plots which may not be sold for two years! That just isn't good accounting. And not only that, but think of the additional income tax you would have to pay under his method. You would be paying tax this year on some income which you wouldn't be receiving until next year or the year after.

BILL COLLINS:

You are right, Frank. Jim's method would show a higher profit figure, but it is not allowed by the tax authorities. The tax code clearly specifies the method of accounting that land development companies are required to use in statement preparation, thus leaving us little leeway in preparing our published statements. The Prentice-Hall Tax Guide states: "The cost should be equitably apportioned to the several lots, and gain or loss calculated on each lot sold. This rule implies that there will be an individual gain or loss on every lot sold and not that the taxpayer shall wait until the capital on the entire tract has been recovered through sales receipts before any taxable income is to be returned. Development costs, including future development costs, may be included in computing gain or loss on sale of lots. Cost apportionment must be made equitably and not ratably, for example, on market price rather than a square foot basis, since front lots would ordinarily bear a greater portion of the cost than those in the rear of the development."

BOB ALLEN (Director of Rocky Mountain and Executive Vice President of the First National Bank of Boulder):

You are probably right on the tax regulations, Bill, but that doesn't mean we have to prepare our published statements in accordance with the tax code. We can prepare them in any manner we desire, and I can't agree with you, Jim, or with the tax code, Bill, when you propose a recognition of profits which may never materialize. Your methods assume that all the land will eventually be sold, and at a profit. However, I think Jim started out on the right track when he said you had to look at the Park as one complete entity, not as nine separate units. I don't think you should show any profit until you have fully recovered all your costs because you just don't make a profit on this development until you have sold enough land to recover all your costs! Then the rest is gravy. I think that all income and all expense from the development should be deferred until the entire project is finished and then you can decide how much profit you made. You aren't grabbing in the dark for estimated this and estimated that, as your method does, Jim. You know, for a fact, exactly how much you made on the project. This is the method my bank uses in recasting corporate financial statements since it doesn't want to loan money to a company on the basis of unearned profits which may never be realized. As you know, Roy, there is considerable risk that actual future costs will not be the same as the estimated costs, and this is *particularly* true in the construction business, and heaven only knows how far off your estimated sales prices might be!

CAMERON BENTHALL (Mr. Benthall's older son and Executive Vice President of Rocky Mountain):

I agree with you, Bob, except that I think only the difference between the sales income and the land costs incurred should be deferred until future periods. This would mean that a deferred income or a deferred expense account would be carried until the entire Park was completed at which time you would then recognize your actual profit or loss. We wouldn't be jumping to any conclusions in recognizing profits which we didn't make.

BRADLEY BENTHALL (Mr. Benthall's younger son and General Construction Manager):

I can't agree with you or Bob, Cam, you're being too conservative. Your method would show no profit for two or three years, and our chance of floating a stock issue would be nil if we presented such a statement to prospective stockholders. I think a combination of methods is what we really need. I agree with Bill when he says we must recognize the profit we made on the plots which were sold in 1961. The land costs could be allocated to these plots on the basis of square footage, expected market price, front footage on an access street, or any other reasonable basis. Further, I think that these plots should also bear some portion of the operating expenses which will be incurred during the next two years, the time we anticipate it will take to completely dispose of all the plots. It seems likely to me that these expenses will remain relatively constant during the life of the development, regardless of the percentage-of-completion or degree of sales saturation. Finally, I think estimated profit should be recognized on those plots which are held under a sales option contract or intended for use by the construction department. It appears likely that these options will be taken up, since land prices are constantly increasing. All costs not allocated to the plots sold in 1961, or under option, should be deferred until future years. This method would provide the most realistic reporting of earnings. The consistent use of this method will provide our stockholders and potential investors with stable revenue and earnings figures on which year to year operating comparisons can be based. I think this is something we should consider before we choose a method of reporting income.

MR. BENTHALL:

It seems to me that the objective of a good income statement should be to match costs and revenues during a given period of time and only then can the true profitability of a firm be judged. I am not sure which of your proposed methods would do this, so I suggest we adjourn until such time as I can gather together the results which would be reported under each of your methods. We will then meet and discuss the merits of each one and decide at that time which one best fulfills our needs relative to internal reporting, external reporting, and tax reporting.

As a result of the confusion and uncertainty created at the board meeting and because of the importance of the company's financial statements, Mr. Benthall contacted Mr. James Reardon, a partner of Gibson and Reardon, Certified Public Accountants, located in Denver, Colorado. He asked Mr. Reardon to evaluate each of the opposing viewpoints presented at the board meeting and to recommend the best method of preparing the income statement.

EXHIBIT 1

Rocky Mountain Construction Company
Land Development Department
Land Layout for Boulder Industrial Park

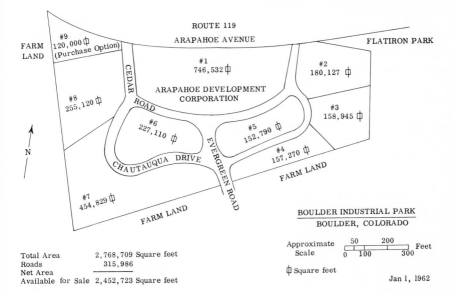

ROUTE 119
ARAPAHOE AVENUE
FLATIRON PARK

FARM LAND

#9
120,000 ⊡
(Purchase Option)

CEDAR ROAD

#1
746,532 ⊡

ARAPAHOE DEVELOPMENT
CORPORATION

#2
180,127 ⊡

#8
255,120 ⊡

#3
158,945 ⊡

#6
227,110 ⊡

#5
152,790 ⊡

N

EVERGREEN ROAD

CHAUTAUQUA DRIVE

#4
157,270 ⊡

FARM LAND

#7
454,829 ⊡

FARM LAND

BOULDER INDUSTRIAL PARK
BOULDER, COLORADO

Total Area	2,768,709	Square feet
Roads	315,986	
Net Area		
Available for Sale	2,452,723	Square feet

Approximate Scale

50   200   Feet
0   100   300

⊡ Square feet

Jan 1, 1962

EXHIBIT 2—PART 1

Rocky Mountain Construction Company
Land Development Department
Improvement Costs to December 31, 1961

	Account Classification	Actual Cost to Date			Estimated to Finish		
		Labor	Invoices	Total	Labor	Invoices	Total
500	SITE WORK[1]						
8	Pile Driving						
10	Temporary Lights						
11	Clearing	$ 2,406	$ 9,037	$11,443			
12	Unclassified Excavation	769	709	1,478			
13	Earth Excavation	34	101	135			
14	Peat Excavation	536	8,131	8,667			
15	Rock Excavation	9,208	19,060	28,268			
16	Temporary Storm Ditches						
17	Temporary Site Work						
18	Temporary (Haul) Roads						
19	Gravel Borrow	2,351	32,493	34,844			
	Total	$15,304	$69,531	$84,835			
520	ROADS						
21	Unclassified Excavation	$ 1,037	$ 2,736	$ 3,773			
22	Earth Excavation	2,034	4,908	6,942			
23	Peat Excavation	68	4,050	4,118			
24	Rock Excavation	2,319	35,680	37,999			
25	Gravel Borrow	677	15,229	15,906			
26	Finish Roadwork—Subcontracted	49	37	86			
30	Granite Curbing	795	4,914	5,709	$ 562	$32,438	$33,000
32	Loam, Spread, and Seed	985	965	1,950	2,400	3,290	5,690
33	Maintenance	293	311	604			
	Total	$ 8,257	$68,830	$77,087	$ 2,962	$35,728	$38,690

[1] Includes site work chargeable directly to specific plots. See Part 2 of this exhibit for details.

EXHIBIT 2—PART 1 (Cont.)

	Account Classification	Actual Cost to Date			Estimated to Finish		
		Labor	Invoices	Total	Labor	Invoices	Total
540	*STORM DRAINS*						
40	10″ R.C. Pipe	$ 2,511	$ 2,882	$ 5,393			
41	18″ R.C. Pipe	305	1,051	1,356			
42	24″ R.C. Pipe	1,122	3,723	4,845			
43	Manholes, Incl. Castings	1,004	1,150	2,154			
44	Catchbasins	2,085	1,749	3,834			
46	21″ R.C. Pipe	32	62	94	$ 11,320	$ 16,860	$ 28,180
47	15″ R.C. Pipe	339	1,544	1,883			
48	30″ R.C. Pipe	864	3,605	4,469			
	Total	$ 8,262	$ 15,766	$ 24,028	$ 11,320	$ 16,860	$ 28,180
550	*SEWERAGE*						
50	8″ Sewer	$ 1,209	$ 5,731	$ 6,940	$ 8,617	$ 17,682	$ 26,299
51	10″ Sewer	1,907	14,371	16,278			
52	Forced Main						
53	Manholes, Incl. Castings	2,607	3,448	6,055			
54	Adjust to Line and Grade	94		94			
55	Pumping Station					22,680	22,680
56	Maintenance of Utilities	392		392	2,436		2,436
57	12″ Sewer		1,542	1,542	3,860	4,120	7,980
58	Exploration for 10″						
	Total	$ 6,209	$ 25,092	$ 31,301	$ 14,913	$ 44,482	$ 59,395
560	*WATER MAINS*						
61	10″ C.I. Pipe	$ 2,567	$ 19,463	$ 22,030	$ 3,110	$ 30,245	$ 33,355
62	12″ C.I. Pipe		295	295		4,820	4,820
63	Hydrants	125	230	355	6,500	15,977	22,477
64	8″ C.I. Pipe	1,072	3,689	4,761	3,700	7,400	11,100
	Total	$ 3,764	$ 23,677	$ 27,441	$ 13,310	$ 58,442	$ 71,752
570	*OPEN DRAINAGE DITCH*	$ 5,609	$ 28,706	$ 34,315			
580	*ENGINEERING*	2,204	6,508	8,712	$ 620	$ 1,416	$ 2,036
590	*INDIRECT GENERAL CONDITIONS²*	5,942	5,903	11,845	4,812	6,237	11,049
	GRAND TOTALS	$ 55,551	$244,013	$299,564	$ 47,937	$163,165	$211,102

² Includes field supervision, watchman's salary, temporary toilets, rain gear, and field telephone.

EXHIBIT 2—PART 2

Rocky Mountain Construction Company
Improvement Costs to December 31, 1961
Site Work Chargeable Directly to Specific Plots

Plot Number	Total Site Work	511 Labor	511 Invoices	514 Labor	514 Invoices	515 Labor	515 Invoices	519 Labor	519 Invoices
							Cost Classification		
1	$25,840		$ 3,012	$ 536	$ 896	$ 3,740	$ 6,579	$ 307	$10,770
3	17,069				2,741	4,313	5,820	979	3,216
5	10,466				3,500	800	420	586	5,160
9	13,911				994	355	6,241	479	5,842
TOTALS	$67,286	0	$ 3,012	$ 536	$ 8,131	$ 9,208	$19,060	$ 2,351	$24,988

Note: Charges under classifications 511, 514, and 519 were for the removal of peat and dumping of general fill on specific plots which were not suitable for construction in raw form. Classification 515 accumulated the cost of blasting and removing a rock shelf under certain plots.

EXHIBIT 3

Rocky Mountain Construction Company
Land Development Department
Individual Plot Specifications and Improved Land Sold During 1961

Plot Number	Square Footage	Front Footage	Anticipated Sales Price Per Sq. Ft.	Sold to	Price Received	Comments
1	746,532	3,025	$1.70	Arapahoe Development Corporation	$632,000	First plot sold. Sold at discount since the proposed shopping center is expected to increase other land values.
2	180,127	375	1.50			
3	158,945	200	1.20	Rocky Mountain Construction Company	158,945	All land used by the construction department is priced at a set rate of $1.00 per square foot.
4	157,270	750	1.30	Rocky Mountain expects to use this plot for plant construction at some future time.		
5	152,790	1,650	1.40			
6	227,110	1,750	1.40			
7	454,829	1,225	1.20			
8	255,120	475	1.20			
9	120,000	675	1.60	Arapahoe Development Corporation (Purchase Option)		Sold purchase option for $5,000. Option must be exercised by January 1, 1964, its expiration date.
TOTALS	2,452,723	10,125			$790,945	

EXHIBIT 4

Rocky Mountain Construction Company
Land Development Department
Profit and Loss Statement for the Year Ended
December 31, 1961

Sales Revenue:

Plot Number	Amount Received		
1	$632,000		
3	158,945		

Total Sales Revenue		$790,945	
Other Income:			
Purchase Option on Plot Number 9		5,000	
Total Income for Period			$795,945
Less Cost of Sales:			
Original Purchase Price of Land	$500,000		
Land Development Costs to			
Dec. 31, 1961 (See Exhibit 2)	299,564		
Total Land Costs			799,564
Gross Profit or (Loss) on Sales:			$ (3,619)
Operating Expenses:[1]			
Advertising		$ 475	
Commissions to Outside Brokers		665	
Park Dedication and Press Conferences		1,140	
Purchase of Signs and Office Equipment		6,226	
Inspection Fees		928	
Legal and Accounting		7,850	
(Includes Legal Fee, Title Fee, and			
Insurance Premium Incurred on			
Original Land Purchase)			
Photographs and Renderings		2,113	
Salaries—Salesmen		12,695	
Salaries—Office		6,620	
Salaries—Engineering		3,113	
Salaries—Gen. Manager, Land Department		10,000	
Sales Commissions		3,480	
Taxes		5,315	
Direct Operating Expenses			$ 60,620
Operating Expense Allocated From the			
Construction Department[2]			8,533
Total Operating Expenses			$ 69,153
Net Loss for Year Ended December 31, 1961			$(72,772)

---

[1] All operating expenses have been computed on an accrual basis and thus include not only cash expenditures made during 1961 but also expenses payable at December 31, 1961.

[2] Allocated on the basis of each department's total sales revenue. This includes heat, light and power, rent on the office building, telephone and telegraph, and other joint expenses.

QUESTIONS:

1. What were the major accounting principles at issue in the discussion at the board meeting?

2. As nearly as you can determine, what amount of net income would be reported in 1961 for the Land Development Department under each of the proposed accounting methods?

3. What accounting method would you use? Why? Consider carefully your treatment of:
   (a) Original purchase price of the land
   (b) Development costs to December 31, 1961
   (c) Estimated remaining development costs
   (d) Operating expenses
   (e) Sale of lot #1 to Arapahoe Development Corporation
   (f) Transfer of lot #3 to Rocky Mountain's Construction Department
   (g) Option of lot #9 to Arapahoe Development Corporation
   (h) Contemplated transfer of lot #4 to the Construction Department

4. Appraise carefully the view that the Boulder Industrial Park be considered as an entity.

5. Do you agree with Mr. Benthall's opening comment that a net loss of $5,000 for the year would result from combining the Construction Department's profit with the Land Development Department's loss? Explain.

Ultrasonic Corporation (B) [1]

In the opinion of the hearing examiner, Ultrasonic's accounting for cost of sales in the Monitor Division was the most controversial and misleading aspect of the case before the SEC.

Monitor's Old Cost System

The Monitor Controller Company, at the time Ultrasonic acquired it in early 1952, was operating without a formal cost system. Cost of sales for a year was based on periodic inventory counts. The inventory at the beginning of a fiscal year plus material, labor and overhead costs incurred during the year less the inventory count at the close of the year was considered cost of sales for the period. The percentage of cost of sales to sales for the year was then used to estimate cost of sales in interim financial statements during the following year. This procedure was continued after Monitor became a division of Ultrasonic.

Development of New Cost System

During 1953, Ultrasonic's management became dissatisfied with the lack of formal cost procedures in the Monitor Division and a cost accountant was hired as an assistant controller to develop a cost system. A cost system was adopted similar to the one used in the corporation's Electronics Division in which actual costs were accumulated by job orders.[2] This was considered appropriate since Monitor's output was largely made to customer orders. It was the accounting department's understanding that costs developed by the

---

[1] See Ultrasonic Corporation (A), page 175, for company history and background information concerning the SEC Hearing.

[2] Government contracts held by the Electronics Division were subject to inspection and audit by government agencies. These agencies required that costs be kept on a job or contract basis.

new system were to be used in all financial statements for the fiscal year beginning October 1, 1953.

Difficulty was encountered in establishing and operating the new cost system. One of the reasons was a decision to centralize Ultrasonic's operations in one large building in Cambridge, Massachusetts. Moving the Monitor Division from a nearby city took almost three months during the first quarter of the 1953-1954 fiscal year. This move made it difficult to cost the large number of inventory parts (in excess of 25,000 individual items). By December, 1953, the system was in operation, but there were delays in getting all of the time and material tickets, collected in the manufacturing departments, to the accounting department in time for preparation of regular monthly income statements.

About the middle of January, a quarterly statement, based on the new system for the first time, was completed for the Monitor Division. The figures showed the following results for the three months ended December 31, 1953:

	October	November	December	First Quarter
Sales	$101,041	$121,268	$109,299	$331,608
Cost of Sales	84,298	102,640	112,243	299,181
Cost of Sales as Percentage of Sales	83.4%	84.6%	102.7%	90.2%

Financial Statement Adjustments

The quarterly report for the entire corporation, including Monitor, showed a net loss of $223,661. This report was to be forwarded to a bank which had extended Ultrasonic a substantial line of credit. Ultrasonic's financial vice president suggested the following adjustments which produced a net profit of $46,858, or approximately 5.1 per cent of quarterly sales:

(1) The first adjustment[3] was a credit to cost of sales and a debit to "Deferred Charges—Moving Expenses" for $68,000, the estimated loss in direct labor efficiency caused by the Monitor Division's transfer to Cambridge.

(2) The second adjustment[3], which was also charged to "Deferred Charges—Moving Expenses," was a credit to various expense accounts for payrolls of supervisory and service employees in connection with the move, $21,310.

(3) The third adjustment[4] was for the unrecorded profit Ultrasonic

---

[3] See Ultrasonic Corporation (C) on page 409.
[4] See Ultrasonic Corporation (A) on page 177.

claimed had accrued on government contract number 174, $110,000. This contract was held by the Electronics Division and was not subject to price redetermination as were most of the corporation's other government contracts.

(4) The final adjustment made in January was a transfer of $94,945 from cost of sales to an asset account entitled "Work in Process—Engineering." This amount represented incurred direct labor and overhead costs to be charged to jobs in process. Management stated this entry was necessary since actual cost allocations to individual jobs were not up to date. Thus, it was decided to defer this amount and write it off over the balance of the fiscal year. Since one fourth of the fiscal year had passed, $23,736, or one fourth of the total, was charged to expense, leaving $71,209 to be expensed over the remainder of the year. Management noted that this type of development cost was usually incurred in the early stages of a contract, and often benefited later stages. Subsequent contracts, calling for similar work, frequently benefited also since additional development work could often be avoided.

In February, 1954, an additional adjustment was made debiting inventory $18,151 and crediting cost of sales, producing total corporate net income *for the four months*, October through January, of $75,305 which was 5.1 per cent of net sales.

Discontinuance of the New Cost System for Reporting Purposes

In early February, 1954, management concluded that Monitor's new cost system produced inaccurate results. Members of top management maintained that it was not their original intention to use the new cost system for book purposes until it could be validated by a physical inventory. They said the assistant controller, who developed the new cost system, had entered the figures produced by that system in the books without authority. It was then decided to determine cost of sales by taking a percentage of sales. The percentage used, 77.3 per cent of sales, was based on the period from February 1, 1952 to December 31, 1952, a period which management felt was comparable to the current one. Use of this formula produced a net profit of 5.1 per cent of sales for the month of February. The new cost system was continued as a means of accumulating cost data, but it was not used for book entries. If monthly results for the second quarter had been based on the new cost system, as originally used from October 1, 1953 through January 31, 1954, the following amounts would have been recorded for cost of sales:

	January	February	March	Quarter
Sales	$113,197	$236,454	$280,539	$630,190
Cost of Sales	109,996	200,687	257,966	568,649
Cost of Sales as Percentage of Sales	97.2%	84.9%	92.0%	90.2%

For the six-month period ended March 31, 1954, which was used in the prospectus and registration statement, the Monitor Division's cost of sales was based on the 77.3 per cent formula. Cost of sales entered on the books from October 1, 1953 to January 31, 1954, originally based on the new cost system, but reduced by the adjustments made in January and February, described above, was further adjusted to conform to the percentage formula.

Management's Position

Management's position may be summarized as follows:
(1) The initial intention was not to use the new cost system for book purposes in fiscal 1954.
(2) The new cost system could not be considered accurate for book purposes until it was validated by a physical inventory. This view was substantiated by the corporation's auditors.
(3) The new cost system could not reflect actual costs when the disruption of the move was considered.
(4) Income statements prepared at the end of the months, October through January, included jobs for which some time and material tickets were missing.

The Examiner's Position

Since the new cost system had been used for book purposes for the first four months of fiscal 1954 and results based on the new system had been available for the entire six-month period, the examiner concluded that management should have used the new system to determine income disclosed on the financial statements in the prospectus and registration statement. He believed convincing testimony showed that management was aware of the difference between cost of sales for the six-month period under the new cost system and under the percentage method.

The examiner refused to place credence in management's position.

It was inconceivable to him that management would not have known the basis for the costs included in the reports covering the first four months. Furthermore, he stressed the fact that the corporation's top accounting personnel felt that the new system did reasonably reflect cost of operations. As to the disruption of the move making the new system unreliable, the examiner replied that this would make equally invalid the use of a formula based on a prior period. The examiner noted that the absence of time and material tickets on jobs completed would only understate cost of sales and make the income statement look better than if all tickets had been included in the final determination.

In his opinion, the most serious item was the use of the 77.3 per cent formula, and the lack of specific reference to this percentage in the prospectus. Referring to a note in the prospectus concerning inventory, he stated that the part explaining inventory determination in the Monitor Division was misleading. He believed that it implied the experience of fiscal 1953 had been used to determine the percentage ratio for cost of sales of the Monitor Division, while in fact, the ratio used was based on the experience from February 1, 1952 to December 31, 1952. He stated that a 15 per cent wage increase in 1953 further invalidated the ratio.

Note A to the financial statements covering inventories, included in the prospectus and registration statement, read as follows:

Inventories of materials and parts are carried at cost, computed on a first-in, first-out basis, which does not exceed current replacement value. Inventories of work in process and finished goods are carried at cost of materials and direct labor plus apportioned factory costs. Inventories used in the computation of costs other than selling and general and administrative expenses were as follows:

Year ended September 30:	Beginning of Period	End of Period
1951	$ 22,321	$ 7,529
1952	7,529	754,875
1953	754,875	1,260,637
Six months ended March 31, 1954 (not audited)	1,260,637	2,113,066

No physical inventory having been taken since September 30, 1953, the amount shown at March 31, 1954 ($2,113,066) represents the book inventory which is considered by the management to represent the fair value of the inventory at that date. The March 31, 1954 inventory was based on the inventory of September 30, 1953, plus increases in inventory at actual cost, minus decreases resulting from sales at actual cost in the Advanced Electronics Division and, in the Monitor Division, at percentages of selling prices determined on the basis of past experience.

On April 4, 1952, Ultrasonic Corporation acquired all the outstanding stock of the Monitor Controller Company. On April 30, 1952, all of Monitor's assets (except its accounts receivable) were transferred to Ultrasonic Corporation, which assumed its liabilities. According to the books of Monitor at that date its inventory was $974,130. In determining the basis at which the assets of Monitor should be carried onto the books of Ultrasonic, based upon a physical count of inventories of the Monitor Division at September 30, 1952, the management estimated that the inventory acquired should be reduced and accordingly stated it at $814,130. The acquired inventory so stated has been used in computing cost ($1,062,526) of goods of the Monitor Division sold from May 1 to September 30, 1952, included in costs of the corporation for the year ended September 30, 1952.

Exhibits 1 and 2 show the corporation's income statements and balance sheets covering the 1953 fiscal year and the six-month period ended March 31, 1954.

EXHIBIT 1

Ultrasonic Corporation (B)
Statements of Income and Deficit

	Year Ended September 30, 1953	Six Months Ended March 31, 1954 (not audited)
Net sales, including progress payments for deliveries under contracts	$5,168,046	$2,443,564
Costs and operating expenses:		
Costs other than selling, general and administrative expenses	$4,111,134	$1,803,564
Selling, general and administrative expenses	757,500	499,217
Total costs and operating expenses	$4,868,634	$2,302,781
Income from operations	$ 299,412	$ 140,783
Other income	12,122	3,890
	$ 311,534	$ 144,673
Income deductions:		
Interest on bonds and mortgage	$ 14,625	$ 18,667
Other interest	12,225	17,685
Miscellaneous	15,866	7,606
	$ 42,716	$ 43,958
Net Income before following charge	$ 268,818	$ 100,715
Portion of moving expenses equal to estimated reduction in federal income taxes resulting therefrom		51,000
Net Income for the Period	$ 268,818	$ 49,715

Statement of Deficit

Balance at beginning of period	$ 339,229	$ 70,411
Net Income for the period	268,818	49,715
Balance at end of period	$ 70,411	$ 20,696

EXHIBIT 2

Ultrasonic Corporation (B)
Condensed Balance Sheets as of September 30, 1953 and March 31, 1954

	September 30, 1953	March 31, 1954 (not audited)
ASSETS		
Current Assets:		
Cash in banks and on hand	$ 127,496	$ 74,568
Accounts receivable:		
U.S. Government contracts	$1,219,948	$1,013,118
Other customers	139,095	354,710
Others	14,536 1,373,579	6,830 1,374,658
Inventories (note A):		
Materials and parts	$ 730,164	$ 686,051
Products in process	296,580	1,004,694
Finished products	14,203	17,771
Accumulated contract costs	219,690 1,260,637	404,550 2,113,066
Costs accumulated pending completion of negotiations for price increases under two government contracts	357,081	413,654
Deposits, unexpired insurance and other prepaid expenses	14,198	31,037
Total current assets	$3,132,991	$4,006,983
Property, plant and equipment, net	1,229,328	1,535,290
Patents and patent applications, net	517,174	521,218
Deferred experimental and development costs	178,213	267,143
Other deferred charges:		
Balance of moving expenses, net of taxes		114,795
Unamortized issue expenses of 6% Income Convertible Bonds	$ 19,789	$ 18,841
Goodwill	9,134 28,923	7,992 26,833
	$5,086,629	$6,472,262
LIABILITIES		
Current Liabilities	$1,187,031	$2,045,756
4½% Mortgage note on land and building	450,000	425,000
6% Income Convertible Bonds	500,000	500,000
CAPITAL		
Common Stock, par value $5 per share	$1,477,485	$1,661,460
Paid-in surplus	1,542,524	1,860,742
	$3,020,009	$3,522,202
Less deficit	70,411 2,949,598	20,696 3,501,506
	$5,086,629	$6,472,262

QUESTIONS:

1. Contrast the three methods used to determine cost of sales in the Monitor Division from its acquisition in 1952 through March 1954. Under what conditions is each method appropriate?

2. Which, if any, of the four adjustments made in January, 1954, do you disagree with? Why? How would you have treated these items?

3. Do you agree with management's contention that the new cost system could not be considered accurate until tested by a physical inventory? Does it follow that the use of the new cost system for book purposes would produce less reliable results than the percentage method actually used? Explain.

4. Was there a material difference between gross profit for the six-month period as determined under the new cost system and under the percentage method?

5. Do you agree with the examiner that the corporation should have used the new cost system for the entire six-month period since it had used it for the first four months? Explain.

6. Do you agree with the examiner's position regarding the missing time and material tickets? Explain.

7. Ultrasonic's auditors expressed opinions on the 1952 and 1953 financial statements in the prospectus. What action, if any, do you think the auditors took in regard to the statements for 1952? for 1953?

Swift & Company (A)

Swift & Company was started in 1855 when G.F. Swift, at age 16, borrowed $20 from his father to buy a heifer. He dressed it and sold the cuts to his neighbors on Cape Cod. From this modest beginning, Swift has grown to become the largest meat packing company in the United States with increasing operations abroad. The company has over 50 packing plants and operates distributing houses in almost every large city in the country. As a national meat packer, its most important function is to move meat from specialized producing areas to distant consuming areas. Swift's principal products are meat, poultry, dairy and other agricultural products, hides and wool.

Meat packing is a highly competitive industry and the company faces constant problems in pricing its products. In its 1957 annual report, management commented on this as follows:

> Most manufacturers take a group of raw materials and assemble them into a finished product. The costs of the various raw materials and processes can be added up in order to arrive at a selling price which will permit a reasonable margin of profit. If that price cannot be obtained immediately, the goods can be held in stock or production cut back.
>
> The meat packer faces a very different situation. His operations consist of "disassembling" a complicated product into its simpler component parts. When he buys a hog or a steer, he must market pork loins, lard, smoked hams and bacon; or beef, hides and other by-products. All these products must be moved into consumption in the quantities and proportions determined by nature and by the farmer and the rancher, not by the meat packer. The flow cannot be controlled by turning a valve or changing a blueprint.
>
> After a meat animal has been dressed and cut into its many products, what can be said about the cost of each product? The meat packer knows how much he paid for the whole animal, but he cannot say that he paid so much for the ham and so much for the lard. This is one reason he cannot base the selling price of each item on a known cost for that product.
>
> If a price has been quoted on a given product, and sales are slow at that price, the meat packer cannot generally accumulate the product

in order to wait for better markets. Most meat is perishable and must be sold within a short period of time. The amount and types of meat that can be profitably stored by canning or freezing are very limited—not more than a few days' supply.

Whatever is stored must meet the competition of fresh supplies coming onto the market later.

For many years, company spokesmen complained of the effect of abrupt inventory price changes on reported net profits and related income taxes. In the President's 1938 Report to Shareholders, Mr. John Holmes stated:

Reserve for Inventory Price Decline

Our company has long realized the nature of inventory profits and losses. We have known that profits due to rising inventory prices are not cash profits because they must be immediately reinvested in high cost inventories to keep our branch houses stocked, our plants operating, and our business going. Recognizing these facts during the years 1933-34-35 when prices were rising, your directors set aside a portion of the reported earnings of those years as a reserve for inventory price declines. It was realized that the time would come when prices would decline and wipe out all or a large portion of these inventory profits. The inventory reserve set up in those three years amounted to a total of $16,767,000.

This year we have drawn $11,000,000 from our inventory reserve account to offset a part of our inventory losses. There remains in the account $5,767,000[1] as a reserve against possible price declines in the future.

I hope that one day our revenue laws will recognize for tax purposes a definition of income which will exclude inventory gains and losses from taxable net income. Such a move on the part of the Federal Government would be definitely in the interest of greater stability in business.

Again, in the 1941 annual report, Mr. Holmes referred to this matter:

We have known that the larger part of profits due to rising inventory prices is not expendable profits. The larger part of this gain is not expendable because it represents an increase in the value of products on hand and appears with the upswing and disappears with the downswing of the price cycle.

Over the past eight years, we have met the situation by setting up reserves for inventory price declines when such inventory profits have accrued. This reserve is represented by the item of $5,767,000 appearing on the balance sheet.

Adoption of Lifo

This year we decided to utilize the elective method of inventory pricing commonly called "Last-in, First-out," as provided for in the Revenue Act of 1939. ... In effect, this method accomplishes the same purpose as inventory reserves.

---

[1] In 1956, this amount was transferred to retained earnings, "because the 'Lifo' method now applies to substantially all of our product inventory ... [and] this reserve [$5,767,000] ... [appears] unnecessary."

In addition, the new method provides a definition of income which removes unrealized inventory gains and losses from current taxable income. Your Directors have adopted this method on certain raw materials, goods in process, and finished products, comprising pork and pork products, fats and oils, hides, wool, dairy and poultry products, etc.

A note to the financial statements in the 1941 annual report stated:

The company and its domestic subsidiaries as of January 1, 1941, the beginning of its current income tax year, adopted the elective method of inventory valuation ("Last-in, First-out" method) provided in the Revenue Act of 1939 . . . to the inventories of certain raw materials, goods in process and finished goods, comprising pork and pork products, fats and oils, hides, wool, dairy and poultry products, etc. Accordingly, at the close of the current fiscal year, November 1, 1941, the inventories of raw materials, goods in process and finished goods in these lines of product, aggregating $53,515,208, have been valued on the "Last-in, First-out" method on the basis of their unit values at January 1, 1941, to the extent of the quantities on hand January 1, 1941, and excess quantities on basis of cost of latest acquisitions. The remainder of the domestic inventories at November 1, 1941, aggregating $46,933,294, has been priced as in the past, that is, products where cost was not ascertainable at approximate market prices, allowing for the estimated selling expenses; other products and ingredients and supplies at the lower of cost or market.

Effect of Lifo

These methods of valuation of certain inventories, as applied . . . for the first time at the close of the current fiscal year, have the effect of reducing the total value of the consolidated inventories at November 1, 1941, $20,650,347 below what it would have been had the method of pricing used in past years been followed and the net profits after income and excess profits taxes, approximately $7,000,000 below what they would have been had the method of pricing inventories used in past years been followed.

The "Reserve for inventory price decline" of $5,767,000 as at October 26, 1940, has been carried forward without change. Appropriations were made to this reserve in the years 1933, 1934, and 1935, when unit inventory values advanced, and a withdrawal was made, restoring $11,000,000 to the surplus account, in 1938, a year of price declines.

Extension of Lifo

In the 1942 annual report, Mr. Holmes commented:

The elective method of inventory pricing, commonly called "Last-in, First-out," which we adopted for certain products last year, has been extended this year to beef, lamb, and veal, thus placing practically all of our major products under this plan. The method, described in last year's report, accomplishes to a large extent the purpose of inventory reserves formerly used and is recognized by the Internal Revenue Department in determining taxable income.

Difference between Fiscal Year and Tax Year

Our fiscal year closes at the end of October and our tax year at the end of December. Therefore, while the taxes shown on the fiscal year statement are correct with respect to the income for the fiscal year, the taxes to be paid may and probably will be different, as the results for November and December will have an effect on the taxable income. Over a period of years such differences tend to equalize themselves.

A note to the 1942 financial statements indicated the effect of "Lifo" on fiscal-year and tax-year profits:

Profits of the years ended November 1, 1941 and October 31, 1942, have been increased as a result of substantial reductions in the inventories during these two years of rising prices, but the increases have been modified by the adoption of the so-called "Lifo" method of inventory valuation, effected as of January 1, 1941, on certain products and also for the Canadian subsidiary in a modified form, and extended to other products as of January 1, 1942. For the year ended October 31, 1942, the adoption of the "Lifo" method to such additional products has reduced profits before taxes by $2,244,015 and after taxes by approximately $400,000. The company's tax year is the calendar year and, therefore, the effective date for determining inventory values under the "Lifo" method is December 31 of each year. It is inherent in the company's business that the inventories are lower at the close of October than at the end of the calendar year. Accordingly, insofar as the quantities under "Lifo" liquidated to the end of October are replaced at costs in excess of the "Lifo" base in the succeeding months of November and December, a profit has been taken to the end of October in each year which would be reversed in arriving at the profits to December 31. This condition obtained in the fiscal year ended November 1, 1941, as well as the current fiscal year.[2]

Replenishment of Depleted Lifo Inventories

If the company should adopt the privilege granted under Section 119 of the Revenue Act of 1942 of reinstating the January 1, 1942, inventory quantities at the "Lifo" base, a further reversal of part of the profit already taken might occur in future years.

A note in the 1948 annual report referred to the replenishment of "Lifo" inventories which were depleted during World War II:

A substantial portion of the product inventories of Swift & Company and its domestic subsidiaries is valued at cost under the "Last-in, First-out" (Lifo) method provided in the Internal Revenue Code, which was adopted effective as at January 1, 1941 and 1942 (the basic dates for quantities and prices), the companies' tax year being the calendar year. Other product inventories of the domestic companies are valued at approximate market, less selling expense. The product inventories of the Canadian subsidiaries are valued in a modified form of the "Lifo" method.

In following the "Lifo" method the domestic companies have also filed for application of the provision of the Internal Revenue Code which permits redetermination of taxable income for the years 1941 to 1946, inclusive, if the inventories at the close of such years were involuntarily reduced below the

---

[2] The method of accounting for this difference between the fiscal year and the tax (calendar) year is considered in question 1.

basic "Lifo" quantities, and if the basic quantities are replaced in a subsequent year to and including December 31, 1950 at prices differing from the basic "Lifo" prices. During the current fiscal year (principally during November and December, 1947) the domestic companies partially replaced the quantities of certain "Lifo" inventories which were involuntarily liquidated during the years 1941 to 1946, inclusive (principally war years). As required for income tax purposes a charge has been made to income of $36,914,407 in writing down such inventory replacements to their basic "Lifo" costs, against which the resulting claims for refund of prior years' Federal income taxes of $24,301,872 have been applied, thereby reducing the net charge to income to $12,612,535. The refundable taxes due to "Lifo" inventory replacements during the current and prior fiscal years are carried in the balance sheet as long term receivables.

Exhibit 1 shows the annual provision for replacement of basic "Lifo" inventories for the years 1950 through 1961. In 1954, approximately $7,000,000 was realized and included in net income for the 1954 fiscal year resulting from replacements of pork inventories in November and December, 1953, being less than was anticipated at October 31, 1953.[3]

---

[3] Apparently this adjustment was unusually large since 1954 was the only year from 1950 through 1961 in which such an adjustment was disclosed.

QUESTIONS:

1. The Schleifer Packing Company's inventory, on a "Lifo" cost basis, consisted of the following "layers" at January 1, 1961, the beginning of its tax year:

        100,000 tons at $170.00 per ton (most recently acquired layer)
        100,000   "   "   165.00   "   "
         50,000   "   "   160.00   "   "

        100,000   "   "   155.00   "   "
         50,000   "   "   152.50   "   "
        200,000   "   "   150.00   "   "

        400,000   "   "   140.00   "   " (basic layer)

Assume that:
(a) Inventory at October 31, 1961, close of the company's fiscal year, is 550,000 tons.
(b) The company is subject to a 52 per cent tax rate.
(c) Based on book income before making any provision for replacement of basic "Lifo" inventory, the company records a debit to income tax expense and a credit to income taxes payable.
(d) After recording the entry in (c), but before closing the 1961 accounts, an entry is made to debit cost of sales for the excess expected to be incurred in November and December of estimated inventory replacement cost over basic "Lifo" cost. Part of the credit portion of this entry is to income tax expense, while the balance is to "Provision for replacement of basic 'Lifo' inventory (net after income taxes)."
(e) As basic "Lifo" stocks are replaced in November and December, cash

EXHIBIT 1

Swift & Company (A)
Selected Financial Data, Years 1950-1961
(in thousands of dollars, except per share figures)

Year Ended	Net Sales	Product Inventory	Provision for Replacement of Basic "Lifo" Inventory (net after income taxes)	Total Net Income	Net Income Per Share
Oct. 28, 1950	$2,215,000	$110,640	$13,590	$16,143	$2.73
Oct. 27, 1951	2,524,000	134,846	9,717	12,109	2.04
Nov. 1, 1952	2,593,000	155,860	7,770	21,698	3.66
Oct. 31, 1953	2,597,000	143,753	11,628	33,903	5.72
Oct. 30, 1954	2,511,000	132,810	2,586	19,051	3.22
Oct. 29, 1955	2,404,000	154,838	698	22,893	3.87
Oct. 27, 1956	2,429,000	160,682	1,416	14,012	2.36
Oct. 26, 1957	2,542,000	139,201	4,081	13,538	2.29
Nov. 1, 1958	2,645,000	158,521	2,064	10,048	1.70
Oct. 31, 1959	2,475,000	134,464	1,226	19,068	3.20
Oct. 29, 1960	2,443,000	157,724	1,323	18,413	3.09
Oct. 28, 1961	2,489,000	154,275	695	12,050	2.01

or accounts payable is credited and the following accounts are debited: inventory (at basic "Lifo" cost), taxes payable, and provision for replacement of basic "Lifo" inventory (net after income taxes).

Given the following estimates at October 31, 1961, of purchases for November and December, show journal entries to record the Provision for replacement of basic "Lifo" inventory (net after income taxes). Treat each part separately.

(1) 450,000 tons at $177.50 per ton.
(2) 350,000 tons at $177.50 per ton.
(3) 550,000 tons at $177.50 per ton.

2. Assume estimate (1) above is made at October 31, 1961. What entry is required in November if 200,000 tons are purchased at $177.50 per ton?

3. Assume that the actual purchases made in November and December were 400,000 tons at $181, but the estimate used at October 31, 1961, was (1) above. What journal entry do you recommend be made as of December 31, 1961, to account for this difference between estimated and actual purchases? How would you disclose the effect of this difference in the financial statements for the fiscal year ending in October, 1962?

4. Can you see any weakness in the method of providing for replacement of basic "Lifo" inventory which might affect the reporting of net income? If so, which period's net income is affected—the one just ending or the one just beginning? Can you recommend any alternative to this procedure?

5. Swift states that "a substantial portion of the product inventories ... is valued at cost under the 'Lifo' method." How would you define the concept of "cost" as used by a meat packing company?

6. Proponents of "Lifo" support its use because it presumably results in better matching of revenue and expense. Swift & Company adopted "Lifo" in 1941. Would you judge that a better matching of revenue and expense has resulted in every year since 1941? Explain.

7. At the close of its fiscal year in 1941, Swift & Company reported product inventories of $107.7 million, while in 1961 it reported $154.3 million. Assuming prices of meat products have at least doubled since 1941, does this mean Swift is now conducting its business with much less physical inventory? Explain.

CHAPTER NINE

Plant and Equipment —Depreciation

Accounting for plant and equipment and related depreciation has probably been the cause of more misunderstanding and disagreement among businessmen, accountants, and U. S. Treasury officials than any other aspect of accounting. Most problems in this important area focus on one or more of the following factors:

(1) Determining the appropriate cost basis for depreciation measurement, such as original cost, current replacement cost, expected replacement cost, or some other basis.

(2) Estimating the useful life of depreciable assets.

(3) Selecting a method of assigning depreciation to accounting periods.

Tax policy has exerted considerable influence—often a dominant influence—on these factors. Differences between the tax treatment and the book treatment of these factors have led to income tax allocation, discussed briefly in Chapter 6, *Income Tax Reporting in Financial Statements*. The present chapter deals with problems of estimating the useful life of depreciable assets, selecting a method of depreciation, and additional income tax allocation problems. The problem of selecting an appropriate cost basis for depreciation measurement is considered in the following chapter.

Estimating Useful Life

Two factors limit useful life: physical deterioration and obsolescence. Actual use is only one element contributing to physical deterioration; the mere passage of time usually brings some decay, rust and so forth. Physical deterioration may be influenced by the intensity of an asset's use and a company's maintenance and repair policies.

The rate of asset obsolescence is usually beyond a company's direct control and is therefore more difficult to estimate than the rate of physical deterioration. Unlike physical deterioration, which usually occurs gradually, obsolescence may occur suddenly when a much improved machine or a new technology is introduced.

U. S. TREASURY POLICY AND DEPRECIABLE LIVES

Since many companies use the same life periods for both book and federal income tax purposes, the Treasury's attitude towards useful-life estimates has played an important role in depreciation accounting. According to the Treasury, taxpayers have been free "to determine reasonable periods of useful life for their depreciable property on the basis of their particular operating conditions, experience, and informed judgment as to technological improvements and economic changes."[1] However, until 1962, the Treasury relied extensively on its Bulletin "F" to measure the propriety of life estimates used by taxpayers. This publication, which listed the average useful life of some 5,000 individual assets, was last revised in 1942 and was frequently criticized by businessmen as containing unrealistically long life estimates.

In July, 1962, Bulletin "F" was superseded by Revenue Procedure 62–21 which represents "a basic reform in the standards and procedures used for the determination of depreciation for tax purposes."[2] In contrast to the thousands of individual assets listed in Bulletin "F," new guideline lives are recommended for about 75 broad classes of assets. In most cases, a single guideline class covers all of the production machinery and equipment used in an industry, such as 14 years for the rubber products industry. Assets in general use, such as office equipment and furniture, are covered by guideline classes applicable to all industries. Three or four classes will typically include all depreciable assets used in any one industry.

The new guideline lives for machinery and equipment average 30 to 40 per cent shorter than the comparable average lives of individual assets listed in Bulletin "F." According to Treasury estimates, this will result in more rapid depreciation deductions than those presently taken on 70 to 80 per cent of the machinery and equipment used by American business.

---

[1] U. S. Treasury Department, "Bulletin 'F,' Tables of Useful Lives of Depreciable Property," Internal Revenue Service Publication No. 173, 1955 (contains tables of useful lives reprinted without change from 1942 edition).

[2] U. S. Treasury Department, "Depreciation Guidelines and Rules," Internal Revenue Service Publication No. 456 (7–62), July, 1962.

Most companies will probably use the new guideline lives for both book and tax-return purposes. While this will reduce income tax expense, at least temporarily, the larger depreciation charges will simultaneously reduce reported income. For example, assuming a 50 per cent income tax rate, $1,000 of additional depreciation expense will reduce *both* income tax expense and reported earnings by $500. For this reason some companies may use the shortened lives for income tax purposes only.

CERTIFICATES OF NECESSITY

An exception to the Treasury's general rule that depreciation must extend over an asset's useful life was made during World War II and again during the Korean War when "certificates of necessity" were issued to encourage construction of certain facilities considered essential to the war effort. Such certificates permitted a company to write off all or a stated percentage of an asset's cost over 60 months, regardless of the asset's probable useful life. The actual percentage for any given asset was determined on the basis of national need and the expected ratio of the asset's military use to its nonmilitary use.

Such certificates were the subject of ARB No. 42, *Emergency Facilities—Depreciation, Amortization, and Income Taxes,* issued in 1952, and included the following year in ARB No. 43 as Chapter 9(C). This bulletin contains an excellent section on depreciation considerations in general and a section on the accounting recognition of income tax effects when the probable economic life of certified facilities exceeded 60 months. Because significant portions of these discussions are relevant to contemporary depreciation problems, the entire bulletin is reproduced below.

CERTIFICATES OF NECESSITY

1. Section 124 A of the Internal Revenue Code, which was added by the Revenue Act of 1950, provides for the issuance of certificates of necessity under which all or part of the cost of so-called *emergency facilities* may be amortized over a period of 60 months for income-tax purposes. In many cases, the amounts involved are material, and companies are faced with the problem of deciding whether to adopt the 60-month period over which the portions of the cost of the facilities covered by certificates of necessity may be amortized for income-tax purposes as the period over which they are to be depreciated in the accounts.

2. Thinking on this question apparently has become confused because many so-called *percentage certificates* have been issued covering less than the entire cost of the facility. This fact, together with the fact that the probable economic usefulness of the facility after the close of the five-year amortization period is considered by the certifying authority in determining the percentage

covered by these certificates, has led many to believe that the percentage used represents the government's conclusion as to the proportion of the cost of the facility that is not expected to have usefulness at the end of five years.

3. In some cases, it is apparent that the probable lack of economic usefulness of the facility after the close of the amortization period must constitute the principal if not the sole basis for determining the percentage to be included in the certificate. However, it must be recognized that the certifying authority has acted under orders to give consideration also to a variety of other factors to the end that the amount certified may be the minimum amount necessary to secure expansion of industrial capacity in the interest of national defense during the emergency period. Among the factors required to be considered in the issuance of these certificates, in addition to loss of useful value, are (a) character of business, (b) extent of risk assumed (including the amount and source of capital employed, and the potentiality of recovering capital or retiring debt through tax savings or pricing), (c) assistance to small business and promotion of competition, (d) compliance with government policies (e.g., dispersal for security), and (e) other types of incentives provided by government, such as direct government loans, guaranties, and contractual arrangements.

DEPRECIATION CONSIDERATIONS

4. The argument has been advanced from time to time that, since the portion of the cost of properties covered by certificates of necessity is amortized over a five-year period for income-tax purposes, it is necessary to follow the same procedure in the accounts. Sound financial accounting procedures do not necessarily coincide with the rules as to what shall be included in "gross income," or allowed as a deduction therefrom, in arriving at taxable net income. It is well recognized that such rules should not be followed for financial accounting purposes if they do not conform to generally accepted accounting principles. However, where the results obtained from following income-tax procedures do not materially differ from those obtained where generally accepted accounting principles are followed, there are practical advantages in keeping the accounts in agreement with the income-tax returns.

5. The cost of a productive facility is one of the costs of the services it renders during its useful economic life. Generally accepted accounting principles require that this cost be spread over the expected useful life of the facility in such a way as to allocate it as equitably as possible to the periods during which services are obtained from the use of the facility. This procedure is known as depreciation accounting, a system of accounting which aims to distribute the cost or other basic value of tangible capital assets, less salvage (if any), over the estimated useful life of the unit (which may be a group of assets) in a systematic and rational manner. It is a process of allocation, not of valuation.

6. The committee is of the opinion that from an accounting standpoint there is nothing inherent in the nature of emergency facilities which requires the depreciation or amortization of their cost for financial accounting purposes over either a shorter or a longer period than would be proper if no certificate of necessity had been issued. Estimates of the probable useful life of a facility by those best informed in the matter may indicate either a shorter or a

longer life than the statutory 60-month period over which the certified portion of its cost is deductible for income-tax purposes.

7. In determining the proper amount of annual depreciation with respect to emergency facilities for financial accounting purposes, it must be recognized that a great many of these facilities are being acquired primarily for what they can produce during the emergency period. To whatever extent it is reasonable to expect the useful economic life of a facility to end with the close of the amortization period the cost of the facility is a proper cost of operation during that period.

8. In determining the prospective usefulness of such facilities it will be necessary to consider their adaptability to post-emergency use, the effect of their use upon economic utilization of other facilities, the possibility of excessive costs due to expedited construction or emergency conditions, and the fact that no deductions for depreciation of the certified portion will be allowable for income-tax purposes in the post-amortization years if the company elects to claim the amortization deduction. The purposes for which emergency facilities are acquired in a great many cases are such as to leave major uncertainties as to the extent of their use during the amortization period and as to their subsequent usefulness—uncertainties which are not normally encountered in the acquisition and use of operating facilities.

9. Consideration of these factors, the committee believes, will in many cases result in the determination of depreciation charges during the amortization period in excess of the depreciation that would be appropriate if these factors were not involved. Frequently they will be so compelling as to indicate the need for recording depreciation of the cost of emergency facilities in the accounts in conformity with the amortization deductions allowable for income-tax purposes. However, the committee believes that when the amount allowed as amortization for income-tax purposes is materially different from the amount of the estimated depreciation, the latter should be used for financial accounting purposes.

10. In some cases, certificates of necessity cover facilities which the owner expects to use after the emergency period in lieu of older facilities. As a result the older facilities may become unproductive and obsolete before they are fully depreciated on the basis of their previously expected life. In such situations, the committee believes depreciation charges to income should be determined in relation to the total properties, to the end that sound depreciation accounting may be applied to the property accounts as a whole.

RECOGNITION OF INCOME TAX EFFECTS

11. In those cases in which the amount of depreciation charged in the accounts on that portion of the cost of the facilities for which certificates of necessity have been obtained is materially less than the amount of amortization deducted for income-tax purposes, the amount of income taxes payable annually during the amortization period may be significantly less than it would be on the basis of the income reflected in the financial statements. In such cases, after the close of the amortization period the income taxes will exceed the amount that would be appropriate on the basis of the income reported in the statements. Accordingly, the committee believes that during the amortization period, where this difference is material, a charge should be made in the income statement to recognize the income tax to be paid in

the future on the amount by which amortization for income-tax purposes exceeds the depreciation that would be allowable if certificates of necessity had not been issued. The amount of the charge should be equal to the estimated amount by which the income tax expected to be payable after the amortization period exceeds what would be so expected if amortization had not been claimed for income-tax purposes in the amortization period. The estimated amount should be based upon normal and surtax rates in effect during the period covered by the income statement with such changes therein as can be reasonably anticipated at the time the estimate is made.

12. In accounting for this deferment of income taxes, the committee believes it desirable to treat the charge as being for additional income taxes. The related credit in such cases would properly be made to an account for deferred income taxes. Under this method, during the life of the facility following the amortization period the annual charges for income taxes will be reduced by charging to the account for deferred income taxes that part of the income tax in excess of what would have been payable had the amortization deduction not been claimed for income-tax purposes in the amortization period. By this procedure the net income will more nearly reflect the results of a proper matching of costs and revenues.

13. There are those who similarly recognize the necessity for giving effect to the amount of the deferred income taxes but who believe this should be accomplished by making a charge in the income account for additional amortization or depreciation. They would carry the related credit to an accumulated amortization or depreciation account as a practical means of recognizing the loss of future deductibility of the cost of the facility for income-tax purposes. If this procedure is followed the annual charges for depreciation will be correspondingly reduced throughout the useful life of the facility following the amortization period. Although this procedure will result in the same amount of net income as the procedure outlined in paragraph 12, and therefore may be considered as acceptable, the committee regards the paragraph 12 procedure as preferable. In any circumstances, there should be disclosure of the procedures followed.

The words "amortize" and "amortization" appear throughout this bulletin. While "depreciation" and "amortization" are frequently used interchangeably, Kohler defines amortization as "the gradual extinguishment of any amount over a period of time."[3] Thus, "amortization" includes depreciation, but it also includes the gradual extinguishment of other amounts such as prepaid insurance. Although the cost of certified facilities was *amortized* over 60 months for income tax purposes, this period was not always considered appropriate for recording depreciation in the books.

The reader should carefully review paragraphs 4 and 5. Paragraph 4 emphasizes possible conflicts between tax rules and generally accepted accounting principles. Paragraph 5 contains the definition of depreciation accounting formulated by the Institute's Committee on

---

[3] Eric L. Kohler, *A Dictionary for Accountants*, 3rd ed. (Englewood Cliffs, N. J.: Prentice-Hall, Inc., 1963), p. 30.

Terminology. Note in the final sentence that depreciation accounting is considered a process of allocation, not of valuation.

Paragraphs 12 and 13 describe alternative methods of accounting for the difference between the amount of income taxes currently payable and the amount of taxes which would be payable on the basis of book income, when the 60-month period is not used in computing depreciation for book purposes. Readers may find it helpful to review pages 119–20 of Chapter 6 where accounting procedures similar to those described in paragraph 13 are discussed.

Methods of Depreciation

Most depreciation methods are based on units of time.[4] The simplest time-based method is the straight-line method, under which an asset's cost (minus its probable salvage value) is written off in equal annual installments over its estimated useful life. This simple method needs no further discussion. More complex alternative methods are discussed in the following sections.

ACCELERATED DEPRECIATION

The term accelerated depreciation refers to the greater amount of depreciation recognized in the early years of an asset's life as compared to the straight-line method. Accelerated depreciation was not widely adopted in this country until its use was authorized for tax purposes by the 1954 Revenue Code on the grounds it would[5]

(1) provide additional incentive for industry to modernize and expand,

(2) offer depreciation tax relief without requiring abandonment of the original-cost basis and the Treasury's established concepts of useful life,

(3) afford a cushion to companies holding certificates of necessity, whose liabilities for postponed taxes would begin to mature in the late 1950's, and

(4) recognize the failure of the straight-line method to measure fairly the rate of decline in the usefulness of many assets.

Two methods of accelerated depreciation, the declining-balance method and the sum-of-the-years-digits method, were specifically

---

[4] When operating activity is clearly a factor, depreciation may be based on some measure of output such as units, miles, operating hours or the like.

[5] Accelerated depreciation has long been accepted for tax purposes in several European countries, notably Britain, Sweden, Denmark and the Netherlands. Canada adopted it in 1949, and one limited type, permitted in the United States since 1939, is described on page 48 of case 3-1, The Kratter Corporation.

authorized in the 1954 Revenue Code.[6] Eligible property included every *new*[7] asset with an estimated useful life of three or more years acquired after January 1, 1954.

ACCELERATED METHODS ILLUSTRATED

When the declining-balance method is used, a constant percentage, equal to twice the appropriate straight-line percentage, is applied each year to whatever part of an asset's original cost remains to be depreciated. Assume, for example, that a property cost $1,000 and its estimated useful life is ten years.[8] Declining-balance depreciation would be 20 per cent of $1,000, or $200, the first year; 20 per cent of $800, or $160, the second; 20 per cent of $640, or $128, the third, etc. To avoid an undepreciated balance at the end of an asset's useful life, a taxpayer may change from the declining-balance method to the straight-line method at any time.

Under the sum-of-the-years-digits method, one adds $1 + 2 + 3$, and so forth, up to the number of years of an asset's estimated useful life. If the life is estimated to be ten years, the sum is $1 + 2 + 3 \ldots + 10$, or 55. Depreciation each year is based on the remaining-years-of-estimated-useful-life divided by this sum. For a $1,000 asset with an estimated useful life of ten years and no estimated salvage value, depreciation would be 10/55 of $1,000, or $181.82, the first year;

---

[6] A taxpayer may use any other method of accelerated depreciation so long as the accumulated depreciation at the end of any year, during the first two-thirds of the useful life of an asset, does not exceed the cumulative depreciation which could have been deducted if the declining-balance method had been used. The term *declining-balance* is used here (and throughout this chapter) to refer to the depreciation method described in the following section. It is sometimes called the *double* declining-balance method.

[7] The exclusion of used property was consistent with the Code's objective of encouraging plant expansion and modernization. This objective had been made clear by the House Ways and Means Committee and the Senate Finance Committee, both of whose reports contained this statement: "More liberal depreciation allowances are anticipated to have far-reaching effects. The incentives resulting from the changes are well timed to help maintain the present high level of investment in plant and equipment." Other countries, seeking the opposite goal, have instituted deferred depreciation; for example, Canada, during the Korean War, enacted a plan that temporarily limited the right to deduct depreciation on certain types of new property.

[8] Salvage value is ignored in applying the declining-balance method, but an asset cannot be depreciated below its estimated salvage value at the end of its useful life. The Revenue Act of 1962 permits estimated salvage value not in excess of 10 per cent of asset cost to be ignored in computing depreciation, regardless of the depreciation method used. If the estimated salvage value exceeds 10 per cent of asset cost, only the excess need be taken into account. This rule applies only to personal property with a life of three or more years acquired after October 16, 1962.

9/55 of $1,000, or $163.64, the second, and so on down to 1/55 of $1,000, or $18.18, the last.

Table 1 shows annual and cumulative depreciation for this asset under the straight-line, declining-balance, and sum-of-the-years-digits methods.

TABLE 1 DEPRECIATION ON A SINGLE ASSET
Cost $1,000, No Salvage Value, Life 10 Years

	Annual Amount			Cumulative Amount		
Year	Straight-Line	Declining-Balance	Sum-of-the-Years-Digits	Straight-Line	Declining-Balance	Sum-of-the-Years-Digits
1	$100.00	$200.00	$181.82	$ 100.00	$ 200.00	$ 181.82
2	100.00	160.00	163.64	200.00	360.00	345.46
3	100.00	128.00	145.45	300.00	488.00	490.91
4	100.00	102.40	127.27	400.00	590.40	618.18
5	100.00	81.92	109.09	500.00	672.32	727.27
6	100.00	65.54	90.91	600.00	737.86	818.18
7	100.00	65.54*	72.73	700.00	803.40	890.91
8	100.00	65.54	54.55	800.00	868.94	945.46
9	100.00	65.53	36.36	900.00	934.47	981.82
10	100.00	65.53	18.18	1,000.00	1,000.00	1,000.00

*Taxpayer switches here to the straight-line method. Declining-balance depreciation, if continued, would be as follows: year 7—$52.43, year 8—$41.94, year 9—$33.55, year 10—$26.84. An undepreciated "tail" of $107.38 would remain at the end of year 10.

FIRST INSTITUTE BULLETIN ON ACCELERATED DEPRECIATION

In October, 1954, following specific approval of declining-balance and sum-of-the-years-digits depreciation methods in the 1954 Revenue Code, the Committee on Accounting Procedure issued ARB No. 44, *Declining-balance Depreciation.* This bulletin follows:

1. The declining-balance method of estimating periodic depreciation has a long history of use in England and in other countries including, to a limited extent, the United States. Interest in this method has been increased by its specific recognition for income-tax purposes in the Internal Revenue Code of 1954.

2. The declining-balance method is one of those which meets the requirements of being systematic and rational. In those cases where the expected productivity or revenue-earning power of the asset is relatively greater during the earlier years of its life, or where maintenance charges tend to increase during the later years, the declining-balance method may well provide the most satisfactory allocation of cost. The conclusions of this bulletin also apply to other methods, including the "sum-of-the-years-digits" method, which produce substantially similar results.

3. When a change to the declining-balance method is made for general accounting purposes, and depreciation is a significant factor in the determination of net income, the change in method, including the effect thereof, should be disclosed in the year in which the change is made.

4. There may be situations in which the declining-balance method is adopted for tax purposes but other appropriate methods are followed for financial accounting purposes. In such cases it may be that accounting recognition should be given to deferred income taxes. However, the committee is of the opinion that, in the ordinary situation, deferred income taxes need not be recognized in the accounts unless it is reasonably certain that the reduction in taxes during the earlier years of use of the declining-balance method for tax purposes is merely a deferment of income taxes until a relatively few years later, and then only if the amounts are clearly material.

The statement entitled "Declining-balance Depreciation" was adopted by the assenting votes of nineteen members of the committee, of whom one, Mr. Stans, assented with qualification. Mr. Burns dissented.

Mr. Stans does not approve the conclusions in the last sentence of paragraph 4. He believes that the reductions in taxes in the earlier years of use in the situations described clearly represent deferments of payment until later years and that the number of years involved has no bearing on the problem. He believes that well-established accounting principles require that deferred income taxes be recognized in every case in which the amounts involved are significant.

Mr. Burns dissents because he believes that the reductions in taxes in the earlier years of use in all cases would clearly represent deferments of payment until later years and that the number of years involved has no bearing on the problem. He believes that compliance with well-established accounting principles requires that deferred income taxes be recognized in every case in which a significant amount is involved in order to avoid a misstatement of reported net income, and he believes that the bulletin should contain a definite statement to that effect.

Income Tax Allocation Problems

Many companies adopted accelerated depreciation for *both* book and tax purposes. This has the advantage of simplicity since only one set of depreciation records is required. Also, as noted in paragraph 2, accelerated depreciation may more accurately measure the decline in usefulness of many assets, especially machinery and equipment.

Other companies adopted accelerated depreciation for tax purposes only, while continuing to use straight-line depreciation in their public reports. A major reason for not using the larger amount of accelerated depreciation in the books was the resulting reduction in reported earnings. Spokesmen for some companies adopting accelerated depreciation for tax purposes only cite the inconsistency of using two methods of depreciation in the books: (1) accelerated depreciation for assets acquired after 1953, and (2) straight-line depreciation for older assets. Also, many businessmen feel accelerated depreciation overstates the real decline in usefulness of some types of property, such as buildings, and is therefore not appropriate for financial reporting purposes.

Paragraph 4 of the bulletin was consistent with the committee's earlier view in Chapter 10 (B) of ARB No. 43 that income tax allocation is unnecessary "where there is a presumption that particular differences between the tax return and the income statement will recur regularly over a comparatively long period of time." (See the last sentence of paragraph 1 on page 123.) In contrast, the committee did recommend accounting recognition of postponed income taxes in the case of certified emergency facilities where the tax postponement was for some *finite* time period.

"NORMALIZATION" vs "FLOW-THROUGH"

Many companies, which adopted accelerated depreciation for tax purposes only, recorded income tax expense on the basis of book income (which reflected use of straight-line depreciation). Most of these companies credited the difference between this amount of recorded tax expense and the tax actually payable currently to a liability account for postponed income taxes. This has been called the "normalization" procedure, because "normal" net income is reported. That is, the amount of net income reported is unaffected by the adoption of accelerated depreciation for income tax purposes only.

Other companies also based book depreciation on the straight-line method, but recorded as income-tax expense only the tax actually payable, as approved in paragraph 4 of ARB No. 44. This has been called the "flow-through" procedure because the tax reduction from using accelerated depreciation in the tax return *only* "flows-through" to—and increases—reported earnings.[9]

In summary, companies which adopted accelerated depreciation for tax purposes followed one of three accounting procedures:

(1) Accelerated depreciation was used for all eligible assets in the books as well as in the income tax return and the amount of taxes actually payable was recorded as income tax expense. As a result, reported earnings were decreased compared to the earnings which would have been reported had the straight-line method been continued for book and tax purposes.

(2) Straight-line depreciation was used in the books and the amount of tax which would have been payable based on book income was recorded as income tax expense. A liability account was established for postponed tax payments. Reported earnings were not affected by using accelerated depreciation for tax purposes only. This is called the "normalization" procedure.

---

[9] The "flow-through" procedure has a different effect in the case of regulated public utilities where the reduction in income taxes usually does not "flow-through" to increase reported earnings, but instead "flows-through" to present customers in the form of lower rates for service.

(3) Straight-line depreciation was used in the books and the amount of income tax actually payable was recorded as income tax expense. As a result, reported earnings were increased. This is called the "flow-through" procedure.

REVISED INSTITUTE BULLETIN ON ACCELERATED DEPRECIATION

Many accountants, including Mr. Burns who dissented to ARB No. 44 and Mr. Stans who objected to the last sentence of paragraph 4, insisted that the "flow-through" procedure was contrary to the accrual basis of accounting and the related matching principle. Furthermore, if the 1954 legislation were ever repealed, the postponed income taxes would become payable over some period of time and, therefore, they should be reflected on the balance sheet as a liability.

In August, 1957, the Institute announced that the 1954 bulletin would be reconsidered, because "there may have been a number of cases in which serious distortion . . . has resulted from the practice of omitting an allocation of the deferred income tax."[10] And in February, 1958, Andrew Barr, chief accountant for the Securities and Exchange Commission, reported in the *Journal of Accountancy* that in some cases use of the "flow-through" procedure had so improved earnings that amendment of financial statements filed with the SEC had "been required on the grounds that failure to do so would make the statements seriously misleading."[11]

In July, 1958, a revised Institute bulletin withdrew approval of the "flow-through" method (except for some regulated companies whose special problems will be discussed later) and recommended that ". . . accounting recognition be given to deferred income taxes if the amounts . . . are material." The revised bulletin follows (except for the first three paragraphs which are identical to the first three paragraphs in the original bulletin):

4. There may be situations in which the declining-balance method is adopted for income-tax purposes but other appropriate methods are used for financial accounting purposes. In such cases, accounting recognition should be given to deferred income taxes if the amounts thereof are material, except in those rare cases, such as are mentioned in paragraph 8, where there are special circumstances which may make such procedure inappropriate. The foregoing provision as to accounting recognition of deferred income taxes applies to a single asset, or to a group of assets which are expected to be retired from service at about the same time; in this case an excess of depreciation taken for income-tax purposes during the earlier years would be followed by the opposite condition in later years, and there would be a tax deferment for a

---

[10] Carman G. Blough, "Subcommittee to Study Experience with Bulletin 44," *Journal of Accountancy*, Vol. 104, August 1957, p. 53.

[11] Andrew Barr, "Financial Reporting for Regulatory Agencies," *Journal of Accountancy*, Vol. 105, February 1958, pp. 29–30.

definite period. It applies also to a group of assets consisting of numerous units which may be of differing lengths of life and which are expected to be continually replaced; in this case an excess of depreciation taken for income-tax purposes during the earlier years would be followed in later years by substantial equality between the annual depreciation for income-tax purposes and that for accounting purposes, and a tax deferment would be built up during the earlier years which would tend to remain relatively constant thereafter. It applies further to a gradually expanding plant; in this case an excess of depreciation taken for income-tax purposes may exist each year during the period of expansion in which event there would be a tax deferment which might increase as long as the period of expansion continued.

5. Where it may reasonably be presumed that the accumulative difference between taxable income and financial income will continue for a long or indefinite period, it is alternatively appropriate, instead of crediting a deferred tax account, to recognize the related tax effect as additional amortization or depreciation applicable to such assets in recognition of the loss of future deductibility for income-tax purposes.

DISCUSSION

6. Following the passage of the Internal Revenue Act of 1954 in August of that year, permitting the use of declining-balance and similar accelerated depreciation methods for federal income-tax purposes, the committee anticipated that many companies would be considering whether such methods should be adopted for general accounting purposes. In October of that year, Accounting Research Bulletin No. 44 was issued in which the committee stated that such accelerated methods met the requirement of being "systematic and rational." The committee also stated that when such methods were adopted for general accounting purposes, appropriate disclosure of the change should be made whenever depreciation was a significant factor in the determination of net income.

7. Since the issuance of Accounting Research Bulletin No. 44, the committee has been observing and studying cases involving the application of the bulletin. Studies of published reports and other source material have indicated that, where material amounts are involved, recognition of deferred income taxes in the general accounts is needed to obtain an equitable matching of costs and revenues and to avoid income distortion, even in those cases in which the payment of taxes is deferred for a relatively long period. This conclusion is borne out by the committee's studies which indicate that where accelerated depreciation methods are used for income-tax purposes only, most companies do give recognition to the resultant deferment of income taxes or, alternatively, recognize the loss of future deductibility for income-tax purposes of the cost of fixed assets by an appropriate credit to an accumulated amortization or depreciation account applicable to such assets.

8. Many regulatory authorities permit recognition of deferred income taxes for accounting and/or rate-making purposes, whereas some do not. The committee believes that they should permit the recognition of deferred income taxes for both purposes. However, where charges for deferred income taxes are not allowed for rate-making purposes, accounting recognition need not be given to the deferment of taxes if it may reasonably be expected that increased future income taxes, resulting from the earlier deduction of declining-balance depreciation for income-tax purposes only, will be allowed in future rate determinations.

9. In those rare situations in which accounting for deferred income taxes is not appropriate, full disclosure should be made of the amount of deferred income taxes arising out of the difference between the financial statements and the tax returns when the declining-balance method is adopted for income-tax purposes but other appropriate methods are used for financial accounting purposes.

10. The committee believes that, in applying the provisions of this bulletin to cases where there was no accounting recognition of deferred income taxes for the years since 1953, the entries made for periods subsequent to the issuance of this bulletin should be based upon all assets acquired after 1953 as to which the declining-balance method has been elected for tax purposes. As is indicated in the "Notes" to each Accounting Research Bulletin, opinions of the committee are not intended to be retroactive unless they contain a statement of such intention. If a retroactive adjustment is made for prior periods, the adjustment may be made in a lump sum, or the deficiency may be systematically accumulated over a reasonable future period of time.

The statement entitled "Declining-balance Depreciation" (July 1958) was adopted unanimously by the twenty-one members of the committee, of whom five, Messrs. Burns, Graham, Halvorson, Jennings, and Powell, assented with qualification.

Mr. Burns objects to the exceptions mentioned in paragraph 4 and discussed in paragraphs 8 and 9. He believes that accounting principles apply equally to all companies operated for profit and that the exceptions referred to are wholly inconsistent with the basic principles stated in paragraph 4; further, that the last sentence of paragraph 8 is based upon an untenable concept, namely, that accounting resulting from the application of an accounting rule prescribed by a regulatory commission may properly be approved by public accountants notwithstanding the fact that the rule is clearly contrary to generally accepted accounting principles.

Mr. Graham objects to the exceptions mentioned in the second sentence of paragraph 4 and discussed in the last sentence of paragraph 8 and in paragraph 9. He believes that accepted accounting principles should be applied uniformly to all corporations, including regulated companies. He does not believe that rate-making rules which are in conflict with these accepted principles constitute a sound basis for sanctioning a departure from these principles in financial reporting. Furthermore, he disagrees with the validity of the assumption which, by implication, forms the basis for this exception; he does not believe that public utility rates will always be adjusted automatically to compensate fully, or even substantially, for increases in future income taxes; he believes that this assumption is not in accord with the known realities of rate regulation and is not, therefore, a proper basis for the anticipation of future revenues.

Mr. Halvorson dissents from the recommendations of paragraph 4 because he believes its requirements for accounting recognition of deferred income taxes should be limited to a requirement for compliance with the recommendations of chapter 10(b) of Accounting Research Bulletin No. 43; he believes that paragraph 4 is effectively a revision of chapter 10(b) and that it is improper thus to make a substantive change in the committee's existing recommendations for tax allocation in the guise of a revision of a bulletin on depreciation.

Messrs. Jennings and Powell dissent from the conclusion (expressed in paragraph 4 and implied in the related discussion) that where the declining-balance method is adopted for income-tax purposes but other appropriate methods are used for financial accounting purposes, there should be accounting recognition of deferred income taxes, except for certain rare cases. They believe this calls for more extensive allocation of income taxes among periods of time than is necessary or desirable, especially where the situation is such that the so-called tax deferment is in effect a permanent tax reduction. Further, they object to the use of a bulletin on depreciation incidentally as a vehicle for making an important change in the committee's views, as set forth in previous bulletins, on accounting for income taxes.

APPLICABILITY OF REVISED BULLETIN

In paragraph 4 the committee advocates recognition of postponed income taxes in three different situations when accelerated depreciation is used in the tax return only and some other depreciation method, usually straight-line, is used for financial accounting purposes. The first situation applies to a single asset, or to a group of assets expected to be retired from service at about the same time. In this situation, which is similar to that for certified emergency facilities, there is tax postponement for a definite time period. This is illustrated in Table 2, in which a *single* asset, having an estimated useful life of 10 years and no salvage value, is purchased at the beginning of year 1. A 50 per cent tax rate is assumed.

TABLE 2   TAX POSTPONEMENT FROM USING SUM-OF-THE-YEARS-DIGITS DEPRECIATION

(assuming purchase of a single $1,000 asset, 10 year useful life, no salvage value, and 50 per cent tax rate)

Year	Excess of SYD Depreciation Over Straight-line Depreciation	Tax Postponement	Cumulative Tax Postponement
1	$81.82	$40.91	$ 40.91
2	63.64	31.82	72.73
3	45.46	22.73	95.46
4	27.27	13.64	109.10
5	9.09	4.55	113.65
6	− 9.09	− 4.55	109.10
7	−27.27	−13.64	95.46
8	−45.46	−22.73	72.73
9	−63.64	−31.82	40.91
10	−81.82	−40.91	none

The second situation applies to a group of assets where continuous replacement is anticipated. In this situation, the total amount of postponed tax increases at first and then tends to stabilize. This is illustrated in Table 3, in which a $1,000 asset, having an estimated useful life of 10 years and no salvage value, is purchased at the beginning of *each* year. A 50 per cent tax rate is assumed.

TABLE 3 TAX POSTPONEMENT FROM USING SUM-OF-THE-YEARS-DIGITS DEPRECIATION

(assuming purchase of a $1,000 asset each year, 10 year useful life, no salvage value, and 50 per cent tax rate)

Year	Excess of SYD Depreciation Over Straight-line Depreciation	Tax Postponement	Cumulative Tax Postponement
1	$ 81.82	$ 40.91	$ 40.91
2	145.46	72.73	113.64
3	190.92	95.46	209.10
4	218.19	109.10	318.20
5	227.28	113.64	431.84
6	218.19	109.10	540.94
7	190.92	95.46	636.40
8	145.46	72.73	709.13
9	81.82	40.91	750.04*
10	none	none	750.04

*Under the assumed conditions, this amount would remain constant beginning at the end of the 9th year.

The third situation applies to a constantly expanding investment in depreciable assets. In this situation, the amount of postponed tax continues to increase indefinitely. This is illustrated in Table 4, in which the purchase of a $1,000 asset is assumed at the beginning of year 1, followed by annual increases of 5 per cent in asset purchases thereafter—$1,050 at the beginning of year 2, $1,102.50 at the beginning of year 3, etc. The annual increases may be attributable to inflation or to physical expansion of depreciable plant. The assets are assumed to have estimated useful lives of 10 years and no salvage value. A 50 per cent tax rate is assumed.

TABLE 4 TAX POSTPONEMENT FROM USING SUM-OF-THE-YEARS-DIGITS DEPRECIATION

(assuming 5 per cent increase each year in asset purchases, 10 year useful life, no salvage value, and 50 per cent tax rate)

Year	Excess of SYD Depreciation Over Straight-line Depreciation	Tax Postponement	Cumulative Tax Postponement
1	$ 81.82	$ 40.91	$ 40.91
2	149.55	74.78	115.69
3	202.47	101.24	216.93
4	239.87	119.94	336.87
5	260.95	130.48	467.35
6	264.91	132.46	599.81
7	250.88	125.44	725.25
8	217.98	108.99	834.24
9	165.23	82.62	916.86*
10	91.59	45.80	962.66

*Under the assumed conditions, this amount would increase at the rate of 5 per cent annually beginning at the end of the 9th year.

CRITICISM OF REVISED BULLETIN

Two members of the committee objected to the extent of income tax allocation recommended in the revised bulletin, and they also objected to using a bulletin on depreciation "as a vehicle for making an important change in the committee's views, as set forth in previous bulletins, on accounting for income taxes." The latter view was shared by a third member of the committee.

A number of other accountants and some businessmen have also criticized the committee's strong position favoring income tax allocation. For example, the chairman of the board and the president of S. S. Kresge Company included the following comment in their 1958 report to the company's stockholders:

[For the years 1954 through 1957 the] tax reduction, and the resulting increase in income through the use of accelerated depreciation permitted by law for income tax purposes, was shown as a footnote to our financial statements. This procedure was approved by our public accountants and permitted under the original bulletin issued in 1954. The revised bulletin requires that, for an unqualified public accountants' opinion, such tax reduction must be recorded within the balance sheet rather than as a footnote.

We continue to believe that the liability now shown on the balance sheet for deferred income taxes is more a contingent liability than a real one and is therefore more properly a footnote item. For a company such as this one, where a continuing relatively level capital expenditure program is a necessity, it is unlikely that any substantial amount of the reserve, if any at all, will require liquidation.

Other critics of the revised bulletin contend there can be no true liability for postponed taxes when both the amount and the time of payment are so uncertain. Also, the creditor, the federal government, recognizes no claim against taxpayers for such taxes.

SUPPORT FOR REVISED BULLETIN

Proponents of the revised bulletin argue that a fair presentation of income is not possible without appropriate income tax allocation. Furthermore, they argue that the ultimate payment of previously postponed income taxes is assured with respect to any *given* asset, or group of assets. That is, after some determinable time interval, the liability account for postponed income taxes will mature with respect to older assets, even though the balance of the account continues to increase because of tax postponements related to recent asset acquisitions. This may be termed the "transaction" concept of postponed income taxes because the tax postponed with respect to depreciation on any given asset-acquisition transaction, or with respect to the transactions of a given year, will definitely become payable in the future.[12] The alternative concept—that postponed income taxes need not be recognized if the total amount of such postponed taxes is likely to stabilize or increase indefinitely—may be termed the "balance-change" concept because the *net change* in the *balance* of postponed income tax is emphasized, rather than the periodic increases and decreases.

In accounting for other liabilities, such as trade accounts payable, the transaction approach is used. The fact that new accounts will replace maturing accounts is not accepted as justification for omitting accounts payable entirely from the balance sheet. Here, of course, different creditors are typically involved in contrast to one, the federal government, in the case of postponed income taxes. However, a maturing debt which is expected to be renewed with the same creditor is never omitted from the liabilities.

One solution to these problems would be to require any company using accelerated depreciation for tax purposes to use it also in its annual reports, as taxpayers using LIFO must do. Such a requirement was written into the 1949 law that first authorized accelerated depreciation in Canada, but it was repealed in 1954 on the grounds that accelerated depreciation is not appropriate for some assets.

ALTERNATIVE TO DEFERRED TAX ACCOUNT

Paragraph 5 presents an alternative accounting treatment which has been used by a few American companies and is favored in Canada. This treatment is also discussed in paragraph 13 of the committee's earlier bulletin on emergency facilities (see page 248 in this chapter). The following note accompanying the 1958 financial statements of the F. W. Woolworth Co. describes the application of this alternative procedure:

Heretofore depreciation has been computed on the straight-line method for both financial statement and income tax purposes. In 1958 the company changed the method of computing depreciation for income tax purposes to the sum-of-the-years-digits method on certain property additions in the U.S.A. and to the declining balance method on properties in Canada. The resulting reduction in income taxes amounted to approximately $1,733,000. Income for 1958 has been charged with depreciation computed on the straight-line method plus an amount equal to the afore-mentioned tax reduction, with the result that net income for the year has not been affected by the change.

REGULATED PUBLIC UTILITY COMPANIES

Paragraph 8 provides an exception for some regulated utilities to

---

[12] Assuming, of course, that the business continues to operate profitably in the future. This assumption is consistent with the going-concern postulate.

the committee's general recommendation concerning accounting recognition of postponed income taxes. Critics of this exception, including Messrs. Burns and Graham who objected to paragraph 8,[13] argue that utilities are not essentially different from other industries; accounting practices unacceptable for other companies should not be condoned for utilities. Further, no utility can "reasonably" predict whether, or when, a decline in its capital outlays will require liquidation of its deferred tax liability, and much less whether the resulting rise in its tax payments will be considered in future rate determinations.

Where utilities have adopted accelerated depreciation for tax purposes only, state and federal regulatory agencies are sharply divided on the need for accounting recognition of the difference between the amount of tax currently payable and the amount which would be payable on the basis of book income. The Federal Power Commission, the Civil Aeronautics Board, and the Securities and Exchange Commission[14] favor such recognition. The Interstate Commerce Commission, which requires use of the "flow-through" method, has stated:[15]

When an available depreciation allowance produces a reduction in federal income taxes, no matter how temporary the benefit may be, the effect on net income should be the same as a reduction in taxes produced by lower tax rates. Possible income taxes to be assessed in the future are not an element of tax expense for the current year. New property units acquired in the future will provide increased depreciation allowances to offset decreasing allowances for older units. The present-day shipper should not be required to provide from current freight rates for possible increased taxes of the indefinite future.

Various state regulatory bodies have been about equally divided in prescribing "normalization" or "flow-through" accounting for utilities subject to state regulation.[16] In general, utilities have opposed rulings which favor "flow-through" accounting, charging that such rulings give present customers an unfair advantage over future customers. Also they claim the "flow-through" method defeats the Congressional purpose of stimulating plant expansion.

ACCOUNTANTS' OPINIONS ON UTILITY FINANCIAL STATEMENTS

Public accounting firms disagree on the type of opinion to render

---

[13] It is interesting to note that of the five qualified assents to ARB No. 44 (Revised), two members, Messrs. Burns and Graham, felt the committee's recommendations were too limited, while three members, Messrs. Halvorson, Jennings, and Powell, felt they were too extreme.

[14] The SEC's position is considered in Chapter 18.

[15] Interstate Commerce Commission, "Accounting for Federal Income Taxes," *Notice to All Carriers Subject to Prescribed Accounting Rules*, February 9, 1959.

[16] Many states requiring "flow-through" accounting in the case of accelerated depreciation have authorized "normalization" for certified emergency facilities.

when a utility is required to use "flow-through" accounting by a state regulatory agency. For example, one firm of certified public accountants included the following comments, after the usual "scope" paragraph, in its opinion of the 1961 financial statements of a large utility company:

> As set forth in Note 1 to the financial statements, the company, in accordance with the policy decision of the Public Service Commission of the State of New York, dated March 30, 1959, does not provide for deferred Federal income taxes resulting from claiming accelerated depreciation for income tax purposes only. The policy of currently claiming higher tax depreciation than is recorded on the books results in lower tax depreciation deductions in later years since the company cannot deduct more than the cost of a piece of property for Federal income tax purposes. Hence, in our opinion, such taxes so deferred constitute current costs unless they can be recovered in the future. Such future recovery cannot be determined at this time.
>
> Subject to the effect of the matter described in the preceding paragraph, in our opinion, . . .

Note 1 read as follows:

> Since January 1, 1954, the company has elected to claim, for Federal income tax purposes, depreciation computed by an accelerated method allowed by the Internal Revenue Code. As a result, depreciation to be claimed for Federal income tax purposes exceeds the amounts recorded on the books which are computed on a straight-line basis. In accordance with the policy decision of the Public Service Commission of the State of New York, dated March 30, 1959, the company does not provide for deferred Federal income taxes resulting from claiming accelerated depreciation for income tax purposes only. The effect of following such accounting treatment has been to reduce Federal income taxes since January 1, 1954, by $3,323,000, of which $922,000 is applicable to 1961 and $746,000 to 1960.

A second firm of certified public accountants rendered a "clean" opinion on the 1961 financial statements of another large utility company, also operating in New York State and therefore subject to the same regulatory commission. The following note accompanied the financial statements of this company:

> Provisions for depreciation in the accounts are made by equal annual charges to income over the estimated useful service lives of the properties as prescribed by the New York Public Service Commission. For federal income tax purposes, depreciation is claimed at rates and on bases different from those used in the accounts.
>
> On certain capital expenditures made subsequent to January 1, 1954, the company has elected to use accelerated depreciation methods provided by Section 167 of the Internal Revenue Code of 1954. The company's method of accounting is in accordance with a statement of general policy adopted by the New York Public Service Commission on March 30, 1959, which is to allow only income taxes currently payable as an expense for accounting

and rate-making purposes. It is the opinion of the company that any future increased income taxes, which might result from using the higher depreciation deductions currently, may reasonably be expected to be allowed in future rate determinations.

DETERMINING THE AMOUNT OF TAX POSTPONED

In accounting for postponed income taxes, most American companies have credited an account called "Deferred Income Taxes"[17] for the difference between the income tax actually payable and the tax which would be payable if accelerated depreciation were not used for tax purposes.

Some accountants contend that the amount of this credit for postponed taxes (and the offsetting debit to income tax expense) should be the estimated amount which will be payable in the future, not the amount which would be payable currently if accelerated depreciation were not used for tax purposes. While these amounts may often be the same, an anticipated change in future tax rates, or a change in the estimated rates to which a particular company will be subject, will cause a difference.

Of much greater significance is the proposal that only the *present value*[18] of the liability for temporarily postponed income taxes should be recorded in the accounts. The estimated rate of return earned on the additional assets made available by postponing payment of income taxes is suggested as an appropriate discount rate. This proposal is based on the argument that the present value (or more properly the "present cost") of a *non-interest bearing* liability, not payable until some future fiscal period, is clearly less than its maturity value. This proposal requires acceptance of the "transaction" concept of asset acquisitions because the present value of an increasing balance of indefinitely postponed income taxes would be zero.

Under this approach, the present or discounted value of estimated future payments of postponed taxes arising from a given year's transactions would be recorded in that year as a debit to income-tax expense and a credit to a liability for postponed income taxes. Thereafter, an entry would be made annually debiting interest expense and crediting the postponed tax liability. This entry would impute an interest cost to the government's "loan" to the taxpayer, and would recognize the gradual increase in the present value of the postponed tax liability. The procedure is analogous to the accounting used for some other liabilities, such as long-term bonds, which are recorded in the books of the issuer at the *present value* of future

---

[17] The classification of this account in the balance sheet is considered in Chapter 18.

[18] The concept of present value is described in an appendix to this chapter, pages 266-69. Pages 624-25 contain present value tables.

principal and interest payments.[19] Postponed income taxes differ from long-term bonds because the federal government specifies no interest on its "loan." Although this proposal is sound in theory, it represents a marked departure from present accounting for postponed income taxes. Also, determination of an appropriate discount rate would be difficult for many companies.[20]

Financial Value Of Accelerated Depreciation

If a company's operations are profitable and its tax rate remains constant, it eventually pays the same total income tax regardless of the depreciation method used. But the difference in *timing* of tax payments may produce a substantial benefit under an accelerated method. This benefit is the amount earned on the additional assets which are temporarily available until payment of the postponed tax is required. For example, assume a company expects to earn 10 per cent on such assets, and also assume the situation described for Table 2, page 257, involving the purchase of a single $1,000 asset. In this situation, use of the sum-of-the-years-digits method rather than the straight-line method produces a *permanent* benefit with a net *present value* of $43.23, as computed in Table 5.[21]

TABLE 5   FINANCIAL VALUE OF USING SUM-OF-THE-YEARS-DIGITS DEPRECIATION

(assuming conditions stated for Table 2 and tax postponements discounted at 10 per cent)

Year	Tax Postponement	Present Value Factor	Present Value of Tax Postponement
1	$40.91	.909	$37.19
2	31.82	.826	26.28
3	22.73	.751	17.07
4	13.64	.683	9.32
5	4.55	.621	2.83
6	− 4.55	.564	− 2.57
7	−13.64	.513	− 7.00
8	−22.73	.467	−10.61
9	−31.82	.424	−13.49
10	−40.91	.386	−15.79
Total			$43.23

[19] This is demonstrated in the appendix to this chapter describing the present value concept, pages 266–69.
[20] Some accountants argue that because the government charges no interest on its "loan," the appropriate discount rate is zero. At a zero discount rate there is no difference between a present and future amount. Therefore, the common practice of recording the full amount of the anticipated future tax payment is sound.
[21] In contrast to the amount of postponed income tax, which *is* recorded in the accounts, the estimated *permanent* benefit (the present value of the postponed tax, as computed in Tables 5, 6, and 7) is not specifically recognized in the accounts.

Assume the situation described for Table 3, page 258, in which a $1,000 asset is purchased *each* year. In this case, the *present value* of the *permanent* benefit from using sum-of-the-years-digits depreciation is $475.85, as computed in Table 6.

TABLE 6   FINANCIAL VALUE OF USING SUM-OF-THE-YEARS-DIGITS DEPRECIATION

(assuming conditions stated for Table 3 and tax postponements discounted at 10 per cent)

Year	Tax Postponement	Present Value Factor	Present Value of Tax Postponement
1	$ 40.91	.909	$ 37.19
2	72.73	.826	60.07
3	95.46	.751	71.69
4	109.10	.683	74.52
5	113.64	.621	70.57
6	109.10	.564	61.53
7	95.46	.513	48.97
8	72.73	.467	33.96
9	40.91	.424	17.35
10	none	.386	—
Total			$475.85

Finally, assume the situation described for Table 4, page 258, in which a $1,000 asset is purchased at the beginning of year 1, followed thereafter by 5 per cent annual increases in asset purchases. In this situation, the *present value* of the *permanent* benefit from using sum-of-the-years-digits rather than straight-line depreciation is $951.77, as shown in Table 7.

TABLE 7   FINANCIAL VALUE OF USING SUM-OF-THE-YEARS-DIGITS DEPRECIATION

(assuming conditions stated for Table 4 and tax postponements discounted at 10 per cent)

Year	Tax Postponement	Present Value Factor	Present Value of Tax Postponement
1	$ 40.91	.909	$ 37.19
2	74.78	.826	61.77
3	101.24	.751	76.03
4	119.64	.683	81.92
5	130.48	.621	81.03
6	132.46	.564	74.71
7	125.44	.513	64.35
8	108.99	.467	50.90
9	82.62	.424	35.03
10	45.80	.386	17.68
11 and thereafter			371.16*
Total			$951.77

*The present value of the tax postponements in all years from the 11th on is $371.16.

Future Problems

This chapter has stressed the complex relationship between tax policy and appropriate financial accounting policy for depreciation of plant and equipment. For a number of reasons, Congress has typically paid little attention to generally accepted accounting principles when establishing tax policy.

While the revision of Bulletin 44 partially resolved (except for regulated utilities) the controversy over accounting for accelerated depreciation, new accounting problems are likely to arise whenever the tax laws pertaining to plant and equipment are changed. For example, in the fall of 1962, Congress approved an investment credit, which provides for an immediate reduction in income taxes by as much as 7 per cent of the cost of eligible assets. The basis of such assets for subsequent tax depreciation is reduced by the amount of the credit—that is, to 93 per cent of the asset's cost if the maximum credit applies.

In December, 1962, the Accounting Principles Board recommended that the effect of the investment credit be spread over the useful lives of assets to which the credit applies.[22] Several members of the board, who favor reflecting a significant portion of the credit in current income, dissented from the majority's opinion. Many businessmen also support this treatment, particularly since the new, shorter guideline lives, if adopted for book purposes, will increase depreciation expense, thus reducing the reported earnings of many companies.

Appendix

PRESENT VALUE CONCEPTS

If $100.00 is invested today at 10 per cent interest, compounded annually, by the end of four years it would grow to $146.41, determined as follows:

	Annual Interest	Accumulated Investment
Invested today		$100.00
End of Year 1	$10.00	110.00
End of Year 2	11.00	121.00
End of Year 3	12.10	133.10
End of Year 4	13.31	146.41

The accumulated investment S at the end of n years is related to the original amount P by the formula,

---

[22] American Institute of Certified Public Accountants, Accounting Principles Board, "Accounting for the 'Investment Credit,'" *Opinions*, No. 2, December 1962. Reprinted in the *Journal of Accountancy*, Vol. 115, February 1963, pp. 70-72.

$$S = P(1 + i)^n,$$

where i is the interest rate per year and the accumulated investment is compounded annually. In the example, $P = \$100.00$, $i = .10$, $n = 4$ years, and

$$S = P(1 + i)^n$$
$$= \$100.00(1 + .10)^4$$
$$= \$100.00(1.4641)$$
$$= \$146.41.$$

In the above illustration, the initial amount P was known, whereas the future amount S was unknown. Frequently this situation is reversed and the amount of a future receipt or payment is known, but its *present value* is unknown. Given S, i, and n, the above formula can be used to find P. Since

$$S = P(1 + i)^n,$$

it follows that

$$P = \frac{S}{(1 + i)^n}.$$

From the above illustration it is evident that the *present value* of $\$146.41$ to be received or paid in four years, with interest at 10 per cent annually, is $\$100.00$.

The *present value* of $\$100.00$ to be received or paid four years hence, with interest at 10 per cent, is $\$68.30$, computed as follows:

$$P = \frac{S}{(1 + i)^n}$$
$$= \frac{\$100.00}{(1 + .10)^4}$$
$$= \frac{\$100.00}{1.4641}$$
$$= \$68.30$$

If $\$68.30$ is invested today at 10 per cent interest, with annual compounding it will grow as follows:

	Annual Interest	Accumulated Investment
Invested today		$68.30
End of Year 1	$6.83	75.13
End of Year 2	7.51	82.64
End of Year 3	8.27	90.91
End of Year 4	9.09	100.00

The calculation of the future value of a present amount is often called *compounding*, while the calculation of the present value of a future amount is generally called *discounting*. Similarly, the rate of interest in the latter situation is usually known as a *discount rate*. Table A, page 624, gives the present value of $1 to be received or paid in the future at various discount rates.

Frequently it is necessary to determine the present value of a *series* of annual receipts or payments. Table A can be used for this purpose. If the series consists of *uniform* payments or receipts over a period of years, however, it is easier and quicker to use Table B, page 625. Table B gives the Present Value of $1 Received or Paid Annually for N Years. Note that the factors in Table B are readily derived from Table A. For example, the present value of $1 *per year* for the next four years, discounted at 10 per cent, is $3.17, as found in Table B. It can also be computed from Table A by adding the present value factors for years 1 through 4; thus, .909 + .826 + .751 + .683 = 3.169.

It can be demonstrated that $1 per year for each of the next four years, discounted at 10 per cent, is the same as $3.17 today. Assume that $3.17 is invested today at 10 per cent interest and $1 is withdrawn from this investment each year beginning one year hence.

	Annual Interest	Annual Withdrawal	Balance of Investment
Invested today			$3.17
End of Year 1	$.32	$1.00	2.49
End of Year 2	.25	1.00	1.74
End of Year 3	.17	1.00	.91
End of Year 4	.09	1.00	—

PRESENT VALUE OF LONG-TERM BONDS

On pages 263–64 it was stated that long-term bonds are recorded in the books of the issuer at the *present value* of the future principal and interest payments. Assume $1,000,000 of ten-year, 5 per cent bonds are sold at par on December 31, 1963. Interest is payable annually on December 31. The issuer would record the sale of these bonds as follows:

Cash	$1,000,000	
Bonds Payable		$1,000,000

The *present value*—the value at the time the bonds are sold—is clearly $1,000,000. This must also be the present value of the future principal and interest payments, discounted at the bond interest rate (5 per cent). This can be proven as follows:

Present value of principal amount of $1,000,000 discounted for ten years at 5 per cent, using Table A (.614 × $1,000,000)	$ 614,000[1]
Present value of ten annual interest payments of $50,000 each, discounted at 5 per cent, using Table B (7.722 × $50,000)	386,000[1]
Total present value of principal and interest payments	$1,000,000

One year later, when nine years remain until maturity, the calculations are as follows:

Present value of principal amount of $1,000,000 discounted for nine years at 5 per cent, using Table A (.645 × $1,000,000)	$ 645,000[1]
Present value of nine annual interest payments of $50,000 each, discounted at 5 per cent, using Table B (7.108 × $50,000)	355,000[1]
Total present value of principal and interest payments	$1,000,000

At any time until maturity the present value of the principal payment and remaining interest payments will be $1,000,000.

REFERENCES

A number of the following references pertain to income tax allocation. They are listed here, rather than in Chapter 6, because they focus primarily on income tax problems of accelerated amortization and accelerated depreciation.

American Institute of Certified Public Accountants, Accounting Principles Board, "New Depreciation Guidelines and Rules," *Interpretive Opinions*, No. 1 (Nov. 1962). Reprinted in the *Journal of Accountancy*, 114 (Dec. 1962), 64–65.

_____, "Accounting for the 'Investment Credit,'" *Opinions*, No. 2 (Dec. 1962). Reprinted in the *Journal of Accountancy*, 115 (Feb. 1963), 70-72.

Bierman, Harold, Jr., "Depreciable Assets—Timing of Expense Recognition," *Accounting Review*, 36 (Oct. 1961), 613–18.

Bodenhorn, Diran, "An Economist Looks at Industrial Accounting and Depreciation," *Accounting Review*, 36 (Oct. 1961), 583–88.

Cerf, Alan Robert, "Tax Allocation and Railroad Accounting," *Journal of Accountancy*, 106 (Oct. 1958), 62–69.

Davidson, Sidney, "Accelerated Depreciation and the Allocation of Income Taxes," *Accounting Review*, 33 (Apr. 1958), 173–80.

---

[1] These amounts are rounded to the nearest thousand dollars. Based upon present value factors carried to eight decimal places, the amounts are: ten years—$613,913.25 + $386,086.75 = $1,000,000.00, nine years—$644,608.92 + $355,391.08 = $1,000,000.00. It is believed that three decimal places, as provided in Tables A and B, are adequate for the present value calculations required in this book.

Dixon, Robert L., "Decreasing Charge Depreciation—A Search for Logic," *Accounting Review*, 35 (Oct. 1960), 590–97.

Dohr, James L., (Correspondence), *Journal of Accountancy*, 107 (Feb. 1959), 19–20.

Drake, David F., "The Service Potential Concept and Inter-Period Tax Allocation," *Accounting Review*, 37 (Oct. 1962), 677–84.

Falls, Glenn, "The Financial Value of Early Tax Deductions for Depreciation," *Accounting Review*, 30 (Jul. 1955), 515–18.

Flewellen, W. C., Jr., "Concept of Depreciation Accounting Held by the United States Supreme Court," *Accounting Review*, 35 (Jul. 1960), 413–21.

Gellein, Oscar S., "The Decreasing-Charge Concept," *Journal of Accountancy*, 100 (Aug. 1955), 56–61.

Goldberg, Louis, "Concepts of Depreciation," *Accounting Review*, 30 (Jul. 1955), 468–84.

Graham, Willard J., "Allocation of Income Taxes," *Journal of Accountancy*, 107 (Jan. 1959), 57–67.

_____, "Income Tax Allocation," *Accounting Review*, 34 (Jan. 1959), 14–27.

Graichen, Raymond E., "Today's Depreciation Deduction," *Journal of Accountancy*, 104 (Dec. 1957), 27–33.

Harrison, William H., "Accounting Alternatives, and Their Consequences, in Handling Charges for Depreciation Under Certificates of Necessity," *Journal of Accountancy*, 94 (Dec. 1952), 716–18.

Harwood, Dale S., Jr., "Yet More on Tax Allocation," *Accounting Review*, 36 (Oct. 1961), 619–25.

Hasbrouck, H. C., "The Public Utility's View of Why the Net-Plant Balance-Sheet Concept Is Wrong," *Journal of Accountancy*, 94 (Oct. 1952), 460–67.

Hill, Thomas M., "Some Arguments Against the Inter-Period Allocation of Income Taxes," *Accounting Review*, 32 (Jul. 1957), 357–61.

"How Should Emergency Facilities Be Treated in Financial Statements?" (Editorial), *Journal of Accountancy*, 94 (Sept. 1952), 294–95.

Jacobsen, Lyle E., "Allocation and Attitudes," *Accounting Review*, 37 (Jul. 1962), 472–74.

Jaedicke, Robert K. and Carl L. Nelson, "The Allocation of Income Taxes—A Defense," *Accounting Review*, 35 (Apr. 1960), 278–81.

Johnson, Arnold W., "'More' on 'Income-Tax-Allocation' Accounting," *Accounting Review*, 36 (Jan. 1961), 75–83.

Lamberton, Ian K., "How Corporations Will Be Affected by the New Depreciation Policy," *The Controller*, 30 (Sept. 1962), 444 ff.

Leonard, W. G., "Accumulated Depreciation—Balance Sheet Presentation," *Accounting Review*, 34 (Oct. 1959), 572–73.

Lorig, Arthur N., "On the Logic of Decreasing Charge Depreciation," *Accounting Review*, 37 (Jan. 1962), 56–58.

Milroy, Robert R., Donald F. Istvan, and Ray M. Powell, "The Tax Depreciation Muddle," *Accounting Review*, 36 (Oct. 1961), 539–47.

Myers, John H., "Accelerated Amortization of Defense Facilities in Annual Reports," *Journal of Accountancy*, 99 (Feb. 1955), 52–55.

Norton, Paul T., Jr., "A Sequel to 'An Engineering Viewpoint on Depreciation Accounting,'" *Journal of Accountancy*, 105 (Jun. 1958), 35–40.

Reno, Edwin S., "The Rules on Depreciation," *Journal of Accountancy*, 101 (May 1956), 59–64.

Reynolds, Isaac N., "Selecting the Proper Depreciation Method," *Accounting Review*, 36 (Apr. 1961), 239–48.

Ross, Myron H., "Depreciation and User Cost," *Accounting Review*, 35 (Jul. 1960), 422–28.

Sands, J. E., "Deferred Tax Credits Are Liabilities," *Accounting Review*, 34 (Oct. 1959), 584–90.

Simon, Sidney I., "The Right Side of Accumulated Depreciation," *Accounting Review*, 34 (Jan. 1959), 97–105.

Singer, Frank A., "'Depreciation'—Better Left Unsaid," *Accounting Review*, 32 (Jul. 1957), 406–12.

Webster, Paul K., "Method of Accounting for Emergency Facilities May Be a Major Factor in Income Determination," *Journal of Accountancy*, 95 (May 1953), 580–87.

Woodward, P. D., "Depreciation—The Development of an Accounting Concept," *Accounting Review*, 31 (Jan. 1956), 71–76.

United Department Stores, Inc.

United was incorporated in 1919 when the former United Stores Corporation was reorganized. The company operates 18 department stores and 40 branch stores. The geographical distribution of total company sales is as follows:

Middle West	45 per cent
South	29 per cent
Far West	20 per cent
Pennsylvania	2 per cent
Canada	4 per cent

The majority of sales consists of women's, men's and children's ready-to-wear clothes and general dry goods.

The Internal Revenue Code of 1954 permitted use of the declining-balance or "sum-of-the-years-digits" depreciation methods for new assets with useful lives of three or more years acquired after December 31, 1953. In October, 1954, the AICPA's Committee on Accounting Procedure issued Accounting Research Bulletin No. 44, titled "Declining-balance Depreciation." In this bulletin the committee recognized the possible use of these accelerated methods in the corporate accounts as well as on the tax returns. ARB No. 44 stated in part:

> 2. The declining-balance method is one of those which meets the requirements of being "systematic and rational."[1] In those cases where the expected productivity or revenue-earning power of the asset is relatively greater during the earlier years of its life, or where maintenance charges tend to increase during the later years, the declining-balance method may well provide the most satisfactory allocation of cost. The conclusions of this bulletin also apply to other methods, including the "sum-of-the-years-digits" method, which produce substantially similar results.
>
> 3. When a change to the declining-balance method is made for general accounting purposes, and depreciation is a significant factor in the determination of net income, the change in method, including the effect thereof, should be disclosed in the year in which the change is made.

---

[1] *Accounting Terminology Bulletin* No. 1, paragraph 56.

272

In 1954, United increased *both* its book and tax depreciation charges to the fullest extent possible under the new Revenue Code. Use of accelerated depreciation increased the company's total depreciation charge for the fiscal year ended January 31, 1955 by about $70,000. Exhibits 1 and 2 give selected financial data related to the company's depreciation policy for the fiscal years ended January 31, 1951 through 1960.

The second paragraph of the auditors' opinion on the 1954–1955 fiscal-year financial statements read as follows:

In our opinion, the accompanying consolidated balance sheet and statements of consolidated profit and loss and earnings retained for use in the business present fairly the financial position of United Department Stores, Inc. and subsidiary companies as of January 31, 1955, and the results of their operations for the year then ended, and were prepared in conformity with generally accepted accounting principles applied on a basis consistent with that of the preceding year.

During the 1956–1957 fiscal year, United undertook the largest expansion program in any year of the company's history, investing $5,462,000 for new stores; $1,579,000 for expanding the size of existing stores; and $2,836,000 for modernizing existing stores, air-conditioning two major stores, and for new fixtures and other improvements.

In its annual report for the fiscal year ended January 31, 1959, management commented on "cash throw-off" as follows:

It is interesting to note that the so-called cash throw-off of our company has been increasing rapidly in recent years. By "cash throw-off" we mean net profit plus depreciation. Depreciation is of course a "non-cash" item. The increased spending for capital assets together with the use of accelerated depreciation and our policy of taking depreciation at as fast a rate as is proper—has pushed up the depreciation charges by about one million dollars per year in the span of the last five years.

Below are given the figures referred to, for the last five years:

Year Ended	Net Profit	Depreciation	Total Cash Throw-Off
January 31, 1959	$4,219,000	$2,706,000	$6,925,000
January 31, 1958	3,996,000	2,388,000	6,384,000
January 31, 1957	4,027,000	1,973,000	6,000,000
January 31, 1956	3,917,000	1,748,000	5,665,000
January 31, 1955	3,551,000	1,617,000	5,168,000

The effect on reported net profit and profit per share of using accelerated depreciation on the books, as well as on the tax return, was of great concern to management. In late 1959, it became apparent that profit per share would be about 22 cents less for the fiscal year ending January 31, 1960 than if accelerated depreciation had not been used in the accounts. Exhibit 3 shows net profit per share and the impact thereon of using accelerated depreciation on the books.

The ratio of pre-tax profit to sales, frequently used when comparing the profitability of several department stores, was also adversely affected by use of accelerated depreciation on the books (See Exhibit 4). Prior to the close of the 1959–1960 fiscal year, management decided to discontinue the use of accelerated depreciation for book purposes, while continuing its use for tax purposes. In recognition of the loss of future tax deductibility of the excess of accelerated depreciation over straight-line depreciation, the company established an account, "Deferred Federal Income Taxes," classified between long-term debt and stockholders' equity, to which $330,000 was credited.

United's management gave the following reasons for the change to straight-line depreciation:

Profit before income taxes amounted to $10,375,430. This was $1,666,369 higher than the year before. The net profit at $4,985,430 was $766,369 higher than the preceding year.

The profit per share this year was increased by about 22 cents per share by a change in the handling of depreciation. The depreciation charged in the accounts this year is on the so-called "straight-line" basis. In prior years, the depreciation reflected in the operations was what is known as "accelerated" depreciation. The company changed its practice on this mainly because it is becoming increasingly difficult to make fair comparisons between our results and the results of other companies in our industry. Practically all of the leading department store companies use straight-line depreciation in their reports. Our company has been using accelerated depreciation since 1954. The resulting difference in per share earnings has grown wider each year— meaning our profit per share earnings were lowered by use of accelerated depreciation by approximately the following amounts: 2 cents in 1954, 6 cents in 1955, 8 cents in the next year, then 14 cents, and then 18 cents for the year ended January 31, 1959. Had we not changed, the difference would have been about 22 cents for the year ended January 31, 1960. Although we have pointed out this difference in each annual report, management has concluded the amount involved has reached the point where it is material. Many people forget or ignore the "explanation" and merely remember or consider the reported profit. Accordingly, to make sure no one is misled, we have changed the method. (No change has been made in handling depreciation in tax returns. This change has no effect of any sort on the taxes we pay.) No retroactive change in depreciation has been made prior to February 1, 1959—meaning the year ended January 31, 1960 has been changed as outlined above, but no change has been made in depreciation of prior years.

There was an increase in earnings of about 28 cents per share, apart from the depreciation change. The sales increase of about $10,000,000 was, of course, the main factor in the increased profit. Our gross margin was up slightly over a year ago, but the expense percentage crept up a small fraction also. Markdowns were even with a year ago. The pre-tax profit per cent to sales was 6.2 per cent compared with 5.5 per cent a year ago.

Elsewhere in the 1959–1960 annual report, management made the following comment:

The cash throw-off of our company has been increasing rapidly in recent years. By "cash throw-off" we mean profit plus depreciation—and plus (in the latest year) the deferred federal income tax relative to "accelerated" depreciation. This deferred tax for the year just closed amounted to $330,000.

To clarify this reference to deferred federal income tax—earlier in this report we explained that the books of the company reflect "straight-line" depreciation. Our federal income tax returns are filed with "accelerated" depreciation deducted. The result is to cut down the federal income tax payable now, because of the larger "accelerated" depreciation deduction. Our auditors have advised us that generally accepted accounting practice is to set aside this tax reduction in a deferred reserve (and not take it into current income)— on the theory that in some future year, the point will be reached where the depreciation per tax return will be less than per books—and additional taxes will be paid. This deferred tax reserve is set aside to cover that situation. All indications are that in our company it will be a considerable number of years into the future, before we reach the point of less depreciation in books than in tax returns.

United received an unqualified opinion on its financial statements for the fiscal year ended January 31, 1960. A note to these statements contained the following information:

With respect to assets which had been depreciated for both book and tax purposes under accelerated methods, the company, effective February 1, 1959, reverted to the use of straight-line depreciation for book purposes. The reduction of $330,000 in federal income taxes currently payable, resulting from the higher depreciation for tax purposes, has been deferred to provide for income taxes payable in future years when book depreciation will exceed the amounts allowable for tax purposes. While the effect that this change in depreciation method had on net profit (after taxes and increases in other charges based on income) cannot be precisely determined, it is estimated that the net profit was increased by approximately $325,000.

EXHIBIT 1

United Department Stores, Inc.
Selected Data from Statement of Profit and Loss
for the Years 1951 through 1960
(000 omitted)

Year Ended January 31	Net Sales	Depreciation Expense	Excess of Accelerated Depreciation Over Straight-line Depreciation	Profit Before Income Taxes	Net Profit After Income Taxes
1951	$125,427	$1,359	—	$9,397	$5,107
1952	124,700	1,351	—	6,442	3,120
1953	128,604	1,454	—	7,081	3,461
1954	130,883	1,515	—	6,933	3,523
1955	130,366	1,617[1]	$ 70[1]	6,971	3,551
1956	138,786	1,748	187	8,037	3,917
1957	148,773	1,973	246	8,087	4,027
1958	153,994	2,388	401	8,178	3,996
1959	157,916	2,706	533	8,709	4,219
1960	167,800	3,045[2]	655[2]	9,720[2]	4,660[2]

[1] Accelerated depreciation adopted during 1954–1955 fiscal year for *both* tax and book purposes.

[2] Assuming use of accelerated depreciation had been continued for book purposes through the 1959–1960 fiscal year.

EXHIBIT 2

United Department Stores, Inc.
Selected Balance Sheet Data for the Years 1951 through 1960
(000 omitted)

As of January 31	Buildings[1]	Accrued Depreciation on Buildings	Store Fixtures	Accrued Depreciation on Store Fixtures
1951	$14,256	$4,876	$7,124	$2,625
1952	17,095	5,357	7,662	2,790
1953	18,058	6,020	8,107	3,075
1954	15,581	6,704	8,526	3,447
1955	16,876	7,193	8,797	3,782
1956	18,555	6,037	9,216	4,238
1957	24,796	6,607	10,358	4,296
1958	28,951	7,601	11,451	4,791
1959	32,581	8,857	12,742	5,545
1960	33,251	10,143	13,989	6,169

[1] Includes land for the period 1951 through 1953.

EXHIBIT 3

United Department Stores, Inc.
Profit per Share and Decrease in Profit per Share
Resulting from Use of Accelerated Depreciation
Years Ended January 31, 1955 through January 31, 1960

Year Ended January 31	Profit per Share Using Accelerated Depreciation	Decrease in Profit per Share Resulting from Use of Accelerated Depreciation
1955	$2.45[1]	$.02
1956	2.70	.06
1957	2.76	.08
1958	2.73	.14
1959	2.88	.18
1960	3.16[2]	.22

[1] Accelerated depreciation adopted during 1954–1955 fiscal year for *both* tax and book purposes.

[2] Profit per share for 1959–1960 fiscal year if accelerated depreciation had been continued for book purposes. Actual profit reported for 1960 was $3.38 per share.

EXHIBIT 4

United Department Stores, Inc.
Effect on Ratio of Pre-tax Profit to Sales of Using
Accelerated Depreciation Instead of Straight-line Depreciation
Years Ended January 31, 1955 through January 31, 1960

Year Ended January 31	Ratio of Pre-tax Profit to Sales Using Straight-line Depreciation	Ratio of Pre-tax Profit to Sales Using Accelerated Depreciation	Decrease in Ratio Resulting from Use of Accelerated Depreciation
1955	5.40%	5.35%[1]	.05
1956	5.93	5.79	.14
1957	5.60	5.44	.16
1958	5.57	5.31	.26
1959	5.85	5.51	.34
1960	6.18	5.79[2]	.39[2]

[1] Accelerated depreciation adopted during 1954–1955 fiscal year for *both* tax and book purposes.

[2] Assuming use of accelerated depreciation had been continued for book purposes through the 1959–1960 fiscal year.

QUESTIONS:

1. Assuming that United's management initially adopted accelerated depreciation for book as well as for tax purposes because it was considered a more realistic method of cost allocation, do you approve of the switch back to straight-line depreciation for book purposes in the 1959–1960 fiscal year? Do you believe it is important for United to determine its profit per share on an accounting basis comparable to that used by other department stores? Explain.

2. Do you think generally accepted accounting practice should conform to various treatments permitted or required under the tax code? If accelerated depreciation does produce a more realistic pattern of cost allocation for many assets, do you believe the Treasury should require its use on the taxpayer's books when it is adopted for tax purposes?

3. Give profit per share retroactive to 1955 assuming the company had used straight-line depreciation. Compute the percentage by which reported earnings were reduced each year as a result of using accelerated depreciation for book as well as tax purposes. By what percentage were reported earnings increased in the 1959–1960 fiscal year as a result of abandoning accelerated depreciation for book purposes?

4. Assume that United's management had wanted to make the change retroactive to 1955. Would you agree with such a treatment? What correcting entry would be necessary? How would the correction be disclosed in the financial statements?

5. Do you agree with management's statements that:
   (a) "The amount involved has reached the point where it is material;"
   (b) "Many people forget or ignore the 'explanation' and merely remember or consider the reported profit;"
   (c) "To make sure no one is misled, we have changed the method"?

6. Examine critically and comment on management's statement that "the [1959–1960] pre-tax profit per cent to sales was 6.2 per cent compared with 5.5 per cent a year ago."

7. Management stated in the 1959–1960 annual report that the change in depreciation policy had "no effect of any sort on the taxes we pay." Do you agree with this statement? Explain.

8. As a result of returning to straight-line depreciation for book purposes, what balance-sheet accounts at January 31, 1960 were different, and by how much, from what they would have been had accelerated depreciation been continued on the books?

9. Do you agree with the auditors' position in 1955 and 1960? Explain.

10. Why is the amount of deferred taxes ($330,000) included in "cash throwoff" for 1959–1960? What is the significance of "cash throw-off"? Why do you suppose this figure was emphasized by United?

11. Comment on the statement that "generally accepted accounting practice is to set aside this tax reduction in a deferred reserve...."

12. Management stated, "It will be a considerable number of years... before we reach the point of less depreciation in books than in tax returns." Under what conditions will this statement be true? If the deferred tax account balance is unlikely to be reduced for many years, what assumptions and estimates are involved in establishing the annual addition to this account?

13. Some accountants propose that the deferred tax account be shown at some discounted present value. Ignoring the problems involved in calculating an appropriate dollar amount, do you agree with this proposal? Explain. Consider carefully how we usually account for long-term debt on which periodic interest is payable.

General Public Utilities Corporation

General Public Utilities, a holding company incorporated in 1906, operates through the following subsidiaries: Pennsylvania Electric Company, Metropolitan Edison Company, Jersey Central Power & Light Company, and New Jersey Power & Light Company. A former subsidiary, Manila Electric Company, was sold to Philippine interests in January, 1962.

The subsidiaries' depreciation charges are based on engineering studies which allocate the original cost of depreciable assets, on a straight-line basis, over the estimated service lives.

In 1956, retroactive to 1954, the domestic subsidiaries adopted the "sum-of-the-years-digits" method of computing depreciation for tax purposes. In its accounts, the corporation did not recognize the loss of future tax deductions from the use of accelerated depreciation on the tax return while using straight-line depreciation in the corporate accounts. The resulting tax reduction "flowed through" to increase reported net income. Exhibit 1 shows operating revenues, depreciation expense, annual and cumulative federal income tax reduction resulting from the use of accelerated depreciation for tax purposes, and reported net income for the years 1954 through 1961.

A note to the 1961 financial statements commented on the tax reductions as follows:

> The domestic subsidiaries are using accelerated depreciation for income tax purposes only. As a result thereof the estimated liabilities for income taxes through December 31, 1961 have been reduced by an aggregate of $23,097,379 of which $5,552,355 and $5,060,887 apply to 1961 and 1960, respectively. In conformity with the Pennsylvania and New Jersey regulatory commissions' rate-making policies and the basic accounting concept of matching of costs and revenues, the subsidiaries account for such income tax effect by reflecting in their accounts only the estimated income taxes actually payable for the period.

In 1954, Pennsylvania Electric Company was granted Certificates of Necessity allowing it to amortize, on a straight-line

basis, approximately $21,500,000 of property over a 60-month period
for federal income tax purposes. Since the estimated useful life of
this property was considerably more than five years, a deferred tax
account was established, classified outside of the stockholders' equity
section "in accordance with the requirements of the Federal Power
Commission." Amortization was completed for tax purposes in 1960.
During 1960 and 1961, the corporation debited the deferred tax account
and credited income tax expense by approximately $373,000 each
year. This amount was 52 per cent of the annual *book* depreciation
applicable to the cost of properties previously amortized over five
years for tax purposes under Certificates of Necessity.

EXHIBIT 1

General Public Utilities Corporation
Selected Consolidated Financial Data for the Years 1954–1961
(000 omitted)

	Operating Revenues	Depreciation Expense[1]	Annual Federal Tax Reduction[2]	Cumulative Federal Tax Reduction[2]	Reported Net Income
1954	$162,875	$15,652	$ 303	$ 303	$23,458
1955	174,137	17,587	971	1,274	26,253
1956	188,671	18,289	1,570	2,844	29,637
1957	202,446	18,647	2,192	5,036	33,264
1958	213,171	19,735	3,186	8,222	33,436
1959	230,715	22,291	4,262	12,484	35,827
1960	204,813[3]	21,294[3]	5,061	17,545	36,773[3]
1961	213,247	22,457	5,552	23,097	36,762

[1] As recorded on the books.
[2] Resulting from use of sum-of-the-years-digits depreciation by domestic subsidiaries
for income tax purposes.
[3] Excluding the Philippine subsidiary in 1960 and 1961.

QUESTIONS:

1. Was the accounting treatment of the income tax effect of using accelerated
   depreciation for tax purposes and straight-line depreciation for book purposes in accordance with "the basic accounting concept of matching of
   costs and revenues," as stated by the corporation? Explain.
2. Contrast General Public Utilities' accounting treatment for accelerated
   depreciation with that for amortization of assets covered by Certificates
   of Necessity. Is there any justification for a different treatment of the
   two? Explain.
3. As an auditor, what kind of an opinion would you give on the 1961
   financial statements?
4. What was the approximate amount of annual depreciation recorded *on
   the books* for the $21,500,000 of property covered by Certificates of Necessity?
   What was the estimated useful life of this property?
5. Assume (a) General Public Utilities expected to earn in the future an

average rate of return of 7 per cent on its total assets; (b) it anticipated a future corporate income tax rate of 52 per cent; (c) the 60-month amortization period began in February, 1954, and ended in January, 1959; and (d) corporate income taxes for any given year are payable early in the following year. As of February 1, 1954, what was the approximate present value of the tax deferrals resulting from tax amortization over 60 months instead of straight-line depreciation over the estimated useful life calculated in question 4? Interpret the meaning of your present value calculations.

Affiliated Department Stores

Affiliated operates large department stores in Boston, New York, Philadelphia, Buffalo, and Cleveland. Total sales in 1944 were $167 million.

Prior to the fiscal year beginning February 1, 1932, the company recorded all fixed assets at cost. Annual depreciation charges, based on asset cost less estimated salvage value, were determined by the straight-line method. On February 1, 1932, the Board of Directors passed the following resolution:

Furniture, fixtures, and equipment will be carried in the company's accounts at 1932 book value of $4,705,122. For all periods ending after January 31, 1932, operations will be charged with the cost of additions and replacements of these assets less any salvage value obtained from retirements. The company will continue to carry land, buildings, and leaseholds at cost less accumulated depreciation.

In the annual report for the fiscal year ended January 31, 1933, the furniture, fixtures, and equipment account was presented as follows:

Furniture, fixtures, and equipment ($4,833,531 on
the basis of cost less depreciation) $4,705,122

The *net* cost of additions to the furniture, fixtures, and equipment account of $158,946 was charged to operations and presented in the income statement just below "Depreciation of buildings and leaseholds" as follows:

Net cost of additions to furniture,
fixtures, and equipment $158,946

The auditors' statement contained the following comment:

In our opinion, the accompanying consolidated balance sheet and related statement of profit and loss present fairly the consolidated financial position of Affiliated Department Stores and subsidiary companies at January 31, 1933 and the consolidated results of their operations for the year then ended, in conformity with generally accepted accounting principles, applied on a basis consistent with that of the preceding year except for the change in accounting for depreciation, which we approve . . . .

Between 1933 and 1943, the company continued to charge operations with the net cost of additions of furniture, fixtures, and equipment. The furniture, fixtures, and equipment account was maintained at the balance established February 1, 1932 with parenthetical disclosure of the current book value of the assets based on cost less depreciation ($4,833,531 at January 31, 1933, as shown above).

The independent auditors issued unqualified opinions on the company's financial statements from 1934 through 1939. In 1940, the auditor's report contained the following explanation:

Furniture, fixtures, and equipment are stated in the balance sheet at a net amount of $4,705,122 and no deductions have been made in the income account for depreciation with respect thereto, but the net cost of additions for the year has been charged against income.

In our opinion, subject to the exception stated in the preceding paragraph relating to the accounting procedure for certain fixed assets, the accompanying consolidated balance sheet and related consolidated statements of income and surplus present fairly the consolidated financial position of Affiliated Department Stores on January 31, 1940 . . . .

The auditors continued to take exception to the depreciation method and included the same paragraph in their reports for the years ended January 31, 1941, 1942, and 1943. (The company had the same auditors between 1932 and 1946.) Selected financial data for the fiscal years ended January 31, 1933 through 1943, are given in Exhibit 1.

Beginning February 1, 1943, the company returned to the customary "reserve" method of recording depreciation. At that time, the cost of furniture, fixtures, and equipment was determined to be $11,690,100. If appropriate periodic debits and credits had been made, the reserve for depreciation would have been $6,632,843 and book value, $5,057,257. These assets were carried on the books at the 1932 book value of $4,705,122.

EXHIBIT 1

Affiliated Department Stores
Selected Data, 1933–1943

Fiscal Years Ended January 31	Net Addition of Furniture, Fixtures, and Equipment Charged to Profit and Loss	Annual Amount of Depreciation Which Would Have Been Charged to Profit and Loss	Reported Profit
1933	$ 158,946	$ 691,773	$ 789,487
1934	144,375	654,628	2,905,365
1935	316,678	616,685	3,301,614
1936	438,767	585,910	3,463,154
1937	615,130	586,650	5,070,458
1938	525,408	583,916	4,917,771
1939	320,595	611,789	3,809,877
1940	1,007,987	615,840	4,402,895
1941	537,209	794,660	5,046,799
1942	987,330	807,557	4,621,788
1943	1,024,845	831,091	4,503,951
Total	$6,077,270	$7,380,499	$42,833,159

QUESTIONS:

1. When the company resumed the "reserve" method of depreciation accounting on February 1, 1943, the following entry was made to restate the accounts:

Furniture, Fixtures, and Equipment	$6,984,978	
Reserve for Depreciation		$6,632,843
Retained Earnings		352,135

The company noted that this entry restated the Furniture, Fixtures, and Equipment account and the Reserve for Depreciation and Retained Earnings accounts as though the "reserve" method had been used between 1933 and 1943. Reconcile this entry (which results in a credit to Retained Earnings) with the apparent overstatement of income of $1,303,229 ($7,380,499 minus $6,077,270) as a result of using the replacement method. You may assume that the company's entry is correct and you may ignore any tax considerations.

2. Comment on the appropriateness of the replacement cost method of depreciation. What are the objections to this method? What arguments are there in support of this method?

3. What reasons might the company have had for changing depreciation methods for the year ending January 31, 1933? For the year ending January 31, 1944?

4. What criticisms do you have of the company's terminology?

5. How might replacement cost depreciation influence the national economy if it were allowed for federal income tax purposes?

Swift & Company (B)[1]

In 1955, retroactive to January 1, 1954, Swift adopted, for income tax purposes only, the "Sum-of-the-Years-Digits" depreciation method (permitted under the 1954 Internal Revenue Code) for computing depreciation on all additions of new depreciable property after January 1, 1954. In October, 1954, the AICPA's Committee on Accounting Procedure stated in Accounting Research Bulletin No. 44, "Declining-balance Depreciation," that this accelerated method (and other accelerated methods) met the requirement of being "systematic and rational." The committee agreed that when they were adopted for general accounting purposes appropriate disclosure of the change should be made, whenever depreciation was a significant factor in determining net income.

When accelerated depreciation was adopted for tax purposes only, the committee stated "that, in the ordinary situation, deferred income taxes need not be recognized in the accounts unless it is reasonably certain that the reduction in taxes during the earlier years of use of the declining-balance method for tax purposes is merely a deferment of income taxes until a relatively few years later, and then only if the amounts are clearly material."

The adoption of accelerated depreciation reduced Swift's income taxes by $1,106,853 for the 1955 fiscal year and $368,668 for the ten months ended October 30, 1954. The latter amount was included in Prior Years' Adjustments in the 1955 Statement of Consolidated Income. (See Exhibit 1.) The total amount of Prior Years' Adjustments, $1,981,000, also reflects an adjustment of property accounts and depreciation reserves for certain expenditures charged to expense in prior years, which were later required to be capitalized for income tax purposes.

In 1956, use of accelerated depreciation reduced federal income taxes by $1,959,559. Prior Years' Adjustments of $550,000 in

---

[1] Refer to Swift & Company (A) on page 236 for company history.

1956 represent a reversal of excess provisions for federal income taxes made in prior years.

Effective August 1, 1958, the company adopted the policy of providing for deferred income taxes equal to the reduction in federal income taxes resulting from use of the "Sum-of-the-Years-Digits" method for tax purposes only. In the 1958 fiscal year, federal income tax payments were reduced by approximately $1,600,000, including $447,597 for the period August 1 to November 1, 1958. Comparable amounts were $2,775,000 for 1957 and $1,876,115 for 1959. At the close of the 1958 fiscal year, $447,597 was credited to accumulated depreciation. On the income statement, this amount was shown separately among the expenses as "Deferred Federal income taxes" between "Federal income taxes" and "Other income taxes." The balance sheet at the close of the 1959 fiscal year disclosed $2,323,712 as "Deferred Income Taxes," shown between "Long Term Debt" and "Capital Stock and Accumulated Earnings." (The credit made in 1958 to accumulated depreciation had been transferred to "Deferred Income Taxes.")

Net income reported in 1955 and 1956 is given in Exhibit 1. In 1954, the company reported $19,051,000. In 1957 and 1958, net income was $13,538,000 and $10,048,000, respectively.

The revision of Accounting Research Bulletin No. 44, issued in July, 1958, states that the declining-balance method may be adopted for income tax purposes, even though other appropriate methods are used for financial accounting purposes. In such cases, accounting recognition should usually be given to deferred income taxes if the amounts are material. In accordance with paragraph 5 of this revised bulletin, it is considered appropriate under some circumstances to record increased depreciation instead of creating a deferred tax account.

EXHIBIT 1

Swift & Company (B)
Consolidated Income Statements for the 52 Weeks
Ended October 27, 1956 and October 29, 1955
(000 omitted)

	52 Weeks Ended	
	October 27, 1956	October 29, 1955
Sales, including service revenues	$2,429,302	$2,404,123
Dividends from foreign subsidiaries, not consolidated	1,132	1,690
Supplemental distribution from mutual casualty company	1,166	1,051
Interest and other dividends	1,577	1,290
Miscellaneous, net	370	441
Total	$2,433,547	$2,408,595
Less:		
Cost of sales and services, including cost of raw materials, provision for inventory replacements, and processing expenses	$2,204,055	$2,174,351
Selling and administrative expenses	153,021	145,612
Depreciation	20,931	19,760
Taxes (other than income taxes)	16,524	16,035
Contributions to Pension Trust	13,573	10,664
Interest charges	3,155	1,802
Federal income taxes	7,209	17,243
Other income taxes	1,617	2,216
Prior years' adjustments	(550)	(1,981)
Total	$2,419,535	$2,385,702
Net Income for the Year	$ 14,012	$ 22,893

QUESTIONS:

1. Why do you suppose the Committee on Accounting Procedure, in its 1954 bulletin, did not recommend the recognition of deferred income taxes when accelerated depreciation was adopted for income tax purposes only?

2. How do you explain the 1958 position of the committee? Explain with reference to Swift & Co., giving the percentage increase in net income caused by not recognizing deferred taxes for the fiscal years 1954 through 1958.

3. Compare the merits of recognizing deferred taxes by (a) a credit to "Deferred Income Taxes," or (b) a credit to "Accumulated Depreciation." What is the appropriate account to debit with each method? Why do you suppose Swift changed from (b) to (a) in 1959?

Ormet Corporation

Ormet, incorporated in 1956, is jointly owned by Olin Mathieson Chemical Corporation and Revere Copper and Brass, Inc., each holding 50 per cent ($8,000,000) of its outstanding common stock. Ormet operates an alumina plant in Louisiana, and an aluminum smelter at Clarington, Ohio, with an annual capacity of 180,000 tons of primary aluminum.

To finance its various facilities, Ormet borrowed $100,000,000 from 10 banks, evidenced by $4\frac{1}{4}$ per cent promissory notes due in annual installments of $20,000,000 beginning March 31, 1959. It also sold to institutional investors $100,000,000 of $4\frac{1}{2}$ per cent first mortgage bonds, of which $6,000,000 mature each year from 1964 through 1973 and $8,000,000 each year from 1974 through 1978.

As long as the bank loan is outstanding, Olin Mathieson has the option to increase its investment in Ormet to 66 per cent by purchase of 32 per cent of Revere's investment at the original cost to Revere.

Ormet started production of aluminum pig in the middle of 1958. Olin Mathieson agreed to purchase 66 per cent, and Revere 34 per cent, of Ormet's entire annual production of primary aluminum at Ormet's cost of production. In determining Ormet's cost of production, it was agreed that annual depreciation charges would include an amount in excess of normal depreciation, so that Ormet's total depreciation would be sufficient to meet its current and future debt maturities. Based on such maturities, Olin Mathieson's share of Ormet's annual "depreciation" charge would be as follows, until the $200,000,000 of debt, held by outside creditors, had been retired:

1959 through 1963	$13,200,000
1964 through 1973	3,960,000
1974 through 1978	5,280,000

In addition, the two companies agreed to provide, in equal amounts, funds required to complete the project and, in the

288

ratio 66 to 34, funds required for replacement of capital equipment and for working capital. At November 30, 1961, the two owners held a total of $25,563,000 of 4½ per cent, 25-year subordinated notes. (See Exhibit 1.)

Olin Mathieson operates its own facilities, using the primary aluminum supplied by Ormet, to produce extrusions, sheet and plate, wire, cable and other aluminum products.

In Olin Mathieson's 1959 and 1960 annual reports to stockholders, it was disclosed that losses from the company's own aluminum operations amounted to 38¢ and 9¢ per share, respectively. Under the heading "Aluminum" the following information was given:

1959:
The most important event of the year was the completion of our entry into the aluminum industry as the nation's fourth largest fully-integrated producer. This was accomplished despite demoralized markets, inadequate prices, and our own start-up problems, which made our initial operating costs abnormally high.

By the year-end, however, costs began to fall into a more normal pattern, and both quality and quantity showed satisfactory improvement. Concurrently, demand and prices headed onto firmer ground. As a result of these developments, and given reasonable business conditions, we can look forward to 1960 as our first profitable year in aluminum.

1960:
Our aluminum operations reached the break-even point in the last quarter of the year, despite absorbing heavy charges for accelerated amortization. This was accomplished in the face of generally poor price conditions throughout the industry.

Losses from aluminum operations during the year were reduced from 38¢ per share in 1959 to 9¢ per share in 1960, of which 7¢ was lost during the first six months. Included in the cost of aluminum, billed by our Ormet affiliate in 1960, were charges for excess depreciation of $3,443,000 after taxes, or 26¢ per Olin share. This, together with regular depreciation, allows repayment of bank loans at the rate of $20,000,000 per year. These loans, originally $100,000,000, are now down to $60,000,000. When payment of these loans is completed in 1963, savings in amortization and interest will increase earnings about 40¢ per Olin share from today's level. Were it not for these special charges, Olin aluminum would have operated profitably in 1960.

Ormet had received Certificates of Necessity permitting amortization of a portion of its plant over 60 months for tax purposes.

Exhibit 1 shows Ormet's condensed balance sheets as of November 30, 1961, 1960 and 1959.

EXHIBIT 1

Ormet Corporation
Condensed Balance Sheets as of November 30, 1961, 1960 and 1959
(000 omitted)

	1961	1960	1959
ASSETS:			
Current Assets:			
Cash	$ 1,019	$ 2,301	$ 1,454
Accounts Receivable	10,837	8,994	10,842
Inventories	15,410	16,628	17,918
Total Current Assets	$ 27,266	$ 27,923	$ 30,214
Property, Plant and Equipment, net	155,545	176,528	195,476
Deferred Expenses	3,602	3,832	3,903
	$186,413	$208,283	$229,593
LIABILITIES AND STOCKHOLDERS' EQUITY:			
Current Liabilities:			
Advances, Accounts Payable and Accrued Expenses	$ 4,850	$ 4,916	$ 6,114
Current Installments—long-term debt	20,000	20,000	20,000
Total Current Liabilities	$ 24,850	$ 24,916	$ 26,114
Long-term Debt	120,000	140,000	160,000
Subordinated Long-term Debt due Stockholders	25,563	27,367	27,479
Common Stock	16,000	16,000	16,000
	$186,413	$208,283	$229,593

QUESTIONS:

1. What is the relationship, if any, between the amount of a company's depreciation charges and its ability to retire debt?
2. What accounting principles are violated by Ormet's depreciation policy? Since Ormet has no public stockholders, can you see any objection to this violation of generally accepted accounting principles?
3. Do you believe Olin Mathieson's auditors should have taken exception to its financial statements because of Ormet's depreciation policies?
4. What was the approximate amount of excess depreciation included in Ormet's charges in 1960 to Olin Mathieson and to Revere?
5. What amount of depreciation has Ormet apparently included in its own accounts?
6. From a tax standpoint, what are the advantages to Olin Mathieson and Revere of the agreement with Ormet?

Marquette Cement Manufacturing Company

Marquette was incorporated in Illinois in 1902. It owns plants in Illinois, Ohio, Iowa, Wisconsin, Missouri, Mississippi, Tennessee, Georgia, New York, Pennsylvania and Maryland, and operates a river fleet of 2 towboats and 28 barges.

In 1957, Marquette began a large-scale plant modernization program expected to last several years. The following expenditures were made from 1957 through 1961:

1957	$3,191,700
1958	6,055,041
1959	6,456,528
1960	6,973,586
1961	6,812,528

The company follows the policy of capitalizing all expenditures for renewals and betterments and charges all expenditures for repair and maintenance directly to profit and loss. In 1959, as part of the modernization program was completed, Marquette stated that "fairly large amounts of plant assets will be abandoned from time to time." Since a write-off of "the values involved in a single year would mask the true operating results for that year and distort the year to year comparisons," management decided to amortize the cost of abandoned assets plus dismantling costs, less accrued depreciation and income tax savings, over a five-year period. The example below illustrates the procedure used for Marquette's Rockmart plant:

Gross value of abandoned plant assets	$2,222,335
Dismantling costs	149,849
	$2,372,184
Less accrued depreciation	606,359
	$1,765,825
Less income tax saving	918,229
Unamortized balance	$ 847,596
Annual amortization (to begin in 1960)	$ 169,519

In the 1960 annual report to stockholders, management made the following disclosure of "Unamortized Values of Abandoned Plant Assets:"

The method, established in 1959, of amortizing remaining values of plant assets abandoned because of large-scale modernization has been continued. Under this method the remaining values, after deducting income tax savings, are amortized over a five-year period starting when the replacements become fully operative. The purpose is to minimize the distortion which would take place in the year to year net income comparisons if the rather large amounts involved were fully charged off in the year in which they occurred. Changes in the account for the current year are shown in the following table:

Unamortized balance, January 1, 1960		$ 847,596
Additions in 1960:		
Cost of abandoned plant assets	$1,835,779	
Dismantling costs	100,770	
	$1,936,549	
Less accrued depreciation	1,063,858	
	$ 872,691	
Less income tax saving	453,799	
Unamortized balance	$ 418,892	418,892
		$1,266,488
Reductions in 1960—Portion amortized		253,298
Unamortized balance, December 31, 1960		$1,013,190
Amortization schedule—Year 1961		$ 253,298
1962		253,298
1963		253,297
1964		253,297
Total as above		$1,013,190

Exhibit 1 shows Marquette's income statements for 1960 and 1959.

EXHIBIT 1

Marquette Cement Manufacturing Company
Income Statements for the Years Ended December 31, 1960 and 1959

	1960	1959
Income		
Sales—products produced, less freight for delivering the products and charges for containers	$56,628,670	$57,422,526
Less discounts and allowances	1,498,398	1,572,977
	$55,130,272	$55,849,549
Receipts from water transportation operations	1,376,119	1,387,179
Miscellaneous receipts	532,984	1,000,394
	$57,039,375	$58,237,122
Expenses		
Production cost of products sold, including packing, package expenses, wear and tear and depletion	32,418,970	33,009,991
Cost of water transportation operations, including wear and tear	1,097,519	1,077,657
Expenses incident to miscellaneous receipts	201,081	655,379
Administrative, selling and general expense	4,858,992	4,583,286
Interest	607,613	640,425
Federal and state taxes on income	8,450,787	8,779,487
	$47,634,962	$48,746,225
Net Income	$ 9,404,413	$ 9,490,897

QUESTIONS:

1. Do you agree with Marquette's accounting treatment of losses from abandoning obsolete plants? What generally accepted accounting principles are involved? How else could you account for these losses? In comparison with alternative methods of accounting, was Marquette's net income materially increased by the accounting treatment used?
2. Do you believe the company's auditors should take exception to this accounting policy? Explain.

National Dairy Products Corporation

National Dairy, which was incorporated in 1923, is primarily engaged in processing and marketing dairy and other food products. Its Kraft Foods Division manufactures cheese, various salad products, margarines, a complete line of jellies and preserves and Kraft's macaroni and spaghetti dinners. The Sealtest Foods Division processes and distributes milk, cream, cottage cheese, buttermilk and ice cream.

The corporation uses the following rates in determining annual depreciation charges:

Buildings	$2\frac{1}{2}$-4%
Machinery and equipment	5-$7\frac{1}{2}$%
Trucks and passenger cars	10-20%
Furniture and fixtures	$6\frac{3}{8}$%
Cabinets, fountains and vending machines	10%
Cans, jackets, cases, etc.	25%

In 1954, the corporation adopted the declining-balance method of depreciation for tax purposes while continuing the straight-line method in the corporate accounts. The resulting reductions in federal income tax payments were divided into two parts: (1) tax reductions applicable to regularly-recurring additions and replacements of machinery and equipment, which were reflected as additional income, and (2) tax reductions applicable to additions in excess of regularly-recurring additions and replacements of machinery and equipment, and tax reductions attributable to buildings, both of which were included in "Provision for federal and Canadian taxes on income," classified, from 1954 through 1956, as a current liability on the balance sheet. Exhibit 1 shows selected financial data pertaining to National Dairy's depreciation policies for the years 1954 through 1961.

A note to the 1955 financial statements explained the adoption of declining-balance depreciation as follows:

The company, for income tax reporting only, has adopted the declining-balance method of computing depreciation (involving increased rates of depreciation) on the major classes of its buildings, machinery and equipment in the United States acquired after December 31, 1953, as permitted by the U.S. Internal Revenue Code of 1954, and on all such assets in Canada whenever acquired as permitted under Canadian tax laws. For all other purposes, including the financial statements, the straight-line method is being continued. The reduction in federal and Canadian income taxes for the year 1955 arising from the additional deduction for depreciation so allowable for income tax reporting is estimated to be $2,850,000. Of this amount, $2,500,000, representing the tax reduction applicable to regularly-recurring additions and replacements of machinery and equipment, as estimated by the management, is reflected as an addition to 1955 earnings through a reduction in the provision for 1955 federal and Canadian taxes on income. The balance of $350,000 of such tax reduction, which is attributable to additional depreciation for tax reporting on machinery and equipment additions in excess of regularly-recurring replacements, and on buildings, has been deferred and is included in the "Provision for federal and Canadian taxes on income" in the accompanying balance sheet.

As of July 1, 1958, National Dairy changed its depreciation accounting policy to conform to the newly-issued Accounting Research Bulletin No. 44 (Revised). The change was explained as follows in the 1958 annual report to stockholders:

The company follows the practice, for income tax reporting only, of using the declining-balance method of computing depreciation (involving increased rates of depreciation) on the major classes of its buildings, machinery and equipment acquired after 1953 in the United States and on all such assets in Canada. For all other purposes, including the financial statements, the straight-line method has been continued. Prior to July 1, 1958, the greater part of the reduction in income tax payments resulting from the additional depreciation deductions has been reflected as additional earnings for the respective years. Effective July 1, 1958, in order to follow the treatment for such tax reductions prescribed by the American Institute of Certified Public Accountants in a revised bulletin dated July, 1958, the company adopted the policy of deferring all tax reductions attributable to declining-balance depreciation and eliminating all such amounts from earnings. Such tax reduction included in earnings amounted to $1,430,000 for the six months ended June 30, 1958, and $3,069,000 for the year ended December 31, 1957. The amounts deferred are included in "Deferred Federal and Canadian Taxes on Income" in the accompanying balance sheets.

EXHIBIT 1

National Dairy Products Corporation
Selected Financial Data for the Years 1954 through 1961
(000 omitted)

	Gross Income	Depreciation Expense	Tax Reduction Applicable to Regularly Recurring Additions and Replacements	Tax Reduction Applicable to Other(Non-recurring) Additions and Replacements
1954	$1,214,230	$22,782	$1,118	$ 292
1955	1,265,623	24,449	2,500	350
1956	1,358,571	26,285	2,763	900
1957	1,438,449	27,917	3,069	1,076
1958	1,457,364	28,285	1,430[1]	N.A.
1959	1,612,047	31,788	—	—
1960	1,673,076	32,771	—	—
1961	1,797,970	34,378	—	—

	Net Income	Cumulative Deferred Income Taxes	Property, Plant and Equipment	Allowance for Depreciation
1954	$37,393	$ 292	$347,655	$156,165
1955	40,347	642	377,561	172,033
1956	41,717	1,542	408,947	187,830
1957	44,058	2,618[2]	438,252	198,577
1958	45,545	4,545	462,321	208,899
1959	49,362	6,385	521,686	231,443
1960	50,667	8,468	542,307	244,204
1961	50,211	10,342	582,082	264,283

[1] Six months to July 1, 1958.
[2] Beginning in 1957, disclosed outside current liabilities as "Deferred Federal and Canadian Taxes on Income."
N.A.—Not Available.

QUESTIONS:

1. By what percentage was National Dairy's net income increased in each year from 1954 through 1958 as a result of using the declining-balance method on the tax return? Do you consider these increases material?

2. What was the logic behind the policy of recognizing deferred taxes only in connection with non-recurring types of asset acquisitions? Do you feel this was a reasonable policy?

3. Do you agree with National Dairy's balance-sheet classification of deferred taxes from 1954 through 1956?

4. What action, if any, do you believe the auditors should have taken in 1954? In 1958?

Celanese Corporation of America

Celanese Corporation of America was incorporated in 1918. It is one of the major chemical companies specializing in the production of synthetic materials which are made by processing petroleum hydrocarbons and cellulose. The corporation's three largest product classes are fibers, plastics and industrial process chemicals, made in 13 plants in various parts of the country. On its 1962 balance sheet, Celanese showed gross plant, property and equipment of $414 million.

Prior to 1953, it had been Celanese's policy to provide for depreciation and obsolescence of site improvements, buildings, machinery and equipment on a straight-line basis over the estimated useful lives of the assets in all but one plant.

In 1953, the corporation adopted, for all machinery and equipment, the policy followed for many years in this plant under which depreciation charges made on a straight-line basis were modified for variations from normal production. Normal production was defined as a percentage of capacity for each plant. While the same percentage was not used for all plants, the percentage remained fixed once it was set for a particular plant. Note that the method did not apply to buildings and site improvements.

The amount charged to operations in any one year could be accelerated to a maximum of 50 per cent in excess of straight-line depreciation or retarded to a minimum of 50 per cent thereof. This "variation from normal production" method of computing depreciation was *not* used for federal income tax purposes. Depreciation expense actually charged to operations, and the difference from straight-line depreciation resulting from use of the "variation from normal production" method, are shown in Exhibit 1 together with other pertinent financial information.

The change to the production method of recording depreciation for machinery and equipment was approved by Celanese's certified public accountants, although an exception was taken regard-

297

ing consistency. A portion of the auditors' opinion in the 1953 annual report read as follows:

.... in conformity with generally accepted accounting principles applied on a basis consistent with that of the preceding year, apart from the change, which has our approval, in the depreciation policy as explained in Note 3 to the consolidated financial statements.

Certificates of Necessity were received in 1953 allowing Celanese to amortize $8,675,000 of emergency facilities over 60 months for income tax purposes. The same period was used in the corporate books.

In 1954, additions to fixed assets were depreciated by use of the declining-balance method for tax purposes only. This change did not affect materially the amount of income reported to stockholders in the 1954 annual report, but again the auditors took exception to consistency. The wording of the auditors' opinion was essentially the same as that used in 1953.

On its 1954 balance sheet, Celanese carried a Reserve for Contingencies of $3,590,675 classified between Funded Debt and Preferred Stock. This reserve, which was created by charges to income, had appeared in varying amounts on the annual balance sheets since before 1940 "to meet any additional liabilities with respect to all unsettled [federal income taxes for prior] years." In 1955, this reserve was eliminated by a credit to income of $90,675 and a credit to a "general reserve against plant facilities" which was included with accumulated depreciation deducted from Fixed Assets on the 1955 balance sheet, as follows:

FIXED ASSETS—AT COST

Factory sites and improvements	$ 6,895,798
Buildings	59,062,869
Machinery and equipment	222,871,448
Plant under construction and mechanical and other supplies	13,061,463
	$301,891,578
Less accumulated depreciation and amortization and general reserve ($3,500,000)	135,201,328
	$166,690,250

In 1956, tax depreciation based on the declining-balance method exceeded straight-line depreciation by approximately $731,000. To absorb anticipated future taxes when straight-line depreciation would exceed depreciation based on the declining-balance method, the corporation made a provision for Deferred Federal Taxes on Income in the amount of $380,000. In reference to the provisions for Deferred

EXHIBIT 1

Celanese Corporation of America
Selected Data for the Years 1948–1959
(000 omitted from column figures)

Year	Sales	Reported Net Income[1]	Book Depreciation[1]	Difference from Straight-line Depreciation Resulting from Use of the "Variation from Normal Production" Method Increase-(Decrease)	Amortization under Certificates of Necessity[2]	Deferred Federal Income Taxes[3]	Deferred Federal Taxes on Income[4]	Fixed Asset Additions
1948	$230,385	$39,484	$ 8,511	—	—	—	—	$41,056
1949	171,292	20,641	10,788	—	—	—	—	11,928
1950	232,484	40,361	11,688	—	—	—	—	9,059
1951	202,651	24,800	12,161	—	—	—	—	35,356
1952	166,711	9,214	12,277	—	—	—	—	30,900
1953	165,981	10,653	13,415	$(2,515)	$1,092	—	—	11,058
1954	147,607	6,590	13,715	(3,143)	1,735	—	—	4,348
1955	177,502	15,303	14,742	(2,320)	1,735	—	—	13,134
1956	188,307	16,863	16,428	(1,164)	1,735	$380	$ 380	25,383
1957	192,297	16,082	18,340	(807)	1,735	964	1,344	19,012
1958	223,709	16,686	18,022	(411)	643	817	2,161	8,193
1959	265,236	22,648	18,882	2,111	—	537	4,798[5]	12,472

[1] As reported in the annual reports.
[2] Included in Book Depreciation.
[3] Annual provisions.
[4] Cumulative amounts as shown on the balance sheet between Current Liabilities and Long-Term Debt.
[5] Increased $2,100,000 by transfer from a current liability account representing an excess provision for taxes in prior years.

Federal Taxes on Income, the following comment was made in a note to the 1959 financial statements:

New fixed assets are depreciated for tax purposes on the declining-balance method. Tax provisions in 1959 and 1958 include $537,000 and $814,000, respectively, to provide for future taxes when the declining-balance method will result in a lesser depreciation charge than the unmodified straight-line method. In addition, as a result of the transfer of an excess provision for taxes accumulated during prior years, Deferred Federal Taxes on Income of $4,797,900 at December 31, 1959, is considered adequate to provide for future taxes resulting from all differences between book and tax methods of computing depreciation in previous periods.

Facilities covered by certificates of necessity became fully amortized in 1958.

QUESTIONS:

1. For each year from 1952 to 1954 inclusive, list the depreciation methods used and the assets subject to depreciation under each method in (a) the corporation's public reports, and (b) its federal income tax returns.
2. Comment on Celanese's change to the "variation from normal production" depreciation method relating it to the matching principle.
3. Based on the information given, compute the apparent percentage variation in actual production from "normal production" for *each* year from 1953 through 1959. Assume that book depreciation consists of the sum of: (a) $2,000,000 of annual depreciation on assets, such as buildings, not subject to the "variation from normal production" method; (b) an amount from amortizing emergency facilities over 60 months; and (c) an amount from using the "variation from normal production" method for all other assets.
4. Can you see any inconsistency in a deferment of federal income taxes in 1956 resulting from the adoption of declining-balance depreciation for tax purposes? If so, what would you have recommended? What effect, if any, would your recommendation have had on reported net income?
5. What effect did the change to the "variation from normal production" method have on reported net income during the period 1953 through 1959? Calculate the percentage by which annual reported net income was increased or decreased from what otherwise would have been reported.
6. Compute the amount of depreciation shown on Celanese's tax returns in 1958 and 1959. Calculate the appropriate tax rate by relating the excess of declining-balance depreciation over straight-line depreciation ($731,000) to the provision for Deferred Federal Taxes on Income ($380,000) in 1956. The same tax rate was applicable in 1958 and 1959 as in 1956.
7. When the company adopted declining-balance depreciation for tax purposes in 1954, its auditors, while approving of the change, took exception to consistency with the previous fiscal period. Since the effect on reported net income in 1954 was considered immaterial, do you believe it was necessary for the auditors to note this change in their opinion?
8. What action, if any, would you take as an auditor if the assets covered by Certificates of Necessity had estimated useful lives of 20 years?

9. Comment on the elimination of the Reserve for Contingencies crediting $90,675 to income and $3,500,000 to a general reserve included on the balance sheet with allowance for depreciation. Why do you think this was done?

10. Straight-line depreciation tends to accentuate fluctuations in a company's net income in contrast to depreciation by units of production or some other method which varies with volume. Assuming it is a desirable national policy to minimize fluctuations in the economy, do you believe our government should encourage such methods of depreciation, perhaps accepting them for tax purposes? Consider carefully the effect of such a policy on both corporate net income and "cash flow."

Aluminum Company of America

The Aluminum Company of America (ALCOA) was incorporated in 1888 under the name of Pittsburgh Reduction Company, the present name being adopted in 1907. The company and its subsidiaries constitute an integrated producer of primary aluminum. The company's products, sold for both military and civilian purposes, are used extensively for building materials, transportation equipment (land, sea and air), household appliances, power transmission, machinery and many other uses.

In 1950, ALCOA undertook a large plant building program, designed to increase the company's aluminum producing capacity by 55 per cent. The four-year program included major enlargements of mining, refining, and smelting facilities, as well as expansion and improvement of fabricating facilities to meet increased demands for aluminum mill products.

During the Korean War more than 70 per cent of the company's aluminum shipments went directly into the defense program. In connection with its expansion program, ALCOA was granted Certificates of Necessity which were issued to encourage construction of certain facilities considered essential to the war effort. Such certificates permitted amortization of some portion of an asset's cost over sixty months for federal income tax purposes, regardless of the asset's probable useful life; the actual portion in each instance was based on national need and the estimated ratio of an asset's military to its nonmilitary use. ALCOA's management also used the amortization claimed for tax purposes in the corporate accounts. Exhibit 1 shows net income before taxes, depreciation charges, federal income taxes, net income after taxes, and other selected data for the years 1950 through 1955.

In 1952, the following note to the financial statements was included in the annual report:

In late 1950, the company and its wholly owned subsidiaries began an expansion program now estimated to cost $350 million, which program

302

will not be completed until late 1954, to increase substantially its United States aluminum producing facilities and to expand its alumina producing, bauxite mining and other operations. Expenditures under this program to December 31, 1952, amounted to $242 million of which $176 million was expended during the year 1952. Certificates of Necessity covering facilities estimated to cost $330 million . . . permit amortization of approximately $240,000,000 of costs over a period of sixty months for United States tax purposes. Allowance for amortization of the emergency facilities which have been put into operation was claimed for tax purposes in 1952 and was recorded in the accounts.

ALCOA's independent auditors rendered unqualified opinions on the financial statements in both 1951 and 1952.

In its 1953 annual report, ALCOA's management disclosed the amount of the reduction in net income resulting from use of accelerated amortization on the books as well as on the tax return. Part of Note C to the 1953 financial statements read as follows:

Most of the facilities constructed under the expansion program are covered by Certificates of Necessity which permit amortization of a part of the costs over a period of sixty months for United States tax purposes. The company has elected to claim such amortization for tax purposes, and, in accordance with its policy consistently applied in the past, such allowances have also been recorded in the accounts. The portion of the costs of these assets which are not certified, as well as the remaining book amounts of all other properties, plants and facilities, are being depreciated in the accounts at annual rates allowed for tax purposes which are based upon the estimated economic useful lives of the respective properties. Had the cost of the portion of these assets certified as emergency facilities been depreciated in the accounts on this same basis, reported net income for 1953, after related tax adjustments, would have been increased by approximately $11.5 million.

The company's auditors took exception to the 1953 financial statements, part of their opinion reading:

As stated in Note C to the financial statements, the company and wholly owned subsidiaries follow the policy of recording amortization of emergency facilities in the accounts in the same amounts as are allowed for tax purposes. Generally accepted accounting principles require that the cost of such facilities be spread over the same period as would be proper if no Certificates of Necessity had been issued.

In our opinion, with the exception set forth in the preceding paragraph, . . .

It was disclosed in the following year's annual report that 1954 net income would have been increased by approximately $15.4 million after taxes if the cost of the portion of assets certified as emergency facilities had been depreciated over the estimated useful lives of the properties. As in the previous year, the auditors took exception to the fairness of the financial statements.

In 1955, ALCOA reversed its accounting policy for emergency facilities covered by Certificates of Necessity. In the "Financial Facts" section of that year's annual report, management commented as follows:

It has been the company's regular policy to report earnings after depreciation based on the estimated economic useful lives of the assets, and after amortization in excess of normal depreciation derived from amortizing over a sixty-month period the cost of certain facilities constructed under Certificates of Necessity. Beginning with 1955, however, the company has changed its method of reporting earnings, whereby the certified portions of the cost of facilities constructed under Certificates of Necessity will be depreciated over their economic useful lives in the same manner as the noncertified assets. Also, an appropriate reserve has been provided for future taxes on income, thereby recognizing the taxes which will be payable when recorded depreciation will exceed the amount deductible for tax purposes. This change has been made retroactive to the years 1951–1954, inclusive, and is more fully described in Note (A) to the financial statements.

Note A read:

The company and its wholly owned domestic subsidiaries, for tax purposes, elected to amortize over a period of sixty months that portion of the cost of facilities constructed under the 1951 expansion program covered by Certificates of Necessity. Prior to November 30, 1955, such allowances were also recorded in the accounts, while the portion of the cost which was not covered by necessity certificates, as well as the remaining book amounts of all other properties, plants and facilities, was depreciated in the accounts at annual rates based upon the estimated economic useful lives of the assets. During the last half of 1955, this accounting policy was re-examined and, on December 22, 1955, the Board of Directors authorized a change, retroactive to and including the calendar year 1951 (the earliest year that any amortization was recorded), whereby, for accounting purposes, the certified portion of the cost of facilities constructed under the program would be depreciated at the same annual rates as noncertified assets. Also, an appropriate reserve has been provided for future taxes on income, thereby recognizing the taxes which will be payable when recorded depreciation will exceed the amount deductible for tax purposes. The accompanying consolidated financial statements have been adjusted to reflect the change in accounting policy.

The following summary reconciles the net income as previously reported with the net income as restated on this basis:

Years	Net Income As Reported	Excess of Amortization Over Depreciation	Adjustment For Future Taxes On Income	Net Income As Restated
1954	$46,471,470	$31,941,960	$16,538,275	$61,875,155
1953	48,848,094	24,131,730	12,484,609	60,495,215
1952	43,527,142	8,015,925	4,180,579	47,362,488
1951	39,301,308	1,117,442	566,456	39,852,294

Amounts shown above are after adjustments for amortization applicable to certified assets retired during the years and other adjustments.

As a result of this change, the auditors rendered an unqualified opinion in 1955. Exhibit 2 shows ALCOA's condensed consolidated balance sheets as of December 31, 1953 and 1952.

EXHIBIT 1

Aluminum Company of America
Selected Income Data for the Years 1950–1955
(000 omitted)

	Net Income Before Taxes	Total Depreciation Charge	Amortization Applicable to Certified Portion of Emergency Facilities[1]	Excess of Amortization Over Depreciation[2]	Federal Income Taxes	Net Income After Taxes
1950	$ 90,857	$19,493	—	—	$44,000[3]	$46,857
1951	115,801	22,775	$ 1,542	$ 1,117	76,500	39,301
1952	92,127	34,103	10,980	8,016	48,600	43,527
1953	104,248	58,179	33,147	24,132	55,400	48,848
1954	87,446	72,595	44,230	31,942	40,975	46,471
1955	176,851	45,114	—	—	89,250	87,600

[1] Included in "Total Depreciation Charge."
[2] Excess of amortization of certified portion of emergency facilities over depreciation based on estimated economic useful lives of such assets.
[3] Includes excess profits taxes from 1950 through 1954.

EXHIBIT 2

Aluminum Company of America
Condensed Consolidated Balance Sheets as of December 31, 1953 and 1952
(000 omitted)

ASSETS

	1953	1952
Current Assets	$ 276,730	$246,852
U.S. Government Securities—Construction Program Financing		40,000
Investments	32,348	32,611
Other Assets and Deferred Charges	8,820	9,966
Properties, Plants and Facilities, at Cost:		
Land and land rights, including mines	$ 25,375	$ 25,572
Structures, machinery, equipment, and other facilities	991,036	878,167
	$1,016,411	$903,739
Less accumulated allowances for amortization, depletion and depreciation	483,379	431,457
	$ 533,032	$472,282
Construction work in progress	52,881	62,044
Patents and other intangible assets, net	1,925	1,878
Total Properties, Plants and Facilities	$ 587,838	$536,204
	$ 905,736	$865,633

LIABILITIES AND CAPITAL

Current Liabilities	$ 187,000	$148,217
Long-Term Debt	294,704	325,941
Deferred Credits to Income and Operating Reserve	4,761	4,543
Capital Stock:		
Preferred Stock	$ 65,991	$ 65,991
Common Stock	9,842	8,162
Additional Capital	27,963	27,957
Retained Earnings	315,475	284,822
Total Capital	$ 419,271	$386,932
	$ 905,736	$865,633

QUESTIONS:

1. Compute the percentage reduction in annual reported net income from 1951 to 1954 as a result of using accelerated amortization for book as well as for tax purposes. Do you consider these differences material?

2. What type of opinion do you feel the auditors should have rendered in each year from 1951 through 1955?

3. From information given in the note to the 1952 financial statements, calculate, in terms of per cent, the portion of the cost of Emergency Facilities certified for amortization over 60 months.

4. Using data for 1953 or 1954 from Exhibit 1, compute to the nearest full year the average economic useful life of properties being amortized over five years for tax purposes.

5. Assume Certificates of Necessity were received by ALCOA covering $123,745,000 of facilities which were placed in service on January 1, 1954.

(This amount is fictitious and not related to any certificates actually received by ALCOA.) The portion of cost "certified" was the same as in the case (calculated in question 3 above). The portion of cost subject to amortization was allocated in equal amounts to each of the following 60 months. Assume the company expected to operate profitably in the future and that federal income taxes are paid on January 1 each year, based on the previous year's taxable income. The effective tax rate was 56 per cent in 1954; it was estimated to be 52 per cent during the period 1955 through 1965 and 48 per cent thereafter. Using the estimated economic life computed in question 4 and assuming straight-line depreciation is normally used, determine the attractiveness of the certificates by computing the present value of the future tax deferrals as of January 1, 1954. Develop a discount rate for your present value calculations from the data in Exhibits 1 and 2. Interpret the meaning of your present value calculations.

CHAPTER TEN

Price-Level Adjustments[1]

Since World War II, no subject has received more attention in professional accounting literature than so-called price-level adjustments. Most of this attention has focused on accounting for plant and equipment because the interval between acquisition and replacement of such assets is often many years. Over long time spans there is considerable likelihood that price levels will change significantly.

During 1947, when prices were rising rapidly, a number of corporations began to recognize the impact of inflation on accounting for plant and equipment by one of two practices. Under the first practice, described in case 10-3, United States Steel Corporation (A), normal depreciation charges, based on the original cost of assets, were increased by an amount estimated to reflect the effect of inflation. Under the second practice, an immediate write-down of the cost of recently-acquired depreciable assets was made against income in an amount estimated to represent excessive or abnormal acquisition costs incurred because of rising prices. Subsequent depreciation was then based on the reduced amount of such assets.

PRONOUNCEMENTS BY THE COMMITTEE ON ACCOUNTING PROCEDURE

In September, 1947, the Institute's Committee on Accounting Procedure, realizing that these growing practices represented a marked departure from generally accepted accounting principles and practices, released an immediate statement rather than take the necessary time to issue a formal bulletin. In December, 1947, the same statement was formally issued as ARB No. 33, *Depreciation and High Costs*. Ten months later, on October 14, 1948, the committee

---

[1] Some aspects of price-level adjustments, mentioned only briefly in the text, are more fully developed in the cases which follow the text.

distributed a letter to the Institute's membership reaffirming the position expressed in ARB No. 33. In 1953, this letter and ARB No. 33 were combined in ARB No. 43 as Chapter 9, Section A, also titled *Depreciation and High Costs*. This section follows:

1. In December, 1947, the committee issued Accounting Research Bulletin No. 33, dealing with the subject of depreciation and high costs. In October, 1948, it published a letter to the membership reaffirming the opinion expressed in the bulletin.

2. The subject is one of continuing importance. The committee once more expresses its approval of the basic conclusions asserted in both publications, but in view of the many requests received for further consideration of various aspects of the problem has placed the subject on its agenda for further study.

3. Accounting Research Bulletin No. 33 read as follows:

4. "The American Institute of Accountants committee on accounting procedure has given extensive consideration to the problem of making adequate provision for the replacement of plant facilities in view of recent sharp increases in the price level. The problem requires consideration of charges against current income for depreciation of facilities acquired at lower price levels.

5. "The committee recognizes that business management has the responsibility of providing for replacement of plant and machinery. It also recognizes that, in reporting profits today, the cost of material and labor is reflected in terms of 'inflated' dollars while the cost of productive facilities in which capital was invested at a lower price level is reflected in terms of dollars whose purchasing power was much greater. There is no doubt that in considering depreciation in connection with product costs, prices, and business policies, management must take into consideration the probability that plant and machinery will have to be replaced at costs much greater than those of the facilities now in use.

6. "When there are gross discrepancies between the cost and current values of productive facilities, the committee believes that it is entirely proper for management to make annual appropriations of net income or surplus in contemplation of replacement of such facilities at higher price levels.

7. "It has been suggested in some quarters that the problem be met by increasing depreciation charges against current income. The committee does not believe that this is a satisfactory solution at this time. It believes that accounting and financial reporting for general use will best serve their purposes by adhering to the generally accepted concept of depreciation on cost, at least until the dollar is stabilized at some level. An attempt to recognize current prices in providing depreciation, to be consistent, would require the serious step of formally recording appraised current values for all properties, and continuous and consistent depreciation charges based on the new values. Without such formal steps, there would be no objective standard by which to judge the propriety of the amounts of depreciation charges against current income, and the significance of recorded amounts of profit might be seriously impaired.

8. "It would not increase the usefulness of reported corporate income figures if some companies charged depreciation on appraised values while others adhered to cost. The committee believes, therefore, that consideration of radical changes in accepted accounting procedure should not be under-

taken, at least until a stable price level would make it practicable for business as a whole to make the change at the same time.

9. "The committee disapproves immediate write-downs of plant cost by charges against current income in amounts believed to represent excessive or abnormal costs occasioned by current price levels. However, the committee calls attention to the fact that plants expected to have less than normal useful life can properly be depreciated on a systematic basis related to economic usefulness."

10. The letter of October 14, 1948, was addressed to the members of the Institute and read as follows:

11. "The committee on accounting procedure has reached the conclusion that no basic change in the accounting treatment of depreciation of plant and equipment is practicable or desirable under present conditions to meet the problem created by the decline in the purchasing power of the dollar.

12. "The committee has given intensive study to this problem and has examined and discussed various suggestions which have been made to meet it. It has solicited and considered hundreds of opinions on this subject expressed by businessmen, bankers, economists, labor leaders, and others. While there are differences of opinion, the prevailing sentiment in these groups is against any basic change in present accounting procedures. The committee believes that such a change would confuse readers of financial statements and nullify many of the gains that have been made toward clearer presentation of corporate finances.

13. "Should inflation proceed so far that original dollar costs lose their practical significance, it might become necessary to restate all assets in terms of the depreciated currency, as has been done in some countries. But it does not seem to the committee that such action should be recommended now if financial statements are to have maximum usefulness to the greatest number of users.

14. "The committee, therefore, reaffirms the opinion it expressed in Accounting Research Bulletin No. 33, December, 1947.

15. "Any basic change in the accounting treatment of depreciation should await further study of the nature and concept of business income.

16. "The immediate problem can and should be met by financial management. The committee recognizes that the common forms of financial statements may permit misunderstanding as to the amount which a corporation has available for distribution in the form of dividends, higher wages, or lower prices for the company's products. When prices have risen appreciably since original investments in plant and facilities were made, a substantial proportion of net income as currently reported must be reinvested in the business in order to maintain assets at the same level of productivity at the end of a year as at the beginning.

17. "Stockholders, employees, and the general public should be informed that a business must be able to retain out of profits amounts sufficient to replace productive facilities at current prices if it is to stay in business. The committee therefore gives its full support to the use of supplementary financial schedules, explanations or footnotes by which management may explain the need for retention of earnings."

Six members of the committee, Messrs. Andrews, Peloubet, Peoples, Smith, Wellington, and Williams, dissented to adoption of section (a) of chapter 9.

The six dissenting members object to the reprinting, in this section, of Bulletin No. 33 of December, 1947, and the reaffirming letter of October 14, 1948. That bulletin was issued to check the extension of certain then-emerging practices and it was successful in that purpose. However, Bulletin No. 33 contains assertions which are not now appropriate and should be eliminated, notably:

(a) " An attempt to recognize current prices in providing depreciation ... would require the serious step of formally recording appraised current values ... and consistent depreciation charges based on the new values" (par. 7 of this section).

Those dissenting believe this is not the only method which may be followed —a conclusion also reached by the Study Group on Business Income (see page 61 of its report).[2]

(b) " ... consideration of radical changes in accepted accounting procedure should not be undertaken, at least until a stable price level would make it practicable for business as a whole to make the change at the same time." (par. 8)

This statement virtually precludes changes in accounting practice in so far as the monetary unit is concerned and is inconsistent with the paragraphs on Accounting and the Corporate System in the introduction to this volume.

(c) The warnings (in paragraphs 5, 6, 16 and 17) to management as to the use of profits.

Such warnings are irrelevant; it is no part of the accountant's function to tell management what it may or may not properly do with income after it has been determined.

Those dissenting believe that acceptable accounting practices should comprehend financial statements to stockholders, employees, and the public designed to reflect those concepts of cost and net income which are recommended in paragraph 5 to management in determining product costs, prices, and business policies. They question whether net income can properly be so designated if appropriations therefrom, as suggested in paragraph 6, are needed to preserve capital invested in plant.

They believe that plant may continue to be carried in the balance sheet at historical cost with deduction for depreciation based thereon. In addition to historical depreciation, a supplementary annual charge to income should be permitted with corresponding credit to an account for property replacements and substitutions, to be classified with the stockholders' equity. This supplementary charge should be in such amount as to make the total charge for depreciation express in current dollars the exhaustion of plant allocable to the period. The supplementary charge would be calculated by use of a generally accepted price index applied to the expenditures in the years when the plant was acquired. The last sentence of paragraph 7 would then be no longer valid; the usefulness of financial statements would be enhanced without sacrifice of presently existing comparability.

From 1953 until it was superseded in September, 1959, by the Institute's new Accounting Principles Board, the Committee on Accounting Procedure reconsidered this bulletin from time to time, but decided against any changes.

---

[2] Study Group on Business Income, *Changing Concepts of Business Income*. New York: The Macmillan Co., 1952.

OTHER PRONOUNCEMENTS

In August, 1951, the Committee on Concepts and Standards Underlying Corporate Financial Statements of the American Accounting Association issued a comprehensive report, *"Price Level Changes and Financial Statements."*[3] The conclusions of this report were as follows:

(1) In periodic reports to stockholders, the primary financial statements, prepared by management and verified by an independent accountant, should, at the present stage of accounting development, continue to reflect historical dollar costs.

(2) There is reason for believing that knowledge of the effects of the changing value of the dollar upon financial position and operating results may be useful information, if a practical and substantially uniform method of measurement and disclosure can be developed.

(3) The accounting effects of the changing value of the dollar should be made the subject of intensive research and experimentation; the specific significance of the basic problem should be determined with as much accuracy as possible; the means of its solution, if its significance warrants, should be thoroughly investigated.

(4) The effects of price fluctuations upon financial reports should be measured in terms of the over-all purchasing power of the dollar—that is, changes in the general price level as measured by a *general* price index. For this purpose, adjustments should not be based on either the current value or the replacement costs of specific types of capital consumed.

(5) The measurement of price level changes should be all-inclusive; all statement items affected should be adjusted in a consistent manner.

(6) Management may properly include in periodic reports to stockholders comprehensive supplementary statements which present the effects of the fluctuation in the value of the dollar upon net income and upon financial position.

    (a) Such supplementary statements should be internally consistent; the income statement and the balance sheet should both be adjusted by the same procedures, so that the figures in such complementary statements are coordinate and have the same relative significance.

    (b) Such supplementary statements should be reconciled in detail with the primary statements reflecting unadjusted original dollar costs, and should be regarded as an extension or elaboration of the primary statements rather than as a departure therefrom.

    (c) Such supplementary statements should be accompanied by comments and explanations clearly setting forth the implications, uses, and limitations of the adjusted data.

While this committee also recommended adherence to the historical cost concept, its report differed in other respects from the statements of the Institute's Committee on Accounting Procedure. Some of these differences will be considered later in this chapter.

---

[3] Committee on Concepts and Standards Underlying Corporate Financial Statements, "Price Level Changes and Financial Statements—Supplementary Statement No. 2," *Accounting Review*, Vol. 26, October 1951, pp. 468-74.

In April, 1961, the Accounting Principles Board stated its interest in price-level changes, as revealed in the minutes of one of its meetings:

...the Board ... agreed that the assumption in accounting that fluctuations in the value of the dollar may be ignored is unrealistic, and that therefore the Director of Accounting Research should be instructed to set up a research project to study the problem and to prepare a report in which recommendations are made for the disclosure of the effect of price-level changes upon the financial statements. In this study, special attention should be paid to the use of supplementary statements as a means of disclosure.[4]

A year later, in the April, 1962, issue of *The CPA*, a bulletin published by the Institute for its members, the Director of Accounting Research reported that the price-level research study was concentrating on:

(1) A clarification of the meaning of price-level adjustments of accounting data by the use of an index of the general price level,

(2) A study of the indexes currently available,

(3) An exploration of the forms that disclosure of price-level changes has taken or could take.

The Securities and Exchange Commission has issued no pronouncements on price-level adjustments. However, it has adopted the position expressed in ARB No. 43, and consequently it rejects financial statements filed with it which include price-level adjustments, except as appropriations of net income or surplus (as approved in paragraph 6 of Chapter 9 (A) of ARB No. 43). Case 10-4, Ayrshire Collieries Corporation, concerns a dispute with the SEC over accounting disclosure of price-level adjustments.

TERMINOLOGY PROBLEMS

One objective of the research study recommended by the Accounting Principles Board is to clarify the meaning of "price-level adjustments." Unfortunately, there has been no uniformity in the terminology used, either by those proposing new techniques to account for changes in the value of the dollar, or by those supporting traditional accounting. The following terms, among others, are frequently used:

Price-level accounting
Price-level depreciation
Uniform dollar accounting
Common dollar accounting
Constant dollar accounting

---

[4] Robert T. Sprouse and Maurice Moonitz, *A Tentative Set of Broad Accounting Principles for Business Enterprises*, Accounting Research Study No. 3 (New York American Institute of Certified Public Accountants, 1962), p. 17.

Fair value depreciation
Replacement value accounting
Replacement value depreciation
While some of these terms refer to different techniques, they all describe some form of price-level adjustment, that is, the restatement of conventional financial statement data to eliminate the effect of changes in the purchasing power of money.

ARGUMENTS FAVORING PRICE-LEVEL ADJUSTMENTS

Proponents of price-level adjustments offer the following arguments:
(1) Revenues in current dollars are matched against adjusted costs, also in current dollars. The resulting net income is more realistic and is more useful for certain decisions cited below in (2).
(2) Decisions concerning dividend distributions and wage negotiations are improved. Net income determined by expressing revenues and expenses in current dollars is a better measure of ability to pay either increased wages or dividends.
(3) Capital is maintained in terms of the purchasing power originally invested and not merely in terms of dollars.
(4) More comparable and equitable accounting will result among different firms. The company with large inventory stocks can to a great extent eliminate the accounting effects of price-level changes from reported net income by using LIFO. However, no similar means is available to the firm with a substantial investment in depreciable assets or other assets susceptible to price-level movements.
(5) Widespread adoption of price-level accounting would improve the chances of its eventual approval for federal income tax purposes.

ARGUMENTS AGAINST PRICE-LEVEL ADJUSTMENTS

Arguments against price-level adjustments, some of which are stated above in Chapter 9 (A) of ARB No. 43, include:
(1) Such methods are not now considered to be generally accepted by the accounting profession and they are rejected by the SEC and by the Treasury.
(2) The cost principle has stood the test of time extremely well. It provides an objective standard and is easily understood.
(3) Price-level adjustments would prove confusing to users of financial statements. This view is stated forcefully by Mr. Ralph E. Kandt, CPA, in the following letter which appeared in the *Journal of Accountancy:*

As a sole practitioner in a small town, serving small businesses, I watch the passing controversy over historical cost versus price-level depreciation, and shudder.

Unfortunately, it seems that the generally accepted accounting principles applicable to the hundred largest corporations are also applicable to the thousand smallest corporations. I can imagine the confusion that would be injected into financial reporting for small businesses if the concept of price-level depreciation were adopted as a generally accepted accounting principle. The relatively simple theory of basing depreciation on historical costs continues to be almost incomprehensible to many of the owners of small businesses. Does not the accounting profession have some obligation to confine accounting principles to practical concepts within the comprehension of the majority of those who must follow them? Surely we must consider more than just the merits of the theory before making such a decision.[5]

(4) There is little demand for price-level adjustments in financial statements. While the business community has constantly protested accounting's failure to cope with the declining value of the dollar and the Treasury's refusal to recognize for income tax purposes the impact of inflation on replacement costs, only a handful of businesses have experimented with supplementary financial statements which incorporate price-level adjustments, as recommended by both the Institute and the American Accounting Association. Part of this hesitation or reluctance may be attributable to management's understandable concern with the level of reported earnings, although, as noted in the previous chapter, many corporations have adopted accelerated depreciation for book purposes despite the resulting significant reduction in reported earnings. This surprising management apathy towards price-level adjustments was noted by Mr. Walter R. Staub, CPA, who participated in a panel discussion, "Accountants and Economists Look at Depreciation," at the December, 1961, annual meeting of the American Economic Association. A portion of Mr. Staub's remarks follow:

I need scarcely argue the obvious point that needed recognition of price-level changes cannot come about by the efforts of accountants alone and without concrete examples showing the interest of the business community. We are endeavoring to serve needs that are of use in our economy, not to pursue theoretical concepts that appear to be regarded as of no practical consequence. Business has done a lot of talking, but it seems extremely loath to experiment in financial statement presentation. If there is a real problem—and I think there is—I would like to see business and the accountants ... developing meaningful supplementary statements, and if certain

---

[5] *Journal of Accountancy*, Vol. 109, March 1960, p. 29.

"rules of the game" could be agreed upon, then they should be used for such period of time as necessary to determine whether they produce a more satisfactory product. If it is then decided (say, by the American Institute's Accounting Principles Board) that a better product has been achieved, I would be inclined to make price-level accounting mandatory.[6]

(5) There is no practical, reasonably uniform method of implementing price-level adjustments. This objection is discussed in the remaining sections of this chapter.

EXTENT OF MEASUREMENT

Even among the proponents of price-level adjustments, there is considerable disagreement concerning the extent of such adjustments and the methods of implementing them. The Committee on Accounting Procedure was concerned only with depreciation and high costs, whereas the AAA's committee recommended in conclusion (5) of its report that *all* financial statement items be included in any measurement of price-level changes.

Supporters of an all-inclusive approach to price-level adjustments contend that adjustment of depreciation only, as suggested in the last paragraph of the dissents to Chapter 9 (A) of ARB No. 43, is inconsistent and results in historical plant costs appearing on the balance sheet with an adjusted amount of depreciation deducted on the income statement. A counter argument is that the resulting differences between the balance sheet and income statement are essentially no different from those arising from the use of LIFO in an inflationary period.

Among those who emphasize adjusting depreciation, there is further disagreement concerning long-term debt. One group argues that the existence of such debt provides a hedge against inflation and therefore should be recognized as an offset to any price-level adjustment of depreciation. For example, if $100,000 of depreciable plant was financed, in part, by $25,000 of long-term debt, this group would adjust only three-fourths of depreciation for any price-level change. A second group would ignore the existence of debt and would include total depreciation in any price-level adjustment. They argue that a "gain" on debt is only realized when the debt is retired, usually not practical during inflation because of increased capital requirements.

The remainder of this chapter considers only the effect of price-level changes on depreciation. For most companies, depreciation is

---

[6] Panel Discussion, "Accountants and Economists Look at Depreciation," Seventy-fourth Annual Meeting, American Economic Association, New York, December 29, 1961. Reproduced, by permission of Lybrand, Ross Bros. & Montgomery, from *The Lybrand Newsletter*, Vol. 4, February 1962, p. 2.

the major item affected by price-level changes, and it is the only item which has been adjusted by several companies, including those described in cases 10-3 and 10-4. The reader should not conclude that all proponents of price-level adjustments would limit such adjustments to depreciation only. However, this limited approach is supported as a logical first step, pending more widespread acceptance and understanding of price-level adjustments. If the reader can comprehend the basic issues involved in the price-level controversy and can understand the methods of measuring price-level changes for depreciation, to be discussed in the following section, he should have no difficulty in visualizing the application of price-level adjustments to *all* financial statement items.

PRICE CHANGES VS. PRICE-LEVEL CHANGES

Price-level adjustments of depreciation may be viewed in two quite different ways. One view is that such adjustments should be related to the changing prices of the particular depreciable assets owned by a business. This view, which emphasizes the problem of replacing *these* assets, is recognized by the Committee on Accounting Procedure in Chapter 9 (A) of ARB No. 43. Note the references to "replacement" and "replaced" in paragraphs 4, 5, 6 and 17.[7] Strictly speaking, adjustments to reflect the price behavior of specific assets would be "price adjustments," not "price-level adjustments."

The second view emphasizes maintenance of the purchasing power of invested capital, as indicated by some general measure of changes in the so-called price-level. This is the view favored by the American Accounting Association's committee in its conclusion (4) above. This view is supported by the fact that initially management was free to invest capital in any way it preferred, and, as such invested capital is recovered through operations, management is again free to use it for reinvestment or other purposes. Both of these views will be considered further in a later section.

CALCULATING PRICE-LEVEL ADJUSTMENTS

A majority of the Committee on Accounting Procedure believed, as stated in paragraph 7, that recognition of "current prices in providing depreciation, to be consistent, would require the serious step of formally recording appraised current values for all properties, and continuous and consistent depreciation charges based on the new values." The majority believed such steps were necessary to establish

---

[7] Elsewhere in Chapter 9 (A), the committee does refer to "price level," "price levels," or "purchasing power of the dollar." However, the committee's statement appears to concentrate on *price* changes, rather than *price-level* changes.

an objective standard or basis for judging the propriety of depreciation charges. A minority of the Committee on Accounting Procedure, the AAA Committee, and more recently the Accounting Principles Board, have recommended that objectivity may be achieved though the use of index numbers.

One technique for using an index number in this way is described in an appendix to case 10-4, Ayrshire Collieries Corporation, page 363. This corporation ends its fiscal year on June 30, and hence the Consumer Price Index for May, released in June, is used each year as the numerator in the formula. As an illustration of the technique described in this appendix, assume the following hypothetical situation. The White Mountain Corporation, which was organized in January, 1961, purchased depreciable assets as follows:

1961	$80,000
1962	$15,000
1963	None

All assets have an estimated useful life of 10 years, with no salvage value anticipated. The corporation computed "price-level depreciation" in 1961 and 1962 by use of an index number (the problem of selecting such an index is considered later). The average level of this index for each year and its year-end level have been as follows:

	Annual Average	Year-End
1961	115	116
1962	117	119
1963	120	121

Note that the base period of the index number is not relevant since depreciation for 1963 will be expressed in current (December 31, 1963) dollars. Assuming straight-line depreciation[8] is applied to historical costs, "price-level depreciation" for the year 1963 is calculated as follows:

Year Assets Acquired	Straight-line Depreciation	Price-level Index Factor	Price-level Depreciation
1961	$8,000	121/115	$8,417
1962	1,500	121/117	1,551
Totals for 1963	$9,500		$9,968

Price-level depreciation, as used here, and as defined by the Ayrshire Collieries Corporation in case 10-4, is the sum of historical cost depreciation and the price-level increment. The price-level adjustment alone is $468. The following entry would be made to record historical cost depreciation:

---

[8] It is not essential that straight-line depreciation be used. Price-level adjustments could also be made to amounts determined by accelerated depreciation.

| Depreciation Expense | $9,500 | |
| Allowance for Depreciation | | $9,500 |

In addition, if the price-level adjustment is formally recorded, an entry such as the following is required:

| Depreciation Expense[9] | $ 468 | |
| Capital Maintained by Recognition of Price-level Depreciation | | $ 468 |

"Capital Maintained by Recognition of Price-level Depreciation" is shown in the stockholders' equity section of the balance sheet. This account would continue to increase during inflation. While it might be reduced during an extended deflation,[10] it is not affected by the periodic retirement and replacement of assets.

Note that the technique illustrated above does not assure that cumulative price-level depreciation will equal the ultimate replacement costs of assets. However, this is not the purpose of such adjustments. Instead, one-tenth of the purchasing power initially invested is charged to depreciation expense each year, expressed in current dollars.

SELECTION OF AN INDEX

Some accountants, while sympathetic to price-level adjustments, are troubled by the selection of an appropriate index. They cite the possible inaccuracy of index numbers and the lack of financial statement comparability which could result from the use of different index numbers by various companies. Those supporting the use of index numbers contend that index numbers are widely used in accounting for LIFO cost inventories, and that inaccuracies inherent in index numbers may be less significant and less variable than inaccuracies in certain accounting judgments, such as depreciation itself.

The late George O. May, a pioneer in the accounting profession, commented on this problem in an interview with Mr. John Lawler, former editor of the *Journal of Accountancy*, on the occasion of Mr. May's eightieth birthday in 1955.

> People seem to look for perfect solutions to every problem. Well, there just aren't any perfect solutions for the problems of accounting. Never was one, never will be. You see I can go back to the days when depreciation was a disputed concept. Exactly the same things were said then about depreciation that are being said today about reflecting monetary fluctuations. They said: "You can't

---

[9] To distinguish this charge from the preceding one, the debit might be to "Price-level Depreciation Adjustment."

[10] The account balance would decrease in a deflation only if the price level fell below the average price level at which depreciable assets were acquired.

measure depreciation. If you use the straight-line method, you will get a figure of X; if you use the diminishing-balance method, you will get 2X. If it can be either X or 2X, it's no good trying at all." Now they are saying: "So you want to adjust by a price index. Well, one index gives you 165; another, 175; still a third gives you 190. Since you can't say which index is best, we won't take any." But, surely, the answer to that kind of comment is that you would be more nearly right if you used any one of the indexes than if you made no adjustment of the figures at all.[11]

Earlier in this chapter the distinction between *price* changes and *price-level* changes was discussed. This distinction is relevant in choosing an appropriate index number. A *general* price-level index was recommended by the AAA committee, and was used by Professor Ralph Jones in his case studies of the effect of price-level changes on four companies.[12] Professor Jones explained his choice of the U.S. Bureau of Labor Statistics Consumer Price Index as follows:

> The conversion of financial statements into uniform current dollars is not a departure from the cost basis of accounting but is rather a recognition of the well-established fact that the basic unit of measurement, the dollar, has changed in value. Since the objective in accounting for inflation is to make adjustments or corrections for changes in the basic unit itself rather than to show current values or replacement costs, a measure of general purchasing power such as the Index of Consumers' Prices of the U.S. Bureau of Labor Statistics must be used.[13]

Professor Jones adjusted all financial statement items of the selected companies for price-level changes. Use of a more specific index number might be acceptable where only depreciation is adjusted, but the movements of such an index may differ significantly from those of a more general price index. For example, since 1957 the Sacramento Municipal Utility District, a large, municipally operated supplier of electricity, has provided additional depreciation "representing the difference between depreciation computed on property adjusted to current price levels and depreciation based on historical cost."[14] The

---

[11] "A Talk with George O. May," *Journal of Accountancy*, Vol. 99, June 1955, p. 41.

[12] Ralph C. Jones, *Price Level Changes and Financial Statements, Case Studies of Four Companies* (Columbus, Ohio: American Accounting Association, 1955). In accordance with the third conclusion of the 1951 AAA report, "Price Level Changes and Financial Statements," (see page 312) Professor Jones conducted these studies for the American Accounting Association with the financial support of the Merrill Foundation for the Advancement of Financial Knowledge. These studies are described briefly in case 10-2, page 334.

[13] *Ibid.*, p. 177.

[14] The technique used differs slightly from that illustrated earlier, but the net result is the same. Although the District refers to *price levels* and *price-level* depreciation, it adjusts depreciation for quite specific *price* changes rather than changes in the general price level.

index used is the Handy-Whitman Index of Public Utility Construction Costs for the Pacific Division. In 1961, when the Consumer Price Index *increased*, the District explained the *reduction* in its additional provision for depreciation as follows:

> The additional provision for depreciation to reflect increases in price level amounted to $646,000 in 1961. This represents a reduction of $95,000 below the 1960 provision. The lesser amount of price-level depreciation in 1961 reflects a sharp drop in utility construction cost indices over the past two years, principally in the categories of line transformers and substation and other equipment.

METHODS OF DISCLOSURE

There are three general methods of disclosing information about price-level changes. They are well described by Mr. May:

> It [the monetary postulate] certainly fails when changes in the value of money become too important to be ignored. When you get such a change, it seems to me that three steps should be considered. The first is to say: "We are still going to adhere to this postulate; but we realize that it is not entirely valid, and we warn you to discount the figures to that extent." The next stage is to say: "We have tried to estimate the effects of this currency fluctuation and are furnishing you with some supplementary information about it. However, we are not yet prepared to embody this data in our formal accounting." The final step might be to say: "Well, we have decided that the monetary changes have now become so significant that we are reflecting them in the formal accounts."[15]

An example of Mr. May's first step is found in a footnote accompanying the 1961 financial statements of the Caterpillar Tractor Co.:

> **Basis of allocating cost of facilities to operations**
>
> The generally accepted accounting principle followed with respect to buildings, machinery and equipment is the systematic allocation to each year's operations of a portion of the *original cost* of these facilities. The "sum-of-the-years-digits" method is used for a substantial portion of the assets acquired after December 31, 1953, and the "straight-line" method for other assets. The plant assets currently in use were, however, acquired over many years at cost levels which were lower than the level of current costs. The portion of the original cost of these assets allocated to 1961 and used in determining profit was therefore substantially lower than if a provision had been made on the basis of current replacement cost levels.

The second method, the use of supplementary statements or schedules, is illustrated in the Reece Corporation case (see **page 334**)

---
[15] *Op. cit.*, p.41.

TABLE 1

HERCULES POWDER COMPANY

Selected Financial Data, 1952-1961
(in thousands of dollars)

	Data as Reported Each Year			Restatement of Reported Data in Dollars of Constant Value		
Year	Net Income	Gross Fixed Assets	Research Expenditures	Net Income (Adjusted to 1961 Consumer Prices)[16]	Gross Fixed Assets (Revalued in Terms of Dec. 31, 1961 Construction Costs)[17]	Research Expenditures (Adjusted to 1961 Costs)[18]
1952	$11,218	$118,688	$ 6,394	$12,600	$300,000	$ 9,000
1953	11,681	125,831	7,905	13,100	306,000	10,600
1954	14,140	144,049	7,578	15,800	327,000	9,900
1955	19,012	153,351	7,903	21,200	335,000	9,900
1956	17,703	182,274	10,523	19,500	366,000	12,500
1957	18,116	198,008	10,172	19,300	379,000	11,500
1958	17,509	208,374	10,816	18,100	386,000	11,900
1959	23,397	224,934	11,602	24,000	399,000	12,300
1960	27,165	285,738	14,090	27,500	460,000	14,400
1961	27,978	319,056	15,409	28,000	488,000	15,400

[16] As measured by the Consumer Price Index of the U.S. Bureau of Labor Statistics.
[17] As measured by the *Engineering News-Record* construction cost index.
[18] As measured by U.S. Bureau of Labor Statistics' index of hourly earnings in all manufacturing industries.

and by the data in Table 1 from the 1961 annual report of the Hercules Powder Company. Note that three different index numbers are used by Hercules to compute the restated data. Use of 1961 as the base year facilitates comparing the restated (adjusted) data with the unadjusted 1961 financial statements. At December 31, 1961, the restated data for gross fixed assets differ from the reported data because the latter are not in 1961 dollars. Instead the reported data represent cumulative costs incurred over many years, stated in the dollars of those years. The restated data reveal that from 1952 through 1961 net income, gross fixed assets, and research expenditures all increased less in "real" terms than indicated in the reported data. This was particularly true for gross fixed assets and research expenditures because the indexes used to measure the change in these two items had increased substantially more than the Consumer Price Index used to measure the change in net income.

The presentation of supplementary statements and schedules to reveal the effect of price-level changes on accounting data has been encouraged by all groups which have studied the price-level problem. The Accounting Principles Board stated in 1961, when announcing its price-level research study, that "special attention should be paid to the use of supplementary statements as a means of disclosure."

Mr. May's final step, the reflection of price-level adjustments in the formal accounts, is illustrated by the Sacramento Municipal Utility District and by the Ayrshire Collieries Corporation in case 10-4. There are only a few other American companies reflecting such adjustments in the formal accounts, although the practice is quite common in a number of other countries where more severe inflation has been experienced than in the United States.

CONTINUING CONTROVERSY

The controversy over the propriety of price-level adjustments is difficult and complex. Beyond the central controversy of whether *anything* should be done, there are numerous related controversies concerning methods of measurement and disclosure. More intensive research and experimentation, such as the studies conducted by Professor Jones and others, and the current project of the Accounting Principles Board, together with greater interest and participation by the business community, should facilitate reaching some generally acceptable conclusions.

REFERENCES

American Accounting Association, Committee on Concepts and Standards Underlying Corporate Financial Statements, "Price Level Changes and Financial Statements—Supplementary Statement No. 2," *Accounting Review*, 26 (Oct. 1951), 468-74. This Statement also appears in *Accounting and Reporting Standards for Corporate Financial Statements and Preceding Statements and Supplements.* Columbus, Ohio: American Accounting Association, 1957.

Andersen, Arthur, & Co., *Accounting and Reporting Problems of the Accounting Profession*, 2nd ed. Chicago: Arthur Andersen & Co. (Oct. 1962), 7-18.

Avery, Harold G., "Depreciation vs. Inflation," *Accounting Review*, 36 (Jan. 1961), 71-74.

Bell, Albert L., "Fixed Assets and Current Costs," *Accounting Review*, 28 (Jan. 1953), 44-53.

Briloff, Abraham J., "Price Level Changes and Financial Statements: A Critical Reappraisal," *Accounting Review*, 33 (Jul. 1958), 380-88.

———, "Price Level Changes and Financial Statements at the Threshold of the New Frontier," *Accounting Review*, 36 (Oct. 1961), 603-7.

Broad, Samuel J., "What Are We Going to Do About Determination of Income Influenced by Inflation?" *Journal of Accountancy*, 93 (Mar. 1952), 300-8.

Brundage, Percival F., "Study Group on Business Income Publishes Its Conclusions After Three Years of Work," *Journal of Accountancy*, 93 (Feb. 1952), 190-98.

Carson, A. B., "A Fund-Change-Statement Approach to the Calculation of Inflationary Distortion in Conventional Income Measurement," *Accounting Review*, 29 (Jul. 1954), 373-82.

Corbin, Donald A., "A Case Study of Price-Level Adjustments," *Accounting Review*, 30 (Apr. 1955), 268-81.

Coughlan, John W., "Two Approaches to the Problem of Changing Prices," *Journal of Accountancy*, 104 (Aug. 1957), 42-47.

Davidson, Sidney, "U.S. Supreme Court Decisions Affecting Public Utility Depreciation," *Journal of Accountancy*, 96 (Sept. 1953), 331-35.

Dein, Raymond C., "Price Level Adjustments: Fetish in Accounting," *Accounting Review*, 30 (Jan. 1955), 3-24.

———, "Price Level Adjustments: Rejoinder to Professor Husband," *Accounting Review*, 31 (Jan. 1956), 58-63.

Dohr, James L., "Limitations on the Usefulness of Price Level Adjustments," *Accounting Review*, 30 (Apr. 1955), 198-205.

Edwards, Edgar O., "Depreciation Policy Under Changing Price Levels," *Accounting Review*, 29 (Apr. 1954), 267-80.

Epps, Max I., "Realistic Accounting Under South American Inflation," *Journal of Accountancy*, 111 (Jan. 1961), 67-73.

Fergusson, D.A., "Accounting and the Price Level," *Accounting Review*, 29 (Oct. 1954), 639-44.

Gordon, Myron J., "The Valuation of Accounts at Current Cost," *Accounting Review*, 28 (Jul. 1953), 373-84.

Goudeket, A., "An Application of Replacement Value Theory," *Journal of Accountancy*, 110 (Jul. 1960), 37-47. An editorial and letters regarding this article appeared in 110 (Jul. 1960), 25-26; 110 (Aug. 1960), 27-31; and 110 (Sept. 1960), 31-33.

————, "How Inflation Is Being Recognized in Financial Statements in the Netherlands," *Journal of Accountancy*, 94 (Oct. 1952), 448-52.

Grady, Paul, "Conservation of Productive Capital Through Recognition of Current Cost of Depreciation," *Accounting Review*, 30 (Oct. 1955), 617-22.

————, "Economic Depreciation in Income Taxation and in Accounting," *Journal of Accountancy*, 107 (Apr. 1959), 54-60.

————, "A Proposal for the Adoption of Standards of Disclosure for Changing Price Levels," *Journal of Accountancy*, 94 (Nov. 1952), 565-69.

Graham, Willard J., "Depreciation and Capital Replacement in an Inflationary Economy," *Accounting Review*, 34 (Jul. 1959), 367-75.

Hendriksen, Eldon S., "Price-Level Adjustments of Financial Statements," *Economic and Business Studies*, Bulletin No. 35. Pullman, Washington: Bureau of Economic and Business Research, School of Economics and Business, Washington State University, 1961.

Herrick, Anson, "Inflation in Accounting," *Journal of Accountancy*, 110 (Sept. 1960), 51-56.

Higgins, Thomas G., "Financial Statements and Inflation," *The New York Certified Public Accountant*, 30 (Mar. 1960), 169-79.

Hill, Thomas M., "An Analysis of Supplementary Statement No. 2," *Accounting Review*, 27 (Jan. 1952), 16-24.

Horngren, Charles T., "Security Analysts and the Price Level," *Accounting Review*, 30 (Oct. 1955), 575-81.

Huizingh, William, "Inflation—Present and to be Accounted for," *N.A.A. Bulletin*, 40 (Apr. 1959), section 1, 43-57.

Husband, George R., "Professor Dein, Mr. Alexander, and Supplementary Statement No. 2," *Accounting Review*, 30 (Jul. 1955), 383-99.

Jones, Ralph C., *Price Level Changes and Financial Statements—Case Studies of Four Companies*. Columbus, Ohio: American Accounting Association, 1955.

————, *Effects of Price Level Changes on Business Income, Capital, and Taxes*. Columbus, Ohio: American Accounting Association, 1956.

Kane, John E., "Relationship Between Depreciation Allowance and Maintenance of Capital During Inflation," *Journal of Accountancy*, 94 (Dec. 1952), 697-701.

MacNeill, James H., "Accounting for Inflation Abroad," *Journal of Accountancy*, 112 (Aug. 1961), 67-73.

Mason, Perry, *Price-Level Changes and Financial Statements*. Columbus, Ohio: American Accounting Association, 1956.

Mathews, Russell, "Inflation and Company Finance," *Accounting Review*, 35 (Jan. 1960), 8-18.

May, George O., "Three Discussions of Financial Accounting and Inflation," *Journal of Accountancy*, 93 (Mar. 1952), 294-99.

McAnly, Herbert T., "Recognizing the Deficiency of Depreciation Provisions Based Upon Historical Costs," *N.A.A. Bulletin*, 39 (Feb. 1958), section 1, 5-15.

Melvoin, Charles, "Depreciation in Accountants' Reports," *Journal of Accountancy*, 108 (Nov. 1959), 34-38.

Paton, William A., "Depreciation—Concept and Measurement," *Journal of Accountancy*, 108 (Oct. 1959), 38-43.

Peloubet, Maurice E., "An Indictment of the Accounting Profession for Failing to Deal with Effects of Inflation," *Journal of Accountancy*, 96 (Dec. 1953), 714-22.

Ray, D.D., "Are Accountants Misstating Profits?" *Business Horizons*, 4 (Fall 1961), 77-84.

Ridilla, Richard A., "A Technique to Adjust Financial Statement Data for Changing Price Levels," *Accounting Review*, 35 (Oct. 1960), 650-58.

_____, "Price Level Adjustments to Financial Statements: A Rejoinder," *Accounting Review*, 36 (Oct. 1961), 608-12.

Sanders, Thomas H., "Inflation and Accounting," *Harvard Business Review*, 30 (May-Jun. 1952), 50-58.

Schiff, Michael, "What Happens to Depreciation," *Journal of Accountancy*, 107 (Mar. 1959), 37-41. Letters regarding this article appeared in 107 (May 1959), 20-25.

Spacek, Leonard, "Inflation in Business," *The Controller*, 25 (Dec. 1957), 578-81.

Stans, Maurice H., "AAA Proposals Offer Practical Suggestions for Dealing with Price Level Changes in Accounting," *Journal of Accountancy*, 93 (Jan. 1952), 52-59.

Steele, Henry M., "Managerial Uses and Limitations of Uniform Dollar Accounting Data," *Accounting Review*, 34 (Apr. 1959), 242-49.

Study Group on Business Income, *Changing Concepts of Business Income*. New York: The Macmillan Company, 1952.

Technical Services Department of the American Institute of Certified Public Accountants, "Opinion Survey On Price-Level Adjustment Of Depreciation," *Journal of Accountancy*, 105 (Apr. 1958), 36-43.

Trumbull, Wendell P., "Price-Level Depreciation and Replacement Cost," *Accounting Review*, 33 (Jan. 1958), 26-34.

Vatter, William J., "Fund-Theory View of Price-Level Adjustments," *Accounting Review*, 37 (Apr. 1962), 189-207.

Wade, Harry H., "Comments on Research Bulletins," *Accounting Review*, 37 (Apr. 1962), 217-22.

Walsh, Francis J., Jr., "Inflation and Corporate Accounting," *Studies in Business Policy*, No. 104. New York: National Industrial Conference Board, 1962.

Warner, George H., "Depreciation on a Current Basis," *Accounting Review*, 29 (Oct. 1954), 628-33.

Weber, G. Fred, "Price Level Accounting," *Accounting Review*, 35 (Oct. 1960), 641-49.

Wilcox, Edward B. and Howard C. Greer, "The Case Against Price-Level Adjustments in Income Determination," *Journal of Accountancy*, 90 (Dec. 1950), 492-505.

Zeff, Stephen A., "Replacement Cost: Member of the Family, Welcome Guest, or Intruder?" *Accounting Review*, 37 (Oct. 1962), 611-25.

Zieha, Eugene L., "Accounting under Conditions of Changing Prices from the Debtor and Creditor Viewpoint," *Accounting Review*, 28 (Oct. 1953), 528-33.

The Wheelock Company

The Wheelock Company, a manufacturer of aluminum products, had experienced rapid, although at times erratic, growth in the postwar period. In February, 1952, Mr. James Wheelock, president and founder of the company, was considering ways of financing future growth. Since he was most anxious to encourage employee interest and participation in the success of the business, he considered an employee stock purchase plan, but concluded that such a plan was not desirable at present for two reasons: (1) Mr. Wheelock, members of his family and a few close associates within the business held all of the outstanding stock and they did not want to dilute their interests, and (2) the record of fluctuating profits coupled with the need to finance a substantial part of the company's growth with retained earnings had made it impossible to establish any regular dividend policy. Mr. Wheelock believed that a policy of more generous and stable dividends would be necessary to make a stock purchase plan attractive to employees.

At a meeting of the Board of Directors on March 2, 1952, Mr. Johnson, treasurer and a stockholder, recommended an issue of debentures. He noted that Wheelock had no long-term debt, but he believed the company was now sufficiently established to consider some of the possible advantages of debt financing. The Wheelock Company had achieved a favorable credit standing through its prompt repayment of periodic seasonal notes at the two local banks.

Mr. Johnson pointed out that debt financing offered a definite tax advantage since interest was a tax-deductible expense. For 1952, the company estimated its average tax liability, including excess profits tax, at 65 per cent of net earnings. Mr. Johnson also noted that debt financing would not affect existing stock holdings. The Board agreed with him and instructed him to develop a proposal for debt financing.

At a meeting on March 10, 1952, Mr. Wheelock, Mr. Johnson, and Mr. Beach, partner of Beach, Wilson and Company,

328

Wheelock's public accountants, discussed the proposed financing. Mr. Beach agreed that a debt issue appeared attractive at this time. Johnson said the possibility of offering debentures to employees had been mentioned at the earlier meeting of the Board of Directors, but that Mr. Wheelock, who was keenly aware of inflation, preferred not to offer "fixed-dollar investments" to employees.

Inflation Provision Debentures

Mr. Beach recalled an article by Richard Goode in *The National Tax Journal* for December, 1951.[1]

The article proposed savings bonds with interest and principal payments related to a price index to eliminate the risk of inflation for bondholders. An appropriate index would be used, and interest payments would rise or fall with the index; principal repayment would provide purchasing power equivalent to that of the original investment.

The concept of a stabilized-purchasing-power bond is not new. As early as the 1880's, the English economist, Alfred Marshall, suggested the idea for long-term debts and other contracts. The experience of American investors with savings bonds since World War II has made "fixed-dollar" investments much less attractive. In real terms, the vast majority of bondholders have earned no interest and instead have suffered a marked loss of principal. To many savers, constant-purchasing-power bonds would probably have considerably wider appeal than stocks as a hedge against inflation because the principal would be safer, and purchase would be simpler and require less knowledge.

Guaranteeing the purchasing power of a bond is in some respects similar to offering a higher interest rate. An important difference is that the value of the purchasing-power guarantee to an individual bondholder varies with his expectations as to the speed and extent of inflation. For those anticipating the greatest inflation, the guarantee would be equal to a very high interest rate.

The idea of such an issue appealed to Mr. Wheelock, and Mr. Johnson agreed to prepare a proposal to be presented to the Board of Directors on May 15, 1952. Exhibit 1 describes the bond issue proposed by Mr. Johnson.

During the discussion at the Directors' meeting, Mr. Wheelock regarded the proposal with enthusiasm. However, questions were raised about the accounting treatment of interest and principal payments and the method of disclosing the debt on the company's balance sheet. The Wheelock Company did not want its auditors to take

---

[1] Richard Goode, "A Constant-Purchasing-Power Savings Bond," *National Tax Journal*, Vol. 4, December, 1951.

exception to any of its accounting procedures, since its financial statements were submitted to the two local banks. Furthermore, the company foresaw the need for public stock financing before maturity of the bonds. In this event, the company's financial statements would be included in registration statements subject to the approval of various state and federal authorities.

In answer to another question, Mr. Johnson stated that interest payments, including amounts attributable to price-level adjustments, would be currently deductible for federal income tax purposes. However, he believed that any adjustment in the principal amount could not be deducted until the debentures were retired in 1972.

Exhibits 2 and 3 give Wheelock's financial statements for the years 1946–1951.

EXHIBIT 1

The Wheelock Company
Description of Debentures

Wheelock Company—$4^1/_2$ per cent Inflation Provision Debentures Dated July 2, 1952, Due July 2, 1972, $100 Face, $300,000 Total. Interest Payable Semi-Annually on January 2 and July 2.

The debentures would be issued on July 2, 1952 in denominations of $100 totaling an original face amount of $300,000. At maturity, July 2, 1972, the aggregate liability of the company would not be less than $300,000 and not more than 150 per cent of face value ($450,000) depending upon fluctuations in the purchasing power of the dollar.

Within these limits, the company would pay interest and principal equal in purchasing power to the value of the money received by the company. To determine the value of the dollar at any interest date or at maturity, the Consumer Price Index would be used. This index is released by the Bureau of Labor Statistics three to four weeks after the end of each month.

The Base Index would be the final official index number for June, 1952. The maturity value would be determined as follows:

$$\frac{\text{Index number for April, 1972}}{\text{Base index}} \times \text{face amount}$$

Interest payments would be computed semi-annually as follows:

$$\frac{\text{Index number for April or October}}{\text{Base index}} \times \text{face amount} \times 4\tfrac{1}{2}\% \times \tfrac{1}{2} \text{ year}$$

EXHIBIT 2

The Wheelock Company
Condensed Statements of Income and Retained Earnings
for Years Ended December 31, 1946 through 1951

	1946	1947	1948	1949	1950	1951
Sales	$784,000	$1,565,000	$2,470,000	$1,170,000	$4,354,000	$8,270,000
Less Cost of Goods Sold	689,000	1,257,000	2,050,000	991,000	3,541,000	7,265,000
Gross Margin	$ 95,000	$ 308,000	$ 420,000	$ 179,000	$ 813,000	$1,005,000
Selling, General & Administrative Expenses	78,400	219,000	322,000	153,000	611,000	745,000
Net Operating Income	$ 16,600	$ 89,000	$ 98,000	$ 26,000	$ 202,000	$ 260,000
Other Income	—	7,800	11,700	—	25,400	71,200
Other Expenses	23,500	23,500	37,700	40,900	40,600	35,900
Net Income (Loss) Before Taxes	$ (6,900)	$ 73,300	$ 72,000	$ (14,900)	$ 186,800	$ 295,300
Federal Income Taxes	—	25,200	27,100	—	91,900	135,000
Federal Excess Profits Taxes	—	—	—	—	—	41,300
Total Taxes	$ —	$ 25,200	$ 27,100	$ —	$ 91,900	$ 176,300
Net Income (Loss) for Year	$ (6,900)	$ 48,100	$ 44,900	$ (14,900)	$ 94,900	$ 119,000
Retained Earnings:						
Balance at Beginning of Year	$(37,500)	$ (44,400)	$ (8,300)	$ 24,600	$ 9,700	$ 48,600
Net Profit (Loss) for the Year	(6,900)	48,100	44,900	(14,900)	94,900	119,000
	$(44,400)	$ 3,700	$ 36,600	$ 9,700	$ 104,600	$ 167,600
Preferred Stock Dividends	—	12,000	12,000	—	24,000	12,000
Common Stock Dividends	—	—	—	—	32,000	20,000
Total Dividends	$ —	$ 12,000	$ 12,000	$ —	$ 56,000	$ 32,000
Balance at End of Year	$(44,400)	$ (8,300)	$ 24,600	$ 9,700	$ 48,600	$ 135,600

EXHIBIT 3

The Wheelock Company
Balance Sheets, as of December 31, 1946 through 1951

	1946	1947	1948	1949	1950	1951
Current Assets						
Cash	$ 30,900	$ 15,200	$ 46,100	$ 42,000	$ 10,000	$ 20,500
Accounts Receivable, net	51,200	69,400	63,200	108,300	112,500	155,000
Inventories	123,000	132,400	181,000	217,900	253,400	342,400
	$205,100	$217,000	$290,300	$368,200	$375,900	$517,900
Long-term Assets						
Land	$ 10,000	$ 10,000	$ 10,000	$ 10,000	$ 10,000	$ 10,000
Buildings and Equipment	476,800	521,400	654,600	790,500	825,800	830,500
Less Depreciation	(149,300)	(168,200)	(193,500)	(220,800)	(243,200)	(245,000)
	$337,500	$363,200	$471,100	$579,700	$592,600	$595,500
Other Assets						
Investments	$ 10,000	$ 10,000	$ 5,000	$ 5,000	—	—
Deferred Charges	11,000	13,800	17,400	19,100	15,500	18,600
	$ 21,000	$ 23,800	$ 22,400	$ 24,100	$ 15,500	$ 18,600
	$563,600	$604,000	$783,800	$972,000	$984,000	$1,132,000
Current Liabilities						
Bank Loans	$ 38,000	—	$ 10,000	$ 60,000	$ 20,000	—
Other Notes Payable	30,300	$ 25,600	50,600	46,000	33,500	$ 24,600
Trade Accounts Payable	125,000	157,400	184,800	217,000	228,200	282,500
Accrued Liabilities	14,700	29,300	13,800	39,300	53,700	89,300
	$208,000	$212,300	$259,200	$362,300	$335,400	$396,400
Stockholders' Equity						
6% Preferred ($100 par)	$200,000	$200,000	$200,000	$200,000	$200,000	$200,000
Common Stock ($2 par)	200,000	200,000	300,000	400,000	400,000	400,000
Retained Earnings	(44,400)	(8,300)	24,600	9,700	48,600	135,600
	$355,600	$391,700	$524,600	$609,700	$648,600	$735,600
	$563,600	$604,000	$783,800	$972,000	$984,000	$1,132,000

QUESTIONS:

1. As Mr. Beach, write a report to the Board of Directors recommending an appropriate accounting treatment for bond interest and principal on the financial statements. The Consumer Price Index for June, 1952, was 113.4 (1947–49 = 100). Compute appropriate information for the financial statements at December 31, 1959, and December 31, 1960, using the following assumed data:

	Consumer Price Index	
	April	*October*
1958	121.0	122.0
1959	124.9	125.7
1960	124.1	123.2

2. In general journal form, give the entries you would record in 1959 and 1960.

The Reece Corporation

In 1955, the American Accounting Association publish-
ed "Price Level Changes and Financial Statements—Case Studies of
Four Companies." The four companies were: New York Telephone
Company, Armstrong Cork Company, The Reece Corporation, and
Sargent & Company, a Connecticut hardware manufacturer. These
studies, which were prepared under the direction of Professor Ralph
C. Jones of Yale University, were made possible by grants from the
Merrill Foundation for the Advancement of Financial Knowledge.

The Reece Corporation was described as follows in
the case studies publication:

The Reece Button Hole Machine Company was founded
and incorporated in 1881 under the laws of the State of Maine for the purpose of producing and marketing John Reece's invention, the first machine
automatically to stitch eyelet-end buttonholes in the high button shoes of
that day. In the following year, a second Maine corporation, The International Button Hole Sewing Machine Company, was separately capitalized
and became the exclusive marketing agent for Reece products in foreign
countries.

From its inception, the company has specialized in automatic
sewing machines for such short cycle stitching operations as button sewing,
tacking, short-seam overedging, and eyelet stitching in addition to the many
varied kinds of buttonhole sewing required by the shoe and garment industries.
The company, it is believed, was among the first to lease exclusively rather
than sell its products. This policy was followed until 1930 when an irrevocable ninety-day option to purchase or lease was granted to customers upon
the installation of new equipment.

In 1948, the two original companies merged to form a new
Massachusetts corporation, The Reece Corporation. In 1949, its manufacturing departments were moved from Boston to Waltham, and in 1954 the administrative, sales, and engineering departments also were moved there. The
company maintains branch offices for sales and service in twenty major
garment producing centers in the United States. Five subsidiary companies
and twenty-eight agents in thirty-three foreign countries sell, lease, and service
its products abroad.

In its seventy-second annual report for the year ended
December 31, 1953, The Reece Corporation, using data gathered in this price

334

level study, presented an analysis of its capital and income, measured in dollars of uniform purchasing power. So far as is known, this is the first American corporation to include such information in its annual report.

Professor Jones presented the following summary of his analysis of The Reece Corporation:

	(*Statements as Reported*)	(*Adjusted Statements*)
The gross income for 1951 was:	almost three times that of 1940	only 1¹/₂ times that of 1940
From 1940 to 1951 income taxes took:	57% of the taxable net income	67% of the taxable net income
From 1940 to 1951 the depreciation charge:	appeared to be adequate to cover the cost of the assets used in operations	was deficient by 22% of book depreciation
The net income from 1940 to 1951 was:	10% of the gross income	6% of the gross income
From 1940 to 1951 the corporation distributed as dividends to common stockholders:	67% of its net income	108% of its net income
From 1940 to 1951 the rate of return on the common stock equity was:	8.1%	4.9%

Since 1953, the annual reports of the company have included price-level data and commentaries, both in the president's letter to the stockholders and in a separate section of the report called "Price Level Study." The following excerpts are taken from the president's letters in the annual reports for the years 1956–1958:

...I wish that all industry would include such [price-level] studies in their reports to stockholders as it would dispel the general illusion that overstated profits are real profits...[1956].

...I... believe that it is an obligation of management to disclose to stockholders a true profit statement, as shown in the Price Level Study in this report, and not a fictitious and enlarged one caused by inflation...

...It is not always easy for small business to borrow and therefore failures and mergers are on the increase. If this keeps on we will end up with big business only. I am not against bigness as such, we all try to get bigger and better, but I am against the policy of making it very difficult for small business to grow. It cannot be otherwise with a tax rate of 52 per cent on earnings fictitiously enlarged through inflation and inadequate depreciation allowances. When smaller manufacturing companies have not the cash to buy up-to-date manufacturing equipment and it is either impossible or inadvisable to borrow, they cannot compete pricewise with the bigger concerns and we get failures or mergers. It is, therefore, the government itself that is causing mergers and due to their increase it is now investigating mergers and making it more difficult to merge...[1957].

...The impact of inflation on a manufacturing organization strikes from many angles. At this point I will mention one impact which limits the ability of manufacturers to purchase new manufacturing equipment. The government allows a deduction from earnings before taxes, spread over a period of years, for the cost of factory equipment such as lathes, grinders, etc., but the replacement cost of these tools is three to four times the original cost, depending on age, therefore the difference shows up as a fictitious profit taxed at 52 per cent. This is one reason why the country's manufacturing plant is less efficient than it should or could be, a rather dangerous result with world conditions as they are. I believe that the replacement cost of manufacturing equipment should be allowed as a deduction from earnings before taxes in order to promote the purchase of new equipment, increase efficiency, lower costs, and improve quality...[1958].

The more technical disclosure was made by Reece's treasurer in the "Price Level Study" section of the annual reports, from which the following excerpts are taken for the years 1955 through 1961:

The purpose of the Price Level Study is to compare the company's financial statements as prepared by conventional accounting with these same statements after adjustment to show the effect of inflation.

In applying the Price Level Study to the company's figures, we compare historical dollars, those with which we are all sadly familiar and which have lost more than half their purchasing power in the last fifteen years, with uniform dollars. The uniform dollar used is defined as a uniform measuring unit whose purchasing power is equal to the 1955 dollar. In order to prepare the accompanying charts, the company's financial statements from 1940 to date have been restated in 1955 uniform dollars by means of index numbers based on the Consumer Price Index. For chart purposes [only], both historical dollar and uniform dollar amounts have been expressed as a percentage of 1940 in order to establish a common point of departure.

From the first chart [see Exhibit 3], it is apparent that, in historical dollars, gross income was almost four times as large in 1955 as it was in 1940, whereas in uniform dollars it is only about twice as large. 1955 net income after taxes in historical dollars is 2.9 times as great as that for 1940, yet in uniform dollars it is only 1.4 times as large.

Studying a company's financial statements when expressed in uniform dollars has a sobering effect in these days of high production, apparently high profits, and general prosperity. The true growth of a company becomes apparent, the false basis of taxable income is high-lighted and, in the case of this company, one finds that earnings plowed back in the business are only about 58 per cent as large as indicated by conventional accounting practice.

The rising cost of machinery and buildings over the last fifteen years is one of the most serious problems that face manufacturing companies. These costs have gone up significantly faster than is indicated by the Consumer Price Index which has been used in preparing this Price Level Study. Unfortunately, we do not know of a price index that could properly be applied to a manufacturing concern so we have used the Consumer Price Index, but we recognize that it falls short of indicating the full effect of inflation on this company. The Price Level Study indicates that the company's reserves for depreciation are 25 per cent or $703,000 less than they should be. No doubt the true inadequacy of the reserves is nearer 40 per cent, or more than $1,000,000. As equipment wears out or becomes obsolete, it must be replaced. Since depreciation reserves are inadequate to provide for replacement, retained earnings or borrowed money must be used to help pay for the replacement equipment.

We believe that the comparison of financial results in historical dollars with those converted to uniform dollars is an invaluable management tool. However, the theory and application of the Price Level Study is difficult to understand even after considerable study. Therefore, we wonder if it is of interest to readers of this report. Would you please note on your proxy whether or not you think we should include this section in future reports [1955].

...During 1956, the underlying pressures of higher and higher wages, and thus higher costs in spite of improving technology, forced prices upward once more, resulting in a 3 per cent increase in the Consumer Price Index. This increase was felt by all of us in our personal purchases of goods and services, yet it did not appear to be an alarming rise. However, the Price Level Study indicates that the rise was sufficient to create serious distortions in the reported figures of industry...[1956].

...If we were permitted to adjust our tax return to allow for a more realistic cost of sales and depreciation expense based on uniform dollars, a 51 per cent tax rate would produce estimated federal and foreign income taxes of $549,000 or $71,000 less than is expected. It probably is not realistic to hope for a change in the tax law that would allow this adjustment in the near future. On the other hand, the apparent 51 per cent tax provision for 1957 is actually 58 per cent of earnings before taxes when expressed in uniform dollars.

The cumulative effect of inadequate depreciation accruals and failure to adjust inventories for the effect of inflation is apparent when the earned surplus account is expressed in uniform dollars. At December 31, 1957 earned surplus as reported by conventional means was $2,180,000, but converted to uniform dollars it was $1,368,000 or 37 per cent less...[1957].

...On an historical dollar basis the company's common dividend of $1.10 for 1958 appears ultra-conservative, but on a uniform dollar basis this dividend leaves very little for the company's growth after payment of approximately $72,000 from retained earnings to purchase preferred stock under the sinking fund provisions and to reduce the principal of its mortgage loan [1958].

...The chart [on the following page] compares changes over the past ten years in certain significant balance sheet items.

Inventories apparently increased 86 per cent during the period, whereas the actual increase expressed in uniform dollars was 52.5 per cent. This increase was required to take care of the company's increased volume of business and greater diversity of product.

Working capital also experienced a substantial increase, but that increase, when expressed in uniform dollars, was much less than historical dollar reporting indicates.

Although on an historical dollar basis fixed assets after depreciation increased $594,000 or 19 per cent, in uniform dollars the company experienced a decrease of $1/2$ of 1 per cent. This is a point of particular significance to the company because it shows that, in spite of investing substantially more

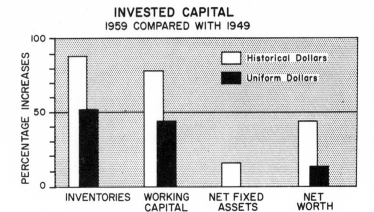

INVESTED CAPITAL
1959 COMPARED WITH 1949

than its depreciation allowances in fixed assets during these years, no real growth in fixed assets occurred.

Net worth has increased 43 per cent in historical dollars but only 17 per cent in uniform dollars. Common stock equity (not shown on the chart) increased $13.16 per share during these ten years as expressed by conventional accounting. However, on a 1959 uniform dollar basis, the increase is $8.55. The $4.61 difference represents the erosion of capital caused by a 17 per cent loss of purchasing power of the dollar and the necessity to provide reserves in excess of normal depreciation allowances in order to replace plant and equipment...[1959].

...It is well to note that although 1960 gross income expressed in historical dollars is more than double that of 1943, in uniform dollars (those of a constant purchasing power) the increase is only 34 per cent. The company's net income before taxes in historical dollars is about twice that of 1943, whereas in true purchasing power it increased 27 per cent.

The Reece Corporation (unconsolidated) shows net profit of $1,002,000 for 1960, but after adjustments for price level changes net profit expressed in 1960 uniform dollars is $906,000. This difference of $96,000 provides for $63,000 additional depreciation and $33,000 additional cost of sales to adjust inventories for the increase in the price level.

Even in a year of relative price stability we find a substantial difference between reported profit, on which income taxes are based, and profit adjusted for price level changes which, in effect, is profit after taking into account the loss of purchasing power of funds invested in fixed assets and inventory. It follows that for 1960 the federal income tax of about $50,000 applicable to the $96,000 necessary to adjust depreciation and inventories is a capital levy, not an income tax.

Extending this example a bit further, it is not hard to imagine a company which reports a low margin of profit in an inflationary period, but which actually suffers a loss after making adjustments for price level changes, being required to pay so-called income taxes.

This company's relatively heavy investment in inventory and fixed assets, including machines leased to customers, requires constant awareness of the effects of price level changes. In periods of inflation, a large share of reported earnings must be reinvested in the business to overcome erosion of capital and provide for reasonable growth. This thought is best illustrated by the fact that during the last ten years the book value of the company's fixed assets has increased 22 per cent in historical dollars but only 2 per cent in uniform dollars [1960].

1961 was a year of relative price stability during which the Consumer Price Index rose 1.1 per cent. On figures adjusted for price level changes, even a moderate rise in prices within a year has some effect on inventory valuation, which is reflected in cost of sales. Coupled with past periods of ever increasing prices, the effect on required depreciation charges is substantial.

In 1961, the company's unconsolidated net profit was $93,000 greater when expressed by conventional means than in uniform dollars. Conversion to uniform dollars required increases in depreciation and cost of sales of $52,000 and $35,000 respectively and a reduction in income of $6,000 caused by the sale of certain assets.

During the past five years, in which price levels increased 10.1 per cent, a very significant difference in growth appears when historical dollar increases are compared with growth expressed in dollars of uniform purchasing power. For ease of comparison, increases in historical and uniform dollars for certain balance sheet items are expressed in percentages below:

Five Year Per Cent Increase

	Historical Dollars	Uniform Dollars
Inventories	39.6	26.8
Working capital	55.8	32.2
Fixed assets	9.0	(.4)
Net worth	34.4	24.4

Exhibits 1 and 2 show Reece's consolidated financial statements for 1960 and 1961. Exhibits 3 and 4 show gross income and net income (before and after taxes) in both historical dollars and uniform dollars as a percentage of 1940 and 1943 figures, respectively. Exhibit 5 gives the effect of price-level changes on unconsolidated net income, cost of sales, and depreciation for the period 1956 through 1961.

EXHIBIT 1

The Reece Corporation
Consolidated Balance Sheets at December 31, 1961 and 1960

	1961	1960
ASSETS:		
Current Assets:		
Cash	$ 899,196	$1,178,244
Short-term securities, at cost, which approximates market value	300,000	—
Receivables, less reserve of $29,500 in 1961, and $28,200 in 1960	1,617,296	1,240,725
Inventories	2,919,456	2,733,352
Prepaid expenses	215,452	189,981
Total current assets	$ 5,951,400	$5,342,302
Municipal Bonds and Miscellaneous Investments, at cost	$ —	$ 200,962
Rental Machines, at cost	$ 6,032,133	$5,955,198
Less—Reserves for depreciation	3,288,566	3,387,863
	$ 2,743,567	$2,567,335
Property, Plant and Equipment, at cost:		
Land	$ 74,188	$ 78,275
Plant	1,739,563	1,615,837
Machinery, equipment, tools and fixtures	1,467,798	1,247,956
	$ 3,281,549	$2,942,068
Less—Reserves for depreciation	1,223,960	1,092,202
	$ 2,057,589	$1,849,866
Patents	$ 1	$ 1
	$10,752,557	$9,960,466
LIABILITIES:		
Current Liabilities:		
Current installments of mortgage note payable	$ 23,333	$ 23,333
Indebtedness to European banks	155,215	150,218
Accounts payable	185,714	192,875
Accrued liabilities	481,250	430,165
Federal and foreign income taxes, less cash reserved in England for tax payments, $314,281 in 1961 and $227,920 in 1960	807,017	754,036
Total current liabilities	$ 1,652,529	$1,550,627
4¼% Real Estate Mortgage Note Payable, due in installments to 1964, less installments due within one year	$ 151,667	$ 175,000

Capital Stock and Surplus:
5% cumulative preferred stock, par value
   $100 per share—
   Authorized, 3,747 shares
   Issued, 2,711 shares in 1960[1] $ — $ 271,100
Common stock, par value $1 per share—
   Authorized, 197,829 shares
   Issued, 192,549 shares   192,549   192,549
Capital surplus   3,772,143   3,774,204
Earned surplus   4,993,346   4,081,829

                                                    $ 8,958,038 $8,319,682
Less—Treasury stock, at cost—
   Preferred, 754 shares in 1960   —   75,166
   Common, 972 shares   9,677   9,677

                                                    $ 8,948,361 $8,234,839

                                                    $10,752,557 $9,960,466

---

[1] Redeemed in 1961. Excess of cost over par value charged to capital surplus.

EXHIBIT 2

The Reece Corporation
Consolidated Statements of Income and Earned Surplus
for the Years Ended December 31, 1961 and 1960

	1961	1960
INCOME:		
Sales, Rentals and Services	$8,901,430	$7,870,560
Costs and Expenses:		
Cost of sales, servicing, selling and engineering expenses	$4,429,134	$4,016,035
General operating expenses	791,892	668,230
Depreciation	874,873	798,556
Taxes, other than federal and foreign income taxes	281,382	241,463
	$6,377,281	$5,724,284
Net income before federal and foreign taxes	$2,524,149	$2,146,276
Provision for federal and foreign income taxes	1,263,000	1,137,000
Net income for the year	$1,261,149	$1,009,276
EARNED SURPLUS:		
Balance, Beginning of Year	$4,081,829	$3,391,620
Add—Net income for the year	1,261,149	1,009,276
	$5,342,978	$4,400,896
Deduct—Cash dividends declared:		
Preferred stock, $2.50 per share in 1961 and $5.00 per share in 1960	$ 4,793	$ 12,544
Common stock, $1.80 per share in 1961 and $1.60 per share in 1960	344,839	306,523
	$ 349,632	$ 319,067
Balance, End of Year	$4,993,346	$4,081,829

EXHIBIT 3

The Reece Corporation
Gross Income and Net Income Before and After
Taxes for 1940-1955 as Percentage of 1940 Figures

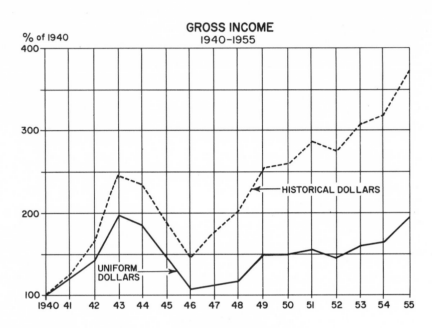

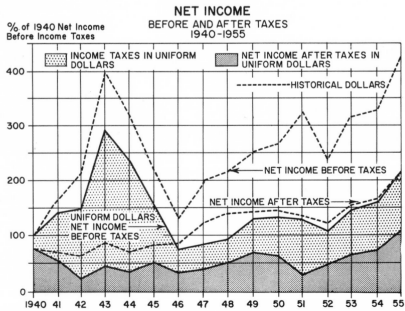

EXHIBIT 4

The Reece Corporation
Gross Income and Net Income Before and After
Taxes for 1943-1961 as Percentage of 1943 Figures

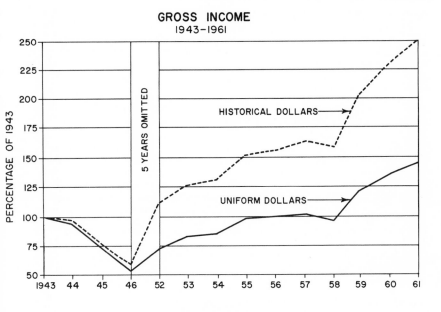

GROSS INCOME
1943–1961

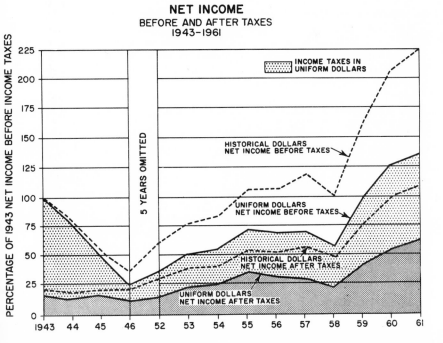

NET INCOME
BEFORE AND AFTER TAXES
1943-1961

EXHIBIT 5

The Reece Corporation
Price-Level Effect on Unconsolidated Net Income, Cost of Sales and Depreciation, 1956-1961
(000 omitted from column figures)

	Net Income		Understatement of	
	Historical Dollars	Uniform Dollars	Cost of Sales	Depreciation
1956	$ 542	$455	$26	$61
1957	594	456	66	72
1958	505	371	58	76
1959	767	675	23	69
1960[1]	1,002	906	33	63
1961[1]	1,089	996[2]	35	52

[1] These data are based on unconsolidated financial statements. Consolidated financial statements are given in Exhibits 1 and 2. Prior to 1960, Reece did not report on a consolidated basis because its investment in subsidiaries and the profits earned by subsidiaries were minor. When the consolidated basis of reporting was adopted in 1960, it was impractical to adjust subsidiary companies' figures in order to report the Price Level Study also on a consolidated basis.

[2] Reflects $6,000 adjustment in income realized from sale of certain assets.

QUESTIONS:

1. Do you consider the differences between reported and adjusted data for The Reece Corporation significant? Explain.
2. In general, the accounting profession has been reluctant to endorse financial statements which reflect price-level changes. What are the reasons for this position?
3. Do you think it is desirable for corporations to present supplementary price-level data in addition to the usual financial statements? Explain.
4. Do you think the disclosure of price-level data is easily understood? Explain.
5. What other disclosure might Reece have used to inform stockholders that not all income should be considered available for dividends because of the effects of inflation?
6. Do you agree with the president's statement that: "It is not always easy for small business to borrow and therefore failures and mergers are on the increase"? Might a more liberal depreciation policy for tax purposes relieve this problem?
7. Reece's president advocates that the replacement cost of equipment should be allowed as a basis for computing depreciation deducted in determining taxable income. What are the pros and cons of replacement cost depreciation? Contrast this with "purchasing power" depreciation.
8. Contrast the effect on various types of businesses (heavy manufacturing, retailing, etc.) of an overall reduction in the corporate income tax rate versus more liberalized depreciation allowances.

United States Steel Corporation (A)

United States Steel Corporation is the nation's largest steel producer, with over 25 per cent of the industry's capacity. The corporation's operations are highly integrated; U. S. Steel produces substantially all of its required iron ore, limestone and coal. The corporation also generates electric power, and operates steamships, barges and dock facilities for transportation of raw materials and steel products.

Management has long been concerned about the effects of inflation on the cost of replacing facilities. In management's judgment, price controls, large wage increases and heavy taxes during World War II had prevented the corporation from retaining sufficient amounts in the business to provide for future needs. After operating at maximum capacity during the war years, U. S. Steel expected to operate at about two-thirds of capacity in 1946 and future years.

1947 Change to Replacement Depreciation

In 1947, management decided to recognize current replacement costs of existing facilities by an increased depreciation charge of $26.3 million in addition to $87.7 million for wear and exhaustion based upon original costs. (See Exhibit 1.) This was disclosed as follows in the income statement:

Wear and Exhaustion of Facilities:
Based on original cost	$ 87,745,483
Added to cover replacement cost	26,300,000
	$114,045,483

On the balance sheet the $26.3 million was classified as a reserve following long-term debt.

Much of the 1947 annual report to stockholders was devoted to an explanation of the impact of inflation on U. S. Steel. Management stated that additional steel price increases of about 40 per cent would have been required to raise 1947 steel prices to the level of wholesale prices of all commodities. The following table was given in support of management's argument:

	Year 1940	December 1947	Per Cent Increase
Wholesale Price of All Commodities	100	208	108
Wholesale Price of All Commodities Other than Farm Products and Foods	100	175	75
Wholesale Price of Iron and Steel	100	150	50
Composite Price of Finished Steel	100	139	39

As examples of cost increases from 1940 to 1947, the following items were cited:

Average hourly earnings	80%
Zinc ore	62
Copper	77
Tin	96
Fuel oil	130
Scrap	93
Coke	111
Wire drawing machines	91
Standard electric cranes	105
Reheating furnaces	108
Blast furnaces	105
By-product coke ovens	150
Mine locomotives	44
Large electric motors	50
Continuous rolling mills	84
Concrete construction	124
Brick construction	250
Cost of construction, general	79

Management contended that additional amounts required for replacements, in excess of original cost, should be recorded as expenses if profits were not to be overstated and capital dissipated. Since Lifo was permitted for short-term inventories, thereby reflecting current costs in the cost of goods sold, managment felt it should be allowed also for "long-term inventories" (machinery, plants and mines). The following statement was made concerning long-term inventories:

Believing that the same principle of recording the cost of short-term inventories consumed is applicable to recording the cost of long-term inventories consumed (wear and exhaustion of machinery, plants and mines), U.S. Steel in 1947 increased its provision for wear and exhaustion from $87.7 million based on original cost to $114.0 million, or by 30 per cent. This was a step toward stating wear and exhaustion in an amount which will recover in current dollars of diminished buying power the same purchasing power as the original expenditure.

If a business is to continue, it is necessary to recover the purchasing power of sums originally invested in tools so that they may be replaced as they wear out. Therefore, this added amount is carried as a reserve for replacement of properties. It is a simple truth that to buy similar tools of production takes many more dollars today than formerly; to count as profits, rather than as cost, the added sums required merely to sustain production is to retreat from reality into self-deception.

The 30 per cent increase in the provision for wear and exhaustion was determined partly through experienced cost increases and partly through study of construction cost index numbers. Although it is materially less than the experienced cost increase in replacing worn-out facilities, it was deemed appropriate in view of the newness of the application of this principle to the costing of wear and exhaustion. The use of index numbers for cost purposes gained recognition early in 1947 in a Tax Court decision...Although this case deals only with costing short-term inventories, the principles set forth are just as applicable to costing the wear and exhaustion of long-term inventories.

While awaiting accounting and tax acceptance, U. S. Steel believed that it was prudent for it to give some recognition to these increased replacement costs rather than to sit idly by and witness the unwitting liquidation of its business should inadequate recording of costs result in insufficient resources to supply the tools required for sustained production.

A note to the financial statements contained essentially the same information. U. S. Steel's auditors took exception to the fairness of the 1947 financial statements and to consistency stating:

During the year 1947, in partial recognition of the increased replacement cost of long-term facilities which are being worn out or exhausted in production, the corporation has included in costs additional depreciation of $26,300,000 (as indicated in the notes to the accounts) in excess of the amount determined in accordance with the generally accepted accounting principle heretofore followed of making provision for depreciation on the original cost of facilities.

In our opinion, except as set forth in the preceding paragraph, the accompanying consolidated statement of financial position and related statement of income, together with the notes thereto, present fairly the position of United States Steel Corporation and its subsidiaries at December 31, 1947, and the results of the year's operations in conformity with generally accepted accounting principles. Except as indicated...[above], the accounting principles were applied during the year on a basis consistent with that of the preceding year.

U. S. Steel was not alone in its concern over the effect of rising prices. In the late 1940's, several other large corporations, among them Crane Company, E. I. du Pont de Nemours & Company and Libbey-Owens-Ford Glass Company, also made accounting provisions for replacement costs.

Carman G. Blough, director of research of the American Institute of Certified Public Accountants (at that time the American Institute of Accountants), commented on this practice as follows:

...Obviously, if present costs continue it will be necessary to replace existing facilities at considerably more than their cost. This will require that additional capital be tied up in plant and equipment. Additional capital can come from only two sources—retained profits or additional investments. Business often seeks new capital for expansion but it does not like to do so merely to hold its own. Nevertheless, there is great reluctance to report the profits that are needed, beyond dividend requirements, to provide enough funds to replace plant and equipment at high price levels. This reluctance is well founded. Stockholders are hard to convince that increased profits should not be distributed as dividends; labor increases its claims for compensation; political demagogues harangue on the excessiveness of corporate income; and enemies of our political order use it to stir up prejudices against private enterprise.

There can be no argument but that a going concern must be able to replace its productive assets as they are used up if it is to continue to do business. It is also important for management to understand that the difference between cost and estimated replacement value may be significant in determining production and pricing policies. It does not follow, however, that the excess of the cost of replacement over the cost of existing assets should be accounted for as current charges to income. All who have dealt with appraisal values know how very difficult it is just to determine current replacement costs but the most striking difficulty in this respect is the impossibility of predicting what will be the eventual cost of replacing a productive asset. How many men are prepared to state what the price level will be two years from today, to say nothing of trying to guess what it will be five or ten years hence when many of these assets are to be replaced?[1]

At a meeting in September, 1947, the problems of basing depreciation on replacement values were considered by the Committee on Accounting Procedure. The committee felt the matter was so important that it released an immediate statement rather than take the time necessary to issue a formal bulletin. This statement was formally issued as ARB No. 33 in December, 1947, and again in 1953 as ARB No. 43, Chapter 9, Section A, paragraphs 4 through 9. (See pages 309–10 of this book.)

1948 Change to Accelerated Depreciation

U. S. Steel continued replacement depreciation during the first three quarters of 1948, and increased the additional charge to 60 per cent of depreciation based on original costs because "the 30 per cent initially adopted was not sufficient to cover the true cost of property currently consumed." However, during the fourth quarter, the corporation changed its policy in light of discussions with the Securities and Exchange Commission and a letter, dated

---

[1] "Replacement and Excess Construction Costs," *The Journal of Accountancy*, Vol. 84, October 1947, pp. 334–35.

October 14, 1948, from the Committee on Accounting Procedure to the Institute's membership reaffirming the opinion expressed earlier in ARB No. 33. (In 1953, this letter was reproduced in ARB No. 43, Chapter 9, Section A, paragraphs 11 through 17. See page 310 of this book.) The SEC rejected depreciation based on replacement cost, referring to its Accounting Series Release No. 4, part of which reads as follows:

In cases where financial statements…are prepared in accordance with accounting principles for which there is no substantial authoritative support, such financial statements will be presumed to be misleading or inaccurate despite disclosures contained in the certificate of the accountant provided the matters involved are material.

Management explained the change as follows in its 1948 annual report to the stockholders:

U. S. Steel believes that the principle which it adopted in 1947 and continued in 1948 is a proper recording of the wear and exhaustion of its facilities in terms of current dollars as distinguished from the dollars which it originally expended for those facilities. However, in view of the disagreement existing among accountants, both public and private, and the stated position of the American Institute of Accountants, which is supported by the Securities and Exchange Commission, that the only accepted accounting principle for determining depreciation is that which is related to the actual number of dollars spent for facilities, regardless of when or of what buying power, U. S. Steel has adopted a method of accelerated depreciation on cost instead of one based on purchasing power recovery. This method is made retroactive to January 1, 1947. The amount of the accelerated depreciation for the year 1948 is $55,335,444, including a deficiency of $2,675,094 in the amount reported in 1947 as depreciation added to cover replacement cost. Such accelerated depreciation is not presently deductible for federal income tax purposes.

The reserve for replacement of properties was eliminated by a transfer to the allowance for depreciation. Part of a note to the 1948 financial statements explained the new depreciation policy as follows:

The accelerated depreciation is applicable to the cost of postwar facilities in the first few years of their lives, when the economic usefulness is greatest. The amount thereof is related to the excess of current operating rate over U. S. Steel's long-term peacetime average rate of 70 per cent of capacity. The annual accelerated amount is 10 per cent of the cost of facilities in the year in which the expenditures are made and 10 per cent in the succeeding year, except that this amount is reduced ratably as the operating rate may drop, no acceleration being made at 70 per cent or lower operations. The accelerated depreciation is in addition to the normal depreciation on such facilities but the total depreciation over their expected lives will not exceed the cost of the facilities.

In its 1949 report, management contended that a business should recover sufficient amounts through depreciation and retained income to replace its plant and equipment, and borrowing should be used only to expand capacity. Management felt that the owners' equity was being diluted by the Treasury's refusal to accept, as tax deductible, the excess of replacement or accelerated depreciation over depreciation based on original cost.

Accelerated Amortization
of Emergency Facilities

During and after the Korean War, U. S. Steel was granted Certificates of Necessity which permitted amortization of designated facilities over a 60-month period for tax purposes regardless of the facilities' probable economic lives. Management decided to depreciate these facilities in the corporate accounts over the 60-month period. (See Exhibit 1.) In 1953, U. S. Steel discontinued its former accelerated depreciation policy, explaining the change in a note to the 1953 financial statements:

> Since 1946 U. S. Steel has followed the policy of reflecting accelerated depreciation on the cost of new facilities in the first few years of their lives when the economic usefulness is greatest. The amounts charged to income for accelerated depreciation have been related to U. S. Steel's rate of operations.
> Under the Internal Revenue Code, that portion of the cost of facilities certified by the Defense Production Administration as essential to the defense effort is covered by a Certificate of Necessity and can be written off for tax purposes at the rate of 20 per cent per year. The effect of amortization of these facilities is to charge to income a greater portion of their cost in the earlier years of life and, therefore, follows the principle of accelerated depreciation.
> U. S. Steel has included in wear and exhaustion in 1953, as a measure of the accelerated depreciation for the year, $105,137,893, representing amortization on its facilities covered by Certificates of Necessity.

In commenting on the effect of accelerated amortization and the tax laws, management pointed out that it had to be regarded as a temporary expedient since "for many companies the addition of amortization on new facilities to so-called regular depreciation on old facilities may approximate, temporarily, a truer total of wear and exhaustion on all facilities based on current dollar value. But it automatically guarantees something of a future crisis." As an example of this, management cited the recently constructed Fairless Works. A portion of this plant's cost was amortized over five years, thus partially offsetting " inadequate " depreciation charges for other facilities. It was stated that this situation would naturally change when the five-year amortization was completed.

Management noted in 1954 that the new methods of accelerated depreciation, first allowed for tax purposes in 1954, would ease the

WEAR AND EXHAUSTION RECORDED vs. WEAR AND EXHAUSTION NEEDED

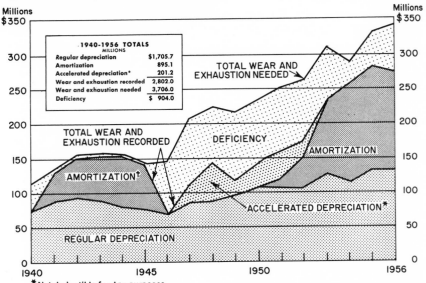

* Not deductible for tax purposes
† Additional amortization due to ending of emergency period allocated to years 1941–1945

future crisis, but even these provisions, applicable to new assets only, would fall far short of providing adequate depreciation on the relatively more numerous and older existing facilities.

In its 1956 report, U.S. Steel included the chart above comparing "wear and exhaustion recorded" with "wear and exhaustion needed."

To calculate "Total Wear and Exhaustion Needed," as shown in the chart, the following statistical procedure was followed: Excluding the amount of non-tax-deductible accelerated depreciation from 1947 through 1952 (see Exhibit 1), and including only regular depreciation on emergency facilities, the amount of wear and exhaustion previously recorded for *each year* included in the chart was subdivided according to the acquisition years of the assets being depreciated. Each yearly subdivision was then adjusted to reflect the change in the *Engineering News-Record*'s index of construction cost from the various earlier acquisition years to any given year included in the chart. The sum of that year's adjusted depreciation amounts gave the "Total Wear and Exhaustion Needed" for that year. The process was repeated for every year in the chart. Notice that each year's deficiency is in dollars of the buying power that prevailed in *that* year.

In 1959, management noted the approaching exhaustion of emergency amortization:

EXHIBIT 1

United States Steel Corporation (A)
Selected Financial Data for the Years 1946-1961
(in millions of dollars)

	Total Cost of Plant and Equipment	Additions and Replacements		Wear and Exhaustion of Facilities					
		Total	Certified Facilities[1]	Accrued Amount	Total Annual Charge	Accelerated Portion[2]	Amortization of Emergency Facilities[3]	Sales	Net Income
1946	$2,568.2	$201.0		$1,741.8	$ 68.7			$1,496.1	$ 88.6
1947	2,725.0	206.6		1,784.5	114.0	$26.3		2,122.8	127.1
1948	2,933.3	275.2		1,632.5[4]	146.0	55.3		2,481.5	129.6
1949	3,067.5	179.1		1,711.5	119.7	22.0		2,301.7	165.9
1950	3,192.7	179.3		1,806.1	143.9	35.5		2,956.4	215.5
1951	3,501.8	352.4	$252.7[5]	1,930.5	162.1	40.4	$ 12.8	3,524.1	184.3
1952	3,914.7	469.2	282.1	2,063.1	176.9	21.6	46.2	3,137.4	143.6
1953	4,198.7	361.4	153.5	2,228.7	236.6		105.1	3,861.0	222.1
1954	4,361.4	227.4	58.3	2,435.7	261.8		142.8	3,250.4	195.4
1955	4,544.3	239.8	31.4	2,670.7	285.2		147.7	4,097.7	370.1
1956	4,768.3	311.8	19.4	2,890.3	277.6		140.2	4,228.9	348.1
1957	5,225.5	514.9	21.3	3,115.9	276.0		115.8	4,413.8	419.4
1958	5,600.2	448.1		3,255.1	204.9		57.2	3,472.1	301.5
1959	5,892.0	366.1		3,380.2	189.9		22.2	3,643.0	254.5
1960	6,303.0	492.4		3,515.4	208.4		13.7	3,698.5	304.2
1961	6,548.5	326.8		3,649.0	210.5		9.0	3,336.5	190.2

[1] Included in Total Additions and Replacements.
[2] Included in Total Annual Charge. Not deductible for tax purposes.
[3] Included in Total Annual Charge. Deductible for tax purposes.
[4] After transfer of $270 million to earned surplus. This amount had been added to the allowance for depreciation in 1935 to cover economic obsolescence of properties. This reserve was not now needed for the purposes anticipated in 1935.
[5] Total of facilities certified in 1950 and 1951.

This [depreciation] deficiency has been aggravated by the running out of 5-year amortization permitted on varying percentages of the total costs of certain defense and defense supporting facilities covered by Certificates of Necessity. The need for revision of the tax laws as they relate to depreciation...continues to be most vital to the maintenance of existing and the addition of new productive capacity.

In 1961, it was stated that the deficiency in recovering the appropriate amount of buying power *each year* from 1946 through 1960 was "$1,605 million, on which taxes were levied as though it were income...[Such tax policy] handicaps all corporations having depreciable property and especially those corporations heavily invested in long-life facilities. It indirectly handicaps all other enterprises who do business with them as their capabilities as customer or supplier are undermined."

QUESTIONS:

1. What is the function of depreciation as viewed by most accountants? Do you consider this a realistic view? Explain. How does U. S. Steel's management define the function of depreciation?
2. Do you agree with U. S. Steel's 1947 change in depreciation policy?
3. Comment on the balance-sheet classification of the $26.3 million additional charge made in 1947.
4. Do you believe, as stated by U.S. Steel's management, that Lifo principles are "applicable to recording the cost of long-term inventories consumed"?
5. Mr. Blough notes in the case "the impossibility of predicting what will be the eventual cost of replacing a productive asset." Is such a prediction necessary to achieve the type of price-level recognition desired by U. S. Steel? Consider carefully the statistical procedures used by the corporation in preparing the chart on page 351.
6. Do you think the 1948 change to accelerated depreciation, related to the rate of operations, was an improvement? Explain. Contrast the 1947 and 1948 depreciation policies.
7. What kind of audit opinion would you have given in 1948? Explain.
8. Comment on the statement that the "annual accelerated amount is 10 per cent of the cost of facilities in the year in which the expenditures are made."
9. Why do you think U. S. Steel preferred the 1947 policy over the one adopted in 1948 even though the latter policy, when applied retroactively to 1947, required an addition of $2.7 million to the provision previously made in 1947?
10. What action, if any, would you have taken as an auditor in 1953?
11. Do you think it was appropriate for U. S. Steel to amortize certified facilities over a five-year period on its books to compensate for inadequate depreciation charges on other assets?
12. Contrast U. S. Steel's accounting treatment of certified facilities with the treatment described in the Aluminum Company of America case, page 302. How do you explain the difference?

Ayrshire Collieries Corporation

Ayrshire Collieries Corporation mines bituminous coal, principally by the stripping method, in Indiana, Illinois and Kentucky. In the late 1940's Ayrshire's management was concerned about the effects of inflation on the adequacy of depreciation provisions based on historical costs.

Proposed Change of Depreciation Accounting

In 1947, the president's message to the stockholders read in part:

The normal method of setting up reserves for depreciation and depletion is based on original cost. The theory is that the total of the depreciation and depletion charges will be sufficient for replacement at the time of exhaustion. This company has followed these accepted principles of accounting.

It seems quite evident to us, however, that the aggregate of these reserves, even if funded with cash or securities retained in the business for that purpose, will no longer be sufficient to provide for necessary replacement, in view of the price trend both as to equipment and coal reserves. Therefore, as a matter of precaution, and so that our balance sheet may be placed on a truly conservative basis, we intend in the coming year to set up an additional reserve in an amount which our accountants and engineers believe to be proper, in order to take care of these excess charges, that is, the difference between the normal reserve accrual and the amount which we feel will actually be required for replacement.

Under present laws, such special appropriations will not be allowable deductions for federal income tax purposes. However, it is the strong opinion of your management that the treatment of depreciation and depletion allowances under the present laws requires extensive revision.

Initial Presentation in Annual Reports

In 1948, Ayrshire began making accounting provisions for "excess replacement cost." An appendix to this case gives a brief description of the statistical method used. On the income statement in the 1948 *annual report*, the provision for excess replacement cost was shown with depreciation and depletion as follows:

Net income before depreciation and other charges deducted below		$6,867,142
Provision for depreciation, depletion and excess replacement cost:		
Depreciation	$471,044	
Depletion	103,601	
Excess replacement cost (Note 4)	221,785	
		796,430
Net income before provision for federal income taxes		$6,070,712
Provision for federal income taxes		2,300,275
Net income for the year (Note 4)		$3,770,437

In Note 4 to the financial statements, management commented as follows:

In accordance with generally accepted accounting practice, the regular provision for depreciation and depletion charged against income during the current and prior years has been made on a basis which will absorb the original cost of the assets over their useful life. However, in view of the marked increase during recent years in the cost of equipping new mines or replacing old equipment, the management has deemed it prudent to make additional provision, by a charge against income, for the year ended June 30, 1948, to a reserve for excess replacement cost of fixed assets.

The same form of presentation was used through 1955.

On the balance sheet, the "Reserve for Excess Replacement Cost of Fixed Assets" appeared in the "Reserves" section between "Long Term Obligations" and "Stockholders' Equity." In his 1948 message to the stockholders, the president stated in part:

Fixed assets, such as buildings and equipment, deteriorate through use; the Depreciation Reserve records on the financial statement the gradual reduction in worth and this "use cost" is charged off annually to expense. When any asset is exhausted through use the accumulated credits therefor to Depreciation Reserve will equal original cost. We shall continue, for the time being, to use this cost method, which is now generally recognized for income tax purposes, in computing Depreciation Reserve. The tie-in of the Reserve to cost, however, presents a special problem in these days of inflation. When a fixed asset wears out, ordinarily it will have to be replaced, at an expenditure which will depend on price levels at that time. The amount included in Depreciation Reserve for the exhausted asset, being based upon original cost, does not imply that it will suffice for replacement. When the dollar is relatively stable, it can be assumed, reasonably, that the amount carried in reserve will approximate the expense of replacement. Now, however, original cost is no longer any criterion of replacement cost, and it is advisable to reflect this fact in the financial statements. Accordingly, we have established this year a "Reserve for Excess Replacement Costs." The amount credited thereto has been considered an additional expense of operation; this recognizes that "use cost," a definite element of the expense of doing business, has reacted to inflationary tendencies in common with all other items of expense. We will continue our studies, and will readjust the special Reserve to conform thereto.

The auditors took exception to this departure from generally accepted accounting principles and their opinion read in part:

As explained in Note 4 to the financial statements, the companies, during the year ended June 30, 1948, have made provision, by a charge against income, to a reserve for excess replacement cost of fixed assets. Such provision, amounting to $221,785, is in addition to the regular provision for depreciation computed in accordance with generally accepted accounting principles on the basis of the original cost of the assets owned and used in operations.

In our opinion, except as set forth in the preceding paragraph, the . . .

(The remainder of the opinion was in the standard form.)

In 1949, the president's message to stockholders stated:

Charges against earnings resulting in this special reserve are not deductible for income tax purposes. We believe that the revenue laws should be revised so as to permit deductions computed on this realistic basis rather than upon the basis of original cost. We are also advised that the present policy of the Securities and Exchange Commission does not permit financial statements, filed with it, to compute depreciation other than on the original cost method. We believe this policy should be revised to recognize that provision for excess replacement costs is proper and necessary.

From 1948 through 1955, the auditors rendered qualified opinions on the financial statements.

Revised Presentation in Annual Reports

In 1956, the corporation changed its accounting treatment on the income statement in its *annual report*. The price-level adjustment was now shown as follows:

Net income for the year	$2,562,030
Appropriation for depreciation adjustment	95,964
Balance of net income	$2,466,066

As a result of this change, the auditors gave an unqualified opinion. A note to the financial statements read:

In accordance with generally accepted accounting practice the regular provision for depreciation and depletion charged against income during the current and prior years has been made on the basis of the historical dollar cost of plant and equipment. Because the purchasing power of the dollar has declined in recent years such provision does not adequately represent a fair expense in terms of current dollars for the use of such plant and equipment. Management has therefore made an appropriation to a reserve for depreciation adjustment (previously titled "Reserve for Excess Replacement Cost of Fixed Assets") in an amount equal to the difference between the regular depreciation provision and the depreciation adjusted on the basis of the change in purchasing power of the dollar.

The "Reserve for Depreciation Adjustment" was shown on the balance sheet in the "Reserves" section between "Long Term Obligations" and "Stockholders' Equity."

Initial SEC Presentation

On financial statements *filed with the Securities and Exchange Commission* as part of Form 10-K, the following accounting treatment was used from 1948 through 1956:

(1) On the balance sheet, the cumulative adjustment was shown following unappropriated "Earned Surplus" as "Appropriated Earned Surplus—Reserve for Excess Replacement Cost of Fixed Assets."

(2) The depreciation adjustment had no effect on any part of the income statement. Ayrshire based its depreciation on historical cost only and made no appropriation from net income for the year.

(3) On the "Statement of Consolidated Surplus" management made the following disclosure for the year ended June 30, 1956:

Earned Surplus [unappropriated]	
Balance at beginning of year	$19,370,678
Net income from Profit and Loss Statement	2,562,030
	$21,932,708
Deductions:	
Appropriated earned surplus—reserve for excess replacement cost of fixed assets	95,964
Cash and stock dividends	1,812,560
	$ 1,908,524
Balance [unappropriated] at close of year	$20,024,184

(4) A note to the financial statements filed with the SEC at the close of the 1954 and 1955 fiscal years stated:

Reserve for Excess Replacement Cost of Fixed Assets: In accordance with generally accepted accounting practices, the regular provision for depreciation and depletion charged against income during the current and prior years has been made on a basis which will absorb the original cost of the assets over their useful life. However, in view of the marked increase during recent years in the cost of equipping new mines or replacing old equipment, the management has deemed it prudent to make additional provision to a reserve for excess replacement cost of fixed assets . . . .

In the accounts of the companies and in the annual reports to stockholders the provision to the reserve for excess replacement cost of fixed assets has been made each year by a charge against income which, in the opinion of the management, is the only proper method of reflecting the actual cost of operations and the true net income for each year. At the insistence of the SEC, however, the financial statements and schedules contained in this report have been prepared on a basis different from that reflected in the accounts of the companies and as reported to stockholders (a) to eliminate the charge against income for the provision to the reserve, . . . and (b) to transfer the balance in the reserve to the equity section of the balance sheet as "appropriated earned surplus."

In a note to the financial statements filed with the SEC for the fiscal year ended June 30, 1956, the second paragraph was changed as follows:

In the accounts of the companies and in the annual reports to the stockholders the provision to a reserve for depreciation adjustment (previously titled "Reserve for Excess Replacement Cost of Fixed Assets") has been made each year by a charge against income or (in the current year) as a direct appropriation out of net income for the year which, in the opinion of the management . . . (remainder same as in 1954 and 1955).

Revised SEC Presentation

In 1957, the following changes were made in *statements filed with the SEC:*

(1) On the income statement:

Income before federal income taxes	$4,419,130
Provision for federal income taxes	1,514,400
Net income for year	$2,904,730
Appropriation for depreciation adjustment	143,587
Balance of net income transferred to Earned Surplus	$2,761,143

(2) On the "Statement of Consolidated Surplus":

Earned Surplus [unappropriated]	
Balance at beginning of year	$20,024,184
Net income (after deducting appropriation for depreciation adjustment)	2,761,143
	$22,785,327
Less cash and stock dividends	1,896,852
Balance [unappropriated] at close of year	$20,888,475

On the balance sheet as of June 30, 1957, *filed with the SEC*, the cumulative price-level adjustment continued to be shown as appropriated earned surplus.

New Auditors and Second Revision of Presentation in Annual Reports

During the 1958 fiscal year Ayrshire changed auditors. In its 1958 *annual report*, the following disclosure was made on the income statement:

Net Income for the year	$2,884,256
Provision for price-level depreciation	195,429
Net earnings	$2,688,827

On the balance sheet, the "Reserve for Depreciation Adjustment" was moved from "Reserves" to "Stockholders' Equity" where it was shown as "Capital Maintained by Recognition of Price-level Depreciation" between "Paid-in Surplus" and "Earned Surplus." The auditors' opinion contained the usual two paragraphs of the standard short-form report with the following addition:

In our opinion, however, the net income for the year is more fairly presented after deducting the provision for price-level depreciation, since current price levels have been recognized in determining the current cost of property consumed in operations. Generally accepted principles of accounting for cost of property consumed in operations are based on historical costs and do not reflect the effect of price-level changes since dates of acquisition or construction of the companies' depreciable property.

SEC's Deficiency Notice

In July, 1958, similar reports were *filed with the SEC*. As in the 1958 annual report, "Capital Maintained by Recognition of Price-level Depreciation" was shown as a separate item in the Stockholders' Equity section, and not as appropriated earned surplus. This, together with the income statement presentation, resulted in a deficiency notice from the SEC in December, 1958, stating that "changes in capital maintained by the recognition of price-level depreciation during the year ended June 30, 1958 should be reported with the other categories of surplus..." The SEC notice concluded:

The statement of earnings for the year ended June 30, 1958 should be revised so as to eliminate the charge for depreciation in excess of the annual provision based on cost. Your attention is drawn to paragraph 12(c), Chapter 8 of Accounting Research Bulletin No. 43, which states, in part:

12. The following, however, should be excluded from the determination of net income under all circumstances:

(c) Amounts deemed to represent excessive costs of fixed assets, and annual appropriations in contemplation of replacement of productive facilities at higher price levels ... [see page 29].

At a later conference with Ayrshire's auditors and the SEC, the corporation requested clarification of the issues involved. It was again referred to the section of Accounting Research Bulletin No. 43, quoted above. The SEC maintained that this was the basis for the deficiency notice. In reply the corporation submitted a quotation from Accounting Research Bulletin No. 43, Chapter 9(A), paragraph 6, reading:

When there are gross discrepancies between the cost and current values of productive facilities, the committee believes that it is entirely proper for management to make annual appropriations of *net income or surplus* [emphasis supplied] in contemplation of replacement of such facilities at higher price levels [see page 309].

The corporation insisted that its provisions were not excessive since the current value of productive facilities substantially exceeded their original cost. The corporation maintained it should be permitted to show the provision for price-level depreciation as a *deduction* at the bottom of the income statement and not merely as a *surplus appropriation* on the balance sheet. It was the corporation's position that it was primarily concerned with showing the proper cost of operations rather than the "contemplation of replacement."

Compromise with the SEC

After some debate, a compromise was reached with the SEC which provided that the item be shown at the bottom of the income statement, but relabeled as an "*appropriation* for price-level depreciation" (instead of "*provision* for price-level depreciation") to prevent its possible interpretation as additional operating expense. It was further required that use of the title "Net Earnings" be discontinued. The new title should indicate that it was the balance of net income after making appropriation for price-level depreciation. The balance sheet designation, "Capital Maintained by Recognition of Price-level Depreciation," and its classification in the "Stockholders' Equity" section, between "Paid-in Surplus" and "Earned Surplus," remained unchanged.

The compromise resulted in the following change in the income statement submitted with Ayrshire's *amended* Form 10-K for the year ended June 30, 1958:

Income after federal income taxes	$2,884,256
Appropriation for price-level depreciation	195,429
Balance of net income transferred to Earned Surplus	$2,688,827

A note to the amended financial statements read:

The appropriation for price-level depreciation represents the excess of depreciation cost measured by the current purchasing power of the dollar over depreciation cost measured by the purchasing power of the dollar at the dates of acquisition or construction of the companies' depreciable property. The company believes such appropriation of net income should be deducted before arriving at net income for the year, but is informed that such treatment is not in accordance with "generally accepted accounting principles" and will not be accepted by the SEC...

Similar disclosure was made in 1959 on the financial statements filed with the Securities and Exchange Commission.

In its 1959 *annual report*, Ayrshire showed the provision for price-level depreciation on the income statement as follows:

Net Income	$3,594,444
Provision for price-level depreciation (See note)	257,278
Net Income, after deducting provision for price-level depreciation	$3,337,166

Note: The provision for price-level depreciation represents the excess of depreciation cost measured by the current purchasing power of the dollar over depreciation cost measured by the purchasing power of the dollar at the dates of acquisition or construction of the companies' depreciable property.

See Exhibits 2, 3, and 4 for Ayrshire's complete 1959 financial statements as they appeared in the corporation's annual report. In his letter to the stockholders, Mr. Norman E. Kelb, president of Ayrshire, attacked generally accepted accounting principles:

We commented in last year's report on the inadequacy of depreciation determined in accordance with the requirements of "generally accepted accounting principles" and the Internal Revenue Code. As a result of the continuing decline in the purchasing power of the dollar, conventional depreciation does not correctly measure the current cost of property used in operations. The dollars we received for our products and the dollars we spent for labor and materials were in current dollars at the time. In our judgment, depreciation cost should also be measured in current dollars both for tax determination and intelligent management and reporting of your company's affairs. We have, therefore, continued to make provision out of income for price-level depreciation in order to provide for the difference between conventional depreciation and depreciation measured in current dollars. Our provision this year was $257,278, compared to $195,429 a year ago.

Chairman's Criticism of the Accounting Profession

In the December, 1959, issue of the *Journal of Accountancy*, Mr. P.F. Goodrich, Chairman of Ayrshire's Board of Directors, was most critical of the accounting profession and the SEC. In commenting upon these issues, he wrote:

> In the annual report of Ayrshire, we did not consider then and we do not consider now that we were making an appropriation of net income. We believe the provision for price-level depreciation is a necessary charge to arrive at the real net earnings of the corporation and to prevent dilution of the equity capital of our stockholders.
>
> We also believe it is abundantly clear from our earnings statement that net income determined in accordance with "generally accepted accounting principles" and net earnings determined in accordance with principles of accounting which give recognition to price-level changes are based on different concepts ... We believe that no reasonably informed person would be misled by our presentation, but that many investors are being misled by the failure of many annual reports to reflect the real cost of property consumed in operations.
>
> Perhaps the failure to make provisions for price-level depreciation which we believe to be in accord with honest reporting rests on the doorstep of the accounting profession. It is my understanding that the Securities and Exchange Commission enforces "generally accepted accounting principles" determined primarily on the basis of pronouncements made by the American Institute of Certified Public Accountants which, in my opinion, has been remiss in its responsibility by not insisting that principles of accounting for cost of property consumed in operations be up-dated to recognize material changes in the purchasing power of the dollar ...
>
> We were required by the SEC to call a "provision for price-level depreciation" an "appropriation for price-level depreciation" and accordingly we changed the note in our amendment to Form 10-K with the belief that informed people would understand what we consider the real net earnings.[1]

In its 1960 and 1961 annual reports, Ayrshire followed the 1959 accounting treatment for price-level depreciation. The 1959, 1960, and 1961 auditors' opinions were similar to the one given in 1958. The corporation considers "Capital Maintained by Recognition of Price-level Depreciation" as a permanent part of its capital structure, and it does not adjust this account when depreciable assets are retired or replaced.

---

[1] From "Letters" column, *Journal of Accountancy*, Vol. 108, December 1959, pp. 23–24. Used by permission.

APPENDIX

Ayrshire Collieries Corporation uses the Consumer Price Index compiled by the Bureau of Labor Statistics in computing price-level depreciation. The procedure is:

1. All depreciable assets are classified according to year of construction or acquisition.
2. Historical cost depreciation, computed on a straight-line basis, is determined for all properties according to year of construction or acquisition.
3. Historical cost depreciation, classified by year of asset construction or acquisition, is then adjusted for price-level changes by use of the following formula:

$$\frac{\text{Consumer Price Index (month of May, current year)}}{\text{Consumer Price Index (year of construction or acquisition)}} \times \frac{\text{historical cost}}{\text{depreciation}}$$

The average index for any given construction or acquisition year is used as the denominator in the above formula. Certain properties are depreciated on an accelerated basis for tax purposes.

EXHIBIT 1

Ayrshire Collieries Corporation
Depreciation Data, 1947–1961

Year Ended June 30	Depreciable Assets	Depreciation on Original Cost	Price-level Adjustment	Price-level Depreciation[1]
1947	$12,554,738	$ 614,753	—	—
1948	15,165,046	574,645	$221,785	$ 796,430
1949	17,670,725	827,008	338,572	1,165,580
1950	17,997,041	763,316	233,471	996,787
1951	21,043,643	920,815	207,683	1,128,498
1952	21,590,318	1,063,313	141,169	1,204,482
1953	22,541,189	1,094,180	125,125	1,219,305
1954	22,199,077	1,230,964	119,785	1,350,749
1955	24,242,978	1,320,298	102,958	1,423,256
1956	27,002,329	1,417,435	95,964	1,513,399
1957	28,733,089	1,772,232	143,587	1,915,819
1958	30,265,383	1,728,577	195,429	1,924,006
1959	30,515,704	1,976,682	257,278	2,233,960
1960	31,002,406	1,653,747	195,585	1,849,332
1961	42,103,714	2,098,346	208,924	2,307,270

---

[1] Sum of Depreciation on Original Cost and Price-level Adjustment.

EXHIBIT 2

Ayrshire Collieries Corporation
Consolidated Income Statement for the Year Ended June 30, 1959

Revenues:

Sales of coal and coke	$45,274,741
Income from other products, royalties, interest, rentals, etc.	929,358
Equity in net income of nonconsolidated affiliates	476,933
	$46,681,032

Expenses:

Coal and coke purchased for resale	$24,166,960
Coal production costs	11,594,147
Depreciation and depletion	1,976,682
Selling, administrative and general expenses	3,498,101
Interest expense	155,248
Federal income taxes	1,695,450
	$43,086,588
Net Income	$ 3,594,444
Provision for price-level depreciation	257,278
Net Income, after deducting provision for price-level depreciation	$ 3,337,166

EXHIBIT 3

Ayrshire Collieries Corporation
Statement of Consolidated Surplus for the Year
Ended June 30, 1959

	Earned Surplus	Paid-in Surplus
Balance, June 30, 1958	$22,686,598	$4,200,976
Net Income, after deducting provision for price-level depreciation	3,337,166	
	$26,023,764	
Deduct:		
Cash dividends, $1.00 per share	687,923	
5% Stock dividend, 34,186 shares—Par value	102,558	
Assigned value in excess of par value	1,559,736	(1,559,736)
Cash—fractional shares	10,280	
	$ 2,360,497	
Balance, June 30, 1959 ($11,990,056 of earned surplus restricted as to payment of cash dividends)	$23,663,267	$5,760,712

EXHIBIT 4

Ayrshire Collieries Corporation
Condensed Consolidated Balance Sheet as of June 30, 1959
(000 omitted)

ASSETS

Current Assets		$14,519
Property, Plant and Equipment, at cost:		
Operating property	$30,516	
Less—Accumulated depreciation and depletion	18,339	$12,177
Mine under construction		8,116
Undeveloped coal lands		3,920
		$24,213
Investments		5,328
Prepaid Expenses and Deferred Charges		3,507
		$47,567

LIABILITIES AND STOCKHOLDERS' EQUITY

Current Liabilities	$ 5,985
Long-term Obligations:	
4½% first mortgage and collateral trust notes, due serially to 1966	$ 2,460
4⅞% unsecured notes, due serially to 1966	3,600
Installment purchase contracts	1,199
Other	84
	$ 7,343
Reserves:	
Work stoppage expense	$ 300
Deferred federal income taxes	159
	$ 459
Stockholders' Equity:	
Common stock	$ 2,172
Paid-in surplus	5,761
Capital maintained by recognition of price-level depreciation	2,183
Earned surplus	23,663
	$33,779
	$47,567

QUESTIONS:

1. In outline form, summarize the accounting disclosure of price-level adjustments on both the income statement and the balance sheet, as these financial statements appeared in Ayrshire's annual reports from 1948 through 1961. Note both the account titles used and the classification of these accounts, that is, where they appeared on the financial statements. Consider the following time periods: (a) 1948 through 1955, (b) 1956 and 1957, (c) 1958, and (d) 1959 through 1961.

2. Prepare a similar outline for financial statements included in Form 10-K, as filed with the SEC. Consider the following time periods: (a) 1948 through 1956, (b) 1957, (c) 1958 (original statements), (d) 1958 (amended statements), and (e) 1959.

3. Contrast the income-statement presentation used in annual reports from 1948 through 1955 with that used in 1956 and 1957. Note both the terminology and the classification used in each period. Why did the auditors render an unqualified opinion in 1956 in contrast to their earlier qualified opinions?

4. Even though the same statistical procedure was used to compute the amount of the adjustment in 1956 as in the years 1948 through 1955, does the change in terminology suggest some change in management's conception of the adjustment's purpose?

5. In 1958, Ayrshire changed auditors and again changed its presentation of the adjustment in the financial statements contained in the annual report. Do you believe the first auditors would have rendered an unqualified opinion on the 1958 financial statements? Explain.

6. Do you agree with the new auditors that "net income for the year is more fairly presented after deducting the provision for price-level depreciation, since current price levels have been recognized in determining the current cost of property consumed in operations"?

7. Contrast the use of the words "provision" and "appropriation," as they appeared in the original and amended financial statements filed with the SEC in 1958. What is your interpretation of each word? Was the main issue in the dispute with the SEC simply the choice between "provision" and "appropriation"?

8. Consider carefully the portions of ARB No. 43 cited by Ayrshire and by the SEC. Is there a conflict between the two citations? Explain.

9. What is Ayrshire's concept of the account, "Capital Maintained by Recognition of Price-level Depreciation"? Is the accounting treatment of this account in accordance with the usual procedures used when assets are replaced or retired?

10. Exhibit 4 shows Ayrshire's balance sheet (somewhat condensed) for the 1959 fiscal year. In what way, in addition to providing for "Capital Maintained by Recognition of Price-level Depreciation," is Ayrshire "protected" from inflation?

CHAPTER ELEVEN

Long-Term Leases

Problems of accounting for *owned* buildings, machinery and equipment were considered in Chapters 9 and 10. Long-term leasing has become an important method of financing the acquisition of asset services in lieu of ownership. The major accounting problem concerns *disclosure* of long-term leases in the lessee's (renter's) financial statements.

INSTITUTE PRONOUNCEMENT

In 1949, the Committee on Accounting Procedure issued ARB No. 38, *Disclosure of Long-Term Leases in Financial Statements of Lessees*, to achieve more uniformity in disclosure of long-term leases. This bulletin was later included in ARB No. 43 as Chapter 14, which follows:

1. The growth in recent years of the practice of using long-term leases as a method of financing has created problems of disclosure in financial statements. In buy-build-sell-and-lease transactions, the purchaser of land builds to his own specifications, sells the improved property, and simultaneously leases the property for a period of years. Similar transactions are the sale and lease of existing properties or the lease of properties to be constructed by the lessor to the specifications of the lessee. The lessee ordinarily assumes all the expenses and obligations of ownership (such as taxes, insurance, interest, maintenance, and repairs) except payment of any mortgage indebtedness on the property.

2. There are many variations in such types of transactions. For example, some leases contain an *option* for acquisition of the property by the lessee, while other leases contain a *requirement* that the lessee purchase the property upon expiration of the lease. In some the price to be paid upon repurchase is related to the fair value of the property or the depreciated book value; in others it is an arbitrary amount with little or no relation to the property's worth, or a nominal sum. Some leases provide for a high initial

367

rental with declining payments thereafter or renewal at substantially reduced rentals.

3. Where long-term leases are used as a substitute for ownership and mortgage borrowing a question arises as to the extent of disclosure to be made in financial statements of the fixed annual amounts payable and other important terms under such leases.[1]

4. Although the types of sell-and-lease arrangements referred to in paragraph 1 differ in many respects from the conventional long-term lease,[2] the principles of disclosure stated herein are intended to apply to both. This chapter does not apply to short-term leases[3] or to those customarily used for oil and gas properties.

5. The committee believes that material amounts of fixed rental and other liabilities maturing in future years under long-term leases and possible related contingencies are material facts affecting judgments based on the financial statements of a corporation, and that those who rely upon financial statements are entitled to know of the existence of such leases and the extent of the obligations thereunder, irrespective of whether the leases are considered to be advantageous or otherwise. Accordingly, where the rentals or other obligations under long-term leases are material in the circumstances, the committee is of the opinion that:

(a) disclosure should be made in financial statements or in notes thereto of:

(1) the amounts of annual rentals to be paid under such leases with some indication of the periods for which they are payable and

(2) any other important obligation assumed or guarantee made in connection therewith;

(b) the above information should be given not only in the year in which the transaction originates but also as long thereafter as the amounts involved are material; and

(c) in addition, in the year in which the transaction originates, there should be disclosure of the principal details of any important sale-and-lease transaction.

6. A lease arrangement is sometimes, in substance, no more than an instalment purchase of the property. This may well be the case when the lease is made subject to purchase of the property for a nominal sum or for an amount obviously much less than the prospective fair value of the property; or when the agreement stipulates that the rental payments may be applied in part as instalments on the purchase price; or when the rentals obviously are so out of line with rentals for similar properties as to negative the representation that the rental payments are for current use of the property

---

[1] Rule 3–18 (b) of Regulation S-X issued by the Securities and Exchange Commission reads: "Where the rentals or obligations under long-term leases are material there shall be shown the amounts of annual rentals under such leases with some indication of the periods for which they are payable, together with any important obligation assumed or guarantee made in connection therewith. If the rentals are conditional, state the minimum annual amounts."

[2] The conventional lease, a straight tenure contract between the owner of property and a lessee, generally does not involve buying, building, and selling of property by the lessee, or special repurchase arrangements.

[3] Three years has been used as a criterion in some cases for classifying leases as short-term or long-term.

and to create the presumption that portions of such rentals are partial payments under a purchase plan.

7. Since the lessee in such cases does not have legal title to the property and does not necessarily assume any direct mortgage obligation, it has been argued that any balance sheet which included the property among the assets and any related indebtedness among the liabilities would be incorrect. However, the committee is of the opinion that the facts relating to all such leases should be carefully considered and that, where it is clearly evident that the transaction involved is in substance a purchase, the "leased" property should be included among the assets of the lessee with suitable accounting for the corresponding liabilities and for the related charges in the income statement.

> *One member of the committee, Mr. Lindquist, assented with quali-*
> *fication to adoption of chapter 14.*

Mr. Lindquist's qualification relates to paragraph 6. He believes that at any time during a long-term lease, other than a reasonable period before its expiration, no determination is possible as to *prospective fair value of the property* for comparison with the purchase price that may be stated in the lease. He also questions the ability of an accountant to carry out the implicit requirement for comparison of the lease rental with *rentals for similar properties* in view of the many physical and other factors on which would rest a conclusion of similarity of properties.

Note that in paragraph 1 the committee refers to "the practice of using long-term leases as a *method of financing* . . . [emphasis added]." With some exceptions,[4] most commonly leased assets can be purchased. Therefore, the decision to lease an asset is not generally made because leasing is the *only* way to acquire the asset, but because leasing is considered an attractive *method of financing* the acquisition.[5] This acceptance of long-term leasing as essentially a method of financing is further indicated by the lessee's usual assumption of "all the expenses and obligations of ownership," as stated in paragraph 1.

ADVANTAGES AND DISADVANTAGES OF LONG-TERM LEASING

Proponents of long-term leasing cite several advantages for this method of financing including one of very direct concern to accountants—that is, avoidance on the balance sheet of long-term debt which would be shown if leased assets were purchased with borrowed funds. Among other advantages claimed for leasing are the following:

1. Provisions of existing debt contracts may restrict additional borrowing, but not long-term leasing.

2. Avoidance of some risks of ownership, such as early obsolescence.

---

[4] An example is urban "downtown" land which cannot be purchased.

[5] Leasing may occasionally be the *only method of financing available to some users*, but *not* the only method of acquiring the asset if it can be purchased outright. This distinction between the asset itself and the method of financing its acquisition is subtle, but important.

3. One hundred per cent external financing because no down payment is required as in the case of most purchased assets.
4. Possible tax advantages in the amount or timing of tax deductions.
5. Freeing of capital from investment in long-term assets for "more profitable" use as working capital.

Some of the claimed advantages cited above are debatable.[6] However, long-term leasing has grown at an extremely rapid rate and the foregoing claims, whether or not entirely justified, have undoubtedly contributed to this growth.

There may be disadvantages to leasing an asset in contrast to outright purchase using debt financing. Lease contracts typically contain "built-in" interest rates about one-half to one per cent higher than would be paid for borrowed funds. A second possible disadvantage of leasing, compared to purchasing, concerns the lessee's status at the expiration of the lease. As stated in paragraph 2 of the bulletin reproduced above, the lessee *may* acquire ownership at the expiration of *some* leases, with the payment then required ranging from a nominal amount to the fair value of the asset. Even though the length of many lease contracts presumably covers the estimated useful life of the leased asset, changing economic conditions, or an unavoidable error in the life estimate, may make ultimate ownership of the asset attractive to the lessee.

The lessor (owner), on the other hand, may desire to retain title to the asset at expiration of the initial lease period. Because rental payments frequently provide for recovery of the lessor's entire capital investment, plus an interest or finance charge, during the initial lease period, proceeds from either selling the property at the expiration of the lease or from renewing the lease, even at much reduced rentals, often influence the lessor's total profit substantially.[7]

PRESENT DISCLOSURE PRACTICES

Paragraph 3 states that the accounting problem is one of disclosure when "long-term leases are used as a substitute for ownership." Paragraph 5 contains the committee's recommendations for disclosure of important information about long-term leases in financial statements. The following note to Sears, Roebuck and Co.'s financial statements for the fiscal year ended January 31, 1962, is an example of current disclosure:

---

[6] See article by Gant listed on page 377.
[7] Because the lease transaction's ultimate profitability to the lessor so often depends on successful completion of the initial lease, lessors tend to emphasize a prospective lessee's general credit standing rather than the leased asset's value. This is, of course, particularly true when assets have been built to the lessee's specifications.

Rentals—Long-Term Leases. Minimum annual fixed rentals, exclusive of taxes, insurance and other expenses paid directly by the company, under long-term leases (over three years) in effect at January 31, 1962, range from approximately $20,205,000 for 1962 to $5,200,000 for 1986. Subject to the right of the company to make rejectable offers, the aggregate minimum rental liability for the entire period subsequent to January 31, 1987 is $26,097,000.

The company is leasing a number of store and warehouse properties from various insurance and educational institutions and from private investors. Most of these leases are for maximum terms ranging from 25 to 99 years with the right, after initial periods ranging from 25 to 45 years, to terminate or continue at reduced rentals, and contain one or both of the following two additional types of options:

The company can, after the initial period of years, purchase the property at the then fair value of the land alone.

The company can, on various specified dates (usually within the first 25 to 35 years), make a rejectable offer to purchase the property at specified prices and, in the event the lessor does not accept the offer, can either terminate or continue the lease.

On first impression, the bulletin seems to provide for adequate disclosure of long-term leases in financial statements. However, many accountants contend that the rather general nature of the recommendations has led to little uniformity of disclosure in published financial reports. A good indication of the extent and method of disclosure is found in the 1962 edition of "Accounting Trends and Techniques."[8] Of 228 companies which referred to, or implied, the existence of long-term leases, 107 merely mentioned or indicated that such leases existed without furnishing any details.

The committee was much more specific in paragraphs 6 and 7 when discussing a "lease" arrangement which is "in substance, no more than an instalment purchase of the property." The committee recommended that failure to possess legal title be ignored where such a purchase transaction is "clearly evident," and "the 'leased' property should be included among the assets of the lessee with suitable accounting for the corresponding liabilities." Such disclosure has been rare in published financial statements. One example is found in the 1958 annual report of Continental Air Lines, in which the following note appeared:

Effective May 23, 1958, the company entered into a sale and leaseback arrangement with respect to its maintenance base located on leased ground at the Los Angeles Airport. Under terms thereof, the property was sold by the company for $750,000 and leased back at a rental of $12,450 per month for a term of 84 months, with an option to repurchase at the end of the term for $20,000. Although the company has thus temporarily divested itself

---

[8] American Institute of Certified Public Accountants, *Accounting Trends and Techniques*, 16th ed. (New York: The Institute, 1962), p. 63.

of legal title to the property, the transaction is in substance a loan arrangement and the company is so treating it in its accounts."[9,10]

Proposed Disclosure

Some accountants feel that the applicability of paragraph 7 should be broadened to include virtually every long-term lease whether or not a transaction is in substance a purchase. They argue that the lessee acquires both possession and control of the leased asset at the time of the transaction, and simultaneously the lessor substantially completes his part of the contract by making the property available. Therefore, the lessee should record an asset and a liability, recognizing the transaction's economic substance rather than its legal form.

Supporters of this view believe that only by recording the lease liability can the accountant fulfill the committee's belief, as expressed in paragraph 5, "that those who rely upon financial statements are entitled to know of the existence of such leases and the extent of the obligations thereunder." "Those who rely upon financial statements" include various groups such as owners, prospective owners, security analysts, and short-term and long-term creditors. These groups frequently use ratios involving long-term debt, total assets, fixed assets, and interest expense to measure a corporation's financial health and to estimate its ability to pay maturing obligations. Examples of such ratios are:

1. Net income before taxes plus interest to interest (the "times-interest-earned" ratio),
2. Debt to equity,
3. Debt to total assets, and
4. Debt to net fixed assets.

Note that under conventional accounting for long-term leases, interest expense, debt, total assets, and net fixed assets are not increased by a decision to lease, as they would be if the leased assets were purchased with borrowed funds.

DISCOUNTING TECHNIQUE

Some accountants favor recording the *present value* of future lease payments in the accounts. The underlying technique of determining the appropriate present value amounts is not difficult. As stated

---

[9] The interest rate for this financing is approximately 7/8 of one per cent per month. That is, the present value of $12,450 per month, discounted for 84 monthly periods at 7/8 of one per cent, plus the present value of a final payment of $20,000, also discounted for 84 months at 7/8 of one per cent per month, is approximately $750,000. The effective annual interest rate is approximately 11 per cent.

[10] The asset continued to be classified under "Operating property and equipment" as "Land, buildings and improvements." The liability was classified under "Long-term debt" as "Other obligations."

earlier, rental payments are established at a level which usually provides, over the initial lease period, for

1. recovery of the lessor's investment in the leased property, and
2. interest on the unrecovered balance of the lessor's investment.

These two components of periodic lease payments emphasize the financial nature of long-term leases where the lessee is, for all practical purposes, acquiring the long-term use of an asset by "borrowing" the lessor's money.

The present value method is supported on the grounds that there is a close similarity between debt and lease financing. Periodic accounting for long-term debt recognizes the two basic components which must be paid by the borrower—principal and interest, but only the *present value* of future principal and interest payments is shown on the balance sheet as a liability. (See Appendix to Chapter 9, pages 268–69.)

If the analogy between debt financing and leasing is accepted, lease obligations should be accounted for in the same manner as debt liabilities. Therefore, the liability disclosed initially should represent future lease payments, discounted to a present value equal to the cost or fair value of the leased asset at the time of the transaction.[11] To determine the discounted amount of future lease obligations, either of two facts must be known:

1. The cost or fair value of the leased property at the time of the lease transaction, or
2. The interest rate used in calculating the amount of periodic lease payments.

If (1) is known, as it would be in a sale and lease-back transaction or where the leased asset is also available for purchase, this amount represents the present value of future lease obligations. This is also the amount of debt which would be incurred currently if the asset were purchased with borrowed funds. If (2) is known (and (1) is not known), it is the appropriate discount rate to use in determining the present value of future rental payments.[12]

---

[11] The discounted (present) value of future lease payments may be somewhat less than the cost or fair value of the leased asset at the time of the transaction if the lessor retains title to the asset at the expiration of the lease and he anticipates material end-of-lease salvage value. Such anticipation may reduce lease payments. In this case, the present value of lease payments will equal the fair value of the asset at the time of the lease transaction less the *present* value of any anticipated salvage value. This present value of end-of-lease salvage value is insignificant under most long-term leases.

[12] In addition to recovery of the lessor's investment and an interest or finance charge, rental payments occasionally reflect services to be provided by the lessor, or costs to be borne by him, such as heat, maintenance, property taxes, etc. The portion of the periodic rental payments attributed to such items should be subtracted from the amount of rental payments to be discounted because this portion is not related to acquiring the right to use the leased asset. Usually this problem does not arise since such costs are customarily borne by the lessee.

ACCOUNTING FOR LEASE RIGHT AND LEASE OBLIGATION

Under traditional accounting for long-term leases, no entry is recorded at the time of the lease agreement and the following entry is made whenever lease rentals are paid:

Rental Expense	xxx	
Cash		xxx

If the present value of future rental payments is disclosed on the balance sheet as a liability, it follows that the asset acquired by the incurrence of this liability, the right to use the leased asset, should also be disclosed on the balance sheet. Those who advocate including leases in the accounting records would make the following journal entry at the time of the lease transaction:

Right to Use Leased Asset	xxx	
Rental Obligations Under Long-Term Lease		xxx

If the leased asset and the liability are recorded at the time of the lease transaction, as in the above entry, a policy must then be adopted for the subsequent accounting treatment of these balances. As previously noted, each rental payment consists of two elements—principal and interest. In the early periods of the lease, the interest element will be relatively large, but will decline as the amount of "debt" declines. Principal repayments will gradually increase because a larger portion of each successive rental payment is applied to principal.[13] The periodic entry would be:

Rental Obligations Under Long-Term Lease	xxx	
Interest Expense	xxx	
Cash		xxx

The liability account, "Rental Obligations Under Long-Term Lease," will be equal to the present value of the *remaining* lease payments at the close of each fiscal period.

A more difficult problem concerns amortization of the asset account, "Right to Use Leased Asset." This asset should be amortized to expense for the same reasons that a purchased asset is depreciated. However, there is disagreement whether the asset should be amortized at the same rate as the liability, or according to the straight-line or

---

[13] This changing relationship between the principal and interest elements of each lease rental payment is similar to that found in any debt which is retired by periodic payments of a level amount, such as the customary mortgage on residential property.

accelerated methods used for comparable depreciable assets. Amortizing the asset at the same rate as the liability would maintain identical balances in the related asset and liability accounts over the term of the lease, but would produce "decelerated" amortization, the very opposite of accelerated depreciation. Regardless of the rate used, the periodic entry would be:

Amortization Expense	xxx	
Allowance for Amortization of		
Right to Use Leased Asset[14]		xxx

Observe that under the present value method of accounting for long-term leases, the *total* amount charged to expense over the life of the lease will not differ from *total* charges to expense under conventional accounting. That is, the sum of charges to "Interest Expense" plus "Amortization Expense" under the present value method will equal the total charges to "Rental Expense" under conventional accounting. However, the timing of expense charges over the life of the lease under the present value method will differ from those under conventional accounting unless the asset is amortized at the same rate as the liability.

OBJECTIONS TO PROPOSED DISCLOSURE

A number of objections have been voiced to the proposed balance-sheet disclosure of long-term lease obligations and the related asset account. Some of these are:

1. Leasing and ownership are fundamentally different and accounting should not overlook the legal fact that the lessor retains title to the leased property. Also, a lessor's position may be inferior to that of long-term creditors should the lessee fail financially.
2. Under many leases, it may be impossible to determine objectively the cost or fair value of the leased property or the appropriate discount rate.
3. It would be inconsistent to adopt the proposed procedure for long-term leases without considering other long-term commitments such as employment and purchase contracts.
4. The method is complex and difficult to understand.
5. The sheer volume of bookkeeping detail for companies with hundreds of leases would be extremely burdensome.
6. Leasing would become less attractive as a method of financing.

---

[14] An alternative would be a direct credit to the asset account, "Right to Use Leased Asset."

METHODS OF DISCLOSURE

Some accountants, who oppose reflecting lease obligations formally on the balance sheet, suggest other methods of disclosing the same information. One method is to disclose the information "short" on the balance sheet (not included in the "money columns"), as in the following balance sheet condensed from the Fairbanks Whitney Corporation's 1961 annual report:

Assets		
Current assets		$ 95,157,743
Property, plant and equipment, net		43,194,696
Rights to use of leased facilities, at December 31, 1961, at discounted amount of related long-term rental obligations—see contra	$13,475,000	
Other assets		7,221,630
		$145,574,069

Liabilities		
Current liabilities		$ 30,062,526
Reserves and deferred credits		13,433,996
Long-term debt		32,467,156
Rental obligations under long-term leases, at December 31, 1961, discounted over period of leases, (including $779,000 due within one year)—see contra	$13,475,000	
Stockholders' equity		69,610,391
		$145,574,069

This "short" disclosure is accepted by the SEC, which has rejected balance sheets filed with it disclosing a leased asset and related liability in the "money columns" because this practice is not in accordance with generally accepted accounting principles at the present time.

A less radical departure from currently accepted practice is disclosure of the discounted amount of long-term lease payments in a footnote, as in the following excerpt from a note to Textron, Inc.'s 1961 financial statements:

> Annual rentals payable under long-term leases are approximately $4,800,000 and the aggregate rentals payable under the leases, discounted to December 30, 1961, are approximately $31,700,000 . . .

REFERENCES

Andersen, Arthur, & Co., *Accounting for Leases*. Chicago: Arthur Andersen & Co. (Aug. 1962).

Boyle, Alexander R. M. and Victor E. Samuelson, "Disclosure of Long-Term Leases—A Problem in Communication," *Financial Analysts Journal*, 18 (Mar.-Apr. 1962), 35–40.

Cohen, Albert H., *Long Term Leases*. Ann Arbor, Michigan: Bureau of Business Research, School of Business Administration, University of Michigan, 1954.

Cook, Donald C., "The Case Against Capitalizing Leases," *Harvard Business Review*, 41 (Jan.-Feb. 1963), 145–62.

Gant, Donald R., "Illusion in Lease Financing," *Harvard Business Review*, 37 (Mar.-Apr. 1959), 121-42. Letters regarding this article appeared in 37 (May-Jun. 1959), 18, 160–165; and 37 (Jul.-Aug. 1959), 19–26, 172–78.

Hennessy, John L., "Recording of Lease Obligations and Related Property Rights," *Journal of Accountancy*, 111 (Mar. 1961), 40–46. Letters regarding this article appeared in 111 (May 1961), 33–35; 111 (Jun. 1961), 28–31; and 112 (Jul. 1961), 25.

"Machines Without Owners," *Fortune*, 66 (Aug. 1962), 112–114.

Myers, John H., *Reporting of Leases in Financial Statements*, Accounting Research Study No. 4. New York: American Institute of Certified Public Accountants, 1962. The Summary and Conclusions from this Accounting Research Study were reprinted in the *Journal of Accountancy*, 113 (Jun. 1962), 63–66.

Rhodes, Jack, "Financial Leases Belong on the Balance Sheet," *N. A. A. Bulletin*, 42 (Dec. 1960), section 1, 83–91.

Rickey, Kenneth R., "Including All Leases in the Balance Sheet—A First," *N.A.A Bulletin*, 41 (Dec. 1959), section 1, 51–60.

Shillinglaw, Gordon, "Leasing and Financial Statements," *Accounting Review*, 33 (Oct. 1958), 581–92.

_____, "Accounting for Leased Property by Capitalization," *N.A.A. Bulletin*, 39 (Jun. 1958), section 1, 31–44.

Simon, Sidney I., "The Lease-Option Plan—Its Tax and Accounting Implications," *Journal of Accountancy*, 113 (Apr. 1962), 38–45.

Vancil, Richard F. and Robert N. Anthony, "The Financial Community Looks at Leasing," *Harvard Business Review*, 37 (Nov.-Dec. 1959), 113–30.

Zises, Alvin, "Disclosure of Long-Term Leases," *Journal of Accountancy*, 111 (Feb. 1961), 37–47. Letters regarding this article appeared in 111 (May 1961), 33–35.

_____, "Long-Term Leases: Case Against Capitalization, For Full Disclosure," *Financial Analysts Journal*, 18 (May-Jun. 1962), 13–20, 63–64.

Manchester Knitting Products Company

Manchester Knitting Products Company manufactures specialized products such as buttons and zippers which it sells to knitting mills in New Hampshire and Massachusetts. During 1961, a brother of the founder and principal stockholder of Manchester formed a separate corporation, Meadows, Inc. This company constructed a building on land purchased from Manchester. The building was completed in December, 1961, and leased to Manchester for office and warehouse space. The lease agreement, which covered a 20-year period, contained no provision for renewal, nor did it contain a purchase-option clause. Annual lease payments were $62,000.

Manchester often used short-term bank borrowings to finance its seasonal inventory requirements. The company's bankers were concerned about the size of the new lease obligation. The bank's president noted that $1,240,000 would be required for lease payments over the 20-year period.

Mr. Santucci, President of Manchester, discussed this matter with the company's independent public accountants in late 1961, and it was agreed to reflect both the lease obligation and the right to use the leased property on the balance sheet at the discounted present value. Manchester's bankers agreed with this presentation and felt that it would facilitate their periodic appraisal of the company's financial statements. In determining the amounts to be reflected in the balance sheet, Manchester used a discount rate of $5\frac{1}{2}$ per cent (the interest rate Meadows, Inc. paid on the mortgage debt it had incurred on the property) and discounted annual rental payments over the 20-year period. The company's balance sheet as of December 31, 1962, one year after execution of the lease, is given in Exhibit 1.

Manchester's controller proposed that the rental obligation liability account and the related leasehold interest asset account be amortized over the 20-year period on a straight-line basis. While he recognized that it would be more correct to amortize these accounts by use of the discount method (only amortizing the decrease in present value and treating the remainder of the current rental payment as interest expense), he thought it more practicable to amortize both accounts on a straight-line basis. He considered this easier for management to understand, and the differences in the amounts produced, compared to those which would appear if amortized under the discount method, were sufficiently insignificant so that the accounts could be considered "discounted." Also, he believed the straight-line method conformed more closely to normal depreciation methods employed on the company's books.

In the company's income statement, the controller did not separate leasehold amortization expense and interest expense, classifying the annual rental payment of $62,000 as rent expense. (See Exhibit 2.) He felt the payment was rent in the legal sense and that it would only be confusing to break it down into amortization and interest.

Note 3 to the company's 1962 balance sheet presented information on certain key facts relating to the lease agreement as follows:

The long-term lease agreement, dated December 31, 1961, and expiring December 31, 1981, covers a building used by the company for office and warehouse space. The lease provides for annual rental payments of $62,000 and, in addition, the company is to pay all property taxes and operating costs applicable to the property.

EXHIBIT 1

Manchester Knitting Products Company
Balance Sheet as of December 31, 1962

ASSETS
Current Assets:

Cash		$ 310,927
Accounts Receivable, net		747,328
Inventories		1,092,543
Prepayments		57,904
		$2,208,702
Investments, at cost		$ 209,300

Property, Plant and Equipment:

Land	$ 20,903	
Buildings, at cost	1,730,852	
Machinery and Equipment, at cost	972,443	
	$2,724,198	
Less: Allowance for Depreciation	1,320,047	
	$1,404,151	
Leasehold Interest in Land and Building at Discounted Amount Related to Long-term Lease Obligation (see contra)	703,855	2,108,006

Other Assets:

Goodwill	$ 715,649	
Unamortized Bond Discount	40,357	756,006
		$5,282,014

LIABILITIES AND NET WORTH
Current Liabilities:

Accounts Payable		$ 467,741
Accrued Liabilities		248,230
Bank Loan		300,000
Income Taxes Payable		315,295
		$1,331,266

Long-term Debt:

4½ per cent Debentures, due 1974		$ 400,000
Rental Obligation Under Long-term Lease, Discounted at 5½ per cent over Period of Lease Expiring in 1981 (see contra)—Note 3		703,855
		$1,103,855

Stockholders' Equity:

Common Stock, par value $1	$ 72,902	
Capital Surplus	901,438	
Retained Earnings	1,872,553	2,846,893
		$5,282,014

EXHIBIT 2

Manchester Knitting Products Company
Statement of Income and Retained Earnings, Year Ended December 31, 1962

Net Sales		$9,347,119
Cost of Goods Sold		7,630,552
		$1,716,567
General, Administrative and Selling Expenses	$729,663	
Depreciation	121,277	
Rent Expense	62,000	912,940
		$ 803,627
Other Expenses:		
Interest	$ 27,305	
Other	16,409	43,714
Income Before Taxes		$ 759,913
Provision for Federal Income Tax		327,206
Net Income		$ 432,707
Retained Earnings, Beginning of Year		1,483,587
		$1,916,294
Dividends		43,741
Retained Earnings, End of Year		$1,872,553

QUESTIONS:

1. Verify the amount of $703,855 which appeared as Leasehold Interest and as Rental Obligation Under Long-term Lease on Manchester's balance sheet at December 31, 1962.

2. Comment on the appropriateness of using $5\frac{1}{2}$ per cent as a discount rate.

3. Do you agree with Manchester's accounting treatment of long-term lease obligations and the related leasehold interest in land and building? Explain. Give the appropriate journal entries for 1962 and 1963 under Manchester's accounting treatment.

4. How would you have treated long-term leases in the 1962 financial statements? Explain. If different from Manchester's treatment, give the journal entries you would make in both 1962 and 1963.

5. Comment critically on the controller's implied analogy between depreciation and amortization of rights acquired under long-term leases.

6. If Manchester had realized a gain on sale of the land to Meadows, Inc., how would you have treated it? Explain.

The Hanover Corporation

The Hanover Corporation is engaged in the wholesale grocery business in Northern New England. The corporation also owns 80 per cent of the common stock of Woodstock Farms, Inc., which processes quick-frozen vegetables and fruits.

Sale and Lease-Back

In 1959, the Hanover Corporation required a new warehouse in order to take advantage of modern materials handling equipment and to provide for recent growth. At that time total fixed assets were $711,698 net of depreciation and amortization. (See Exhibit 1.) In early 1960, the corporation authorized construction of a 350,000 square foot combined warehouse and office building in White River Junction, Vermont. Hanover agreed (1) to sell the completed building with land to the Valley Insurance Company for $2,500,000, the estimated cost of the building plus the value of the land, and (2) to lease back the property for an original term of 25 years with a renewal option for an additional 25 years. Management intended to finance construction of the building by short-term borrowing which would be repaid with the funds received from sale of the property to the insurance company.

Construction of the new warehouse and office building was completed towards the close of the 1960–1961 fiscal year. Upon completion, the building and land were sold to the insurance company and leased back by the corporation at an annual rental of $175,500 for the initial period of 25 years. If Hanover chose to renew the lease for the second 25-year period, the annual rental from the 26th through the 50th year would be $86,100. Hanover reserved the right to terminate the lease at the end of the 11th or the 20th year of the *renewal* period. Real estate taxes and maintenance were to be paid by Hanover.

The total construction cost of the building exceeded

the estimated cost by $390,000. Costs of relocating to the new facilities were estimated at $300,000. This included moving of inventories, $30,000; retraining employees to use the new equipment, $70,000; duplication of overhead during the transition period resulting from occupancy of both plants for a period of several months, $130,000; and the cost of financing the new building until its sale to the Valley Insurance Company, $70,000.

Change in Inventory Valuation

At the end of the 1961–1962 fiscal year, total inventories were shown at $10,728,513 on the *consolidated* balance sheet (including Woodstock Farms). Of this total, inventories of $5,378,358 were stated at cost determined by the Lifo method, which was substantially the same as replacement cost. The remaining inventories were stated at the lower of cost or market, cost being determined by the Fifo method. During the 1961–1962 fiscal year, Hanover had transferred part of its inventories to Woodstock Farms, which used only Lifo. The method of pricing all transferred inventories was changed from the lower of cost or market, based on Fifo valuation, to cost determined by the Lifo method. This change did not materially affect the reported net income for the fiscal year.

During the 1962–1963 fiscal year, Woodstock Farms, Inc. changed its method of valuing finished product inventories by including transportation charges that were incurred to place the inventory at points of distribution. Warehousing costs were also included, but limited to include the first month's storage and handling charges. As a result of this change, consolidated net income before taxes for the period was increased approximately $86,000 to $463,121.

EXHIBIT 1

The Hanover Corporation
Balance Sheet as of June 30, 1959

ASSETS

Current Assets:

Cash on hand and in bank		$ 885,588
Customers accounts receivable (less reserve of $20,135)		1,993,448
Sundry accounts receivable		47,658
Merchandise inventories:		
At the lower of cost or market	$3,855,674	
At cost, determined on the last-in, first-out method	1,350,881	5,206,555
Total Current Assets		$8,133,249
Other Assets		5,050
Fixed Assets—at cost:		
Land	$ 60,682	
Building and equipment, less reserves for depreciation of $564,087	176,631	
Leasehold improvements, less reserves for amortization of $201,513	474,385	711,698
Deferred Charges and Prepaid Expenses		81,322
Goodwill		1
		$8,931,320

LIABILITIES

Current Liabilities:

Notes payable—banks		$ 800,000
Note payable—other		500,000
Accounts payable—trade		461,149
Accrued state income and other taxes		72,664
Accrued payrolls and expenses		339,930
Reserve for federal taxes on income		312,000
Total Current Liabilities		$2,485,743
Long-Term Liability:		
Notes payable to bank	$1,300,000	
Less: Amounts due within one year	300,000	1,000,000
Capital Stock and Earned Surplus:		
Common Stock—no par value		
Authorized and issued—312,600 shares	$1,667,200	
Earned Surplus	3,889,289	
	$5,556,489	
Less: 7,600 shares of Common Stock at cost—held in treasury	110,912	5,445,577
		$8,931,320

QUESTIONS:

Sale and Lease-Back

1. Approximately what rate of interest does the insurance company earn before income taxes on its investment if Hanover does not renew the lease for the second 25-year period and the building has an estimated salvage value at the end of the initial lease period of $1,100,000?

2. What accounting treatment do you recommend for the $390,000 of cost which the corporation did not recover when the building was sold?

3. How would you account for the $300,000 of relocation costs? Consider separately each of the four types of costs incurred.

4. In 1961, how would you disclose Hanover's annual lease obligation of $175,500 in compliance with Chapter 14 of ARB No. 43, "Disclosure of Long-Term Leases in Financial Statements of Lessees"?

5. Using present value analysis and the discount rate calculated in question 1, give journal entries for (a) and (b) below. Consider only the initial 25-year lease.

   (a) The entry required to disclose the lease as both an asset and a liability on the corporation's balance sheet at the close of its fiscal year, June 30, 1961.

   (b) The entry, or entries, required during the 1961–1962 fiscal year.

   (c) Is the rate of interest inherent in the lease (calculated in question 1) the most appropriate rate for Hanover to use in establishing the dollar amounts for the entries required in questions 5(a) and 5(b)? Explain.

6. Comment on the contrast in disclosure between the methods you have used in questions 4 and 5. Can you suggest any other means of disclosure?

Change in Inventory Valuation

1. What action would you take as the corporation's auditor regarding the change in inventory valuation?

2. Do you agree with the inclusion of transportation charges and warehousing cost in inventories? Explain. What action, if any, should you take as the auditor? Explain.

Empire Television Corporation

Empire Television Corporation produces live and taped TV shows for sale to various sponsors. Under long-term leases it also acquires films specifically produced for television by independent producers as well as older films originally made for motion picture audiences. These lease contracts permit Empire to use the films over a period of from one to seven years. However, rentals are normally payable in fixed installments over a period significantly shorter than the use period.

When lease contracts are signed, Empire records the full amount of the liability, with an offsetting debit to prepaid film expenses on the balance sheet. Prepaid film expenses are subsequently amortized to income on a usage basis. Since films are used over a period longer than the payment period, the prepaid expenses always exceed unpaid liabilities.

Although the corporation separates the asset and liability accounts in the books, management prefers, for financial reporting purposes, to net the liability against the prepayment and show the difference as a current asset. Empire follows this method of presentation because of a small saving in state franchise taxes, which are based on total capitalization including debt.

Prior to 1962, the auditors did not object to the corporation's preference in this matter because the amounts involved were considered immaterial. However, in 1962, Empire signed a $1,200,000 contract for use of 708 feature films over a seven-year period with rentals payable from 1962 through 1964. This contract, together with several medium-size contracts entered into during the year, increased prepaid film expenses to $1,698,000 and film contracts payable to $1,352,000 at the end of the 1962 fiscal year.

The auditors felt that the two accounts should no longer be offset. They proposed that the asset and the liability be disclosed separately on the balance sheet and that long-term portions of each account be excluded from current assets and current liabilities.

The corporation did not object to such disclosure and used it on its balance sheet at October 31, 1962. (See Exhibit 1.)

The current portion of prepaid film expenses was determined by applying to each of the film contracts Empire's estimated percentage of total use during the next year. This estimate was reviewed by the corporation's auditors for reasonableness in light of their knowledge of Empire's business and expected future plans, and by comparing similar statistics for previous years. There was no problem in determining the current portion of film contracts payable since, in almost every instance, the contract called for payment in fixed installments.

EXHIBIT 1

Empire Television Corporation
Condensed Balance Sheet as of October 31, 1962

ASSETS
Current Assets:

Cash	$1,238,000
Prepaid film expenses (current portion)	516,000
Other current assets	514,000
Total current assets	$2,268,000
Property and equipment	2,106,000
Prepaid film expenses (excluding current portion of $516,000)	1,182,000
Goodwill	1,602,000
Total assets	$7,158,000

LIABILITIES AND STOCKHOLDERS' EQUITY
Current Liabilities:

Note payable to bank	$3,150,000
Amounts payable within one year on long-term debt and film contracts	1,562,000
Accounts payable and accrued liabilities	238,000
Total current liabilities	$4,950,000
Serial notes payable (excluding $900,000 payable within one year)	1,900,000
Film contracts payable (excluding $662,000 payable within one year)	690,000
Capital stock and retained earnings (deficit)	(382,000)
Total liabilities and stockholders' equity	$7,158,000

QUESTIONS:

1. Is there any generally accepted accounting principle which requires Empire to record lease obligations prior to the time when payments become due?

2. How do these transactions resemble long-term leases? In what respects are they different from long-term lease transactions?

3. Do you approve of Empire's practice prior to 1962 of offsetting the contract liabilities against the asset, prepaid film expenses? Explain.

4. Do you have any reservations concerning the terminology used on the balance sheet? Explain.

5. Consider the problem of amortizing prepaid film expenses. Do you favor the seven-year use period provided by the lease contract, the three-year period over which rentals are payable, or some other period?

Mohasco Industries, Inc.

Mohasco Industries, Inc. was the name adopted in 1955 when Alexander Smith, Inc. merged with Mohawk Carpet Mills, Inc. Mohasco's major business is the manufacture and sale of wool and synthetic rugs and carpets.

In 1958, in accordance with a policy of minimizing its investment in land and buildings, Mohasco sold substantially all of its Amsterdam, New York properties (about 2,200,000 sq. ft.), simultaneously leasing the same properties for 18 years. The assets sold were carried on Mohasco's books at $2,049,077. This excluded machinery and equipment which remained in the company's possession. The selling price was $10,500,000—$2,500,000 payable in cash and $8,000,000 in a mortgage note secured by the property. By December 31, 1958, the note had been reduced to $7,877,389. (See Exhibit 1.)

Management decided to treat the gain on the sale as a special item in the 1958 income statement and to establish a liability for future lease obligations by a special charge, net of future taxes. (See Exhibit 2.) Lease rental payments of $388,455 in 1958, and $388,333 in subsequent years, were charged against this liability.

Note 4 to the 1958 financial statements described the transaction as follows:

> 4. *Sale and lease of Amsterdam properties:* In December 1958 certain land and buildings in Amsterdam, New York... were sold for cash of $2,500,000 and a 5 per cent purchase money mortgage receivable of $8,000,000 and thereupon these properties were leased to Mohasco Industries, Inc. The gain on this sale, $8,450,923 net of applicable state taxes and expenses (no federal income taxes payable [because of tax loss carryforward]) is included as a special item in the statement of income. The mortgage receivable and interest thereon are due in equal quarterly instalments of $130,084 from April 1, 1959 to October 1, 1966 and $219,282 thereafter to October 1, 1976, which sums are to be applied first to interest and the balance to principal.
>
> The liability for rentals due over the term of the lease, net of the estimated future tax effect, has been provided by a special charge in the statement of income.

At December 31, 1955, the date of the merger, Mohasco acquired Alexander Smith's tax loss carryover of $33,275,000. Of this amount, $10,490,000 remained to be used in 1959 and 1960. Without benefit of such loss carryover, 1958 net income before special charges would have been subject to federal income taxes of approximately $2,990,000 and the gain on sale of Amsterdam properties subject to taxes of about $1,975,000. Net income reported in 1956 and 1957, not subject to federal income taxes, was $3,653,638 and $3,266,078, respectively.

EXHIBIT 1

Mohasco Industries, Inc.
Condensed Balance Sheet as of December 31, 1958

ASSETS	
Current Assets	$46,575,082
Mortgage and other notes receivable, non-current:	
Secured by properties in Amsterdam (note 4)	$ 7,877,389
Other	3,060,797
Total Mortgage and other notes receivable, non-current	$10,938,186
Investments and advances	$ 914,946
Operating property, plant and equipment (note 4)	$57,292,408
Less accumulated depreciation and amortization	24,632,574
Operating property, plant and equipment—net	$32,659,834
	$91,088,048
LIABILITIES	
Current Liabilities:	
Long-term debt due within one year	$ 1,832,695
Accounts payable	3,969,619
Accrued expenses	3,299,221
Total current liabilities	$ 9,101,535
Long-term debt	$14,583,929
Other non-current liabilities:	
Long-term rentals on Amsterdam properties (note 4)	$ 6,601,545
Estimated liability under pension plans	1,408,980
Other liabilities and deferred credits	251,397
Total other non-current liabilities	$ 8,261,922
Shareowners' equity:	
Capital stock:	
Cumulative preferred, par value $100:	
3½ per cent series	$ 3,794,800
4.20 per cent series	4,004,000
Common, par value $5	15,334,625
Capital surplus	3,629,518
Earned surplus	32,377,719
Total shareowners' equity	$59,140,662
	$91,088,048

EXHIBIT 2

Mohasco Industries, Inc.
Income Statement for the Year Ended December 31, 1958

Net sales	$89,698,979
Cost of sales	69,693,763
Gross profit on sales	$20,005,216
Selling, general and administrative expenses	13,880,938
Operating income	$ 6,124,278
Interest on borrowings	1,069,443
	$ 5,054,835
Other income—net:	
Interest and royalties	$ 1,024,181
Gain on disposal of property, plant and equipment	1,164
Other	71,660
	$ 1,097,005
Net income before special items	$ 6,151,840
Special credit—gain on sale of Amsterdam properties (note 4)	8,450,923
	$14,602,763
Special charge—provision for long-term rentals on Amsterdam properties (note 4)	6,990,000
Net income after special items	$ 7,612,763

QUESTIONS:

1. Using data given in the case, verify how the $6,990,000 provision for long-term rentals was determined.

2. Do you agree with the accounting treatment used for the sale and lease-back transactions? Consider both the gain and the long-term lease.

3. Was the accounting treatment used for recording the long-term lease consistent with that used for recording the mortgage note?

4. Consider all other possible ways of accounting for the sale and lease-back transactions. Which do you prefer? Explain.

5. Was it appropriate to record the future lease obligation net of federal income taxes when the company still had a substantial tax loss carryover?

6. Why was it particularly advantageous for the company to complete the sale and lease-back transactions in 1958?

7. Verify as closely as you can that the quarterly mortgage and interest receipts ($130,084 and $219,282) will retire the balance ($7,877,389) of the mortgage note receivable by 1976. Assume such payments are received annually and use the interest rate given in the case as a discount rate. Do you increase or decrease the present value amount by assuming annual payments instead of quarterly payments? Explain.

CHAPTER TWELVE

Intangible Assets

An intangible asset may be defined as "an asset intended for long-continued use or possession having no physical existence, its value being dependent on the rights that possession confers upon the owner."[1] Intangibles include such assets as patents, copyrights, goodwill, franchises, trade names, secret processes, leases and leasehold improvements. Problems may arise in determining appropriate accounting for

1. the initial acquisition cost of intangible assets,
2. subsequent amortization to expense, and
3. write-downs or complete write-offs when there are indications of a substantial and permanent decline in the value of such assets.

INSTITUTE PRONOUNCEMENTS

The first Institute pronouncement dealing with intangible assets was ARB No. 24, issued in December, 1944. This bulletin, somewhat revised, was included in ARB No. 43 as Chapter 5, *Intangible Assets*, which follows:

1. This chapter deals with problems involved in accounting for certain types of assets classified by accountants as intangibles, specifically, those acquired by the issuance of securities or purchased for cash or other consideration. Such assets may be purchased or acquired separately for a specified consideration or may be purchased or acquired, together with other assets, for a lump-sum consideration without specification by either the seller or the purchaser, at the time of purchase, of the portions of the total price which are applicable to the respective assets thus acquired. In dealing with the intangible assets herein considered, important questions arise as to

---

[1] Eric L. Kohler, *A Dictionary for Accountants*, 3rd ed. (Englewood Cliffs, N. J.: Prentice-Hall, Inc., 1963), pp. 82 and 269.

the initial carrying amount of such assets, the amortization of such amount where their term of existence is definitely limited or problematical, and their write-down or write-off at some later time where there is a substantial and permanent decline in the value of such assets. These questions involve basic accounting principles of balance-sheet presentation and income determination and this chapter is designed to promote a fuller consideration of those principles. It does not, however, deal with the problems of accounting for intangibles developed in the regular course of business by research, experimentation, advertising, or otherwise.

CLASSIFICATION OF INTANGIBLES

2. The intangibles herein considered may be broadly classified as follows: (a) Those having a term of existence limited by law, regulation, or agreement, or by their nature (such as patents, copyrights, leases, licenses, franchises for a fixed term, and goodwill as to which there is evidence of limited duration);
(b) Those having no such limited term of existence and as to which there is, at the time of acquisition, no indication of limited life (such as goodwill generally, going value, trade names, secret processes, subscription lists, perpetual franchises, and organization costs).
3. The intangibles described above will hereinafter be referred to as type (a) and type (b) intangibles, respectively. The portion of a lump-sum consideration deemed to have been paid for intangible elements when a mixed aggregate of tangible and intangible property is acquired, or the excess of a parent company's investment in the stock of a subsidiary over its equity in the net assets of the subsidiary as shown by the latter's books at the date of acquisition, in so far as that excess would be treated as an intangible in consolidated financial statements of the parent and the subsidiary, may represent intangibles of either type (a) or type (b) or a combination of both. [This paragraph and paragraph 10 refer, in part, to intangibles which may arise when a parent company's investment in a subsidiary exceeds its equity in the subsidiary's net assets (book value) at the date of acquisition. The reader may find it helpful to refer to paragraph 7 of ARB No. 51, *Consolidated Financial Statements*, page 92, which also discusses such intangibles.]

INITIAL CARRYING AMOUNT

4. The initial amount assigned to all types of intangibles should be cost, in accordance with the generally accepted accounting principle that assets should be stated at cost when they are acquired. In the case of non-cash acquisitions, as, for example, where intangibles are acquired in exchange for securities, cost may be considered as being either the fair value of the consideration given or the fair value of the property or right acquired, whichever is the more clearly evident.

AMORTIZATION OF INTANGIBLES

Type (a)

5. The cost of type (a) intangibles should be amortized by systematic charges in the income statement over the period benefited, as in the case of

other assets having a limited period of usefulness. If it becomes evident that the period benefited will be longer or shorter than originally estimated, recognition thereof may take the form of an appropriate decrease or increase in the rate of amortization or, if such increased charges would result in distortion of income, a partial write-down may be made by a charge to earned surplus.

Type (b)

6. When it becomes reasonably evident that the term of existence of a type (b) intangible has become limited and that it has therefore become a type (a) intangible, its cost should be amortized by systematic charges in the income statement over the estimated remaining period of usefulness. If, however, the period of amortization is relatively short so that misleading inferences might be drawn as a result of inclusion of substantial charges in the income statement a partial write-down may be made by a charge to earned surplus,[2] and the rest of the cost may be amortized over the remaining period of usefulness.

7. When a corporation decides that a type (b) intangible may not continue to have value during the entire life of the enterprise it may amortize the cost of such intangible by systematic charges against income despite the fact that there are no present indications of limited existence or loss of value which would indicate that it has become type (a), and despite the fact that expenditures are being made to maintain its value. Such amortization is within the discretion of the company and is not to be regarded as obligatory. The plan of amortization should be reasonable; it should be based on all the surrounding circumstances, including the basic nature of the intangible and the expenditures currently being made for development, experimentation, and sales promotion. Where the intangible is an important income-producing factor and is currently being maintained by advertising or otherwise, the period of amortization should be reasonably long. The procedure should be formally approved and the reason for amortization, the rate used, and the shareholders' or directors' approval thereof should be disclosed in the financial statements.

WRITE-OFF OF INTANGIBLES

8. The cost of type (b) intangibles should be written off when it becomes reasonably evident that they have become worthless. Under such circumstances the amount at which they are carried on the books should be charged off in the income statement or, if the amount is so large that its effect on income may give rise to misleading inferences, it should be charged to earned surplus.[2] In determining whether an investment in type (b) intangibles has become or is likely to become worthless, consideration should be given to the fact that in some cases intangibles acquired by purchase may merge with, or be replaced by, intangibles acquired or developed with respect to other products or lines of business and that in such circumstances the discontinuance of a product or line of business may not in fact indicate loss of value.

---

[2] See Chapter 8, paragraphs 11, 12, and 13 [pages 28–30].

LIMITATION ON WRITE-OFF OF INTANGIBLES

9. Lump-sum write-offs of intangibles should not be made to earned surplus immediately after acquisition, nor should intangibles be charged against capital surplus. If not amortized systematically, intangibles should be carried at cost until an event has taken place which indicates a loss or a limitation on the useful life of the intangibles.

PURCHASE OF SUBSIDIARY'S STOCK OR BASKET PURCHASE OF ASSETS

10. A problem arises in cases where a group of intangibles or a mixed aggregate of tangible and intangible property is acquired for a lump-sum consideration, or when the consideration given for a stock investment in a subsidiary is greater than the net assets of such subsidiary applicable thereto, as carried on its books at the date of acquisition. In this latter type of situation there is a presumption that the parent company, in effect, placed a valuation greater than their carrying amount on some of the assets of the subsidiary in arriving at the price it was willing to pay for its investment therein. The parent corporation may have (a) paid amounts in excess of carrying amounts for specific assets of the subsidiary or (b) paid for the general goodwill of the subsidiary. In these cases, if practicable, there should be an allocation, as between tangible and intangible property, of the cost of the mixed aggregate of property or of the excess of a parent's investment over its share of the amount at which the subsidiary carried its net assets on its books at the date of acquisition. Any amount allocated to intangibles should be further allocated to determine, if practicable, a separate cost for each type (a) intangible and for at least the aggregate of all type (b) intangibles. The amounts so allocated to intangibles should thereafter be dealt with in accordance with the procedures outlined in this chapter.

Note that this bulletin is concerned only with intangibles "acquired by the issuance of securities or purchased for cash or other consideration. It does not . . . deal with problems of accounting for intangibles developed in the regular course of business by research, experimentation, advertising, or otherwise." However, despite this disclaimer, much of the committee's discussion appears applicable to accounting for internally developed intangibles, except for the problem of determining the cost of such assets. In general, the bulletin leaves management considerable discretion in accounting for most acquired intangibles. As a result, there is little uniformity in practice. An example of such discretion is found in the following notes to the 1960 and 1961 financial statements of the Colgate-Palmolive Company:

Goodwill, trade-marks, etc. at December 31, 1960 represents the excess of cost over the book value of net assets of companies acquired in 1959 and 1960, less amortization to date. This goodwill is being amortized over a period of 15 years and, accordingly, $573,000 in 1960 and $494,000 in 1959 have been charged to operations.

In 1961, Colgate-Palmolive revised its policy of amortizing goodwill. The following notes appeared in the 1961 annual report:

During the year, the company acquired the assets and business of Reefer-Galler, Inc. and of the Consumer Products Division of Unexcelled Chemical Corporation for $4,760,000 in cash. The excess ($3,046,000) of the amounts paid over the net assets acquired was recorded as goodwill.

Goodwill, trade-marks, etc. at December 31, 1961 represents the excess of cost over the book value of net assets of companies acquired in 1959 and subsequent years, less amortization to December 31, 1960. In 1961, the Board of Directors discontinued the practice of amortizing goodwill by annual charges to earnings. Goodwill charged to 1960 operations amounted to $573,000.

Although a change, such as that made by Colgate-Palmolive, in the classification of an intangible from type (a) to type (b) is not specifically mentioned by the committee, there appears to be no objection against it. The committee does suggest in paragraph 5 that an appropriate decrease be made in the rate of amortization of a type (a) intangible "if it becomes evident that the period benefited will be longer ... than originally estimated."

An example of treating the excess of a parent's cost over its equity in subsidiaries' net assets at dates of acquisition as a type (b) intangible is described in the following note to the Ford Motor Company's 1961 financial statements:

The excess of cost of investments in consolidated subsidiaries over equities in net assets at the dates of acquisition is not being amortized because in the opinion of management there has been no decrease in value. Substantially all of the increase during 1961, $224.6 million, was the result of additional investment in Ford Motor Company Limited (Britain).

Paragraph 7 states that type (b) intangibles *may* be amortized by charges to income even though there are no indications of limited existence or loss of value. This view reflects the widely-held belief that conservative balance sheets should reflect only assets having "real" value. On the other hand, amortization of type (b) intangibles may violate the basic matching and going-concern concepts.

A partial write-down of either type (a) or type (b) intangibles is discussed in paragraphs 5 and 6, while a complete write-off of type (b) intangibles is considered in paragraph 8. The committee favors showing such charges in the income statement except where it might mislead users of the financial statements. In such cases, the committee approves charges against retained earnings. There is an understandable tendency for management to favor the latter procedure because it does not reduce reported net income. At present, with the wide latitude of accounting treatments sanctioned by the bulletin, the independent public accountant must rely on experience, prudent judgment and the sound application of accounting principles when examining the propriety of management's accounting for intangibles. An illustration of a write-down of type (a) intangibles, as discussed in paragraph 5, is contained in the following excerpt from a note to the 1958 financial statements of the U. S. Hoffman Machinery Corporation:

> It has been the policy of the corporation to amortize goodwill resulting from the acquisition of new subsidiaries over periods not in excess of 20 years by charges to income. However, a recent review of the operations of certain of these subsidiaries indicated reasonable evidence that a loss in value of the goodwill applicable thereto had been sustained and, accordingly, the Board of Directors deemed it prudent to authorize the elimination of the goodwill applicable to such subsidiaries as of January 1, 1958,... which writeoff is shown as a Special Item in 1958. The amortization policy will be continued with respect to the remaining goodwill applicable to subsidiaries where no loss in value of the goodwill was indicated.

ARB No. 24, *Accounting for Intangible Assets* (1944), stated the committee's belief that the long-accepted practice of eliminating type (b) intangibles immediately after acquisition against any existing surplus, capital or earned, should be discouraged. In paragraph 9, the 1953 committee took a more positive stand, stating that "lump-sum write-offs of intangibles should not be made to earned surplus immediately after acquisition, nor should intangibles be charged against capital surplus." An example of the earlier practice is described in the following note to the financial statements from the American Home Products Corporation's 1961 annual report:

> INTANGIBLE ASSETS at December 31, 1961 include the cost, $19,692,734, of good will, trade-marks, formulae, etc., acquired since January 1, 1954 and $226,005 for patents and patent rights acquired since January 1, 1950, which are stated at cost less amortization. In accordance with generally accepted accounting practice at the time, good will, trade-marks, formulae, etc., acquired prior to January 1, 1954, aggregating approximately $40,000,000, were written down to $1 by charges against retained earnings and capital surplus; however, such amount should be recognized in any determination of total invested capital.

ACCOUNTING TREATMENT OF INTERNALLY DEVELOPED INTANGIBLES

As noted earlier, intangible assets may be developed internally in the course of doing business. Examples are patents, copyrights, and deferred research and development costs. Many intangible assets may be either purchased or developed internally. However, goodwill should not be recorded in the accounts unless it results from a purchase transaction.

In most instances, management charges the cost of research and development and similar activities to expense each year as incurred. Such a policy is described in the following statement from the 1961 annual report of the Corn Products Company:

Consistent with our policy, ... research, advertising, and promotion costs were all charged to expense in the year in which they were incurred. Although it is permissible to capitalize major research and introductory costs of new products and amortize such costs over the profitable years of such products, the company charges current earnings with *all* such expenses. As in prior years, this enables us to face the future with a "clean slate," benefiting from future earnings of new products without the offsetting amortization of introductory costs. The net effect of these product introductions was a penalty on 1961 earnings.

The following notes to the financial statements of Fairbanks Morse & Co. (1961) and J. I. Case Company (1960) show two different alternatives of treating engineering costs; in the first, an intangible asset is recognized, while in the second, similar costs are charged to expense as incurred.

Fairbanks Morse & Co.:
Effective January 1, 1961, the company adopted the policy of capitalizing pattern and tool costs (included in machinery and equipment) and deferring engineering costs applicable to new products, and amortizing such costs over a period not to exceed three years from the time the new product is placed in production. In the opinion of management, this policy will provide a more accurate matching of revenues and expenses. Under the previous policy of charging these costs to expense as incurred, the net loss would have been increased by approximately $480,000.

J. I. Case Company:
In 1960 the company adopted a policy of charging all engineering and product development costs to expense as incurred, a change from its previous policy of deferring major costs relating to products scheduled for future production and amortizing those costs over the two years following the year in which they were incurred. Such costs in the amount of $4,140,964 (included in cost of goods sold), deferred at the beginning of the year, less related deferred income taxes of $1,933,165 (included in credit for taxes on income), were also charged to expense in 1960.[3]

The decision whether to defer such costs or charge them to expense as incurred involves questions of conservatism and matching. Under the matching concept, costs should be allocated to the fiscal periods benefited. When there is doubt about the extent or duration of future benefits, conservatism calls for current charges to expense. Presently, most corporations charge research and development and

---

[3] J. I. Case incurred a loss in 1960.

similar costs to expense as incurred rather than deferring them.[4] This treatment may not fairly reflect costs applicable to later fiscal periods, and some unrecorded intangible assets may be more vital to a company's success than many tangible assets which are recorded in the accounts.

REFERENCES

Andersen, Arthur, & Co., *Accounting and Reporting Problems of the Accounting Profession*, 2nd ed. Chicago: Arthur Andersen & Co. (Oct. 1962), 91–95, 103–5, 149–59.

Belser, Anthony A., Jr., "Deferred Development Expense," *Journal of Accountancy*, 97 (Apr. 1954), 441–42.

Blake, Matthew F., "Accounting for Research and Development Costs," *New York Certified Public Accountant*, 29 (Jan. 1959), 32–46.

Blough, Carman G., "Engineering and Development Costs in Contractors' Balance Sheets," *Journal of Accountancy*, 114 (Aug. 1962), 69–70.

Higgins, Thomas G., "Deferral vs. Charge-Off of Research and Development Costs," *1954 Annual Meeting Papers*. New York: American Institute of Accountants, 1954. Also included in *Controversial Areas In Accounting*, a booklet published by the Institute, 1954.

Hill, Gordon, M., "Wanted: Solutions to Three Major Technical Problems," *Journal of Accountancy*, 100 (Aug. 1955), 44–48.

McFadden, J. A., Jr. and C. D. Tuska, *Accounting and Tax Aspects of Patents and Research*. Princeton, New Jersey: D. Van Nostrand Company, Inc., 1960.

National Association of Cost Accountants, "Accounting for Research and Development Costs," *N.A.C.A. Bulletin*, 36 (Jun. 1955), section 3, Research Series No. 29, 1373–1437.

Nelson, Robert H., "The Momentum Theory of Goodwill," *Accounting Review*, 28 (Oct. 1953), 491–99.

Research Department of the American Institute of Accountants, "Should Goodwill Be Written Off?" *Journal of Accountancy*, 93 (Apr. 1952), 464–65.

Simon, Sidney I., "Court Decisions Concerning Goodwill," *Accounting Review*, 31 (Apr. 1956), 272–77.

Trumbull, Wendell P., "Case Study in Writing Off Intangibles," *Accounting Review*, 31 (Oct. 1956), 599–607.

Walker, George T., "Why Purchased Goodwill Should Be Amortized on a Systematic Basis," *Journal of Accountancy*, 95 (Feb. 1953), 210–16.

---

[4] For income tax purposes, research and development costs may be either deducted currently or amortized over a period of 60 months or longer. The choice, once made, can be changed only with permission of the Internal Revenue Service.

Continental Baking Company

Continental Baking, which was incorporated in Delaware in 1925, makes bread, cakes and other bakery products sold under the names Wonder, Profile and Daffodil Farm Bread and Hostess Cake. It operates more than 75 bakeries throughout the United States.

On November 30, 1955, Continental acquired the Morton Packing Company, one of the country's largest producers of frozen meat and fruit pies, by issuing 179,357 shares of Continental common stock for Morton's net assets. The fair market value of these shares exceeded the book value of Morton's net assets by $3,814,753 at the date of acquisition. This amount was classified as goodwill on the consolidated balance sheet, to be charged to income over a 20-year period. Exhibit 1 shows Continental's net sales, annual amortization charges and net income for the years 1955 through 1960.

During 1960, management decided to write off the remaining balance of goodwill. This decision was explained as follows in the 1960 annual report to stockholders:

Included in the item of goodwill at the end of the year 1959 was an amount of $3,051,776, resulting from the acquisition in 1955 of the assets of Morton Packing Company. During each of the years 1956 to 1960, inclusive, an amount equivalent to one-twentieth of such [initial] amount was being taken down as a charge to income. From a study made during 1960, it was found that over 53 per cent of the items sold by the Morton Frozen Foods Division during the preceding year consisted of items which had been developed since Morton's acquisition by Continental Baking Company, and that since its acquisition by Continental Baking Company expenditures for fixed assets had been greater than the total value of the fixed assets at the date of acquisition. From this study it was determined that the profits now being experienced by our Morton Frozen Foods Division had resulted from operating efficiencies because of new equipment purchases and sales increases resulting from new product items. Therefore, the Board of Directors decided that there was not any goodwill remaining at the end of the year 1960 from the acquisition of Morton Packing Company and the balance at the foregoing date of $2,861,040 was written off by a special charge shown in the Statement of Consolidated Income and Earned Surplus.

Exhibit 2 gives Continental's Statement of Consolidated Income and Earned Surplus for the year ended December 31, 1960.

EXHIBIT 1

Continental Baking Company
Selected Income Data for the Years 1955-1960
(000 omitted from column figures)

	Net Sales	Amortization of Goodwill[1]	Net Income
1955	$244,014	$ —	$7,737
1956	284,207	196	7,512
1957	307,877	191	7,762
1958	328,004	191	8,855
1959	385,941	198	9,323
1960	410,642	198	9,311

[1] Includes amortization of $190,738 due to goodwill arising from Morton acquisition.

EXHIBIT 2

Continental Baking Company
Statement of Consolidated Income and Earned Surplus for the Year Ended
December 31, 1960

Net Sales	$410,642,040
Deduct:	
Cost of goods sold	240,639,226
Delivery, selling and advertising expenses	136,882,093
Depreciation	5,193,819
General and administrative expenses	3,172,261
Contribution to Pension Funds:	
Company Plan	992,000
Jointly administered union management plans	3,341,556
	390,220,955
	20,421,085
Add: Other income	280,542
	20,701,627
Deduct:	
Interest on debentures	299,779
Interest on notes payable	194,310
Miscellaneous	11,840
	505,929
	20,195,698
Deduct: Provision for federal income tax	10,687,000
	9,508,698
Deduct: Amortization of goodwill	197,552
Net Income for Year	9,311,146
Deduct: Special charge to write-off unamortized goodwill	2,861,040
Net Income for Year Less Special Charge	6,450,106
Add:	
Earned Surplus at Beginning of Year	38,111,650
	44,561,756
Deduct:	
Dividends:	
On $5.50 dividend cumulative preferred stock	704,000
On common stock—$2.20 per share	4,216,256
	4,920,256
Earned Surplus at End of Year	$ 39,641,500

QUESTIONS :

1. Comment on management's reasons for eliminating goodwill from the balance sheet. Do you agree with this decision even though frozen meat and fruit pies were still sold under the Morton trade name? Explain.

2. Was the balance of the goodwill account at the end of the 1960 fiscal year written off against earned surplus or income for the year? What treatment do you recommend? Why?

3. What earnings per common share would you have disclosed for 1960 under (1) the accounting treatment used by the company and (2) the treatment you would have used?

4. Why do you suppose "Amortization of goodwill" was shown after "Provision for federal income tax" in Exhibit 2?

5. Do you have any objection to the terminology used in Exhibit 2? Explain.

Trans World Airlines[1]

TWA, incorporated in 1934, is a well-established and progressive airline, with an excellent reputation. It is one of the major domestic carriers, and is second only to Pan American Airways in international operations. It provides extensive overseas service to Western Europe, the Middle East and Southeast Asia.

Jet Acquisition Program

In 1955, TWA (and other major airlines) began planning the acquisition of jet aircraft. Its final decision was to order a total of 33 Boeing 707's and 30 Convair 880's. Delivery of the planes was not expected before 1959 and 1960.

These jet orders involved commitments of approximately $300 million, including necessary spare parts. In 1957, $90 million was invested in Lockheed Super Constellations and other piston aircraft to fill out TWA's fleet until delivery of the jets. TWA financed a major part of the Lockheed purchase through bank loans and a stock issue.

Early in 1959, the first jets were delivered by Boeing to TWA's holding company, the Hughes Tool Company, which in turn leased the planes to TWA on a short-term basis. This leasing arrangement was considered temporary until TWA could arrange for long-term financing needed to cover direct purchase of the full fleets. It was apparent from comparing the company's balance sheets at December 31, 1958 and December 31, 1957 (see Exhibit 1) that such financing had not been completed.

TWA's financial staff realized that the airline's ability to raise a substantial amount of long-term capital might be impaired

---

[1] Adapted with permission from a case prepared by Professors Neil E. Harlan and Richard F. Vancil, copyright by the President and Fellows of Harvard College.

by its recent profit history (Exhibit 2) even though a marked improvement was expected in 1959. It was therefore extremely important that any improvement in the 1959 profit situation be not only substantial and impressive, but also strong enough to carry through to subsequent years.

In February, 1959, Mr. John Smith,[2] controller of Trans World Airlines, reviewed the company's policy concerning amortization of acquisition and integration costs incurred in introducing new aircraft into revenue service. TWA had placed its first jet, a Boeing 707, in service the previous month, and expected further rapid additions to its jet fleet. The airline planned to complete its jet acquisition program by the end of 1960.

From 1955 to 1959, a considerable amount of corporate time and energy was used to prepare for the introduction of jet planes. The planning and technical staffs were involved in the program right from the start in consultations with manufacturers and in the many other necessary preparations. Now when jets were coming into service, the program required intensive advertising, considerable training, and numerous other expensive activities all connected with integration of the jet planes. The nature and details of these costs are discussed in more detail below. Briefly, TWA expected to have spent nearly $17 million on such activities before the jet fleet was completely integrated.

Previous Policy for Deferred Costs

Prior to 1956, TWA had not capitalized acquisition and integration costs. Such costs had been immaterial and were expensed as incurred. In 1956, however, TWA spent $4,000,000 in acquisition and integration costs in connection with its new Lockheed planes. It was felt that deferral of such a large amount was required under a Civil Aeronautics Board regulation.[3] Consequently, the company decided to amortize these costs in its accounts on a straight-line basis over a five-year period beginning at the estimated mid-point of the period when new planes were integrated into revenue service. For federal income tax purposes, TWA decided to write off the costs as incurred and establish an account for deferred taxes.

---

[2] All names of persons in the case are fictitious.

[3] Paragraph 241.2-4(c) of the "Uniform System of Accounts and Reports for Air Carriers," as published in the Federal Register of June 23, 1956, stated as follows: "Expenditures incurred during the current accounting year which demonstrably benefit operations to be performed during subsequent accounting years to a significant extent shall be deferred and amortized to the period in which the related operations are performed when of sufficient magnitude to distort the accounting results of the year in which incurred."

Need for Policy Revision in 1959

Exhibits 3 and 4 give detailed information on acquisition and integration costs. They were prepared by Mr. Smith based on actual accruals to date and budgeted estimates of future expenditures.

Exhibit 3 shows acquisition costs from the time jets were first considered until the planes were delivered.

Exhibit 4, integration costs, includes all activities from receipt of the jets until the time when they were placed in revenue service. For example, a considerable sum of money was spent on introductory advertising to acquaint the public with the availability, comfort and advantages of jet flights. Some of the other important categories included in integration activities were training of personnel (ground and air staff), publicity and proving flights, maintenance and other operating costs during the integration period, and direct administrative costs while the integration took place.

Prior to 1959, TWA had presumed that the same amortization policy would be followed for the jets as had been developed when the new Lockheed planes were introduced. The fact that total deferrals up to that time were a small part of the anticipated total was probably the reason why no serious attention was paid to the matter before 1959. When Mr. Smith began to study the question in 1959, however, he did so with the full expectation that 1959 and 1960 would see large acquisition and integration expenditures.

Mr. Smith's first impulse (to use the same five-year amortization basis as had been used on the Lockheed integration costs) was checked when he learned that another major airline had chosen a seven-year basis. Furthermore, there was talk that another airline had chosen a ten-year period. Mr. Smith started wondering just what basis TWA should use to amortize the deferred costs. Should they be deferred at all? Since jet service was coming in quite fast in 1959, he felt he could probably argue that the expenditures made in that year were "current" operating expenses, even though they would also benefit future periods.

Another question concerned the possibility of using different accounting treatments for the different classes of deferred costs. Additional problems might arise if TWA purchased some or all of the planes during the integration period. In that event, there would be no rentals paid, but TWA would bear interest and depreciation expenses. In the opinion of his assistant, Mr. Jones, depreciation was something that was quite clearly "gone," and Mr. Jones didn't like the idea of deferring any depreciation.

Mr. Smith noted the following facts that might help him in his decision. First, the "mid-point" of the integration period of the jet fleet could probably be said to be around December 1959-January 1960. Second, if and when TWA took over the planes from the holding company, the lives used in calculating depreciation on the planes would probably be ten years for the airframes and five years for some engines and seven years for others.

EXHIBIT 1

Trans World Airlines
Condensed Consolidated Balance Sheets at December 31, 1958 and 1957
(in millions)

	1958	1957
Current Assets:		
Cash and U. S. Government securities	$ 41.2	$ 30.0
Accounts receivable	23.9	24.0
Inventory of spare parts, etc.	12.5	13.8
Prepayments	2.6	2.3
Total Current Assets	$ 80.2	$ 70.1
Noncurrent Assets and Investments	$ 3.0	$ 1.9
Property and Equipment—at cost	$339.0	$324.0
—less depreciation	177.8	151.9
—net	$161.2	$172.1
Deferred Debits:		
Long-term prepayments	$ 1.7	$ 1.7
Costs relating to new overhaul base	2.0	2.7
Training and other costs applicable to new aircraft acquired or to be acquired	4.7	4.2
Miscellaneous	1.5	0.9
Total Deferred Debits	$ 9.9	$ 9.5
TOTAL	$254.3	$253.6
Current Liabilities:		
Short-term notes payable to banks	—	$ 12.0
Current maturities of long-term debt	$ 14.2	12.2
Accounts payable, deposits and accruals	44.6	34.4
Accrued income taxes	0.2	0.5
Unearned revenue	5.7	5.8
Total Current Liabilities	$ 64.7	$ 64.9
Long-term Debt[1]	$ 67.1	$ 63.2
Deferred Federal Income Taxes	12.3	13.6
Stockholders' Equity:		
Capital stock, $5 par	$ 33.4	$ 33.4
Paid-in surplus	48.9	48.9
Retained earnings[2]	27.9	29.6
Total Stockholders' Equity	$110.2	$111.9
TOTAL	$254.3	$253.6

[1] Includes notes payable to Hughes Tool Company, $18.1 million in 1958 and $5.8 million in 1957.

[2] Debt agreements prohibited payment of cash dividends in both years.

EXHIBIT 2

Trans World Airlines

Operating Results, 1950-1958, and Estimate for 1959

($ millions)

	1959 (est.)	1958	1957	1956	1955	1954	1953	1952	1951	1950
Passenger Revenue	$300	248	231	210	189	174	160	135	114	88
Other Revenue	50	37	33	30	28	30	27	26	28	29
Total Operating Revenue	$350	285	264	240	217	204	187	161	142	117
Wages and Salaries	$125	115	110	101	85	77	74	63	53	45
Depreciation, Amortization, Obsolescence	35	32	27	20	20	22	23	17	12	11
Other Expenses	170	139	132	123	100	82	79	66	61	50
Total Operating Expenses	$330	286	269	244	205	181	176	146	126	106
Operating Income (loss)	$20	(1)	(5)	(4)	12	23	11	15	16	11
Income Taxes (credit)	$11	1	(3)	(2)	7	13	6	7	8	3
Net Income (loss)	$9	(2)	(2)	(2)	5	10	5	8	8	8
Revenue Passengers (thousands)	5,500	4,723	4,818	4,428	4,048	3,594	3,140	2,573	2,223	1,706
Seat Miles Flown (millions)	8,000	7,256	6,985	6,202	5,405	4,768	4,110	3,155	2,577	2,264
Revenue Ton Miles (millions)	650	514	492	452	405	373	336	274	234	186
Payload Factor (per cent)	62.5	57.8	57.2	60.7	61.8	64.2	65.7	67.8	66.8	61.2

EXHIBIT 3

Trans World Airlines
Jet Aircraft Acquisition Costs, 1956–1960[1]
(000 omitted)

	1960	1959	1958	1957	1956	Total
Salaries						
Planning & Research	$275	$350	$150	$ 75	$ 10	$ 860
Technical Services	100	100	50	25	5	280
Traveling	25	30	20	15	10	100
Communications	20	15	10	5	—	50
Other	45	50	5	—	—	100
	$465	$545	$235	$120	$25	$1,390

[1] 1959 and 1960 estimated.

EXHIBIT 4

Trans World Airlines
Jet Aircraft Integration Costs, 1957–1960[1]
(000 omitted)

Advertising and Promotion	$ 3,600
Salaries and Wages (crew maintenance, sales and administration)	6,600
Travel	1,000
Communications	50
Maintenance Materials	300
Outside Services	150
Stationery and Supplies	300
Plane Rentals	1,600
Insurance and Taxes	450
Maintenance Provision	600
Fuel and Oil	950
	$15,600

Annual breakdown available only in total, as below:

1957	$ 100
1958	850
1959[1]	10,400
1960[1]	4,250
	$15,600

[1] 1959 and 1960 estimated.

QUESTIONS:

1. What is the criterion for deferring costs on the balance sheet?

2. What basis should TWA use to amortize deferred costs? Should they be deferred at all? Explain.

3. Should management differentiate between different classes of costs? Explain.

4. Using the amortization period or periods you have selected, give the

annual changes in the deferred costs and deferred tax accounts, applicable to amounts given in Exhibits 3 and 4, from 1956 and 1957, respectively, until the balances are eliminated. Use a 52 per cent tax rate.

5. If TWA purchased some or all of the jet aircraft during the integration period, instead of leasing them, would you agree with Mr. Jones that depreciation is something that is clearly "gone" and therefore non-deferable? Explain.

Ultrasonic Corporation (C)[1]

One of the primary accounting issues in the Ultrasonic hearings concerned the method of determining and accounting for $89,310 of moving costs which had been deferred to an account entitled "Deferred Charges—Moving Expenses."

Purchase and Transfer of Monitor

In 1952, Ultrasonic acquired the Monitor Controller Company of Baltimore, Maryland, a small manufacturer of electrical motor controls and switchgears. Shortly after it was acquired, Monitor was moved to Braintree, Massachusetts. In the summer of 1953, Ultrasonic purchased a large, five-story building in Cambridge, Massachusetts, to consolidate its scattered operations. The transfer to the new building, which began in the fall of 1953, was completed in December, 1953. A major moving problem was Monitor's inventory of over 25,000 individual parts, which had to be transferred, catalogued and placed in new bins.

Accounting Treatment of Moving Costs

Ultrasonic calculated the costs of moving its facilities at $165,795. Since management believed economies would result from centralization, benefiting future periods, it was decided to defer the total moving cost and amortize it systematically over a five-year period beginning April 1, 1954. On the balance sheet[2] at December 31, 1953, the end of the first quarter in the 1953-1954 fiscal year, $165,795 was shown under "Deferred Charges—Moving Expenses." Since the corporation planned to deduct the total amount on its tax return

---

[1] See Ultrasonic Corporation (A) on page 175 for company history and information concerning the SEC hearing.

[2] This statement was distributed internally and also externally to the corporation's banks.

for the 1953–1954 fiscal year,[3] it was decided in the second quarter to credit the deferred moving expense account and charge income by $51,000, the estimated tax saving from currently deducting the full amount of moving costs. This left a balance of $114,795 as a deferred charge on the balance sheet at March 31, 1954. (See Exhibits 1 and 2 to Ultrasonic Corporation (B) on pages 233–34.)

Included in total moving costs were two controversial items. The first concerned $68,000 which management maintained was a "loss of efficiency" of direct labor in the Monitor Division caused by the general disruption of the move. This amount was based on estimated percentages of direct labor inefficiency; 50 per cent of direct labor was charged to the deferred moving expense account in October, 75 per cent in November and 75 per cent in December. These charges to deferred moving expense reduced cost of sales by credits to that account.

The second disputed item included in deferred moving expense was the cost of supervisory wages and salaries incurred during the move, $21,310.

Amortization of Deferred Moving Expenses

A partner of the public accounting firm[4] which had audited the corporation's 1953 financial statements questioned the propriety of the five-year amortization period. He testified that there was no evidence the corporation would benefit from the move long enough to justify deferment over five years. The examiner noted that the partner "did not quarrel with the principle of deferring costs of the move over an appropriate period, but rather felt that the period selected should not be without demonstrable evidence of benefit." The partner suggested an alternative of writing off the costs over the remaining months of the 1953–1954 fiscal year. Although his alternative was not accepted, it was largely through his efforts that management agreed to credit deferred moving expense and charge income with $51,000, the tax reduction resulting from the current deduction of total moving costs for tax purposes.

Method of Determining Loss of Efficiency

The public accounting firm partner testified that, in his opinion, sufficient factual evidence had not been provided to

---

[3] By December, 1953, Ultrasonic had exhausted tax loss carryover benefits.
[4] Ultrasonic changed auditors in August, 1954.

support the amount claimed as loss of efficiency. He pointed out that there were no direct labor time tickets to support the charge.

There was disagreement on how the percentages were derived. Both the controller and his assistant stated they were told by the financial vice president that the percentages were determined by the president and executive vice president, the latter being in direct charge of the Monitor Division. However, the executive vice president testified that he was not consulted in determining the loss of efficiency and stated that he "just wouldn't know how to measure it." Similarly, the president disagreed with the financial vice president, testifying that he did not determine or authorize use of the percentages. However, the estimates were supported as reasonable by the chief engineer of the Monitor Division, although he had no part in determining them.

After considering the testimony, the examiner set forth the following opinion concerning the method used:

> ... while the percentages may be open to question in a technical sense, it is nevertheless believed that a high degree of disruption would inevitably attend the moving of a manufacturing establishment from one location to another—particularly when it is considered that the parts inventory alone contained 25,000 items, not to mention tools and machinery, plus finished and unfinished products and raw materials. Accordingly, although management may not have used the best judgment and foresight in handling this aspect of the move, nevertheless it does not appear that the company should be penalized thereby, in absence of a showing of bad faith or a deliberate intention to falsify; nor be deprived on technical grounds of reasonable recognition of a self-evident fact. Indeed, it would appear that the investor is no worse off with an informed judgment figure being utilized in this connection than he would be in a similar estimate of valuation of various kinds of physical assets as done by appraisers every day, everywhere throughout the world. There is no evidence that the [financial vice president] did not use his best judgment, even though he might perhaps have done better had he instructed the accountants to plan and take charge of this aspect of the move. And being a man of mature years and experience in manufacturing, his honest judgment is believed to be entitled to recognition.

Statements Made by Ultrasonic's Controller[5]

Although the examiner believed the judgment figure of $68,000 valid, he opposed the entries used to place that amount in the moving expense account. He contended that Ultrasonic should have credited the $68,000 to inventory, since he believed the "loss of efficiency" cost was lodged there, not in cost of sales. He noted that management had made the following entries, as testified by Ultrasonic's controller:

---

[5] The controller resigned on April 30, 1954.

EXAMINER: Are you familiar with the entry made on the books of
               the company with respect to moving expenses?
CONTROLLER: I remember this journal entry in principle and the amounts
               approximately as they are here because this is one of the
               major areas where we [management] differed. In fact, the
               entry is marked that management determined this journal
               entry so it was not my determination. At the time I did
               not approve of this journal entry. This journal entry was
               based on the theory that the cost of this move included
               not only direct loss of direct labor ... as developed by
               actual time tickets, but in addition to that, certain labor
               people who were working on the jobs could not work as
               efficiently ... So by conference they decided a certain
               amount of that was not a proper charge to cost of sales.
EXAMINER: What was the amount of this last figure?
CONTROLLER: For $68,000. But they moved it through in several phases.
               The first part of it increased moving and decreased in-
               ventory:

                         Dr. Moving Expense
                               Cr. Inventory.

               The second thing, they increased inventory which wiped
               out the reduction—the inventory ended up the way it was—
               and reduced cost of sales:

                         Dr. Inventory
                               Cr. Cost of Sales.

EXAMINER: Now, as an accountant, there was actually a loss of ef-
               ficiency?
CONTROLLER: That is right.
EXAMINER: How would you recommend treating that as an accountant?
               I mean, if you were left entirely on your own?
CONTROLLER: Well, it would have to be an estimate.
EXAMINER: What I wanted to know is, would you, as an accountant,
               applying the principles you live by, say this thing should
               be completely disregarded or do you think some value
               could justifiably be assigned to it and, if so, how would
               you arrive at it?
CONTROLLER: I would do it the same as it was done, except I believe
               I'd come up to a smaller inventory.
EXAMINER: Do I understand your present objection to be you thought
               the percentage too high, you didn't quarrel with the
               principles, you quarrelled with the way in which it was
               applied?
CONTROLLER: Yes, but further, this journal entry as it ends up doesn't
               carry the thing through because the net effect of this
               journal entry does not affect inventory, puts it in inventory
               and takes it out of inventory and the combined effect of
               these two operations is that your increase is in your mov-
               ing expense capital item and reduces your cost of sales
               which increased your profit and surplus.
               If this theory was carried through, the theory is that this
               direct labor was not efficiently used, and therefore, it did

not add value to the inventory as shown on its face. In other words, this $68,000 of direct labor did not add to the value, was not added to the value of inventory due to this disruption, so what the effect should be, the first part of this should be—well, if you want to transfer something from your inventory to this cost of the move there would be no harm in that. But then when you put back your labor and put your inventory back up and reduce your cost of sales, I don't think it is sound accounting. I can't go along with that.

EXAMINER: What do you think should have been the final entry?

CONTROLLER: If you care to apply the principle and give effect to this type of thing, should have been a reclassification and transferring $68,000, granting these percentages, added to inventory—excuse me, a correction on that,—$68,000 added to moving and reduce inventory value.

Examiner's Conclusion

The examiner concluded that without the $68,000 credit to cost of sales, the profit of $49,715 reported for the period ended March 31, 1954 would have been eliminated and a loss of $18,285 would have resulted. He deemed the item to be materially misleading, and rejected a statement by Ultrasonic's counsel that investors were not seriously concerned with either a small income or small loss when a corporation is essentially a growth enterprise. The counsel stressed that investors would be more interested in growth of sales from $40,000 in 1950 to over $5,000,000 in 1953.

Counterarguments by Ultrasonic's Counsel

Ultrasonic's counsel claimed that the examiner was mistaken in concluding that a net loss for the six-month period ended March 31, 1954 would have resulted if the $68,000 had not been credited to cost of sales. In his brief of exceptions to the examiner's findings, he advanced the following argument:

Little thinking that the examiner would fasten upon an accounting technicality dealt with only in the testimony of a single witness, we saw no reason to argue the point now at issue in our trial brief or reply brief. Had we done so, the necessity for its consideration by the Commission might well have been precluded. The matter can, at all events, be quickly disposed of.

The fact is that it would have made no net difference whatever to the March 31, 1954 results of operation of the Monitor Division, as reflected in the financial statements, whether as of December 31, 1953, $68,000 was credited to inventory rather than to cost of sales. The result of what was actually done, it is true, was to produce a cost of sales figure for the Monitor Division for the three months ended December 31, 1953, lower by this amount than would have been shown if it had been credited to inventory. It was later determined, however, that the books should be adjusted as of March 31, 1954 to reflect cost of sales in the Monitor Division for the entire six months period in an amount determined by use of a percentage-ratio formula.[6] To carry out this adjustment it was necessary to make offsetting entries as between cost of sales and inventory, crediting the former and debiting the latter. To the extent that the company's treatment of the $68,000 item had already reduced the cost of sales, the amount necessary to adjust cost of sales so as to bring it into line with the amount arrived at by use of the formula was thereby reduced. By the same token, the amount by which it was necessary to debit inventory was also smaller.

Conversely, had inventory been initially credited and cost of sales left unaffected, as advocated in the testimony quoted by the hearing examiner, it would have been necessary in order to give effect to the formula to credit cost of sales by a larger amount and debit inventory by that same amount.

Under the circumstances, it is clear that it made no net difference to the operating results of the Monitor Division reflected in the March 31, 1954 statements whether the deferred charge of $68,000 was initially arrived at by crediting inventory or by crediting cost of sales. As of March 31, 1954 the inventory figure and the cost of sales figure for the Division shown on the books would have been exactly the same no matter which course had been followed. The result of the course actually chosen, therefore, could not have been to mislead an investor by overstatement of Monitor inventory, as the examiner concluded.

Cost of Supervisory Time During Transfer

The SEC's Division of Corporation Finance, which reviewed all evidence presented at the hearing, contended there was no basis in fact for deferring $21,310, the cost of time spent by supervisory personnel in the move. The Division claimed that this amount, like the $68,000 item, was not supportable by adequate evidence of time records.

QUESTIONS:

1. What basis, if any, was there for capitalizing moving costs of $165,795? What accounting principles apply? Explain.

2. Comment on the appropriateness of the $51,000 charge to income and credit to the account for deferred moving expenses.

3. Does the lack of supporting time tickets preclude deferral of moving cost? Explain.

4. Do you agree with the controller's position? If not, how would you have accounted for the $68,000 loss of efficiency? Explain.

5. Do you believe Ultrasonic's counsel was right in stating that investors stress growth more than "a small income or small loss"? Explain.

---

[6] See Ultrasonic Corporation (B) on pages 230-31.

6. If the $68,000 had been expensed, would this have resulted in a loss for the six-month period of $18,285 as purported? Ultrasonic's Statement of Income for this period is given in Ultrasonic Corporation (B), Exhibit 1, page 233.

7. Was Ultrasonic's counsel correct in claiming that accounting for the $68,000 of moving cost did not affect the income statement for the six-month period because the company had used the percentage-ratio formula to determine cost of sales? See Ultrasonic Corporation (B), pages 230–33, for a description of the percentage-ratio formula.

8. Would you treat the $21,310 cost of time spent by supervisory personnel in the move differently from the $68,000? Explain.

9. Do you think the auditors had any responsibility with respect to moving costs, considering that their last opinion on the financial statements was given as of September 30, 1953? The opinion at that time was unqualified. Explain.

Vitreometals, Inc.[1]

Vitreometals, Inc., was organized in the early 1920's to produce porcelain enamel products for one principal customer. It had not been particularly successful but managed to remain on the business scene until after World War II. In 1946, C.R. Newton learned of the company while seeking a good post-war business in which he could try out some of his ideas on management and product development. He was impressed with the favorable qualities of porcelain enamel on metal as a durable product with strength, beauty, and flexibility in use. He felt potential markets had not been tapped and that companies manufacturing and marketing such products were unimaginative and lacking in managerial know-how.

Newton acquired a 50 per cent interest in Vitreometals and became vice president in 1947. That year showed a small profit, but, more important, Newton was convinced that many unexploited possibilities existed for the product line. In 1950, he acquired the remaining outstanding stock, thus removing outside ownership and giving him a free hand, as president of the company, to carry out his long-range plans.

Seasoned and skilled men, who shared Newton's philosophy of managing a small company, joined the organization. Once the management group was formed, an aggressive program was begun to develop new products and to exploit new markets.

---

[1] Adapted with permission from a case prepared by Professor Henry Key, The School of Business, Texas Christian University. This case also appears in Robert N. Anthony, *Management Accounting—Text and Cases*, Revised edition (Homewood, Illinois: Richard D. Irwin, Inc., 1960).

New Products Through Research and Development

Newton and his associates realized that a growing, dynamic company would require a product line combining diversification, flexibility, and market depth. Every conceivable use for ceramic coated metals was examined, without limitation as to the engineering and production problems involved. Total research and development costs were more than $3,000,000 over a twelve-year period, and in 1961 more than 90 per cent of sales consisted of products not in the 1950 line.

Expansion Program

Between 1955 and 1961 two companies were wholly acquired and voting control was purchased in a British company. Penetration of foreign markets had been effected principally through licensing agreements under which Vitreometals furnished technical and production know-how.

In 1961, Vitreometals leased a modern plant to turn out a wide range of products for its rapidly expanding domestic and world market. The company invested over $400,000 in new machinery and equipment for this plant and incurred heavy moving and start-up costs as operations were transferred.

Financing Problems

In March, 1962, Mr. Newton and W. P. Mason, treasurer, discussed some problems encountered in securing funds for working capital and other purposes. A pending agreement with financial institutions provided $720,000 in mortgage money and $480,000 from sale of prior preferred stock. Before the agreement was concluded, several questions arose concerning its terms and conditions.

Vitreometals and the financial institutions had tentatively agreed that net assets, defined as net worth less appraisal surplus and goodwill, were to be maintained at a minimum of $2 million. However, when counsel for the institutions prepared the customary loan and purchase covenants, it was stipulated that not only appraisal surplus and goodwill, but also the cost of blueprints and drawings related to plans for a "package [prefabricated] building," moving and start-up costs, and deferred research and development costs should all be deducted from total equity to arrive at "net tangible assets" to be maintained.

Newton and Mason both felt that the earlier definition should be honored. They proposed these values: the package building plans, $48,000; moving and start-up costs, $143,996; and deferred research and development costs, $564,187. They stated that no further additions would be made to these accounts if these amounts were accepted. Also, these accounts would be reduced by appropriate amortization in the future. If the more restrictive definition were used, it was apparent that Vitreometals might find it difficult to maintain net tangible assets at the minimum level specified.

Part of the discussion between the two executives went as follows:

NEWTON: Bill, I don't think these lawyers, or the professional accountants, understand some of the problems a small and growing company like ours is up against. Those package building plans are just as hard assets as the machinery in our plant and ought to be included in determining the minimum net tangible assets requirement. As a matter of fact, you know that those plans and engineering drawings are the main assets we acquired from the Builtwell Company. The other assets were insignificant, yet those boys want to throw out the best assets we acquired as if they have no value at all. Sometimes I think public accountants and lawyers hinder a growing business more than they help.

MASON: Yes, I know what you say is largely true, Bob. The accountants and the lawyers have developed a lot of so-called generally accepted principles and conventions that are applied to financial statements in a rather indiscriminate manner. It grows out of practices of the past that have largely disappeared from the business scene, but the attitude of accountants toward these soft assets is still prevalent. The bulletins of the American Institute of Certified Public Accountants have a great deal of weight and influence in such matters, in fact, perhaps too much.

NEWTON: I think it is time some of these concepts that have no real validity in fact ought to be changed. If someone would bring these matters out into the open and get them thoroughly examined and discussed, maybe some helpful changes could be brought about.

And while we are on the subject, I have often wondered why the accounting profession has never developed some way to show on the balance sheet the value of such intangibles as our licensing agreements with Foreco, Ltd. of Canada, Sollingen-Stahlblechbau of Germany, Emailleries-Girondaux of Belgium, Ceramic Enamel Corp. of South Africa, Lesperes Réunies of France, Smalterie Lombardi, S.A. of Italy and the others. These licensing and royalty agreements represent tremendous asset values in terms of future income to the company, yet they are hidden away in an obscure footnote to the balance sheet if they are mentioned at all. They ought to be quantified in monetary terms on the balance sheet. That would give a truer picture of the sound going-concern value of a company like ours than present accounting and legal practices permit.

In commenting on the company's financing problems Mr. Newton stated:

> In a small growing company engaged simultaneously in production and product research and development, there is always an acute problem of working capital shortage. Research and development costs overbalance the nominal income from limited product sales, hence reinvestment is inadequate as a source of funds. Such a situation places a strain on the credit position of a company.

Vitreometals might have followed the conventional method of meeting its pressing financial needs with heavy mortgage debt. Instead, it chose to follow the less common route of equity financing through public sale of stock. The company wanted to establish a public market for its shares to be in a better position for meeting future needs. A modest offering of common stock in 1952 was absorbed by the public with good distribution. A second offering of common stock with warrants for purchase of additional common was successfully distributed in 1955. Almost all of the warrants had been exercised before the expiration date in 1958. The most recent public offering was in 1961, when $329,712 was raised. Outstanding common shares were also increased in 1961 by the conversion of $420,000 of convertible debentures.

Exhibits 1 through 6 show the company's financial statements and other financial information.

EXHIBIT 1

Vitreometals, Inc.
Sales and Net Income for the Years 1950-1961

Year	Sales	Net Income (Loss) After Taxes
1950	$ 465,440	$ 11,760
1951	689,520	15,490
1952	726,850	(25,790)
1953	891,325	5,391
1954	1,267,146	23,227
1955	1,690,093	23,405
1956	2,382,215	48,611
1957	2,409,026	49,895
1958	2,435,702	(141,913) strike
1959	3,473,588	102,818
1960	3,387,107	108,083
1961	2,886,580	8,586

EXHIBIT 2

Vitreometals, Inc.
Statements of Consolidated Income
For the Years Ended December 31, 1961 and 1960

	1961	1960
Total Revenues	$2,886,580	$3,387,107
Cost of Goods Sold	2,412,712	2,810,266
Gross Profit	$ 473,868	$ 576,841
Selling and Administrative Expenses	440,743	396,348
Income from Operations	$ 33,125	$ 180,493
Other Income (Charges), net	(37,015)	(66,487)
Net Income (Loss) before Federal Income Taxes	$ (3,890)	$ 114,006
Federal Income Taxes (Note 6)		5,923
Net Income (Loss) after Provision for Federal Income Taxes	$ (3,890)	$ 108,083
Refund of Federal Income Taxes due to Net Operating Loss Carry-backs	12,476	
Consolidated Net Income	$ 8,586	$ 108,083

EXHIBIT 3

Vitreometals, Inc.
Consolidated Balance Sheets
December 31, 1961 and 1960

ASSETS	1961	1960
Current Assets:		
Cash	$ 167,882	$ 169,487
Accounts and Notes Receivable (Note 1)	796,979	769,638
Inventories, at lower of cost or market	687,032	749,754
Claim for Refund of Prior Years' Federal Income Taxes	12,476	
Prepaid Expenses (Note 1)	41,506	50,738
Total Current Assets	$1,705,875	$1,739,617
Investment in Unconsolidated Subsidiary, at cost (Market—December 31, 1961, $84,000) (Notes 1-2)	27,420	27,420
Plant and Equipment (Notes 3-4):		
Land, Buildings, Machinery, Equipment	$2,107,946	$1,648,099
Less: Accumulated Depreciation	443,869	533,796
Net Plant and Equipment	$1,664,077	$1,114,303
Other Assets:		
Goodwill from Acquisition of Subsidiary	152,653	152,653
Package Building Plans	48,000	48,000
Cash Surrender Value of Life Insurance (Note 4)	25,991	22,625
New Plant—Moving and Start-up Costs	143,996	
Deferred Charges—Research and Development Costs	564,187	322,576
Unamortized Bond Discount		42,738
Total Other Assets	$ 934,827	$ 588,592
TOTAL ASSETS	$4,332,199	$3,469,932

EXHIBIT 3 (continued)

LIABILITIES AND STOCKHOLDERS' EQUITY

	1961	1960
Current Liabilities:		
Notes and Mortgages Payable, current		
portion (Notes 1 and 4)	$ 694,884	$ 368,647
Accounts Payable and Accrued Liabilities	933,149	702,895
Federal Income Taxes Payable		8,051
Total Current Liabilities	$1,628,033	$1,079,593
Long-term Notes and Mortgages Payable,		
less current portion above (Notes 1 and 4)	408,927	289,903
Convertible Subordinated Debentures,		
5³/₄%, Due 1971		420,000
Stockholders' Equity		
Capital Stock, par value $1.00 per share—		
authorized 600,000, issued and outstand-		
ing 476,474 (1961), 306,362 (1960) (Note 5)	$ 476,474	$ 306,362
Capital in Excess of Par Value of		
Common Shares	1,316,485	736,885
Appraisal Surplus	355,031	457,667
Retained Earnings	147,249	179,522
Total Stockholders' Equity	$2,295,239	$1,680,436
TOTAL LIABILITIES AND STOCKHOLDERS' EQUITY	$4,332,199	$3,469,932

EXHIBIT 4

Vitreometals, Inc.
Statement of Changes in Stockholders' Equity
For the Year Ended December 31, 1961

	Common Stock, Par $1	Capital in Excess of Par Value	Appraisal Surplus	Retained Earnings
Balance, January 1, 1961	$306,362	$ 736,885	$457,667	$179,522
Consolidated net income for				
year ended December 31, 1961				8,586
Amortization and write-off				
of appraisal increment (Note 3)			(102,636)	
Write-off of unamortized bond				
discount on conversion to stock				(40,859)
Proceeds of issue of 170,112				
shares of common stock	170,112	579,600		
Balance, December 31, 1961	$476,474	$1,316,485	$355,031	$147,249

EXHIBIT 5

1. Accounts receivable of $401,040 are assigned as security for notes payable—bank in the amount of $328,740. 24,000 shares of Haynes, Ltd. are assigned as security for notes payable in the amount of $60,000. Unexpired insurance premiums of $23,200 are pledged against notes payable of $18,500.

2. Investment in unconsolidated subsidiary of $27,420 consists of 58 per cent of the outstanding ordinary shares of Haynes, Ltd., London, England.

3. As a result of independent appraisals, the fixed assets are shown at cost plus an appraisal increment of $355,031 (net of amortization). Amortization of the appraisal increment has been charged in the amount of $34,110 to appraisal surplus. In addition, the balance of the appraisal increment on the A-plant, which was sold in 1961, was charged to appraisal surplus in amount of $68,526.

4. Plant and equipment having a book value of $1,664,077 together with cash surrender value of life insurance amounting to $25,991 are pledged to secure notes and mortgages of $471,220.

5. Of the 123,526 shares of Vitreometals, Inc. common stock unissued at December 31, 1961, 17,140 shares are held for the redemption of warrants which expire September 1, 1965.

6. Certain costs, deferred in the company's accounts, have been deducted in computing Federal Income Taxes.

EXHIBIT 6

To the Board of Directors
Vitreometals, Inc.
Alton, Connecticut

We have examined the consolidated balance sheet of Vitreometals, Inc. and its wholly owned subsidiaries, Super Finish, Inc. and Metal Surface Products Co., as of December 31, 1961, and the related statements of consolidated income and changes in stockholders' equity for the year then ended. Our examination was made in accordance with generally accepted auditing standards and accordingly included such tests of the accounting records and such other auditing procedures as we considered necessary in the circumstances, except that inventories of Super Finish, Inc. amounting to $173,090 were taken by responsible employees of that company and priced at the lower of cost or market. We did not verify the condition or quantities of these inventories at December 31, 1961, such quantities and values being stated at company figures. However, a responsible officer of the company did certify to the quantities, condition, and valuation of these inventories.

Subject to the foregoing, in our opinion, the statements mentioned above present fairly the consolidated financial position of Vitreometals, Inc., and its wholly-owned subsidiaries at December 31, 1961, and the results of consolidated operations for the year then ended, in conformity with generally accepted accounting principles applied on a basis consistent with that of the preceding year.

Alfred D. Sessions and Company
Certified Public Accountants
February 16, 1962

QUESTIONS:

1. What determines whether deferral of moving and start-up costs is in accordance with generally accepted accounting principles? Do deferred charges on the balance sheet add to or detract from the usefulness of financial statements in measuring annual earnings and otherwise?

2. Under what circumstances may goodwill arise on a balance sheet? What principles govern the treatment of goodwill? Does it make sense to exclude it in determining "net assets" under the loan agreement?

3. What may have been the objective of the lawyers and accountants for the financial institutions in excluding appraisal surplus, goodwill, deferred research and development costs, moving and start-up costs, and the cost of blueprints and drawings for the package building plan in arriving at "net tangible assets"?

4. Would it be in accordance with generally accepted accounting principles to attach a value to foreign licensing agreements and disclose these as assets on the balance sheet? Explain. What principle applies?

5. What are the reasons for Newton's criticism of accountants and lawyers? Is this criticism valid? What do accounting principles have to do with the problem from (a) Newton's standpoint and (b) from the standpoint of external suppliers of capital?

6. Comment on Vitreometals' financing dilemma. Are such problems typical for companies of this size? Do currently accepted accounting principles serve or hinder Vitreometals in its financing efforts?

7. Do you think adding the appraisal increment to the cost of fixed assets and establishing an account for Appraisal Surplus is an appropriate way of recognizing price-level changes? Consider the effect of the initial accounting and subsequent amortization, as it was apparently handled by Vitreometals, on both the balance sheet and the income statement.

8. Are the financial facts given in the case adequately reflected in the financial statements and in the notes thereto? Explain.

9. Consider carefully the auditors' report on the financial statements. What kind of an opinion would you have given based on the information available?

The Gillette Company

Gillette's history began in 1901 when King C. Gillette invented the safety razor. The company's main business is the manufacture and sale of safety razors, safety razor blades, and brushless shaving creams. Gillette diversified its operations in 1948 by the acquisition of The Toni Company which produces home permanent wave kits, shampoos, deodorants, and cosmetics. In 1955, Gillette acquired the Paper Mate Companies whose main products are ball point pens and refills. Gillette products are manufactured in several countries and are distributed throughout the world outside of the "Iron Curtain." During the three years, 1959 through 1961, shaving products, the Toni line, and Paper Mate products accounted for approximately 69 per cent, 24 per cent and 7 per cent, respectively, of total company sales. Toni's and Paper Mate's contributions to company profits were somewhat less than their contributions to sales.

Acquisition of The Toni Company

The 1948 acquisition of the outstanding stock of The Toni Company, adding Toni Home Permanent Wave Kits, Toni Creme Rinse, and Toni Creme Shampoo to Gillette's shaving products, was described as follows in the 1947 annual report to the stockholders, dated April 21, 1948:

On January 2, 1948 the company acquired all of the outstanding capital stock of The Toni Company, manufacturers of Toni Home Permanent Wave Kits and Toni Creme Shampoo. The purchase price of the stock was fixed at the net worth of The Toni Company at December 31, 1947 (estimated on the basis of a preliminary audit at $4,650,493.86) plus $8,000,000. A total of $11,500,000 cash was paid by Gillette on January 2, 1948 and the balance (less a reserve for contingencies) will be paid on July 1, 1948. As a further part of the purchase price, it was agreed that after Toni has earned $8,000,000 for Gillette after taxes assessed on The Toni Company, Gillette will pay to the former stockholders of Toni additional

424

sums equivalent to 50 per cent of Toni's earnings after taxes earned there-after, until an additional $8,000,000 has been paid.

Contemporaneously with the acquisition of the stock of The Toni Company, and in order to preserve Gillette's cash position, $5,000,000 was borrowed from banks at $2\frac{1}{2}$ per cent per annum with installment payments spread over a period of three years. Prior to the date of this report $1,000,000 of the loans has been repaid by anticipation of payments not yet due.

The permanent wave business is seasonal in character, January, February, and March being periods normally expected to produce sales at a rate lower than the average for the year. In the period January 1, 1948 to March 31, 1948, Toni's net earnings after provision for taxes are estimated to be $1,244,000 compared with $463,081.66 for the similar period in 1947. Earnings for the calendar year 1947 amounted to $4,464,354.83.

While the Toni Home Permanent Wave Kits have been on the market only slightly over three years, acceptance by the trade and consumers has been most satisfactory. Aggressive sales efforts have been backed by vigorous advertising, consisting of the use of newspapers, more than 30 leading mag-azines and 16 nation-wide radio network broadcasts each week. These activities will be continued and expanded.

In this short period Toni Kits have reached a dominant position in the trade, progress having been steady and rapid since introduction. It is realized that Toni will meet increased competition in its field as time goes on. How-ever, having in mind the position now held by Toni and the prospects of an increase in the use of home permanents, it would seem that prospects for the continuance of profitable operations are good. Toni Creme Shampoo has been introduced to the market within the past six months. That market is highly competitive but preliminary results are encouraging.

Until August 1947, Toni operations were confined to the United States. At that time arrangements for manufacturing in Canada were made and ac-ceptance of the Toni products in Canada has compared favorably with acceptance upon introduction in the United States. Other foreign markets are currently being studied.

In June, 1952, a Fortune Magazine article, "Gillette Looks Sharp Again,"[1] touched upon the acquisition of The Toni Company:

[By 1947] the proportion of the market occupied by the "regulars" (Gillette, Schick, American, and Pal) had become fairly static, and further sales in-creases for Gillette would have to come from raiding the competition or getting more people to shave more often—a slow business. The company decided the time had come to go into other fields with some new product that would counterbalance the terrific blade-and-razor peak of the September World Series promotion. It settled on Toni.

The Wave of the Present

Toni, a dynamic little company set up in 1944 by the brothers Neison and Irving Harris, had started late in a field of four. By the beginning of 1947 it had fought its way to first place. The Harrises, then seriously considering equity financing, decided they'd come off better from the tax standpoint by an outright sale. An agreement was reached with Lever Brothers in the

---

[1] Richard Austin Smith, "Gillette Looks Sharp Again," *FORTUNE*, Vol. 45, June 1952, pp. 164–66. Used by permission.

spring of 1947 for the sale of Toni at $7,500,000, but when President Charles
Luckman forwarded the proposal to Lever headquarters in London without
his recommendation, the deal fell through.

It was lucky for the Harrises that it did. The next quarter Toni sales
began the dramatic spurt that was to carry the company's share of the market
from 50 per cent to 90 per cent by the close of the year. Procter and Gamble
made a try for Toni in the fall of 1947 with an offer of $12,000,000 for the
stock and net worth, and a percentage of earnings over the next three years
that would have produced a total of about $18,000,000. The $12,000,000 was
all right with the Harrises, but other matters were not. The three-year cut
off not only let them out at the end of that period but seemed to assure the
golden egg at the expense of the Toni goose: there would be great pressure
on the Toni management to take all the profits possible, cut back advertising,
and in general operate hand to mouth. Moreover, the Harrises found P. &
G. exasperatingly slow; to get a decision through the chain of command,
matters had to go from the vice president in charge of the Toni negotiations
to the executive vice president to the president, to the executive committee,
and finally to the Board of Directors.

The Harrises decided to go over the P. & G. offer with A. G. Becker &
Co., Inc., Chicago investment banker, which had previously advised them on
equity financing. David B. Stern, Becker's chairman and a Gillette director,
suggested Gillette—that company had been quietly investigating Toni since
October, 1947. (Becker later collected a $330,000 broker's fee on the sale.)
There was no nonsense or red tape about Gillette's negotiations. Neison
Harris met [Joseph P.] Spang [Gillette President] in November in the latter's
suite at the New York Ritz-Carlton and both parties laid their cards on the
table. Spang, too shrewd a trader to want any part of competitive bidding,
made it clear that any offer from Gillette would be on a take-it or leave-it
basis. In the two weeks following, the Harrises and their staff got their presentation ready; the first week in December, Spang and William A. Barron,
Jr., Chairman of the Board, went to Chicago for a four-day palaver with Toni
at the Palmer House. When it was over, Gillette had all the important answers—and a condition: the Harrises, chary of delay and anxious about next
year's taxes, wanted the deal concluded within twenty-four hours. Spang and
Barron got back to Boston the next morning just in time to walk into the
directors' meeting. Most boards don't like settling a $20,000,000 proposition
on a few hours' notice, but after Spang and Barron had made their sales talk
(supplemented by the estimate of market-research director Bernard Gould that
Toni had a long-term holding power of 50 to 60 per cent of the market),
the directors voted unanimously to approve the purchase. The terms: $8,000,000
for the stock, something over $4,000,000 for Toni's 1947 net worth, and
another $8,000,000 to be paid to the former stockholders (after the company
had earned $8,000,000 net) at the rate of 50 per cent of Toni profits.

Toni turned out to be almost solid gold. Within two and a quarter years
it earned the $8,000,000 net for the parent company and Gillette was able to
prepay the $5,000,000 borrowed for the purchase.

The inclusion of Toni's accounts in Gillette's 1948 consolidated
financial statements was disclosed as follows in a note:

The accounts of The Toni Company, acquired on January 2, 1948, are
included in the consolidated statements for the first time with the result that
consolidated goodwill has been increased by $8,000,000 representing the amount

initially paid for The Toni Company applicable to intangibles. The substantial earnings of The Toni Company for the year 1948 have been included in the Consolidated Statement of Income and not segregated.

No plans were disclosed in the 1948 annual report concerning subsequent accounting for the $8,000,000 of goodwill.

In its 1949 annual report to stockholders, management gave further details pertaining to the acquisition and disposition of intangibles (see also Exhibit 1):

It will be recalled that the initial portion of the purchase price for the acquisition of The Toni Company was an amount equal to its net assets plus $8,000,000. The contract under which The Toni Company stock was purchased calls for additional payments contingent on Toni earnings, to be made to the former stockholders of The Toni Company. These payments are not to exceed a total of $8,000,000 and are to equal 50 per cent of the net earnings of The Toni Company after Toni shall have earned $8,000,000 under Gillette ownership. During the period January 2, 1948, the date of acquisition by Gillette, to December 31, 1949, Toni earned $7,550,567. By the end of the first quarter of 1950 Toni had produced earnings greater than the sum paid for it in excess of its net assets and therefore additional payments to the former stockholders may be expected to accrue under this provision of the contract in 1950.

Since the close of the year the amount of this contingent liability has been reduced to $7,547,600 through the release of the interests of one of the former shareholders of The Toni Company. Accordingly annual payments under this provision of the contract will be proportionately reduced. [Further payments are to accrue in subsequent years in amounts equivalent to 47.1725 per cent (reduced from 50 per cent) of Toni's net earnings after taxes.]

On December 31, 1949, the corporate structure was simplified by eliminating The Toni Company as a separate corporation. The Toni Company is currently operating as a Division of Gillette Safety Razor Company maintaining, however, its identity as a separate organization under the same management.

At the time of the acquisition of Toni on January 2, 1948, the company borrowed $5,000,000 from banks, payable in installments over a period of three years. On October 26, 1949, the company prepaid the remaining installments on these notes in full.

Accounting

While confident that a conservative valuation of the company's going concern value, represented by goodwill, trademarks and patents, would result in amounts in excess of those at which such items were carried on the company's accounts in prior years, nonetheless in line with current accounting practice, the company, as at December 31, 1949, wrote down to a nominal figure [$3] all intangibles appearing on its consolidated balance sheet and the additional amount which would appear if non-consolidated subsidiaries were included. The Gillette goodwill of $15,955,967,[2] arising in the main from the acquisition of The Auto-Strop Company and its subsidiaries in 1930, has been eliminated by charges of $15,302,922 against the available Capital Surplus and $653,045 against Earned Surplus. The goodwill of $8,000,000 arising out

---

[2] [Including $900,760 of other intangibles applicable to subsidiaries not consolidated at December 31, 1949.]

of the acquisition of The Toni Company has been eliminated by a charge to Earned Surplus. The charge to Earned Surplus to write off the so-called Toni goodwill was approximately equivalent to the earnings of The Toni Company since its acquisition.

The accounting policy of the company will be to write off annually any increases in goodwill resulting from further payments to the former stockholders of The Toni Company under the contract described above. This will be accomplished by special annual charges to be reflected in the combined statements of Income and Earned Surplus. Interim reports will, of course, state earnings before any such special charges. Annual reports will be on a comparative basis with prior years, reporting earnings before such charges but will state the amount of each such charge.

The table below shows the portion of Toni's earnings payable to Toni's former stockholders, the contingent liability at the beginning of the year and the amounts actually paid.

TABLE 1

	Contingent Liability at the Beginning of the Year	Portion of Toni Earnings Payable to Toni's Former Stockholders	Amounts Paid During the Year	Current Liability at End of Year
1948	$8,000,000	—	—	—
1949	8,000,000	—	—	—
1950	8,000,000	$1,402,293	$ 998,355*	$ 632,485
1951	6,145,307	1,006,010	1,458,004	180,491
1952	5,139,297	2,156,445	580,491	1,756,445
1953	2,982,852	Not given	4,739,297	—

Includes $228,547 paid to former Toni stockholder in settlement of $452,400 of contingent liability.

Under the heading "Supplementary Information" in the 1953 annual report, management discussed completion of payments for The Toni Company:

Since at the current level of earnings of The Toni Division there would appear to be only a relatively short time before the remaining portion of the purchase price for the stock of The Toni Company which was contingent on future Toni earnings would become due and payable under the terms of the contract, the company exercised its option to prepay the entire balance of $2,982,852 to become due under the contract....

It will be recalled that the company acquired all of the stock of The Toni Company on January 2, 1948 pursuant to a contract with the former stockholders of that company pursuant to which the company paid to the former stockholders the sum of $12,719,891 (being the net worth of The Toni Company determined as provided in the contract plus $8,000,000). Under the contract the company agreed to pay an additional $8,000,000 (subsequently reduced to $7,547,600 by the acquisition on a discounted basis of the interest of one of the former stockholders) on the conditions prescribed in the contract. Under the contract, once the Toni business had earned $8,000,000 under Gillette ownership, the second $8,000,000 of the purchase price would become due and payable in annual installments equal to fifty per cent of the previous year's earnings from Toni business until paid in full. Payments on account of this part of the purchase price began in 1950 and by December 31, 1952 the portion still contingent on future earnings of The Toni Division had been reduced to $2,982,852 which has now been paid in full.

The acquisition of The Toni Company was a most important step in the company's progress. Today this aggressive, closely knit organization constitutes one of the real strengths of the company. Its earning power and strong competitive position in its field provide the broadening of the base of Gillette operations and earnings which was hoped for when the acquisition was made. In the six years that Gillette has owned Toni, the total of Toni contributions to Gillette net earnings after taxes has substantially exceeded the price paid by Gillette for the stock of The Toni Company, $20,496,038.

Exhibit 2 shows Gillette's total assets, intangibles, and stockholders' equity for the years 1946 through 1961.

Acquisition of the Paper Mate Companies

In 1955, Gillette continued its product diversification by acquiring the Paper Mate Companies, a leader in the ball point pen field. Details pertaining to the acquisition were disclosed in the 1955 annual report in a special section entitled "Paper Mate" as follows:

The various companies located in the United States and Puerto Rico engaged in the manufacture and distribution of Paper Mate pens were acquired as of September 30, 1955, by two newly created subsidiaries of the company for a total cash purchase price of $15,100,523. Of the total purchase price, $6,000,000 was borrowed by Paper Mate of Puerto Rico, Inc., one of the subsidiaries, from a bank in Puerto Rico at $3^3/_4$ per cent per annum for a period of three years with a right of prepayment, and the remainder of the funds required by these subsidiaries for the purchase was supplied by the company from cash in its treasury.

Paper Mate's net worth at September 30, 1955, the date of acquisition, was $7,588,735, including goodwill on the books of one of the acquired companies of $233,024. The balance of goodwill attributable to Paper Mate amounted to $7,601,742 representing the cost of acquisition and that portion of the Paper Mate purchase price applicable to the intangibles of a going business. Consistent with the company's policy to carry goodwill of existing properties at a nominal value, Paper Mate intangibles are being amortized over a period of 36 months. The annual amounts required to write-off Paper Mate goodwill will be reflected in the consolidated statement of income and earned surplus as a special charge. A write-off representing a proportionate charge for the three months ended December 31, 1955, amounting to $652,897 has been made in the 1955 consolidated statements, leaving a balance of $7,181,869[3] to be amortized over the remaining 33-month period.

Earnings of Paper Mate for the three months ended December 31, 1955, have been included in consolidated income.

---

[3] Increased to $7,231,869 by $50,000 of additional goodwill recorded in 1956. See (C) in Exhibit 3.

Exhibit 3 shows the relevant portion of "Schedule VII—Intangible Assets," part of Form 10-K filed with the Securities and Exchange Commission for the years 1954, 1955, and 1956. Subsequent details of amortization of goodwill are found in Exhibits 1 and 2.

Acquisition of Harris Research Laboratories, Inc.

In its 1956 annual report, Gillette's management disclosed the acquisition in November, 1956, of the Harris[4] Research Laboratories, Inc.:

The scope of research and development activities in all of the company's laboratories is being broadened and important contributions in the form of new and improved products and processes continue to be made.

The company's interests embrace an unusually wide range of sciences, including such diverse fields as mechanics, metallurgy, physics, chemistry, radiochemistry, biochemistry and medicine. To serve such a diversity of interests and to meet accelerated competitive activity, continued emphasis is being placed on more effective coordination among the company's various research centers and on longer range planning in research programs.

The growing shortage of research and engineering personnel gives great importance to the procurement, effective utilization, and continued training of scientific personnel.

The acquisition of the Harris Research Laboratories, Inc., of Washington, D. C., in November 1956 is an important step toward broadening the company's research effort. An independent research laboratory of international reputation, its staff of scientists with broad experience in many research fields of importance to the various divisions and subsidiaries of the company is expected to perform valuable services for the various divisional research groups. The company contemplates that the Harris Laboratory will continue to carry on substantial consulting work for third parties in fields not competitive with the company's business.

In another section of the 1956 report it was stated that patents, acquired with the Harris purchase and valued at $700,000, would be amortized over their remaining lives, whereas $184,944 of goodwill applicable to the purchase was written off as a special charge to income.

In the 1958 annual report, management stated that amortization of the goodwill arising from the purchase of the Paper Mate Companies had been completed by a special charge of $1,971,192 to 1958 income. The unamortized balance in the asset account, Goodwill, Patents and Trademarks, was applicable to patents of Harris Research Laboratories, Inc., increased during 1959 by the acquisition cost of additional patents and trademarks.

---

[4] Not related to the Harris brothers from whom Gillette purchased Toni.

EXHIBIT 1

The Gillette Company
Selected Income Data for the Years 1946-1961
(000 omitted from column figures except for per share amounts)

	Net Sales	Net Income Before Special Charges	Net Income Before Special Charges per Share of Common Stock[4]	Special Charges	Dividends Paid on Common Stock	Dividends Paid per Share of Common Stock[4]
1946	$ 51,757	$10,501	$ .38	—	$ 6,839	$ .21
1947	59,560	11,627	.43	—	7,395	.20
1948	85,883	15,001	.57	—	7,899	.25
1949	90,795	13,918	.52	$23,956[1]	8,401	.27
1950	99,346	16,630	.64	1,631[2,3]	9,895	.41
1951	102,723	15,739	.60	1,006	11,395	.42
1952	120,485	14,713	.56	2,156	11,395	.42
1953	140,839	18,832	.73	2,983	12,897	.46
1954	162,189	26,138	.92	—	16,833	.58
1955	176,929	29,031	1.04	653	19,625	.67
1956	200,715	31,544	1.13	2,817[5]	20,871	.75
1957	194,929	25,941	.93	2,628	20,879	.75
1958	193,865	27,565	.99	1,971	20,882	.75
1959	209,277	31,152	1.11	—	24,450	.83
1960	224,737	37,123	1.33	—	28,025	1.00
1961	253,502	42,761	1.52	—	30,896	1.10

[1] $15,302,922 against Capital Surplus (balance of account).
$ 8,653,045 against Earned Surplus.
[2] Excess over $1,402,293 due to payment of $228,547 to former Toni shareholder in settlement of $452,400 of contingent liability.
[3] Special charges made to income beginning in 1950.
[4] Based upon the number of shares outstanding at the end of the year, as adjusted for two-for-one stock splits in 1950 and 1955, and a three-for-one split in 1961.
[5] Includes $2,632,000 of Paper Mate Goodwill and $185,000 of Harris Research Laboratories Goodwill.

EXHIBIT 2

The Gillette Company
Selected Balance Sheet Data 1946-1961
(000 omitted from column figures)

	Total Assets	Goodwill, Trademarks and Patents	Stockholders' Equity
1946	$ 51,970	$15,055	$ 34,574
1947	61,364	15,055	39,051
1948	78,310	23,055	45,977
1949	54,788	— [1]	26,778
1950	52,276	—	31,376
1951	54,599	—	35,402
1952	66,889	—	43,044
1953	58,017	—	46,246
1954	69,567	—	56,798
1955	88,040	7,182	66,193
1956	90,376	5,294	73,016
1957	90,990	2,600	74,899
1958	94,814	562	78,934
1959	106,861	875	87,494
1960	114,682	740	94,436
1961	132,161	604	106,601

[1] Recorded at $3 for the years 1949 through 1954.

EXHIBIT 3

The Gillette Company
Schedule VII of SEC Form 10-K—Intangible Assets
Years Ended December 31, 1954-1956

Description	Balance at Beginning of Period	Additions at cost	Deductions Charged to Profit and Loss	Balance at Close of Period
Year ended December 31, 1954				
Goodwill, trademarks and patents:				
Goodwill, trademarks and trade names	$ 1	—	—	1
Patents and patent rights	2	—	—	2
Total	$ 3	—	—	3
Year ended December 31, 1955				
Goodwill, trademarks and patents:				
Goodwill, trademarks and trade names	$ 1	7,834,766 (A)	652,897[1]	7,181,870
Patents and patent rights	2	—	—	2
Total	$ 3	7,834,766	652,897	7,181,872
Year ended December 31, 1956				
Goodwill, trademarks and patents:				
Goodwill, trademarks and trade names	$7,181,870	50,000 (C) / 184,944 (B) / 700,000 (B)	2,817,366[1]	4,599,448
Patents and patent rights	2		5,506	694,496
Total	$7,181,872	934,944	2,822,872	5,293,944

(A) Goodwill attributable to Paper Mate acquisition.
(B) Goodwill and patents arising from acquisition of Harris Research Laboratories, Inc.
(C) Additional costs of acquiring Paper Mate Companies.
[1] Special charges to amortize Goodwill.

QUESTIONS:

1. (a) What kind of intangibles do you think Gillette acquired in the Toni purchase? Refer to the comments about the acquisition quoted from the 1947 annual report.

   (b) Based on your answer to 1(a), how would you amortize the intangibles (over what period and to which accounts), if at all?

2. Should Gillette have shown the entire $16 million excess of purchase price over Toni's net worth as goodwill in 1948?

3. Gillette stated in its 1949 report that its accounting treatment was "in line with current accounting practice" even though "a conservative valuation . . . would result in amounts in excess of those at which such items were carried on the company's accounts in prior years." Do you agree with this interpretation? Explain.

4. Can you find any justification for differences in (a) the timing and (b) the treatment used in accounting for the two amounts of $8 million?

5. Can you suggest an alternative method of amortizing the second $8 million which would be more in compliance with matching revenues and expenses?

6. Why do you suppose Gillette changed to a 36-month amortization period for intangibles arising from the purchase of the Paper Mate Companies?

7. Since Paper Mate's earnings were included with those of Gillette's, was there a mismatching of revenues and expenses when amortization of intangibles resulting from the Paper Mate purchase was shown as a special charge? Explain.

8. Do you agree with Gillette's procedure of computing earnings per common share without inclusion of the special charges? Explain. Had special charges been included, what earnings per common share would have been reported annually from 1950 through 1958? Are the differences in the earnings per common share figures material? Explain.

9. In the acquisition of Harris Research Laboratories, Inc., contrast the accounting treatment used for the cost of patents with that used for goodwill.

CHAPTER THIRTEEN

Investments in Unconsolidated Subsidiaries and Jointly-Owned Companies

In Chapter 5, *Consolidated Statements*, appropriate criteria were discussed for the inclusion or exclusion of a subsidiary in consolidated financial statements. As noted in Chapter 5, there may be valid reasons for not consolidating certain subsidiaries. The present chapter will focus on the accounting treatment in consolidated financial statements of (1) unconsolidated subsidiaries,[1] (2) fifty per cent jointly-owned companies, and (3) less than fifty per cent jointly-owned companies.

Investments in Unconsolidated Subsidiaries

There are two methods of accounting for unconsolidated subsidiaries in consolidated financial statements : (1) the cost method, and (2) the equity method. Under the cost method, the investment in unconsolidated subsidiaries is disclosed on the consolidated balance sheet at cost, and only dividends actually remitted by such subsidiaries are included in consolidated net income. Under the equity method, the investment in unconsolidated subsidiaries is disclosed on the consolidated balance sheet at cost *plus* the controlling company's (or companies') proportional interest in the unconsolidated subsidiaries' undistributed net income *since acquisition*, and the consolidated income statement includes the controlling company's (or companies')

---

[1] A subsidiary is a corporation more than fifty per cent of whose voting stock is held, directly or indirectly through other subsidiaries, by one of the corporations included in the consolidation.

proportional interest in the unconsolidated subsidiaries' net income for the period, regardless of the amount of any dividends remitted by such subsidiaries.

INSTITUTE PRONOUNCEMENT

The Committee on Accounting Procedure commented on accounting for unconsolidated subsidiaries in paragraphs 19 through 24 of ARB No. 51,[2] *Consolidated Financial Statements,* issued in August, 1959. These paragraphs follow:

Unconsolidated Subsidiaries in Consolidated Statements

19. There are two methods of dealing with unconsolidated subsidiaries in consolidated statements. Whichever method is adopted should be used for all unconsolidated subsidiaries, subject to appropriate modification in special circumstances. The preferable method, in the view of the committee, is to adjust the investment through income currently to take up the share of the controlling company or companies in the subsidiaries' net income or net loss, except where the subsidiary was excluded because of exchange restrictions or other reasons which raise the question of whether the increase in equity has accrued to the credit of the group. (Adjustments of the investment would also be made for "special" debits or credits shown on the income statements of the unconsolidated subsidiaries below the net income for the period, and for similar items shown in the schedule of earned surplus.) The other method, more commonly used at present, is to carry the investment at cost, and to take up income as dividends are received; however, provision should be made for any material impairment of the investment, such as through losses sustained by the subsidiaries, unless it is deemed to be temporary. When the latter method is followed, the consolidated statements should disclose, by footnote or otherwise, the cost of the investment in the unconsolidated subsidiaries, the equity of the consolidated group of companies in their net assets, the dividends received from them in the current period, and the equity of the consolidated group in their earnings for the period; this information may be given in total or by individual subsidiaries or groups of subsidiaries.

20. Whichever method of dealing with unconsolidated subsidiaries is followed, if there is a difference between the cost of the investment and the equity in net assets at the date of acquisition, appropriate recognition should be given to the possibility that, had the subsidiaries been consolidated, part of such difference would have been reflected in adjusted depreciation or amortization. Also, appropriate recognition should be given to the necessity for an adjustment for intercompany gains or losses on transactions with unconsolidated subsidiaries. If sales are made to unconsolidated subsidiaries and the investment in the subsidiaries is carried at cost plus the equity in undistributed earnings, an elimination of unrealized intercompany gains and losses should be made to the same extent as if the subsidiaries were consolidated. The same applies where intercompany sales are made by the uncon-

---

[2] See pages 90-95 for paragraphs 1 through 18 of ARB No. 51.

solidated subsidiaries. If, however, the investment is carried at cost, it is not necessary to eliminate the intercompany gain on sales to such subsidiaries, if the gain on the sales does not exceed the unrecorded equity in undistributed earnings of the unconsolidated subsidiaries. If such gain is material, it should be appropriately disclosed. Where the sales are made by the unconsolidated subsidiaries to companies included in the consolidated group, the intercompany gains or losses should be eliminated in arriving at the amount of the equity in the undistributed earnings of the unconsolidated subsidiaries which will be disclosed in a footnote or otherwise. (See paragraph 19.)

21. Where the unconsolidated subsidiaries are, in the aggregate, material in relation to the consolidated financial position or operating results, summarized information as to their assets, liabilities and operating results should be given in the footnotes, or separate statements should be presented for such subsidiaries, either individually or in groups, as appropriate.

Combined Statements

22. To justify the preparation of consolidated statements, the controlling financial interest should rest directly or indirectly in one of the companies included in the consolidation. There are circumstances, however, where combined financial statements (as distinguished from consolidated statements) of commonly controlled companies are likely to be more meaningful than their separate statements. For example, combined financial statements would be useful where one individual owns a controlling interest in several corporations which are related in their operations. Combined statements would also be used to present the financial position and the results of operations of a group of unconsolidated subsidiaries. They might also be used to combine the financial statements of companies under common management.

23. Where combined statements are prepared for a group of related companies, such as a group of unconsolidated subsidiaries or a group of commonly controlled companies, intercompany transactions and profits or losses should be eliminated, and if there are problems in connection with such matters as minority interests, foreign operations, different fiscal periods, or income taxes, they should be treated in the same manner as in consolidated statements.

Parent-Company Statements

24. In some cases parent-company statements may be needed, in addition to consolidated statements, to indicate adequately the position of bondholders and other creditors or preferred stockholders of the parent. Consolidating statements, in which one column is used for the parent company and other columns for particular subsidiaries or groups of subsidiaries, often are an effective means of presenting the pertinent information.

The statement entitled "Consolidated Financial Statements" was unanimously adopted by the twenty-one members of the committee, of whom nine, Messrs. Bedford, Dunn, Graese, Graham, Halvorson, Hoyler, Kent, Powell, and Werntz, assented with qualification.

[Qualified assents pertaining to paragraphs 1 through 18 are given on pages 94–95.]

Mr. Kent believes the consolidation policy section [See paragraphs 1 through

5 of ARB No. 51, pages 90–91.] is deficient since it fails to restrict the increasing practice of not including certain subsidiaries in consolidated financial statements. He suggests that the bulletin may possibly result in further increasing such practice as a consequence of the preference expressed in paragraph 19 for the inclusion of the equity in earnings of unconsolidated subsidiaries in consolidated statements. It is his belief that in the usual situation a full consolidation policy as implied in paragraph 1 is generally preferable, supplemented by such summarized financial information, in footnotes or otherwise, as may be appropriate.

Messrs. Dunn and Graham believe that the "preferable" method in paragraph 19 should be recognized as the only acceptable method of dealing with unconsolidated subsidiaries in consolidated statements, and that the method which carries the investment in unconsolidated subsidiaries at cost, and takes up as income only the dividends received, should be discontinued as rapidly as is practicable. They feel that the "preferable" method conforms to the purpose of consolidated statements as set forth in paragraph 1—to present the results of operations and the financial position essentially as if the group were a single company, and that its uniform adoption would increase the comparability of the financial statements of different companies, and would avoid the possibility of manipulation of reported consolidated earnings through the control of dividends received by the parent.

Mr. Dunn believes that paragraph 20 should require the elimination of intercompany gain on sales to unconsolidated subsidiaries if the failure to do so would have a material effect on the reported consolidated income, regardless of whether the gain on intercompany sales exceeds the unrecorded equity in undistributed earnings of the unconsolidated subsidiaries.

Observe that paragraphs 19, 20, and 21 are concerned only with the treatment of unconsolidated subsidiaries in *consolidated statements.* A paragraph in an earlier draft of this bulletin which recommended use of the equity method for unconsolidated subsidiaries in *parent company* financial statements was deleted. This deletion recognized that *parent company statements* pertain to a single legal entity, while consolidated statements represent an economic entity subject to common ownership and control rather than a separate legal entity. Since the equity method likewise ignores the existence of separate legal entities, use of the equity method of accounting for unconsolidated subsidiaries is considered appropriate only in consolidated statements and not in parent company statements. Accordingly, *some* of the entries given below to illustrate the equity method would not be recorded in a parent corporation's accounts. Such entries would be made only in the preparation of consolidated statements.

Although the committee preferred the equity method, it also approved the cost method, the result being that both methods are used to account for unconsolidated subsidiaries in consolidated financial statements, even under similar circumstances. Of 600 corporations surveyed by the Institute in 1962,[3] 286 disclosed unconsolidated

---

[3] American Institute of Certified Public Accountants, *Accounting Trends and Techniques,* 16th ed. (New York : The Institute, 1962), p. 70.

subsidiaries in their 1961 annual reports. About 20 per cent of the 286 used some form of the equity method to account for unconsolidated subsidiaries, whereas 80 per cent used the cost method. In 1955, the equity method was employed by less than 10 per cent of the companies then disclosing unconsolidated subsidiaries.

THE EQUITY METHOD

Assume that an unconsolidated subsidiary, 80 per cent owned, reported earnings of $3,000,000 for a fiscal period and paid cash dividends of $1,000,000. When the equity method is used, the entry to recognize the unconsolidated subsidiary's undistributed earnings for the period is:

Investment in Unconsolidated Subsidiary	$1,600,000	
Equity in Undistributed Earnings of		
Unconsolidated Subsidiary[4]		$1,600,000

Dividends received from the unconsolidated subsidiary are recorded by the following entry:

Cash	$ 800,000	
Dividend Income		$ 800,000

An acceptable alternative treatment would require the following entries:

Investment in Unconsolidated Subsidiary	$2,400,000	
Equity in Earnings of Unconsolidated		
Subsidiary		$2,400,000
Cash	$ 800,000	
Investment in Unconsolidated Subsidiary		$ 800,000

Note that the credit in the first entry under the *alternative* treatment is to "Equity in Earnings of Unconsolidated Subsidiary," *not* "Equity in *Undistributed* Earnings of Unconsolidated Subsidiary." Under this alternative method, no distinction is made between the subsidiary's remitted and unremitted earnings.

If the equity method is followed, the investment account should not only reflect changes in undistributed earnings of an unconsolidated subsidiary but also, as noted in paragraph 19, " 'special' debits or credits shown on the income statement of the unconsolidated subsidiary below the net income for the period, and for similar items shown·in the [unconsolidated subsidiary's] schedule of earned surplus." An example of accounting for both the undistributed net income and a special credit of unconsolidated subsidiaries is found in the 1961

---

[4] There is no general agreement where this item should appear on the consolidated income statement. It is sometimes shown immediately after "Sales." More often it is one of the last items, if not *the* last item, before "Net Income."

financial statements of the Reynolds Metals Company. Part of the statement of consolidated income is shown below :

Income before taxes	$29,554,913
Provision for taxes on income	8,374,719
	$21,180,194
Equity in undistributed[5] net income and special credit of unconsolidated subsidiaries	$ 3,919,459
Net income	$25,099,653

On Reynolds' *consolidated* balance sheet, the asset account, "Investments in and receivables from related companies," was increased by $3,919,459.

Consolidated net income for a fiscal period and consolidated retained earnings at the close of the period are the same whether *all* subsidiaries are consolidated or the equity method is used to account for subsidiaries which are not consolidated.[6] When the equity method is used, however, the individual revenue and expense items of *unconsolidated subsidiaries* are not disclosed in the consolidated income statement. Similarly, the consolidated balance sheet does not reflect the individual asset and liability accounts of such subsidiaries, or the interests of any minority stockholders in the unconsolidated subsidiaries.

THE COST METHOD

When the cost method is used, unconsolidated subsidiaries are maintained at cost on the consolidated balance sheet and only the earnings of such subsidiaries remitted as cash dividends are included in consolidated income. The entry to record the receipt of dividends is :

Cash	xxx	
Dividend Income		xxx

There is no formal accounting recognition for any *undistributed* earnings of the subsidiary.

The bulletin notes that under the cost method, "provision should be made for any material impairment of the investment [in unconsolidated subsidiaries], such as through losses sustained by the

[5] Dividends received from unconsolidated subsidiaries were shown elsewhere on the income statement classified as "Dividends."

[6] Occasionally the equity interest in unconsolidated subsidiaries' undistributed earnings is not included in consolidated retained earnings, but is classified separately in the "Stockholders' Equity" section of the consolidated balance sheet as "Equity in Undistributed Earnings of Unconsolidated Subsidiaries Since Acquisition."

subsidiaries." In its 1961 annual report, Deere & Company disclosed the following policy concerning losses of unconsolidated subsidiaries :

The Company follows the conservative practice of charging consolidated net income with the loss of any subsidiary not consolidated but does not include in consolidated net income any earnings of unconsolidated subsidiaries, other than income offsetting prior losses charged to income, until they are received as dividends; no dividends were received from any unconsolidated subsidiary during 1961.

According to the last sentence of paragraph 19, when the *cost method* is followed, "the consolidated statements should disclose, by footnote or otherwise:"

(1) cost of the investment in the unconsolidated subsidiaries,
(2) equity in the unconsolidated subsidiaries' net assets,
(3) dividends received from unconsolidated subsidiaries in the current period, and
(4) equity in the unconsolidated subsidiaries' earnings for the current period.

Usually item (1) will be disclosed in the consolidated balance sheet, although the investment account may have been reduced below cost through recognition of unconsolidated subsidiaries' losses. Item (3) will generally be disclosed separately on the consolidated income statement. Items (2) and (4) are often disclosed in a footnote, or the necessary information for calculating these items is provided as in the following example from the National Steel Corporation's 1961 annual report.

The Corporation's equity in the recorded net assets of the unconsolidated subsidiaries exceeded the carrying amount of investments in the subsidiaries by $2,699,532 at December 31, 1961. The Corporation's equity in the net earnings of such subsidiaries for 1961 was $620,237 less than the dividends received from the unconsolidated subsidiaries during the year; its equity in the undistributed net earnings of such subsidiaries for the year 1960 was $1,037,548.

If a corporation does not disclose its equity in the undistributed earnings of unconsolidated subsidiaries, the corporation's auditors may call attention to this lack of disclosure in their report. For example, the following paragraph appeared between the "scope" paragraph and the "opinion" paragraph in the auditors' report on the 1961 financial statements of the Ingersoll-Rand Company.

The Company's equity in the earnings for the year 1961 of foreign subsidiary companies not consolidated, as shown by their books, converted at rates of exchange in effect at December 31, 1961, was substantially in excess of the dividends received from those companies and credited to other income in 1961. The remittance of earnings from certain foreign countries is, however, subject to exchange restrictions.

Although the cost method of accounting for unconsolidated subsidiaries is widely used and can be defended as conservative, the resulting consolidated net income is subject to the controlling interest's ability to manipulate the amount of dividends remitted by the unconsolidated subsidiaries.[7] Also, footnote disclosure of significant information about unconsolidated subsidiaries is inferior to inclusion of such information in the consolidated financial statements, either by use of the equity method or by full consolidation of all subsidiaries.[8] The major advantage of the equity method is that income of unconsolidated subsidiaries is recognized when it is *earned* by the subsidiary, whereas under the cost method, income is recognized when dividends are *remitted* by the subsidiary.

The contrast between the equity method and the cost method is highlighted in the following note from the International Harvester Company's 1961 annual report explaining the Company's use of the equity method in accounting for its unconsolidated finance subsidiary:

The financial statements presented herein include the consolidation of the Company and all its subsidiaries except International Harvester Credit Corporation. The Credit Corporation's full equity value (instead of International Harvester Company's investment in this subsidiary) is shown as an investment in the Statement of Consolidated Financial Condition; its net income (instead of the dividends which it paid to the Company) is combined with the consolidated net income; and its accumulated net income retained is combined with the consolidated accumulated net income retained.

TECHNICAL PROBLEMS

Paragraph 20 deals with several technical problems in accounting for unconsolidated subsidiaries. These are similar to problems in preparing consolidated financial statements. For example, if the cost of an investment in an unconsolidated subsidiary differed from the equity acquired in the subsidiary's net assets (book value) *at the date of acquisition*, this difference should be analyzed as it would be for a consolidated subsidiary. (See paragraphs 7 and 8 of ARB No. 51 on page 92.) After applying the recommendations made in these two paragraphs, the amount of an unconsolidated subsidiary's undistributed earnings included in consolidated net income (equity method) or disclosed in a footnote (cost method) may be reduced or increased by depreciation, amortization, or other adjustments which

---

[7] In Chapter 8 of ARB No. 43, *Income and Earned Surplus,* the Committee on Accounting Procedure states in paragraph 2: "An important objective of income presentation should be the avoidance of any practice that leads to income equalization." (See page 26.)

[8] To give shareholders "a broader and more informative picture of world-wide operations," Ingersoll-Rand presented consolidated financial statements in 1962.

would have been made had the subsidiary been consolidated.

When the investment in unconsolidated subsidiaries is carried at *cost plus equity* in undistributed earnings since acquisition (equity method), gains and losses on intercompany sales should be eliminated. This is true whether the sales are made to unconsolidated subsidiaries or made by them to other companies included in the consolidation.

When the investment in unconsolidated subsidiaries is *carried at cost* (cost method), it is not necessary to eliminate from consolidated net income the gain on intercompany sales to unconsolidated subsidiaries *if* the gain on such sales is *less* than the equity in the unconsolidated subsidiaries' *undistributed* current-year earnings. However, gains or losses on sales made by unconsolidated subsidiaries to other companies included in the consolidation should be eliminated under the cost method when disclosing (usually in a footnote) the equity in the undistributed earnings of unconsolidated subsidiaries.

FINANCIAL STATEMENTS OF UNCONSOLIDATED SUBSIDIARIES

Paragraph 3 of ARB No. 51 (see page 91) notes that "separate [financial] statements or combined [financial] statements would be preferable for a subsidiary or group of subsidiaries if the presentation of financial information concerning the particular activities of such subsidiaries would be more informative to shareholders and creditors of the parent company than would the inclusion of such subsidiaries in the consolidation." Paragraphs 21, 22 and 23 concern such statements.

An example of the disclosure recommended in paragraph 21 is found in the General Electric Company's 1961 annual report in which the information on the following page was disclosed for the Company's wholly-owned, unconsolidated credit subsidiary.

GENERAL ELECTRIC CREDIT CORPORATION

		December 31	
Financial Position		*1961*	*1960*
Cash		$ 27,513,079	$ 26,810,555
Receivables, less reserve		635,220,386	522,943,804
Prepaid interest and discount		1,677,062	1,893,316
Other assets		1,465,060	838,840
	Total assets	665,875,587	552,486,515
Notes payable to:			
General Electric Company		20,000,000	20,000,000
General Electric Company—subordinated		39,000,000	33,000,000
Others		414,617,500	342,049,156
Accounts and drafts payable		24,754,517	17,291,587
Deferred payments to dealers		27,071,407	22,792,365
Accrued Federal taxes on income		6,995,121	5,252,306
Other accrued liabilities		2,679,608	2,519,205
Deferred income		61,665,518	50,029,940
	Total liabilities	596,783,671	492,934,559
Assets less liabilities—equity		$ 69,091,916	$ 59,551,956
Equity represented by:			
Common stock (par value $100 a share)		$ 10,000,000	$ 10,000,000
Investment in excess of par value of common stock		1,100,000	1,100,000
Reinvested earnings		57,991,916	48,451,956
Equity—held by General Electric Company		$ 69,091,916	$ 59,551,956

Current and Reinvested Earnings	*1961*	*1960*	*1959*
Volume of time sales and inventory financing	$820,615,545	$756,577,498	$649,985,671
Gross earned income	$ 65,177,962	$ 57,805,179	$ 48,707,142
Expenses—Operating and administrative	30,455,192	27,875,177	22,760,078
—Interest and discount	14,912,810	14,709,520	10,400,171
—Federal income taxes	10,270,000	7,895,000	7,980,000
Net earnings for the year	9,539,960	7,325,482	7,566,893
January 1 reinvested earnings	48,451,956	41,126,474	33,559,581
December 31 reinvested earnings	$ 57,991,916	$ 48,451,956	$ 41,126,474

General Electric follows the equity method in accounting for its interest in the credit subsidiary. At December 31, 1961, the investment in the credit subsidiary was carried at $69,091,916 on the consolidated balance sheet. Similarly, the consolidated income statement included "Net Earnings of General Electric Credit Corporation—$9,539,960."

General Electric presented the following *combined* statements for its unconsolidated foreign subsidiaries in accordance with paragraph 22.[9]

FOREIGN NONCONSOLIDATED SUBSIDIARIES—COMBINED STATEMENTS

Financial Position	September 30	
	1961	*1960*
Customer receivables	$102,702,000	$ 86,960,000
Inventories	83,710,000	69,582,000
Fixed assets	51,578,000	46,123,000
Other assets	93,694,000	59,683,000
Total assets	331,684,000	262,348,000
Borrowings	55,752,000	51,776,000
Other liabilities	141,538,000	104,097,000
Total liabilities	197,290,000	155,873,000
Equity of, and advances by, General Electric	134,394,000	106,475,000
Carrying value at September 30	84,900,000	55,446,000
Excess of equity over cost	$ 49,494,000	$ 51,029,000
Operations (twelve months ended Sept. 30)		
Net sales billed	$215,949,000	$159,838,000
Earnings on these sales	$ 5,448,000	$ 6,309,000
Provision for the effect on net assets, except fixed assets, of net decline in local currency values	5,415,000	1,407,000
Net earnings	$ 33,000	$ 4,902,000
Dividends for calendar years 1961 and 1960, included in General Electric Company's earnings	$ 2,602,548	$ 2,151,312

General Electric uses the cost method to account for its investment in unconsolidated foreign subsidiaries. The company noted in its 1961 annual report that "only dividends received from foreign nonconsolidated subsidiaries are included in the company's statement of current earnings, and carrying value of these subsidiaries represents cost of investment . . . in these companies."

Investments in Fifty Per Cent Jointly-Owned Companies

Corporate expansion through investment in fifty per cent jointly-owned companies has increased significantly in recent years. The chief advantage of such an arrangement to the two owners is the sharing of risk and capital requirements. Jointly-owned companies may be formed for various reasons such as exploiting a source of raw materials needed by both companies or utilizing the productive capacities of one co-owner and the marketing know-how of the other.

---

[9] Combined financial statements are discussed briefly in Chapter 5, *Consolidated Statements*, pages 95-96.

Four methods of accounting for investments in fifty per cent jointly-owned companies are briefly considered :

1. the cost method,
2. the equity method,
3. consolidation, and
4. inclusion of one-half of the jointly-owned company's specific accounts—cash, receivables, sales, etc.—in each owner's financial statements.

The cost method has been most widely used, but the substantial size of some fifty per cent jointly-owned companies and the common practice of financing much of their growth through their retained earnings has led to increased interest in the equity method. Technically, the preference expressed in ARB No. 51 for the equity method does not apply to fifty per cent jointly-owned companies since the bulletin pertains only to unconsolidated subsidiaries in which there is a *controlling* interest. In a fifty per cent jointly-owned company, neither owner has a controlling interest. While the bulletin does not deal specifically with the problem of accounting for fifty per cent jointly-owned companies, the equity method is growing in acceptance, as illustrated by the following note to the 1960 financial statements of Chemetron Corporation:

The accompanying consolidated financial statements include all domestic subsidiaries. All significant intercompany sales, profits, and other items have been eliminated. In recognition of the increasing significance of foreign operations and of the 50 per cent owned domestic affiliates, the policy was adopted in 1960 of recording investments in unconsolidated foreign subsidiaries and in foreign and domestic 50 per cent owned companies at cost plus the related share of undistributed earnings since dates of acquisition. Heretofore, such investments were carried at cost and the earnings thereof included in the accounts only to the extent of dividends received. For comparative purposes, the consolidated financial statements for 1959 have been restated in accordance with the new accounting policy. No provision has been made for additional taxes that might result from the distribution of these earnings as dividends.

While the equity method does not disclose the individual asset and liability account balances of the fifty per cent jointly-owned company, it comes closer than the cost method to reflecting the economic reality of the relationship.

Since *control* is normally considered an essential prerequisite for consolidation, the possible consolidation of fifty per cent jointly-owned companies has not received serious consideration. A major objection to consolidation is the resulting "minority" interest of fifty per cent. Another possible method, number 4 in the above list, is for each owner to add half of the jointly-owned company's income statement and balance sheet accounts to its own. This method, which is a hybrid presentation bearing some resemblance both to the equity method and to consolidation, is considered in Case 13–3, Monsanto Chemical Company.

Investments in Less Than Fifty Per Cent Jointly-Owned Companies

Joint ownership of a company may involve three or more owners each of whom holds a significant minority ownership interest. While the cost method is the generally accepted way of accounting for such investments, some accountants believe that the equity method is appropriate where the owners conduct a significant amount of business with the jointly-owned company and participate actively in its management.

Future Accounting Treatment of Intercorporate Investments

ARB No. 51, issued in August, 1959, was the last bulletin prepared by the Committee on Accounting Procedure before it was superseded on September 1, 1959, by the new Accounting Principles Board. In 1961, the Board announced a research study concerned with intercorporate investments. This is an area in which significant changes in accounting procedure appear likely.

REFERENCES

Andersen, Arthur, & Co., *Accounting and Reporting Problems of the Accounting Profession*, 2nd ed. Chicago: Arthur Andersen & Co. (Oct. 1962), 183–94.

Halvorson, N. T., "Current Accounting Problems." *Proceedings of the Seventh Annual Institute on Accounting*, University of Colorado, Boulder, Colorado, (Oct. 1960), 65–67.

Kocan, Peter, "Reporting the Operations of Jointly Owned Companies," *Journal of Accountancy*, 113 (Feb. 1962), 54–59.

Peoples, John, "The Preparation of Consolidated Statements," *Journal of Accountancy*, 104 (Aug. 1957), see especially pp. 35–36.

Zieha, Eugene L., "Accounting for Investments in Jointly-Owned Associated Companies," *New York Certified Public Accountant*, 26 (Dec. 1956), 703–8.

E. I. DuPont de Nemours & Company

When DuPont was founded as a partnership in 1802 its main business was the manufacture of explosives. Since then, the company has grown rapidly to a position where today it is the country's largest producer of commercial explosives, dyes, cellophane, and synthetic fibers and one of the leaders in plastics, basic chemicals, finishes, and pigments.

In 1917, DuPont acquired a common stock interest in General Motors Corporation.[1] By 1925, after having sold a substantial part of this interest to General Motors executives, DuPont held about 26 per cent of General Motors' common stock which had cost $57,304,304.

Since 1925, DuPont has revalued this investment annually to an amount which closely corresponds to its interest in G.M.'s common stockholders' equity as disclosed on G.M.'s consolidated balance sheet at December 31 of the preceding year. In 1946, the company's investment consisted of 10,000,000 shares, carried on DuPont's books at $264,500,000, representing 22.7 per cent of G.M.'s outstanding common stock. (See Exhibit 1.)

Until 1952, the offsetting credit (or debit) to the annual increase (or decrease) in the investment account was reflected in an unsegregated surplus account, which combined earned surplus, paid-in surplus, and surplus arising from revaluation of security investments.

---

[1] In 1949, the government filed suit against DuPont claiming violation of the Sherman Act (charging that DuPont exerted an influence whereby it was favored in some purchases by G. M.) and the Clayton Act (charging that DuPont's investment in G. M. could result in a monopoly position for DuPont in supplying G. M. with automotive fabrics and finishes). The case was finally settled in 1961 by a U. S. Supreme Court decision ordering DuPont to divest itself of its investment in G. M.

447

In 1952, to comply with a new requirement of the Securities and Exchange Commission, DuPont segregated its surplus account into the following three classes:

Earned Surplus	$ 534,680,163
Paid-in Surplus	63,313,909
Surplus Arising from Revaluation of	
Security Investments	455,742,355[2]

Dividends from G.M. have constituted a substantial portion of DuPont's net income after taxes. Exhibit 1 shows G.M. dividends, net of taxes, received by DuPont from 1946 through 1961, and the percentage of total DuPont after-tax income represented by such dividends.

Exhibits 2, 3 and 4 show how investments, investment income and surplus adjustments from revaluation of security investments were reflected in DuPont's 1961 financial statements.

---

[2] $451,378,242 applicable to the investment in General Motors.

EXHIBIT 1

E. I. DuPont de Nemours & Company, Inc.

Selected Data Pertaining to Investment in General Motors Corporation Common Stock

(in millions except per cent figures)

	As of December 31						Year Ended December 31		
	Number of G.M. Common Shares Held by DuPont	% Outstanding G.M. Common Shares Held by DuPont	G.M. Common Stockholders' Equity	DuPont Carrying Value of G.M. Investment	DuPont Total Assets	DuPont Operating Income[3]	DuPont Total Net Income	DuPont Net Income From G.M. Investment[4]	% DuPont Net Income From G.M. Investment
1946	10	22.7%	$1,144	$265	$1,264	$649	$113	$21	19%
1947	10	22.7	1,297	259	1,438	796	120	28	23
1948	10	22.7	1,517	292	1,585	978	157	42	27
1949	10	22.7	1,809	344	1,749	1,032	214	75	35
1950	20[1]	22.7	2,104	410	1,974	1,310	308	113	37
1951	20	22.7	2,257	477	2,163	1,546	221	74	33
1952	20	22.7	2,444	509	2,371	1,613	224	74	33
1953	20	22.6	2,699	554	2,567	1,765	236	74	31
1954	20	22.6	3,056	609	2,747	1,709	344	92	27
1955	63[2]	22.6	3,971	763	3,030	1,941	432	125	29
1956	63	22.5	4,298	895	3,318	1,917	383	116	30
1957	63	22.4	4,622	968	3,552	2,000	397	116	29
1958	63	22.3	4,733	1,033	3,754	1,859	341	116	34
1959	63	22.2	5,087	1,055	3,970	2,144	419	116	28
1960	63	22.1	5,531	1,131	4,232	2,170	381	116	30
1961	63	22.1	5,742	1,222	4,517	2,223	418	145	35

[1] G. M. Common Stock split two for one.

[2] One million shares bought in February, 1955 through exercise of rights. Subsequently, G. M. split its Common Stock three for one.

[3] Consists of Net Sales plus Other Operating Revenues (see Exhibit 3).

[4] After taxes. In recent years, 85 per cent of intercorporate dividends have been tax-free. The remaining 15 per cent is taxed at the usual corporate tax rate of 52 per cent (for all taxable income in excess of $25,000). The effect is to produce a tax rate on such dividends of 7.8 per cent (52 per cent×15 per cent). In 1961, DuPont received dividends of $157.5 million from General Motors on which DuPont's income tax was approximately $12.3 million.

EXHIBIT 2

E. I. DuPont de Nemours & Company, Inc.
Consolidated Balance Sheet as of December 31, 1961

ASSETS

CURRENT ASSETS:	
Cash	$ 92,892,528
Marketable Securities	258,389,251
Accounts and Notes Receivable, less reserve	243,565,112
Inventories	309,821,145
Prepaid Expenses	9,764,791
Total Current Assets	$ 914,432,827
PLANTS AND PROPERTIES (At approximate cost)	$ 2,301,169,016
OTHER ASSETS:	
Investments in Majority-owned Companies not consolidated	$ 28,744,666
Other Securities and Investments	8,506,445
Goodwill, Patents, Trademarks, etc.	41,883,749
Total Other Assets	$ 79,134,860
INVESTMENT IN GENERAL MOTORS CORPORATION	
63,000,000 Shares Common Stock	$ 1,222,200,000
Total	$ 4,516,936,703

LIABILITIES

CURRENT LIABILITIES:	
Accounts Payable	$ 90,960,328
Estimated Federal Taxes on Income, less U. S. Government Securities – $201,297,440	—
Other Accrued Liabilities	48,336,159
Total Current Liabilities	$ 139,296,487
BONUS AWARDED IN CASH – PAYABLE BEYOND ONE YEAR	$ 37,414,387
"B" BONUS FUND – UNAWARDED BALANCE	$ 1,690,899
RESERVES:	
Depreciation and Obsolescence	$ 1,387,052,030
Insurance and Contingencies	7,726,104
Total Reserves	$ 1,394,778,134
CAPITAL STOCK AND SURPLUS:	
Preferred Stock	$ 238,885,000
Common Stock	229,863,480
Surplus	2,475,008,316
Total Capital Stock and Surplus	$ 2,943,756,796
Total	$ 4,516,936,703

EXHIBIT 3

E. I. DuPont de Nemours & Company, Inc.
Statement of Consolidated Income, Year Ended December 31, 1961

OPERATING INCOME:

Net Sales	$ 2,190,960,318
Other Operating Revenues	31,778,667
	$ 2,222,738,985

Less:

Cost of Goods Sold and Other Operating Charges	$ 1,273,306,665
Selling, General and Administrative Expenses	244,053,626
Provision for:	
Depreciation and Obsolescence	168,960,624
"B" Bonus (credited to Fund)	33,548,000
Federal and Foreign Taxes on Operating Income	244,910,000
	$ 1,964,778,915
OPERATING INCOME – NET	$ 257,960,070

OTHER INCOME:

Dividends from General Motors Corporation Common Stock	$ 157,500,000
Income from Investments in Majority-owned Companies not consolidated	6,225,437
Miscellaneous Other Income	16,497,008
	$ 180,222,445
Less – Provision for Federal and Foreign Taxes on Other Income	20,020,000
OTHER INCOME – NET	$ 160,202,445

NET INCOME FOR THE YEAR	$ 418,162,515

EXHIBIT 4

E. I. DuPont de Nemours & Company, Inc.
Statement of Consolidated Surplus, Year Ended December 31, 1961

EARNED SURPLUS

BALANCE AT BEGINNING OF YEAR	$ 1,151,278,492
Add—Net Income for the Year	418,162,515
	$ 1,569,441,007
Less—Dividends:	
Preferred Stock	
$ 4.50 Series	$ 7,599,825
$ 3.50 Series	2,450,000
Total Preferred Dividends	$ 10,049,825
Common Stock (1961—$ 7.50)	344,644,673
Total Dividends	$ 354,694,498
BALANCE AT END OF YEAR	$ 1,214,746,509

PAID-IN SURPLUS

BALANCE AT BEGINNING OF YEAR	$ 146,981,171
Add—Adjustments arising out of disposition of common stock	19,338,281
BALANCE AT END OF YEAR	$ 166,319,452

SURPLUS ARISING FROM REVALUATION
OF SECURITY INVESTMENTS

BALANCE AT BEGINNING OF YEAR	$ 1,002,592,355
Add—Adjustment resulting from revaluation of Investment in General Motors Corporation	91,350,000
BALANCE AT END OF YEAR	$ 1,093,942,355
TOTAL SURPLUS AT END OF YEAR	$ 2,475,008,316

QUESTIONS:

1. Do you agree with DuPont's method of accounting for its investment in G.M.? Consider carefully (a) how the revaluation is done, (b) the basis used in calculating the investment amount, and (c) alternative accounting methods which DuPont might have used. Is DuPont using the "cost" or "equity" method, or some other method, of accounting for its investment in General Motors? Explain.

2. Could the amount of periodic revaluation have been reflected on DuPont's income statement? Explain.

3. What effect did the company's disclosure of taxes payable have on the current ratio? Do you agree with such a treatment? Explain.

4. Comment on DuPont's disclosure of plants and properties and related reserves for depreciation and obsolescence.

5. Comment on the company's disclosure of taxes on the income statement. Do you consider this a desirable method of disclosure? Explain.

6. What suggestions do you have regarding the terminology used in the financial statements?

Mission Development Company

Mission Development Company, which is controlled by the Getty Oil Company, was incorporated in 1948. After its incorporation, the company acquired 2,467,113 shares of Tidewater Oil Company common stock from the Mission Corporation (also controlled by the Getty Oil Company) in exchange for 4,934,226 shares of Mission Development common stock. Subsequently, Mission Corporation distributed all of these Mission Development shares as dividends to its stockholders. Mission Development has in excess of 14,000 stockholders, although over 60 per cent of its outstanding shares are held by the Getty Oil Company.

The number of Tidewater shares held by Mission Development has increased as a result of the following stock dividends issued by Tidewater:

Year	Percentage of Tidewater Stock Dividend	Additional Tidewater Shares Received by Mission Development	Tidewater Shares Held by Mission Development at December 31
1952	100%	2,467,113	4,934,226
1954	5%	246,711	5,180,937
1955	5%	259,047	5,439,984
1956	5%	272,000	5,711,984
1957	5%	285,601	5,997,585
1958	5%	299,882	6,297,467
1959	5%	314,873	6,612,340
1960	5%	330,617	6,942,957

Mission Development is entirely a holding company. Of total assets of $60,684,249 at December 31, 1959, the investment in Tidewater accounted for $60,612,392, disclosed on the balance sheet as follows:

Investment in Common Stock of Tidewater Oil Company—6,612,339[1] shares (after stock dividends of 100 per cent or 2,467,113 shares in 1952 and 5 per

---

[1] Less than the 6,612,340 shares given above because of excluding fractional shares received in stock dividends.

453

cent in each of the years 1954 to 1959, inclusive—carrying value not changed);
a 47.73 per cent interest. This investment was acquired in 1948 and 1951
from Mission Corporation by issuance of 4,934,226 shares of the Company's
common stock and is carried at fair value as determined by the Board of
Directors in those years. The quoted market price as of December 31,
1959, was $24.00 per share, aggregating $158,696,136 for the shares owned . . .

Management stated that it did not contemplate selling the investment, but that if it were sold, the company would incur a tax liability
of $27,943,864—25 per cent of the excess of the market value
($158,696,136) over the tax basis of the stock ($46,956,680—the tax
basis acquired from Mission Corporation).

Effective January 1, 1960, Mission Development decided to account
for its Tidewater investment in accordance with the equity method.
Consequently, Mission Development increased the account, "Investment
in Common Stock of Tidewater Oil Company," by $137,428,446, its
share of Tidewater's consolidated earnings retained in the business
from the dates of acquisition, and credited a new account included
in the "Stockholders' Interest" section of the balance sheet called
"Share of consolidated earnings retained by Tidewater Oil Company."
At December 31, 1960, the company's share of Tidewater's 1960
earnings retained in the business, amounting to $15,385,607, was
added to these accounts. Mission Development's 1960 financial statements are given in Exhibits 1 and 2.

In November, 1960, Tidewater offered certain of its stockholders
an opportunity to convert common stock into $1.20 cumulative pre-
ferred stock in the ratio of one share of preferred for one share of
common. Tidewater stated that cash dividends on its common stock
were unlikely for at least five years, and that it was ceasing to distribute stock dividends.

Hence, Tidewater submitted the conversion plan to accommodate its
common stockholders who relied on current income. When the conversion offer expired on January 11, 1961, 777,688 shares had been
surrendered for conversion. Mission Development did not convert
any of its Tidewater common, but, as a result of conversions made
by other Tidewater shareholders, its percentage holding of Tidewater's
outstanding common shares increased from 47.91 per cent at December 31, 1960, to 50.62 per cent at January 11, 1961.

EXHIBIT 1

Mission Development Company
Balance Sheet as of December 31, 1960

ASSETS

CURRENT ASSETS:		
Cash		$ 19,767
U. S. Treasury bills, at cost (approximating market)		99,018
Total current assets		$ 118,785

INVESTMENT IN COMMON STOCK OF TIDEWATER OIL COMPANY—6,942,957 shares; a 47.91[1] per cent interest (increased to 50.62 per cent in January, 1961), at cost......plus share of subsequent consolidated earnings retained by Tidewater Oil Company. The quoted market price at December 31, 1960, was $20.75 per share, aggregating $144,066,358

	213,426,464
	$ 213,545,249

LIABILITIES AND STOCKHOLDERS' INTEREST

CURRENT LIABILITIES			$ 5,051
NOTE PAYABLE TO GETTY OIL COMPANY (PARENT COMPANY), Interest at prime rate			100,000
STOCKHOLDERS' INTEREST:			
Common stock, $5 par value —			
Authorized, 6,000,000 shares			
Issued and outstanding, 4,934,226 shares		$ 24,671,130	
Excess of fair value assigned by the Board of Directors to the shares of Tidewater Oil Company common stock acquired over the par value of common stock issued in exchange therefor (no change during the year)		35,941,147	
Earnings retained in the business			
Balance, December 31, 1959	$ 67,213		
Less — Net loss for the year	53,345	13,868	
		$ 60,626,145	
Share of consolidated earnings retained by Tidewater Oil Company		152,814,053	$ 213,440,198
			$ 213,545,249

---

[1] The increase in the percentage of Mission Development's ownership of outstanding Tidewater common shares from 47.73 per cent at December 31, 1959, to 47.91 per cent at December 31, 1960, was due entirely to a reduction in the total number of Tidewater common shares outstanding as a result of treasury stock transactions by Tidewater.

EXHIBIT 2

Mission Development Company
Statements of Income and Share of Consolidated
Earnings Retained by Tidewater Oil Company
For the Year Ended December 31, 1960

INCOME

INCOME:

5% stock dividend, 330,617 shares of Tidewater Oil Company common stock		$ ——
Interest		1,663

EXPENSES:

Office and administrative expenses	$ 19,992	
Stock transfer and registration fees and expenses	11,728	
Stationery and printing	10,316	
State franchise tax	8,145	
Postage and mailing	3,527	
Directors' fees	1,300	55,008
Net loss		$ 53,345

SHARE OF CONSOLIDATED EARNINGS RETAINED BY TIDEWATER OIL COMPANY ($ 3.12 per share)	15,385,607
Share of consolidated earnings retained by Tidewater Oil Company less net loss	$ 15,332,262

SHARE OF CONSOLIDATED EARNINGS RETAINED
BY TIDEWATER OIL COMPANY

BALANCE, DECEMBER 31, 1959	$ ——
ADD:	
Share of consolidated earnings retained by Tidewater Oil Company from dates of acquisition of investment to December 31, 1959	$ 137,428,446
Share of consolidated earnings retained by Tidewater Oil Company for the year	15,385,607
BALANCE, DECEMBER 31, 1960	$ 152,814,053

QUESTIONS:

1. Was the 1960 carrying value of Mission Development's interest in Tidewater determined in accordance with generally accepted accounting principles? Explain.

2. Do you think the change resulted in improved disclosure? Explain.

3. Do you agree with disclosing the investment in 1960 at $213,426,464 when the market value was only $144,066,358? Also, would you recognize the capital gains tax which Mission Development would incur if it disposed of its Tidewater investment? Explain.

4. In 1960, Tidewater's earnings retained in the business, after preferred dividends, were $32,174,000. Reconcile this figure with the amount of $15,385,607 shown by Mission as its share of Tidewater's retained earnings for the year.

5. What percentage interest, 47.91, 50.62, or some other, would you use in recording Mission Development's share of Tidewater's 1961 retained earnings? Explain.

6. In January, 1961, Tidewater transferred $19,442,000 on its books from retained earnings to the preferred capital stock account, representing $25.00 par value per share for the 777,688 preferred shares issued in exchange for surrendered common stock. What adjustment, if any, would you make in the total amount recorded by Mission Development as its share of Tidewater's earnings retained since acquisition ($152,814,053) to reflect this transaction? Explain.

Monsanto Chemical Company

Monsanto Chemical Company, established in 1901 as the Monsanto Chemical Works, sells a widely diversified line of chemical products including fibers, plastics, phosphate products, detergents, medicinals and various synthetics.

In 1949, Monsanto and American Viscose Corporation, as joint and equal owners, formed the Chemstrand Corporation to produce nylon and acrylic fibers. By 1960, Chemstrand had grown to become the nation's second largest producer of the two items, the latter sold under the trademark Acrilan.

Prior to 1960, Monsanto consolidated only its majority-owned domestic and Canadian subsidiaries for financial reporting purposes. Monsanto's interest in foreign subsidiaries and its 50 per cent interest in associated companies were carried as investments valued at cost; only the dividends received from these companies were included in income. Monsanto did, however, clearly disclose its equity in the unremitted earnings and in the net assets of such companies.

Beginning in 1955, the Company included *supplementary, unaudited* financial statements in its annual reports which reflected the "Shareholders' Net Interests in Parent Company, Domestic and Foreign Subsidiaries and 50 per cent Owned Associated Companies." This was done because a substantial part of Monsanto's post-war investment and growth had been in jointly-owned companies and in overseas subsidiaries.

The treatment of Monsanto's 50 per cent interest in associated companies, which included Chemstrand and several smaller companies, was unique. After elimination of intercompany transactions, half of these companies' assets, liabilities, sales, income and other financial data were included; that is, the financial statements of the 50 per cent-owned companies were split, with 50 per cent of their cash being added to Monsanto's cash, 50 per cent of their sales to its sales, and so forth, after eliminating intercompany transactions.

Monsanto explained that its shareholders' true assets and true earnings included these portions of 50 per cent-owned companies' assets and profits "which are not given full effect in normal consolidations."

Below is a tabulation (in millions of dollars) of the net income reported by Monsanto from 1955 through 1959 in both its formal, audited income statements and in the supplementary, unaudited statements:

	Parent, Domestic and Canadian Subsidiaries (audited)	Parent, All Subsidiaries and Share of 50 Per Cent-Owned Companies (unaudited)
1955	$ 42.2	$ 50.3
1956	38.6	45.3
1957	37.4	48.9
1958	34.6	42.9
1959	49.0	61.7

These supplementary statements included a provision for the additional income taxes which would have been payable had Monsanto's share of the unremitted earnings of foreign subsidiaries and 50 per cent-owned companies been received as dividends.

The supplementary, unaudited financial statements for 1959 are given in Exhibits 1 and 2. The formal audited statements for 1959 are given in Exhibits 3 and 4.

In its report for the first quarter of 1960, management noted that since 1955 it had reported to shareowners the audited balance sheet and income statement of the parent company and its domestic and Canadian subsidiaries, and, in addition, it had presented supplementary statements of the shareowners' interests in the parent company, *all* subsidiaries *and* 50 per cent-owned companies. The latter supplementary presentations were made in the belief that they more adequately disclosed the total interests of Monsanto shareowners.

Beginning with the first quarter of 1960, management decided to report *formally* on the combined basis used previously for the supplementary reports. The major effect of this change arose from the inclusion of Monsanto's 50 per cent interest in Chemstrand, which in 1959 had sales in excess of $200 million. Exhibits 5 and 6 show the balance sheet and income statement, respectively, for the first quarter of 1960. The same procedure was followed in preparing the financial statements for the second and third quarters of 1960. Since these interim statements were not audited, the methods followed were not reviewed by Monsanto's auditors.

On January 16, 1961, Monsanto became the sole owner of Chemstrand through an exchange of 3,540,000 shares of its common stock for American Viscose Corporation's entire investment in Chemstrand.

This transaction was treated as a pooling of interests[1] and because of Chemstrand's size and the merger's consummation immediately following the close of the year, Monsanto's financial statements at December 31, 1960 were recast to reflect the merger.

Management commented on 50 per cent-owned companies as follows in the 1960 annual report:

> For several years, in order to reflect the total interests of Monsanto shareowners, we have been including in our Annual Reports, in addition to certified financial statements, a supplementary presentation which combined the assets, liabilities and income for the parent company, its subsidiaries, and its proportionate share of our 50 per cent-owned associated companies.
>
> The significance of our interests in associated companies, relative to Monsanto's total interests, has been greatly reduced through acquisition of full ownership of Chemstrand. Consequently, the supplementary presentation is being discontinued, and the extent of our interest in the net worth and income of such remaining associated companies is indicated in the Financial Review . . .

As it had done in the 1960 interim quarterly financial statements and in the previous supplementary annual statements, Monsanto consolidated all foreign, majority-owned subsidiaries in the final 1960 balance sheet and income statement. The provision for additional income taxes on unremitted earnings of consolidated subsidiaries, previously included in the unaudited supplementary statements, was discontinued. In explaining the change, management stated that "since the undistributed earnings of these companies are retained to finance future growth, a continuation of this practice would result in the accumulation of a substantial tax reserve which under normal circumstances would never be required."

---

[1] Pooling of interests is described in Chapter 16.

EXHIBIT 1

Monsanto Chemical Company
Supplementary 1959 Financial Statements[1]
Balance Sheet as of December 31, 1959
(in millions)

ASSETS
Current Assets:

Cash	$ 32.5
Marketable securities	106.7
Net receivables	115.5
Inventories	125.7
	$ 380.4
Investments, etc.	40.5

Property:

Land	$ 15.4
Buildings	140.5
Machinery and equipment	649.2
Phosphate deposits	6.9
Producing oil and gas properties	76.6
Undeveloped oil and gas leaseholds	10.0
Accumulated depreciation, etc.	(358.9)
Accumulated depletion	(25.6)
Net property	$ 514.1
Deferred Charges	16.0
	$ 951.0

LIABILITIES
Current Liabilities:

Accounts payable and accruals	$ 71.6
Income taxes less tax notes	49.4
Sinking funds and notes payable	13.2
Employes' bonus awards	3.1
	$ 137.3
Debentures, Bonds, etc.	118.0
Income Debentures	141.0

Other Liabilities:

Deferred income taxes	$ 28.6
Pensions, etc.	1.2
Employes' bonus—unawarded	1.4
	$ 31.2
Minority Interests in Subsidiaries	20.5

Capital Stock and Surplus:

Common shares	$ 46.3
Paid-in surplus	225.9
Earned surplus	230.8
	$ 503.0
	$ 951.0

---

[1] Showing stockholders' net interests in parent company, domestic and foreign subsidiaries and 50 per cent-owned associated companies.

EXHIBIT 2

Monsanto Chemical Company
Supplementary 1959 Financial Statements[1]
Income Statement for the Year Ended December 31, 1959
(in millions)

Income :	
Net sales	$ 811.4
Other	9.9
	$ 821.3
Deductions :	
Cost of goods sold	$ 584.0
Selling, administrative, research	98.4
Provision for employes' bonus	2.5
Income charges	14.5
Minority interests	1.5
	$ 700.9
Income Before Income Taxes	$ 120.4
Provision for Income Taxes	58.7
Net Income	$ 61.7

[1] Showing stockholders' net interests in parent company, domestic and foreign subsidiaries and 50 per cent-owned associated companies.

EXHIBIT 3

Monsanto Chemical Company
Audited Income Statement for the Year Ended December 31, 1959

Income:	
Net sales	$ 615,377,078
Dividends	4,337,151
Other	7,425,912
	$ 627,140,141
Deductions:	
Cost of goods sold	$ 458,323,515
Selling, administrative and research expenses	71,997,690
Provision for employes' bonus	1,884,502
Interest	6,356,721
Other	2,804,556
	$ 541,366,984
Income Before Income Taxes	$ 85,773,157
Provision for Income Taxes	36,796,000
Net Income	$ 48,977,157

EXHIBIT 4

Monsanto Chemical Company
Audited Balance Sheet as of December 31, 1959

ASSETS
Current Assets:

Cash	$ 21,814,084
Marketable securities	91,439,192
Net receivables	84,412,412
Inventories	88,732,867
	$ 286,398,555

Investments and Miscellaneous Assets:

Investment in and advances to subsidiaries	$ 15,256,512
Investment in and advances to associates	42,291,292
Common shares held for bonus awards	907,438
Miscellaneous investments and receivables	30,945,352
	$ 89,400,594
Property, Plant and Equipment	$ 662,306,737
Less accumulated depreciation and depletion	306,953,818
Net property	$ 355,352,919
Deferred Charges	$ 10,554,688
	$ 741,706,756

LIABILITIES
Current Liabilities:

Accounts payable and accruals	$ 52,927,443
Income taxes	31,829,265
Sinking fund payments	1,790,000
Employes' bonus awards	2,713,791
	$ 89,260,499

Debentures and Bonds—Less Current Portion Above:

$3\frac{1}{4}\%$ Debentures, due 1968	$ 13,750,000
2.65% Debentures, due 1971	24,000,000
$3\frac{5}{8}\%$ Debentures, due 1972	12,000,000
Other	290,500
	$ 50,040,500

Income Debentures:

$3\frac{3}{4}\%$, due 2002	$ 91,000,000
$4\frac{1}{4}\%$, due 2008	50,000,000
	$ 141,000,000

Other Liabilities:

Deferred income taxes	$ 15,055,317
Pensions	802,126
Employes' bonus—unawarded	722,462
	$ 16,579,905

Capital Stock and Surplus:

Common shares—authorized, 25,000,000 shares, par value $2 each; outstanding, 23,156,857 shares	$ 46,313,714
Surplus:	
Paid-in	215,860,588
Earned	182,651,550
	$ 444,825,852
	$ 741,706,756

EXHIBIT 5

Monsanto Chemical Company
Unaudited Balance Sheet as of March 31, 1960[1]
(000 omitted from column figures)

	The Company and Subsidiaries Consolidated	The Company's Proportionate Share of Fifty Per Cent-Owned Companies	Combined Total
ASSETS			
Current Assets:			
Cash	$ 22,976	$ 5,570	$ 28,546
Marketable securities	67,397	12,956	80,353
Net receivables	105,361	19,405	122,848
Inventories	110,408	19,147	129,397
	$ 306,142	$ 57,078	$ 361,144
Investments and Miscellaneous Assets:			
Investment in and advances to associates	$ 43,358		
Miscellaneous investments and receivables	44,327	$ 2,396	$ 47,106
	$ 87,685	$ 2,396	$ 47,106
Property, Plant and Equipment	$ 754,203	$ 162,998	$ 917,201
Less accumulated depreciation and depletion	345,586	54,060	399,646
Net property	$ 408,617	$ 108,938	$ 517,555
Deferred Charges	$ 17,649	$ 2,127	$ 23,462
Total	$ 820,093	$ 170,539	$ 949,267
LIABILITIES			
Current Liabilities:			
Notes payable		$ 6,297	$ 6,297
Accounts payable and accruals	$ 62,373	12,070	72,525
Income taxes	27,597	8,875	36,472
Sinking fund payments	1,790	3,878	5,668
	$ 91,760	$ 31,120	$ 120,962
Long Term Debt—Less Current Portion	$ 209,793	$ 64,279	$ 258,313
Other Liabilities:			
Deferred income taxes	$ 19,230	$ 7,556	$ 26,786
Other	2,036	814	2,850
	$ 21,266	$ 8,370	$ 29,636
Minority Interests in Subsidiaries	$ 20,570		$ 20,570
Shareowners' Equity:			
Common shares—authorized, 35,000,000 shares, par value $2 each; outstanding, 23,170,315 shares	$ 46,341	$ 8,807	$ 46,341
Paid-in surplus	224,053	15,915	226,231
Retained earnings	206,310	42,048	247,214
	$ 476,704	$ 66,770	$ 519,786
Total	$ 820,093	$ 170,539	$ 949,267

[1] All intercompany transactions have been eliminated in the financial statements. As a result, the columns do not necessarily add to the combined totals.

EXHIBIT 6

Monsanto Chemical Company
Unaudited Income Statement for the Three Months Ended March 31, 1960[1]
(000 omitted)

	The Company and Subsidiaries Consolidated	The Company's Proportionate Share of Fifty Per Cent- Owned Companies	Combined Total 1960	Combined Total 1959
Income:				
Net sales	$ 178,288	$ 37,228	$ 212,114	$ 197,842
Dividends	217		5	15
Other	1,868	91	1,776	1,759
	$ 180,373	$ 37,319	$ 213,895	$ 199,616
Deductions:				
Cost of goods sold	$ 132,543	$ 23,679	$ 152,796	$ 141,129
Selling, administrative and research expenses	22,054	4,878	26,932	23,248
Interest	2,041	644	2,526	2,464
Minority interests	400		400	193
Other	224	196	420	255
	$ 157,262	$ 29,397	$ 183,074	$ 167,289
Income Before Income Taxes	$ 23,111	$ 7,922	$ 30,821	$ 32,327
Provision for Income Taxes	10,530	4,160	14,690	15,712
Net Income	$ 12,581	$ 3,762	$ 16,131	$ 16,615

---

[1] All intercompany transactions have been eliminated in the financial statements. As a result, the columns do not necessarily add to the combined totals.

QUESTIONS :

1. Why was Monsanto so concerned about adequate disclosure of its investment in 50 per cent-owned companies and in foreign subsidiaries?

2. Do you agree with the policy used in preparing 1960 quarterly financial statements and supplementary annual financial statements from 1955 through 1959 for 50 per cent-owned associated companies? Explain. Do you think such statements are easily understood by stockholders and other users of corporate financial statements? As an auditor, what action, if any, would you have taken had the company's final 1960 statements been presented on the combined basis as in Exhibits 5 and 6?

3. What was the amount of intercompany receivables at March 31, 1960? What was the amount of intercompany sales in the first quarter of 1960?

4. In addition to the two methods used by Monsanto in its audited and unaudited statements, in what other ways might you account for 50 per cent-owned companies? Do these methods create any new disclosure problems?

5. In 1960, do you believe Monsanto should have continued its earlier policy of providing for additional taxes which would have been payable had its share of subsidiaries' and associated companies' unremitted earnings been received as dividends? Explain.

Allied Stores Corporation

Allied Stores operates over 85 stores in 25 states throughout the country. Most of these are full-line department stores selling women's, men's and children's clothing, dry goods, furniture, housewares and other items generally carried by department stores. Allied maintains buying offices in New York, Chicago and Los Angeles, and foreign buying offices in London, Paris, Brussels, Frankfurt, Vienna, Florence and Tokyo.

Total sales for the 1960 fiscal year, ended January 31, 1961, were divided as follows:

Cash and will-calls	43.2%
Regular charge accounts	37.5%
Deferred charge accounts	7.8%
Revolving credit accounts	11.5%

Investment in Alstores Realty Corporation

In 1947, Allied organized Alstores Realty Corporation as a wholly-owned subsidiary to take advantage of favorable financing arrangements while still conforming to the corporation's long-established policy "of keeping its equity capital invested primarily in merchandising activities." In adherence to this policy, the corporation leased most of its store facilities, a practice followed by many department stores.

In its 1950 annual report to stockholders (for the fiscal year ended January 31, 1951), management discussed its policy regarding store facilities as follows:

The principal function or purpose of Allied Stores Corporation is that of selling merchandise to the consumer. Its principal capital requirements are for working capital to finance merchandise inventories and customers' accounts receivable and for fixed assets such as store fixtures and equipment and store premises. In order that the maximum amount of its stockholders'

467

capital may be used more directly in the field of merchandising, it has long been the policy of the company to keep its investment in real estate to the minimum practical amount.

Real estate occupied by stores acquired has often been retained by the seller and leased to the company. From time to time the company has sold real estate to investors and continued to occupy it under long term lease arrangements. In more recent years, however, the financial markets have been such that mortgage money has been readily available on terms that were quite favorable to the borrower. As a consequence, it has been possible to finance a very substantial part of the purchase price of real estate through institutional borrowings and thereby obtain an over-all carrying cost more advantageous to the company than could be obtained by leasing.

Alstores Realty Corporation was organized in 1947 as a real estate holding company. It is a wholly owned subsidiary of Allied Stores Corporation devoted exclusively to the ownership and operation of real estate . . . The common stock of, and the advances to, Alstores Realty Corporation are considered as investments by Allied Stores Corporation.

Due to fundamental differences in purpose, methods of operation, financial structure and policies as contrasted with other subsidiaries of the company, Alstores Realty Corporation is not consolidated therewith. It is believed that to do so would certainly be confusing and might be misleading. Under the company's long term note issue, Alstores Realty Corporation is not subject to the restrictions on funded debt which apply to Allied Stores Corporation and its other subsidiaries.

Alstores Realty Corporation finances its property acquisitions primarily by obtaining loans from insurance companies. Such obligations are secured by liens on the properties and by pledges of rentals . . .

This real estate subsidiary has acquired property from Allied Stores Corporation and its other subsidiaries. It has acquired properties which were under long term leases to them from outside owners. It has also carried on substantial construction activities. Most of the properties owned by Alstores Realty Corporation are leased to Allied Stores Corporation or its other subsidiaries. Leases to such subsidiaries are guaranteed by Allied Stores Corporation just as is frequently the case with outside landlords.

Alstores has been used as a vehicle for financing "some of . . . [Allied's] present investment in land, buildings and improvements as well as for future plant expansion activities." In addition, much of Allied's depreciable property has been sold to Alstores. For example, in 1949, Alstores purchased property and equipment from Allied at its depreciated value of $15,469,079.

Other advantages derived from organizing the subsidiary included control of properties for which there was an apparent future need. In many cases, such control could be obtained most advantageously by purchase. Similarly, major improvements could be more easily arranged for owned property. Another important consideration was the likelihood of substantial future appreciation in the market value of owned real estate, which would benefit Allied's stockholders since Alstores was a wholly-owned subsidiary.

Alstores' Capital Structure

Alstores' sources of long-term capital consist of borrowings, chiefly from institutional investors, and Allied's interest in the form of advances, stock investment and retained earnings. Exhibit 1 contains selected financial data for Alstores, including the amount of capital supplied by the above sources, for the fiscal years 1947 through 1960. Exhibits 2 and 3 show Alstores' condensed balance sheet as of January 31, 1961, and its statement of earnings and retained earnings for the 1960–1961 fiscal year.

Allied's Disclosure of Investment in Alstores

As stated earlier, for annual reporting purposes, Allied does not consolidate Alstores' financial statements. On its statement of financial position in the 1960–1961 annual report, Allied made the following disclosure:

Investment in and Advances to Alstores
Realty Corporation:
Investment (Equity in net assets in
excess of cost—$3,436,906) —Note A $ 5,703,315
Advances   14,160,690
   $ 19,864,005

Less excess of sales price over net
carrying value of properties sold
to Alstores Realty Corporation   588,546
   $ 19,275,459

Note A read as follows:

The consolidated financial statements include the accounts of all subsidiaries except Alstores Realty Corporation (100 per cent owned) and its subsidiaries.

Exhibit 4 shows selected financial data for Allied Stores for the fiscal years 1946 through 1960. Exhibits 5 and 6 show condensed financial statements of Allied Stores and its consolidated subsidiaries for the 1960-1961 fiscal year.

SEC Accounting and Disclosure
Requirements

Regulation S-X under the Securities Act of 1933 and the Securities Exchange Act of 1934 states the requirements regarding the form and content of financial statements filed with the Securities and Exchange Commission. Article 4, Rule 4.02, of Regulation S-X, pertaining to consolidated statements of the registrant and its subsidiaries, requires that the registrant shall follow, in the consolidated statements, principles of inclusion or exclusion which will clearly exhibit the financial condition and results of operations of the registrant and its subsidiaries.

Rule 4.03 on "Group Statements of Subsidiaries Not Consolidated" states:

For majority-owned subsidiaries not consolidated with the registrant there may be filed statements in which such subsidiaries are consolidated or combined in one or more groups pursuant to principles of inclusion or exclusion which will clearly exhibit the financial condition and results of operations of the group or groups. If it is essential to a properly summarized presentation of the facts, such consolidated or combined statement shall be filed.

In a prospectus, dated November 16, 1960, filed with the SEC, Allied Stores consolidated Alstores' balance sheet but not its statement of earnings.

Elsewhere in the prospectus, the following tabulation disclosed real estate leases, as of July 31, 1960, on properties occupied by Allied Stores:

Year of Lease Expiration	Leases from Alstores		Leases from Outside Interests	
	No. of Leases	Minimum Annual Rents	No. of Leases	Minimum Annual Rents
1960	4	$ 72,800	33	$ 116,748
1961	—	—	18	144,908
1962	—	—	10	58,750
1963	—	—	10	142,009
1964	—	—	5	63,718
1965	—	—	2	11,400
1966	—	—	3	77,000
1967	—	—	1	900
1968–1972	2	65,000	15	325,143
1973–1977	3	94,000	24	851,115
1978–1982	14	934,926	20	1,682,749
1983–1987	21	2,425,700	21	544,313
1988–1992	16	1,469,400	6	598,000
1993–1998	3	1,280,000	2	25,400
1999–2059	12	2,692,500	32	882,000
Total	75	$ 9,034,326	202	$ 5,524,153

A note to the financial statements explained lease arrangements as follows:

At July 31, 1960, the corporation and its consolidated subsidiaries were lessees under 212 leases having terms of more than three years from that date. The rentals under these leases at the present fixed or minimum annual rentals amount to a minimum of $14,165,273 (of which $8,961,526 is payable to Alstores Realty Corporation and subsidiaries), plus in most cases, real estate taxes and other expenses and, in certain instances, increased amounts based on percentages of sales.

All long-term leases which have annual rentals in excess of $100,000 each expire between 1971 and 2010, except for one expiring in 2027.

EXHIBIT 1

Alstores Realty Corporation
Selected Financial Data 1947-1960[1]
(000 omitted from column figures)

Fiscal Year	Total Assets	Property and Equipment, net	Long-term Debt	Advances From Allied Stores	Stockholders' Equity	Total Revenues	Revenues From Allied Stores	Net Income
1947	$ 3,381	$ 3,256	$ 2,500	$ 508	$ 259	$ 49	$ 49	$ 9
1948	13,003	12,829	10,553	2,020	274	356	356	15
1949	37,909	35,679	30,436	5,478	1,043	1,270	1,270	19
1950	47,745	46,690	39,704	6,218	1,104	2,772	2,682	61
1951	70,158	69,279	59,573	8,473	1,328	4,522	4,117	224
1952	79,044	78,008	71,606	4,889	1,606	5,461	4,611	278
1953	81,883	80,897	71,320	7,262	1,979	6,091	5,102	373
1954	89,821	88,705	81,652	4,444	2,583	6,268	5,195	250
1955	96,981	95,671	91,592	1,070	3,552	6,712	5,527	266
1956	106,581	105,157	92,331	8,477	3,926	7,432	6,204	374
1957	149,351	147,059	126,923	14,442	4,206	8,561	7,026	281
1958	160,011	157,191	133,980	19,706	4,458	10,987	8,550	252
1959	158,084	155,095	135,890	15,267	4,915	12,206	8,892	457
1960	160,270	157,177	135,642[2]	14,160	9,140	12,517	9,122	225

[1] The corporation's fiscal year ends on January 31. Reference to any fiscal year is to the calendar year in which 11 months of the corporation's fiscal year fall. Thus, the 1960 fiscal year ended on January 31, 1961.
[2] Includes $8,437,796 classified as Current Liabilities in Exhibit 2.

EXHIBIT 2

Alstores Realty Corporation
Condensed Balance Sheet as of January 31, 1961

ASSETS:

Current Assets	$ 2,109,664
Property and Equipment, net	157,177,353
Unamortized Long-Term Debt Expense	983,396
	$ 160,270,413

LIABILITIES AND NET WORTH:

Current Liabilities	$ 9,765,714[1]
Long-Term Debt	127,203,788
Advances from Allied Stores Corporation and its Subsidiaries	14,160,690
Stockholders' Equity:	
Capital Stock	$ 5,000,000
Capital Surplus	703,315
Retained Earnings	3,436,906
	$ 9,140,221
	$ 160,270,413

[1] Includes $8,437,796 classified as long-term debt in Exhibit 1.

EXHIBIT 3

Alstores Realty Corporation
Statement of Earnings and Retained
Earnings, Year Ended January 31, 1961

Rental Income (including $9,122,315 from Allied Stores Corporation and its Subsidiaries)	$ 12,516,874
Operating Expenses :	
Depreciation and amortization	3,721,029
Interest (including $852,299 to Allied Stores Corporation)	6,899,444
Taxes, other than Federal income taxes	851,189
Maintenance and repairs	295,116
Rent	198,531
Other expenses—net of service charges to tenants	474,012
	$ 12,439,321
	$ 77,553
Gain on sale of properties	197,544
Earnings before Federal Income Taxes	$ 275,097
Federal Income Taxes	50,000
Net Earnings	$ 225,097
Retained Earnings at Beginning of Year	3,211,809
Retained Earnings at End of Year	$ 3,436,906

EXHIBIT 4

Allied Stores Corporation
Selected Financial Data 1946-1960[1]
(000 omitted)

Fiscal Year	Total Assets	Property and Equipment, net	Long-term Debt	Stockholders' Equity	Total Rental Payments	Rentals Paid to Alstores	Net Sales	Net Income
1946	$ 125,273	$ 19,105	$ None	$ 86,235	$ —[2]	$ —	$ 361,712	$ 18,379
1947	156,245	32,885	25,000	92,436	7,610	49	392,199	13,623
1948	165,399	37,989	24,250	102,972	8,272	356	419,228	15,805
1949	170,776	34,708	23,500	110,290	8,506	1,270	407,838	12,227
1950	201,144	40,438	29,750	122,716	9,636	2,682	439,909	14,944
1951	212,920	40,931	39,800	127,638	10,401	4,117	476,693	8,258
1952	220,810	39,317	37,600	131,577	11,355	4,611	501,841	12,137
1953	226,598	43,603	39,900	136,807	11,971	5,102	515,830	11,809
1954	235,957	44,406	39,950	142,720	12,271	5,195	543,984	13,231
1955	267,167	51,353	37,750	168,574	12,887	5,527	581,901	13,972
1956	283,350	62,096	50,300	173,562	14,096	6,204	615,773	14,262
1957	283,389	61,343	47,850	176,684	14,850	7,026	632,814	12,351
1958	283,299	61,230	45,400	180,009	15,945	8,550	643,778	12,004
1959	290,087	62,908	42,800	185,716	16,604	8,892	679,488	14,637
1960	286,717	62,103	39,551	188,554	16,532	9,122	680,492	10,888

[1] The corporation's fiscal year ends on January 31. Reference to any fiscal year is to the calendar year in which 11 months of the corporation's fiscal year fall. Thus, the 1960 fiscal year ended on January 31, 1961.

[2] Not disclosed separately. Included in total operating expenses.

EXHIBIT 5

Allied Stores Corporation and Consolidated Subsidiaries
Condensed Statement of Financial Position as of January 31, 1961

Current Assets	$ 201,573,591
Current Liabilities	58,612,063
	$ 142,961,528
Investments and Other Assets	3,489,239
Investments In and Advances to Alstores Realty Corporation	$ 19,864,005
Less excess of sales price over net carrying value of properties sold to Alstores Realty Corporation	588,546
	$ 19,275,459
Property and Equipment, net	62,102,914
Unamortized Long-Term Debt Expense	275,952
	$ 228,105,092
Long-Term Debt	39,551,319
STOCKHOLDERS' EQUITY	$ 188,553,773
Preferred Stock	$ 22,164,700
Common Stockholders' Equity:	
Common Stock	$ 2,688,365
Capital Surplus	53,063,366
Retained Earnings	110,637,342
Total Common Stockholders' Equity	$ 166,389,073
STOCKHOLDERS' EQUITY	$ 188,553,773

EXHIBIT 6

Allied Stores Corporation and Consolidated Subsidiaries
Statement of Earnings and Retained
Earnings, Year Ended January 31, 1961

Net Sales (including leased departments)	$ 680,492,329
Costs and Expenses:	
Cost of goods sold	446,345,375
Selling, general and administrative expenses (less credit service income)	168,436,234
Rent (including $9,122,315 to Alstores Realty Corporation)	16,531,586
Taxes, other than federal income taxes	15,483,537
Depreciation and amortization	6,993,581
Maintenance and repairs	3,968,912
Interest (less interest received from Alstores Realty Corporation: $852,299)	945,362
	$ 658,704,587
Earnings Before Federal Income Taxes	$ 21,787,742
Federal Income Taxes	10,900,000
Net Earnings	$ 10,887,742
Retained Earnings at Beginning of Year	108,654,398
Cash Dividends:	
Cumulative Preferred Stock—$4.00 per share	920,698
Common Stock—$3.00 per share	7,984,100
	$ 8,904,798
Retained Earnings at End of Year	$ 110,637,342

QUESTIONS:

1. Do you agree with Allied's policy of not consolidating Alstores? Do you agree with management's statement that it would "certainly be confusing and might be misleading" if Alstores' accounts were consolidated with Allied's accounts? Give reasons for and against consolidation.

2. Prepare consolidated financial statements (statement of financial position at January 31, 1961, and income statement for year ended January 31, 1961) for Allied and Alstores based on the information in Exhibits 2, 3, 5 and 6. You may assume that all intercompany relationships, both at the year-end and during the year, are disclosed in the case.

3. The 1961 edition of a financial reference service disclosed the following ratios for Allied Stores for its fiscal year ended January 31, 1961:

   1. Times interest earned before income taxes   24.05
   2. Total assets less current liabilities per $1,000 of long-term debt $5,767
   3. Net current assets per $1,000 of long-term debt $3,615
   4. Capitalization:
      a. Per cent long-term debt   17.34%
      b. Per cent preferred stock   9.72%
      c. Per cent common stock and surplus   72.94%
   5. Per cent sales to net property   1,095.75%
   6. Per cent sales to total assets   237.34%
   7. Per cent net income to total assets   3.80%

   Compute these same ratios using the consolidated financial statements developed in question 2. Are the resulting differences significant? How and by whom do you suppose such ratios are used? Which set of ratios—those given above or those you calculated—do you consider better reflects the financial position and operating results of Allied Stores? Explain.

4. Why do you suppose a consolidated balance sheet including Alstores, but not a consolidated income statement, was included in the prospectus mentioned in the case?

5. Is Allied Stores able to use "the maximum amount of its stockholders' capital . . . more directly in the field of merchandising" by limiting "its investment in real estate to the minimum practical amount"? Consider this question in light of Allied's policy of leasing store facilities, particularly from Alstores Realty Corporation.

6. Assume that Allied Stores amortized the "excess of sales price over net carrying value of properties sold to Alstores Realty Corporation" to income over the term of the lease. Would this be a desirable accounting procedure? Explain.

7. Do you believe Allied's investment in Alstores was adequately disclosed in the 1960–1961 annual report? Consider the disclosure in Allied's Statement of Financial Position at January 31, 1961, and Note A, both of which are given on page 469. How else, short of consolidation, might Allied have accounted for its Alstores investment?

8. Are lease arrangements adequately disclosed in the prospectus? Explain.

9. In Exhibit 6, do you approve of deducting credit service income from "Selling, general and administrative expenses"? Explain.

CHAPTER FOURTEEN

Pensions

The main growth in the number and size of pension plans has occurred since 1935 when passage of the Social Security Act focused public attention on pensions. Growth of such plans was further encouraged during World War II by the exemption of pensions and other so-called fringe benefits from government wage stabilization controls. After World War II, the Supreme Court upheld a lower court's decision that pensions were included in the definition of "wages . . . or other conditions of employment" in the National Labor Relations Act, and thus were a proper subject for collective bargaining between industry and labor. Following this decision, there was a marked growth in the number of corporate pension plans as more and more unions won pensions at the bargaining table.

TYPES OF CORPORATE PENSION PLANS

Most corporate pension plans involve the accumulation of funds during employees' working years followed by distribution of these funds during retirement. Under an insured plan, an insurance company receives periodic contributions[1] which are invested until needed to pay pension benefits. Such pension benefits are usually guaranteed by the insurance company.

Under another common type of pension plan, a trustee, often a bank or trust company, is designated to receive and manage pension contributions and to pay pensions to retired employees. These plans are known as trusteed plans. An advantage of a trusteed plan, in contrast to an insured plan, is the trustee's freedom in investing pension funds. Insurance company investments are frequently limited

---

[1] Contributions may be received from the employer only, or from both the employer and employees.

by state regulatory authorities, usually to bonds and mortgages, while a trustee is free to invest in common stocks where the possibility of higher yields and price appreciation may reduce the employer's pension costs. The trustee makes no guarantees, his function being limited to investment and administration of the pension fund.

At the end of 1962, the book value of assets held by trustees for corporate pension plans was $36.0 billion, while the figure for insured plans was $21.6 billion. Comparable amounts at the end of 1950 were $5.5 billion and $5.6 billion, respectively.[2]

ACCOUNTING PROBLEMS

Accounting for the cost of pension plans, particularly trusteed plans, has created several problems. One problem concerns the proper accounting treatment of so-called "past-service costs." Frequently, when a pension plan is adopted, or an existing plan is liberalized, employees' future pensions are partially based on services performed in the past. In November, 1948, the Committee on Accounting Procedure issued ARB No. 36, *Pension Plans—Accounting for Annuity Costs Based on Past Services*, which was later included in ARB No. 43 as Section A of Chapter 13, *Compensation*. This section follows:

1. This section deals with the accounting treatment of costs arising out of past service which are incurred under pension plans involving payments to outside agencies such as insurance companies and trustees. Self-administered and informal plans which do not require payments to outside agencies are not dealt with because of their special features and lack of uniformity. The principles set forth herein, however, are generally applicable to those plans as well.

2. Charges with respect to pension costs based on past service have sometimes been made to surplus on the ground that such payments are indirectly compensation for services and that since the services upon which computation of the payments is based were performed in the past, the compensation should not be permitted to affect any period or periods other than those in which the services involved were performed. In other cases all annuity costs based on past service have been charged to income in the period of the plan's inauguration as a current cost of originating the plan. In still other cases the position has been taken that a pension plan cannot bring the hoped-for benefits in the future unless past as well as future services are given recognition and, accordingly, annuity costs based on past service have been spread over a period of present and future years. The last method is the one permitted under provisions of the Internal Revenue Code.

3. The committee believes that, even though the calculation is based on past service, costs of annuities based on such service are incurred in contemplation of present and future services, not necessarily of the individual affected but of the organization as a whole, and therefore should be charged to the present and future periods benefited. This belief is based on the assumption that

---

[2] Securities and Exchange Commission, "Corporate Pension Funds, 1962," *Statistical Series*, Release No. 1902, May 24, 1963.

although the benefits to a company flowing from pension plans are intangible, they are nevertheless real. The element of past service is one of the important considerations in establishing pension plans, and annuity costs measured by such past service contribute to the benefits gained by the adoption of a plan. It is usually expected that such benefits will include better employee morale, the removal of superannuated employees from the payroll, and the attraction and retention of more desirable personnel, all of which should result in improved operations.

4. The committee, accordingly, is of the opinion that:

(a) Costs of annuities based on past service should be allocated to current and future periods; however, if they are not sufficiently material in amount to distort the results of operations in a single period, they may be absorbed in the current year;

(b) Costs of annuities based on past service should not be charged to surplus.

5. This opinion is not to be interpreted as requiring that charges be made to income rather than to reserves previously provided, or that recognition be given in the accounts of current or future periods to pension costs written off prior to the issuance of an opinion on this subject.

According to this bulletin, a corporation receives benefits from a pension plan only in fiscal periods *following* the plan's adoption and these periods should therefore be charged with the related costs. Even though employees' past services may be a factor in calculating pension costs, these costs are not literally *past* costs. For accounting purposes such costs are merely a form of current and future costs based upon employees' past services. Other pension accounting problems, including choice of a time period over which past-service costs should be charged off, were not considered in this first bulletin. Some of these problems were discussed in ARB No. 47, *Accounting for Costs of Pension Plans*, issued in September, 1956. This bulletin follows:

1. Variations in the provisions of pension plans in the United States, in their financial arrangements, and in the circumstances attendant upon their adoption, have resulted in substantial differences in accounting for pension costs. This bulletin indicates guides which, in the opinion of the committee, are acceptable for dealing with costs of pension plans in the accounts and reports of companies having such plans. It is not concerned with funding as such.

2. The term *pension plan* is here intended to mean a formal arrangement for employee retirement benefits, whether established unilaterally or through negotiation, by which commitments, specific or implied, have been made which can be used as the basis for estimating costs. It does not include profit-sharing plans or deferred-compensation contracts with individuals. It does not apply to informal arrangements by which voluntary payments are made to retired employees, usually in amounts fixed at or about the time of an employee's retirement and in the light of his then situation but subject to change or discontinuance at the employer's will; where such informal arrangements exist, the pay-as-you-go method of accounting for pension costs generally is appropriate, although the accrual method is equally appropriate in cases where costs can be estimated with reasonable accuracy.

3. When a pension plan is first adopted, it is customary to provide that pensions for covered employees will give recognition not only to services which are to be rendered by them in the future, but also to services which have been rendered by them prior to the adoption of the plan. The costs of the pensions to the employer, therefore, usually are based in part on past services and in part on current and future services of the employees. The committee considers that all of such costs are costs of doing business, incurred in contemplation of present and future benefits, as are other employment costs such as wages, salaries, and social security taxes. It, therefore, is of the opinion that past service benefit costs should be charged to operations during the current and future periods benefited, and should not be charged to earned surplus *at the inception of the plan.* The committee believes that, in the case of an *existing plan* under which inadequate charges or no charges for past services have been made thus far and the company has decided to conform its accounting to the preferred procedure expressed in this bulletin, it may be appropriate to charge to earned surplus the amount that should have been accumulated by charges to income since inception of the plan.

4. In addition to the basic features of a pension plan relating to employee eligibility and the level of pension payments, other factors enter into the determination of the ultimate costs of pensions. Some of these are:

(a) other benefits (such as social security) where amounts of pension payments are integrated therewith;

(b) length of life of employees both before and after retirement;

(c) employee turnover;

(d) in some cases, alternatives as to age at which employees may retire;

(e) future compensation levels; and

(f) in a funded plan, future rates of earnings on the fund and the status of fund investments.

Because of these factors, the total cost of the pensions that will be paid ultimately to the present participants in a plan cannot be determined precisely in advance, but, by the use of actuarial techniques, reasonably accurate estimates can be made. There are other business costs for which it is necessary to make periodic provisions in the accounts based upon assumptions and estimates. The committee believes that the uncertainties relating to the determination of pension costs are not so pronounced as to preclude similar treatment.

5. In the view of many, the accrual of costs under a pension plan should not necessarily be dependent on the funding arrangements provided for in the plan or governed by a strict legal interpretation of the obligations under the plan. They feel that because of the widespread adoption of pension plans and their importance as part of compensation structures, a provision for cancellation or the existence of a terminal date for a plan should not be the controlling factor in accounting for pension costs, and that for accounting purposes it is reasonable to assume in most cases that a plan, though modified or renewed (because of terminal dates) from time to time, will continue for an indefinite period. According to this view, costs based on current and future services should be systematically accrued during the expected period of active service of the covered employees, generally upon the basis of actuarial calculations. Such calculations may be made as to each employee, or as to categories of employees (by age, length of service, or rate of pay, for example), or they may be based upon an average of the expected service lives of all covered employees. These calculations, although made primarily for funding purposes, may be used also for accounting purposes. They should, of course,

be revised at intervals. Also according to this view, costs based on past services should be charged off over some reasonable period, provided the allocation is made on a systematic and rational basis and does not cause distortion of the operating results in any one year. The length of the period benefited by costs based on past services is subject to considerable difference of opinion. Some think that the benefits accrue principally during the early years of a plan; others feel that the period primarily benefited approximates the remaining service life of the employees covered by a plan at the time of its adoption; still others believe that the benefits of such costs extend over an indefinite period, possibly the entire life of a plan and its successors, if any. In practice, costs based on past services have in many instances been charged off over a ten- to twelve-year period, or over a fixed longer period such as twenty or thirty years. (The minimum period presently permitted for tax purposes is ten years if the initial past-service cost is immediately paid in full, or about twelve years if one-tenth of the initial past-service cost plus interest is paid each year.)

6. In the view of others, the full accrual of pension costs may be unnecessary. They point out that in some cases accounting for such costs in the manner indicated in paragraph 5 would result, as to a given year or cumulatively or both, in the accrual of costs under a pension plan in amounts differing materially from the payments made under the plan into a pension fund or to retired employees, and in other cases it would require the employer to record pension costs in amounts varying widely from his legal liabilities. They say that a company would in all probability never be called upon to utilize the entire amount of an actuarially calculated full accrual, and that, in the event of liquidation of the business, any amounts accrued with respect to employees who have not at the time acquired vested rights would, except for a voluntary act of grace, revert to the surplus of the company. They also believe that in the case of an unfunded or partially funded plan the accumulation of a substantial accrual would lead to pressure for full funding, possibly to the detriment of the company and its security holders, and that fear of this might deter management from entering into pension arrangements beneficial to employees. They also feel that the method of accounting envisioned in paragraph 5 disregards the probability that future unfavorable changes in a company's economic position undoubtedly would lead to changes in the pension arrangements it would make for its employees. According to this view, management should have wider discretion in accounting for pension costs, provided there is adequate disclosure as to the method followed.

7. The committee regards the method outlined in paragraph 5 as being the method most likely to effect a reasonable matching of costs and revenues, and therefore considers it to be preferable. However, the committee believes that opinion as to the accounting for pension costs has not yet crystallized sufficiently to make it possible at this time to assure agreement on any one method, and that differences in accounting for pension costs are likely to continue for a time. Accordingly, for the present, the committee believes that, as a minimum, the accounts and financial statements should reflect accruals which equal the present worth, actuarially calculated, of pension commitments to employees to the extent that pension rights have vested in the employees, reduced, in the case of the balance sheet, by any accumulated trusteed funds or annuity contracts purchased.

8. The committee believes that the costs of many pension plans are so material that the fact of adoption of a plan or an important amendment to

it constitutes significant information in financial statements. When a plan involving material costs is adopted, there should be a footnote to the financial statements for the year in which this occurs, stating the important features of the plan, the proposed method of funding or paying, the estimated annual charge to operations, and the basis on which such annual charge is determined. When an existing plan is amended to a material extent, there should be similar disclosure of the pertinent features of the amendment. When there is a change in the accounting procedure which materially affects the results of operations, there should be appropriate indication thereof. If there are costs of material amount based on past or current services for which reasonable provision has not been, or is not being, made in the accounts, appropriate disclosure should be made in a footnote to the financial statements as long as this situation exists.

The statement entitled "Accounting for Costs of Pension Plans" was adopted unanimously by the twenty-one members of the committee, of whom six, Messrs. Flatley, Jennings, Lindquist, Luther, Powell and Staub, assented with qualification.

The six members assenting with qualification object to that part of paragraph 3 which appears to sanction the charging to earned surplus in some circumstances of pension costs based on past service. They believe this to be in conflict with section A of Chapter 13 of Accounting Research Bulletin No. 43, in which the committee expresses the opinion that costs of annuities based on past service should not be charged to surplus. They consider the conclusions expressed in Chapter 13 to be sound for the reasons therein stated.

Observe in paragraph 1 that the bulletin is not concerned with funding, the actual payment of cash or other assets to a pension fund, but with the measurement of pension costs during a fiscal period. Because of legal, tax, and actuarial considerations, which are discussed later, the amount of cash actually *paid* into a pension fund during a fiscal period may differ substantially from pension expense allocable to the period in accordance with the accrual method of accounting. Since management may have some leeway in determining the amount of such cash payments, there is an opportunity to increase or decrease reported profit or loss if pension expense is based on the amount of cash payments.

On a *cash* basis, the journal entry to record pension expense would be :

        Pension Expense   xxx
            Cash   xxx

On an *accrual* basis, the journal entry to record pension expense would be :

        Pension Expense   xxx
            Estimated Liability for Pensions   xxx

When a cash payment is made to the trustee, the entry would be :

        Estimated Liability for Pensions   xxx
            Cash   xxx

In the last two entries the actual payment of cash has no effect on the *timing* or the *amount* of charges to pension expense.

In paragraph 3 the committee repeats the position expressed in the earlier bulletin that costs based on past service are "incurred in contemplation of present and future benefits" and "should be charged to operations during the current and future periods benefited." However, to encourage use of the accounting procedures recommended in later paragraphs of the bulletin, a majority of the committee did sanction charges to retained earnings for past service costs in the case of an *existing* plan where inadequate charges or no charges had been made in the past.

Factors influencing pension costs and considered by an actuary in determining funding requirements are listed in paragraph 4. The actuary plays a vital role in the pension area, although his primary interest is directed towards the adequacy of funding and not the problem of accounting for pension costs.

Paragraphs 5 and 6 present two contrasting views of accounting for pension costs. Advocates of the view expressed in paragraph 5 do not believe the *funding arrangements* or the employer's *legal obligations* under a pension plan should necessarily govern the accrual of pension costs. They believe a business realizes benefits from a pension plan during the "expected period of active service of the covered employees" and therefore pension costs, whether based on past, or present and future services, should be systematically accrued by periodic debits to pension expense and credits to estimated liability for pensions.

Advocates of the view expressed in paragraph 6 rely on the extent of the employer's *legal liability*. They also note that full accrual of pension costs will frequently exceed actual payments to the fund for many years. They favor wider management discretion in accounting for pension costs, provided there is adequate disclosure.

The committee favored full accrual of pension costs. To facilitate a smooth transition to this method, however, the committee included "for the present" a minimum procedure, as stated in the last sentence of paragraph 7. This minimum procedure recommended recognition of accruing pension costs "to the extent that pension rights have vested in the employees." An employee is, of course, entitled to any pension benefit purchased with his own payments to the pension fund even if he terminates his employment. Under some pension plans, an employee is similarly entitled to benefits purchased by the employer's payments. Such benefits are "vested" in, or owned by, the employee. Usually vesting of benefits purchased by employer payments does not take place until an employee has worked a certain number of years or attained a stated age. Some pension plans provide for no vesting until the employee actually retires or is eligible to retire.

INCOME TAX CONSIDERATIONS

A pension plan is said to be "qualified" if it meets certain Internal Revenue Code requirements concerning the purpose and operation of the plan and the eligibility of employees to participate. Most pension plans are designed to meet these requirements because of a qualified plan's income tax advantages. Under such a plan, an employer's payments to a pension trust are tax deductible when paid to the trust, but are not taxable as income to the employee until he receives them as a pension following retirement. That is, the tax law governing pension plans follows *cash accounting*, not *accrual accounting*. This use of cash accounting for tax purposes has contributed to its use in reporting pension expense on the income statement. There are distinct advantages to the employee in not being taxed until retirement. Most employees are then subject to a lower effective tax rate because of reduced income and increased personal tax exemptions available at age 65. Another tax advantage concerns the trust itself. The earnings of a qualified pension trust are not taxable. This increases the accumulation of invested funds and substantially reduces the cost of providing pension benefits.

To continue as a qualified plan for tax purposes, annual contributions to the pension fund must fall within rather wide maximum and minimum limits. If a company has contributed more than the minimum amount in the past, it may temporarily reduce or even eliminate contributions without jeopardizing the status of its qualified plan. Such flexible provisions may be desirable from management's standpoint and may encourage the formation of qualified plans, but basing the periodic charge to pension expense on varying cash payments does not follow the accrual method of accounting.

ACTUARIAL FACTORS

Strict adherence to a corporation's legal rights and obligations under a pension plan and the influence of tax considerations have resulted in frequent use of either the cash or limited accrual basis of accounting for pension costs instead of the full accrual method preferred by the committee. In the preferred view, pension costs should be systematically accrued on "the basis of actuarial calculations." These calculations *may* be the same calculations used for funding purposes. However, if such calculations do not produce results useful for the systematic accrual of pension costs because of the influence of legal or tax considerations, separate actuarial calculations may be required for accounting purposes.

In discussing these actuarial calculations, the bulletin states that "they should, of course, be revised at intervals." Such revisions, based on the actual experience of a pension plan, reflect "actuarial gains and losses." "Actuarial gains" may result from several factors including a higher than estimated rate of return on pension fund investments or greater than anticipated employee turnover or mortality (note that high mortality is a *favorable* factor for a pension plan). Of course, contrary changes will produce "actuarial losses."

As a result of "actuarial gains," a plan may be temporarily "overfunded" and current contributions to the trustee may be reduced or eliminated. An example of this situation is described in the General Electric Company's 1961 annual report:

Earnings of the General Electric Pension Trust have shown steady improvement, amounting in 1961 to approximately 4.2 per cent on invested assets (excluding net profits on disposition of investments). As a result, the estimated future earnings rate used in the computation of pension liabilities was increased from 3 per cent to $3^{1}/_{2}$ per cent effective January 1, 1961. A reappraisal of liabilities for participants' service since 1946 using the new $3^{1}/_{2}$ per cent interest assumption indicated an excess of applicable Trust assets over such liabilities, since Company contributions in prior years were determined so as to maintain assets equal to liabilities computed at the earnings rates then being used. The Company's contribution to the Trust for the cost of pension credits earned by participants in 1961 takes into account about one-half of such excess.

Pension Trusts for Employees of General Electric Company and its Subsidiaries
(in millions)

Operating Statement	1961	1960
Total assets—January 1	$1,097.3	$1,003.8
Plus : Company contributions	27.4	65.0
Employee contributions	13.2	10.8
Investment income	46.2	44.0
	1,184.1	1,123.6
Less : Pensions paid	32.5	26.3
Total assets—December 31	$1,151.6	$1,097.3
Financial Position—December 31		
Investments	$1,126.1	$1,068.3
Cash	3.2	1.9
Other assets—net	22.3	27.1
Total assets	$1,151.6	$1,097.3
Liability to pensioners	$ 249.5	$ 205.6
Reserve for pensions to participants not yet retired	902.1	891.7
Liabilities and reserves	$1,151.6	$1,097.3

Note that General Electric apparently could have omitted any contribution to the pension trust in 1961. It recognized one-half of the total effect of increasing the estimated future earnings rate from 3 to $3^{1}/_{2}$ per cent. Company contributions, which were also the amount charged to expense, declined by over one-half from $65.0 million in 1960 to $27.4 million in 1961. General Electric reported net earnings after taxes of $242.1 million in 1961, up from $200.1 million in 1960.

The committee did not specifically discuss appropriate methods of accounting for the effect of actuarial gains and losses. Three possible methods might be considered: (1) adjustment of retained earnings to recognize excessive (or deficient) contributions in the past, (2) immediate recognition in the current fiscal period of the entire excess or deficiency in accordance with the cash basis of accounting which is widely used for pension accounting purposes, and (3) deferred recognition over future fiscal periods. Methods (1) and (3), which are similar to acceptable methods used to account for changes in the estimated lives of depreciable assets, can be supported by sound arguments. Method (2) is difficult to support on any rational basis.

DISCLOSURE

Three of the disclosure provisions described in paragraph 8 pertain to important events which may have a material effect on pension costs. The committee specifically notes the *adoption* or *amendment* of a pension plan or *change* in accounting procedure. There is no problem in identifying such events and it is usually fairly evident when disclosure is required.

The last sentence of paragraph 8 concerns a more troublesome problem of disclosure. Should a "reasonable provision" for pension costs be based only on the accrual method? As indicated earlier in this chapter, this question has not been satisfactorily answered and there is substantial variation in the accounting procedures used for pension costs. Until the profession has resolved some of the problems in this difficult area, more comprehensive disclosure than recommended in paragraph 8 would appear desirable. Such disclosure would at least permit the sophisticated reader to judge for himself the adequacy of pension provisions. The following information might be disclosed:

1. The amount charged to pension expense during the fiscal period. This amount is often included in total employee compensation and not separately disclosed.
2. The estimated present value of vested pension benefits and the estimated present value of all pension benefits earned to date disregarding any vesting provision. The first estimate indicates the current *legal* liability while the second indicates the *going-concern* or *economic* liability. Under full accrual accounting, the latter amount, reduced by contributions already paid to a trustee, would appear as a liability on the balance sheet.
3. A summary of the actuarial factors used by the actuary and the date of the most recent actuarial review.

4. Any change in actuarial factors or methods indicating both the accrual accounting effects and the tax effects of such a change.

REFERENCES

Andersen, Arthur, & Co., *Accounting and Reporting Problems of the Accounting Profession*, 2nd ed. Chicago: Arthur Andersen & Co. (Oct. 1962), 19–26.

———, *Accounting for the Costs of Pension Plans*. Chicago: Arthur Andersen & Co. (Apr. 1962).

Blough, Carman G., "Accounting for Pensions," *Journal of Accountancy*, 89 (Mar. 1950), 251.

———, "Disclosure of Pension Plan Liability," *Journal of Accountancy*, 90 (Oct. 1950), 351–52.

———, "AIA Committee Continues Discussion of Pension Accounting Problems," *Journal of Accountancy*, 92 (Aug. 1951), 219–20.

———, "The Minimum Liability for Pension Costs," *Journal of Accountancy*, 103 (Jun. 1957), 69–70.

———, "Elimination of Provision for Pension Costs Unjustified," *Journal of Accountancy*, 106 (Dec. 1958), 74–75.

———, "More About the Elimination of Provision for Pension Costs," *Journal of Accountancy*, 107 (Jan. 1959), 80–81.

Brundage, Percival F., "Pension Plans from an Accountant's Point of View," *Journal of Accountancy*, 89 (Jan. 1950), 8–15.

Dean, Arthur H., "Accounting for the Cost of Pensions—A Lien on Production," *Harvard Business Review*, 28 (Jul. 1950), 25–40, and 28 (Sept. 1950), 102–22.

Friest, Philip L., "Accounting Treatment of Pension Plan Costs," *N.A.A. Bulletin*, 43 (May 1962), section 1, 19–30.

Huizingh, William, "Accounting Principles and Pension Costs," *N.A.C.A. Bulletin*, 36 (Jan. 1955), section 1, 722–28.

Kurtz, Cornelius, "The Cost of Human Depreciation—Ostrich Liability?" *Accounting Review*, 32 (Jul. 1957), 413–18.

Lorensen, Leonard, "Pension Costs in Selected Financial Statements," *Journal of Accountancy*, 113 (Mar. 1962), 57–61.

Matthews, Roy M., Jr., "Accounting for Pension Costs," *N.A.A. Bulletin*, 41 (Aug. 1960), section 1, 19–26.

"Must Companies Tell All on Pensions?" *Business Week* (Dec. 10, 1955), 29.

Ogden, Warde B., "Survey of 260 Pension Plans Reveals Wide Variety of Accounting for Costs, Plus Some Hazards," *Journal of Accountancy*, 93 (Jan. 1952), 44–47.

"The Startling Impact of Private Pension Funds," *Business Week* (Jan. 31, 1959), 88–105.

Werntz, William W., "Accountant's Responsibility in Reporting Corporate Profits," *Journal of Accountancy*, 107 (Mar. 1959), 48–49.

Williams, John, H., "Actuarial Principles and Pension Plans," *New York Certified Public Accountant*, 29 (Jul. 1959), 505–15, and 29 (Aug. 1959), 578–84.

American Sugar Refining Company

The American Sugar Refining Company was incorporated in 1891, when it acquired the property of the Sugar Refineries Company which controlled a number of sugar refining plants. American Sugar is a refiner of raw cane sugar, which it purchases, refines, packs and sells. The company's bulk business is of primary importance, but it also sells packaged sugar under the trade names Domino, Franklin and Sunny Cane.

Under the company's first pension plan, started in 1912, only certain employees were entitled to benefits. Part of the liability for such payments was recognized by charges to operations and credits to a "reserve" for pensions. This credit account was considered part of "Sundry reserves for pensions, insurance and contingencies," classified between current liabilities and capital stock.

In 1943, a proposal was made to up-date the plan. American Sugar's president, Mr. Joseph F. Abbott, commented on the proposal as follows in the company's 1943 annual report:

Your Board of Directors at its meeting on December 15, 1943, approved for submission to the stockholders for action at their annual meeting on April 19, 1944, an amendment to our present pension plan which would bring into the plan all employees of the company and of its domestic constituent companies. On October 12, 1924, the Directors discontinued the application of our pension plan to employees entering the service of the company after that date. We have a situation today under which part of our employees are entitled to pension benefits on reaching the required age or completing the required years of service, while other employees have no pension rights. The proposed amendment to the plan will afford uniform recognition to all of our employees for their loyal service and provide additional security in their old age. The amendment proposes substantially the same benefits as provided in the old pension plan, except that certain deductions are to be made because of old age benefits [from the Federal Insurance Contributions Act] and increases are to be made in both the minimum and maximum pensions. The amendment, as in the case of the present plan, provides that the pensions will be without cost to the employees.

To meet increased financial demands upon the company in carrying out the amended plan, the Directors have authorized the transfer of the sum of $2,000,000, the amount formerly carried in Reserve for Pensions, from Sundry Reserves to a special Pension Fund Reserve. To this amount has been added $500,000 out of the 1943 net income of the company. It is hoped that in good years this fund may be increased, and that in any year in which the net income of the company might be strained by pension payments, some part, or all, of such payments may be defrayed from the principal of the fund, or from the income which will accrue to it through the investment thereof under the direction of the Board of Directors. This Pension Fund Reserve has been established as a matter of convenience in administering the pension plan, and the company reserves the right to make it available for other corporate purposes at any time.

The $500,000 addition to *both* the pension fund and the related pension fund reserve was disclosed on the 1943 income statement as follows:

Net income	$4,821,327.51
Provision for pension fund	$ 500,000.00
Provision for war contingencies	271,336.51
	$ 771,336.51
Balance of net income added to surplus	$4,049,991.00

At the annual meeting in April, 1944, the stockholders approved the amendment to the pension plan, giving all of the company's employees protection without cost to them. At the close of 1944, an additional provision, $512,950,[1] was appropriated from 1944 net income and credited to the Pension Fund Reserve. Exhibit 1 shows the changes in the Pension Fund Reserve for the years 1943 through 1960.

Pension Fund assets were disclosed on the company's balance sheet at December 31, 1944, as follows:

Pension fund (see Note):

U. S. Government securities, at cost plus accrued interest	$1,859,281.25
5,000 shares of company's own preferred stock	
reacquired and held in pension fund, at cost	632,650.00
Cash in bank	544,952.62
	$3,036,883.87

Note: The pension fund and reserve have been established as a matter of convenience in administering the company's pension plan, but the company reserves the right to make the fund and the reserve available for other corporate purposes at any time.

---

[1] Consisted of $500,000 (as in previous year) plus $12,950, the amount of dividends which would have been paid on the preferred stock of the company acquired for the Pension Fund had such stock been outstanding.

Exhibit 2 shows the composition of Pension Fund assets at December 31, from 1944 through 1960.

In American Sugar's annual reports for the years 1947 through 1949, Mr. Abbott stated, in part:

[1947]

There has been added to the Pension Reserve during the year the sum of $2,095,166. Of this amount $2,000,000 was transferred from "Earned Surplus." The sum of $60,166 represents the equivalent of interest on government securities in the Pension Fund[2] and $35,000 represents the equivalent of the dividend which would have been paid on the preferred stock of the company acquired for the Pension Fund had this stock been outstanding.

Our 1943 report explained our old pension plan and the amendment of it subsequently approved by the stockholders at their annual meeting on April 19, 1944. We stated that the Pension Fund and Reserve were established as a matter of convenience in administering the pension plan and that the company reserved the right to make them available for other corporate purposes at any time. However, the fund and reserve have now reached a figure which is about 75 per cent of the company's estimate of the total pensions expected to be paid eventually, under the company's *original* pension plan, both to present pensioners and (based on services rendered up to the end of 1947) to old employees still actively employed.

[1948]

There has been added to the Pension Fund Reserve and to the Pension Fund during the year the sum of $1,622,507. Of this amount $1,500,000 was transferred from Earned Surplus. The sum of $87,507 represents the equivalent of interest on government securities in the Pension Fund and $35,000 represents the equivalent of the dividend which would have been paid on the preferred stock of the company acquired for the Pension Fund had this stock been outstanding.

The Pension Fund and Reserve have now reached a figure, net of tax deductions, which approximates our estimate of the amount now required to provide (1) pensions to those now on the pension roll and (2) the accrual to date toward future pension costs of all present employees.

[1949]

It was pointed out in last year's annual report that the Pension Fund and Reserve of $6,927,300 approximated our estimate of the amount then required, net of tax deductions, to provide pensions for those then on the pension roll plus the accrual up to that time toward the future cost of pensions for all persons then employed. In the light of further study and subsequent developments, it has seemed desirable to add another $1,000,000 to the Pension Fund and Reserve, and this has been done by a transfer of this amount from Earned Surplus.

We have also revised our accounting procedure for pension costs so that beginning in 1949 we will provide each year an addition to our Pension Fund and Reserve sufficient to maintain it at a level representing our best estimate of our pension costs accrued to date.

---

[2] Through 1948, income from government securities in the Pension Fund was credited, as received, to the company's regular interest income account. At the year-end, the same amount was credited to the Pension Fund Reserve, accompanied by a charge to operations (see Exhibit 1). Beginning in 1949, such income was credited directly to the Pension Fund Reserve as received.

Accordingly, in addition to the provision of $1,000,000 mentioned above, we added to our Reserve in 1949 the total sum of $603,341. Of this amount $170,569 was provided by the income from Pension Fund investments. The balance of $432,772 was charged to operations. Actual payments made for pensions during the year, amounting to $373,465, were charged directly to our Pension Fund Reserve and not to operations as in preceding years. (Had we followed the same accounting method as in preceding years, our charge to operations would have been $59,307 less.)

The net result of these adjustments was to increase our Pension Fund Reserve by $1,229,876.

In 1955, American Sugar adopted an improved plan which qualified under Internal Revenue Code regulations. In the 1955 annual report, Mr. W. F. Oliver, president since 1954, commented as follows in his message to the company's stockholders:

At a special meeting of stockholders on December 14, 1955, approval was given to the adoption of an improved pension plan providing greater benefits at normal retirement age for regular full-time employees of the company.

The company has established a tax-exempt trust fund with The First National City Bank of New York for the purpose of providing benefits to pension plan members and their beneficiaries in accordance with the terms of the new plan. Income to the trust fund from securities held by it is not taxable. Contributions to the trust fund, within certain maximum limitations, are deductible in determining the company's taxable income for federal income tax purposes.

For a number of years the company had maintained a pension reserve on its books by making annual provisions from earnings. A fund in an amount equal to the reserve was also maintained. These provisions were not permitted as deductions for purposes of determining taxable income, however, since only the actual payments of pension benefits are so recognized if a tax-exempt trust or other qualified funding arrangement does not exist.

Our pension fund and reserve will be confined hereafter to the undeposited past service cost, adjusted for the amount of tax reduction to be obtained when deposits are made. Accruals for each year's current service cost for pensions will not be reflected in the reserve, as the related sums will be deposited directly in the trust fund.

In December, a deposit of 10 per cent of the past service cost was made to the tax-exempt trust fund. A portion of this deposit represented a charge to 1955 earnings in recognition of the higher past service cost of the improved trusteed plan as estimated by independent actuaries. The pension reserve aggregated $10,656,415 at December 31, 1955.

Provisions for pension costs charged to 1955 earnings amounted to $1,188,309 after reflecting the applicable reduction in taxes. Of this amount, $778,309 represents the provision for current service cost and $410,000[3] an additional provision toward past service.

---

[3] From 1955 through 1960, $410,000 of the annual contribution towards undeposited past service costs was made from unsegregated company assets and charged to current *after-tax* earnings (the actual contribution was approximately $850,000, but the *after-tax* expense was $410,000). The balance of the annual contribution towards past service costs was made from assets segregated in the company's Pension Fund (see Exhibit 2) and charged to Pension Fund Reserve (see Exhibit 1).

EXHIBIT 1

American Sugar Refining Company
Selected Data from the Company's Annual Reports, 1943-1960

Year Ended	Sales (000 omitted)	Net Income (000 omitted)	Pension Costs Charged to Operations	Provision for Pension Costs from Net Income	Appropriation from Earned Surplus to Pension Reserve	Balance of Pension Fund Reserve	Income from Pension Fund Investments	Pension Payments[3]	Number of Employees Receiving Pensions
1943	$150,545	$ 4,821	$238,693	$500,000		$ 2,500,000		$238,693	401
1944	201,609	5,903	263,390	512,950[1]		3,036,884	$ 23,934[2]	239,456	392
1945	174,084	4,540	332,247			3,118,762	81,878	250,369	413
1946	169,886	4,735	377,018			3,209,627	90,865	286,153	474
1947	302,161	10,245	411,134		$2,000,000	5,304,793	95,166	315,968	492
1948	245,124	7,648	461,181		1,500,000	6,927,300	122,507	338,674	522
1949	277,188	7,951	432,772		1,000,000	8,157,176	170,569	373,465	593
1950	287,292	10,007	736,978			8,669,641	196,064	420,577	613
1951	282,557	7,499	862,214			9,277,096	217,170	471,929	646
1952	292,391	7,807	853,791			9,851,622	225,727	504,992	678
1953	306,866	6,552	948,286			10,486,723	236,316	549,501	694
1954	308,837	7,623	984,485			11,133,310	251,915	589,813	726
1955	325,894	8,330	1,188,309[4]			10,656,415	N.A.	640,693	745
1956	338,055	9,886	1,155,195			9,883,668	173,586[4]	709,293	807
1957	330,802	9,947	1,249,007			8,367,373	N.A.	N.A.	921
1958	350,233	11,591	1,302,050			7,113,238	N.A.	1,000,869	965
1959	335,768	10,055	1,252,527			5,839,351	N.A.	N.A.	1,016
1960	338,179	9,388	1,345,841			5,480,205	N.A.	N.A.	1,208

[1] $12,950 equals dividend payment which would have been paid on the preferred stock of the company acquired for the Pension Fund had it been outstanding.

[2] Charged to operations through 1948.

[3] Charged to operations through 1948; 1949 through 1954 charged to Pension Fund Reserve. From 1955, payments were made by the Trustee.

[4] After 1954, amounts shown are net of taxes.

N.A.—Not Available.

EXHIBIT 2

American Sugar Refining Company
Composition of Pension Fund on the Company's Books
December 31, 1944-1960

	Cash	Government Securities	Company's own Preferred Stock	Total
1944	$ 544,953	$ 1,859,281	$632,650	$ 3,036,884
1945	78,440	2,407,672	632,650	3,118,762
1946	26,977	2,550,000	632,650	3,209,627
1947	2,047,143	2,625,000	632,650	5,304,793
1948	1,624,650	4,670,000	632,650	6,927,300
1949	1,086,526	6,438,000	632,650	8,157,176
1950	98,991	7,938,000	632,650	8,669,641
1951	1,446	8,643,000	632,650	9,277,096
1952	320,972	8,898,000	632,650	9,851,622
1953	75,073	9,779,000	632,650	10,486,723
1954	91,660	10,409,000	632,650	11,133,310
1955	729,765	9,294,000	632,650	10,656,415
1956	526,367	8,724,651	632,650	9,883,668
1957	37,106	7,697,617	632,650	8,367,373
1958	82,776	6,397,812	632,650	7,113,238
1959	51,027	5,155,674	632,650	5,839,351
1960	51,329	4,796,226	632,650	5,480,205

QUESTIONS:

1. Using the data in Exhibit 1, prepare a schedule to reconcile the yearly changes in the column headed "Balance of Pension Fund Reserve" from 1944 through 1954. (Start with $2,500,000, the balance at the beginning of 1944, and show the increases and decreases for 1944. Do the same thing for each year through 1954.)

2. Carefully analyze the company's accounting treatment of pension costs for each of the following periods: 1943, 1944–1948, 1949–1954, 1955–1960. Would you say the company used the accrual method, the cash method, or some other method of accounting in each of these periods? Explain.

3. In the 1943 annual report, the president stated that it was hoped the pension fund might be increased in good years (resulting in charges to income) and decreased in bad years (no charges to income). Is this in accordance with generally accepted accounting principles? Is there any indication that the company followed this procedure?

4. Do the transfers from Earned Surplus to the Pension Fund Reserve from 1947 to 1949 conform with AICPA recommendations as expressed in the appropriate Accounting Research Bulletin? Is there any significant difference between making appropriations from net income or earned surplus?

5. Comment on the appropriateness of disclosure made regarding the pension plan. Is it clear to you? Do you believe the typical stockholder would understand it? If not, what changes would you propose?

6. What advantages, if any, did the company derive from the change in its pension plan made in 1955?

7. Explain how the company planned to account for past service costs under the 1955 plan. Is this a reasonable procedure?

Swift & Company (C)[1]

Swift & Company established a noncontributory pension plan in 1916 which was embodied in an irrevocable pension trust in 1925. Annual contributions to the trust, which are determined by the Board of Directors, are shown in Exhibit 1 for the years 1950 through 1961. During 1957, management decided to reduce its pension contributions to $1.1 million from a level of $13.6 million in 1956. The decline was explained by President Porter Jarvis in "The Year in Review" section of the 1957 annual report:

Our noncontributory pension plan has been in effect since 1916. The pension plan is in excellent condition, the annual income from investments in the fund currently being in excess of annual pension payments. Because of this the directors felt justified in reducing the pension contributions for the current year.

This statement by Mr. Jarvis was the only reference made to pensions in the 1957 annual report. In the 1960 annual report, he commented as follows:

The Swift & Company Pension Trust is paying pensions to 12,994 people. Included are 8,606 retired employees and 4,388 widows and minor children. The Trust is in excellent financial condition. It embodies the company's 44-year-old noncontributory pension plan, which is one of the oldest among industrial firms. In 1960 the income from invested funds, plus the company contribution to the Trust, exceeded total pension payments by $6,479,398. This amount was applied toward the liability for service of employees not yet on pension.

In 1961, the following note to the financial statements explained Swift's pension contributions:

Swift & Company established a noncontributory pension plan in 1916 which was embodied in an irrevocable pension trust in 1925. While the plan is not

---

[1] Refer to Swift & Company (A) on page 236 for company history.

fully funded based upon actuarial computations using cost of assets and an assumed interest rate of $3\frac{1}{2}\%$, the plan is substantially funded if recognition is given to market value of the plan's investments. Contributions made to the trust over the years have accumulated so that the assets of the trust are substantially in excess of the amount needed (determined actuarially) to meet future pension payments to present pensioners. For the past several years, the directors of the company have authorized contributions in amounts which, while substantially lower than amounts determined actuarially for current service costs, are considered reasonable and adequate in light of the trust's current financial status.

The "Auditors' Report" for 1957 through 1961 was unqualified.

Exhibit 2 shows the text of an article which appeared in *The Wall Street Journal* on May 6, 1960.

EXHIBIT 1

Swift & Company (C)
Selected Financial Data, Years 1950-1961
(in thousands of dollars, except per share figures)

Year Ended	Net Sales	Contributions to Pension Trust	Net Income	Net Income per Share
Oct. 28, 1950	$2,214,000	$12,049	$16,143	$2.73
Oct. 27, 1951	2,524,000	10,179	12,109	2.04
Nov. 1, 1952	2,592,000	14,169	21,698	3.66
Oct. 31, 1953	2,597,000	15,716	33,903	5.72
Oct. 30, 1954	2,510,000	13,400	19,051	3.22
Oct. 29, 1955	2,404,000	10,664	22,893	3.87
Oct. 27, 1956	2,429,000	13,573	14,012	2.36
Oct. 26, 1957	2,542,000	1,139	13,538	2.29
Nov. 1, 1958	2,645,000	4,675	10,048	1.70
Oct. 31, 1959	2,475,000	5,196	19,068	3.20
Oct. 29, 1960	2,443,000	5,853	18,413	3.09
Oct. 28, 1961	2,489,000	4,722	12,050	2.01

EXHIBIT 2

Swift & Company (C)
Reprint of an Article Appearing in
The Wall Street Journal on May 6, 1960[1]

Swift & Co. disclosed details of its employee pension fund, one of the oldest in industry.

Assets of the 44-year-old pension plan are valued at cost at $209 million, according to R. W. Reneker, vice president, and pension board chairman. The market value is greater, but was not disclosed.

Dividends, interest and profits from securities sold added nearly $8,750,000 to the fund during 1959, Mr. Reneker said. This addition, together with the

---

[1] Reproduced with permission of *The Wall Street Journal.*

company's contribution,...exceeded 1959 pension payments by about $4 million, he said.

The plan is supported wholly by company contributions, and the big meat packer has never before stated its size. No reason was given for the change in policy other than a decision that employees and the public would be interested.

About 28 per cent of the assets are invested in common stocks, with only a "minute" portion of Swift stock, the statement said. The bulk of the investment is in non-government bonds and preferred stocks.

Receiving pensions are 8,118 retired workers and 4,389 widows and minor children, Mr. Reneker said. Annual benefits are computed on the basis of $1\frac{1}{8}$ per cent of total accrued wages, and employees become eligible at age 65 after 20 years of continuous service. The average monthly pension, including Social Security payments, amounts to more than $200 for a retired married couple.

The plan began in 1916 and funds were placed in an irrevocable trust in 1925; since 1925, $122 million has been paid out in benefits. The trustee is the Bankers Trust Co. of New York. "The Swift pension trust is in excellent financial condition," Mr. Reneker commented, and is stronger than indicated by the assets, "which are reported at cost rather than today's higher market values."

QUESTIONS:

1. Do you approve of the Board of Directors' decision in 1957 to reduce pension contributions from $13.6 million for the previous year to $1.1 million? Explain.

2. Did the decrease in contributions from 1956 to 1957 have a material effect on reported net income? Assuming contributions in 1957 had been maintained at the 1956 level, what amount of net income after taxes would have been reported in 1957?

3. Do you consider disclosure of the change in contributions to the pension plan trustee in 1957 adequate? Comment.

4. In *The Wall Street Journal* article, reproduced as Exhibit 2, Mr. Reneker, Swift & Company vice president and pension board chairman, commented that the pension trust was stronger than indicated by the assets, "which are reported at cost rather than today's higher market values." Do you believe the financial condition of a pension trust is enhanced by an excess of market value over cost in the trust's assets? Explain.

5. Would it result in more useful and realistic reporting if the trustee maintained the trust's investment account on a market instead of a cost basis?

6. In the note to the 1961 financial statements, quoted in the case, two references are made to "determined actuarially." Consider each of these references carefully with particular attention to the employees involved. As nearly as you can tell, what was the status of the pension trust at the close of the 1961 fiscal year?

The Hampshire Company

The Hampshire Company is a large New England textile manufacturer. Its pension plan calls for contributions by both employees and the company, based on all compensation received by the employee. Part of the Pension Plan Agreement states that:

> The contributions of the company are determined by actuarial valuation to meet the annual accruing liability on account of benefits of the fund not covered by employees' contributions and such additional payment as may be made from time to time against any unfunded accrued liability.

As of December 31, 1956, actuarially-computed unfunded past service costs amounted to $1,165,000. Table 1 shows the company's net sales, net income and pension costs for the years 1955-1961 (in thousands of dollars):

TABLE 1

Year Ended Dec. 31	Net Sales	Net Income or (Loss)	Pension Costs[1]	Number of Employees
1955	$79,409	$2,867	$1,135	9,401
1956	84,119	2,190	721	8,173
1957	72,068	1,285	759	7,039
1958	59,367	939	—	5,363
1959	43,572	(9,775)	—	4,326
1960	37,789	(2,465)	—	3,657
1961	43,362	1,156	—	4,466

In 1956 and 1957, the company omitted contributions towards past service costs; the pension costs shown in Table 1 for these two years reflect current service costs only. Hampshire changed auditors in 1957. Since the effect on net income of the omission of a contribution towards past service costs in 1956 was not considered

---

[1] These amounts were actually contributed by the company to the Pension Plan Trustee.

material, disclosure had not been made nor a qualification taken by the former auditors. Consequently, the accounting procedure in 1957 was consistent with that of the previous year, but, because of reduced net income, the effect of the omission was relatively greater. The new auditors were concerned about what action, if any, they should take.

If the company had continued its previous policy, a contribution of approximately $225,000 would have been made for past service costs in both 1956 and 1957. Total pension costs would have been $946,000 in 1956 and $984,000 in 1957.

Securities held by the Pension Plan Trustee on December 31, 1956, had a market value of $24.9 million compared with a book value of $21.4 million. Most of this excess was due to appreciation in the market value of common stocks. Since the market value of the securities exceeded the book value by $3.5 million, three times the actuarially computed unfunded past service costs, the company justified omitting the contribution towards past service costs. It also did not disclose any amount for unfunded past service costs.

From 1957 through 1961, the market value of securities held by the Pension Plan Trustee increased an additional $5.2 million, which, when added to the contribution made in 1957, was somewhat more than cumulative contributions would have been over the five years for current service costs plus past service costs. As a result, no contributions were made after 1957, no pension costs were recorded in the accounts, and no pension liability was disclosed.

Exhibit 1 shows a portion of the 1957 income statement as it appeared in (a) the 1957 annual report and (b) the 1958 annual report. The company presents a comparative income statement for the current and prior year in its annual report. Hence the 1957 income statement appeared in both the 1957 and 1958 annual reports.

EXHIBIT 1

The Hampshire Company
Portion of 1957 Income Statement as it Appeared
in the 1957 and 1958 Annual Reports
(000 omitted)

	In 1957 Annual Report	In 1958 Annual Report
Costs and Expenses		
Cost of goods sold	$53,952	$55,159
Advertising, selling, general and administrative expenses	13,952	13,504
Pension fund contribution[1]	759	
Interest expense and other charges	857	857
	$69,520	$69,520

[1] This caption did not appear in the 1958 annual report.

QUESTIONS:

1. What action, if any, do you believe the auditors should have taken at the end of 1956, 1957, and 1958? Why?

2. Do you agree with management's argument that a contribution towards past service costs, or disclosure of any past service liability, is unnecessary in 1956 because the market value of pension fund securities exceeded book value by three times the year-end liability for past service costs? Explain. What would you do if market value fell below cost? What accounting concepts and conventions are relevant in answering these questions?

3. Explain why the company might have rearranged the 1957 cost figures before including them in the 1958 annual report for comparative purposes.

United States Steel Corporation (B)

In the spring of 1959, the representatives of the United Steelworkers of America and the major steel companies met to negotiate a new wage contract to replace the contract expiring in June. The Union requested sizable increases in wages and fringe benefits, contending that large steel profits would permit these increases without affecting the prices of finished steel. The Steel Industry spokesmen argued this was not possible; any *sizable* wage increase would have to be passed along in the form of higher prices. There was considerable government pressure for a settlement without the need for a price increase in order to avoid the threat of further inflation.

In May of 1959, the Union paid for a series of full-page newspaper advertisements stating its position. A portion of one of these ads, which cites financial data from the United States Steel Corporation's 1952 and 1958 annual reports, is reproduced below.

STEELWORKERS SHARE OF
STEEL INDUSTRY'S INCOME HAS
NOT INCREASED SINCE 1952[1]

TRUE, there have been wage increases, but because fewer men are making more steel, the total labor costs have remained the same.

Please examine these LABOR COSTS

1952	42.1¢	of each sales dollar
1958	42.8¢	of each sales dollar

(notice they are about the same)

now examine the NET PROFITS

1952	$143,678,740
1958	301,558,231

(profits have *DOUBLED*)

---

[1] *Wall Street Journal*, May 14, 1959. Reproduced by permission.

Because neither side would compromise its position, a nation-wide steel strike resulted, lasting from July until mid-November. The union's advertisement, while failing to arouse sufficient public reaction to prevent the strike, raised some questions about the pension accounting practices of the United States Steel Corporation.

Accounting for Pension Costs

As a result of wage-contract bargaining, U.S. Steel had substantially revised its pension plan in 1950. At that time, past service costs of the revised plan were estimated on an actuarial basis at $496 million. For each year, 1950 through 1957, U.S. Steel funded the annual current service costs, interest on past service costs, and the approximate maximum amount of past service costs permitted by the United States Treasury Department. These past service cost payments totaled $297 million by December 31, 1957 (see Exhibit 1).

On its income statement, the corporation reported as pension costs the amounts actually paid to the Trustee of the Fund. Since these amounts were charged to income and paid to the Trustee annually, no accruals were carried on the balance sheet.

Change in Policy

In 1958, the corporation changed its policy and made reduced payments to the Trustee. Such a change was within the discretion of the Board of Directors. A proxy statement prepared for a special meeting of stockholders, held on February 27, 1958, stated:

There are many factors relating to financing the cost of pensions . . . which may make desirable, from time to time, changes in the method of making financial provision for these costs and in the amounts set aside in any year. The Board of Directors of the corporation proposes to use its discretion from time to time with respect to such financing.

The independent auditors' report, as it appeared in U.S. Steel's 1958 annual report, read as follows:

February 24, 1959

To the Stockholders of
United States Steel Corporation:

As independent auditors elected at the annual meeting of stockholders of United States Steel Corporation held on May 5, 1958, we have examined the consolidated statement of financial position of United States Steel Corporation and subsidiaries at December 31, 1958 and the consolidated statement of income for the year 1958. Our examination was made in accordance with generally accepted auditing standards and accordingly included such tests of the accounting records and such other auditing procedures as we considered necessary in the circumstances.

Under the practice being followed by the Corporation in accounting for pension costs, the amounts charged to income annually have been equal to the amounts paid to the Trustee of its pension funds. With respect to non-contributory pensions, prior to 1958 such amounts included the annual current service costs (including interest on past service costs) and, in addition, the approximate maximum amount permitted by United States Treasury Department tax regulations for past service costs. Such additional payments for past service costs totaled $297 million to December 31, 1957. In view of these earlier payments, in 1958 the Board of Directors determined that, under the business conditions and the reduced steel operating rate existing during the first three quarters of the year, $61 million of the additional $297 million would be applied against current service costs for the first three quarters of 1958 and that no payment would be made for the year for past service costs; provision and payment have been made for current service costs for the fourth quarter.[2] While the amount paid to the Trustee for 1958 for noncontributory pension costs is less than the related current service costs which accrued during the year, the aggregate of all amounts paid to the Trustee to date, for both current and past service costs, exceeds all current service costs accrued since the adoption of the plan in 1950. The assets held by the Trustee at December 31, 1958 were adequate to cover the estimated cost of all pensions for those then entitled to receive them.

As indicated in the preceding paragraph, the charges to income for non-contributory pension costs for 1958 were not comparable in amount with the charges for 1957, although the amounts for each year were equal to the amounts paid to the Trustee. If the Corporation had made payments to the Trustee and charged such amounts to income for 1958 on the same basis as for 1957, the additional pension costs charged against 1958 income would have amounted to approximately $97 million before the effect of income taxes and $46.6 million after such taxes.

In our opinion, with the foregoing explanation, the accompanying consolidated statement of financial position and related statement of income, together with the notes thereto, present fairly the position of United States Steel Corporation and subsidiaries at December 31, 1958 and the results of the year's operations, in conformity with generally accepted accounting principles applied on a basis consistent with that of the preceding year.

In 1959, current service costs and interest on the unfunded amount of past service costs were contributed on the same basis as in 1957 and prior years. However, no provision was made for past service costs. Mr. Roger M. Blough, Chairman of the Board of Directors, explained this in the 1959 annual report:

...the Board of Directors, in the exercise of its discretion with respect to making financial provisions for pension costs, determined that because of the reduced steel operating rate which was brought about by the steelworkers' strike, no payments be made toward the funding of past service cost for the year 1959.

---

[2] See Exhibit 2: Quarterly Sales and Net Income, 1957–1961.

Change in Actuarial Factors

Certain actuarial factors were changed in 1960, explained as follows in the annual report:

During 1960, in the light of a review of U.S. Steel's actual experience, certain actuarial service and mortality tables and the interest rate were refined, and costs were more directly related to the level of operations. If these refinements had not been made, total pension costs in 1960 would have been increased to approximately $122 million because of increased pension benefits made effective following negotiations with labor unions during the year.

Although full provision was made for current service pension costs for the year 1960, it was determined that because of the reduced level of steel operations no payments be made toward funding of past service cost. In 1959 it was also determined that no payments be made in that year toward the funding of past service pension cost. Past service cost applies against the actuarial cost of noncontributory pensions for service rendered prior to March 1, 1950, the effective date of the present plan.

The effects of the changes made in 1958 and 1959 are shown on the comparative statements presented in Exhibit 3 and 4. Exhibit 3 presents selected consolidated income statements (including the data used by the Union in preparing the advertisement); Exhibit 4 includes the details of the pension cost figures. Exhibit 5 presents the Trustee's Statement of Changes in the Pension Trust for the years 1957 through 1961.

EXHIBIT 1

United States Steel Corporation
Selected Data for the Years 1948–1961
(dollar figures in millions; employees in thousands)

		Pension Costs			
Year	Wages & Salaries	For Current Service[1]	For Past Service	Total Pension Costs	Other Employee. Benefit Costs
1948	$1,005.8	$ 10.2	$ —	$ 10.2	$ 19.7
1949	906.4	7.1	—	7.1	32.4
1950	1,018.5	59.0	50.0	109.0	51.9
1951	1,217.6	59.6	37.0	96.6	60.3
1952	1,176.6	62.7	26.0	88.7	56.7
1953	1,397.4	69.4	36.0	105.4	66.4
1954	1,218.2	66.1	36.0	102.1	66.6
1955	1,415.0	79.5	36.0	115.5	84.4
1956	1,455.6	87.2	38.0	125.2	100.1
1957	1,596.8	102.2	38.0	140.2	124.9
1958	1,344.5	94.3	(61.0)	33.3	110.7
1959	1,355.0	104.4	—	104.4	116.8
1960	1,453.3	87.2	—	87.2	159.4
1961	1,382.4	85.5	—	85.5	154.9

	Total Employment Costs	Average No. of Employees	Sales	Net Income
1948	$1,035.7	297	$2,481.5	$129.6
1949	945.9	291	2,301.7	165.9
1950	1,179.4	288	2,956.4	215.5
1951	1,374.5	301	3,524.1	184.5
1952	1,322.1	294	3,137.4	143.7
1953	1,569.2	302	3,861.0	222.1
1954	1,386.9	268	3,250.4	195.4
1955	1,614.9	273	4,097.7	370.1
1956	1,680.9	261	4,228.9	348.1
1957	1,861.9	271	4,413.8	419.4
1958	1,488.5	223	3,472.2	301.6
1959	1,576.2	200	3,643.0	254.5
1960	1,700.0	225	3,698.5	304.2
1961	1,622.7	199	3,336.5	190.2

[1] Includes provision for interest on unfunded past service costs from 1950 through 1961.

EXHIBIT 2

United States Steel Corporation
Quarterly Sales and Net Income for the Years 1957–1961
(in millions)

		Sales	Net Income
1957:	1st quarter	$1,166.5	$115.3
	2nd quarter	1,170.3	115.9
	3rd quarter	1,042.8	97.7
	4th quarter	1,034.2	90.2
1958:	1st quarter	800.1	62.4
	2nd quarter	863.1	73.2
	3rd quarter	872.2	74.9
	4th quarter	937.0	90.7
1959:	1st quarter	1,077.6	106.6
	2nd quarter	1,448.7	148.4
	3rd quarter	368.4	(31.1)[1]
	4th quarter	748.9	30.2
1960:	1st quarter	1,187.6	112.6
	2nd quarter	1,002.4	80.9
	3rd quarter	785.2	52.4
	4th quarter	723.3	58.6
1961:	1st quarter	708.7	32.0
	2nd quarter	869.1	59.0
	3rd quarter	861.3	51.8
	4th quarter	897.3	47.4

[1] Steel strike July 15—November 7

EXHIBIT 3

United States Steel Corporation
Comparative Income Statements for the Years 1952 and 1957–1959
(in millions)

	1952	1957	1958	1959
Products and services sold	$3,137.4	$4,413.8	$3,472.2	$3,643.0
Costs				
Employment costs				
Wages and salaries	$1,176.6	$1,596.8	$1,344.5	$1,355.0
Pensions and other benefits	145.5	265.1	144.0	221.2
	$1,322.1	$1,861.9	$1,488.5	$1,576.2
Products and services bought	1,312.1	1,324.2	1,085.6	1,278.2
Wear and exhaustion of facilities	172.4	276.0	204.9	189.9
Interest and other costs on debt	1.9	7.0	11.5	17.6
State, local & miscellaneous taxes	68.3	119.3	95.1	93.6
Estimated U.S. & foreign income taxes	117.0	406.0	285.0	233.0
Totals	$2,993.7	$3,994.4	$3,170.6	$3,388.5
Income	$ 143.7	$ 419.4	$ 301.6	$ 254.5

EXHIBIT 4

United States Steel Corporation

Comparative Costs of Employee Benefits for the Years 1952 and 1957–1961

(000 omitted)

	1952	1957	1958	1959	1960	1961
Pension Costs						
Funding of current service costs (including interest on unfunded past service costs):	$ 62,745	$102,193	$ 94,280	$104,357	$ 87,226	$ 85,451
Funding of portion of past service costs:	26,000	38,000	—	—	—	—
Funding of past service costs in prior years used for current service costs:	—	—	(60,984)	—	—	—
Total pension cost	$ 88,745	$140,193	$ 33,296	$104,357	$ 87,226	$ 85,451
Other Employee Benefits:						
Social Security, Insurance, Supplemental Unemployment Benefits, etc.	56,733	124,926	110,696	116,812	159,444	154,929
Total Costs	$145,478	$265,119	$143,992	$221,169	$246,670	$240,380

508 UNITED STATES STEEL CORPORATION (B)

EXHIBIT 5

United States Steel Corporation
Statement of Changes in Pension Trust for the Years 1957–1961
(000 omitted)

	1957	1958	1959	1960	1961
Balance at beginning of year	$ 894,729	$1,051,087	$1,103,018	$1,228,793	$1,338,436
Additions					
Receipts from employing companies	140,193	33,296	104,357	87,226	85,452
Receipts from participating employees	6,215	6,392	7,188	6,796	7,092
Income from investments	38,593	43,148	46,925	55,516	58,649
Gain on disposition of investments	1,780	492	2,040	3,555	8,336
	$1,081,510	$1,134,415	$1,263,528	$1,381,886	$1,497,965
Deductions					
Pension payments	21,371	30,690	33,972	42,516	48,658
Refunds to withdrawing employees	629	707	763	934	1,446
Transfers to reserves for investments	8,423	—	—	—	—
	$ 30,423	$ 31,397	$ 34,735	$ 43,450	$ 50,104
Balance at end of year	$1,051,087	$1,103,018	$1,228,793	$1,338,436	$1,447,861

QUESTIONS:

1. Analyze the Union's newspaper advertisement. Why do you suppose 1952 was selected as the year with which to compare 1958 profits and labor costs? How did the corporation's 1958 change in pension funding and accounting affect the Union's advertisement?

2. Do you consider U.S. Steel's accounting treatment of pension costs for 1957, 1958 and 1959 to be in keeping with the principles of consistency and matching of revenue and expense? Explain.

3. Do you consider the auditors' 1958 report adequate? On what basis, if any, might the auditors have taken exception to U.S. Steel's accounting treatment of pension costs?

4. Do you agree with the 1960 reduction in pension costs of approximately $35 million resulting from actuarial refinements? Explain. Would this call for any action on the auditors' part?

5. Comment on U.S. Steel's policy of charging operations with the amount of actual *contributions* to the pension trust. Is this in accordance with ARB No. 47? Explain.

ACF Industries

ACF Industries was incorporated in 1899 as American Car & Foundry Co., the present name being adopted in 1954. Over the years it diversified and considerably expanded its operations. The company has four manufacturing divisions producing electronic and electro-mechanical equipment, railroad cars, carburetors, and valves. Two other divisions are service oriented, one associated with the Atomic Energy Commission's laboratories, and the other leasing more than 16,000 tank and special railroad cars to industry.

In its annual report for the fiscal year ended April 30, 1958, ACF's management stated that for several years the company had made pension contributions of approximately the maximum amount permitted by the Treasury as tax deductible. In the opinion of the company's consulting actuary, it was not necessary to continue funding at this maximum rate to maintain the plan on an actuarially sound basis. Management noted that "to do so causes a drain on working capital."

Upon the consulting actuary's recommendation, the company based its 1957-1958 pension contribution on the step-rate method instead of the level premium method which it had previously used. (See Appendix on page 510 for a description of these methods.) This change resulted in total contributions in the 1957-1958 fiscal year of $2,675,000 compared with the maximum allowable for tax purposes of $4,913,000. The reduced 1957-1958 contributions included $728,000 towards funding past service credits.

The auditors' opinion covering the 1958 fiscal year read as follows:

June 26, 1958

To the Board of Directors and the
Shareholders of ACF Industries, Incorporated

In our opinion, the [financial] statements . . . present fairly the financial position of ACF Industries, Incorporated and its consolidated subsidiaries at April 30, 1958 and the results of their operations for the year then ended, in conformity with generally accepted accounting principles. With the comments in Note 5 regarding pension expense, these principles were applied on a basis consistent with that of the preceding year. Our examination of such statements was made in accordance with generally accepted auditing standards, and accordingly included such tests of the accounting records and such other auditing procedures as we considered necessary in the circumstances.

Exhibit 1 shows pension contributions and other selected data for the fiscal years ended April 30, 1956 through 1961. Exhibit 2 gives Note 5 to the 1958 Financial Statements.

The increase in unfunded past service credits of $6,400,000 from 1958 to 1959 resulted primarily from a revision in the pension plan which provided increased benefits for past service. Contributions were made during the 1959 and 1960 fiscal years for current service costs and interest on unfunded past service credits; no contributions were made towards funding past service credits.

For the 1961 fiscal year, current service costs and interest on unfunded past service credits amounted to $2,890,000. This amount was reduced by realized actuarial gains of $1,543,000, leaving $1,347,000 which was contributed and charged to operations.

During the 1961 fiscal year, the company's consulting actuary extended the recalculations begun in 1958. Based on the step-rate method for the first time, unfunded past service credits were estimated to be $17,100,000 at April 30, 1961.

From 1959 through 1961, the auditors made no further reference to pensions in their opinions on the financial statements.

APPENDIX

The step-rate and level premium methods are methods of funding. Both are designed to achieve the same goal—the accumulation of a fund which, based on actuarial estimates, will be sufficient to provide the benefits granted in a pension plan.

Under the step-rate method, a contribution is made *each year* equal to the present value of the future amount required to provide additional retirement benefits "earned" *during that year*. Such annual contributions made on behalf of younger employees will be substantially less than those made for older employees since discounting takes place over a longer period. As an employee, or a group of employees, grows older, the discount period is shortened and annual contributions per employee increase in a "step-rate" pattern.

Under the level premium funding method, a constant "level" amount is contributed each year sufficient to accumulate exactly the same future sum as under the step-rate method. Compared to the step-rate method, the higher payments at younger ages are used to offset the deficiency in payments in later years.

Although the difference in annual contributions under the two methods may be quite significant at the outset, it tends to narrow with passage of time, particularly if the average age and other employee group characteristics are reasonably stable.

EXHIBIT 1

ACF Industries
Selected Financial Data 1956–1961
(000 omitted)

Year Ended April 30	Net Sales	Net Income	Pension Contributions[1]	Unfunded Past Service Credits
1956	$245,585	$8,008	$4,061	[2]
1957	294,592	9,033	4,102	$18,400
1958	294,894	7,851	2,675	16,800
1959	178,726	1,714	1,825	23,200
1960	263,611	3,933	2,585	24,300
1961	215,852	3,248	1,347	17,100

[1] Also amount charged to expense.
[2] Not given.

EXHIBIT 2

ACF Industries
Note 5 to the 1958 Financial Statements

Pension Contributions:

For the past several years the Company has contributed approximately the maximum permitted by the United States Internal Revenue Service as tax deductible under its retirement and pension plans. In the opinion of the consulting actuary, it is not necessary to continue funding at this maximum rate in order to maintain the programs on an actuarially sound basis. To do so causes a drain on working capital. Upon the recommendations of the consulting actuary, using an alternative computation, contributions for the fiscal year ended April 30, 1958 totaled $2,675,000 as compared with $4,913,000 which represents the maximum allowable as a tax deduction for the period. The unfunded past service credits of employees at April 30, 1958 amounted to $16,800,000 after deducting amounts provided during the year.

QUESTIONS:

1. Do you feel that the change made during the 1958 fiscal year from the level premium funding method to the step-rate method was proper? Explain.

2. Comment on the company's decision to discontinue contributions towards unfunded past service credits in the 1959 fiscal year.

3. Do you agree with the auditors' position in 1958? In 1959? In 1961? Explain.

4. Is there any need for pension funding and pension accounting policies to be directly related to one another? Explain.

5. What accounting disclosure do you recommend for unfunded past service credits?

6. What are actuarial gains?

The Colorado Fuel and Iron Corporation

Colorado Fuel and Iron Corporation (C.F. & I.) was incorporated in 1936. Its principal business is manufacturing and distributing iron, steel and certain fabricated steel products, and mining or quarrying iron ore, limestone, dolomite, and coal, chiefly for use in its own plants.

In July, 1949, the United Steel Workers of America— C.I.O. demanded increased pay rates and non-contributory pension and social insurance plans for its members. Negotiations between the industry and the union failed and the United Steel Workers struck the major steel companies including C.F. & I.

After a 42-day strike, an agreement was reached which provided, among other things, for the establishment of (1) a non-contributory pension plan and (2) a contributory social insurance program. Both items were approved for C.F. & I. employees at a special stockholders' meeting in February, 1950, and became effective on March 1, 1950. Under the agreement, the plan would continue in effect until December 31, 1951, and, unless terminated by the corporation after that date, until October 31, 1954.

The plan provided pensions at age 65 to any present and future employee who had at least 15 years' continuous service. The pensions were based upon one per cent of the employee's average monthly compensation during the 10 years before retirement multiplied by the total years of service. The minimum pension for employees reaching age 65, and having 25 years or more of continuous service, was $100 per month. The minimum granted an employee who had between 15 and 25 years of continuous service was determined by multiplying $4 by the number of continuous service years. Disability pensions were granted to permanently and totally disabled employees, with at least 15 years' continuous service, until they reached the age of 65, after which they were eligible for retirement pensions.

Actuarial estimates were made of the liabilities resulting from the plan, based on the plan's continuation until 1954 and certain assumptions concerning dates of retirement, continuity of employment, future compensation, and future old-age insurance benefits under the Federal Social Security Act. Pensions provided by the corporation were reduced by the amount of Social Security pension benefits received by retired employees. The *maximum* cost for the five-year period (January 1, 1950 through December 31, 1954) was estimated at $10,000,000, part of which related (1) to employees who had retired prior to December 31, 1949, and (2) to current employees who had already met the age and service requirements of the plan but had not yet retired. The corporation did not compel employees to retire at age 65.

The following accounting objectives were established:

(1) Allocate the $10,000,000 of maximum estimated cost over the five-year period, 1950 through 1954.
(2) Record the estimated actuarial liability for employees who (a) have been granted pensions, or (b) are eligible to retire.
(3) Record a deferred charge to future operations for the excess of the liability, as recorded in (2) above, plus cash already paid to the trustee over amounts charged to Pension Expense since January 1, 1950.

Exhibit 1 contains data for the years 1950 through 1961 for the following accounts which were established to meet these accounting objectives:

(1) "Payments to pension trust due within one year—estimated" (classified as a current liability),
(2) "Estimated present liability under pension plan—portion due after one year" (classified separately between long-term debt and stockholders' equity), and
(3) "Portion of estimated present liability under pension plan to be allocated against future operations" (classified as a deferred charge).

Effective November 1, 1954, the corporation agreed to increase benefits and extend the pension plan until October 31, 1957. This agreement was substantially similar to settlements made by other major steel companies. The minimum monthly pension to an employee who had reached age 65 and had at least 30 years of continuous service at the date of his retirement was $140. The minimum monthly pension granted to employees with between 15 and 30 years of continuous service was $140 less $2 for each year by which the number of years was less than 30. The minimum amount of disability pensions was also increased. No change was made in the minimum amount of pensions for any employees retired prior to November 1, 1954.

When an employee was granted a pension, the corporation *funded* it in five annual installments beginning in the year the employee retired. It was not the corporation's policy to fund pension benefits prior to an employee's retirement. The corporation's independent actuaries had prepared a table comparing the annual funding requirement of the present plan with and without the 1954 amendment. Note that in each of the succeeding years the total funding requirement consisted of the first annual installment for employees who retired in that year plus applicable unpaid installments for pensioners who retired in prior years and for whom five installments had not been paid. The actuaries' table is shown below:

First Annual Installment (similar annual installments required during next four years)	Without Amendment	With Amendment
Active Employees over Age 65 on 1/1/1955	$318,612	$839,172
Employees who will reach Age 65 between 1/1/1955 and 1/1/1956	77,651	206,555

Estimates shown in the table were based on the assumption that all employees eligible for retirement would retire at the date of earliest eligibility. Management noted that funding requirements would be lower if some employees did not retire when eligible.

Beginning in the 1955 fiscal year, for *accounting* purposes, as contrasted to the *funding* policy described above, charges to Pension Expense were made on the basis of averaging over the following *ten* years the estimated funding requirements for employees retired or who might be expected to retire during that period if the present plan continued in effect. The pension liability accounts shown on the balance sheet continued to represent the *unfunded* amount of the actuarial liability for employees retired or eligible to retire at the balance-sheet date. Likewise, the deferred charge account continued to represent the excess of amounts credited to the liability accounts, or paid in cash to the trustee, over amounts charged to Pension Expense since January 1, 1950.

In 1958 and 1960, benefits were again increased and it was necessary for the corporation to increase substantially its liability for pensions (and related costs applicable to future periods).

Selected financial and employment data for the years 1950 through 1961 are given in Exhibit 2.

EXHIBIT 1

The Colorado Fuel and Iron Corporation
Selected Balance Sheet Data as of June 30, 1950–1956
and as of December 31, 1957–1961

	Payments to pension trust due within one year—estimated	*Estimated present liability under pension plan—portion due after one year*	*Portion of estimated present liability under pension plan to be allocated against future operations*
1950	$ 650,000	$ 1,500,000	$ 1,374,395
1951	560,000	2,586,652	1,451,794
1952	690,200	2,487,577	1,009,196
1953	782,300	2,465,062	—
1954	1,149,100	2,399,961	—
1955	1,480,514	3,830,076	1,766,356
1956	1,602,889	4,761,825	1,989,661
1957	2,731,361	7,163,706	4,092,428
1958	3,297,147	14,267,792	10,953,400
1959	3,145,900	14,176,071	10,446,891
1960	4,670,677	20,189,771	17,939,572
1961	4,944,601	21,249,570	19,130,203

EXHIBIT 2

The Colorado Fuel and Iron Corporation
Selected Financial and Employment Data, 1950–1961

	Sales (000 omitted)	Net Income or (Loss) (000 omitted)	Total Wages and Salaries (000 omitted)	Pension Expense	Number of Employees	Number of Pensions Granted During Year for	
						Retirement	Disability
Year Ended June, 1950	$112,643	$ 4,406	$ 43,689	$1,012,549	13,963	352	26
1951	191,444	10,382	61,688	1,947,547	16,857	95	6
1952	195,757	5,762	67,120	1,901,395	17,127		
1953	248,836	8,031	89,810	1,714,639	22,215	844	53
1954	250,236	7,052	97,392	1,481,135	21,102	251	26
1955	257,543	10,887	102,246	2,006,280	20,652	318	35
1956	341,630	16,663	124,721	2,607,339	22,333	252	19
Dec., 1956[1]	148,367	5,131	60,000	N.A.	N.A.	N.A.	
Year Ended Dec., 1957	340,755	14,239	131,773	3,335,404	22,512	265[2]	
1958	276,164	2,147	116,459	3,937,011	19,001	404	
1959	280,288	4,365	111,337	4,408,063	20,053	358	
1960	249,109	(1,197)[3]	111,661	5,093,917	17,620	367	
1961	230,278	2,006[3]	105,218	4,910,823	15,364	359	

[1] Six months ended December 31, 1956. Fiscal year changed to calendar year.
[2] Retirement and disability pensions not separated after June, 1956.
[3] Before non-recurring losses of $3,606,104 in 1960 and $1,450,023 in 1961.
N.A. Not Available.

EXHIBIT 3

The Colorado Fuel and Iron Corporation
Working Capital Changes, Years Ended June 30, 1950–1952

	1950	1951	1952
Additions to Working Capital:			
Net income from operations	$ 4,406,226	$10,382,228	$ 5,761,965
Non-cash charges to income:			
Amounts provided for normal wear of facilities	3,436,047	3,913,896	5,064,010
Amounts charged to pension expense, less portion paid in year or payable within one year	125,605	1,009,253	343,523
Net book value of assets retired	193,032	279,867	510,937
Increase in operating reserves		446,150	
Amounts provided for mine stripping in excess of actual expenditures			610,693
Net increase in long-term debt	2,948,477		10,601,464
Purchase money notes payable		7,900,000	
Net Current assets of E. & G. Brooke Iron Company acquired through issuance of preferred and common stock			2,512,008
Other increases	95,511		1,206,694
Total Additions	$11,204,898	$23,931,394	$26,611,294
Deductions from Working Capital:			
Expenditures for property, plant and equipment	$ 4,098,551	$ 8,470,255	$20,040,585
Deferred expenditures for mine stripping	524,128	105,556	
Expenditures for rolls, moulds, etc.		583,774	573,672
Portion of bond indebtedness due under sinking fund requirements	250,000		
Purchase of preferred stock	51,784	365,801	250,083
Dividends declared on preferred and common stock	2,229,468	3,417,304	3,172,956
Other items	57,098	9,757,993	944,840
Total Deductions	$ 7,211,029	$22,700,683	$24,982,136
Increase in Working Capital	$ 3,993,869	$ 1,230,711	$ 1,629,158

QUESTIONS:

1. Give the journal entries pertaining to the pension plan which would have been made either during or at the close of the fiscal years ending (a) June 30, 1950, (b) June 30, 1951, and (c) June 30, 1952. Some information helpful in making these entries is found in Exhibit 3. Prove that total charges made to Pension Expense for the fiscal years 1950 through 1952 *plus* the balance of the deferred charge account at June 30, 1952, equals total cash payments to the trustee during the three years *plus* the balances of the two pension liability accounts at June 30, 1952.

2. Give an appraisal of the accounting procedures used by Colorado Fuel and Iron Corporation for its pension and social insurance plans from 1950 through 1954.

3. Comment on the accounting policy begun in 1955 of making charges to Pension Expense on the basis of averaging over the following *ten* years the estimated funding requirements for employees retired or who might be expected to retire during that period if the present plan continued in effect. Contrast this policy to the one used from 1950 through 1954. Do you believe the corporation should have changed its funding procedures in 1955 also to correspond with the change in accounting? Do you approve of the change in accounting policy? Explain.

The Michigan Salt Corporation

Michigan Salt is a large producer of various salt compounds used in many diverse fields ranging from metal treatment to antibiotic drugs. For many years, the corporation had been paying retirement benefits to former employees, but no formal plan existed and the benefits were not guaranteed. Recognizing the corporation's moral obligation to employees who had devoted a great portion of their lives to its service, the Board of Directors wanted to establish a qualified pension trust which would meet the requirements of the Internal Revenue Code.

In July, 1961, the Board of Directors met with the corporation's accounting and finance officers to discuss a proposed pension plan to be presented for stockholder approval at the annual meeting on October 21, 1961.

At the July meeting, the Board of Directors agreed that the plan should be non-contributory and provide lifetime pensions for participants. Certain benefits would also be provided in case of death, permanent disability or termination of employment. All pension contributions were to be irrevocable; the plan was to be administered by a Retirement Committee appointed by the Board of Directors; and, all assets of the trust were to be held by a bank acting as Trustee. The corporation would reserve the right to amend, modify, or terminate the plan at any time.

Tentatively it was agreed that the plan would become effective on June 30, 1962, if approved. Thus, the first fiscal year of the pension trust would end on June 29, 1963. The present value of the liability for past service costs had already been estimated by independent actuaries at $8,133,121. Current service costs *for the corporation's fiscal year ending June 30, 1963* (the first complete corporate fiscal period in which the plan would be in operation) would be $599,711.

At this point Mr. Smith, one of the Board members, suggested that pension costs attributable to past services should be charged to retained earnings because such payments were compensation for past services, and they should not be permitted to affect any period other than those in which the services were performed. Mr. Darr, Chairman of the Board, took the position that any contributions made in recognition of past services would benefit present and future periods and therefore should be charged to present and future periods.

After a short discussion, Mr. Jackson, Michigan's Treasurer, proposed an initial contribution to the Retirement Plan Trustee of the corporation's interest in 1,150 acres of land located in New York State. The land, which contained a deposit of high-grade salt rock, was independently appraised at $5,353,000. Because of increasing transportation costs to its existing recovery facilities, Michigan had discontinued mining the property some 10 years ago. At that time, the initial cost had been fully amortized and the property was now carried on the corporation's books at no value. Although it was not economical for Michigan to re-mine it, the property could be profitably worked by two recently-established, smaller mining firms with recovery facilities in the area.

For corporate purposes only (not for tax purposes), Mr. Jackson suggested the following accounting treatment for the contribution. The appraised value of the land was to be classified on the balance sheet under *Other Assets and Deferred Charges* as "Prepaid prior service benefit costs—Retirement Plan for Employees." A credit of like amount would be carried on the balance sheet as "Deferred credit resulting from transfer of property to Retirement Plan for Employees." Beginning with the corporate fiscal year ending *June 30, 1962*, and each subsequent year until the $5,353,000 contribution was exhausted, $813,312, representing the annual amortization of *past service cost* over a 10-year period, would be charged to expense and credited to "Prepaid prior service benefit costs—Retirement Plan for Employees." At the same time, an entry would be made to transfer a similar amount of the deferred credit to income. Royalty income from mining the property would be received directly by the Trustee. No current service costs would be recognized on the corporation's books for the year ended June 30, 1962, since the plan would be operative for only one day of that fiscal period. During the 1962–1963 fiscal year, the company would contribute $599,711 in cash to the Trustee and charge "Retirement Plan expense."

For income tax purposes only, the amount of $5,353,000 would be applied to *both* past and current service costs for the corporation's tax year ending June 30, 1962. Thus, the corporation would deduct *on its tax return* 10 per cent of the past service cost, $813,312, *plus* current service costs, $599,711, for the pension trust's 1962–1963 fiscal period (beginning June 30, 1962 and ending June 29, 1963). Provision would be made in the corporation's 1961–1962 accounts for $311,850, the estimated reduction in income taxes actually payable attributable to the excess pension expense deduction to be taken on the tax return *over* the amount recorded in the corporate accounts. This amount would be shown on the corporation's balance sheet under *Reserves* as "Deferred Federal income taxes."

For the tax year ending June 30, 1963, the corporation would again deduct $813,312 for past service costs. In addition, it would deduct the cash payment of $599,711 to be made to the Trustee during 1962–1963. *For income tax purposes,* this cash payment would apply to current service costs of the pension trust's *second* fiscal year (beginning June 30, 1963). *For income tax purposes,* current service costs of the trust's *first* fiscal year would be treated as explained above.

After this presentation, several questions were raised. Although he believed there would be no capital gains tax on the contribution, Mr. Edwards, Michigan's Comptroller, doubted that $599,711 of the $5,353,000 contribution could be taken as deduction for current service costs on the corporation's 1961–1962 tax return. In reply, Mr. Jackson stated that Michigan's tax counsel thought this procedure would be approved by the tax authorities since the pension plan would become effective within the corporation's 1961–1962 tax year.

Mr. Koenig, President of Michigan Salt, was concerned about both the accounting and tax aspects of the proposal. Assuming pre-tax net income of $3,000,000 for the year ending June 30, 1962, *before* inclusion of any income or expense attributable to the proposed pension plan and *before* considering the tax effects of the proposal, he said net income after taxes would be $1,440,000. Mr. Koenig was uncertain how the proposed transaction would affect reported net income. He was also concerned about the effect, if any, on the corporation's cash position since substantial capital expenditures were planned for the next few years. Exhibits 1 and 2 show the corporation's 1960 and 1961 financial statements.

The president wanted the various issues clarified and appointed Mr. Edwards to write a memorandum to the Board of Directors after consultation with the corporation's auditors and tax counsel.

EXHIBIT 1

The Michigan Salt Corporation
Consolidated Statement of Earnings and Retained Earnings
Fiscal Years Ended June 30, 1961 and June 30, 1960

	1961	1960
Net Sales	$81,481,965	$67,523,085
Cost and expenses:		
Cost of sales	$69,980,619	$58,518,458
Selling, general and administrative expenses	6,783,075	5,354,513
Research and development expenses	583,251	607,949
	$77,346,945	$64,480,920
Operating profit	$ 4,135,020	$ 3,042,165
Other deductions—net:		
Royalties on salt lands	$ 1,237,849	
Interest	142,199	$ 196,590
Loss (gain) on disposition of fixed assets	32,841	(222,631)
Miscellaneous	64,141	274,962
	$ 1,477,030	$ 248,921
Earnings before federal income taxes	$ 2,657,990	$ 2,793,244
Federal income taxes—estimated	1,306,000	1,128,000
Net earnings from operations	$ 1,351,990	$ 1,665,244
Special credits and charges:		
Special credit	$ 702,055	
Less special charges	(888,917)	$(1,000,000)
	$ (186,862)	$(1,000,000)
Net earnings and special charges (net)	$ 1,165,128	$ 665,244
Retained earnings at beginning of year	26,271,600	26,884,674
	$27,436,728	$27,549,918
Deduct dividends on preferred stock		
1961: $1.50 per share	319,579	
1960: $6.00 per share		1,278,318
Retained earnings at end of year	$27,117,149	$26,271,600

EXHIBIT 2

The Michigan Salt Corporation
Consolidated Balance Sheet as of June 30, 1961 and June 30, 1960

	1961	*1960*
Assets:		
Current Assets		
Cash	$ 6,861,443	$ 6,900,448
Accounts receivable	$21,361,565	$16,823,862
Less allowances for discounts and doubtful receivables	528,035	352,012
Net receivables	$20,833,530	$16,471,850
Inventories	$12,052,730	$11,990,112
Prepaid expenses	817,220	—
	$40,564,923	$35,362,410
Investments in non-consolidated subsidiary and affiliated companies	$ 72,251	$ 54,001
Other assets		48,881
Property, plant and equipment—substantially at cost	$59,433,620	$60,171,627
Less accumulated depletion, depreciation and amortization	36,325,116	35,795,083
	$23,108,504	$24,376,544
Other deferred charges	$ 1,261,982	$ 3,383,044
Patents	1	1
	$ 1,261,983	$ 3,383,045
	$65,007,661	$63,224,881
Liabilities:		
Current Liabilities		
Dividends payable on preferred stock		$ 319,579
Current installment of long-term obligations	$ 1,044,396	1,051,568
Accounts payable	2,955,203	2,057,345
Accrued liabilities	1,935,208	1,146,809
Federal and State income taxes—estimated	2,204,855	1,955,481
	$ 8,139,662	$ 6,530,782
Long-term obligations	$ 5,380,086	$ 6,347,333
Reserves for:		
Fire and tornado insurance, accident compensation, etc.	$ 163,028	$ 157,855
Deferred Federal income taxes	927,213	711,913
	$ 1,090,241	$ 869,768
Stockholders' equity:		
6 per cent Cumulative Participating Preferred Stock, $100 par	$21,305,215	$21,305,215
Common Stock—no par value	552,188	477,063
Capital in excess of amounts assigned to capital stock	1,423,120	1,423,120
Retained earnings	27,117,149	26,271,600
	$50,397,672	$49,476,998
	$65,007,661	$63,224,881

QUESTIONS:

1. As Mr. Edwards, prepare the memorandum to the Board of Directors explaining:
    (a) The appropriate accounting treatment of
        (1) past and current service costs of any pension plan, and
        (2) Michigan Salt's proposed contribution of the property to the Pension Plan Trustee;
    (b) The effect of the proposed transaction and the proposed accounting treatment on reported 1961–1962 net income assuming net income of $3,000,000 is realized for the year *before* taxes and *before* inclusion of any income or expense attributable to the pension plan;
    (c) The effect, if any, of the proposed transaction on the corporation's cash position in 1962 and in future years;
    (d) The probable reaction of the corporation's auditors to this transaction as expressed in their opinion on the financial statements.

2. At the annual meeting of stockholders on October 20, 1962, management was accused of making a number of accounting changes to reduce reported earnings. Based on the information given in the case, do you believe this allegation is correct regarding the accounting changes for pension costs? Explain.

CHAPTER FIFTEEN

Stock Options

Since 1950, the restricted stock option has become a popular method of compensating corporate executives. In that year, only 13.7 per cent of 525 companies surveyed[1] by the American Institute mentioned the existence of stock option plans. By 1962, such plans were used by 75 per cent of the 600 companies then surveyed.[1] Major problems in accounting for stock options involve determining (1) the amount of any compensation expense which should be recognized by a corporation granting stock options, and (2) the appropriate method of recording such compensation.

THE NATURE OF STOCK OPTIONS

A stock option entitles a corporate employee to purchase a specified number of his employer's common shares at a fixed price (the option price) over a period of years designated in the option agreement.[2] The option price is usually equal to or less than the market price (or other measure of fair value) on the *grant date*, the date of the option agreement between the corporation and the employee.

Before liberalization of the tax law in 1950, the difference between the option price and the market price on the *exercise date*, the date on which an employee purchases stock from the corporation at the option price, was taxable as ordinary income to the employee and was tax-deductible to the corporation. This tax treat-

---

[1] American Institute of Certified Public Accountants, *Accounting Trends and Techniques,* 5th ed. and 16th ed. (New York: The Institute, 1951 and 1962), p. 88 and p. 132, respectively.

[2] There is considerable variation in the terms of option agreements. In some, the employee can purchase all of the option shares at one time; in others, he can purchase shares only in periodic installments.

525

ment, which dated from 1945, gave options little added attraction as a means of compensation compared to regular salaries.

In 1950, Congress enacted a tax law creating the "restricted stock option" which later became Section 421 of the 1954 Internal Revenue Code. Under this section, no taxable income is realized by an employee upon exercise of a "restricted stock option." Furthermore, any gain realized on the sale of such stock after a specified time is subject to capital gains tax only. However, the code prohibits a tax deduction to the corporation for any element of employee compensation involved.

Under the tax laws, the basic requirements for a "restricted stock option" are:

1. The optionee must be an employee.
2. The option price must be at least 85 per cent of the fair market price at the time of grant.
3. The option must be nontransferable except by death and may be exercised only by the employee to whom granted during his lifetime.
4. The term of the option must not exceed 10 years.
5. If the optionee owns, directly or indirectly, more than 10 per cent of the outstanding voting stock of the employer corporation, the option price must be at least 110 per cent of the fair market price at the time of grant, and the option period must not exceed 5 years.
6. The option must be exercised while the option holder is still an employee or within three months after termination of employment.
7. After exercise of an option, the stock must be held for at least two years from the date of grant and six months from the date of exercise.
8. If an option is granted at an option price between 85 and 95 per cent of fair market price, upon sale of such shares the lesser of the difference between the option price and the fair market value on the date of grant or the fair market value on the disposition date is taxable at ordinary rates.

Some early stock option plans were viewed chiefly as a means of closing the growing gap between corporate owners and managers. It was believed that the opportunity to acquire an ownership interest in the corporation would provide management with added incentive to enhance corporate success and progress. However, rising stock prices during the 1950's and the tax advantages of restricted stock options have contributed to the current view that stock options are primarily a *compensation device* and only secondarily a means of encouraging executives' proprietary interests.

Two features of restricted stock options make them extremely attractive to executives of expanding corporations. One, the opportunity to exercise options at a fixed price for as long as ten years, limits the executive's risk by not requiring any commitment of capital until the market price of the stock substantially exceeds the option price. The other attractive feature is the tax treatment of restricted stock options—the avoidance of income tax when options are exercised and capital gains treatment on gains realized from selling option shares after the prescribed holding period.

A possible disadvantage both to the granting corporation and the executives concerned is the unfavorable reaction of some stockholders and other critics to the apparent high levels of compensation which may result from gains realized through stock option plans. Some stockholders feel the use of such plans dilutes their equity, especially when unissued, rather than reacquired, shares are used.

INSTITUTE PRONOUNCEMENTS

The proper accounting for stock options is a controversial subject. There is general agreement that the amount of compensation expense, if any, incurred by the granting corporation is the excess of the fair market price over the option price. However, there is disagreement regarding the date on which this excess should be measured. The three dates most commonly advocated are the (1) *grant date*, (2) *exercisable date*, or (3) *exercise date*. Only the second of these dates needs clarification. Many plans require that the recipient of a stock option fulfill certain conditions, such as continued employment for a specified time from the grant date, before the option will become exercisable. Thus, the exercisable date is usually the date on which such conditions are satisfied and the corporation is legally required to issue the stock if and when the employee desires to exercise his option.[3]

The first Institute pronouncement on stock options was ARB No. 37, *Accounting for Compensation in the Form of Stock Options*, issued in November, 1948. It advocated measuring compensation as the difference between the option price and the fair market price on the date the option became a legal obligation of the corporation, usually the *exercisable date*. Accordingly, there would be a charge to "Compensation expense"[4] and a credit to a capital account, such as "Capital

---

[3] In some plans, the exercisable date may follow the date on which such conditions are satisfied.

[4] If the time interval between the grant date and the exercisable date includes more than one fiscal period, accrual of compensation expense would be recognized in the appropriate fiscal periods to the extent feasible.

arising from grant of stock options." This entry would be made regardless of whether the option were exercised in the future.[5]

When restricted stock option plans became more common in the early 1950's, there were objections to the 1948 bulletin, particularly to its provision concerning the appropriate charge to compensation expense. In January, 1953, ARB No. 37 was revised and later included in ARB No. 43, Chapter 13, *Compensation*, as Section B, *"Compensation Involved in Stock Option and Stock Purchase Plans."* This section follows:

1. The practice of granting to officers and other employees options to purchase or rights to subscribe for shares of a corporation's capital stock has been followed by a considerable number of corporations over a period of many years. To the extent that such options and rights involve a measurable amount of compensation, this cost of services received should be accounted for as such. The amount of compensation involved may be substantial and omission of such costs from the corporation's accounting may result in overstatement of net income to a significant degree. Accordingly, consideration is given herein to the accounting treatment of compensation represented by stock options or purchase rights granted to officers and other employees.[6]

2. For convenience, this section will discuss primarily the problems of compensation raised by stock option plans. However, the committee feels that substantially the same problems may be encountered in connection with stock purchase plans made available to employees, and the discussion below is applicable to such plans also.

RIGHTS INVOLVING COMPENSATION

3. Stock options involving an element of compensation usually arise out of an offer or agreement by an employer corporation to issue shares of its capital stock to one or more officers or other employees (hereinafter referred to as grantees) at a stated price. The grantees are accorded the right to require issuance of the shares either at a specified time or during some determinable

---

[5] If the option were not subsequently exercised, the amount credited to "Capital arising from grant of stock options" might be transferred to "Contributed capital arising from nonexercised stock options."

[6] Bulletin 37, "Accounting for Compensation in the Form of Stock Options," was issued in November, 1948. Issuance of a revised bulletin in 1953 and its expansion to include stock purchase plans were prompted by the very considerable increase in the use of certain types of option and purchase plans following the enactment in 1950 of Section 130A of the Internal Revenue Code. This section granted specialized tax treatment to employee stock options if certain requirements were met as to the terms of the option, as to the circumstances under which the option was granted and could be exercised and as to the holding and disposal of the stock acquired thereunder. In general, the effect of Section 130A is to eliminate or minimize the amount of income taxable to the employee as compensation and to deny to the issuing corporation any tax deduction in respect of such restricted options. In 1951, the Federal Salary Stabilization Board issued rules and regulations relating to stock options and purchase rights granted to employees whereby options generally comparable in nature to the restricted stock options specified in Section 130A might be considered for its purposes not to involve compensation, or to involve compensation only in limited amounts.

period. In some cases the grantee's options are exercisable only if at the time of exercise certain conditions exist, such as that the grantee is then or until a specified date has been an employee. In other cases, the grantees may have undertaken certain obligations, such as to remain in the employment of the corporation for at least a specified period, or to take the shares only for investment purposes and not for resale.

RIGHTS NOT INVOLVING COMPENSATION

4. Stock option plans in many cases may be intended not primarily as a special form of compensation but rather as an important means of raising capital, or as an inducement to obtain greater or more widespread ownership of the corporation's stock among its officers and other employees. In general, the terms under which such options are granted, including any conditions as to exercise of the options or disposal of the stock acquired, are the most significant evidence ordinarily available as to the nature and purpose of a particular stock option or stock option plan. In practice, it is often apparent that a particular option or plan involves elements of two or more of the above purposes. Where the inducements are not larger per share than would reasonably be required in an offer of shares to all shareholders for the purpose of raising an equivalent amount of capital, no compensation need be presumed to be involved.

5. Stock purchase plans also are frequently an integral part of a corporation's program to secure equity capital or to obtain widespread ownership among employees, or both. In such cases, no element of compensation need be considered to be present if the purchase price is not lower than is reasonably required to interest employees generally or to secure the contemplated funds.

TIME OF MEASUREMENT OF COMPENSATION

6. In the case of stock options involving compensation, the principal problem is the measurement of the compensation. This problem involves selection of the date as of which measurement of any element of compensation is to be made and the manner of measurement. The date as of which measurement is made is of critical importance since the fair value of the shares under option may vary materially in the often extended period during which the option is outstanding. There may be at least six dates to be considered for this purpose: (a) the date of the adoption of an option plan, (b) the date on which an option is granted to a specific individual, (c) the date on which the grantee has performed any conditions precedent to exercise of the option, (d) the date on which the grantee may first exercise the option, (e) the date on which the option is exercised by the grantee, and (f) the date on which the grantee disposes of the stock acquired.

7. Of the six dates mentioned two are not relevant to the question considered in this bulletin—cost to the corporation which is granting the option. The date of adoption of an option plan clearly has no relevance, inasmuch as the plan per se constitutes no more than a proposed course of action which is ineffective until options are granted thereunder. The date on which a grantee disposes of the shares acquired under an option is equally immaterial since this date will depend on the desires of the individual as a shareholder and bears no necessary relation to the services performed.[7]

---

[7] This is the date on which income or gain taxable to the grantee may arise under Section 130A. Use of this date for tax purposes is doubtless based on considerations as to the ability of the optionee to pay taxes prior to sale of the shares.

8. The date on which the option is exercised has been advocated as the date on which a cost may be said to have been incurred. Use of this date is supported by the argument that only then will it be known whether or not the option will be exercised. However, beginning with the time at which the grantee may first exercise the option he is in effect speculating for his own account. His delay has no discernible relation to his status as an employee but reflects only his judgment as an investor.

9. The date on which the grantee may first exercise the option will generally coincide with, but in some cases may follow, the date on which the grantee will have performed any conditions precedent to exercise of the option. Accordingly this date presents no special problems differing from those to be discussed in the next paragraph.

10. There remain to be considered the date on which an option is granted to a specific individual and the date on which the grantee has fulfilled any conditions precedent to exercise of the option. When compensation is paid in a form other than cash the *amount* of compensation is ordinarily determined by the fair value of the property which was agreed to be given in exchange for the services to be rendered. The time at which such fair value is to be determined may be subject to some difference of opinion but it appears that the date on which an option is granted to a specific individual would be the appropriate point at which to evaluate the cost to the employer, since it was the value at that date which the employer may be presumed to have had in mind. In most of the cases under discussion, moreover, the only important contingency involved is the continuance of the grantee in the employment of the corporation, a matter very largely within the control of the grantee and usually the main objective of the grantor. Under such circumstances it may be assumed that if the stock option were granted as a part of an employment contract, both parties had in mind a valuation of the option at the date of the contract; and accordingly, value at that date should be used as the amount to be accounted for as compensation. If the option were granted as a form of supplementary compensation otherwise than as an integral part of an employment contract, the grantor is nevertheless governed in determining the option price and the number of shares by conditions then existing. It follows that it is the value of the option at that time, rather than the grantee's ultimate gain or loss on the transaction, which for accounting purposes constitutes whatever compensation the grantor intends to pay. The committee therefore concludes that in most cases, including situations where the right to exercise is conditional upon continued employment, valuation should be made of the option as of the date of grant.

11. The date of grant also represents the date on which the corporation foregoes the principal alternative use of the shares which it places subject to option, i.e., the sale of such shares at the then prevailing market price. Viewed in this light, the *cost* of utilizing the shares for purposes of the option plan can best be measured in relation to what could then have been obtained through sale of such shares in the open market. However, the fact that the grantor might, as events turned out, have obtained at some later date either more or less for the shares in question than at the date of the grant does not bear upon the measurement of the compensation which can be said to have been in contemplation of the parties at the date the option was granted.

MANNER OF MEASUREMENT

12. Freely exercisable option rights, even at prices above the current market price of the shares, have been traded in the public markets for many years, but there is no such objective means for measuring the value of an option which is not transferable and is subject to such other restrictions as are usually present in options of the nature here under discussion. Although there is, from the standpoint of the grantee, a value inherent in a restricted future right to purchase shares at a price at or even above the fair value of shares at the grant date, the committee believes it is impracticable to measure any such value. As to the grantee any positive element may, for practical purposes, be deemed to be largely or wholly offset by the negative effect of the restrictions ordinarily present in options of the type under discussion. From the viewpoint of the grantor corporation no measurable cost can be said to have been incurred because it could not at the grant date have realized more than the *fair value* of the optioned shares, the concept of fair value as here used encompassing the possibility and prospect of future developments. On the other hand, it follows in the opinion of the committee that the value to the grantee and the related cost to the corporation of a restricted right to purchase shares at a price *below* the fair value of the shares at the grant date may for the purposes here under discussion be taken as the excess of the then fair value of the shares over the option price.

13. While market quotations of shares are an important and often a principal factor in determining the fair value of shares, market quotations at a given date are not necessarily conclusive evidence.[8] Where significant market quotations cannot be obtained, other recognized methods of valuation have to be used. Furthermore, in determining the fair value of shares for the purpose of measuring the cost incurred by a corporation in the issuance of an option, it is appropriate to take into consideration such modifying factors as the range of quotations over a reasonable period and the fact that the corporation by selling shares pursuant to an option may avoid some or all of the expenses otherwise incurred in a sale of shares. The absence of a ready market, as in the case of shares of closely-held corporations, should also be taken into account and may require the use of other means of arriving at fair value than by reference to an occasional market quotation or sale of the security.

OTHER CONSIDERATIONS

14. If the period for which payment for services is being made by the issuance of the stock option is not specifically indicated in the offer or agreement, the value of the option should be apportioned over the period of service for which the payment of the compensation seems appropriate in the existing circumstances. Accrual of the compensation over the period selected should be made by means of charges against the income account. Upon exercise of an option the sum of the cash received and the amount of the charge to income should be accounted for as the consideration received on issuance of the stock.

15. In connection with financial statements, disclosure should be made as

---

[8] Whether treasury or unissued shares are to be used to fulfill the obligation is not material to a determination of value.

to the status of the option or plan at the end of the period of report, including the number of shares under option, the option price, and the number of shares as to which options were exercisable. As to options exercised during the period, disclosure should be made of the number of shares involved and the option price thereof.

One member of the committee, Mr. Mason, assented with qualification to adoption of section (b) of chapter 13. One member, Mr. Knight, did not vote.

Mr. Mason assents only under the assumption that if an option lapses after the grantee becomes entitled to exercise it, the related compensation shall be treated as a contribution by the grantee to the capital of the grantor.

Despite the warning contained in the first paragraph that "the amount of compensation involved [in stock option plans] may be substantial and omission of such costs from the corporation's accounting may result in overstatement of net income to a significant degree," the practical effect of the revised bulletin favoring the grant date has been that no compensation cost is recognized in the vast majority of option plans.[9] In most plans, the option price is either 100 per cent or 95 per cent of the market price on the grant date. In the latter case, the difference is considered immaterial, involving a discount no larger than would be true of most public share offerings.

The committee notes in paragraph 2 that the bulletin is applicable both to stock option and stock purchase plans. Stock purchase plans are used by many corporations to encourage a proprietary interest among employees and, in some cases, to raise substantial amounts of equity capital.[10] Such plans differ significantly from most stock option plans. Typically, all or a majority of employees are eligible to participate, and shares are purchased on an installment basis at some nominal discount under the fair market price. Generally these plans are not considered to result in employee compensation and therefore no compensation expense is recorded by the corporation.

The distinction drawn between the plans mentioned in paragraphs 3 and 4 is largely academic since, as already noted, use of the grant date as the time to measure compensation has resulted in the recognition of no compensation expense under most plans. Nevertheless, it may be helpful to discuss briefly these two paragraphs. The primary intent of a plan may be revealed by certain conditions imposed on the employee. The emphasis would appear to be on compensation when the corporation, in exchange for the stock option, requires a

---

[9] Note that under a restricted stock option plan net income *after taxes* is reduced by the *full amount* of any compensation recognized because such compensation is not a tax-deductible expense to the corporation.

[10] From 1946 through September 30, 1962, the American Telephone and Telegraph Company sold $1.8 billion of common stock to employees, approximately 19 per cent of all equity capital raised from investors during this period.

stated or minimum period of employee services. On the other hand, conditions limiting the employees' right to dispose of shares acquired through options, or requiring the employee to sell such stock to the corporation at no gain if he desires to dispose of his investment within a required holding period, would emphasize the proprietary investment nature of a plan, and not the compensation nature. Such restrictions on disposal of option stock are uncommon.

Because the revision represented such a marked departure from the earlier bulletin, the Institute's Research Department prepared the following statement which appeared in the April, 1953, issue of *The Journal of Accountancy*:[11]

Accounting for Stock Options:
Why Accounting Research Bulletin 37
Was Revised

Selection of a date on which to measure the compensation involved in stock-option and stock-purchase plans, under which corporate employers grant to employees options to buy corporation shares at favorable prices, has long been a troublesome problem. Accounting for this type of compensation to corporate employees has been dealt with on two occasions by the American Institute of Accountants committee on accounting procedure—first in Accounting Research Bulletin No. 37 and more recently in Accounting Research Bulletin No. 37 (Revised), "Accounting for Compensation Involved in Stock Option and Stock Purchase Plans," issued in January, 1953. In the latter bulletin the committee effected several changes and improvements over the predecessor bulletin.

DIFFERENCE BETWEEN NEW AND OLD BULLETINS

The most important difference between the revised bulletin and its predecessor is in the choice of the date as of which the compensation element, if any, of the option or purchase plan is measured. The manner of measuring the compensation cost to the employer—difference between option and fair market price—remains unchanged. Previously the date on which an option right became the property of the employee was considered to be the preferable time to measure the compensation. In the revised bulletin, the committee recognizes the date on which an option is granted to a specific individual as being the appropriate time to measure compensation cost to the employer.

FALLACY OF THE "PROPERTY" DATE

In the 1948 bulletin, selection of the date on which an option right became the "property" of the employee as the date on which to measure the compensation under the option was based primarily on the consideration that at such date the employee had met all conditions precedent to receiving the option, and the corporation had an unqualified obligation to issue shares if

---
[11] Research Department, American Institute of Accountants, "Accounting for Stock Options: Why Accounting Research Bulletin 37 Was Revised," *Journal of Accountancy*, Vol. 95, April 1953, pp. 436-39.

the employee elected to exercise the option. However, the committee has concluded from experience with the old bulletin that this was not a satisfactory approach in that it introduced irrelevant factors which frequently could result in an unforeseeable and unreasonable impact on corporation accounting, and in any event the principle of the bulletin could be nullified by simple changes in the form of agreement.

In essence, a stock-option arrangement is an optional grant of a portion of the future equity of the corporation at what may be a favorable price. If the option price is below fair market value at the grant date, a charge equivalent to the difference reasonably reflects the advantage accorded the grantee, except for such value as may be assignable to his "call" on the stock for a period of time.

An option to purchase stock, even at a price above the market or fair value at the grant date, undoubtedly has some "value." Stock options which are not conditional upon personal factors and which are freely transferable can be and have been valued by customary market machinery on the basis of the then existing factors. However, it is impossible to "value" in such a manner an option which carries a variety of personal contingencies such as employment and nontransferability. Investment bankers have stated that such options have no "market" that can be evaluated. Accordingly, the committee is of the opinion that it is impracticable to measure any such value and that corporate accounting for such options should be based upon the cost of the option to the corporation.

It should be noted that option plans are not profit-sharing devices dependent upon hindsight but, rather, are a forward-looking medium entered into by the parties in advance of services. It is at the date on which an option is granted to a specific individual that the employer and employee reach a meeting of the minds as to the basis of the option. Where a stock-option plan is made generally available to substantial groups of existing employees, it is similarly current conditions and current estimates of the future which are given consideration.

The date of grant also represents the date on which the corporation foregoes the alternative use of the shares placed subject to the option; namely, the sale of such shares at the then-prevailing market price.[12] It follows that the *cost to the corporation* of thus utilizing the shares can best be measured in relation to what could have been obtained through sale of the optioned shares at that time.

Prior to revision, Bulletin 37 employed a measure of compensation (difference between option and market price at the "property" date) which was not only of an unknown amount at the date of grant, but which was also affected by subsequent vagaries of the market, including the effects of forces completely unrelated to the operations of the issuing corporate employer and the efforts of the employees involved.

OLD BULLETIN NOT APPLICABLE TO MODERN PLANS

The undesirable accounting impact of old Bulletin No. 37 has for some time been avoided by draftsmen of option plans by (a) drawing plans so that the "property," or exercisable, date coincides with the grant date or falls very

---

[12] The fact that a corporation may easily be able to increase its authorized capital to obtain additional shares is not relevant to the question of determining cost here involved.

shortly thereafter, and (b) providing for an integral or simultaneous employment agreement [containing conditions or restrictions, such as continued
employment for a specified period, which otherwise would have been contained in the option agreement, but were excluded from it to make the
options immediately exercisable]. The form of an option and the "property
date" are essentially questions of law, and the accountant is obviously dependent upon the legal effect of option documents and upon interpretations
as to what constitutes the "property date," although he is not necessarily
controlled by such recitals as that the option "is not to be compensatory."
While such avoidance may have been inadvertent, it was nonetheless real.

Serial option plans are attractive because they are well adapted to the
purposes of sound corporate management and the establishment of incentives
in that the number of shares periodically made available to the employee
can be appropriately related to successive periods of service. However, the
old bulletin tended to bar or discourage the use of serial option plans because it required the corporation to accept a series of indeterminate future
income charges. The revised bulletin treats in the same way, both (a) the
immediately or soon exercisable single option, and (b) the serial option,
thereby promoting use of the latter more desirable form.

The adoption in 1950 of Section 130A of the Internal Revenue Code has
popularized an entirely new type of option plan, generally called the "restricted" option plan. Application of old Bulletin No. 37 to such plans
presented a special problem because of nondeductibility of any expense by
the corporation in augmenting such a plan, for which an equitable solution was needed.[13] Restricted stock options are conditioned upon a number
of personal factors, are not transferable, and contain other terms and conditions such that a market price for the option is not determinable. It is
obvious that the existence of such conditions result in lesser value than the
market would set for a similar option free of such conditions. It is reasonable to value a restricted option at the excess of market (or 95 per cent of
market) at the grant date over the option price and to consider that any
additional value inherent in the restricted option is approximately offset by
the conditions and restrictions.[14]

Both the Congress, in enacting Section 130A, and the Salary Stabilization
Board, in implementing the salary stabilization provisions of the Defense
Production Act, have selected the grant date as the time for determining
whether compensation exists and have followed substantially the procedure
indicated by the revised bulletin in measuring the compensation involved, if
any.

OTHER CONSIDERATIONS

It seems in the light of experience basically illogical to consider a date
other than the date of grant in measuring compensation cost. Once an
option is granted to a particular employee, it is largely within his personal
control whether the option becomes exercisable (since his continued employment is a prime corporate objective) and is in fact exercised. Variations in

---

[13] No expense appears to be deductible by the corporation even where an employee
fails to comply with the requirements of Section 130A and so loses his special
tax status.

[14] In retrospect of course, this may or may not be accurate because of subsequent
market changes.

price while the employee is unable to or delays exercise represent changes in the option value to him, and may reflect the results of his personal speculation, but they should not be deemed to affect the cost of the option to the corporation.

Further, stockholders of the issuing corporation are likely to be unduly penalized if the compensation cost is not determined as of the date the option is granted. They, of course, sustain the contemplated dilution of their equity when additional shares are issued. They may also suffer from an unpredictably large income charge as the result of a substantial increase in the market price of the shares. In fact, there have been instances in which the size of the charge required by the old bulletin was so great (as a sole result of unforeseeable increases in the level of stock prices generally) as to produce a negative net income.

It seems clear that market prices subsequent to the grant date should not be compared with the option price to determine the cost of the option to the corporation because:

a. Future prices of shares are dependent on events not determinable or foreseeable at the grant date.

b. The value of an option at a given date is unrelated to subsequent increases or decreases in the price of the shares involved. Changes in market prices after the grant date are not a logical basis on which to determine the value assignable to the option when granted and consequently to the amount of "compensation" involved in an option.

c. It is particularly illogical to select some future date, arbitrarily set long in advance, as the date on which to compare the then market price with the option price for the purpose of retroactively determining the cost of an option. This is true whether the first date on which the option became exercisable or any later date, such as the date of actual exercise, is selected for such purpose.

ADDITIONAL FEATURES OF REVISED BULLETIN

Revised Bulletin 37 also deals specifically with the accounting for two types of situations not clearly covered in the old bulletin—stock-option plans and stock-purchase plans for the purpose of raising capital or obtaining wider employee stock ownership or both. The new bulletin gives general criteria for distinguishing such plans from those in which the primary consideration is compensation of employees.

Finally revised Bulletin 37 furthers the trend toward more complete and adequate disclosure by calling for disclosure of the status of the option plan at the end of the period of report, including the number of shares under option, their option price, and the number of shares as to which options were *exercisable*. In addition, as to options *exercised* during the period, the revised bulletin calls for disclosure of the number of shares involved and the option price of such shares.

SUMMARY

Revised Bulletin 37 represents an advance and improvement over its predecessor in accomplishing the following:

a. It is applicable to all types of stock-option and purchase plans including the newest and most popular types based on Section 130A.

b. It provides for a more realistic accounting treatment of compensatory options by making the measure of compensation cost the value of the option determined on the basis of information available to the employer and the employee when the option plan was put into effect. In so doing it avoids charges which could not be contemplated when the agreement was made, with a resultant greater equity to stockholders.

c. It provides for more adequate disclosure of the status of option plans with resultant safeguards to stockholders and the investing public.

DISCLOSURE

After release of ARB No. 37 (Revised) in January, 1953, the Securities and Exchange Commission requested views on its tentative plan to continue the requirements of the original bulletin in financial statements filed with it. Subsequently, "in the light of comments received, the Commission deemed it inappropriate to prescribe a procedure for determining the amount of cost, if any, . . . to be reflected in [financial statements filed with it]. However, in order that investors may be apprised of the monetary significance of the concessions made by [corporations] to [their] officers and employees through the granting of stock options,"[15] the Commission adopted the following disclosure rule :[16]

(1) A brief description of the terms of each option arrangement shall be given, including (i) the title and amount of securities subject to option; (ii) the year or years during which the options were granted; and (iii) the year or years during which the optionees became, or will become, entitled to exercise the options.

(2) State (a) the number of shares under option at the balance sheet date, and the option price and the fair value thereof, per share and in total, at the dates the options were granted; (b) the number of shares with respect to which options became exercisable during the period, and the option price and the fair value thereof, per share and in total, at the dates the options became exercisable; and (c) the number of shares with respect to which options were exercised during the period, and the option price and the fair value thereof, per share and in total, at the dates the options were exercised. The required information may be summarized as appropriate with respect to each of these categories.

(3) State the basis of accounting for such option arrangements and the amount of charges, if any, reflected in income with respect thereto.

The SEC's disclosure requirement, in contrast to the disclosure recommendations contained in paragraph 15 of the revised Institute bulletin, enables the reader to compute the compensation cost, if any, which would be recorded using any of three dates—the grant date, the exercisable date, and the exercise date. The following notes from the 1961 annual report of the National Dairy Products Corpo-

---

[15] Securities and Exchange Commission, *Nineteenth Annual Report of the Securities and Exchange Commission, Fiscal Year Ended June 30, 1953.*

[16] Securitites and Exchange Commission, *Accounting Series Release 76,* November, 1953.

ration and from a prospectus filed with the SEC by the Corporation on March 22, 1962, both pertain to stock options. The note in the annual report, which complies with the disclosure recommendations of paragraph 15 of the revised Institute bulletin and also with the generally similar requirements of the New York Stock Exchange, follows:

EMPLOYEES' STOCK OPTION PLAN

Under the Employees' Stock Option Plan approved in 1952 and amended in 1958, there were 492,503 shares of the authorized and unissued common stock of the Company reserved at December 30, 1961, for sale to officers and other key employees. At that date 1,614 employees held options to purchase a total of 448,738 shares at prices ranging from $25.975 to $74.25 per share, with an aggregate purchase price of $21,064,048, and 43,765 shares remained available for future grants. All options become exercisable in cumulative periodic installments extending over the terms of such options (generally ten years or to earlier retirement date), commencing not earlier than one year from date of grant. Options became exercisable during 1961 with respect to 71,513 shares having an aggregate purchase price of $2,677,585. On October 5, 1961, options were granted to purchase 65,675 shares at $74.25 per share. During the year 100,606 shares were issued under the Plan and the proceeds of $3,382,030 were credited to the common stock and capital surplus accounts.

The note in the prospectus filed with the SEC stated:

The Employees' Stock Option Plan, approved by the stockholders of the Corporation on April 17, 1952, authorized the granting, from time to time to April 17, 1957, of options and the sale thereunder to key employees of the Corporation and its subsidiaries of 300,000 shares of the Corporation's common stock. At December 30, 1961 (after giving effect to the two-for-one split of the Corporation's common stock on August 17, 1954) there were 206,516 shares of the Corporation's authorized and unissued common stock reserved for sale under options outstanding at that date which were granted prior to April 17, 1957.

The stockholders of the Corporation on April 17, 1958 approved an amendment of the Employees' Stock Option Plan authorizing the granting of options and sale thereunder to key employees of the Corporation and its subsidiaries of an additional 300,000 shares of the Corporation's common stock. Options under the Plan as amended may be granted by the Board of Directors from time to time through April 17, 1963 at option prices fixed by the Board of Directors but to be not less than the closing sale price of such stock on the New York Stock Exchange on the day the option is granted. On December 30, 1961 there were outstanding options to purchase 242,222 of such shares.

Under the Plan, which is a restricted stock option plan, all options are nonassignable and are exercisable in cumulative periodic installments, the first of which is not exercisable earlier than one year from the date of the option grant. The term of each option is to a date ten years from the date it is granted, or to a date three months after the normal retirement age of 65 of the employee to whom it was granted, whichever is the shorter period.

Further information relating to shares subject to options under the Plan and the prices therefor is summarized on the following page:

	Number of Shares	Option Price		Market Value[17]	
		Range of Option Prices	Total Option Price	Range of Market Values	Total Market Value
				at dates options were granted	
Authorized and unissued shares reserved for sale, under the Plan, at December 30, 1961	492,503				
Options outstanding December 30, 1961	448,738	$25.975 to $74.25	$21,064,048	$ 26.50 to $74.25	$21,386,957
				at dates options became exercisable	
Options becoming exercisable during period :					
1957	59,292	$25.975 to $38.60	$ 1,833,664	$ 34.50 to $38.25	$ 2,124,269
1958	63,124	25.975 to 38.60	1,989,046	38.625 to 48.25	2,803,164
1959	72,797	25.975 to 48.25	2,540,516	47.50 to 53.50	3,688,250
1960	69,755	25.975 to 48.25	2,436,729	47.75 to 63.00	3,784,653
1961	71,513	25.975 to 61.50	2,677,585	62.25 to 77.375	4,888,878
				at dates options were exercised	
Options exercised during period :					
1957	24,976	$25.975 to $38.60	$ 688,790	$33.125 to $38.125	$ 908,207
1958	49,478	25.975 to 38.60	1,436,010	38.625 to 49.375	2,203,530
1959	62,386	25.975 to 48.25	1,827,888	47.25 to 54.375	3,167,048
1960	54,456	25.975 to 48.25	1,679,674	46.00 to 63.00	2,978,809
1961	100,606	25.975 to 61.50	3,382,030	60.00 to 78.375	6,821,228

No charges have been reflected in the Corporation's earnings statements for any year with respect to the Employees' Stock Option Plan. The proceeds from the sale of stock which has been issued under this Plan have been credited to the Corporation's common stock and capital surplus accounts.

---

[17] Based on reported quotations on the New York Stock Exchange using the last quoted sale on the day in which the event occurred.

CONTINUING CRITICISM OF ACCOUNTING FOR STOCK OPTIONS

As in the problem of accounting for pension costs, discussed in Chapter 14, tax considerations appear to have exerted considerable influence on accounting for stock options. The granting and exercise of a *restricted* stock option have no tax consequences for either the employee or the employer corporation. Under this interpretation, the employee has received no income; therefore, the corporation cannot have incurred an expense. Some accountants and other critics who have studied the problem continue to argue that stock options clearly involve compensation in excess of any difference between the option price and the fair market value on the grant date. One group proposes a return to use of the exercisable date, another favors the exercise date, while a third group accepts the logic of the grant date, but rejects the committee's view that compensation expense can best be measured by what could have been obtained from selling option shares in the open market on the grant date. This last group proposes various methods for determining an appropriate value of either the option itself or of the future services for which the option is compensation. Because such methods[18] are inevitably quite subjective they have received only limited attention from the accounting profession.

REFERENCES

Andersen, Arthur, & Co., *Accounting and Reporting Problems of the Accounting Profession*, 2nd ed. Chicago: Arthur Andersen & Co. (Oct. 1962), 77–83.

Baker, John C., "Stock Options at the Crossroads," *Harvard Business Review*, 41 (Jan.–Feb. 1963), 22 ff.

Bomeli, Edwin C., "Stock Option Plans—Full Disclosure," *Accounting Review*, 37 (Oct. 1962), 741–45.

Campbell, Edwin D., "Stock Options Should Be Valued," *Harvard Business Review*, 39 (Jul.–Aug. 1961), 52–58.

Ford, Henry, II, "Stock Options Are in the Public Interest," *Harvard Business Review*, 39 (Jul.–Aug. 1961), 45–51.

Griswold, Erwin N., "Are Stock Options Getting Out of Hand?" *Harvard Business Review*, 38 (Nov.–Dec. 1960), 49–55. Letters of particular interest to accounting students regarding this article appeared in 39 (Mar.–Apr. 1961), 17, and 39 (May–Jun. 1961), 22–28.

Holland, Daniel M. and Wilbur G. Lewellen, "Probing the Record of Stock Options," *Harvard Business Review*, 40 (Mar.–Apr. 1962), 133–50.

Lent, George E. and John A. Menge, "The Importance of Restricted Stock Options in Executive Compensation," *Management Review*, 24 (Jun. 1962), 6–13.

---

[18] For examples, see articles by Campbell and Raby on this and the following page.

Raby, William L., "Accounting for Employee Stock Options," *Accounting Review*, 37 (Jan. 1962), 28–38.

"SEC Proposes New Accounting Rule on Stock Options," (Official Releases), *Journal of Accountancy*, 95 (Apr. 1953), 503–5.

Sheehan, Robert, "The Stir over Stock Options," *Fortune*, 66 (Oct. 1962), 131 ff.

Sweeney, Daniel L., *Accounting For Stock Options*. Ann Arbor, Michigan: Bureau of Business Research, School of Business Administration, University of Michigan, 1960.

Radio Corporation of America

Radio Corporation of America (RCA) was incorporated in 1919 by the General Electric Company. Its principal business is the development and manufacture of radio, television, and allied products. It also manufactures consumer, commercial, and military electronic apparatus, operates television and radio stations, and supplies programs for broadcasting.

When the Revenue Act of 1950 clarified the tax status of stock options, the corporation granted options for 100,000 common shares to David Sarnoff, Chairman of RCA's Board of Directors, and for 50,000 shares to President Frank M. Folsom. The options were exercisable at $17.75 per share, the closing price of RCA common stock on the New York Stock Exchange on the day before the options were granted. The options were nontransferable and exercisable in whole or in part at any time until November 3, 1955, as long as the optionee remained employed by RCA.

The following disclosure was made in the stockholders' equity section of the balance sheet in the 1950 annual report:

Common stock, no par, shares authorized 18,500,000,
    outstanding 13,881,016 (Note 5), at a stated value of $27,762,032

Note 5 read as follows:

On November 3, 1950 the Board of Directors granted, subject to stockholders' approval, options entitling two officers to purchase a total of 150,000 shares of common stock on or before November 3, 1955 at $17.75 per share, representing the market price on November 2, 1950.

At the annual meeting on May 1, 1951, the stockholders approved the two grants.

In February, 1953, the two officers exercised their options and common stock was issued in exchange for $2,662,500 paid by the officers to the corporation. For each share sold, the stated value of $2.00 per share was credited to common stock and the re-

542

maining $15.75 per share was added to capital surplus. The closing market price of RCA common stock on the exercise date was $25.50 per share.

In a proxy statement dated March 5, 1954, it was stated that the difference between the option price and the market price at the time of exercise did not represent a realizable profit because under law the stock had to be held for at least six months before any gain could be realized by the optionee.

Mr. Sarnoff reached RCA's normal retirement age in 1956. As an inducement to retain his services for a longer period, the Board of Directors proposed that an additional stock option for 100,000 shares be granted to Mr. Sarnoff. A reference to this proposal in the 1956 proxy statement read in part:

> On July 1, 1955 the Board of Directors ... authorized an employment agreement with David Sarnoff providing, among other things, for his services to RCA for a period of ten years past his normal retirement date of March 1, 1956, for his present rate of compensation continuing during such ten year period and for his waiving participation in the RCA Incentive Plan. In consideration of David Sarnoff executing the employment agreement, the Board of Directors on July 1, granted him an option qualifying as a 'restricted stock option' under the 1954 Internal Revenue Code to purchase 100,000 shares of Common Stock of the Corporation at $49.64 per share, representing 95 per cent of the market price of $52.25 per share on the date of grant.
>
> The option is exercisable ... in whole or in part at any time on or before June 30, 1965 ....

RCA did not intend to issue new stock, as it had previously, but instead planned to use treasury stock purchased on the New York Stock Exchange, deducting from capital surplus the excess of cost of such treasury shares over the proceeds from sale of optioned shares.

In its 1955 annual report, management made the following disclosure:

a) On the balance sheet as of December 31, 1955, under "Investment":

RCA Common stock held in treasury,
at cost—89,540 shares (Notes 8 and 9) $3,861,143

b) In Note 8:

Stock option: On July 1, 1955 the Board of Directors granted, subject to ratification by stockholders at their next annual meeting on May 1, 1956, a stock option entitling the Chairman of the Board to purchase a total of 100,000 shares of common stock on or before June 30, 1965 at $49.64 per share, representing 95 per cent of the market price on July 1, 1955. The closing market price of RCA Common Stock on the New York Stock Exchange on February 14, 1956 was $41⅜ per share.

Note 9 referred to the RCA Incentive Plan.

The second stock option was approved by the stockholders at their 1956 annual meeting.

In 1957, the stock option program was expanded and options for 233,000 shares were granted to 59 officers and other key employees. The option price was the market value on the grant date and the options, most of which did not expire for 10 years, were exercisable in cumulative annual installments of 20 per cent. Accordingly, options for 46,600 shares were exercisable at December 31, 1957. Treasury stock was still used when options were exercised and the excess of cost of treasury stock over proceeds received upon exercise of stock options was deducted from capital surplus.

Exhibit 1 shows selected financial data from RCA's annual reports for the years 1950 through 1958.

EXHIBIT 1

Radio Corporation of America
Selected Financial Data for the Years 1950 through 1958
(000 omitted from dollar amounts)

	Net Income	Number of Common Shares Issued	Stockholders' Equity			
			Preferred Stock	Common Stock	Capital Surplus	Retained Earnings
1950	$46,250	13,881,016	$14,574	$27,762	$6,652	$123,802
1951	31,193	13,881,016	14,574	27,762	6,652	137,984
1952	32,325	13,881,016	14,574	27,762	6,652	153,299
1953	35,022	14,031,016	14,574	28,062	9,014	164,068
1954	40,525	14,031,016	14,574	28,062	9,014	182,549
1955	47,525	14,031,022	14,574	28,062	9,025[1]	206,020
1956	40,031	14,031,100	14,574	28,062	9,030[1]	222,087
1957	38,549	14,031,114	14,574	28,062	9,019[1]	236,727
1958	30,942	14,031,114	14,574	28,062	9,019	243,783

[1] Capital Surplus Changes (in *actual* dollar amounts, 000 *not* omitted):

	1955	1956	1957
(a) Award value over (under) cost of treasury stock distributed under RCA Incentive Plan	$10,938	$ 921	$(11,860)
(b) Excess paid in over stated value of common stock issued upon conversion of debentures	292	3,808	684
	$11,230	$4,729	$(11,176)

QUESTIONS:

1. For accounting purposes, should the excess of market value over the option price be determined at (1) the grant date, (2) the exercisable date, or (3) the exercise date, in estimating the amount of compensation paid the employee? What are the merits of using (1), (2), and (3) above?

2. Assume that options for 1,000 shares of $2.00 par common stock are exercisable at $10 per share and the market price at the exercisable date is $20. Assuming compensation expense is measured as of the exercisable date, give journal entries when:

(a) authorized but unissued shares are used;

(b) shares are purchased by the corporation on the market on the exercisable date;

(c) shares are purchased by the corporation between the grant date and the exercisable date (assume shares are purchased at $15).

3. Assume that market value exceeds the option price on the exercise date. From an accounting viewpoint, do you agree with RCA's management that no profit is realized by the optionee upon exercise of the option? Explain.

4. Why do you suppose RCA changed from the use of authorized but unissued stock to treasury stock in meeting option obligations?

5. In its expanded 1957 stock option plan, RCA charged capital surplus with the excess of treasury stock cost over the proceeds from sale of option shares. Do you support this accounting? If not, what procedure would you use?

6. Do you approve of RCA's balance-sheet classification for shares held in the treasury at December 31, 1955? Explain.

Standard Oil Company
(New Jersey)

The Standard Oil Company of New Jersey (referred to often as "Jersey") is primarily a holding company. Several of its subsidiaries are engaged in the acquisition, exploration, and exploitation of oil and gas lands. Other subsidiaries buy and sell crude oil and operate huge pipe-line systems and a large tanker fleet to distribute petroleum products.

The Board of Directors proposed a stock option plan in the 1951 proxy statement to be voted on at the annual meeting of the stockholders in June. The plan was intended to provide additional incentives for executives of the company and its wholly-owned subsidiaries. The main provisions of the incentive stock option plan were:

1. No more than 1,800,000[1] shares could be sold,
2. No more than 600,000 shares could be sold to directors,[2]
3. Options granted to directors could not exceed 180,000 shares in any calendar year,
4. Options granted to any one director could not exceed 24,000 shares in any calendar year,
5. Options granted to any one director could not exceed 72,000 shares during the term of the plan,
6. Each option would be exercisable after one year of continued employment following the grant date,
7. The option price would be 95 per cent of the fair market value on the grant date,[3]
8. All options would expire prior to December 31, 1961,

---

[1] This figure and all others pertaining to number of shares have been adjusted, where appropriate, for the following stock splits: two for one on June 12, 1951, and three for one on February 10, 1956. As a result of these adjustments, all share figures are in terms of shares outstanding at December 31, 1961.

[2] Standard Oil has no "outside" directors. All directors are full-time executives of the company.

[3] Determined as the mean between the low and high quotations on the New York Stock Exchange.

9. Previously issued shares, reacquired by purchase, would be used to meet the options, and
10. Shares purchased by company executives through the exercise of options should be for investment purposes.

On June 29, 1951, eighty key executives were granted options for a total of 491,400 shares at a price of $19.02 per share. Of this total, 167,280 were granted to directors. In 1951, Jersey purchased 380,100 shares of its outstanding stock for $8,516,568. These shares were carried at cost under the caption "Prepaid Charges and Other Assets" following the "Fixed Assets" category on the company's balance sheet. In the financial section of the 1951 annual report, management explained in detail the number of shares optioned under the plan. The number of shares subject to outstanding options was reduced to 486,567 in 1952 by the exercise of options for 4,833 shares. Exhibit 1 shows various data pertaining to Jersey's stock option plan for the years 1951 through 1960. When options were exercised, the excess of the cost to the company of the reacquired shares over the option price was charged as additional compensation expense.

Some of Jersey's shareholders did not approve of the stock option plan, referring to the high salaries that key employees already received (Exhibit 2). In 1951, a shareholder instituted two suits against the company seeking to restrain the operation of the stock option plan and to invalidate options already granted. However, the suits were not successful and the Superior Court of New Jersey rendered a decision in 1952 which sustained the validity of the plan.

At March 15, 1959, options for 1,752,260 shares of Jersey's capital stock had been granted from the 1,800,000 shares authorized by the 1951 plan. At the annual meeting on May 27, 1959, management presented a new plan for stockholder approval. The proposed plan *differed* from the 1951 plan in the following respects:

1. Number of shares provided under the 1959 plan as compared with the 1951 plan:

	1951 Plan	1959 Plan
Maximum shares that could be sold:		
Total	1,800,000	3,000,000
To all company directors	600,000	500,000
Maximum shares that could be optioned:		
By all company directors during one year	180,000	150,000
By one company director during one year	24,000	20,000
By one company director during term of plan	72,000	60,000

2. The option price could not be less than 100 per cent of the fair market value on the grant date,
3. Each option would be exercisable only after two years of continued employment following the grant date,
4. Options could be granted up to May 27, 1964. Options would expire no later than ten years after the grant date, and

5. Either previously issued and reacquired shares or authorized but unissued shares could be used to meet the options.

At the stockholders' meeting on May 27, 1959, several shareholders supported the plan. One stockholder, noting that he had studied the option plans of other large corporations, stated that half of these had bonus or deferred incentive compensation plans in addition to stock option plans. Also, he stated that salaries of many of Jersey's top executives were below the average for the corporations he had studied.

This discussion followed his statement:

SHAREHOLDER: We should not compare with other companies in other industries, but with oil companies, and I call to the attention of the stockholders that one of the very large ones has no stock option plan.

Also, the new plan provides something which the old plan, as I understand it, did not provide. It provides that unissued shares may be used for options. If those shares are issued and used for options, this is definitely a dilution of your equity. You are cutting more pieces of pie for the dividend, which does not seem to be increasing and even may be threatened.

I would like to speak also about the inflationary aspect of the plan. If we give these options, labor is going to want its round robin. This is going to add to the cost of gasoline, the cost of our doing business, and is, in my opinion, particularly unwise at this time when management should be tightening its belt as an example to labor if we are not going to have another round of price increases and inflation.

CHAIRMAN: I think I made it clear that this isn't any new experiment with us. We started this in '51, and it worked. You can argue what causes inflation many different ways. I don't think our particular plan is inflationary. I think, as I have stated before, that this is a good thing for the company and good for the stockholders. We respect your views on it, and thank God that we're living in a country where we can still disagree with each other and debate things.

SHAREHOLDER: In this intellectual argument I feel hesitant to say what I have to say because it's purely emotional. Speaking for the average woman, any management which keeps an unfailing policy of clean washrooms deserves all the incentives we can give them.

Stockholders approved the second incentive stock option plan, 96.1 per cent of the voted shares favoring the new plan. In 1959 and 1960, options for 1,643,900 shares were granted under the new plan including options to directors for 213,500 shares.

In the 1960 proxy statement, some stockholders made the following resolution:

RESOLVED: That the stockholders of Standard Oil Company (New Jersey) assembled in annual meeting in person and by proxy, hereby request that any extension of the Stock Option Plan taking the form of an increase in the total number of shares subject to option under the Plan, be made subject to the following provisions:

1. All shares purchased through the exercise of the option shall be held by the optionee for at least three years subsequent to exercising the option.
2. The purchase price per share under the option shall not be less than 100 per cent of the fair market value of the common stock of the corporation at the time such option is granted.
3. Shares to be optioned shall be optioned in yearly installments as nearly equal as possible over a period of not more than ten (10) years (such period to be determined by the Board of Directors or its Committee), and that the right to purchase shares in each installment shall not be cumulative and will *expire to the extent not exercised during the applicable installment period.*

REASONS: Mandatory holding period makes option privilege abuse more difficult. Last year, 5,523,014 shares were voted in favor of the proposal. Dean Erwin N. Griswold of Harvard Law School recently testified before the Mills Committee that option plans permit executives to play "Heads I win, tails you lose" in [the] stock market. Dr. Griswold added: "This is a one way lottery, understandably attractive to those favored by it."
If you agree please mark your proxy FOR this reform, otherwise it will be voted against it.

Management recommended a vote against this resolution. At the 1960 stockholders' meeting Mr. Rathbone, President of Standard Oil Company (New Jersey), argued against the proposal as follows:

A resolution substantially the same as the one now being proposed was considered by the shareholders last year and was defeated by a vote of something around 167,000,000 shares.

In the present stock option plan, we did adopt one of the provisions the shareholders have included in this resolution—namely that the purchase price of the shares constitutes 100 per cent of the market value of the stock at the time that the option is issued.

The management, as you have noted from the proxy statement, does oppose restrictions 1 and 3 in the shareholder proposal.

We oppose them on the grounds that this program is, as the name implies, an incentive program—a program which is provided for under the tax law of the United States and under the Treasury Department's regulations. And when you put in an incentive plan—which this is—and then diminish materially the incentive factors associated with the plan, it doesn't seem very farsighted.

I would like, if I may, to take a few moments to talk about this stock option plan in more general terms. We in the Jersey Company feel that it is very important to command the best caliber of personnel that we can. We think we have the best oil company in the business, and we think that the best oil company in the business ought to have the best people in the business.

In our wage-earner ranks we try to keep the total compensation package, the total incentive package, competitive with that offered by other companies. I think that any reasonable appraisal of our compensation package for our wage-earner group and our clerical group would indicate that we are right at the top in that respect. If a wage earner is getting a certain rate from most other employers, you have to equal or exceed it.

The same situation exists in the executive ranks—except that the competition there, I think it's fair to say, is even more keen and intense because the supply is not equal to the demand for top-flight executive people.

A stock option for the executive group is a part of the general incentive package which we use to attract and retain top-flight executives. Most other oil companies and most other industrial companies do the same. Compared to other stock option plans, we feel that ours is reasonably conservative. It is certainly not the most generous; neither is it the poorest.

One of the stockholders supporting the resolution stated:

Our President spoke as though this resolution were opposed to option stock in any amount and under any circumstances. If you read it carefully, you will see that this is not the case.

Now, mind you, our tax setup today leaves a great deal to be desired. But the man or the woman who finances his own business—who does not have the money of outsiders invested in his business—has no such thing as option stock. This can only be done with publicly owned corporations.

All of this talk about incentive—a $250,000 salary is an incentive. Everybody in the United States is subject to the same set of income tax laws. They hurt all of us. None of us enjoy them.

But if a man takes up his option stock on Monday and throws it on the market on Tuesday, this is, to use the vernacular, shooting crap, playing the market. We strongly feel that the gentlemen should keep their stock for a reasonable time. I don't think that this is asking too much.

And then to have ten years in which to sit back and hold an option!

We are not opposed to option stock. But we are opposed, in many instances, to the amounts that option stock runs into and to the way it is exercised.

Stockholders rejected the resolution, 96.2 per cent of the voted shares opposing it.

Exhibit 3 shows the quarterly range of Jersey's common stock on the New York Stock Exchange from 1952 through 1961.

EXHIBIT 1

Standard Oil Company (New Jersey)
Selected Stock Option Data for the Years 1951-1960
(dollar amounts in thousands except option price and dividends per share)

Year	Grant Date	Number of Executives Granted Options	Option Price	Number of Option Shares			Shares Held by Standard Oil Company at 12/31		Charge to Income	Dividends per Share
				Granted	Exercised[1]	Unexercised at 12/31	Number	Dollar Cost		
1951	6/29	80	$19.02	491,400	4,833(51)	491,400	380,100	$ 8,517		$1.38
1952					110,640(51)	486,567	384,267	8,627		1.42
1953						374,427	273,627	6,028	$ 495	1.50
1954	6/24	97	27.95	229,080	256,302(51)	347,205	208,725	4,857	2,103	1.52
1955	6/9	112	36.85	229,200	76,164(51)	419,616	418,116	16,875	81	1.75
	12/22		48.55	1,500	78,495(54)					
1956	7/5	184	54.75	250,820	26,352(51)	517,126	483,816	24,017	728	2.10
	12/20		56.00	4,430	79,959(54)					
					49,089(55)					
1957	4/18	232	56.95	1,730	6,870(51)	689,939	470,759	24,875	1,238	2.25
	9/5		59.32	302,080	35,715(54)					
					83,685(55)					
					4,727(56)					
1958	6/5	260	51.42	2,500	2,379(51)	898,425	697,055	37,863	204	2.25
	9/18		54.87	252,610	13,248(54)					
					21,954(55)					
					4,123(56)					
1959	12/3	567	49.25	703,700	32,439	1,852,531[2]	865,206	47,349	394	2.25
1960	7/7	578	41.50	3,000	12,623	2,800,922[3]	1,043,200	55,870	116	2.25
	9/23		40.38	924,900						
	12/29		41.00	12,300						

[1] Numbers in brackets refer to year in which options were granted. In addition to options exercised, approximately 100,000 options had expired without being exercised or had been canceled by December 31, 1960.
[2] Includes options for 299,625 shares assumed upon merger of Humble Oil with Jersey.
[3] Includes options assumed upon purchase of Monterey Oil Company.

EXHIBIT 2

1950

Standard Oil Company (New Jersey)
Remuneration of Company Directors in 1950[1] and 1958[2]

F. W. Abrams	Chairman; Director	$158,638
F. H. Bedford, Jr.	Director	82,150
J. W. Brice	Director	72,412
S. P. Coleman	Director	77,881
J. E. Crane	Vice President; Director	101,096
Orville Harden	Vice President; Director	136,682
R. T. Haslam	Vice President; Director	96,337
H. H. Hewetson	Director	71,038
Eugene Holman	President; Director	186,013
B. B. Howard	Director	90,200
F. W. Pierce	Director	90,200
M. J. Rathbone	Director	80,673
C. F. Smith	Vice President; Director	123,925
E. E. Soubry	Director	80,538
J. R. Suman	Vice President; Director	117,494

1958

H. H. Baker	Executive Vice President (to September); Director (full year)	$137,927
M. W. Boyer	Director	95,128
S. P. Coleman	Vice President; Director	144,565
L. W. Elliott	Executive Vice President (from March); Director	158,589
H. H. Hewetson	Vice President; Director	144,370
Eugene Holman	Chairman; Director	273,775
P. T. Lamont	Director	103,888
H. W. Page	Director	103,888
A. T. Proudfit	Director	114,838
M. J. Rathbone	President; Director	219,025
D. A. Shepard	Director	114,838
E. E. Soubry	Executive Vice President (from March); Director	158,800
W. R. Stott	Director	87,463
L. D. Welch	Executive Vice President (from April); Director	147,606
M. A. Wright	Director (from May)	48,194

---

[1] Year preceding adoption of First Incentive Stock Option Plan.
[2] Year preceding adoption of Second Incentive Stock Option Plan.

EXHIBIT 3

Standard Oil Company (New Jersey)
Quarterly Range of Common Stock, 1952-1961[1]

	1952	1953	1954	1955	1956
1st quarter	$24.46–$28.33	$24.17–$26.21	$23.92–$27.25	$35.54–$39.96	$47.38–$60.75
2nd quarter	24.38– 26.88	22.67– 24.42	26.67– 30.04	37.29– 43.38	54.13– 62.63
3rd quarter	25.00– 27.33	22.33– 25.04	28.00– 33.75	42.58– 48.17	52.88– 60.75
4th quarter	24.00– 25.96	22.71– 24.63	32.21– 37.42	40.50– 51.33	52.25– 60.00

	1957	1958	1959	1960	1961
1st quarter	$53.38–$60.00	$47.50–$51.88	$50.13–$59.13	$43.00–$50.50	$40.75–$46.75
2nd quarter	57.13– 68.25	50.63– 55.88	49.63– 54.88	40.00– 45.38	43.25– 49.75
3rd quarter	56.00– 68.50	51.38– 58.38	48.13– 55.13	39.75– 42.38	42.75– 46.50
4th quarter	47.50– 51.88	54.88– 60.25	45.63– 50.50	38.00– 41.75	43.00– 52.00

[1] Price range per share on the New York Stock Exchange, adjusted for three-for-one stock split on February 10, 1956.

QUESTIONS:

1. Assume that the options exercised in 1958 relate to the following grant dates, as given in Exhibit 1: ('51) to 6/29/51; ('54) to 6/24/54; ('55) to 6/9/55; and ('56) to 7/5/56. Compute the amount of compensation involved under (a) the grant date method, (b) the exercisable date method, and (c) the exercise date method. Use the mean between the appropriate high and low quotations for part (b) and the mean for the third quarter for part (c).

2. In connection with the stock option plan, what amount did the company actually charge to compensation in 1958? How was this amount determined? Using the assumptions for question 1, what price (weighted average) did the company receive for options exercised in 1958? What was the excess of the company's cost per share over this price?

3. Contrast the method used by Jersey in recording compensation under its option plan with methods (a), (b), and (c) in question 1.

4. Comment on the appropriateness of using (1) the grant date, (2) the exercisable date and (3) the exercise date in determining any compensation expense which may be involved in a stock option plan. State which one you believe should be used and give supporting reasons for your choice.

5. The AICPA recommends the use of the grant date. In ARB No. 43, Chapter 13, section B, its Committee on Accounting Procedure states in part:

> Where the inducements are not larger per share than would reasonably be required in an offer of shares to all shareholders for the purpose of raising an equivalent amount of capital, no compensation need be presumed to be involved.

Do you agree? Explain.

6. Do you think stock options would have any significant market value if they were traded on a stock exchange? What would such value represent? Do you know of anything comparable to a stock option which is traded by the public? Does this suggest a possible way of measuring and accounting for compensation *on the grant date* other than taking the difference between the option price and the market price of the stock?

7. Do you approve of the company's balance-sheet classification for the shares reacquired to meet the needs of the stock option plan?

8. The following is quoted from Jersey's 1957 annual report:

> This [exercise of options] resulted in a charge to income of $1,237,774, which represented the excess of Jersey's cost of such [optioned] shares over the proceeds received. However, dividends of $1,033,811 were not required to be paid during the year on the shares of capital stock held for the exercise of options.

Do you agree with the implication that the $1,237,774 of compensation expense was largely offset by dividends not paid on the reacquired stock? Explain.

9. At the 1959 stockholders' meeting, a stockholder stated that the use of unissued, rather than reacquired, shares to meet option requirements dilutes the stockholders' equity. Do you agree with this statement? Explain.

10. It was stated in the 1959 annual report that no more options would be granted under the 1951 plan. All options under the 1951 plan expired on December 31, 1961. How would you appraise the success of this plan?

11. Do you agree with management's counterargument to the 1960 stockholder resolution? Give reasons pro and con.

PART FIVE

Accounting for Owners' Equity

CHAPTER SIXTEEN

Business Combinations

In Chapters 5 and 13, methods of accounting for a corporation's ownership interest in one or more other corporations were considered. This chapter focuses on accounting for the combination of two or more corporations. It is included in the book's final section, *Accounting for Owners' Equity*, because the effect of a business combination on the various ownership interests influences the accounting treatment to be followed. In some business combinations only the owners of one of the combining corporations continue as owners after the combination. In other combinations essentially all owners of the combining corporations retain ownership interests after the combination.

Throughout the history of business combinations, which in the United States dates primarily from the trust era of the 1890's, the major accounting problems have been the treatment of asset and stockholders' equity accounts. The first problem involves the selection of an appropriate basis for recording the assets of the combined businesses. Among the possible choices are book value, appraisal value, replacement value, or the fair market value of any stock or other consideration exchanged by the parties to a combination. If a choice is available, most managements prefer to record assets subject to depreciation or amortization at relatively low values because this favorably affects future net income.

The second accounting problem concerns the proper treatment of the retained earnings balances of the combining corporations. Depending on the nature of the combination, retained earnings of all, one, or none of the combining corporations may be carried forward. Management would usually prefer the first treatment because it implies successful operations in the past and, subject to the availability of cash, may enhance future dividends.

557

ACCOUNTING TREATMENT

For accounting purposes, a business combination may be treated either as a pooling of interests or as a purchase. Under a pooling-of-interests treatment, comparable accounts of the constituent corporations are combined *at their book values* to arrive at the financial statements of the combined enterprise. Under a purchase treatment, the assets of the acquired corporation are stated *at their fair values* in accordance with the cost principle as applied to purchased assets. If cash is paid, there is no problem in determining the total fair value of acquired assets. If the acquiring company issues stock or uses some other non-cash consideration, then the fair market value of this consideration or of the acquired assets, whichever is more readily determinable, is used.

If the total fair value of the acquired assets exceeds their book value (on the acquired corporation's books), this excess should be allocated to specific assets whenever the excess can be identified with such assets. Any remaining excess which cannot be so identified is recorded as goodwill,[1] subject to the accounting treatment for intangibles discussed in Chapter 12. Certain types of such goodwill should be amortized in the future for accounting purposes. Also, future depreciation expense will be increased to the extent that a portion of the excess is identified with depreciable assets. Thus, reported net income of later periods is affected by recognizing the excess of fair value over book value in the accounts of the acquiring company.

If the combination qualifies as a tax-free reorganization[2] under the Internal Revenue Code, as do most combinations, the tax basis of the acquired assets remains unchanged. This means that the extra depreciation expense, related to any excess of fair value over book value, *cannot* be deducted for tax purposes.[3]

The pooling-of-interests treatment is particularly attractive when a combination would otherwise result in the accounting recognition of a material excess of fair value over book value. The following example illustrates the significance of the different accounting treatments. Selected accounts of the Stamford Corporation follow:

---

[1] A more precise classification would be "goodwill arising from excess of cost over book value of purchased assets."

[2] In general, a business combination qualifies as a tax-free reorganization if not more than 20 per cent of the consideration exchanged is cash, the remainder being voting stock.

[3] Amortization of goodwill is also not allowed for tax purposes.

	Book Value, Net	Fair Value
Net Current Assets	$50,000,000	$50,000,000
Buildings	11,000,000	16,500,000
Furniture and Fixtures	1,500,000	2,500,000
Machinery	5,000,000	7,500,000
Other Asset Accounts	7,500,000	7,500,000
Total (equal to stockholders' equity)	$75,000,000	$84,000,000

Assume that in a business combination consideration of $95 million was exchanged for these assets. Under a purchase treatment, $84 million would be allocated on the purchaser's books to the above assets and $11 million to goodwill as follows:

Net Current Assets	$50,000,000
Buildings	16,500,000
Furniture and Fixtures	2,500,000
Machinery	7,500,000
Goodwill	11,000,000
Other Asset Accounts	7,500,000
Total	$95,000,000

Assume further that: (1) Stamford's operations in the year following the combination earn $10 million before income taxes and before recognizing any accounting effects of the business combination, (2) the remaining useful life of Stamford's depreciable assets is 10 years, and (3) any goodwill will be amortized over 10 years. If the combination is treated as a *purchase*, Stamford's operations would make the following contribution to the reported net income of the combined enterprise:

Net income before taxes	$10,000,000
Federal income tax	(5,200,000)
	$ 4,800,000
Items not deductible for tax purposes:	
Depreciation expense related to restating	
assets at fair value	(900,000)
Amortization of goodwill	(1,100,000)
Net income contribution	$ 2,800,000

Had the combination been treated as a *pooling of interests* (and Stamford's assets carried forward *at their book value*), the contribution to net income would be:

Net income before taxes	$10,000,000
Federal income tax	(5,200,000)
Net income contribution	$ 4,800,000

Although the choice of the proper accounting treatment between a purchase and a pooling of interests must be made at the time of the combination,[4] it is the impact on *future earnings* which makes the choice so vitally important.

INSTITUTE PRONOUNCEMENTS

ARB No. 40, *Business Combinations*, was issued in 1950. This bulletin, substantially unchanged, was incorporated as Chapter 7, Section C, in ARB No. 43 in 1953. Since the requirements for a pooling-of-interests treatment were only described briefly in the first bulletin, ARB No. 48, *Business Combinations*, was issued in January, 1957, as follows:

1. Whenever two or more corporations are brought together, or combined, for the purpose of carrying on the previously conducted businesses, the accounting to give effect to the combination will vary depending largely upon whether an important part of the former ownership is eliminated or whether substantially all of it is continued. This bulletin differentiates these two types of combinations, the first of which is designated herein as a *purchase* and the second as a *pooling of interests*, and indicates the nature of the accounting treatment appropriate to each type.

2. For accounting purposes, the distinction between a *purchase* and a *pooling of interests* is to be found in the attendant circumstances rather than in the designation of the transaction according to its legal form (such as a merger, an exchange of shares, a consolidation, or an issuance of stock for assets and businesses), or in the number of corporations which survive or emerge, or in other legal or tax considerations (such as the availability of surplus for dividends).

3. For accounting purposes, a *purchase* may be described as a business combination of two or more corporations in which an important part of the ownership interests in the acquired corporation or corporations is eliminated or in which other factors requisite to a pooling of interests are not present.

4. In contrast, a *pooling of interests* may be described for accounting purposes as a business combination of two or more corporations in which the holders of substantially all of the ownership interests[5] in the constituent corporations become the owners of a single corporation which owns the assets and businesses of the constituent corporations, either directly or through one or more subsidiaries, and in which certain other factors discussed below are present. Such corporation may be one of the constituent corporations or it may be a new corporation. After a pooling of interests, the net assets of all of the constituent corporations will in a large number of cases be held by a single corporation. However, the continuance in existence of one or more of the constituent corporations in a subsidiary relationship to another of the constituents or to a new corporation does not prevent the combination from being a pooling of interests if no significant minority interest remains out-

---

[4] Some combinations, originally treated as purchases, have been retroactively restated to poolings of interests. See case 16-4, Providence Breweries, Inc.

[5] As used in this bulletin, the term "ownership interests" refers basically to common stock, although in some cases the term may also include other classes of stock having senior or preferential rights as well as classes whose rights may be restricted in certain respects.

standing, and if there are important tax, legal, or economic reasons for maintaining the subsidiary relationship, such as the preservation of tax advantages, the preservation of franchises or other rights, the preservation of the position of outstanding debt securities, or the difficulty or costliness of transferring contracts, leases, or licenses.

5. In determining the extent to which a new ownership or a continuity of old ownership exists in a particular business combination, consideration should be given to attendant circumstances. When the shares of stock that are received by the several owners of one of the predecessor corporations are not substantially in proportion to their respective interests in such predecessor, a new ownership or purchase of the predecessor is presumed to result. Similarly, if relative voting rights, as between the constituents, are materially altered through the issuance of senior equity or debt securities having limited or no voting rights, a purchase may be indicated. Likewise, a plan or firm intention and understanding to retire a substantial part of the capital stock issued to the owners of one or more of the constituent corporations, or substantial changes in ownership occurring shortly before or planned to occur shortly after the combination, tends to indicate that the combination is a purchase. However, where a constituent corporation has had two or more classes of stock outstanding prior to the origin of the plan of combination, the redemption, retirement, or conversion of a class or classes of stock having senior or preferential rights as to assets and dividends need not prevent the combination from being considered to be a pooling of interests.

6. Other attendant circumstances should also be taken into consideration in determining whether a purchase or a pooling of interests is involved. Since the assumption underlying the pooling-of-interests concept is one of continuity of all of the constituents in one business enterprise, abandonment or sale of a large part of the business of one or more of the constituents militates against considering the combination as a pooling of interests. Similarly, the continuity of management or the power to control management is involved. Thus, if the management of one of the constituents is eliminated or its influence upon the over-all management of the enterprise is very small, a purchase may be indicated. Relative size of the constituents may not necessarily be determinative, especially where the smaller corporation contributes desired management personnel; however, where one of the constituent corporations is clearly dominant (for example, where the stockholders of one of the constituent corporations obtain 90% to 95% or more of the voting interests in the combined enterprise), there is a presumption that the transaction is a purchase rather than a pooling of interests.

7. No one of the factors discussed in paragraphs 5 and 6 would necessarily be determinative and any one factor might have varying degrees of significance in different cases. However, their presence or absence would be cumulative in effect. Since the conclusions to be drawn from consideration of these different relevant circumstances may be in conflict or partially so, determination as to whether a particular combination is a purchase or a pooling of interests should be made in the light of all such attendant circumstances.

8. When a combination is deemed to be a purchase, the assets acquired should be recorded on the books of the acquiring corporation at cost, measured in money, or, in the event other consideration is given, at the fair value of such other consideration, or at the fair value of the property acquired, whichever is more clearly evident. This is in accordance with the procedure applicable to accounting for purchases of assets.

9. When a combination is deemed to be a pooling of interests, a new basis of accountability does not arise. The carrying amounts of the assets of the constituent corporations, if stated in conformity with generally accepted accounting principles and appropriately adjusted when deemed necessary to place them on a uniform accounting basis, should be carried forward; and the combined earned surpluses and deficits, if any, of the constituent corporations should be carried forward, except to the extent otherwise required by law or appropriate corporate action. Adjustments of assets or of surplus which would be in conformity with generally accepted accounting principles in the absence of a combination are ordinarily equally appropriate if effected in connection with a pooling of interests; however, the pooling-of-interests concept implies a combining of surpluses and deficits of the constituent corporations, and it would be inappropriate and misleading in connection with a pooling of interests to eliminate the deficit of one constituent against its capital surplus and to carry forward the earned surplus of another constituent.

10. Where one or more of the constituent corporations continues in existence in a subsidiary relationship, and the requirements of a pooling of interests have been met, the combination of earned surpluses in the consolidated balance sheet is proper since a pooling of interests is not an acquisition as that term is used in paragraph 3 of Chapter 1 (a) of Accounting Research Bulletin No. 43 which states that earned surplus of a subsidiary corporation created prior to acquisition does not form a part of the consolidated earned surplus. Under the pooling-of-interests concept, the new enterprise is regarded as a continuation of all the constituent corporations and this holds true whether it is represented by a single corporation or by a parent corporation and one or more subsidiaries. If, however, prior to the origin of a plan of combination one party to the combination had been acquired by another such party as a subsidiary in circumstances which precluded the transactions from being considered a pooling of interests, the parent's share of the earned surplus of the subsidiary prior to such acquisition should not be included in the earned surplus of the pooled corporations.

11. Because of the variety of conditions under which a pooling of interests may be carried out, it is not practicable to deal with the accounting presentation except in general terms. A number of problems will arise. For example, if a single corporation survives in a pooling of interests, the stated capital of such corporation may be either more or less than the total of the stated capitals of the constituent corporations. In the former event, the excess may be deducted first from the total of any other contributed capital (capital surplus), and next from the total of any earned surplus, of the constituent corporations. When the stated capital of the surviving corporation is less than the combined stated capitals of the constituent corporations, the difference should appear in the balance sheet of the surviving corporation as other contributed capital (capital surplus), analogous to that created by a reduction in stated capital where no combination is involved.

12. When a combination is considered to be a pooling of interests, statements of operations issued by the continuing business for the period in which the combination occurs should ordinarily include the combined results of operations of the constituent interests for the part of the period preceding the date on which the combination was effected; if combined statements are not furnished, statements for the constituent corporations prior to the date of combination should be furnished separately or in appropriate groups. Results of operations of the several constituents during periods prior to that

in which the combination was effected, when presented for comparative purposes, may be stated on a combined basis, or shown separately where, under the circumstances of the case, that presentation is more useful and informative. Disclosure that a business combination has been, or in the case of a proposed combination will be, treated as a pooling of interests should be made and any combined statements clearly described as such.

The statement entitled "Business Combinations" was unanimously adopted by the twenty-one members of the committee.

Observe the continued emphasis on *ownership* and *attendant circumstances* throughout the bulletin. The distinction between a purchase and a pooling of interests is found in the attendant circumstances rather than in the transaction's legal form. The accounting treatment itself does not determine, but instead *follows*, the nature of the combination.

Where the owners of the predecessor corporations substantially become the owners of the combined enterprise, the combination should be treated as a pooling of interests if certain secondary requirements also support the pooling treatment. Where there is little or no continuity of ownership, the combination is considered a purchase even if all secondary requirements are met. Continuity of ownership and the preservation of relative voting rights require that a combination be completed primarily through an exchange of common stock rather than cash, preferred stock, or debt securities. Also, there must be no intent or plan of one group of owners to dispose of such exchanged stock shortly after the combination.

RELATIVE SIZE

The fulfillment of the continuity of ownership requirement is in itself not sufficient justification for treating a combination as a pooling. Other secondary requirements must be considered. Individually, their presence or absence does not negate a pooling treatment, but, as their effect is cumulative, the exercise of sound judgment becomes of paramount importance. The requirement that neither party be dominant in size has been widely disputed. The bulletin indicates that a purchase is presumed where one group of owners obtains less than 5–10 per cent of the voting interest in the combined enterprise. This requirement was strictly followed for a time after the release of ARB No. 48 in January, 1957. In July, 1957, Carman G. Blough, then the AICPA's Director of Research, offered the following reasons for not treating a proposed combination as a pooling of interests :[6] (1) a relative voting interest of about eight per cent obtained by one corporation's owners was not sufficient, and (2) the influence of the

---

[6] See Reference on page 567.

smaller corporation's management on the management of the combined enterprise was not significant enough to warrant a pooling-of-interests treatment.

It was difficult to sustain such an arbitrary criterion as the 5–10 per cent rule. Larger corporations logically argued that they were subject to discrimination. Such a criterion would virtually make it impossible for industry giants to participate in a pooling of interests. However, large corporations could circumvent this requirement by having their subsidiaries, which qualified from a size standpoint, enter into such combinations. The importance of the relative size criterion has decreased substantially since the issuance of ARB No. 48. Poolings in which the voting interest of one ownership group was only a fraction of one per cent occurred in the early 1960's.

CONTINUITY OF MANAGEMENT

The importance attached to continuity of management has likewise diminished. Since the relative size factor has declined in importance, it has become unrealistic to require that the smaller corporation's management be represented on the board of directors or be active in the top management of the combined enterprise. It is now apparently considered sufficient if the influence of the constituent corporations' managements in the over-all management of the combined enterprise is in reasonable relationship to relative ownership interests and to the business and assets contributed by the combining corporations.

ACCOUNTING ADJUSTMENTS

Even though a combination is treated as a pooling of interests, some accounts may be adjusted before being carried forward, as mentioned in paragraph 9 of the bulletin. Adjustments may be necessary to achieve uniform accounting where, for example, one corporation uses FIFO and the other LIFO, or where one uses accelerated and the other straight-line depreciation. Certain states prohibit the addition of retained earnings accounts, even when a combination is treated as a pooling of interests. If a combination is treated as a pooling of interests for accounting purposes in these states, the retained earnings of the smaller party will be added to the paid-in-capital of the combined enterprise.

As noted in paragraph 11, the stated capital of the combined enterprise under a pooling-of-interests treatment may be more or less than the sum of the constituent corporation's stated capital. Assume the following facts for companies A and B:

	Company A	Company B
Common Stock: Company A, par value $10.00—outstanding shares—100,000;	$1,000,000	
Company B, par value $20.00—outstanding shares—5,000		$100,000
Other paid-in capital	500,000	25,000
Retained earnings	2,000,000	300,000
Stockholders' Equity	$3,500,000	$425,000

Assume a combination of A and B is treated as a pooling of interests, with A as the only surviving corporation. If A issues 15,000 shares in exchange for B's 5,000 shares, $150,000 should be added to the combined common stock account. Since B has only $100,000 in its common stock account, $50,000 is transferred from the combined balance of other paid-in capital of $525,000. If the combined balance of other paid-in capital had been insufficient, the remaining transfer would be made from retained earnings. Had A only exchanged 5,000 shares instead of 15,000, the addition to A's common stock account would be $50,000. The difference between the $100,000 shown by B prior to the combination and the $50,000 issued by A would then be added to the combined other paid-in capital.

An illustration of the provisions of both paragraphs 11 and 12 is found in a note to the 1961 financial statements of the National Biscuit Company describing a pooling of interests between that company and The Cream of Wheat Corporation.

The Cream of Wheat Corporation was acquired August 9, 1961 for 360,000 shares of National Biscuit Company common stock, which acquisition has been treated as a pooling of interests. Consequently, the statement of income and retained earnings includes the results of Cream of Wheat operations for both 1960 and 1961. The statement of financial position at December 31, 1960 has been restated to include amounts applicable to Cream of Wheat at that date. The details of restated additional paid-in capital at December 31, 1960 are as follows:

National Biscuit Company	$2,593,787
The Cream of Wheat Corporation	1,240,953
	3,834,740
Less excess of par value of 360,000 shares of National Biscuit Company common stock over par value of the capital stock of The Cream of Wheat Corporation	2,400,000
	$1,434,740

Business combinations are usually major events which should be disclosed in notes to the financial statements. Terminology is often misused in describing a combination in such notes. Although the bulletin states that "a pooling of interests is not an acquisition," notes to the financial statements frequently refer to poolings as "acquisitions."

SUMMARY OF ACCOUNTING DIFFERENCES

The difference between the two accounting treatments for business combinations can be summarized as follows :

(a) Purchase treatment :

The acquired assets are recorded at their current *fair* value, retained earnings of the acquired corporation are not carried forward and paid-in capital of the acquiring corporation is increased only to the extent that equity capital is used as a means of payment. All or most of any excess of fair value over book value must be depreciated or amortized depending on its allocation between tangible and intangible assets.

(b) Pooling-of-interests treatment :

The assets, paid-in capital, and retained earnings of the constituent corporations are combined at their *book* values, subject to changes necessary to achieve uniform accounting. This accounting treatment has no effect on future periods' income statements.

BASIC CONTROVERSY

One of the most controversial aspects of business combinations has been the treatment of assets in the combined balance sheet. Opponents of the pooling concept claim that it ignores the cost principle. They argue that in most poolings a dominant party "acquires" the other party or parties. Appropriate accounting treatment should be based on the fair market value of either the stock issued or the assets acquired. Management of the dominant corporation should be held accountable for assets recorded at this value, not at their previous book value.

Supporters of the pooling concept claim that use of book values, rather than fair market values, is proper because the corporations merely pool their interests to carry on business together without any material change in the ownership, management, or assets of the combined corporations. Therefore, it would be inconsistent to restate the assets of the smaller party to a fair market value basis while the assets of the larger party remained unchanged.

When there is no single dominant party in a business combination, some accountants argue that an entirely new entity is created. They claim that the nature and characteristics of the new entity differ from those of the former entities, that these former entities cease to exist as going concerns, and that the accounting treatment for a new business is most appropriate. All assets of the new entity should be recorded at their current fair value and no retained earnings should be carried forward. These accountants advocate use of only the purchase treatment, as previously described in this chapter, when a combination is clearly dominated by one corporation which, for all practical purposes, is the only surviving entity. They would abolish the pooling-of-interests treatment, as it now exists. At this writing, these proposals have not been considered by the Accounting Principles Board.

REFERENCES

Andersen, Arthur, & Co., *Accounting and Reporting Problems of the Accounting Profession*. Chicago : Arthur Andersen & Co. (Oct. 1962), 69–75.

Barr, Andrew, "Accounting Aspects of Business Combinations," *Accounting Review*, 34 (Apr. 1959), 175–81.

Blough, Carman G., "Business Combinations : 'Pooling' or Purchase?" *Journal of Accountancy*, 104 (Jul. 1957), 55–56.

————, "Some Observations on Pooling of Interests," *Journal of Accountancy*, 110 (Sept. 1960), 73-74.

Jaenicke, Henry R., "Ownership Continuity and ARB No. 48," *Journal of Accountancy*, 114 (Dec. 1962), 57–63.

————, "Management's Choice to Purchase or Pool," *Accounting Review*, 37 (Oct. 1962), 758–65.

May, George O., "Business Combinations : An Alternate View," *Journal of Accountancy*, 103 (Apr. 1957), 33–36.

McCarthy, George D., "Premeditated Merger," *Harvard Business Review*, 39 (Jan.–Feb. 1961), 74–82.

Rappaport, Louis H., "Business Combinations : Purchase vs. Pooling," *New York Certified Public Accountant*, 28 (Oct. 1958), 745–46.

Research Department of the American Institute of Accountants, "Business Combinations," *Journal of Accountancy*, 103 (Feb. 1957), 51–53.

Sapienza, Samuel R., "Distinguishing Between Purchase and Pooling," *Journal of Accountancy*, 111 (Jun. 1961), 35–40.

————, "Pooling Theory and Practice in Business Combinations," *Accounting Review*, 37 (Apr. 1962), 263–78.

Schrader, William J., "Business Combinations," *Accounting Review*, 33 (Jan. 1958), 72–75.

Werntz, William W., "Intangibles in Business Combinations," *Journal of Accountancy*, 103 (May 1957), 46–50.

Tuck Manufacturing Company

The Tuck Manufacturing Company was incorporated in Massachusetts in 1951 to design and manufacture wire-wound potentiometers for use in military aircraft, missile systems, and computers. Other products include a line of small torque measuring devices and several other electronic instruments for general laboratory use and product testing.

On April 30, 1962, the last day of its fiscal year, Tuck merged with the Chase Company through an exchange of common stock. At the time of the merger, Chase, a manufacturer of panel meters, had a tax loss carry-forward of $366,520 which could be applied against future profits of the combined enterprise. The excess of the fair value of Tuck stock issued over amounts attributable to Chase's net assets was $149,011, which was disclosed in the 1962 balance sheet as goodwill. (See Exhibit 1.)

On October 31, 1962, Tuck continued its expansion program by purchasing the Woodbury Corporation. Woodbury maintained an extensive testing laboratory in the vicinity of Tuck's plant and had formerly conducted performance tests for Tuck on a contract basis. Tuck issued 86,723 shares of its common stock in exchange for all of the outstanding capital stock of Woodbury. Woodbury's net assets exceeded the fair value of the 86,723 Tuck shares by $154,666.

In his 1963 message to the stockholders, Tuck's president stated that net sales showed an increase of 11 per cent and that net income as a percentage of net sales was 8.2 per cent. Exhibit 2 gives Tuck's income statements for the fiscal years ended April 30, 1963 and 1962. Exhibit 3 shows the Statement of Capital Surplus for the fiscal year ended April 30, 1963.

EXHIBIT 1

Tuck Manufacturing Company
Condensed Balance Sheets as of April 30,
1963 and 1962

	1963	1962
Assets:		
Current Assets	$1,261,413	$ 711,938
Plant and Equipment, net	186,667	158,082
Other Assets:		
Deposits Receivable	24,680	24,680
Cash Surrender Value of Life Insurance	24,709	19,562
Goodwill	—	149,011
	$1,497,469	$1,063,273
Liabilities and Stockholders' Equity:		
Current Liabilities	$ 203,210	$ 302,878
Long Term Debt	—	57,600
Stockholders' Equity:		
Common Stock	$ 361,985	$ 226,514
Capital Surplus	418,615	180,563
Retained Earnings	513,659	295,718
Total Stockholders' Equity	$1,294,259	$ 702,795
	$1,497,469	$1,063,273

EXHIBIT 2

Tuck Manufacturing Company
Income Statements for the Fiscal Years Ended April 30,
1963 and 1962

	1963	1962
Net Sales	$2,651,842	$2,386,614
Cost of Goods Sold	1,707,018	1,485,582
Gross Margin	$ 944,824	$ 901,032
Selling and Administrative Expenses	725,093	701,850
Net Operating Income	$ 219,731	$ 199,182
Other Deductions	1,790	2,474
Net Income Before Taxes	$ 217,941	$ 196,708
Federal Income Taxes	—[1]	93,941
Net Income After Taxes	$ 217,941	$ 102,767

---

[1] No provision was made because of tax loss carry-forward obtained through merger.

EXHIBIT 3

Tuck Manufacturing Company
Statement of Capital Surplus for the Fiscal Year
Ended April 30, 1963

Balance at April 30, 1962		$180,563
Add: Excess of net assets over cost in merger with the Woodbury Corporation		154,666
Excess over par value of proceeds received on sale of capital stock	$277,376	
Less expense of marketing capital stock	44,979	232,397
		$567,626
Less elimination of goodwill		149,011
Balance at April 30, 1963		$418,615

QUESTIONS:

1. What is the usual accounting treatment for goodwill resulting from an excess of "fair market value" of stock issued over net assets acquired? What are the pertinent factors and what accounting principles apply?

2. Do you agree with Tuck's accounting treatment of the goodwill recognized in the Chase merger? What action would you take as an auditor?

3. Do you agree with Tuck's accounting treatment for the excess of Woodbury's net assets over the fair value of Tuck shares issued to purchase Woodbury?

4. Can you see any justification for unusual accounting treatments in this case?

5. Do you consider the president's disclosure of sales and earnings figures in the 1963 annual report as being appropriate? How would you disclose net income as a percentage of net sales in 1963?

6. Comment critically on the use of the terminology "capital surplus" and "goodwill" in financial statements.

Bedford Laboratories

In early 1963, Bedford Laboratories learned that Davitron, Inc. was interested in a possible merger with a larger company. The two companies, which were located in Boston suburbs, produced electronic equipment for both defense and civilian needs.

Davitron's stock was entirely held by the two Davis brothers, their wives and children. The company, which was founded in 1947, grew at a modest rate until 1959; then sales increased rapidly from $7 million to $18 million in 1962. While the Davises were optimistic about the future of the company, they were concerned over the lack of a public market for their stock. For example, neither of their families could pay federal and state estate taxes without sale of stock should one of the brothers die. They favored a merger with a larger company whose stock was listed on an exchange. Also, they were anxious to add some diversification to their products, which were chiefly related to the boom in quality high-fidelity equipment.

Since R. Fred Webster had become president of Bedford Laboratories in 1956, he had broadened the company's product lines through several mergers. Final arrangements for the merger between Bedford and Davitron took place during the summer and it was agreed that the merger would become effective on September 1, 1963. Exhibit 1 shows Bedford's and Davitron's balance sheets as of August 31, 1963. In early 1963, Davitron's plant and equipment had been appraised at $5,125,000 for insurance purposes. The Davis brothers believed this was approximately the fair market value of the property at the time of the merger. The book value of Davitron's inventory at August 31, 1963 approximated its market value. Bedford's and Davitron's income statements for the *eight months* ended August 31, 1963, are given in Exhibit 2.

The merger agreement stated that Bedford would exchange 410,000 shares of its common stock for all of the common stock of Davitron. Davitron would then be dissolved with Bedford continuing as the surviving corporation. On August 31, 1963, Bedford's common stock closed at $33\frac{1}{2}$ on the New York Stock Exchange.

Mr. Kenneth R. Davis, president of Davitron, was to become manager of the new Davitron Division and a member of Bedford's Board of Directors.

For income tax purposes, the merger constituted a tax-free exchange of stock. The corporations and their stockholders did not incur any tax liability as a result of the merger. Also, the tax basis of Davitron's assets was assumed by Bedford.

EXHIBIT 1

Bedford Laboratories
Balance Sheets of Bedford Laboratories and Davitron, Inc.
as of August 31, 1963
(000 omitted)

	Bedford Laboratories	Davitron Corporation
ASSETS:		
Current Assets:		
Cash	$ 10,021	$ 621
Accounts Receivable	14,832	987
Inventories	38,456	2,508
Total Current Assets	$ 63,309	$ 4,116
Plant and Equipment, at cost	$130,820	$10,126
Less: Allowance for Depreciation	70,212	7,286
	$ 60,608	$ 2,840
Other Assets	9,045	912
TOTAL ASSETS	$132,962	$ 7,868
LIABILITIES AND STOCKHOLDERS' EQUITY:		
Current Liabilities:		
Accounts Payable	$ 7,121	$ 302
Other	12,381	682
Total Current Liabilities	$ 19,502	$ 984
Long-term Debt	40,500	2,000
Stockholders' Equity:		
Capital Stock, Par Value $5.00	$ 24,485	—
Capital Stock, No Par Value	—	$ 1,330
Capital Surplus	10,397	—
Retained Earnings	38,078	3,554
Total Stockholders' Equity	$ 72,960	$ 4,884
TOTAL LIABILITIES AND STOCKHOLDERS' EQUITY	$132,962	$ 7,868

EXHIBIT 2

Bedford Laboratories
Income Statements of Bedford Laboratories and Davitron, Inc. for the
Eight Months Ended August 31, 1963
(000 omitted)

	Bedford Laboratories	*Davitron Corporation*
Net Sales	$223,982	$15,086
Cost of Goods Sold	149,025	7,521
Gross Margin	$ 74,957	$ 7,565
Selling and Administrative Expenses	56,255	3,752
Earnings Before Provision for Income Taxes	$ 18,702	$ 3,813
Federal Income Taxes	9,720	1,978
Net Earnings for the Period	$ 8,982	$ 1,835

QUESTIONS:

1. Considering the major criteria used to distinguish a pooling of interests from a purchase, how would you account for the merger of Bedford and Davitron? Based on the information given in the case, develop relevant material to support your argument.

2. Develop Bedford's balance sheet as of September 1, 1963, immediately after the merger, assuming that the merger is treated (a) as a pooling of interests, and (b) as a purchase.

3. Assume monthly sales and expenses for Bedford and the new Davitron Division continue at approximately the same level for the remainder of 1963 as in the first eight months. Develop Bedford's income statement for the year 1963, if the merger is treated (a) as a pooling of interests, and (b) as a purchase. Any "goodwill" recognized as a result of the merger will be amortized over a ten-year period beginning September 1, 1963. The excess of appraisal value over book value of Davitron's depreciable assets, if recognized in the accounts, will be depreciated, beginning September 1, 1963, over six years, the estimated remaining useful life of these assets.

4. Based on the income statements derived in question 3, calculate the amount of earnings per share which Bedford would report in 1963 if the merger is treated (a) as a pooling, and (b) as a purchase. Consider carefully the appropriate number of Bedford common shares to use as a divisor in these calculations.

5. What will be the *difference* in earnings per common share *for 1964* as a result of the choice made in 1963 between the pooling and purchase accounting treatments?

6. As Mr. Webster, which procedure would you prefer to use in accounting for the merger of Bedford and Davitron? Explain.

7. Some accountants question the pooling concept on the grounds that it ignores appropriate accounting for *costs*. What is the cost principle? Do you believe the pooling concept ignores the cost principle? Explain with reference to Bedford Laboratories.

Continental Can Company, Inc.

Continental Can Company, Inc. was incorporated in New York in 1913. The company has expanded its operations and diversified its product lines through a series of mergers. By 1963, Continental Can produced metal, glass, and paper containers, polyethylene bottles, paper and plastic-coated paper plates and cups, "twist-off" closures for glass jars and bottles, and other complementary products.

In 1956, shortly after it had merged with Hazel-Atlas Glass Company and the White Cap Company, Continental's management proposed a merger with Robert Gair Company, Inc. The merger with Gair, a manufacturer of folding cartons, shipping containers, and Kraft bags, would permit Continental to offer its customers a complete line of packaging materials and services.

An affirmative vote of at least two-thirds of the outstanding common stock of Continental Can and at least two-thirds of the outstanding $3.75 cumulative preferred stock would be required for approval of the merger agreement.

In a letter dated September 25, 1956, General Lucius D. Clay, Chairman of Continental Can Company, requested stockholder support at a meeting to be held October 26, 1956, to consider the proposed merger. Part of his letter follows:

Your company has been making good progress in building its business as a leader in the packaging field. Our economic system of mass production and distribution depends to a large extent on packaging to protect and to help sell its products. The demand for packaging continues to increase each year. Our metal containers are still the major part of your company's business; through diversification our objective has been to provide a "tailor-made" packaging service for nearly every product. To do so, the management believes that such service could not be complete without being able to offer glass containers, and Kraft paper bags. To bring about our entry into the glass container field, the company acquired the Hazel-Atlas Glass Company on September 13 .... The merger of Robert Gair Company, Inc., into your company will provide the necessary facilities for the production of folding cartons, shipping containers, and Kraft paper bags to round out the company's line of products in the packaging field.

It is anticipated that, in addition to bringing to the company further diversification in packaging, the merger will permit many economies in administration, financing, manufacturing, and merchandising of the combined companies' products.

The following excerpts from the proxy statement give background information pertaining to the merger.

TERMS OF MERGER

The total number of shares which Continental will be authorized to issue will be 15,385,832, of which 15,000,000 shares will be common stock having a par value of $10 each, 150,000 shares will be preferred stock without par value and 235,832 shares will be new second preferred stock having a par value of $100 each. The present par value of Continental's common stock, of which 10,000,000 shares are now authorized, is $20. On September 14, 1956, Gair had outstanding 2,989,510 shares of common stock of the par value of $1 per share and 235,832 shares of preferred stock of the par value of $100 per share. Upon the completion of the merger, assuming that all of said outstanding shares of common stock of Gair are changed into common stock of Continental, that all of said outstanding shares of preferred stock of Gair are changed into new second preferred stock of Continental, and that Continental will have the same number of shares of common stock outstanding as on September 14, 1956, Continental will have outstanding and in treasury 11,165,796 shares of common stock and 235,832 shares of new second preferred stock, in addition to the 150,000 shares of $3.75 cumulative preferred stock presently outstanding. However, each share of the present preferred stock of Gair is convertible into three shares of the present common stock of Gair and will continue to be so convertible until the merger becomes effective. Consequently, each time a share is so converted the outstanding Gair preferred stock will be reduced by one share and the outstanding Gair common stock will be increased by three shares. Accordingly, upon completion of the merger the outstanding common stock of Continental will be increased by 2.4 shares [see explanation below] and the outstanding new second preferred stock of Continental will be decreased by one share in respect of each share of Gair preferred stock so converted. Continental has in the past from time to time issued its common stock in exchange for businesses acquired, and may do so in the future, but at present it has no other plans for issuing additional common stock, except such as may be issued pursuant to its employees' stock purchase plans.

On the effective date of the merger, shares of capital stock of Gair and Continental will be changed into or constitute shares of capital stock of Continental, as the surviving corporation, as follows:

Each share of the then outstanding common stock of Gair will be changed into eight-tenths (8/10) of one share of common stock of Continental.

Each share of the then outstanding preferred stock of Gair will be changed into one (1) share of new second preferred stock of Continental.

Each share of common stock of the par value of $20 per share of Continental then outstanding or in the treasury of Continental will be changed into one (1) share of common stock of the par value of $10 per share of Continental.

Each share of outstanding $3.75 cumulative preferred stock of Continental will continue to be one (1) share of $3.75 cumulative preferred stock of Continental.

The change in the par value of the common stock of Continental from $20 per share to $10 per share is a change made desirable by the difference in the respective par values of the common stock of Gair and Continental.

On the basis of the shares of capital stock of Gair and Continental outstanding on September 14, 1956, ... the capitalization of Continental upon the effective date of the merger will be as follows:

$3.75 Cumulative preferred stock		
(Authorized—150,000)		
Shares of Continental previously outstanding		150,000
New second preferred stock		
(Authorized—235,832)		
Issued in respect of preferred stock of Gair		235,832*
Common stock		
(Authorized—15,000,000*)		
Shares of common stock of Continental previously outstanding or in treasury	8,774,188	
Issued in respect of common stock of Gair	2,391,608	
Total shares outstanding and in treasury		11,165,796

Of the authorized common stock, 565,996.8 shares are to be reserved for the conversion of shares of the new second preferred stock and 235,784 shares are to be reserved for issue pursuant to employees' stock purchase plans.

The outstanding common stock of Continental, as shown in the foregoing tabulation, will be increased by 2.4 shares and the outstanding new second preferred stock of Continental, decreased by one share, in respect of each share of Gair preferred stock converted after September 14, 1956, and prior to the merger.

BUSINESS OF GAIR

Gair was incorporated under the laws of the State of Delaware on April 6, 1932. Its principal executive offices are located at 155 East 44th Street, New York 17, New York.

The principal business of Gair and its subsidiaries is the manufacture and sale of folding paperboard cartons for packaging goods for consumer sale, corrugated shipping containers, paper bags, and wrapping and specialty papers, and the production, both for conversion into finished products and for sale to others, of paperboard and paper.

In 1955 sales of folding cartons and shipping containers each accounted for approximately one-third of the total sales in dollar volume of Gair. The balance was derived from sales of paper bags and wrapping and other papers, paperboard and other products. With respect to each of the major lines of products produced by Gair, there are many other important producers of the same or similar products. Thus, in each case Gair must meet keen competition in price, quality and service.

BUSINESS OF CONTINENTAL

Continental was incorporated under the laws of the State of New York on January 17, 1913. The principal business of Continental and its subsidiaries is the manufacture and sale of metal cans and other metal containers. Other products include paper containers, fibre drums, kraft linerboard, flexible packaging materials, crown and vacuum caps, plastic products, and can closing machinery. In addition, as described under the heading "Acquisition of Hazel-Atlas Glass Company," Continental has entered the glass container field. In 1955 sales of cans and other metal containers accounted for between two-thirds and three-fourths of the total sales in dollar volume of Continental. With respect to each of the major lines of products manufactured by Continental, there are several other important suppliers of the same or similar products. Thus, in each case Continental must meet vigorous competition in price, quality and service.

The major portion of the business is conducted directly by Continental. Its principal subsidiaries, all of which are wholly-owned, are The Container Company, Continental Can Company of Canada Limited, Continental Can Corporation, Continental-Shellmar Incorporated, Continental-Shellmar International Company, Inc. and White Cap Company. It also has subsidiaries, wholly or partially owned, in Mexico, Columbia, Venezuela, Panama and Brazil. References herein to the business of "Continental" are to the business as conducted by the enterprise as a whole. Continental operates through the following divisions: Metal, Crown and Cork, Paper Container, Fibre Drum, Paperboard, Shellmar-Betner, Canadian, Overseas, Equipment Manufacturing and Hazel-Atlas. Each operating division is headed by either a vice president or a general manager, who is responsible for all phases of the operation of the particular division. Continental also operates through the White Cap Company, a wholly-owned subsidiary which Continental acquired on January 4, 1956.

ACQUISITION OF HAZEL-ATLAS GLASS COMPANY

On September 13, 1956 Continental acquired all of the assets, properties, business and goodwill of Hazel-Atlas Glass Company, a West Virginia corporation (herein called "Hazel-Atlas") in exchange for an aggregate of 999,140 shares of common stock of Continental and the assumption by Continental of all of the liabilities of Hazel-Atlas, as provided in a Reorganization Agreement and Plan dated June 29, 1956, between Continental and Hazel-Atlas.... The Hazel-Atlas operations are now being conducted as a division of Continental.

The division manufactures glass containers and glassware, including tumblers, tableware and kitchenware and articles of special design for industrial use. It also manufactures metal closures for glass containers. It operates plants at 13 locations and maintains leased warehouses at six locations. Its principal customers are manufacturers and packers of cosmetics, medicinal preparations and food and other products and wholesalers and distributors of glass jars for home canning.

The management of Hazel-Atlas believed it to be the third largest glass container manufacturer in the United States in terms of dollar volume of sales, but the leader in the industry had a sales volume several times that of Hazel-Atlas.

SUMMARIES OF EARNINGS

The following summary shows the net sales and net income, the earnings applicable to common stock and the earnings per share of common stock of

Continental and consolidated subsidiaries (including, for the entire period of five years and six months, the accounts of Hazel-Atlas ...) for the years 1951 to 1955, inclusive, and for the six months ended June 30, 1956....

Year ended December 31	Net Sales*	Cost of Goods Sold and Operating Expenses*	Selling and Administrative Expenses*	Income before Taxes*	Taxes on Income*	Net Income*	Earnings Applicable to Common Stock*	Earnings per share of Common Common Stock[1]
1951	$530,479	$463,961	$25,338	$41,393	$22,812	$18,581	$17,952	$2.45
1952	547,796	486,873	27,708	33,432	16,088	17,344	16,337	2.22
1953	633,687	559,235	36,834	38,011	19,218	18,793	17,945	2.27
1954	695,338	606,631	40,651	48,368	24,003	24,365	23,744	2.86
1955	746,186	643,951	47,283	55,267	27,702	27,565	27,003	3.24
Six months ended June 30, 1956	393,478	334,083	27,676	31,719	16,524	15,195	14,914	1.70

*000 omitted

[1] Based on the number of shares outstanding at the end of the periods indicated, adjusted where necessary to reflect the distribution by Continental on February 15, 1956 of one additional share of its common stock for each share then outstanding, plus 999,140 shares issued to Hazel-Atlas....

The following summary shows the net sales and net income, and the earnings applicable to common stock and the earnings per share of common stock of Gair and consolidated subsidiaries ... for the years 1951 to 1955, inclusive, and for the six months ended June 30, 1956....

Year ended December 31	Net Sales and Operating Revenues*	Cost of Goods Sold and Operating Expenses*	Selling and Administrative Expenses*	Income before Minority Interest and Taxes*	Taxes on Income*	Minority Interest in Income of Subsidiaries*	Net Income*	Earnings per share of Common Stock[1]
1951	$137,565	$ 94,087	$11,028	$32,450	$21,115	$ 842	$10,493	$3.76
1952	135,654	97,068	13,193	25,393	15,789	733	8,871	2.81
1953	145,969	108,228	14,830	22,911	12,884	768	9,259	2.92
1954	144,366	110,602	15,538	18,226	9,660	918	7,648	2.29
1955	160,662	121,266	16,690	22,706	12,073	1,313	9,320	2.80
Six months ended June 30, 1956	85,853	64,897	8,562	12,394	6,520	509	5,365	1.62

*000 omitted

[1] Based on the average number of shares outstanding during the period....

RANGE OF SECURITY PRICES

The common and preferred stocks of Gair and the common stock of Continental are listed on the New York Stock Exchange. The high and low sales prices of such stock on such exchange by quarterly periods during the calendar years 1954 and 1955 and for the first two quarters of 1956, as reported in *Bank & Quotation Record*, and for the period from July 1, 1956 to September 14, 1956 were:

	GAIR				CONTINENTAL	
	Common		Preferred[1]		Common[2]	
	Low	High	Low	High	Low	High
1954						
First Quarter	19	23			27 1/4	31
Second Quarter	21	23 3/4			30 15/16	35 11/16
Third Quarter	23	27 5/8			34 1/4	38 5/8
Fourth Quarter	25	31 3/4			34	39 7/8
1955						
First Quarter	26 1/4	31 7/8			36 3/16	41 1/2
Second Quarter	26 3/4	34	104 1/4	110	37 9/16	42 1/2
Third Quarter	28	34	105	113	36 1/16	40 7/8
Fourth Quarter	27 1/2	30 1/2	105 3/4	110	36 1/8	44 1/4
1956						
First Quarter	28 3/4	34 1/2	107 1/4	112 1/2	39	44 3/4
Second Quarter	28 5/8	36 3/8	109 1/4	117 7/8	42 3/4	50
July 1 to Sept. 14	34 1/2	40 3/4	112	124	47	56 1/2

---

[1] Issued in May, 1955.

[2] All prices prior to February 15, 1956 are adjusted to give effect to 100 per cent stock distribution on outstanding common stock of Continental made on that date.

MANAGEMENT

The Merger Agreement provides that the Board of Directors of Continental, as the surviving corporation, shall consist of 18 Directors including George E. Dyke, President and a Director of Gair, Raymond F. DeVoe, Senior Vice President in Charge of Finance and a Director of Gair, Robert L. Fitts, Vice President and a Director of Gair, and Parker Newhall, a Director of Gair. The other 14 Directors will be selected from the present 15 Directors of Continental by the Board of Directors of Continental prior to the Special Meeting of Stockholders.

No changes are to be made in the officers of Continental. It is contemplated that Gair will continue after the merger as a Division of Continental; that the Divisional management will be the same as the present executive management of Gair; and that initially the compensation of the present officers of Gair, as employees of Continental, will be substantially the same as their current compensation.

OTHER MATTERS

Continental is subject to a court decree rendered in antitrust proceedings brought by the Department of Justice. The Department of Justice has requested from both Continental and Gair information related to their respective businesses and to the proposed transactions. The Department of Justice has not, however, implied that the transaction would violate the antitrust laws or the existing court decree. Insofar as the information requested is available to Continental and Gair, it has been or will be furnished to the Department of Justice.

At the stockholders' meeting held on October 26, 1956, Continental Can's stockholders voted as follows:

	Preferred		Common	
	Shares Voted	As Per Cent of Outstanding Shares	Shares Voted	As Per Cent of Outstanding Shares
For the Merger	126,404	84.2%	7,248,682	82.6%
Against the Merger	125	.1	27,789	.3

Exhibit 1 shows Continental Can's and Gair's condensed balance sheets as of June 30, 1956, and the pro forma combined balance sheet giving effect to the merger.

EXHIBIT 1

Continental Can Company, Inc.
Condensed Balance Sheets as of June 30, 1956 and Pro Forma
Combined Balance Sheet Giving Effect to the
Transactions Described in the Accompanying
Notes (Unaudited)
(000 omitted from column figures)

	Continental Can Company, Inc. and Consolidated Subsidiaries (Note 1)	Robert Gair Company, Inc. and Consolidated Subsidiaries	Pro Forma Combined (Note 2)
ASSETS			
Current Assets	$298,384	$ 46,928	$345,312
Investments	8,624	382	9,006
Property, Plant, and Equipment:			
Land	$ 6,586	$ 1,959	$ 8,545
Buildings and equipment	297,267	120,528	417,795
Timberlands	9,081	21,642	30,723
Other	3,562	998	4,560
Construction in progress	32,269	—	32,269
	$348,765	$145,127	$493,892
Less Reserves for depreciation and depletion	122,104	53,131	175,235
	$226,661	$ 91,996	$318,657
Prepaid Expenses and Deferred Assets	$ 7,608	$ 3,150	$ 10,758
Less Reserve for deferred accounts receivable	202	—	202
	$ 7,406	$ 3,150	$ 10,556
Deposits with Mutual Insurance Companies	$ 1,471	—	$ 1,471
	$542,546	$142,456	$685,002

EXHIBIT 1 (continued)

	Continental Can Company, Inc. and Consolidated Subsidiaries (*Note 1*)	Robert Gair Company, Inc. and Consolidated Subsidiaries	Pro Forma Combined (*Note 2*)
LIABILITIES AND STOCKHOLDERS' EQUITY			
Current Liabilities	$171,419	$ 17,646	$189,065
Long-Term Debt	80,396	38,013	118,409
Operating Reserves	1,544	—	1,544
Minority Interest in Subsidiaries	—	8,705	8,705
Capital Shares Issued:			
Continental Can Company, Inc.:			
150,000 shares $3.75 cumulative preferred stock, without par value	$ 15,000	$ —	$ 15,000
238,348 shares second preferred stock, $100 par value	—	—	23,835
8,758,782 shares common stock, $20 par value	175,176	—	—
11,144,351.6 shares common stock, $10 par value	—	—	111,444
Robert Gair Company, Inc.:			
238,348 shares $4.50 cumulative preferred stock, $100 par value	—	23,835	—
2,981,962 shares common stock, $1 par value	—	2,982	—
	$190,176	$ 26,817	$150,279
Capital Surplus	6,421	214	73,349
Earnings Retained in the Business:			
Appropriated for excess replacement costs of fixed assets	9,700	—	9,700
Appropriated for inventory price decline or other contingencies	6,170	—	6,170
Unappropriated	76,874	51,061	127,935
	$289,341	$ 78,092	$367,433
Less common stock in treasury, at cost—5,616 shares	154	—	154
	$289,187	$ 78,092	$367,279
	$542,546	$142,456	$685,002

Notes to Balance Sheets as of June 30, 1956

1. The balance sheet of Continental Can Company, Inc. and consolidated subsidiaries gives effect, as of June 30, 1956, to the acquisition of the business and assets of Hazel-Atlas Glass Company in consideration of the issuance of 999,140 shares of common stock of Continental, the assumption by Continental of all of the liabilities of Hazel-Atlas, the merging of the earnings retained in the business and the other adjustments resulting from the Reorganization Agreement and Plan, dated June 29, 1956. . . .
2. The pro forma combined balance sheet gives effect, as of June 30, 1956, to the Agreement of Merger dated September 19, 1956, between Robert Gair Company, Inc. and Continental Can Company, Inc., as more fully described elsewhere herein. In the preparation of this combined balance sheet the excess, namely $20,874,000, of the par value of the common stock of Continental to be issued to Gair over the par value of the common stock of Gair to be retired has been charged to capital surplus.

QUESTIONS:

1. Was the merger of Continental Can and Gair treated as a purchase or a pooling of interests? Explain.

2. Which, if any, of the accounting requirements for a pooling of interests does the merger between Continental Can and Gair meet? Comment on the relevance of each criterion you cite.

3. What are the advantages to management of a pooling-of-interests treatment over a purchase treatment? Would a pooling-of-interests treatment always be more attractive than a purchase treatment? Explain.

4. If this merger had been treated as a purchase, approximately what amount of goodwill might have appeared on Continental Can's balance sheet? What assumption(s) have you made in your calculations?

5. Was it appropriate for Continental Can to include the earnings of Hazel-Atlas from 1951 in its summary of earnings, considering that the two companies did not merge until September 13, 1956? Explain.

6. In the "Terms of Merger" section of the proxy statement, it was stated that 565,996.8 shares of Continental Can's common stock were reserved for the conversion of the new second preferred stock. Continental Can's common stock would be increased by 2.4 shares and the outstanding new second preferred stock of Continental Can decreased by one share for each share of Gair preferred stock converted after September 14, 1956, and prior to the merger. Was this provision necessary from an accounting point of view in determining whether the merger was a pooling or a purchase? Explain.

7. One of the criteria for a pooling-of-interests treatment concerns the relative size of the parties to a merger. Consider this criterion in light of the quotation in the case under "Other Matters" that "a court decree [has been] rendered in antitrust proceedings brought by the Department of Justice." Does this help explain why the size criterion has diminished in importance? Explain.

Providence Breweries, Inc.

Providence Breweries, Inc. was incorporated in 1922. Its products are marketed in the northeastern United States. In 1958, Providence considered a merger with the Eastern Beverage Company as part of a diversification program into the soft drink field.

A merger agreement, effective at the close of business on September 30, 1958, was concluded during the summer. Part of a listing application to the New York Stock Exchange described the transaction as follows:

Pursuant to an Agreement and Plan of reorganization dated July 29, 1958 (the "Agreement"), Providence Breweries, Inc. ("Providence") will acquire substantially all of the assets of Eastern Beverage Company ("Eastern"), in exchange solely for 177,889 shares of Providence common stock of the par value of $1 per share, and the assumption by Providence of all liabilities and obligations of Eastern. Eastern is engaged principally in the production and marketing of nonalcoholic beverages.

Under the Agreement, and as part thereof, Eastern will take appropriate steps to effect its corporate dissolution promptly after the closing and to distribute the shares of Providence stock received by it to its stockholders in complete liquidation of Eastern.

Providence favorably regards the acquisition of the net assets of Eastern because it will provide for Providence a line of products which complement and strengthen Providence's present activities in the growing beverage market. Providence knows of no officer, director, or principal stockholder of Providence, or any of its affiliates, who has any direct or indirect beneficial interest in Eastern.

The closing of the transaction contemplated by the Agreement is scheduled to take place on September 30, 1958. The Providence stock to be issued pursuant to the Agreement will be recorded on the books of Providence at $1 per share, the par value thereof, or a total of $177,889, and there will be credited to additional paid-in capital the difference between the amount determined in the next following sentence and said total of $177,889. The net assets of Eastern acquired, under the Agreement, from Eastern will be recorded on the books of Providence at the fair market value of the Providence stock to be issued. The fair market value of the Providence stock to be issued will be determined by using the per share closing price on the

New York Stock Exchange as of the last business day preceding the closing date. The value so ascertained, plus Eastern's liabilities assumed by Providence, will be allocated among the various Eastern assets according to the respective fair appraisal values of said assets as of the date of closing. Any excess of the market value of the Providence stock determined as aforesaid over the fair appraisal value of the assets of Eastern at the date of closing will be recorded as an intangible asset and will be amortized over a ten-year period. This accounting treatment has been reviewed and approved by Providence's independent accountants, Messrs. John Holland & Co., as being in accordance with generally accepted accounting principles.

Balance sheets and income statements for Providence and Eastern before the merger are shown in Exhibits 1 through 4. On September 29, 1958, Providence common closed at $63\frac{7}{8}$ on the New York Stock Exchange. The fair value of Eastern's assets was determined as follows at the time of the merger:

	(000 omitted)
Cash	$1,585
Government Bonds	518
Accounts Receivable, net	4,835
Inventories	6,622
Cash Surrender Value of Life Insurance	241
Prepaid Expenses and Deferred Charges	184
Land, Buildings, and Equipment, net	2,571

The excess of the fair appraisal value over the book value of Eastern's land, buildings, and equipment at September 30, 1958, consisted of $140,000 assigned to land and $660,000 applicable to buildings and equipment. The average remaining useful life of these buildings and equipment was $8\frac{1}{4}$ years at the time of the merger.

For income tax purposes, the exchange of Providence stock for Eastern's net assets was tax-free. The corporations and their stockholders did not incur any tax liability as a result of the merger, and the tax basis of Eastern's assets was assumed by Providence.

In December, 1961, Mr. William R. Johnson, financial vice president of Providence and a CPA, learned of another merger which was accounted for as a purchase when it took place in 1958, but recently had been reconsidered and the original purchase treatment changed to a pooling of interests. Mr. Johnson wondered whether such a change would be possible for Providence. He consulted the appropriate Accounting Research Bulletins, current accounting literature, and a number of corporate annual reports and New York Stock Exchange listing applications in which mergers were disclosed. As a result of this research, he felt reasonably sure that a retroactive change would be acceptable to the company's auditors. He wrote John Holland & Co. the following letter to ascertain if his interpretations were correct:

December 27, 1961

Mr. J. B. Quinn, Partner
John Holland & Co.
22 Rayton Road
Boston, Massachusetts

Dear Jim:

Before we prepare our 1961 financial statements, prior to your usual year-end audit, we would appreciate your opinion on a contemplated change in accounting for our 1958 merger with the Eastern Beverage Company from a purchase treatment to a pooling-of-interests treatment.

In 1958, we agreed that the transaction was properly treated as a purchase rather than a pooling of interests in accordance with generally accepted accounting principles, as then defined.

We have recently reviewed the situation and find that, in light of all the circumstances, the transaction could more appropriately be considered a pooling of interests, rather than a purchase, because of the following:

(1) *Relative Size of the Constituents*

Accounting Research Bulletin No. 48 provides that where one of the corporations is clearly dominant, there is a presumption that the transaction is a purchase rather than a pooling of interests. In practice, relative size has become less significant since the bulletin was issued in 1957. During the past year several mergers were treated as poolings despite very substantial disparity in the relative size of the merged companies. American Machine Company concluded a merger several years ago which was originally considered a purchase, but its statements were recently revised to show the transaction as a pooling of interests. In our case, if size were the only factor involved, it now appears the transaction could have been treated as either a purchase or a pooling.

(2) *Continuity of Management or Power to Control Management*

In September, 1958, there was no clear indication of continuity of Eastern management. Since then, management of Eastern has been continued. In addition, one of the former major stockholders of Eastern has become an active member of Providence's Board of Directors.

Your early attention to this matter will be greatly appreciated as we would like to make the necessary accounting changes prior to your audit.

Sincerely yours,
(Signed) W. R. Johnson

WRJ:bs

Providence Breweries' *tentative* 1961 financial statements, which *do not* reflect the proposed change in accounting for the merger with Eastern, are given in Exhibits 5 and 6.

EXHIBIT 1

Providence Breweries, Inc.
Condensed Balance Sheet at September 30, 1958
(000 omitted)

Current Assets:	
Cash and Short-term Securities	$ 25,064
Receivables, net	40,569
Inventories	72,397
Total Current Assets	$138,030
Total Current Liabilities	28,380
Working Capital	$109,650
Investments	14,796
Land, Buildings, and Equipment, net	45,140
Prepaid Expenses	3,427
Total Assets less Current Liabilities	$173,013
Long-term Debt	38,362
Excess of Assets over Liabilities	$134,651
Stockholders' Equity:	
Common Stock, $1 par value	$ 4,112
Additional Paid-in Capital	39,836
Retained Earnings	90,703
Stockholders' Equity	$134,651

EXHIBIT 2

Providence Breweries, Inc.
Statement of Income and Retained Earnings
for the Year Ended December 31, 1957 and Nine Months Ended September 30, 1958
(000 omitted)

	Year Ended December 31, 1957	*Nine Months Ended September 30, 1958*
Net Sales	$205,931	$159,915
Costs and Expenses:		
Cost of Sales	$148,302	$112,065
Depreciation and Amortization	5,893	4,828
Selling, Administrative, and General Expenses	33,580	25,988
	$187,775	$142,881
Operating Income	$ 18,156	$ 17,034
Other Income, less other Deductions	1,414	1,518
Net Income Before Taxes on Income	$ 19,570	$ 18,552
Provision for Taxes on Income	9,987	9,468
Net Income	$ 9,583	$ 9,084
Retained Earnings, Beginning of Period	91,223	89,291
	$100,806	$ 98,375
Dividends Declared	11,515	7,672
Retained Earnings, End of Period	$ 89,291	$ 90,703

EXHIBIT 3

Eastern Beverage Company
Condensed Balance Sheet at September 30, 1958
(000 omitted)

Assets:

Current Assets:

Cash	$ 1,585
Government Bonds	518
Accounts Receivable, net	4,835
Inventories	6,622
Total Current Assets	$13,560
Cash Surrender Value of Life Insurance	$ 241
Prepaid Expenses	184
Land, Buildings, and Equipment, net	1,771
Total	$15,756

Liabilities and Stockholders' Equity:

Current Liabilities	$ 7,805
Long-term Debt	1,104
Stockholders' Equity:	
Common Stock, $5 par value	$ 400
Capital Surplus	2,190
Retained Earnings	4,257
Total Stockholders' Equity	$ 6,847
Total	$15,756

EXHIBIT 4

Eastern Beverage Company
Statement of Income and Retained Earnings
for the Year Ended December 31, 1957 and Nine Months Ended September 30, 1958
(000 omitted)

	Year Ended December 31, 1957	Nine Months Ended September 30, 1958
Operating Revenues	$21,719	$16,453
Costs and Expenses:		
Cost of Sales	$18,648	$14,779
General and Administrative Expenses	1,695	942
	$20,343	$15,721
Operating Income	$ 1,376	$ 732
Discounts, Interest, and Miscellaneous Income	133	169
	$ 1,509	$ 901
Interest Expense	55	42
Net Income Before Taxes	$ 1,454	$ 859
Provision for Taxes on Income	835	414
Net Income	$ 619	$ 445
Retained Earnings, Beginning of Period	3,903	4,122
	$ 4,522	$ 4,567
Dividends Declared	400	310
Retained Earnings, End of Period	$ 4,122	$ 4,257

EXHIBIT 5

Providence Breweries, Inc.
Tentative Condensed Balance Sheet at December 31, 1961
(000 omitted)

Current Assets:	
Cash and Short-term Securities	$ 24,109
Receivables, net	45,651
Inventories	81,312
Total Current Assets	$151,072
Total Current Liabilities	35,017
Working Capital	$116,055
Investments	13,934
Land, Buildings, and Equipment, net	52,606
Prepaid Expenses	2,052
Goodwill (net of amortization)	2,508
Total Assets less Current Liabilities	$187,155
Long-term Debt	36,726
Excess of Assets over Liabilities	$150,429
Stockholders' Equity:	
Common Stock, $1 par value	$ 4,290
Additional Paid-in Capital	51,021
Retained Earnings	95,118
Stockholders' Equity	$150,429

EXHIBIT 6

Providence Breweries, Inc.
Tentative Statement of Income and Retained Earnings
for the Year Ended December 31, 1961
(000 omitted)

Net Sales	$261,753
Costs and Expenses:	
Cost of Sales	$186,450
Depreciation and Amortization[1]	7,949
Selling, Administrative, and General Expenses	42,336
	$236,735
Operating Income	$ 25,018
Other Income, less other Deductions	(3,285)
Net Income Before Taxes on Income	$ 21,733
Provision for Taxes on Income	10,610
Net Income	$ 11,123
Retained Earnings, Beginning of Period	94,291
	$105,414
Dividends Declared	10,296
Retained Earnings, End of Period	$ 95,118

[1] Includes amortization of goodwill arising from merger with Eastern Beverage Company.

QUESTIONS:

1. In his letter to Mr. Quinn, Mr. Johnson refers to "generally accepted accounting principles, as then defined." In general, what forces or factors lead to changes in "generally accepted accounting principles"? Specifically, what seems to have produced the alleged change in this case? Do you approve of Mr. Johnson's use of the word "principles"? Explain. What principles of accounting, if any, do you believe are considered in deciding between a pooling-of-interests treatment and a purchase treatment?

2. As Mr. Quinn, would you approve of the proposed change in the original accounting treatment of the Providence-Eastern merger? Explain.

3. Exhibits 5 and 6 show Providence's 1961 financial statements as they would appear if no change were made in the method of accounting for the merger with Eastern. Using these exhibits, calculate Providence's earnings per share for 1961.

4. How much total net income would Providence report for 1961 if the pooling-of-interests method were adopted retroactive to September 30, 1958? What amount of earnings per share would then be reported in 1961? As an officer of Providence Breweries, would you consider this amount to be materially different from the amount determined in question 3? Explain.

5. Give the entry or entries required at December 31, 1961, to restate the accounts retroactively to September 30, 1958, if the pooling-of-interests method is adopted. You may assume the 1961 accounts are still open.

CHAPTER SEVENTEEN

Stock Dividends
and Stock Splits

A stock dividend is a distribution of a corporation's own stock to its stockholders without any payment being made by the stockholders to the corporation. The type of stock dividend considered in this chapter, a distribution of common stock to present holders of common stock in proportion to their share holdings, does not change a stockholder's equity interest in the corporation. The only effect of a stock dividend on the issuing corporation's books is a transfer from retained earnings to one or more permanent capital accounts.

Stock splits also take the form of share distributions without any payment being made by stockholders to the corporation. However, in contrast to stock dividends, there is no effect on the corporation's accounts. The usual purpose of a stock split is to reduce the market price per share to a price range that improves marketability of the shares. For example, a 2 for 1 split of stock selling for $100 per share will reduce the market price to about $50 per share, a range more likely to attract investors with limited funds who wish to diversify their stock holdings.

INSTITUTE PRONOUNCEMENTS

The American Institute of Certified Public Accountants first expressed an opinion on accounting for stock dividends and stock splits in ARB No. 11, issued in November, 1941. In November, 1952, this bulletin was revised and in the following year included in ARB No. 43, Chapter 7, *Capital Accounts*, Section B, "*Stock Dividends and Stock Split-Ups*." This section follows:

1. The term *stock dividend* as used in this chapter refers to an issuance by a corporation of its own common shares to its common shareholders without consideration and under conditions indicating that such action is prompted mainly by a desire to give the recipient shareholders some ostensibly separate evidence of a part of their respective interests in accumulated corporate earnings without distribution of cash or other property which the board of directors deems necessary or desirable to retain in the business.

2. The term *stock split-up* as used in this chapter refers to an issuance by a corporation of its own common shares to its common shareholders without consideration and under conditions indicating that such action is prompted mainly by a desire to increase the number of outstanding shares for the purpose of effecting a reduction in their unit market price and, thereby, of obtaining wider distribution and improved marketability of the shares.

3. This chapter is not concerned with the accounting for a distribution or issuance to shareholders of (a) shares of another corporation theretofore held as an investment, or (b) shares of a different class, or (c) rights to subscribe for additional shares or (d) shares of the same class in cases where each shareholder is given an election to receive cash or shares.

4. The discussion of accounting for stock dividends and split-ups that follows is divided into two parts. The first deals with the problems of the recipient. The second deals with the problems of the issuer.

AS TO THE RECIPIENT

5. One of the basic problems of accounting is that of income determination. Complete discussion of this problem is obviously beyond the scope of this chapter. Basically, income is a realized gain and in accounting is recognized, recorded, and stated in accordance with certain principles as to time and amount.

6. In applying the principles of income determination to the accounts of a shareholder of a corporation, it is generally agreed that the problem of determining his income is distinct from the problem of income determination by the corporation itself. The income of the corporation is determined as that of a separate entity without regard to the equity of the respective shareholders in such income. Under conventional accounting concepts, the shareholder has no income solely as a result of the fact that the corporation has income; the increase in his equity through undistributed earnings is no more than potential income to him. It is true that income earned by the corporation may result in an enhancement in the market value of the shares, but until there is a distribution, division, or severance of corporate assets, the shareholder has no income. If there is an increase in the market value of his holdings, such unrealized appreciation is not income. In the case of a stock dividend or split-up, there is no distribution, division, or severance of corporate assets. Moreover, there is nothing resulting therefrom that the shareholder can realize without parting with some of his proportionate interest in the corporation.

7. The foregoing are important points to be considered in any discussion of the accounting procedures to be followed by the recipient of a stock dividend or split-up since many arguments put forward by those who favor recognizing stock dividends as income are in substance arguments for the recognition of corporate income as income to the shareholder as it accrues to the corporation, and prior to its distribution to the shareholder; the acceptance

of such arguments would require the abandonment of the *separate entity* concept of corporation accounting.

8. The question as to whether or not stock dividends are income has been extensively debated; the arguments pro and con are well known.[1] The situation cannot be better summarized, however, than in the words approved by Mr. Justice Pitney in *Eisner* v. *Macomber*, 252 U.S. 189, wherein it was held that stock dividends are not income under the Sixteenth Amendment, as follows:

"A stock dividend really takes nothing from the property of the corporation and adds nothing to the interests of the stockholders. Its property is not diminished and their interests are not increased . . . the proportional interest of each shareholder remains the same. The only change is in the evidence which represents that interest, the new shares and the original shares together representing the same proportional interests that the original shares represented before the issue of the new ones."

9. Since a shareholder's interest in the corporation remains unchanged by a stock dividend or split-up except as to the number of share units constituting such interest, the cost of the shares previously held should be allocated equitably to the total shares held after receipt of the stock dividend or split-up. When any shares are later disposed of, a gain or loss should be determined on the basis of the adjusted cost per share.

AS TO THE ISSUER

Stock Dividends

10. As has been previously stated, a stock dividend does not, in fact, give rise to any change whatsoever in either the corporation's assets or its respective shareholders' proportionate interests therein. However, it cannot fail to be recognized that, merely as a consequence of the expressed purpose of the transaction and its characterization as a *dividend* in related notices to shareholders and the public at large, many recipients of stock dividends look upon them as distributions of corporate earnings and usually in an amount equivalent to the fair value of the additional shares received. Furthermore, it is to be presumed that such views of recipients are materially strengthened in those instances, which are by far the most numerous, where the issuances are so small in comparison with the shares previously outstanding that they do not have any apparent effect upon the share market price and, consequently, the market value of the shares previously held remains substantially unchanged. The committee therefore believes that where these circumstances exist the corporation should in the public interest account for the transaction by transferring from earned surplus to the category of permanent capitalization (represented by the capital stock and capital surplus accounts) an amount equal to the fair value of the additional shares issued. Unless this is done, the amount of earnings which the shareholder may believe to have been distributed to him will be left, except to the extent otherwise dictated by legal requirements, in earned surplus subject to possible further similar stock issuances or cash distributions.

11. Where the number of additional shares issued as a stock dividend is

---

[1] See, for instance, Freeman, "Stock Dividends and the New York Stock Exchange," *American Economic Review*, December, 1931 (pro), and Whitaker, "Stock Dividends, Investment Trusts, and the Exchange," *American Economic Review*, June, 1931 (con).

so great that it has, or may reasonably be expected to have, the effect of materially reducing the share market value, the committee believes that the implications and possible constructions discussed in the preceding paragraph are not likely to exist and that the transaction clearly partakes of the nature of a stock split-up as defined in paragraph 2. Consequently, the committee considers that under such circumstances there is no need to capitalize earned surplus, other than to the extent occasioned by legal requirements. It recommends, however, that in such instances every effort be made to avoid the use of the word *dividend* in related corporate resolutions, notices, and announcements and that, in those cases where because of legal requirements this cannot be done, the transaction be described, for example, as a *split-up effected in the form of a dividend.*

12. In cases of closely-held companies, it is to be presumed that the intimate knowledge of the corporations' affairs possessed by their s'areholders would preclude any such implications and possible constructions as are referred to in paragraph 10. In such cases, the committee believes that considerations of public policy do not arise and that there is no need to capitalize earned surplus other than to meet legal requirements.

13. Obviously, the point at which the relative size of the additional shares issued becomes large enough to materially influence the unit market price of the stock will vary with individual companies and under differing market conditions and, hence, no single percentage can be laid down as a standard for determining when capitalization of earned surplus in excess of legal requirements is called for and when it is not. However, on the basis of a review of market action in the case of shares of a number of companies having relatively recent stock distributions, it would appear that there would be few instances involving the issuance of additional shares of less than, say, 20% or 25% of the number previously outstanding where the effect would not be such as to call for the procedure referred to in paragraph 10.

14. The corporate accounting recommended in paragraph 10 will in many cases, probably the majority, result in the capitalization of earned surplus in an amount in excess of that called for by the laws of the state of incorporation; such laws generally require the capitalization only of the par value of the shares issued, or, in the case of shares without par value, an amount usually within the discretion of the board of directors. However, these legal requirements are, in effect, minimum requirements and do not prevent the capitalization of a larger amount per share.

Stock Split-Ups

15. Earlier in this chapter a stock split-up was defined as being confined to transactions involving the issuance of shares, without consideration moving to the corporation, for the purpose of effecting a reduction in the unit market price of shares of the class issued and, thus, of obtaining wider distribution and improved marketability of the shares. Where this is clearly the intent, no transfer from earned surplus to capital surplus or capital stock account is called for, other than to the extent occasioned by legal requirements. It is believed, however, that few cases will arise where the aforementioned purpose can be accomplished through an issuance of shares which is less than, say, 20% or 25% of the previously outstanding shares.

16. The committee believes that the corporation's representations to its shareholders as to the nature of the issuance is one of the principal considerations in determining whether it should be recorded as a stock dividend

or a split-up. Nevertheless, it believes that the issuance of new shares in ratios of less than, say, 20% or 25% of the previously outstanding shares, or the frequent recurrence of issuances of shares, would destroy the presumption that transactions represented to be split-ups should be recorded as split-ups.

Three members of the committee, Messrs. Knight, Calkins, and Mason, assented with qualification, and one member, Mr. Wilcox, dissented to adoption of section (b) of chapter 7.

Mr. Knight assents with the qualification that he believes the section should recognize the propriety of treating as income stock dividends received by a parent from a subsidiary. He believes the section should have retained from the original Bulletin No. 11 the statement, "It is recognized that this rule, under which the stockholder has no income until there is a distribution, division, or severance, may require modification in some cases, or that there may be exceptions to it, as, for instance, in the case of a parent company with respect to its subsidiaries . . . ."

Messrs. Calkins and Mason approve part one, but believe part two is inconsistent therewith in that the former concludes that a stock dividend is not income to the recipient while the latter suggests accounting procedures by the issuer based on the assumption that the shareholder may think otherwise. They believe it is inappropriate for the corporate entity to base its accounting on considerations of possible shareholder reactions. They also believe that part two deals with matters of corporate policy rather than accounting principles and that the purpose sought to be served could be more effectively accomplished by appropriate notices to shareholders at the time of the issuance of additional shares.

Mr. Wilcox dissents from the recommendations made both as to the recipient and as to the issuer. He believes that, with proper safeguards, stock dividends should be regarded as marking the point at which corporate income is to be recognized by shareholders, and denies that the arguments favoring this view are in substance arguments for the recognition of corporate income as income to the shareholder as it accrues to the corporation. He believes that the arguments regarding severance and maintenance of proportionate interest are unsound, and cannot logically be invoked as they are in this section, since they are widely ignored with respect to distributions of securities other than common stock dividends. Mr. Wilcox believes the recommendations as to the issuer are inconsistent with the rest of the section, involve arbitrary distinctions, hamper or discourage desirable corporate actions, result in meaningless segregation in the proprietorship section of balance sheets, and serve no informative purpose which cannot be better served by explanatory disclosures. He therefore also dissents from the omission of requirements for information and disclosures which were contained in the original Bulletin No. 11 issued in September, 1941.

Note that the committee's statement consists of two major parts, the first pertaining to the recipient of a stock dividend or stock split and the second to the issuer. The bulletin supports the generally-held view among accountants that stock dividends are not income to the recipient.[1] Despite this viewpoint, the committee recommends that the issuing corporation's accounting treatment recognize that

---

[1] For opposing views see articles by Husband and Wilcox listed on page 598.

shareholders may believe they are receiving income equivalent to the fair value of the dividend shares, particularly in the case of small stock dividends having relatively little effect on stock market prices.

A number of accountants, including Messrs. Calkins and Mason, members of the Committee on Accounting Procedure when ARB No. 43 was released in 1953, object to the apparent inconsistency between the recommended accounting procedures, which assume that stockholders may view stock dividends as income, and the committee's view that stock dividends are not income to the recipient. A second objection is directed towards the propriety of the accountant's concern with a matter primarily of corporate policy, and not of accounting policy. Critics contend that the amount of retained earnings capitalized in a stock dividend, in excess of any legal requirement, should properly be within the discretion of the issuing corporation's board of directors.

DISCLOSURE

Some accountants suggest discontinuing use of fair market values in accounting for stock dividends because such use tends to confirm shareholder beliefs that income is received. At the same time, they advocate a continuing effort to inform shareholders about the nature of stock dividends. The following paragraph concerning information to be supplied shareholders was contained in the original (1941) bulletin on stock dividends, but deleted from the revised (1952) version (which contains no recommendations on disclosure):

> In the case of any stock dividend, the issuing corporation should inform its stockholders by notice at the time of issuance, as to the amount capitalized per share and the aggregate amount thereof, as well as to the account or accounts to which such aggregate has been charged and credited, whether or not such notification is required by statute or regulation. In addition, the corporation should inform the stockholder as to the percentage by which the interest which he had in the corporation before the issuance of the stock dividend will be reduced if he should decide to dispose of his dividend shares.

The effect of this disclosure recommendation can best be analyzed by considering each of the paragraph's two sentences separately. The first sentence recommends that stockholders be advised of the amount capitalized, both per share and in total. Since the original bulletin, as well as the revision, recommended that this amount should have a reasonable relationship to the fair value of the dividend shares, information concerning the amount capitalized may imply to stockholders that a stock dividend results in receipt of income equal to the fair market value of the dividend shares. Having arrived at this false, but happy, conclusion, the stockholder is then advised, according to the recommendations of the paragraph's second sentence, "if you sell your dividend shares, you're worse off than you were before receiving them because your percentage interest in the corporation will decline."

The New York Stock Exchange requires essentially the same disclosure to stockholders as recommended in the original Institute bulletin. In addition, the notice to stockholders required by the Exchange should indicate the relationship of the total amount capitalized to the current year's undistributed earnings and "the reason for paying the stock dividend." The following comments, relating to both a stock dividend and a stock split, are from a letter, mailed on December 30, 1960, to the common shareholders of the International Paper Company. These comments illustrate the Exchange's disclosure requirements.

To Holders of Our Common Stock :

The enclosed certificate for International Paper Company $2.50 par value common stock represents (i) the additional two shares resulting from the 3-for-1 split of each $7.50 par value share that you held of record immediately before the split became effective December 6, 1960 plus, if you then held seventeen or more such $7.50 par value shares, (ii) any whole $2.50 par value shares resulting from the 2 per cent stock dividend payable on your holdings of record at the close of business December 6, 1960. . . .

Effect of Stock Dividend

The purpose and effect of the stock dividend is to capitalize a portion of the earnings which the Company has been investing in capital assets and working capital. The 3-for-1 split became effective on the Company's books before the close of business on December 6, 1960 and increased outstanding Common Stock to 40,026,495 shares of $2.50 par value each. The stock dividend is being paid to holders of record at the close of business that day and further increases that total by 800,530 additional $2.50 par value shares. Neither the stock split nor the stock dividend increases the percentage of your interest in the Company. Sale by you of all the dividend shares accruing to you, including any fractional interest, would reduce your interest in the Company by one fifty-first (1/51st).

Entries made to reflect this stock dividend on the Company's books have reduced Retained Earnings by $23,215,370 ($29.00 per $2.50 par value share), and have increased the Common Stock Account by $2,001,325 ($2.50 a share, the par value) and Capital Surplus by $21,214,045 ($26.50 per $2.50 par value share). The reduction in Retained Earnings was more than covered by the balance, after cash dividends, of consolidated net earnings for the twelve months ended June 30, 1960. The stock split did not occasion changes in the dollar amounts of any of these accounts.

Tax Status

Counsel for the Company advise that neither the stock split nor the stock dividend gives rise to any taxable income to the recipient under the U. S. Federal income tax law. However, if any Common Stock held at the close of business on the record date or any stock or fractional interest received on the stock dividend is sold, both the stock split and the stock dividend must be taken into consideration in calculating tax basis (cost) in order to determine gain or loss for Federal income tax purposes. . . .

TERMINOLOGY PROBLEMS

Paragraph 10 states that the description of stock distributions as *dividends* leads many stockholders to "look upon them as distributions of corporate earnings and usually in an amount equal to the fair value of the additional shares received." Although they are not used in the bulletin, words such as *pay, paid, paying, payable,* and *payment* are similarly confusing when applied to a stock distribution. Unfortunately, their use is just as commonplace as the term *stock dividend.* The Exchange, for example, refers to "the reason for *paying* the stock dividend," and the letter to International Paper Company common shareholders refers to "stock dividend *payable,*" and *"paid* to holders." A few accountants, such as Mr. Wilcox who dissented to the committee's statement on accounting for stock dividends, have no reservation about using words such as *dividend* or *pay* (and its derivatives) because they believe a stock dividend *does* represent income to the recipient. Similarly, Mr. Knight would recognize income in the case of stock distributions from a subsidiary to its parent, presumably because the parent has *control* over the subsidiary's dividend policy. However, the chief controversy among accountants does not focus on whether stock dividends constitute income to the recipient. Most accountants agree they do not, but many feel that the accounting procedures recommended for the issuing corporation imply the receipt of income to stockholders.

REFERENCES

Barker, C. Austin, "Evaluation of Stock Dividends," *Harvard Business Review,* 36 (Jul.–Aug. 1958), 99–114.

―――――, "Are Accounting Requirements for Stock Dividends Obsolete?" *Analysts Journal,* 14 (Nov. 1958), 69–72.

Blough, Carman G., "Valuing Shares of Stock Issued as a Dividend," *Journal of Accountancy,* 108 (Aug. 1959), 76.

Burke, John T., "Stock Dividends—Suggestions for Clarification," *Accounting Review,* 37 (Apr. 1962), 283–88.

Chambers, R. J., "Asset Revaluations and Stock Dividends," *Journal of Accountancy*, 106 (Aug. 1958), 55–68.

Graham, Benjamin, "Stock Dividends: An Analysis of Some of the Major Obstacles," *Barron's*, 33 (Aug. 10, 1953), 5–6.

Horngren, Charles T., "Stock Dividends and the Entity Theory," *Accounting Review*, 32 (Jul. 1957), 379–85.

Hunter, Robert V., (Correspondence), *Journal of Accountancy*, 95 (May 1953), 543–46.

Husband, George R., "The Entity Concept in Accounting," *Accounting Review*, 29 (Oct. 1954), 552–63.

May, George O., "Stock Dividends and Concepts of Income," *Journal of Accountancy*, 96 (Oct. 1953), 427–31.

"New York Stock Exchange Issues New Policy on Accounting for Stock Dividends," *Journal of Accountancy*, 95 (May 1953), 604.

Porterfield, James T. S., "Dividends, Dilution, and Delusion," *Harvard Business Review*, 37 (Nov.–Dec. 1959), 56–61.

Ray, J. C., "Amount to be Capitalized for a Stock Dividend," *New York Certified Public Accountant*, 32 (Aug. 1962), 511–17.

Sussman, M. Richard, *The Stock Dividend*. Ann Arbor, Michigan: Bureau of Business Research, School of Business Administration, University of Michigan, 1962.

Wilcox, Edward B., "Accounting for Stock Dividends: A Dissent from Current Recommended Practice," *Journal of Accountancy*, 96 (Aug. 1953), 176–81.

International Business Machines Corporation

IBM was incorporated in 1911 as the Computing-Tabulating-Recording Company, the present name being adopted in 1924. By 1963, the Corporation had become the world's largest manufacturer of electronic computers and business machines for commercial and scientific data processing. The majority of the corporation's income is derived from leasing and servicing this equipment. IBM has sales and service offices located in all principal cities of the United States and a wholly-owned subsidiary, IBM World Trade Corporation, operates sales, service, manufacturing, and laboratory facilities in over 90 foreign countries.

Prior to 1946, IBM had distributed an annual stock dividend to its stockholders for 11 consecutive years. The New York Stock Exchange's regulations governing stock dividends in 1946 stated in part:

> . . . the Exchange, in authorizing the listing of additional shares for such stock dividend: (1) will consider the relationship between the amount of the earnings and the fair market value of the number of shares to be issued for this purpose; and (2) will expect that the amount of earnings or earned surplus to be capitalized for each dividend share would be at least the fair market value per share, it being understood that it is impracticable to define exactly "fair market value" but it would appear that this term would ordinarily mean an amount which bears a reasonable relationship to the range of market prices established on the Exchange over the period during which the income to be capitalized by the stock dividend was earned.

In 1946, IBM's stock dividend policy was interrupted when a stock split of 25 per cent was declared. The New York Stock Exchange distinguishes between a stock dividend and a stock split by the percentage of the share distribution. If the distribution is less than 25 per cent it is considered a stock dividend, while distributions of 100 per cent or more are recognized as stock splits.

If a distribution ranges between 25 and 99 per cent, the Exchange evaluates each issue individually before determining how the distribution should be treated.

IBM's common stock was split again in 1948 when three additional shares were issued for each four shares held. In the following year, the corporation resumed its stock dividend policy at an annual rate of five per cent, the same rate as declared from 1937 through 1945.[1] This policy was continued through 1953. The combined reduction in retained earnings for the years 1951 through 1953 from cash dividend payments and transfers to capital stock as a result of stock dividends exceeded reported net income for these years. In general, the stock dividends were declared in October to be distributed in January. For example, the five per cent stock dividend declared on October 28, 1952 was issued on January 29, 1953. No formal recognition was made in the accounts in 1952, the transfer of $28,923,206 from retained earnings to no-par capital stock being made on January 29, 1953. Disclosure was made on the balance sheet at December 31, 1952, as follows:

> Earned surplus[2] $96,962,516.19
>   Subject to a charge of
> $28,923,206.00 in respect
>   of stock dividend payable
>   January 29, 1953 to stockholders
>   of record January 5, 1953.

Exhibit 1 gives selected data from IBM's income statements and statements of retained earnings pertaining to stock dividends and stock splits for the period 1946 through 1961.

In February, 1953, the New York Stock Exchange amended its accounting regulations for stock dividends. The Exchange now explicitly required that the amount transferred from retained earnings to capital stock, based on the fair market value of the dividend shares, could not exceed the balance of net income for the year after deducting any cash dividends. As a result of this amendment, IBM could no longer distribute stock dividends of five per cent and it was forced to reduce the stock dividend distributed in 1954 to $2^1/_2$ per cent. No stock dividend was distributed in 1955 even though net income was the highest in the corporation's history. In July, 1955, the New York Stock Exchange issued a new statement on stock dividends discontinuing the requirement that the amount transferred from retained earnings to capital stock must be covered by current undistributed earnings. The requirement that the transfer be

---

[1] Stock dividends of two per cent and three per cent were issued, respectively, in 1935 and 1936.

[2] "Retained Earnings" used in place of "Earned Surplus" beginning in 1957.

based on the fair market value of the stock was continued. Subsequent to this change, IBM declared a $2^1/_2$ per cent stock dividend on October 25, 1955, to be distributed on January 27, 1956.

IBM's ratio of debt to equity had reached such a level by 1956 that management deemed it desirable to raise approximately $200 million through an issue of common stock. Since 1925, the corporation had been able to finance its rapid expansion by long-term borrowing and retained earnings. The 1956 public offering of common stock was well received and IBM raised $226 million to finance the corporation's continued growth.

IBM's management was becoming concerned about the increasing size of the transfers from retained earnings to capital stock attributable to stock dividends. The increases were caused by a larger number of shares outstanding coupled with a continued rise in the market price of the corporation's stock. In its 1958 annual report to stockholders, management explained this as follows:

> The purpose of stock dividends is to capitalize a portion of the corporation's retained earnings. Corporations following a policy of declaring successive stock dividends must transfer from retained earnings to the capital stock account an amount equal to the approximate current market price of the stock, adjusted to reflect the issuance of the shares to be distributed.
>
> For the stock dividend declared October 28, 1958, 296,123.97 shares will be issued which, priced at $410 per share (representing the approximate adjusted market value on October 27, 1958, the day prior to the declaration of the stock dividend), equals $121,410,830, the amount to be transferred on January 28, 1959 on the books of the corporation from retained earnings to the capital stock account.
>
> The company wishes to inform stockholders that although accumulated retained earnings are adequate for this stock dividend, the effect of the transfer of $121,410,830 results in a reduction of accumulated retained earnings. For the 11,849,023 shares outstanding at December 31, 1958, the corporation earned $10.65 per share in 1958, and paid cash dividends of $2.60 per share, leaving a balance of $8.05 per share. Relating the $121,410,830 to the 11,849,023 shares equals $10.24 per share which, together with $2.60 cash dividends, totals $12.84, or $2.19 per share ($25,983,964) more than the amount earned during 1958.
>
> While the Board of Directors believe that stock dividends can be in the best interest of our company and the stockholders, they wish to emphasize that the corporation cannot continue to reduce retained earnings in this manner. Depending upon the future market value of IBM stock, therefore, future stock dividends may be declared on a less frequent basis or in amounts less than $2^1/_2$ per cent.

Exhibit 2 shows IBM's total assets, long-term debt, capital stock, retained earnings, and the number of common shares outstanding at December 31, 1946 through 1961.

EXHIBIT 1

International Business Machines Corporation
Selected Data Pertaining to Stock Dividends and Stock Splits
for the Years 1946 through 1961

	Gross Income from Sales, Service, and Rentals in United States ($000)	Net Income ($000)	Cash Dividends ($000)	Cash Dividends Per Share[1]	Stock Dividends Distributed ($000)	Stock Dividends Distributed	Price Range[1]	Stock Splits
								25%
1946	$ 115,645	$ 18,766	$ 8,587	$ .35	—	—	—	
1947	139,404	23,554	8,590	.35	—	—	—	
1948	156,398	28,101	10,023	.41	—	—	—	75
1949	183,465	33,277	10,519	.43	$ 12,530	5%	24 7/8- 15 1/2	—
1950	214,917	33,301	11,044	.45	13,154	5	26 3/4- 20 5/8	—
1951	266,798	27,892	11,577	.47	17,263	5	27 1/2- 23 1/4	—
1952	333,728	29,875	12,173	.49	21,748	5	30 1/4- 22 3/4	—
1953	409,989	34,119	12,779	.51	28,923	5	33 5/8- 29 5/8	—
1954	461,350	46,537	15,558	.63	17,979	2 1/2	61 7/8- 32 1/2	25
1955	563,549	55,873	16,386	.66	—	—	74 1/4- 58 3/8	—
1956	734,340	68,785	19,937	.80	37,897	2 1/2	116 3/8- 63 1/8	25
1957	1,000,432	89,292	25,407	.93	—	—	159 1/4-105 3/8	100
1958	1,171,788	126,192	30,765	1.13	80,847	2 1/2	239 3/8-130 1/8	—
1959	1,309,788	145,633	37,074	1.35	121,411	2 1/2	325 3/8-219 3/8	50
1960	1,436,053	168,181	54,852	2.00	—	—	400 -271 1/2	—
1961	1,694,296	207,228	63,266	2.30	—	—	607 -386 3/4	50

[1] Adjusted for all stock splits and stock dividends through 1961.

EXHIBIT 2

International Business Machines Corporation
Selected Financial Data at December 31, 1946 through 1961
(dollar amounts in thousands)

	Total Assets	Long-Term Debt	Capital Stock	Retained Earnings	Number of Common Shares
1946	$ 148,405	$ 30,000	$ 36,918	$ 46,091	1,432,407
1947	184,270	50,000	36,918	60,539	1,432,407
1948	241,977	85,000	36,918	78,616	2,506,712
1949	267,345	85,000	49,448	88,845	2,632,007
1950	299,953	85,000	62,602	101,652	2,763,548
1951	394,119	135,000	82,285	101,009	2,901,652
1952	428,229	175,000	104,033	96,963	3,046,641
1953	520,438	215,000	132,957	89,380	3,198,868
1954	565,475	250,000	150,936	92,393	4,098,471
1955	629,511	295,000	150,936	131,879	4,098,471
1956	769,049	330,000	188,833	142,829	5,251,118
1957	1,086,969	375,000	415,804	206,714	11,552,460
1958	1,261,147	425,000	498,928	221,294	11,849,023
1959	1,390,637	425,000	635,077	208,442	18,268,943
1960	1,535,366	425,000	651,019	321,771	18,310,954
1961	1,768,649	425,000	678,558	506,633[1]	27,561,531

[1] Includes $40.9 million of undistributed net earnings of IBM World Trade Corporation.

QUESTIONS :

1. What are the advantages to IBM of declaring regular stock dividends?

2. Can you see any reason for not *distributing* a $2^1/_2$ per cent stock dividend *in 1955* even though current undistributed earnings were sufficient to warrant it?

3. Do you think the New York Stock Exchange requirements in effect from February, 1953 to July, 1955 were realistic? Do you think this requirement was desirable from the standpoint of (a) a corporation and (b) its stockholders? Relate your answers to accounting requirements for cash dividends. Also, consider the distinction, if any, made by a stockholder between receipt of cash and stock dividends.

4. Do you believe that a transfer from retained earnings based on the fair market value is realistic considering the wide fluctuations in stock prices?

5. Do you agree with management's reasoning as explained in the 1958 annual report?

6. What criteria do you think the Exchange would use to determine whether a distribution in the range between 25 and 99 per cent was to be treated as a stock dividend or a stock split?

7. How would you disclose, on the financial statements at December 31, a stock dividend declared in October to be issued in January? Contrast your recommendation with IBM's disclosure of such a dividend. Do you have any suggestions regarding the language used by IBM in its balance-sheet disclosure?

CHAPTER EIGHTEEN

Classification
of Deferred Income Taxes
as Equity

There has been little uniformity in the classification and description of the account for postponed income taxes when accelerated depreciation is used for income tax purposes only and some other depreciation method, usually straight-line, is used for book purposes. This has been particularly true of regulated public utilities following the "normalization" procedure.[1] Among both these utilities and other companies, a common practice has been to establish a separate *major* classification on the balance sheet between Long-Term Debt and Stockholders' Equity, usually described as "Deferred Income Taxes."

This chapter consists of a single case in which the classification of such an account as part of stockholders' equity is the major issue. The court decision rendered in the case supported procedures considered sound by most accountants, but the decision was also significant for other reasons. An editorial in the August, 1959, issue of the *Journal of Accountancy*[2] noted that the decision "established an important precedent upholding the authority of an Institute committee to express opinions on accounting principles." The editorial concluded that "this legal affirmation of the Institute's rights and obligations comes at an opportune time, as the new Accounting Principles Board prepares to take up its duties."

---

[1] The "normalization" procedure is described on page 253.
[2] "Institute's Right to Issue Accounting Opinions Upheld by Courts " (Editorial), *Journal of Accountancy*, Vol. 108, August 1959, pp. 23-24.

REFERENCES

Andersen, Arthur, & Co., *The AICPA Injunction Case Re: ARB No. 44 (Revised)*. Chicago: Arthur Andersen & Co., 1960, (*Cases in Public Accounting Practice*—Vol. 1).

_____ *SEC Administrative Policy Re: Balance-Sheet Treatment of Deferred Income-Tax Credits*. Chicago: Arthur Andersen & Co., 1961, (*Cases in Public Accounting Practice*—Vols. 5 & 6).

Blough, Carman G., "Tax Allocation and the SEC," *Journal of Accountancy*, 109 (Jun. 1960), 65–66.

"Institute's Right to Issue Accounting Opinions Upheld by Courts," (Editorial), *Journal of Accountancy*, 108 (Aug. 1959), 23–24.

News Reports, *Journal of Accountancy*, 107 (May 1959), 8; 108 (Aug. 1959), 7; 108 (Sept. 1959), 7; 110 (Nov. 1960), 16; 110 (Dec. 1960), 20–22; 111 (Mar. 1961), 11.

Perry, Bernard T., (Correspondence), *Journal of Accountancy*, 109 (Jan. 1960), 23–24.

U. S. Securities and Exchange Commission, "Statement of Administrative Policy regarding Balance Sheet Treatment of Credit Equivalent to Reduction in Income Taxes," *Accounting Series Release*, No. 85 (Feb. 29, 1960).

_____ "Response to Comment on Statement of Administrative Policy regarding Balance Sheet Treatment of Credit Equivalent to Reduction in Income Taxes," *Accounting Series Release*, No. 86 (Apr. 12, 1960).

_____ "Findings and Opinion of the Commission in the Matters of Kentucky Power Company and American Electric Power Company, Inc.," *Holding Company Act Release*, No. 14353 (Jan. 13, 1961).

American Electric Power Company, Inc.

The American Electric Power Company, Inc.[1] (AEP) is a holding company whose operating subsidiaries form an integrated electric utility system. AEP's operating companies are:

> Appalachian Power Company
> Indiana & Michigan Electric Company
> Kentucky Power Company
> Kingsport Utilities, Inc. (Tenn.)
> Ohio Power Company
> Wheeling Electric Company (West Virginia)

AEP serves an area of 49,000 square miles with a population of about 5½ million people in the States of Indiana, Michigan, Ohio, Kentucky, West Virginia and Tennessee. The system leads the nation's private power industry in the sale of electric energy.

Company management is proud of the dynamic growth of the system. Electric sales increased from 14 billion kilowatt hours (kwh) in 1951 to 28.6 billion kwh in 1961. During this period, annual expenditures for new construction averaged $115 million. Despite increased operating costs, the company reduced the average price of power to the consumer by over 10 per cent, from 1.36 cents per kwh in 1951 to 1.22 cents per kwh in 1961.

Company Financing

In 1952, the company issued $20 million of 3⅜ per cent Sinking Fund Debentures due June 1, 1977. An application to the SEC in connection with this issue contained a commitment by the company agreeing to the following restrictions on its capital structure:

---

[1] Name changed from American Gas and Electric Company in 1958.

(1) Maintenance of consolidated common stock equity of at least 30 per cent of total consolidated capitalization including surplus. (See Exhibit 3 for items classified as "common stock equity" and "capitalization.")
(2) Maintenance of consolidated funded debt of less than 60 per cent of total capitalization including surplus.

In November, 1957, the company completed arrangements with ten banks to borrow up to $52 million with maturity in November, 1959. Interest was one-fourth of one per cent above the prime commercial. rate.

In 1959, AEP requested approval of regulatory authorities to extend the bank loan maturity into 1960 when it expected to sell common stock. Approval of the loan extension was denied, and 1,200,000 shares of common stock were sold in October, 1959 to meet the maturing bank loan.

Depreciation Policy

The company uses straight-line depreciation for financial reporting purposes. For federal income tax purposes, it (a) amortizes over 60 months facilities covered by Certificates of Necessity, (b) uses declining-balance depreciation on non-certified assets constructed or acquired since December 31, 1953, and (c) uses the straight-line method for all other depreciable assets.

Where required by state regulatory authorities, AEP has made provision for deferred income taxes resulting from the use of accelerated amortization and declining-balance depreciation for tax purposes. By the end of 1961, these provisions totaled $126,829,000 (see Exhibit 1) and were estimated to exceed $200,000,000 by 1970. Exhibit 2 shows AEP's Statement of Income for 1959, 1960, and 1961, while Exhibits 3 through 5 show the "liability" side of AEP's consolidated balance sheets for the years 1958 through 1961.

AICPA Injunction

On December 30, 1958, the SEC issued a "Notice of Intention to Announce Interpretation of Administrative Policy." In this notice, the SEC proposed an order disallowing the inclusion of deferred income taxes within the equity section of balance sheets filed with it. Hearings of interested parties were announced for the spring of 1959.

In April, 1959, Mr. Carman G. Blough, Director of Research of the AICPA, testified at the SEC hearing. Mr. Blough stated that in view of the controversy and uncertainty over the classification of deferred income tax accounts, the Committee on Accounting Procedure of the AICPA was about to distribute a letter of opinion and clarification of the committee's intent in issuing Accounting Research Bulletin Number 44 (Revised). Mr. Blough read excerpts from the letter into the record of the hearing. The entire letter follows:

AMERICAN INSTITUTE OF CERTIFIED PUBLIC ACCOUNTANTS
270 Madison Avenue, New York 16, New York

April 15, 1959

To the Members of the American Institute of Certified Public Accountants

Gentlemen:

Question has been raised with respect to the intent of the committee on accounting procedure in using the phrase "a deferred tax account" in Accounting Research Bulletin No. 44 (revised), *Declining-balance Depreciation*, to indicate the account to be credited for the amount of the deferred income tax (see paragraphs 4 and 5). [See pages 254–55.]

The committee used the phrase in its ordinary connotation of an account to be shown in the balance sheet as a liability or a deferred credit. A provision in recognition of the deferral of income taxes, being required for the proper determination of net income, should not at the same time result in a credit to earned surplus or to any other account included in the stockholders' equity section of the balance sheet.

Three of the twenty-one members of the committee, Messrs. Jennings, Powell and Staub, dissented to the issuance at this time of any letter interpreting Accounting Research Bulletin No. 44 (revised).

COMMITTEE ON ACCOUNTING
PROCEDURE

By William W. Werntz, Chairman

The Complaint

On April 15, 1959, three operating subsidiaries of the American Electric Power Company filed a complaint in the U. S. District Court of the Southern District of New York against the American Institute of Certified Public Accountants, its President, Director of Research, and the Chairman of its Committee on Accounting Procedure.

Plaintiffs: Appalachian Power Company
               Ohio Power Company
               Indiana & Michigan Electric Company

Defendants: American Institute of Certified Public Accountants
               L. H. Penney, President
               William W. Werntz, Chairman, Committee on Accounting Procedure
               Carman G. Blough, Director of Research

Plaintiffs sought to delay publication or distribution of the proposed letter for 60 days to provide for the usual "exposure" procedure normally followed by the Institute and the Committee before publishing bulletins. They complained that the defendants had not followed proper procedures and were acting in undue haste in publishing the proposed letter.

These companies, which also opposed issuance of the SEC's ruling on "Interpretation of Administrative Policy," emphasized the great weight generally attached to the opinions of the Institute by the SEC, state regulatory agencies, and many financial institutions. In view of this widespread influence, the complaint noted, the AICPA had previously circulated exposure drafts of proposed opinions to interested parties for a preliminary opinion before final adoption and publication. The companies pointed out that the balance-sheet classification of deferred income tax credits influenced the ratio of debt to equity, a measure widely used in appraising the attractiveness of debt and equity securities, particularly those of public utilities.

Court Action

The District Court granted a temporary order restraining the circulation of the letter.

On May 20, 1959, Judge Richard H. Levet dismissed the complaint. Parts of his opinion are quoted below:

... There is no allegation that the method of accounting proposed by defendants is inherently false or fraudulent. On the contrary, it is supported by respectable authority. Neither is there any allegation of special damages, except in the most general and speculative terms.

This action is not to prevent interference with plaintiffs' contracts, their sales or their property. It seeks to delay the distribution of an adverse opinion relative to accounting procedures. True, it may ultimately affect plaintiffs' application for credit. However, such a result is collateral, not direct, an effect which incidentally flows from a justifiable act. The plaintiffs may have grievances, but they relate to the distribution of honest opinions, not facts. No threat of intentional, unjustifiable harm to plaintiffs' business rights or property exists.

This court has been unable to find any precedent under the doctrine of prima facie tort or otherwise for a preliminary or final injunction forbidding a group from publishing and distributing opinions under circumstances equivalent or even similar to these.

Accordingly, the application for preliminary injunction must be denied and the complaint dismissed and summary judgment granted.

The power companies appealed Judge Levet's decision and were granted a stay until the U. S. Court of Appeals could hear the motion.

On June 17, 1959, the Court of Appeals upheld Judge Levet's

opinion and went even further in establishing the right of the Institute, as a professional organization, to issue statements in the area of its professional competence. The Court of Appeals stated:

On the merits we agree with Judge Levet's reasoned opinion . . . . We think the courts may not dictate or control the procedures by which a private organization expresses its honestly held views. Defendants' action involves no breach of duty owed by them to the plaintiffs. *On the contrary, every professional body accepts a public obligation for unfettered expression of views and loses all right to professional consideration, as well as all utility, if its views are controlled by other criteria than the intellectual conclusions of the persons acting* [emphasis added]. Absent a showing of actual malice or its equivalent, the courts would be making a great mistake, contrary indeed to their own ideals and professions, if they assumed to restrict and denigrate this widely recognized and assumed professional duty.

On July 7, 1959, an appeal to the U. S. Supreme Court was denied and the original letter interpreting ARB No. 44 (revised) was mailed together with a letter from Mr. Penney, President of the Institute, explaining the delay.

AEP's 1959 Annual Report

For the year ended December 31, 1959, AEP maintained the same depreciation policies and accounting procedures as in 1958, but changed the classification of the deferred tax accounts on the balance sheet as follows (see Exhibit 4):

Retained Income Restricted for Deferred Federal Income Taxes	$83,256,000
Reserve for Deferred Federal Income Taxes[2]	5,196,000

The following is quoted from a note to the 1959 statements:

In 1958, largely as a result of orders of the Public Service Commission of West Virginia, which does not recognize for rate-making purposes provisions relating to the tax effects of the declining-balance method of computing depreciation, three subsidiaries made no provision in the accounts maintained for purposes of state regulatory authority for certain deferred Federal income taxes . . . . If provisions for such deferred taxes had been made for the years 1959 and 1958 they would have aggregated $723,000 and $629,000 respectively, and the amount shown as Consolidated Earnings for Common Stock of Parent Company for each of those years would have been correspondingly less.

In another note, the company stated:

---

[2] This account, instead of "Retained Income Restricted for Deferred Federal Income Taxes," was required by Ohio regulatory authorities for deferred income taxes resulting from use of *declining-balance depreciation* for income tax purposes.

Retained Income Restricted for Deferred Federal Income Taxes represents amounts restricted under orders of state regulatory authorities, ... $76,804,000 relating to amortization of emergency facilities and $6,452,000 relating to liberalized [declining-balance] depreciation.

In addition to the information cited above, the company also disclosed the position of the Federal Power Commission and the SEC with regard to the treatment of the deferred tax account. In May, 1958, the FPC had ordered that deferred taxes be classified in a separate account ("Accumulated Deferred Taxes on Income"), not to be identified as either a reserve or restricted retained income. AEP then adopted the procedure of allowing the reduction in income taxes to "flow through" to unrestricted earned surplus for FPC reporting purposes *only*. This procedure was challenged by the FPC. As part of a note in the 1959 annual report, AEP made the following statement regarding controversies with regulatory commissions and the AICPA:

The company is unable at this time to predict the outcome of the FPC action or to state what action the SEC may take to require a change in the subsidiaries' accounting and reporting practices, nor can the company state whether any such action may lawfully be taken by either commission as applied to the subsidiaries of a registered holding company.[3]
... The American Institute of Certified Public Accountants released a letter of its Committee on Accounting Procedure to the effect that it was the committee's view that provisions for deferred income taxes should not be shown in the balance sheet as retained income or as any other account included in the stockholders' equity section of the balance sheet.
It is the opinion of the company and its independent certified public accountants that the methods used by the subsidiaries of the company in accounting for the credits resulting from provisions for deferred income taxes in accordance with orders of State regulatory authorities are among several acceptable alternatives commonly in use in the public utility industry.

The company's auditors gave an unqualified opinion on the 1959 financial statements.

SEC Action Against AEP

On February 29, 1960, the SEC issued a "Statement of Administrative Policy Regarding Balance Sheet Treatment of Credit Equivalent to Reduction of Income Taxes." The statement provided:

... any financial statement filed with this commission which designates as earned surplus (or its equivalent) or in any manner as a part of equity capital

---

[3] The dispute with the FPC was still unsettled as of February 15, 1963.

(even though accompanied by words of limitation such as "restricted" or "appropriated") the accumulated credit arising from accounting for reductions in income taxes resulting from deducting costs for income tax purposes at a more rapid rate than for financial statement purposes will be presumed by the commission to be misleading or inaccurate despite disclosure contained in the certificate of the accountant or in footnotes to the statements, provided the amounts involved are material.

The following was contained in a footnote to the SEC's statement:

So far as this commission is concerned, since it believes that classifying the item as a component part of common stock equity is misleading for financial statement purposes, it does not intend to consider the item as a part of common stock equity for analytical purposes, although it *may give consideration to the item as one of a number of relevant factors in appraising the overall financial condition of a company* [emphasis added].

In the spring of 1960, the Kentucky Power Company, one of AEP's operating subsidiaries, proposed to issue $40 million of promissory notes to four commercial banks. At that time, the latest balance sheet of the Kentucky Power Company, dated March 31, 1960, contained $731,441 designated as "Earned Surplus Restricted for Future Federal Income Taxes." On the same date, AEP's consolidated balance sheet disclosed $86,976,332 classified in the same manner. The SEC instituted proceedings to determine what action should be taken with regard to the deferred tax accounts in light of its Statement of Administrative Policy.

After discussions between the SEC and AEP officials, a compromise, acceptable to both parties, was made public on January 13, 1961.

On the balance sheets the deferred tax credit would be captioned:

Accumulated Amount Invested in the Business Equivalent to Reduction in Federal Income Taxes Resulting from Accelerated Amortization and Liberalized [Declining-balance] Depreciation, Which is Recorded as Earned Surplus Restricted, or as a Reserve, for Future Federal Income Taxes in Accounts Maintained Pursuant to State Regulatory Requirements.

In addition, this amount was not to be considered as either long-term debt or common stock equity, as is indicated by the following agreement which was reached regarding AEP's capital structure:

[So long as there is a substantial amount of accumulated tax reductions arising from the use of accelerated amortization or liberalized depreciation for federal income tax purposes], ... the commission will not impose any terms and conditions ... or make adverse findings ... in respect to capitalization ratios with respect to any proposed financing of the American system where upon completion of the financing:
(a) Common stock equity is not less than 30 per cent of total capitalization, including surplus.

(b) Mortgage debt is not in excess of 60 per cent of total capitalization, including surplus.

(c) Long-term debt is not in excess of 65 per cent of total capitalization, including surplus.

For purposes of these tests:

(i) The computation of common stock equity, mortgage debt and long-term debt ratios is to be on a system consolidated basis or on a subsidiary corporate basis as is appropriate;

(ii) The terms "common stock equity" and "total capitalization, including surplus" are not to include any accumulated tax reduction resulting from charges against income as an operating revenue deduction in respect of accelerated amortization or liberalized [declining-balance] depreciation for federal income tax purposes;

(iii) The term "long-term debt" is to include all indebtedness for borrowed money having, at the date of issuance, renewal or the guaranty thereof, a maturity of more than 12 months; and

(iv) The term "total capitalization, including surplus" is to include long-term debt, the aggregate of the par value of, or stated capital represented by, the outstanding shares of all classes of stock, any premium on stock, and surplus.

In the 1960 and 1961 annual reports, AEP captioned the deferred tax accounts as prescribed by the SEC. (See Exhibits 5 and 6.) The auditors rendered an unqualified opinion on the 1960 and 1961 financial statements.

AEP's Position

On February 2, 1961, after the compromise with the SEC had been announced, Philip Sporn, President of AEP, and Donald C. Cook, Executive Vice President[4], addressed the New York Society of Security Analysts. Mr. Sporn spoke first and discussed the effects of the SEC decision on AEP and its customers.

... I pointed out [in hearings before the SEC] that the foundation of our case was the fact that we were a unique company in a unique industry, that in an industry that was highly dynamic we were especially so, that we had expanded for many years at a greater rate than the industry, and that there were solid reasons for this, and these were *tied up with this accounting order* [emphasis added] ....

... A very interesting question is how we have been able to keep the price of our product going down when our costs have been going up. This has not been an easy job, by any means. [See Exhibits 7 and 8.]

There are a number of solid reasons: because of expansion of plant to meet the growth of the system, we have been able to introduce advance design concepts, larger generators, larger boilers, higher system temperatures, higher steam pressures, higher transmission voltages resulting in more eco-

---

[4] In November, 1961, Mr. Cook was elected President of AEP upon Mr. Sporn's retirement.

nomical transmission costs, more economical distribution and more efficient use of labor. And to all these must be added the very important fact of our being able to reduce costs of capital through our methods of financing....

...During the past several years we have had substantial help from the amount of restricted surplus as a base for maintaining our equity ratios. It has therefore served the same purpose as new equity capital. It has enabled us to sell more debt securities than would otherwise have been possible and it has served to reduce both our capital costs and our federal income taxes.

This substantial help in financing has redounded to the benefit of both investors and consumers and, to the extent that it has helped in the growth and development of our territory, it has also furthered the general public interest.

In this next chart [Exhibit 9] I have shown the pronounced effect of the debt ratio on annual costs of charges required to carry investment in plant and property. Based on the assumptions in the chart, which are conservative, annual cost declines from 9.77 per cent to 9.32 per cent when debt ratio increases from 45 per cent to 50 per cent; from 9.32 per cent to 8.86 per cent when the debt ratio increases from 50 per cent to 55 per cent; from 8.86 per cent to 8.41 per cent when debt ratio increases from 55 per cent to 60 per cent; and, finally, from 8.41 per cent to 7.94 per cent when the debt ratio increases from 60 per cent to 65 per cent. A change of five percentage points in the debt ratio increases annual carrying charges about $4,500 for each $1-million of invested capital. In the case of AEP System companies, with about $1.3-billion of invested capital, a change of 5 per cent in the capital structure would mean an increase in annual cost of almost $6-million.

In the next chart [Exhibit 10] I have made a calculation of the effect on the AEP System costs if the restricted surplus at the time it totaled $86-million—it is greater than that now—had been replaced by common stock. You will notice that the difference between equity costs and debt costs is a difference of some 6.8 per cent and this difference in terms of $86-million represents $5,848,000 a year. For the annual kwh sold at that date of almost 26 billion, this represents a difference in cost of .226 mills. One of our aluminum customers takes approximately 3.2 billion kwh from us annually and a difference of .226 mills per kwh means an additional annual cost to him of over $723,000....

Mr. Cook, a CPA and a former member and chairman of the SEC, discussed the significance of the SEC decision from the financial community's viewpoint. Mr. Cook felt that the caption adopted recognized the following:

1. The credit measures the accumulated amount at the balance sheet date *actually invested* in the business, that is, that either assets have been increased, liabilities decreased, or a combination of the two.

   This is easily demonstrated as a fact and is of the first importance.

   Incidentally, many accounting authorities prefer to characterize equity in terms of amounts invested in the business.

2. The credit represents net reductions to date of federal income taxes.

   We think this concept is of very great importance because, if reductions in federal income taxes have occurred, the effect can only be to increase proprietorship.

3. There is no present liability of any kind created as a result of the use of accelerated amortization and liberalized [declining-balance] depreciation for tax purposes while using straight-line depreciation for book purposes.

Although the liability concept was at one time advanced in some quarters, I think it is now generally agreed that where there is no debt, no debtor and no creditor, there can be no liability.

Such is the case here, and the Commission agreed with this position.

4. The State regulatory bodies regard the item as being Earned Surplus.

The orders of the State regulatory bodies so provide and were placed in the record.

It has always been our view, and we had highly qualified and respected experts prepared to testify to this effect, that the most meaningful financial statements are those prepared on the basis of the requirements of the regulatory body having major rate jurisdiction. In our case this is the State Commissions.

5. We not only have the right and the duty to keep our books as required by State regulatory bodies but we have the right to disseminate financial statements which clearly show how the books are kept.

At a minimum this is a matter of full and fair disclosure.

6. The accumulated amount will furnish the basis of future accretions to Unrestricted Earned Surplus.

This is also a matter of clear and easy proof. The recognition of this principle drastically narrows the area of argument about the character of the item. In effect, the argument is limited to the question of whether it is *income already received which may be recognized as earned*, or whether it is *income already received, the recognition of which should be deferred*. The fact that income has been received, in the sense that accretions have come into the enterprise and increased net assets, is admitted. The only remaining question, therefore, is *when* this income should be recognized as having been earned . . . .

In connection with this last point, Mr. Cook referred to the following footnote in the SEC Opinion on the Kentucky Power action:

It should also be borne in mind that, by the very nature of the accumulated tax reduction, whether it be in respect of accelerated amortization or liberalized [declining-balance] depreciation, the amounts which have heretofore been, and which will hereafter be, credited to this account through charges to the income account, will be returned to income during the remaining life of the related physical assets, generally in proportion to the increased amount of income taxes to which a company will become subject in later years as the depreciation deductions for income tax purposes applicable to such assets become less than the straight-line depreciation deductions taken as depreciation in the accounts. In that sense, therefore, the accumulated tax reduction may properly be regarded as a deferred credit to income in that it represents a source of enhancement of future income by way of mitigation, for financial accounting purposes, of a future expense—namely, income tax expense. It will thus furnish the basis for future accretions to unrestricted earned surplus. While this may be more readily apparent where the accumulated tax reduction relates to accelerated amortization where necessity certificates are no longer being issued by the federal government than where it relates to liberalized [declining-balance] depreciation where, in a growing company, the balance in the accumulated tax reduction account may be expected to grow, nevertheless the existing balance as of any given time in the accumulated tax reduction account, regardless of the nature of the credits, will ultimately be returned to income and thence to unrestricted earned surplus.

Mr. Cook concluded his remarks with the following summary of the agreement:

What is the significance of this agreement to the financial community having an interest in American Electric Power? It can be stated in a nutshell. On the basis of our present forecasts it appears that the American Electric Power System should now be able to rely largely upon debt financing to meet its capital requirements for many years to come. Certainly for the next six or seven years, and perhaps for ten years or longer, we should not have to sell any additional shares of common stock whatsoever. This is as it should be, for the System has a large and solid equity. [See Exhibit 11.]

The formula properly recognizes that whatever the capitalization ratios seem to be when calculated exclusive of the increase in proprietorship due to accumulated tax reductions, the fact is that the physical property and other net assets resulting from the accumulated tax reduction are available for the protection and enhancement of all of the security holders. Thus, the opinion gives express recognition to the fact that the technical answer to the accounting question is not determinative of how the item should be viewed for analytical purposes. Indeed, an examination of the opinion shows that the Commission evaluated the Kentucky capital structure, which was specifically before the Commission because of the Kentucky financing, in terms of assets...

The formula also recognizes that long-term unsecured debt may be issued in substantial amounts under the Holding Company Act. This latter concept, while not entirely new, has now been strengthened and given new vitality. In view of the high cost of preferred stock capital and the desirability of substituting debt for it, this favorable recognition is of extreme importance.

While long-term unsecured debt may now become a permanent part of our financing program in substantial amounts, this will in no way reduce our reliance upon short-term bank credit for financing the System. It will only affect the character of the securities to be issued at the time when our bank loans are retired from the proceeds of long-term financing.

In conclusion, I would like to express the opinion that the decision of the Commission was statesmanlike. When the Commission disposed of this case it faced up to its responsibilities, clearly set out under the Holding Company Act, to protect the interests of consumers and investors and took appropriate action to do so. It rejected an abstract and controversial accounting theory that had been enunciated without adequate study or consideration and instead accepted hard legal and financial facts of life, readily recognizable, as the appropriate basis for determining financial condition and security structures. It declined to go down a road which could only have resulted in using the Public Utility Holding Company Act as a sword against consumers and investors and the general public interest rather than as a shield to protect them.

EXHIBIT 1

American Electric Power Company, Inc.
Selected Financial Data for the Years 1951-1961
(000 omitted)

	Construction Expenditures	Net Income (after Dividends on Preferred Stock)	Depreciation[1]	Annual Provision for Future Federal Income Taxes	Cumulative Provision for Deferred Federal Income Taxes[2]
1951	$ 95,600	$24,300	$19,664	$ 337	$ 337
1952	112,700	27,346	21,838	1,549	1,886
1953	137,400	30,956	24,047	3,217	5,103
1954	85,500	32,465	27,823	8,516	13,619
1955	73,800	38,488	30,518	12,100	25,719
1956	127,000	40,466	31,941	13,053	38,772
1957	164,100	44,483	34,406	13,759	52,531
1958	153,400	46,294	38,223	17,553	70,084
1959	116,100	49,253	42,341	18,368	88,452
1960	97,200	53,972	44,882	17,734	106,186
1961	96,600	55,098	49,620	20,643	126,829

[1] Amounts reported in income statements.

[2] Cumulative amount provided whether classified (a) as a "Reserve," (b) as "Restricted Retained Income" or (c) under the new caption adopted in accordance with the SEC compromise of January, 1961.

EXHIBIT 2

American Electric Power Company, Inc.
Consolidated Statement of Income for the Years 1959-1961
(000 omitted)

	1961	1960	1959
Operating Revenues	$352,443	$337,596	$323,092
Operating Expenses:			
Operation	$112,606	$110,376	$105,578
Maintenance	27,854	28,064	27,907
Depreciation	49,620	44,882	42,341
Taxes, Other Than Federal Income Taxes	30,402	29,387	28,790
Federal Income Taxes	27,143	28,265	24,728
Provision for Future Federal Income Taxes	23,199	20,169	20,160
Portion of Current Federal Income Taxes Provided for in Prior Years (Credit)	−2,556	−2,435	−1,792
Total Operating Expenses	$268,268	$258,708	$247,712
Operating Income	$ 84,175	$ 78,888	$ 75,380
Other Income Less Miscellaneous Income Deduction	453	489	642
Income Before Interest Charges	$ 84,628	$ 79,377	$ 76,022
Interest Charges:			
Long-term Debt and Miscellaneous	$ 27,424	$ 26,928	$ 27,874
Interest Charged to Construction (Credit)	−2,226	−5,859	−5,446
Total Interest Charges	$ 25,198	$ 21,069	$ 22,428
Consolidated Net Income, Before Preferred Stock Dividend Requirements of Subsidiaries	$ 59,430	$ 58,308	$ 53,594
Deduct Preferred Stock Dividend Requirements of Subsidiaries	4,332	4,336	4,341
Consolidated Net Income, Applicable to Common Stock of American Electric Power Company, Inc.	$ 55,098	$ 53,972	$ 49,253

EXHIBIT 3

American Electric Power Company, Inc.
Condensed "Liability" Side of Balance Sheet, December 31, 1958
(000 omitted from column figures)

Capitalization:	
Long-Term Debt	$ 714,990
Preferred Stocks of Subsidiaries	$ 101,925
Common Stock Equity:	
Common Stock—$10 par	$ 201,699
Premium on Common Stock	10,705
Retained Income (including $86,900,000 restricted at December 31, 1958, of which $66,629,000 represents deferred federal income taxes)[1]	206,222
Other Paid-In Capital	22
Total Common Stock Equity	$ 418,648
Total Capitalization	$1,235,563
Reserve for Deferred Federal Income Taxes[2]	$ 3,455
Current Liabilities	143,772
Other Items	8,107
Total	$1,390,897

[1] $20,271,000 restricted by mortgage covenants from use for cash dividends on common stock.

[2] Classification required by Ohio regulatory authorities for deferred income taxes resulting from use of *declining-balance depreciation* for income tax purposes.

EXHIBIT 4

American Electric Power Company, Inc.
Condensed "Liability" Side of Balance Sheet, December 31, 1959
(000 omitted from column figures)

Long-Term Debt	$ 723,149
Preferred Stocks of Subsidiaries	101,776
Common Stock—$10 par	213,699
Premium on Common Stock	54,217
Other Paid-In Capital	32
Retained Income Other Than Amounts Restricted for Deferred Federal Income Taxes	154,032
Retained Income Restricted for Deferred Federal Income Taxes	83,256
Reserve for Deferred Federal Income Taxes[1]	5,196
Current Liabilities	114,349
Other Items	8,104
Total	$1,457,810

[1] Classification required by Ohio regulatory authorities for deferred income taxes resulting from use of *declining-balance depreciation* for income tax purposes.

EXHIBIT 5

American Electric Power Company, Inc.
Condensed "Liability" Side of Balance Sheet as of
December 31, 1961 and December 31, 1960
(000 omitted from column figures)

	1961	1960
Long-Term Debt	$ 750,876	$ 718,297
Preferred Stocks of Subsidiaries	101,573	101,728
Common Stock—$10 par	219,041	213,699
Stock Dividend Distributed January 10, 1961	—	26,711
Premium on Common Stock	75,586	54,217
Other Paid-In Capital	43	36
Earned Surplus as Recorded in Unrestricted Accounts Maintained, in the Case of the Principal Electric Utility Subsidiaries, Pursuant to State Regulatory Requirements	158,696	144,854
Accumulated Amount Invested in the Business Equivalent to Reduction in Federal Income Taxes Resulting from Accelerated Amortization and Liberalized [Declining-balance] Depreciation, Which is Recorded as Earned Surplus Restricted ($119,940,000 at 12/31/61 and $99,214,000 at 12/31/60), or as a Reserve ($6,889,000 at 12/31/61 and $6,972,000 at 12/31/60), For Future Federal Income Taxes in Accounts Maintained Pursuant to State Regulatory Requirements	126,829	106,186
Current Liabilities	120,433	133,474
Other Items	8,033	7,987
Total	$1,561,110	$1,507,189

EXHIBIT 6

American Electric Power Company, Inc.

Consolidated Statement of Accumulated Amount Invested in the Business Equivalent to Reduction in Federal Income Taxes Resulting from Accelerated Amortization and Liberalized [Declining-balance] Depreciation, Which is Recorded as Earned Surplus Restricted, or as a Reserve, for Future Federal Income Taxes in Accounts Maintained Pursuant to State Regulatory Requirements, Years Ended December 31, 1961 and December 31, 1960 (000 omitted)

	1961	1960
Balance at Beginning of Year	$106,186	$ 88,452
Additions—Amounts Equal to Provision for Future Federal Income Taxes	23,199	20,169
	$129,385	$108,621
Deductions—Amounts Equal to Portion of Current Federal Income Taxes Provided for in Prior Years	2,556	2,435
Balance at End of Year	$126,829	$106,186

EXHIBIT 7

American Electric Power Company, Inc.
Average Revenue per Kilowatt Hour, Years 1951-1961[1]

Year	Cents per Kilowatt Hour
1951	1.36
1952	1.36
1953	1.35
1954	1.38
1955	1.25
1956	1.28
1957	1.31
1958	1.29
1959	1.23
1960	1.22
1961	1.22

[1] This tabulation includes all customers—residential, commercial, industrial, and all others—while the data in Exhibit 8 pertain to residential customers only.

EXHIBIT 8

American Electric Power Company, Inc.
AEP vs. United States—Use and Price of
Residential Electric Power for the Years 1950 through 1961

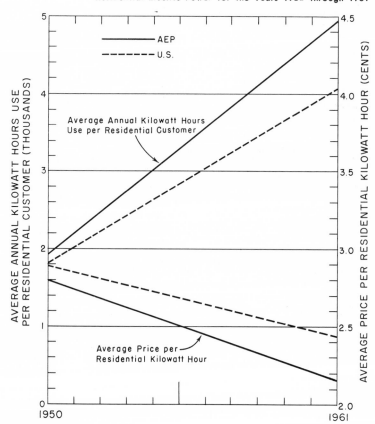

EXHIBIT 9

American Electric Power Company, Inc.
Effect of Debt Ratio on Annual Charges
Required to Carry Investment
(in Per Cent of Original Investment)[1]

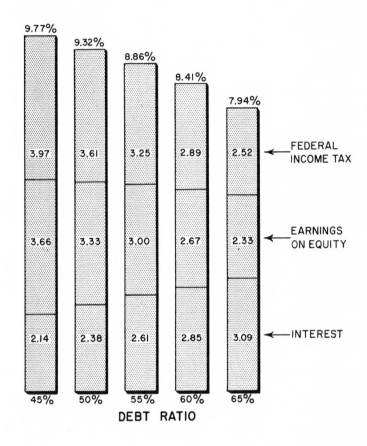

[1] Based on 4¾ per cent bonds, 6⅔ per cent earnings on equity, and 52 per cent federal income tax rate.

EXHIBIT 10

American Electric Power Company, Inc.
Difference in Cost Between Debt and Equity Financing
and Effect on Power Costs
(Prepared September, 1960)

	Per cent
Equity at 18 times earnings	5.50
Federal Income Taxes (52% rate)	6.05
Total	11.55
Less: Debt	4.75
Difference	6.80

Assume:

$86 million in restricted surplus transferred to reserve account and replaced by equity. Then:

Added financing costs (6.8% times $86 million)	$5,848,000
Total kwh sold in 1959	25,866,000,000
Added cost per kwh sold (mills)	.226

EXHIBIT 11

American Electric Power Company, Inc.
Estimated Total Capitalization and Estimated Tax
Reduction Resulting from Use of Accelerated Amortization
and Liberalized Depreciation for Income Tax Purposes
(000 omitted from dollar amounts in columns)

		Accumulated Tax Reduction					
	Estimated Total	*Accelerated Amortization*[2]		*Liberalized Depreciation*[3]		*Total*	
Year End	*Capitalization Including Surplus*[1]	*Amount*	*%*	*Amount*	*%*	*Amount*	*%*
1961	$1,440,207	$108,241[4]	7.5	$ 20,301[4]	1.4	$128,542[4]	8.9
1965	1,799,546	137,251	7.6	48,923	2.7	186,174	10.3
1970	2,409,204	104,420	4.3	104,612	4.3	209,032	8.6

[1] Includes accumulated tax reduction (both that recorded as "Earned Surplus Restricted" and that recorded as a "Reserve for Future Federal Income Taxes").

[2] Resulting from use of accelerated amortization for income tax purposes as permitted under certificates of necessity.

[3] Resulting from use of declining-balance depreciation for income tax purposes for assets constructed or acquired after December 31, 1953 (other than those assets subject to accelerated amortization).

[4] These estimates were prepared in 1960. The actual accumulated tax reduction at December 31, 1961 was $126,829,000, consisting of $108,596,000 related to accelerated amortization and $18,233,000 related to liberalized [declining-balance] depreciation. A regulatory change in Ohio, effective January 1, 1961, reduced the estimated tax reduction related to liberalized depreciation at December 31, 1961 by $2,140,000.

QUESTIONS:

1. What are the arguments for presenting the deferred tax credit outside of the equity section on a balance sheet? Relate your comments to the points made by Mr. Cook in his speech before the security analysts.

2. (a) Do you think the compromise caption is consistent with the SEC's Statement of Administrative Policy?
   (b) How would you classify the new account?
   (c) Is the new account caption easily understood?

3. The amount of $2,435,000 appears in both Exhibit 2 and Exhibit 6. What does this figure represent? Why do you suppose the company used this form of presentation? Have you encountered it before? Do you approve of it? Explain. Reconcile the amounts of $20,169,000 and $2,435,000 from Exhibits 2 and 6 with the amount of $17,734,000 in Exhibit 1.

4. What action, if any, should the company's auditors have taken in 1959? In 1960? Explain.

5. (a) Describe "flow-through" accounting. Was American Electric Power using flow-through accounting in 1958? Explain.
   (b) What is the effect of flow-through accounting on the customers of a public utility?
   (c) Should auditors take exception to the use of flow-through accounting where prescribed by State regulatory authorities? Explain.
   (d) Comment on the soundness of flow-through accounting in terms of generally accepted accounting principles.

6. Using information available in the case, estimate the total amount of depreciation and accelerated amortization claimed in AEP's 1959 federal income tax return.

7. Using the data in Exhibit 3, calculate the percentage of total capitalization represented by common stock equity, preferred stock, and long-term debt, treating the $66,629,000 of deferred taxes as (a) part of common stock equity (as classified in Exhibit 3), (b) excluded entirely from capitalization, and (c) as part of long-term debt.

8. Do you consider the differences in the ratios calculated in question 7 to be significant? Explain.

9. Contrast the classification of accounts on the "Liability" side of the company's balance sheets from 1958 to 1960, as given in Exhibits 3, 4, and 5.

10. In Exhibit 9, prove the 8.86 per cent annual charge for a debt ratio of 55 per cent. Do you agree with Mr. Sporn's conclusions, given in the case, that the annual charges required to carry investment, expressed as a per cent of original investment, decline about 0.45 per cent for each 5 per cent increase in the debt ratio? Explain.

11. Contrast Exhibit 9 with Exhibit 10 noting the similarities and differences. How do you explain the differences?

APPENDIX TABLE A, PRESENT VALUE OF $1.00

Years Hence	1%	2%	3%	4%	5%	6%	7%	8%	9%	10%	11%	12%	13%	14%	15%	16%	17%	18%	19%	20%
1	.990	.980	.971	.962	.952	.943	.935	.926	.917	.909	.901	.893	.885	.877	.870	.862	.855	.847	.840	.833
2	.980	.961	.943	.925	.907	.890	.873	.857	.842	.826	.812	.797	.783	.769	.756	.743	.731	.718	.706	.694
3	.971	.942	.915	.889	.864	.840	.816	.794	.772	.751	.731	.712	.693	.675	.658	.641	.624	.609	.593	.579
4	.961	.924	.888	.855	.823	.792	.763	.735	.708	.683	.659	.636	.613	.592	.572	.552	.534	.516	.499	.482
5	.951	.906	.863	.822	.784	.747	.713	.681	.650	.621	.593	.567	.543	.519	.497	.476	.456	.437	.419	.402
6	.942	.888	.837	.790	.746	.705	.666	.630	.596	.564	.535	.507	.480	.456	.432	.410	.390	.370	.352	.335
7	.933	.871	.813	.760	.711	.665	.623	.583	.547	.513	.482	.452	.425	.400	.376	.354	.333	.314	.296	.279
8	.923	.853	.789	.731	.677	.627	.582	.540	.502	.467	.434	.404	.376	.351	.327	.305	.285	.266	.249	.233
9	.914	.837	.766	.703	.645	.592	.543	.500	.460	.424	.391	.361	.333	.308	.284	.263	.243	.225	.209	.194
10	.905	.820	.744	.676	.614	.558	.508	.463	.422	.386	.352	.322	.295	.270	.247	.227	.208	.191	.176	.162
11	.896	.804	.722	.650	.585	.527	.475	.429	.388	.350	.317	.287	.261	.237	.215	.195	.178	.162	.148	.135
12	.887	.788	.701	.625	.557	.497	.444	.397	.356	.319	.286	.257	.231	.208	.187	.168	.152	.137	.124	.112
13	.879	.773	.681	.601	.530	.469	.415	.368	.326	.290	.258	.229	.204	.182	.163	.145	.130	.116	.104	.093
14	.870	.758	.661	.577	.505	.442	.388	.340	.299	.263	.232	.205	.181	.160	.141	.125	.111	.099	.088	.078
15	.861	.743	.642	.555	.481	.417	.362	.315	.275	.239	.209	.183	.160	.140	.123	.108	.095	.084	.074	.065
16	.853	.728	.623	.534	.458	.394	.339	.292	.252	.218	.188	.163	.142	.123	.107	.093	.081	.071	.062	.054
17	.844	.714	.605	.513	.436	.371	.317	.270	.231	.198	.170	.146	.125	.108	.093	.080	.069	.060	.052	.045
18	.836	.700	.587	.494	.416	.350	.296	.250	.212	.180	.153	.130	.111	.095	.081	.069	.059	.051	.044	.038
19	.828	.686	.570	.475	.396	.331	.277	.232	.194	.164	.138	.116	.098	.083	.070	.060	.051	.043	.037	.031
20	.820	.673	.554	.456	.377	.312	.258	.215	.178	.149	.124	.104	.087	.073	.061	.051	.043	.037	.031	.026
21	.811	.660	.538	.439	.359	.294	.242	.199	.164	.135	.112	.093	.077	.064	.053	.044	.037	.031	.026	.022
22	.803	.647	.522	.422	.342	.278	.226	.184	.150	.123	.101	.083	.068	.056	.046	.038	.032	.026	.022	.018
23	.795	.634	.507	.406	.326	.262	.211	.170	.138	.112	.091	.074	.060	.049	.040	.033	.027	.022	.018	.015
24	.788	.622	.492	.390	.310	.247	.197	.158	.126	.102	.082	.066	.053	.043	.035	.028	.023	.019	.015	.013
25	.780	.610	.478	.375	.295	.233	.184	.146	.116	.092	.074	.059	.047	.038	.030	.024	.020	.016	.013	.010
30	.742	.552	.412	.308	.231	.174	.131	.099	.075	.057	.044	.033	.026	.020	.015	.012	.009	.007	.005	.004
35	.706	.500	.355	.253	.181	.130	.094	.068	.049	.036	.026	.019	.014	.010	.008	.006	.004	.003	.002	.002
40	.672	.453	.307	.208	.142	.097	.067	.046	.032	.022	.015	.011	.008	.005	.004	.003	.002	.001	.001	.001
45	.639	.410	.264	.171	.111	.073	.048	.031	.021	.014	.009	.006	.004	.003	.002	.001	.001			
50	.608	.372	.228	.141	.087	.054	.034	.021	.013	.009	.005	.003	.002	.001	.001	.001				

These tables are condensed with permission from tables which will appear in *Managerial and Engineering Economics: Executive Decision-Making,*

624

Years	1%	2%	3%	4%	5%	6%	7%	8%	9%	10%	11%	12%	13%	14%	15%	16%	17%	18%	19%	20%
1	0.990	0.980	0.971	0.962	0.952	0.943	0.935	0.926	0.917	0.909	0.901	0.893	0.885	0.877	0.870	0.862	0.855	0.847	0.840	0.833
2	1.970	1.942	1.913	1.886	1.859	1.833	1.808	1.783	1.759	1.736	1.713	1.690	1.668	1.647	1.626	1.605	1.585	1.566	1.547	1.528
3	2.941	2.884	2.829	2.775	2.723	2.673	2.624	2.577	2.531	2.487	2.444	2.402	2.361	2.322	2.283	2.246	2.210	2.174	2.140	2.106
4	3.902	3.808	3.717	3.630	3.546	3.465	3.387	3.312	3.240	3.170	3.102	3.037	2.974	2.914	2.855	2.798	2.743	2.690	2.639	2.589
5	4.853	4.713	4.580	4.452	4.329	4.212	4.100	3.993	3.890	3.791	3.696	3.605	3.517	3.433	3.352	3.274	3.199	3.127	3.058	2.991
6	5.795	5.601	5.417	5.242	5.076	4.917	4.767	4.623	4.486	4.355	4.231	4.111	3.998	3.889	3.784	3.685	3.589	3.498	3.410	3.326
7	6.728	6.472	6.230	6.002	5.786	5.582	5.389	5.206	5.033	4.868	4.712	4.564	4.423	4.288	4.160	4.039	3.922	3.812	3.706	3.605
8	7.652	7.325	7.020	6.733	6.463	6.210	5.971	5.747	5.535	5.335	5.146	4.968	4.799	4.639	4.487	4.344	4.207	4.078	3.954	3.837
9	8.566	8.162	7.786	7.435	7.108	6.802	6.515	6.247	5.995	5.759	5.537	5.328	5.132	4.946	4.772	4.607	4.451	4.303	4.163	4.031
10	9.471	8.983	8.530	8.111	7.722	7.360	7.024	6.710	6.418	6.145	5.889	5.650	5.426	5.216	5.019	4.833	4.659	4.494	4.339	4.192
11	10.368	9.787	9.253	8.760	8.306	7.887	7.499	7.139	6.805	6.495	6.207	5.938	5.687	5.453	5.234	5.029	4.836	4.656	4.487	4.327
12	11.255	10.575	9.954	9.385	8.863	8.384	7.943	7.536	7.161	6.814	6.492	6.194	5.918	5.660	5.421	5.197	4.988	4.793	4.611	4.439
13	12.134	11.348	10.635	9.986	9.394	8.853	8.358	7.904	7.487	7.103	6.750	6.424	6.122	5.842	5.583	5.342	5.118	4.910	4.715	4.533
14	13.004	12.106	11.296	10.563	9.899	9.295	8.745	8.244	7.786	7.367	6.982	6.628	6.302	6.002	5.724	5.468	5.229	5.008	4.802	4.611
15	13.865	12.849	11.938	11.118	10.380	9.712	9.108	8.559	8.061	7.606	7.191	6.811	6.462	6.142	5.847	5.575	5.324	5.092	4.876	4.675
16	14.718	13.578	12.561	11.652	10.838	10.106	9.447	8.851	8.313	7.824	7.379	6.974	6.604	6.265	5.954	5.669	5.405	5.162	4.938	4.730
17	15.562	14.292	13.166	12.166	11.274	10.477	9.763	9.122	8.544	8.022	7.549	7.120	6.729	6.373	6.047	5.749	5.475	5.222	4.990	4.775
18	16.398	14.992	13.754	12.659	11.690	10.828	10.059	9.372	8.756	8.201	7.702	7.250	6.840	6.467	6.128	5.818	5.534	5.273	5.033	4.812
19	17.226	15.678	14.324	13.134	12.085	11.158	10.336	9.604	8.950	8.365	7.839	7.366	6.938	6.550	6.198	5.877	5.584	5.316	5.070	4.844
20	18.046	16.351	14.877	13.590	12.462	11.470	10.594	9.818	9.129	8.514	7.963	7.469	7.025	6.623	6.259	5.929	5.628	5.353	5.101	4.870
21	18.857	17.011	15.415	14.029	12.821	11.764	10.836	10.017	9.292	8.649	8.075	7.562	7.102	6.687	6.312	5.973	5.665	5.384	5.127	4.891
22	19.660	17.658	15.937	14.451	13.163	12.042	11.061	10.201	9.442	8.772	8.176	7.645	7.170	6.743	6.359	6.011	5.696	5.410	5.149	4.909
23	20.456	18.292	16.444	14.857	13.489	12.303	11.272	10.371	9.580	8.883	8.266	7.718	7.230	6.792	6.399	6.044	5.723	5.432	5.167	4.925
24	21.243	18.914	16.936	15.247	13.799	12.550	11.469	10.529	9.707	8.985	8.348	7.784	7.283	6.835	6.434	6.073	5.746	5.451	5.182	4.937
25	22.023	19.523	17.413	15.622	14.094	12.783	11.654	10.675	9.823	9.077	8.422	7.843	7.330	6.873	6.464	6.097	5.766	5.467	5.195	4.948
30	25.808	22.396	19.600	17.292	15.372	13.765	12.409	11.258	10.274	9.427	8.694	8.055	7.496	7.003	6.566	6.177	5.829	5.517	5.235	4.979
35	29.409	24.999	21.487	18.665	16.374	14.498	12.948	11.655	10.567	9.644	8.855	8.176	7.586	7.070	6.617	6.215	5.858	5.539	5.251	4.992
40	32.835	27.355	23.115	19.793	17.159	15.046	13.332	11.925	10.757	9.779	8.951	8.244	7.634	7.105	6.642	6.234	5.871	5.548	5.258	4.997
45	36.094	29.490	24.519	20.720	17.774	15.456	13.606	12.108	10.881	9.863	9.008	8.283	7.661	7.123	6.654	6.242	5.877	5.552	5.261	4.999
50	39.196	31.424	25.730	21.482	18.256	15.762	13.801	12.233	10.962	9.915	9.042	8.305	7.675	7.133	6.661	6.246	5.880	5.554	5.262	4.999

Case Index

Subject Index

N

O

P